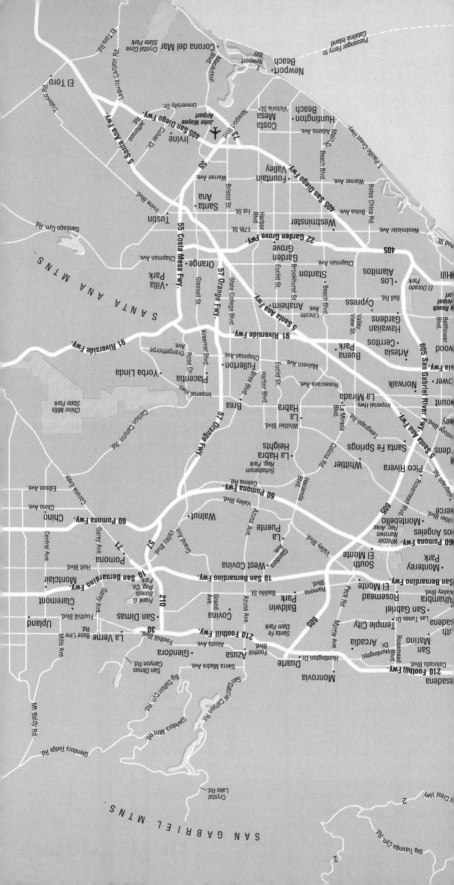

# Orientation

Big breaks happen here. Hopes and schemes are played out like the screenplays scribbled by thousands of aspiring writers, and people from around the world arrive in LA looking for the American Dream. Why? Because Los Angeles is a city where anything can happen—and almost everything does happen here. This is where TV game-show contestants spin fortunes, movie stars drive Harleys, and Zsa Zsa Gabor slugs a Beverly Hills cop. This is where snow dusts the mountain ranges at the same time sandy-haired, suntanned surfers take to the beach. And for those who've never felt the earth tremble and shake beneath their feet, this is where you can thrill to a fake earthquake courtesy of Universal Studios, and where lucky youngsters can make all their dreams come true with a journey through one of the grandest theme parks of them all, Disneyland.

Part movie and entertainment capital, part social experiment, LA is a vast megalopolis where every lifestyle and culture converge in a puzzle of head-spinning contrasts. Whatever your pleasure, be it cutting-edge architecture, fantastic food, or warm, sandy beaches, LA has it all.

For a taste of the diversity that radiates in all directions in this City of Angels, cruise the storied boulevards—Wilshire, Sunset, Santa Monica, and Olympic—that snake like tributaries to the Pacific and its legendary beaches. Heading west on Olympic, stop for crab soup in Koreatown and spy the Beverly Hills High School's oil rig as you approach the striking twin towers of Century City. On Sunset, pull over for a drink at the Art Deco St. James's Club, indulge on Wolfgang Puck's famous gourmet pizza at Spago, pick up a movie-star map for a tour of the estates of the rich and famous, or turn off at Will Rogers State Historic Park to tour the Rogers' home and hike the chaparral-covered hills. You can also ponder the beasts of millennia at the La Brea Tar Pits along

RIK OLSON

*Los Angeles City H*

Wilshire, browse through the Los Angeles County Museum of Art's gallery of German Expressionism, and peruse haute couture at the exclusive boutiques on Beverly Hills' Rodeo Drive. When you reach the coast, where towering palm trees line the palisades overlooking the Pacific in Santa Monica and seagulls pester people for handouts, you can pedal the bike path or stroll the pier, but don't miss the Third Street Promenade, where movie theaters, trendy restaurants, and bookstores draw throngs of pedestrians every day and night of the year.

All this, and you still haven't even entered LA's notorious freeway system. Everything you've heard about the horrible highways is true: Interchanges are piled like concrete pick-up sticks, and more than one thousand on-ramps and 511 miles of tarmac are clogged daily. But burning fuel is part of the Southern California experience. So if you're ready to venture beyond city limits, fill up your tank, grab a roadmap, and buckle up for an extended tour of the most motorized region in the world.

Travel north up the coastal highway and sink your feet into the Malibu beaches mythologized in film and song. Travel south and stroll the Venice Beach boardwalk, where New Age hippies, bikini-clad roller skaters, well-oiled bodybuilders, and chain-saw jugglers have found the end point of the Western Frontier. Or venture even farther south to Anaheim in Orange County and shake hands with Mickey Mouse at the venerable Disneyland. What makes it all worthwhile is the balmy weather (it's practically perfect year-round) and the fact that this is LA, where almost anything can happen.

## How To Read This Guide

LOS ANGELES ACCESS® is arranged by neighborhood so you can see at a glance where you are and what is around you. The numbers next to the entries in the following chapters correspond to the numbers on the maps. The type is color-coded according to the kind of place described:

Restaurants/Clubs: Red        Hotels: Blue

Shops/ Outdoors: Green    Sights/Culture: Black

### Rating the Restaurants and Hotels

The restaurant ratings take into account the quality, service, atmosphere, and uniqueness of the restaurant. An expensive restaurant doesn't necessarily ensure an enjoyable evening; however, a small, relatively unknown spot could have good food, professional service, and a lovely atmosphere. Therefore, on a purely subjective basis, stars are used to judge the overall dining value (see the star ratings at right). Keep in mind that chefs and owners often change, which sometimes drastically affects the quality of a restaurant. The ratings in this guidebook are based on information available at press time.

The price ratings, as categorized at right, apply to restaurants and hotels. These figures describe general price-range relationships between other restaurants and hotels in the area. The restaurant price ratings are based on the average cost of an entrée for one person, excluding tax and tip. Hotel price ratings reflect the base price of a standard room for two people for one night during the peak season.

### Restaurants

| ★ Good | |
|---|---|
| ★★ Very Good | |
| ★★★ Excellent | |
| ★★★★ An Extraordinary Experience | |
| $ The Price Is Right | (less than $15) |
| $$ Reasonable | ($15-$25) |
| $$$ Expensive | ($25-$45) |
| $$$$ Big Bucks | ($45 and up) |

### Hotels

| $ The Price Is Right | (less than $80) |
|---|---|
| $$ Reasonable | ($80-$125) |
| $$$ Expensive | ($125-$185) |
| $$$$ Big Bucks | ($185 and up) |

### Map Key

1 Entry Number        Freeway

City/Town ●     Highway   [ Tunnel ----

Point of ■          Tertiary Road
Interest

# Getting to Los Angeles

## Airports

### Los Angeles International Airport (LAX)

The principal hub of the Western Pacific Rim, Los Angeles International Airport (LAX) is the world's

third busiest airport. Revamped for the 1984 Summer Olympics, LAX features more than 75 air carriers located in eight terminals, and each terminal is equipped with hotel/motel information boards, cafeterias, snack bars, cocktail lounges, newsstands, restrooms, gift shops, and lockers.

The central complex houses seven terminals around the perimeter of a two-level loop, with parking, a restaurant, a heliport, and a control tower within the loop. The five-level, million-square-foot **Tom Bradley International Terminal** (named after LA's mayor) is in the middle of the loop, between American Airlines and United Airlines terminals. Airlines frequently merge and change terminals, so call 310/646.5252 for up-to-date information.

The **West Imperial Terminal,** a separate terminal just south of the central complex, handles charter flights and supplemental carriers. A free blue-and-green bus connects you with the main terminal every half-hour from 7AM to 12:30AM. Take the bus from the center island in front of each baggage-claim area.

Flight departures are made from the upper level (a few airlines, such as **MGM Grand Air,** use the West Imperial Terminal located on the south side of the airfield), where you can purchase tickets and check in. A number of restaurants, newsstands, and general and duty-free gift stores are found here, too.

Arrivals may be picked up at the lower level, where you'll also find the baggage-claim areas, car-rental agencies, information on hotels, and other ground transportation. Free blue, green, and white **Airline Connections** buses link each terminal at both levels. Other complimentary buses will take you to satellite parking lots and the West Imperial Terminal. **Handicapped Connections** is a free minibus with extra-wide doors and a ramp for wheelchairs. For additional airport information, pick up the yellow courtesy telephones inside the terminal to contact the **Airport Information Aides.**

### LAX Information

| | |
|---|---|
| Airport Security | 310/646.4269 |
| Currency Exchange | 310/417.0366 |
| Customs and Immigration | 310/215.2414 |
| First Aid Station | 310/215.6000 |
| Information | 310/646.5252 |
| Lost and Found | 310/417.0440 |
| Traveler's Aid | 310/646.2270 |
| Wheelchair/Handicap Service | 310/646.6402 |

**Getting to the Airport by Car** From downtown LA, take the Santa Monica Freeway (I-10) west to the San Diego Freeway (I-405) south and exit at either La Tijera or Century boulevards. In mid-1993 the new Glenn M. Anderson Freeway (I-105) will funnel drivers into LAX, connecting the 605, 710, 110, and 405 freeways between Norwalk to the east and the airport.

**Airport Parking** There are a number of parking options. The **Central Terminal** lots cost $3 for the first two hours, and $16 maximum for each 24-hour period. The **West Imperial Terminal** lot charges $1 per hour, and a maximum of $6 for each 24-hour period. **Metered parking** is available for 25¢ per 15 minutes (for a two-hour maximum). There is also **short-term airport parking** (8,300 spaces in eight central lots) at reasonable rates; these lots are often full on holidays and during peak periods.

**Long-term parking** is available at two major satellite lots (16,400 spaces): **Lot C** (at the corner of Sepulveda Boulevard and 96th Street) and **Lot B** (at the corner of La Cienega Boulevard and 111th Street). Both of these lots have 24-hour bus service running every 10 to 20 minutes to each of the eight terminals. And for greater convenience at a higher cost, leave your car at one of the privately owned lots scattered around the airport. For more information about airport parking, call 310/646.5707.

To avoid the hassle of driving and parking altogether, door-to-door airport shuttles offer 24-hour service to all Los Angeles area airports.

**Ground Transportation** A bewildering array of buses and vans circle the airport loop, stopping at the center island outside each baggage-claim area. Be sure to stand at the correct pick-up site. Major services include:

**SuperShuttle** Bright blue vans offer door-to-door service from LAX to most destinations in Los Angeles and Orange counties, including the other major airports. Prices range from $4 to $25, depending on your destination. For pick-up at the airport, call 310/338.1111 after you have collected your baggage; for service from your home or hotel, call 800/258.3826 24 hours in advance.

### Other Shuttles

| | |
|---|---|
| Airport Flyer | 800/244.5755 |
| All-American Shuttle | 310/641.4090 |
| Best Shuttle | 310/670.7080 |
| Metropolitan Express | 800/338.3898 |
| Prime Time | 310/558.1606 |

### Limousines

| | |
|---|---|
| Diamond Limousine | 310/271.4836 |
| Executive Transit Inc. | 800/540.0224 |
| Fox Limousine | 800/274.4369 |
| Pacific Limousine | 310/649.5466 |

### RTD Airport Service

Regular public bus service links many parts of town with the bus terminal at Lot C. A free 24-hour connector bus stops at each of the airline terminals every 10 to 20 minutes.

For other ground-transportation services, check with the ticket/information booths on the sidewalk outside each baggage-claim area.

### Major Airlines

| | |
|---|---|
| Alaska Airlines | 800/426.0333 |
| American Airlines | 800/433.7300 |
| Delta Air Lines | 800/221.1212 |
| Northwest Airlines | 800/447.4747 |
| United Airlines | 800/241.6522 |

**Other Airports Serving Southern California**

# Getting around Los Angeles

If you haven't heard already, you'll quickly learn that the traffic in LA is *always* unpredictable. For example, the trip from downtown Los Angeles to LAX on the Santa Monica Freeway (I-10) and the San Diego Freeway (I-405) could take 20 minutes or it could take one hour (or even several hours if there's an accident). So bear in mind this essential rule of the road: **Always allow plenty of time to get anywhere in LA.** Tune into local radio stations in the morning and late afternoon for minute-to-minute traffic reports. The state transportation department often publishes schedules of upcoming road construction in local newspapers, or you can call 213/628.7623 for information on highway conditions.

## Bicycles

There are more than 200 miles of bicycle trails in Los Angeles County. The most popular is the **South Bay Bicycle Trail,** which runs along 22 miles of shoreline from Santa Monica to Torrance Beach. Long Beach's three-mile **ocean-side bike path** offers a picturesque ride from Shoreline Village to Belmont Shore. The **San Gabriel River Trail** follows a 37-mile course from Santa Fe Dam in Azusa to Long Beach's Shoreline Village. And the eight-mile **Griffith Park Trail** takes in the LA Zoo, Travel Town, and the Gene Autry Western Heritage Museum. Detailed maps are available; contact the **Los Angeles City Department of Transportation** at 213/485.2265.

## Boats

You can charter a boat to watch whales, cruise to Catalina Island, or fish for barracuda, and they all depart from Long Beach and San Pedro harbors. A two-hour, blues-and-jazz brunch tour of the Los Angeles Harbor departs from Seaport Village in Long Beach at 11AM every Sunday. Fishing charters usually leave at 7AM, but check with the tour operator for specific departure time. A nonstop trip to Catalina takes about an hour, and a more leisurely trip lasts twice as long. For more information, contact the following companies:

## Buses

It may surprise many visitors and even some local Angelenos, but public transportation *does* exist in Los Angeles. More than 1.3 million people commute on public transportation daily. The **Rapid Transit District (RTD)** operates 208 bus routes in the greater metropolitan area. The fare is $1.10 and each transfer is 25¢. From Spring Street in downtown, bus no. 27 takes you nonstop into Beverly Hills. Also from down-

town, bus no. 439 travels to LAX and Manhattan, Hermosa, and Redondo beaches. For trips to and from the beaches along Santa Monica's coast, take bus no. 20 on Wilshire Boulevard or bus no. 4 on Santa Monica Boulevard. Both of these buses offer 24-hour services. For more information, call 213/626.4455.

To obtain a copy of RTD's *Self-Guided Tours* and a tourist kit, write to: RTD, 425 South Main Street, Los Angeles 90013-1393. Municipal bus information is available through each city's chamber of commerce.

The downtown **DASH** shuttle runs Monday through Saturday 6AM to 6PM and takes riders to nearby Chinatown, Union Station, City Hall, the Music Center, Little Tokyo, and Olvera Street for 25¢. For more information, call 800/2.LA.RIDE.

## Car Rentals

More than 30 national and local car-rental agencies are located around LAX, and all major hotels have car-rental counters. You can rent a Rolls Royce, Ferrari, a classic two-seater T-Bird, or just your basic Ford—the choice is yours. Weekly (a minimum of five days) or three-day weekend rates are usually the best deals, but you should always shop around. Contact the following major companies for their current rates:

Or for the extremely budget conscious:

And for the excessively status conscious:

## Metro Rail

A new 22-mile **Metro Rail Blue Line** can be boarded at any of its 22 stations between downtown Los Angeles and Long Beach. Scheduled to open early in 1993, the long-awaited **Red Line** will provide service between Union Station and MacArthur Park; and by 1996 it is expected to extend westbound to Westwood Village along the Wilshire Boulevard corridor. In 1994 the 20-mile **Green Line** will transport riders from Norwalk in the east to El Segundo and the LAX area. Metro Rail's long-term goal is a 400-mile system that incorporates light rail, subway, and commuter rail through Los Angeles County and other surrounding communities. For more information, see the **Metro Rail map** on the inside of this book's back cover or call 213/620.7245.

## Taxis

Hailing a cab in LA is virtually unheard of, but you can find taxis waiting for customers in front of hotels and at LAX, Union Station, the Greyhound/Trailways terminal, and other major ports of entry. Once inside a cab, you're obligated to pay $1.90. Afterward, the

metered rate is $1.60 per mile. If you prefer door-to-door service, radio dispatchers can send a cab to your home or business in about 20 minutes.

| | |
|---|---|
| Independent Cab Company. | 800/821.8294 |
| LA Taxi | 213/627.7000 |
| United Independent Taxi Drivers | 213/653.5050 |

## Trains

Thousands of passengers arrive daily in Los Angeles via the historic Union Station depot, an elegant hybrid of Art Deco and Spanish Mission architectural traditions, located in downtown at 800 North Alameda Street. **Amtrak** provides frequent service from LA to San Diego, with stops in several cities along the way. Great day trips by rail are the coastal routes to Santa Barbara ($25 to $40), San Francisco ($113 to $150), the old mission in San Juan Capistrano ($22 to $30), and the Del Mar Racetrack ($31 to $48). The fare to Disneyland in Anaheim is $12 to $16. For information and reservations, call 800/USA.RAIL.

Tourist information is available near main points of interest throughout the city. In LA's downtown financial district, the **Los Angeles Convention and Visitors Bureau** provides maps, information on lodging, and discount tickets to amusement parks and cultural attractions. Their office hours are Monday through Friday 8AM to 5PM, and Saturday 8:30AM to 5PM; 695 South Figueroa Street, Los Angeles 90071; 213/689.8822.

In Hollywood, tour guides and brochures also are available at the **Janes House** (6541 Hollywood Boulevard; 213/461.4213); or stop by the office between 9AM and 5PM Monday through Saturday. Contact the following visitor information centers for more information:

| | |
|---|---|
| Beverly Hills | 310/271.8174 |
| Long Beach | 310/436.3645 |
| Palm Springs | 619/346.8800 |
| Pasadena | 818/795.9311 |
| Santa Monica | 310/393.7593 |

Chambers of commerce in these surrounding cities also provide free information:

| | |
|---|---|
| Catalina Island (in Avalon) | 310/510.1520 |
| Hermosa Beach | 310/376.0951 |
| Marina del Rey | 310/821.0555 |
| Monterey Park | 818/280.3864 |
| Santa Barbara | 805/965.3021 |
| West Hollywood | 213/654.9213 |

## Banks

Most banks are open Monday through Friday 9AM to 6PM and Saturday mornings. If you need to exchange money, check with the major banks.

Automatic Teller Machines (ATMs), where you can withdraw cash instantly, are available at most banks.

## Distances

From downtown Los Angeles to:

| | |
|---|---|
| Anaheim (Disneyland) | 26 miles |
| Beverly Hills | 10 miles |
| Big Bear Lake | 100 miles |
| Burbank-Glendale-Pasadena Airport | 13 miles |
| Griffith Park | 6 miles |
| Hollywood | 6 miles |
| Los Angeles International Airport (LAX) | 17 miles |
| Pasadena | 9 miles |
| Santa Monica | 15 miles |
| Universal City (Universal Studios) | 9 miles |
| Valencia (Six Flags Magic Mountain) | 30 miles |
| Venice Beach | 16 miles |

## LA Freeways

| Number | Name(s) |
|---|---|
| 2 | Glendale Freeway |
| 5 | Santa Ana Freeway<br>Golden State Freeway |
| 10 | Santa Monica Freeway<br>San Bernardino Freeway |
| 22 | Garden Grove Freeway |
| 57 | Orange Freeway |
| 60 | Pomona Freeway |
| 90 | Marina Freeway |
| 91 | Artesia Freeway<br>Riverside Freeway |
| 101 | Ventura Freeway<br>Hollywood Freeway |
| 105 | Glenn M. Anderson Freeway |
| 110 | Pasadena Freeway<br>Harbor Freeway |
| 118 | Simi Valley-San Fernando Freeway |
| 210 | Foothill Freeway |
| 405 | San Diego Freeway |
| 605 | San Gabriel Freeway |
| 710 | Long Beach Freeway |

## Parking

Tickets for parking violations can cost you the price of a dinner for two (with wine), so read all parking signs for restrictions before you enter into an agreement with the curb. Most meters in high-traffic commercial areas have a one-hour limit at a rate of 25¢ for 20 or 60 minutes. A **red curb** means no parking; a **green curb** permits parking for 20 minutes; and a **white curb** means loading and unloading only. For periods longer than 60 minutes, a parking garage, which may charge a $3 to $15 maximum, is less painful on the pocketbook than a $38 (or more) ticket.

## Publications

The *Los Angeles Times* newspaper is the only major metropolitan daily in the area. It offers in-depth coverage on international news, business, entertainment, and the arts, and it has suburban zone editions for local news. For the most thorough arts and entertainment information, pick up the free *LA Weekly*, distributed on Thursday at restaurants and book, record, and convenience stores; it's the nation's largest alternative weekly. Los Angeles' daily *La Opinion* is the largest Spanish newspaper in the country. And if you're looking for bargains, from used cars to computers, pick up the free *Recycler* at liquor stores or corner markets.

## Radio Stations

Nowhere does radio boast a more captive audience than in LA, where the average commuter is trapped in his or her car an hour a day. Morning talk shows range from racy Mark and Brian on KLOS 95.5 FM to shock radio with Howard Stern on KLSX 97.1 FM to light rock and pop on KOST 103.5 FM. The major LA stations include:

| | | |
|---|---|---|
| KALI | Spanish | 1430 AM |
| KCRW | Public Radio | 89.9 FM |
| KGFJ | Country | 1230 AM |
| KIIS | Top 40 | 102.7 FM/1150 AM |
| KKGO | Classical | 105.1 FM |
| KLOS | Rock | 95.5 FM |
| KLSX | Classic Rock | 97.1 FM |
| KOST | Light Rock/Pop | 103.5 FM |
| KROQ | New Wave/Rock | 106.7 FM |
| KRTH | Oldies | 101.1 FM |
| KTWV | New Age | 94.7 FM |

## Restaurants

Reservations are essential at most trendy or expensive restaurants. Reserve weeks ahead, if possible, or else prepare to eat dinner at 6PM or 10PM. Many popular tourist spots take reservations for parties of six or more only. And for walk-ins, expect a long wait.

## Shopping

You'll find boutique shopping in Westwood (home to the University of California, Los Angeles), Old Pasadena, trendy Melrose Avenue, Santa Monica's chic Third Street Promenade, Montana Avenue, and Main Street, which is south of the civic center.

For those who prefer the all-inclusive shopping center, there are several malls to choose from. The most massive is the 350-store **Del Amo Fashion Center** in Torrance. The open-air **Century City Shopping Center and Marketplace** and the indoor **Beverly Center** are the most chic. In Orange County, Costa Mesa's 200-store **South Coast Plaza** has everything from Chanel and Mark Cross to a full-size merry-go-round; and the outdoor, upscale **Fashion Island** shopping complex is located in Newport Beach.

Wholesale shopping can be found in the garment district between Seventh and Los Angeles streets in downtown or at the new **Citadel** complex in the City of Commerce. For haute couture, head for Rodeo Drive in Beverly Hills.

## Telephones

Public pay phones can be hard to find in LA, and phone books are even scarcer. Many merchants have given the heave-ho to nearby phones because they attract drug dealers. Most restaurants, however, have them installed for their customers' convenience.

Carry a handful of change before dialing—calls within the city can be costly. Directory assistance is available by dialing 411.

## Weather

Raincoats are rarely needed here: rain falls an average of 35 days a year between the months of November and April. Typically, the sun shines 186 days a year in the city and 137 days at the beach. The average temperature in LA is 74°F, with summer highs typically in the mid-80s and winter lows in the mid-60s. In the desert, winter temperatures hover in the 70s, and summer highs range between 103° to 110°F.

## Phone Book

**Emergency**

| | |
|---|---|
| **Ambulance/Fire/Police/Sheriff** | **911** |
| AAA Motor Club (road service) | 800/336.4357 |
| AIDS Hot Line | 800/922.2437 |
| Beach Information | 310/479.9701 |
| Child Abuse | 800/540.5200 |
| Disabled Riders Hot Line | 800/621.7828 |
| Earthquake Preparedness | 213/237.1927 |
| Missing Children | 800/222.3463 |
| Poison Control Center | 800/777.6476 |
| Surf and Weather | 213/451.8761 |
| Time | 213/853.1616/1212 |
| Transit Information | 800/252.7433 |
| USC Medical Center | 213/226.3164 |

RIK OLSON

The Día de los Muertos (Day of the Dead) Mexican religious celebration is held every November at El Pueblo de Los Angeles Plaza. For more information, see page 13.

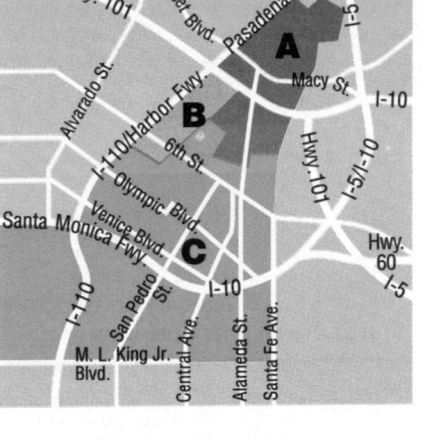

# Downtown

Although it's a surprise to many people—even resident Angelenos—the mammoth, sprawling city of LA *does* have a downtown district. It's a large, rich area, and to make it easier to explore, it is divided in this book into three sections (see regions A, B, and C on the map at left), much of which can be explored on foot:

**A.** The **Historic Core**, including **El Pueblo de Los Angeles** (site of the first settlement), **City Hall, Chinatown,** and **Little Tokyo;**

**B.** The **Business and Financial** district, a corridor of high-rise offices to the east of the Harbor Freeway (see page 39); and
**C.** The **Commercial and Exposition Park** area, with LA's classic commercial buildings, movie palaces, and markets, extending south to the **University of Southern California** and the museums (see page 36).

Throughout the downtown area, the streets are crowded and active by day (more than 210,000 people commute here daily) and they're often deserted at night (the resident population is less than 20,000, but it is now slowly increasing). In fact, most stores close just as the office workers head home.

Driving in downtown is a penance: streets are clogged with traffic or construction crews, the one-way street system is confusing, and parking garages charge extortionate rates. If you arrive by car, it is best to leave it in your hotel garage. From the airport, there is frequent coach service to the major hotels. Cruising cabs are rare; call ahead for service. The best ways to get around during the day are on foot and by **DASH** shuttle, a minibus that runs every six to 15 minutes on weekdays from 6:30AM to 6:30PM, and on Saturday from 10AM to 5PM. It only costs a quarter for each of two loops that, together, stop at most of the major landmarks. Route A runs from Little Tokyo west to the business corridor, south on Flower Street to Wilshire Boulevard, and east to the Garment District. Route B crosses the Harbor Freeway to Library Square, heads north on Grand to the Civic Center, and north again to El Pueblo and Chinatown. For more information on the DASH shuttle, call 800/252.7433. Work has begun on the **Metro Rail Red Line** subway and, if funds don't run out, a four-mile stretch to mid-Wilshire Boulevard will be completed this year; eventually, the first line may extend through Hollywood and into the San Fernando Valley.

# A. Downtown/Historic Core

This is where Los Angeles began. Ever since the founding of the city by a handful of Spanish settlers on 4 September 1781, the central core has remained close to its origins around El Pueblo de Los Angeles. Within a short walk of City Hall, you can explore more than 200 years of history and an extraordinary ethnic and economic diversity. Los Angeles became a Mexican city in 1822 after Mexico won its independence from Spain. In 1847 the Stars and Stripes was raised, and a small stream of Yankee immigrants began arriving. Local boosters roamed the nation singing the praises of a promised land. In 1887, when two competing railroads established links to the midwest and briefly dropped the fare to a dollar, the trickle became a flood. Immigrants slept in tents and bathtubs. But the land boom quickly went bust, leaving downtown with twice as many permanent residents, and only a third of the newly planted communities survived.

The more affluent residents began to relocate to the west of downtown, leaving the center and east to new arrivals. Over the years the influx took its toll, and the area around City Hall became a civic embarrassment. Urban renewal began in the 1930s, with the creation of **Olvera Street** as a symbol of the original Spanish pueblo. In the late '40s the city created the **Community Redevelopment Agency (CRA)**, which began to acquire properties for renovation and renewal, notably in Little Tokyo, Chinatown, and El Pueblo de Los Angeles. Today ethnic traditions flourish as strongly as ever, here and in surrounding neighborhoods, and you can enjoy the culture and cuisine of almost every country in Latin America and along the Pacific Rim. Los Angeles is home to 3.6 million Hispanics, making it one of the largest Spanish-speaking cities in the United States. There are two centers of Latino activity downtown: Olvera Street for tourists, and **Broadway** (in the Downtown/Commercial and Exposition Park section of this chapter) for locals.

---

*Area code 213 unless otherwise noted.*

**1 El Pueblo de Los Angeles Historic Monument and Olvera Street** Bounded by Sunset Boulevard and Spring, Arcadia, and Alameda streets, this is the founding site of the city of Los Angeles, comprising the Plaza, Olvera Street, a park, and 27 historic or architecturally significant buildings. The city has recently taken over responsibility from the state and is pondering a major redevelopment of the surrounding area. Docent-led tours are held Tuesday through Saturday hourly from 10AM to 1PM. Olvera Street (pictured below) is named for **Augustin Olvera,** a Los Angeles County judge and supervisor, and was rebuilt in 1930 in the style of a Mexican marketplace. The brick-paved block is lined with shops and *puestos* (stalls), which sell Mexican handicrafts and confections. Food is served at a number of stands and cafes along the street. For dessert go to the Plaza, where a fruit vendor sells peeled mangoes, papayas, and other tropical fruit. The confectioners at the center of Olvera Street carry Mexican sweets such as candied squash or brown sugar cones. Delicious Mexican *churros* (donuts) can be found at the bakery near the north-center side of the street. ♦ Daily 10AM-7PM winter; daily 10AM-10PM summer. 628.1274

**2 La Luz del Dia** $ You can watch women skilled in the fast-disappearing art of making tortillas by hand. ♦ Mexican ♦ Tu-Su 11AM-10PM. 107 Paseo de la Plaza. 628.7495

**2 Sepulveda House** This red-brick business block building and former boardinghouse was built in 1887 by **Eliosa Martinez de Sepulveda.** It now houses a **Visitor Information Center.** An 18-minute film chronicling the history of El Pueblo is

available on request, and a 50¢ walking tour guide is available in a variety of languages. ♦ M-F 10AM-3:30PM; Sa 10AM-4:30PM. 624 N. Main St. 628.1274

**3 Pelanconi House** Constructed in 1855, this is one of the first brick buildings in Los Angeles. The two-story balconied structure was built as a residence with a large wine cellar. It is named for its second owner, **Antonio Pelanconi,** and is still a private residence. ♦ 17 W. Olvera St

Within the Pelanconi House:

**Casa La Golondrina** $$ Mariachis and dancers entertain you while you enjoy Mexican food. ♦ Mexican ♦ Daily 10AM-9PM. 628.4349

**3 Bazaar de Mexico** Taxco silver jewelry and Mexican clothing and costumes are sold here. ♦ Daily 9AM-8PM. W-7 Olvera St. 620.9782

**3 Casa de Sousa** This shop carries Mexican and Central American folk art. ♦ Daily 10AM-8PM. 634 N. Main St. 626.7076

**4 Zanja Madre** A fragment of the city's original irrigation ditch, this was built in 1781 to carry water from the LA River near Elysian Park into LA. ♦ Off Olvera St

**5 Avila Adobe** LA's oldest adobe was built in 1818 by **Don Francisco Avila,** one-time mayor of the pueblo. Parts of the original two-foot-thick walls survive. The simple one-story structure is of characteristic Mexican design, with a garden patio in the rear. ♦ Free. Tu-F 10AM-3:30PM; Sa 10AM-4PM. 10 Olvera St. 628.7164

*Olvera Street*

**6 El Pueblo de Los Angeles Plaza (Old Plaza)** The center of **El Pueblo Historic Park** and the hub of community life through the 1870s, the plaza is now the setting for public festivals that bring back the spirit of the Mexican era. Most notable are **Cinco de Mayo** (5

May, a Mexican Independence holiday); **Día de los Muertos** (Day of the Dead), a religious festival in which the souls of the dead return to visit their living relatives in early November; and **Las Posadas** (the week before Christmas). At the center of the plaza is the **Kiosko,** a hexagonal bandstand with filigree ironwork. ♦ SE end of Olvera St

**7 Pico House** This Italian palazzo was built by **Ezra F. Kysor** in 1870 for **Pio Pico,** the last Mexican governor of California. During its heyday the Pico House was the finest hotel in California south of San Francisco. ♦ 430 N. Main St

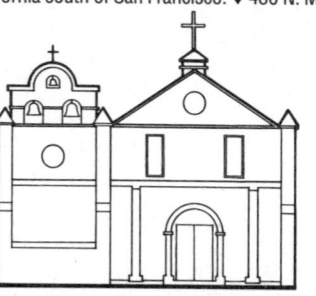

**8 Plaza Church (Church of Our Lady the Queen of the Angels)** The Plaza Church (pictured above) was originally a simple adobe built by Franciscan padres and local Indians between 1818 and 1822. The first structure to be built in the pueblo was the jail, and it was rushed to completion. However, it took the town 40 years to build the church. It is the oldest religious structure in Los Angeles. ♦ Daily 24 hours. 535 N. Main St

**9 Merced Theatre** Ezra F. Kysor designed this three-story 1870 Italianate masonry building with a theater, no longer in use. The interior is being restored. ♦ 420 N. Main St

**10 Masonic Hall** Designed in 1858, this is the city's first lodge, a two-story Italian Renaissance structure with a cast-iron balcony and three arched openings on each floor. Call for group tours. ♦ Free. Tu-F 10AM-3PM. 416 ½ N. Main St. 626.4933

**11 Garnier Block** Philippe Garnier built this block in 1890 as commercial stores and apartments for the city's Chinese businessmen. It is constructed of buff brick with sandstone trim and has an unusual cornice of Victorian Romanesque design. ♦ 415 N. Los Angeles St

**12 Old Plaza Firehouse** Once a castellated brick structure, the 1884 firehouse is now a museum containing only firefighting equipment and photographs of 19th-century fire stations. ♦ Free. Tu-F 10AM-3PM; Sa 10AM-4:30PM. Tours: Tu-Sa 10AM, noon. 535 N. Main St. 625.3741

**13 Union Station** One of LA's greatest, least appreciated architectural treasures and the last of the grand railroad passenger terminals, Union Station (pictured above) was designed by **John & Donald Parkinson** in 1939 and built jointly by the Southern Pacific, Union Pacific, and Santa Fe railroad companies. It is a free interpretation of Spanish Mission architecture, combining enormous scale with moderne and Moorish details. The wood-beamed ceiling of the waiting room is 52 feet high, the floors are of marble, and deep scalloped archways lead to two atmospheric patios. **Fred Harvey's** restaurant is shuttered but available for receptions and special events. There are daily departures of the *Desert Wind* to Las Vegas and Chicago and the *Coast Starlite* to Seattle, plus busy short-distance runs to San Diego and to New Orleans tri-weekly. As the conductor calls "all aboard," the ghosts of past glories stir. ♦ 800 N. Alameda St. 683.6875; for schedule and ticket information, call 800/872.7245; Fred Harvey's: 625.5865

**14 City Archives** You'll find a treasury of maps, papers, photos, and council records documenting LA since 1827. The archives are almost unknown, except to city officials, but anyone can make an appointment to do research. They're located one-half mile east of Union Station. ♦ M-F 8AM-5PM. 555 Ramirez St, Space 320. 485.3512

**15 Terminal Annex** Formerly LA's principal mail distribution center, this handsome building, with its 1930s **Works Progress Administration (WPA)** murals by **Boris Deutsch,** continues to operate a full-service post office. ♦ 900 N. Alameda St. Counter service: M-F 8AM-7PM; Sa 8AM-4PM. 617.4641

**16 Philippe's Original Sandwich Shop** ★$ Legend has it that the French-dip sandwich was invented here in 1908. Since then, the faithful have been coming here for simple, honest food and 10¢ coffee. The crowd, waiting for a seat at the linoleum-topped tables on the sawdust floor, is a cross section of LA society, from ballplayers to stockbrokers. Be sure to have your sandwich double-dipped. The restaurant is across the street from the Terminal Annex. ♦ American ♦ Daily 6AM-10PM. 1001 N. Alameda St. 628.3781

# Chinatown

LA's Chinatown is located on the 700 to 1000 blocks of North Broadway in an area bordered approximately by Ord, Alameda, Bernard, and Yale streets. In 1850 only two Chinese people lived in this area; about 9,600 people now live here, and this is the cultural center for more than 200,000 Chinese Americans living in the Southland. **Chinese New Year** is celebrated in this part of the city with parades, beauty pageants, and lots of traditional food (the date varies from year to year because the Chinese follow a lunar calendar, but it is usually held in February or March).

The original settlement on Alameda Street was moved northwest in the 1930s to clear the site for Union Station. Civic leaders saw the tourist potential in a "new Chinatown"; in 1938 the theme buildings on the 900 block of North Broadway were built in a *Chu Chin Chow* style, with exaggerated, curved roof lines and abundant ornamentation. Behind these gaudy facades you'll find a food shopper's paradise. Chickens squawk, ducks quack, fish swim—and you know the food is fresh. Gift shops sell everything from Hong Kong kitsch to fine art. Try **Sam Ward Co.,** 959 North Hill Street, for chinaware; **Fong's,** 939-943 Chung King Road, for art; **China Cultural Center, Inc.,** 970 North Broadway #103, for Chinese paintings, books, and acupuncture and art supplies; **Jin Hing & Co.,** 412 Bamboo Lane, for jade; and **Sincere Importing,** 483 Gin Ling Way, for baskets.

**17 Mon Kee** ★★$$$ It's chaotic and crowded, but this restaurant still serves the freshest seafood, superbly prepared. Specialties, including whole crab and shrimp in spicy salt, are worth the wait. ♦ Chinese/Seafood ♦ Daily 11:30AM-9:45PM. 679 N. Spring St. 628.6717

**17 Young Sing** ★$$ Located down the block from Mon Kee, this establishment also features the same tank-fresh seafood. It lacks the reputation of Mon Kee, and it also lacks the crowds. ♦ Chinese/Seafood ♦ Daily 11:30AM-1AM. 643 N. Spring St. 623.1724

**17 Dragon Inn Seafood** ★$ Prawns with lobster sauce and wok-charred oysters are seafood favorites in this budget-priced yet elegant restaurant. ♦ Chinese/Seafood ♦ M-F 10AM-9:30PM; Sa-Su 9AM-9:30PM. 700 N. Spring St. 617.2323

**18 ABC Seafood** ★★$$ Cantonese seafood is served in a bustling dining room. Dim sum are served for lunch, but the best choices are at dinner time: fresh crab, calamari, or your favorite fish in season. ♦ Cantonese/Seafood ♦ Daily 8AM-9:45PM. 708 New High St. 680.2887

**19 Thanh-Vi** ★★$ Some of the best Vietnamese food in LA is served in this raffish noodle bar, which might have been imported from Saigon. ♦ Vietnamese ♦ Daily 8AM-7PM. 422 Ord St. 687.3522

**20 Mandarin Deli** ★$ You've arrived in dumpling heaven: painless on the pocket but murder on the waistline. Everything is fresh. There are branches in Monterey Park and the San Fernando Valley, too. ♦ Chinese ♦ Daily 11AM-9PM. 727 N. Broadway. 623.6054

**20 Ocean Seafood Restaurant** ★★$$ Tasty dim sum and fresh fish from a tank are featured in the spacious upstairs dining room with contemporary Chinese decor. Try the dumplings, prawn dishes, or the pricier Peking duck that's carved at the tableside. ♦ Cantonese/Seafood ♦ Daily 8:30AM-10PM. 747 N. Broadway. 687.3088

**21 Fortune Seafood** ★$$ Delicious, original renditions of standard and exotic Cantonese dishes (don't miss the crab in garlicky black bean sauce) are served by unusually cheerful waiters in a spare room decorated with fish tanks. Fortune Seafood is run by a former manager of the Hop Li. ♦ Cantonese/Seafood ♦ Daily 11:30AM-1AM. 750 N. Hill St. 680.0640

**21 Green Jade** ★$$ They serve very spicy Hunanese cooking, so if you don't want a skin transplant on your throat, ask them to moderate the spices. Hot-and-sour soup and braised shrimp are highly recommended. ♦ Hunanese/Mandarin ♦ M-Th, Su 11:30AM-3PM, 4:30-9PM; F-Sa 11:30AM-3PM, 5-9:30PM. 750 N. Hill St. 680.1528

**22 Hop Li** ★$$ A good seafood place, this is one of the many founded by renegade chefs from Mon Kee. The food is similar to Mon Kee's—and less expensive. ♦ Chinese/Seafood ♦ Daily 11:30AM-10PM. 528 Alpine St. 680.3939

**23 Won Kok** ★$ This bustling Cantonese restaurant stays open and busy until the wee hours. Particularly fine after a night of carousing are their noodle dishes or a bowl of *jook,* a bland but wonderfully soothing thick rice porridge. ♦ Cantonese ♦ Daily 11:30AM-3AM. 208 Alpine St. 613.0700

**24 Yang Chow** ★$$ It's the Szechuan dishes that draw crowds to this rather tacky-looking restaurant. Special kudos go to pan-fried dumplings, *kung pao* chicken, spicy Szechuan beef, and slippery shrimp. ♦ Szechuan ♦ M-Th, Su 11:30AM-9:30PM; F-Sa 11:30AM-10:30PM. 819 N. Broadway. 625.0811

**25 Dragon Gate Inn** $$ This Best Western-affiliated lodge is strategically located in the heart of Chinatown. ♦ 818 N. Hill St. 617.3077, 800/528.1234

**26 Plum Tree Inn** ★$$ Peking duck and *kung pao* chicken are specialties of this stylish restaurant. ♦ Chinese ♦ M-Th, Su 11AM-11PM; F-Sa 11AM-1AM. 937 N. Hill St. 613.1819

**26 Foo Chow** ★$$ Distinctive dishes to taste at this restaurant include braised sea bass in red wine sauce, fried crab with a spicy bean sauce, and deep-fried oysters. ♦ Chinese ♦ M-Th, Su 11AM-11PM; F-Sa 11AM-1AM. 949 N. Hill St. 485.1294

**Downtown/Historic Core**

**26 Full House** ★$ A favorite of the late night crowd, the pan fried scallops in spicy Szechuan style make a peppery midnight snack. ♦ Chinese ♦ Daily 11:30AM-3AM. 963 N. Hill St. 617.8382.

**27 Empress Pavilion** ★$$ Cantonese and Szechuan specialties are served in this spacious second-story restaurant in the Bamboo Plaza. Take-out food is available. ♦ Chinese ♦ M-F 9AM-10PM; Sa-Su 8AM-10PM. 988 N. Hill St. 617.9898

**28 Chiu Chow** ★$$ The cuisine here is named after a section of Canton called, not surprisingly, Chiu Chow. The tastes are milder and more subtle than most Cantonese cooking. Try the duck or steamed chicken. ♦ Cantonese ♦ Daily 11AM-11PM. 935 Sun Mun Way. 628.0097

**29 Mandarin Shanghai** $ The contemporary cuisine is enhanced by an appealing neon wall sculpture in the dining room. ♦ Chinese ♦ Daily 11:30AM-3PM, 4-9:30PM; F-Sa 4-10:30PM. 970 N. Broadway #114. 625.1195

**29 Golden Plum** ★$ Check out this hot spot in terms of the crowds and the spices used in such dishes as Chinese cabbage, *kung pao* chicken, and meatballs. Bring plenty of beer. ♦ Szechuan ♦ M-Th, Su 11:30AM-2:30PM, 5-9:30PM; F-Sa 11:30AM-2:30PM, 5-10PM. 980 N. Broadway. 687.3238

**30 San Antonio Winery** This is a working winery in an old industrial section of town. The three-acre site includes tasting rooms, a restaurant, and the original buildings made from wooden boxcars in 1917. Italian sandwiches are the restaurant's specialty. ♦ M-Tu 9AM-6:30PM; W-Sa 9AM-7PM; Su 10AM-6PM. 737 Lamar St. 223.1401

**Restaurants/Clubs:** Red
**Shops/ 🌳 Outdoors:** Green

**Hotels:** Blue
**Sights/Culture:** Black

**15**

**31 Civic Center** LA has the second largest governmental center in the United States outside of Washington, DC, and it's pompous and lifeless. Look for a sign that says, "Abandon hope all ye who enter here." ◆ Bounded by Temple, Main, First, and Grand Sts

**Downtown/Historic Core**

**32 Hall of Records** Designed in 1962, this is one of **Richard Neutra's** last and slightest works. ◆ M-F 8AM-5PM. 320 W. Temple St. 974.6616

**33 Hall of Justice Building** The Municipal Court of the Los Angeles Judicial District, County of Los Angeles, and State of California are housed in this building designed by **Allied Architects** in 1925. ◆ M-F 8AM-5PM. 210 W. Temple St. 974.6141, 974.6143

**34 United States Federal Courthouse Building** The United States District Court is housed in this handsome WPA-style structure, designed by **Louis Simon & Gilbert Underwood**. ◆ 312 N. Spring St. 894.3650

**35 City Hall** The classic monument, designed by **Austin, Parkinson, Martin & Whittlesey** in 1928, is now undergoing a long overdue facelift by **Hardy Holzman Pfeiffer,** which may also bring back nighttime illumination. Until 1957 this was the only exception to the city's 13-story height limit. The stepped-back building (pictured above), with its pyramid-crowned tower, is crammed with historical references, but it is unmistakeably Jazz Age American in its brash self-confidence. Inside, luxurious marble columns and an inlaid tile dome give the public areas the feel of a cathedral—don't miss the Easter concert of Renaissance choral music, which exploits the rotunda's acoustics to dazzling effect. Another offbeat attraction is the holographic portrait of **Mayor Tom Bradley.** On a clear day you can see forever from the 27th-floor observation deck. A 45-minute escorted tour offers a capsule history of Los Angeles and California. Tours are by reservation only; call at least two weeks in advance. There are changing exhibitions in the **Bridge Gallery** weekdays from 8AM to 5PM. ◆ Free. Observation deck: M-F 8AM-1PM. 200 N. Spring St. 485.2121

**36 Los Angeles Children's Museum** Children and adults alike will enjoy this touch-and-play experience of exceptional quality. Changing exhibitions on the city's streets, African-American roots, and a kids' television station encourage participation. Classes and workshops are regularly scheduled; call the museum for current availability. Labels on the exhibitions are in Spanish and English. Weekday parking is available in the Los Angeles Mall garage. ◆ Admission; children under two free. W-Th 2-4PM; Sa-Su 10AM-5PM. Summer: M-F 11:30AM-5PM; Sa-Su 10AM-5PM. 310 N. Main St. 687.8800 (recording), 687.8801 (office)

**37 Parker Center** Named after a former chief of police, this is the headquarters of the Los Angeles Police Department. ◆ 150 N. Los Angeles St. 485.2121. Tours: 485.3281

**38 Los Angeles Times** Gordon Kaufmann designed this stodgy moderne block in 1935; the 1973 steel-and-glass addition is by **William Pereira & Associates**. A free tour allows you to see the making of the newspaper from press room to printing. Children must be 10 or over. Meet the guide at the First Street entrance. Also available is a tour of the Olympic Plant, their production facility, by reservation. ◆ Free. Tours: M-F 11:15AM, 3PM. 202 W. First St. 237.5757

**39 St. Vibiana's Cathedral** Another design by **Ezra F. Kysor,** this is the seat of the Archbishop of Los Angeles, **Cardinal Roger Mahoney.** The 1876 cathedral (pictured above) was modeled after a baroque church in Barcelona; the facade's pilasters and volutes are crowned with a tower and cupola. Inside, relics of the Early Christian martyr, St. Vibiana, are preserved in a marble sarcophagus. ◆ Daily 11:30AM-12:30PM. 114 E. Second St. 624.3941

The Brooklyn Dodgers baseball team moved to LA in 1957. More than 78,000 people flocked to the team's opening day doubleheader the following year, where the Dodgers beat the New York Yankees and the San Francisco Giants.

# Little Tokyo

This is the heart of Southern California's Japanese-American community of more than 200,000 people. It's bounded by First and Third streets from Main to Alameda streets, southeast of the Civic Center. First settled one hundred years ago, the community began to flourish after World War I, but was devastated by the forced evacuation of Japanese-Americans from the Pacific Coast during World War II. Little Tokyo has emerged in the past decade as an active and cohesive area, a mix of late 19th-century commercial buildings and modern structures. **"Nisei Week,"** held annually in August, is a major community event, with a parade, street dancing, festival food, and public demonstrations of such Japanese arts as flower arranging, *sumi* brush painting, and the traditional tea ceremony.

**40 New Otani Hotel** $$$ A symbol of the area's vigorous redevelopment since 1977, the hotel features American- and Japanese-style rooms. The "Japanese Experience" is a pricey but memorable night for two in a garden suite that has a sitting room with shoji screens, a Japanese bed, and a soaking tub, plus sauna, massage, and dinner in **A Thousand Cranes/Sen Bazuru.** A quality shopping arcade includes the **Kinokuniya Bookstore** (687.4480) for books on Japanese culture, and **Marukyo** (628.4369) for textiles, kimonos, and futons. In the center of the main lobby is the 24-hour **Rendezvous Lounge.** South of the hotel is a three-level shopping courtyard, whose primary appeal is to the local community. It gives access to a fourth-story Japanese garden, a haven of tranquility with a dramatic backdrop of new office towers. The **Genji Bar** at this level is a lovely place to watch twilight deepen. ♦ First St at Los Angeles St. 629.1200, 800/273.2294 (CA), 800/421.8795 (US/Canada); fax 622.0980

Within the New Otani Hotel:

**A Thousand Cranes/Sen Bazuru** ★★$$$ The stylish hotel restaurant overlooking the roof garden has separate rooms for sushi, tempura, and the teppan grill. The service is excellent. ♦ Japanese ♦ Daily 11:30AM-2PM, 6-10PM. 629.1200

**Azalea Restaurant and Bar** ★$$$ The hotel's American restaurant serves steak, seafood, and pasta. ♦ American ♦ Daily 24 hours. 629.1200

**41 Astronaut Ellison S. Onizuka Street** Formerly **Weller Court** and renamed to commemorate a member of the *Challenger* disaster, this is a handsome pedestrian precinct. The major tenant is **Matsuzakaya,** a branch of Japan's oldest department store. ♦ Off Weller St (at Second St)

On Astronaut Ellison S. Onizuka Street:

**Nanban-Tei** $$ They specialize in *yakitori*—savory barbecued meats and vegetables served on skewers. ♦ Japanese ♦ M-F 11:30AM-2PM, 6-9:30PM; Sa-Su 5:30-9PM. 620.8743

**42 Horikawa** ★★$$$ This is a favorite with Japanese businessmen for its sushi bar, teppanyaki grill, and handsome dining room. Horikawa's chef, **Tatsuo Tanaka,** worked for 14 years in one of the best *kaiseki* restaurants of Osaka, and he will prepare a 10-course *kaiseki* dinner or five-course lunch with two days' advance notice. Your group should ask for one of the teahouse rooms, where the decor is as

artfully calculated as each dish. ♦ Japanese ♦ M-Th 11:30AM-2PM, 6-10PM; F 11:30AM-2PM, 6-10:30PM; Sa 5:30-11PM; Su 5:30-9:30PM. 111 S. San Pedro St. 680.9355

**43 Tokyo Kaikan** ★$$ A re-creation of an old Japanese inn, this restaurant has an excellent sushi bar and teppan grill. ♦ Japanese ♦ M-F 11:30AM-2PM, 6-10:30PM; Sa 6-10:30PM. 225 S. San Pedro St. 489.1333

# The Raw Deal

If you already rave about raw fish, Little Tokyo—birthplace of the California sushi craze—will be your idea of *Hamachi* heaven. But novices who feel intimidated by such exotic dishes, much less the thought of eating with chopsticks, may want to prep a little before dinner. Try walking around the neighborhood and looking at the sushi displays—most of the Japanese restaurants set up plastic models of their meals. If these tingle your tastebuds but their foreign names leave you tongue-tied, you can always bring your waiter outside and point. To make ordering easier, here is a glossary of the most common sushi terms:

| | |
|---|---|
| Aji | Spanish mackerel |
| Akagai | Ark shell (red clam) |
| Amaebi | Sweet shrimp |
| Anago | Sea eel |
| Aoyagi | Round clam |
| Awabi | Abalone |
| California roll | Avocado and crab |
| Hamachi | Yellowtail |
| Hashira | Scallop |
| Hirami | Halibut |
| Ika | Squid |
| Ikura | Salmon eggs |
| Kaki | Oyster |
| Kani | King crab |
| Kappa maki | Cucumber roll |
| Kazunoko | Herring roe |
| Kohada | Gizzard shad |
| Maguro | Tuna |
| Masago | Smelt eggs |
| Mirugai | Geoduck (jumbo clam) |
| Nizasakana | Cooked fish |
| Saba | Mackerel |
| Sake | Salmon |
| Shako | Squilla |
| Tai | Red Snapper |
| Tako | Octopus |
| Tamago | Cooked egg |
| Tekka maki | Tuna roll |
| Toro | Fatty tuna (or tuna belly) |
| Umeshiso maki | Plum roll |
| Unagi | Freshwater eel |
| Uni | Sea urchin |
| Yakisakana | Broiled fish |

**17**

# Race, Rage, and the LA Riots

The multiracial harmony touted by LA's civic leaders was no more real than a movie set. In fact, what little harmony did exist went up in smoke on 29 April 1992

Downtown/Historic Core

in a maelstrom of violence. When four white Los Angeles police officers, who had been caught on videotape brutally beating black motorist Rodney King, were found not guilty of felony assault by a jury of almost all-white suburbanites, the news of the verdict spread like wildfire. Rage and frustration exploded in South-Central Los Angeles, unleashing violence that crossed all ethnic lines. For three days, LA became a war zone in the country's most deadly civil disturbance of the century.

There were 51 people killed and 2,383 injured, more than 1,200 buildings damaged or burned down, and thousands of businesses destroyed. Television viewers—transfixed by the horrifying images of the beatings, looting, and arson that were broadcast live—and the thousands of victims caught in the urban holocaust witnessed more than retribution.

It was revolt, social upheaval, anarchy, mass hysteria, and a moral breakdown exposed. Families with children were looting Kmart. Firefighters squelching flames were dodging bullets fired by angry passersby. The white officers' beating of King came full circle. Inner-city neglect, the widening gap between the rich and the poor, segregation, and the Los Angeles Police Department's reputation for civil abuses were laid bare in the rebellion that spread from South Central to Midtown to Hollywood.

In the aftermath, thousands of people gathered with mops and brooms and money to help clean up, but the task of rebuilding the city and establishing racial

harmony could take years, if not decades. Peter Ueberroth, former baseball commissioner and president and organizer of the 1984 LA Olympic Games, was chosen by Mayor Tom Bradley to head a "Rebuild LA" committee. The group of business and civic leaders plans to help revitalize the inner-city areas through economic development. Early strides include Vons Supermarkets' $100 million plan to build 12 grocery stores in South-Central Los Angeles, and General Motors' pledge to launch an $18 million program that includes moving a business to the area.

Tourism in LA—the second largest industry in the county—was also severely damaged by the unrest. Forecasters, who predicted a $1 billion loss in tourist dollars the first year after the riots, said tourism probably won't fully recover until 1996.

But while the rebuilding is slow, reform in the disheveled police department began on 28 June 1992, when the city's first black police chief, Willie L. Williams, took the helm. He replaced Daryl Gates, who many claimed poorly managed the King uproar, not to mention racial tensions that led up to the riots. Though most residents polled after the riots said they expect another outbreak of violence in a few years, many have set their sights on Williams, who has won high marks in the past for his brand of community-based policing. By the fall of 1992, Williams had begun to set his policies in motion, and more police officers are patrolling the riot-torn areas than ever before.

Establishing a safe environment and creating economic opportunities are paramount concerns to this region of LA, although they are just the beginning of what will be required to bring peace and harmony to the scorched neighborhoods. Some doubt that the racial tensions and anger will ever be completely eased in South-Central LA, but many leaders and residents have vowed never to stop trying.

---

**44 The Japanese American Cultural and Community Center** The center houses many cultural groups and activities and is a major resource for the entire city. Special events and displays are organized in conjunction with annual community festivals, including *Hanamatsuri* (birth of the Buddha) in early April, Children's Day in early May, *Obon* (Festival of the Dead) in June and July, *Nisei* in early August, and *Oshogatsu* (New Year's festivities). ♦ 244 S. San Pedro St. 628.2725

Within the Japanese American Cultural and Community Center:

**George J. Doizaki Gallery** This gallery features regular exhibitions of historical treasures and new art and graphics. They also sell posters and distinctive crafts. ♦ Tu-F 11AM-5PM; Sa-Su noon-4PM. 628.2725

**Franklin D. Murphy Library** Japanese magazines and books on Japan and Japanese-Americans are sold here. ♦ Tu-F noon-5PM; Sa 10AM-4PM. 628.2725

**Japan America Theater** The best in traditional and contemporary performing arts from

Japan, including the Grand Kabuki, Bugaku, and Noh dramas are presented here, plus Bunraku puppet theater and Western dance and chamber music. ♦ Box office: daily noon-5PM. 680.3700

**The JACCC Plaza** Designed by **Isamu Noguchi**, is the monumental rock sculpture in the plaza dedicated to the *Issei* (first generation of Japanese immigrants).

**James Irvine Garden** (*Seiryu-en* or Garden of the Clear Stream) This garden won the prestigious **National Landscape Award** in 1981. It is a fusion of the two cultures, a sunken green oasis for strolling and meditation. ♦ Call ahead for hours. 628.2725

**45 Rafu Bussan** An unusually large selection of lacquerware and ceramics is sold here. ♦ M-F 9:30AM-6PM; Sa-Su 10:30AM-6PM. 326 E 2nd St. 614.1181

**46 Japanese Village Plaza Mall** This shopping complex, constructed in 1979, uses white stucco with exposed wood framing to set off the blue sanchu tile roofs and incorporates a traditional fireman's lookout tower as

marker. Inset stone paths, rocks, and pools give a rural feeling. ♦ 335 E. Second St. Parking on Central Ave. 620.8861

Within the Japanese Village Plaza Mall:

**Yagura Ichiban** $$ Grilled snacks are served with drinks alongside a conventional dining room in this *robata* bar. ♦ Japanese ♦ Tu-F 11AM-2:30PM, 5-10:30PM; Sa-Su noon-11:30PM. 623.4141

**Naniwa Sushi** ★$$ This is one of the better sushi bars in the area. The dining room serves other Japanese dishes. ♦ Japanese ♦ Daily 11AM-10PM. 623.3661

**Oiwake** $$ This sushi bar with live *minyo*—Japanese country-and-western music—encourages customers to come up on stage and sing along with the band, which colors its songs with such instruments as Chinese bells and maracas. ♦ Japanese ♦ M, W-Su 5PM-2AM. 628.2628

**Hama Sushi** ★★$$ If it's great sushi you're yearning for, look no further. This place is crowded and full of beer and plenty of bantering between customers and sushi chefs. ♦ Japanese ♦ M-Sa noon-2PM, 5:30PM-midnight; Su 5:30-10:30PM. 680.3454

**47 Suehiro** $ Reliable teriyaki, tempura, and noodles for Little Tokyo denizens are dished up here. ♦ Japanese ♦ M-F 11AM-3AM; Sa-Su 11AM-1AM. 337 E. First St. 626.9132

**48 Japanese American National Museum** The new private facility is housed in the historic 1925 **Nishi Hongwanji Buddhist Temple** building designed by architect **Edgar Cline** in a mix of styles, including Japanese and Middle Eastern. The museum documents the Japanese experience in the United States through exhibitions in a 5,000-square-feet gallery and education and research. ♦ Admission. Tu-Th, Sa-Su 10AM-5PM; F 11AM-8PM. 119 N. Central Ave. 625.0414

**49 The Museum of Contemporary Art (MOCA) at the Temporary Contemporary (TC)** The transformation of two city-owned warehouses by architect **Frank Gehry** in 1983 was intended as a stop-gap while MOCA's new building was being readied, but the 55,000-square-foot loft space has now become a permanent facility, presenting some of the museum's most ambitious exhibitions. Highlights have included *Blueprints for Modern Living* (on the Case Study House program), *The Automobile and Culture*, and *Tokyo: Form and Spirit*. The building would be worth seeing without the art: Gehry has skillfully preserved the raw character of the interiors, adding a steel-and-chain-link canopy over the street to create an outdoor lobby. **Barbara Kruger's** mural enlivens the south front. The admission fee covers the TC and MOCA on Grand Avenue. Admission is free for members, children under 12, and on Thursday from 5PM to 8PM. There's

low cost parking and easy access from the **DASH** shuttle. The TC is temporarily closed to accommodate the First Street Plaza project and will reopen in spring 1994. ♦ Admission. Tu-W, F-Su 11AM-6PM; Th 11AM-8PM. 152 N. Central Ave. 626.6222

### Downtown/Historic Core

**50 Avery Services Corporation** Equip a restaurant or buy a single chef's pan at this discount emporium. ♦ M-F 8AM-5PM; Sa 9AM-2PM. 905 E. Second St (at Alameda St). 624.7832, 800/877.0905 (US)

**51 Yoro-no-Taki** ★$ Businesspeople crowd this wood-paneled room and down large quantities of sake and beer as they nibble on grilled fish, pickled vegetables, and *oden*, a fish cake stew. ♦ Japanese ♦ Daily 5PM-1AM. 432 E. Second St. 626.6055

**52 Hana Ichimonme** ★$ If you saw the movie *Tampopo*, you will know how seriously the Japanese take *ramen*, and here the noodles are fresh and carefully cooked, the broth rich and delicately spiced. ♦ Japanese ♦ Tu-Sa 11:30AM-9PM; Su 11:30AM-8:30PM. 333 S. Alameda St. 626.3514

**52 Shibucho** ★★$$ Don't miss this very good sushi bar on the fourth (restaurant) floor of **Little Tokyo Square,** a cavernous shopping center. ♦ Japanese ♦ M-Sa 11:30AM-2:30PM, 5:30-10:30PM; Su noon-8:30PM. 333 S. Alameda St. 626.1184

**52 Kappo Kyara** ★$$ *Kappo* is the Japanese equivalent of tapas: imaginative nibbles to accompany sake and beer. ♦ Japanese ♦ M-F 11:30AM-2PM, 6-10PM; Sa noon-2:30PM, 6-10:30PM; Su noon-8PM. 333 S. Alameda St. 626.5760

**52 Issenjoki** ★$$ This cozy, family run, antique-filled restaurant offers colorful specialties as well as fine salads, noodles at lunch, and *kushiyaki* (grilled kebabs) at dinner. ♦ Japanese ♦ Daily 11:30AM-3PM, 5:30-10:30PM. 333 S. Alameda St. 680.1703

**52 Karaoke Fantasy** Serious crooners who aspire to fame as lounge lizards come to this place on the second floor of Yaohan Plaza. ♦ M-Tu 11AM-midnight; W-Th, Su 11AM-2AM; F-Sa 11AM-3AM. 333 S. Alameda St. 620.1030

**53 Higashi Hongwangji Buddhist Temple** This traditional structure by **Kajima Associates** in 1976 was designed for the **Jodo Shinshu Sect**. A broad flight of stairs leads to the entrance; the blue-tile roof is protected by two golden dragons. ♦ 505 E. Third St. 626.4200

**54 Tasuki** ★★$$$ **Mashiko,** one of the top local sushi masters, presents fresh and flavorful sushi as well as other authentic and sometimes unusual dishes. In winter he serves *mushi sushi* (warmed sushi). ♦ Japanese ♦ M-F 11:30AM-2PM, 5:30-10PM; Sa 5:30-10PM. 416 Boyd St. 613.0141

# B. Downtown/Business and Financial

High-rise banks and corporate offices dominate a now-flattened **Bunker Hill** and a narrow corridor flanking the Harbor Freeway. Unlike the business and financial centers of many major US cities, the architecture in this part of downtown is generally undistinguished and little has been done to make the pedestrian feel welcome. It is a monument to local boosters who confuse growth with greatness. Massive urban redevelopment has obliterated neighborhoods and landmarks. The process began in the 1960s, and one of the latest installments, **California Plaza**, is only marginally better than what currently exists.

At the turn of the century, Bunker Hill was the most desirable residential neighborhood in the city, with its Victorian gingerbread mansions that look down on what was even then the city's business district. Over the years the neighborhood fell into disrepair. In 1959 the **Community Redevelopment Agency** proposed

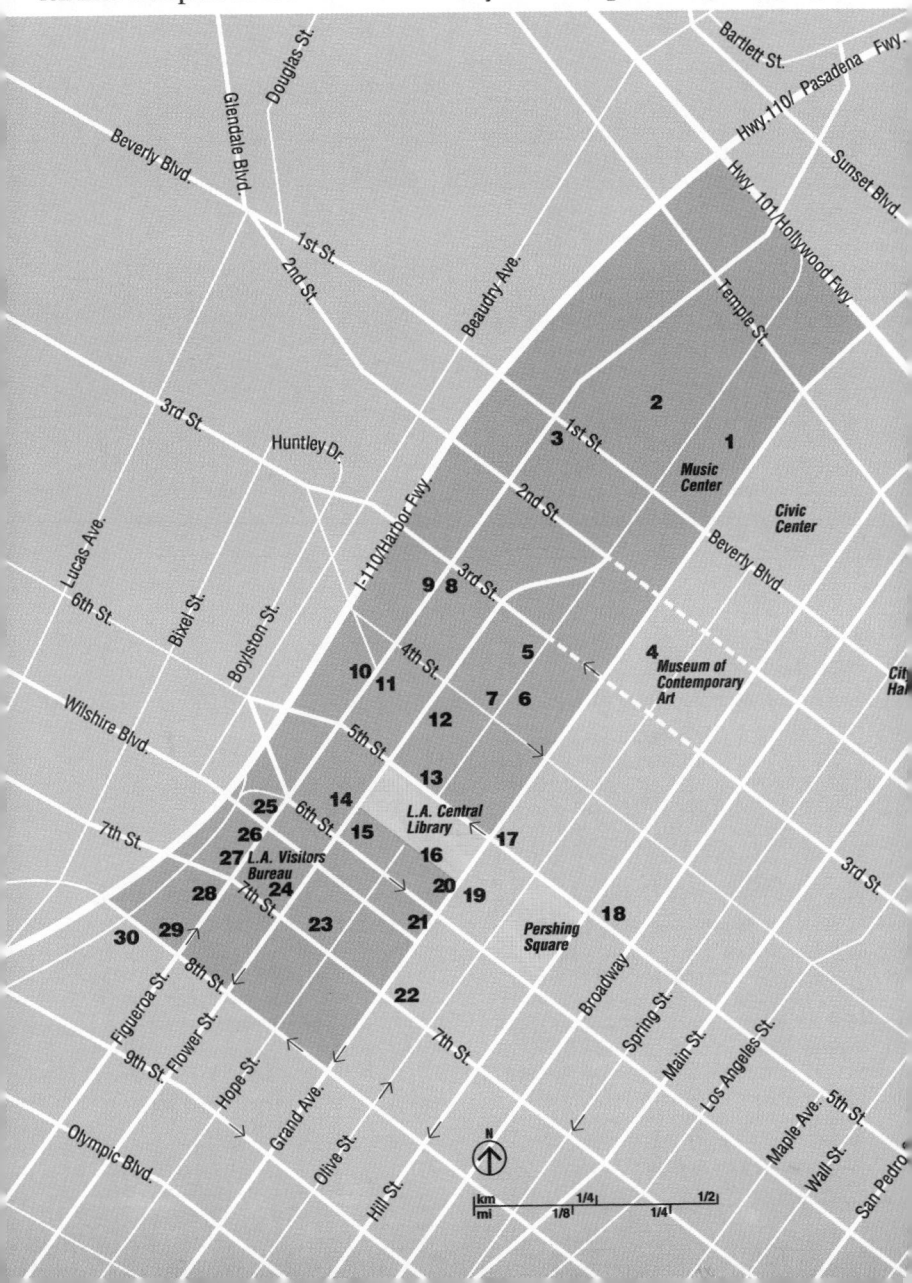

hat the dilapidated Victorian structures, many of which had been converted nto seedy boardinghouses, be demolished and the top of the hill be leveled (no hought of rehabilitation or adaptive reuse back then!). The resulting open space, plus the elimination in 1957 of the 13-story height limitation on buildings, en- iced several major corporations to relocate, thus creating the present cluster of leek towers.

**Flower Street** is the main avenue of this burgeoning financial district. The boom has been fueled by the widespread popularity of branch banking in Southern Cali- ornia and the emergence of Los Angeles as the American capital of the Pacific Rim. Of the six largest banks in California, four have built high-rise headquarters n LA, while the other two maintain their Southern California headquarters here. Overseas companies have invested heavily in downtown, too, for real estate in his area is a fraction of the cost of similar districts in Tokyo and Hong Kong.

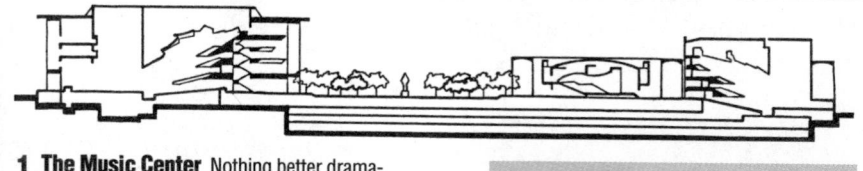

**1 The Music Center** Nothing better drama- tizes LA's growing sophistication in the visual arts than the plans for the 2,400-seat **Walt Disney Concert Hall**, a $200 million project scheduled to open in 1996. The original Music Center (pictured above) was designed in 1969 by LA's big corporate firm, **Welton Becket & Associates**—with no public debate—and is as life enhancing as a mausoleum. The new hall—future home of the **Los Angeles Philhar- monic**—was the subject of a widely publicized international architectural competition, won by architect **Frank Gehry.** The old center is defen- sive and bleak; the new Disney hall will look out to the street through waves of glass. Gehry radically changed his winning plan when To- kyo-based **Minoru Nagata** took over as acous- tic consultant. The new, more controversial design looks like a sculpture of curving and folding French limestone, with a concave cop- per roof and inward tilting walls. ♦ 135 N. Grand Ave (at First St). 972.7211

Within The Music Center:

**Dorothy Chandler Pavilion** When **Esa- Pekka Salonen** or a celebrated guest is con- ducting the **LA Philharmonic,** when the **LA Opera** is presenting one of its landmark pro- ductions, or when the **La Master Chorale** is at the top of its form, this big barn (see the plan at right) can be the most exciting place in the city. ♦ LA Philharmonic: 850.2000; LA Opera: 972.7211; La Master Chorale: 972.7211

**Mark Taper Forum** For 20 years **Gordon Davidson** has made this one of America's most adventurous theaters, beginning with a produc- tion of *The Devils,* which was denounced by **Cardinal McIntyre** and provoked a walk-out by **Governor Ronald Reagan**—as auspicious a send-off as being banned in Boston. Since then the Taper has offered more than 600 produc- tions, including *The Trial of the Catonsville Nine, Zoot Suit,* and *Children of a Lesser God.* The horseshoe-plan Taper, with its open stage (see the plan at right) is the only theater in the

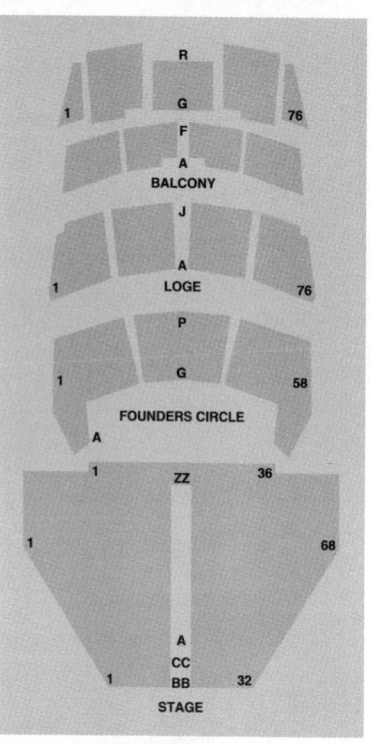

*Dorothy Chandler Pavilion*

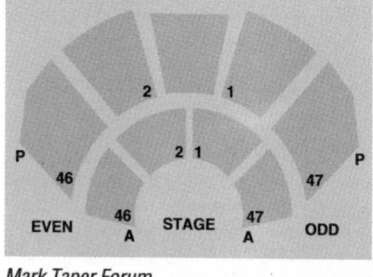

*Mark Taper Forum*

Music Center where you can see and hear well from every seat in the house. Readings and a literary cabaret are presented at the **Itchey Foot** restaurant down the street; experimental productions take place at the **Taper, Too** in the **John Anson Ford Theater** in Hollywood. ♦ 972.7211

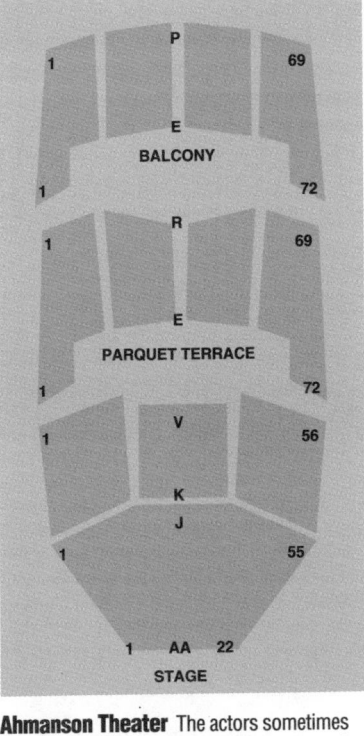

**Ahmanson Theater** The actors sometimes seem to be on a different planet than the audience in this cavernous playhouse (see the plan above). Unless you are a faithful subscriber or have lucked into good seats, you had best bring a telescope to see the stars. ♦ 972.7211
**Preconcert Dining** Within the Dorothy Chandler Pavilion, at street level, is the **Otto Rothschild Bar & Grill** (972.7322), offering moderately priced fare. On the fifth floor is the **Pavilion Restaurant** (972.7333), which offers elegant dining and a lavish buffet. It's a good place to know about if you've just won your case at the County Courthouse across the street.

Other choices for pretheater dining include **Chinatown, Little Tokyo,** and **Bernard's** in the Biltmore (612.1580). Three blocks south is the **Taipan** (626.6688), the **California Pizza Kitchen** (626.2616), **Stepps on the Court** (626.0900) in the **Wells Fargo Center,** and **Rex-II Restaurant** (627.2300) in the Oviatt Building.

The 1984 Summer Olympics, held in Los Angeles, were the most widely watched ever. At least 2,500 technicians, 56 cameras, 660 miles of cable, and 2 communications satellites brought the Olympics to more than 120 nations. About 187½ hours of Olympic events were televised, nearly two-and-a-half times as many as the Montreal Games in 1976.

**2 Department of Water and Power Building** West of the Music Center is the headquarters of the largest utility company in the United States. The glass-and-steel building, designed by **A.C. Martin & Associates** in 1964, is an elegant stack of horizontal planes that looks its best when lit up at night. ♦ 111 N. Hope St

**3 Bunker Hill Towers** These three high-rise blocks, designed by **Robert Alexander** in 1968, were the first residential structures on redeveloped Bunker Hill. ♦ 800 W. First St (between Second and Figueroa Sts)

**4 4 California Plaza** The last open area of Bunker Hill, this 11.5-acre site is being developed by **Bunker Hill Associates** in congruence to a master plan by **Arthur Erickson Architects.** So far, two slick-skinned office towers with curving walls of glass anchored by granite, a residential tower, a spiral amphitheater, a museum, and a 1.5-acre outdoor performance space and garden have been built. Soon to come are a restored version of the historic **Angel's Flight Railway** (the world's shortest railway, which chugs up a steep grade for only 335 feet between Hill and Olive streets), a Metro Rail station, shops, restaurants, and a hotel. Plans for a dance gallery were scrapped when promised donor money dried up. Architecturally, this is a stiff, conventional scheme that won a limited competition; the runner-up was a marvelously inventive collaboration by architects **Cesar Pelli, Charles Moore, Frank Gehry, Hardy Holzman Pfeiffer,** and others, backed by developer **Robert Maguire.** It would have "leavened the dough" of downtown LA. However, the city did insist that the developer pay for the new art museum. ♦ Between First and Third Sts

**4 Hotel Inter-Continental at California Plaza** This 17-story, 469-room hotel is designed to look residential in contemporary sandstone with neoclassical overtones. Amenities include a full-service health spa with lap pool, 24-hour room service, and two restaurants: the **Grand Cafe** and the **Angel's Flight Restaurant & Lounge.** ♦ At Second and Olive Sts. 617.3300

The Los Angeles Conservancy is a preservation group that has attracted widespread support and has helped combat LA's mania for destroying the best of its past. The organization's efforts saved the Sunset Tower (now known as the St. James's Club), the Wiltern Theater, and Engine Company No. 28. Members and visitors enjoy a lively program of tours and special events focusing on the city's architectural heritage and diverse neighborhoods. Weekly tours include 11 downtown areas and houses from different decades. For more information, call 213/623.CITY or write to 727 West Seventh Street, Suite 955, Los Angeles, CA 90017.

The first elevator in LA was installed more than one hundred years ago at the four-story Nadeau Hotel in downtown.

**Restaurants/Clubs:** Red  **Hotels:** Blue
**Shops/ ♣ Outdoors:** Green  **Sights/Culture:** Black

## 4 Museum of Contemporary Art (MOCA)

The 1986 building (illustrated below) is a dazzling fusion of Western geometry, clad in red sandstone with pyramidal skylights, and the Eastern tradition of solid and void. The first major United States building by Japan's leading architect, **Arata Isozaki,** it is also one of the city's finest. A sequence of luminous galleries with exposed vaults open off a sunken courtyard. Isozaki has even indulged his fascination with **Marilyn Monroe** in the sensuous curve of the parapet overlooking the courtyard.

Under the leadership of director **Richard Koshalek,** MOCA has come far in less than a decade, accumulating a major collection of international scope that includes the works of such artists as **Franz Kline, Claes Oldenburg, Louise Nevelson,** and **Mark Rothko,** and presenting some challenging exhibitions that are also displayed in the **Temporary Contemporary** (scheduled to reopen after renovation in 1994), a few blocks away in Little Tokyo.

In the courtyard is a well-stocked shop and the elegant **MOCA Cafe,** both designed by **Brent Saville.** Below the galleries is a steeply raked 162-seat auditorium used for film, video, and performing arts. Every Thursday night the museum stays open late. There is a bar, free hors d'oeuvres, and, in the summer, live entertainment in the courtyard. Artists, critics, and curators give informative tours of current exhibitions. Parking is available at First and Grand (lot 16) and the Music Center; rates in the garages below MOCA are astronomical on weekdays before 5PM. MOCA is also served by the **DASH** shuttle. ♦ Tu-W, F-Su 11AM-6PM; Th 11AM-8PM. 250 S. Grand Ave. 626.6222 (recording), 621.2766 (office)

*Museum of Contemporary Art*

## 5 Security Pacific National Bank Headquarters Building and Plaza

The well-detailed 55-story tower was designed in 1974 by **A.C. Martin & Associates.** It is set at an angle to the street and is anchored by the red **Alexander Calder** stabile outside the main entrance. Regular art shows take place in the main lobby. ♦ Gallery: daily 10AM-4:30PM. Building: daily 6AM-7PM. 345 S. Hope St. 345.6211

### Downtown/Business and Financial

## 6 Wells Fargo Center

The twin knife-edge towers clad in polished brown granite and tinted glass were designed by **Skidmore, Owings & Merrill** in 1983 and developed by **Maguire Thomas Partners**. Between the towers is **The Court,** an exciting glass-walled garden designed by **Lawrence Halprin,** with sculpture by **Jean Dubuffet, Joan Miró, Louise Nevelson,** and **Robert Graham.** More art, by contemporary Californians, is displayed in the upper-level **Court Cafeteria,** a popular lunch spot for office workers. ♦ 350 S. Hope St

Within Wells Fargo Center:

**Wells Fargo History Museum** From the company that helped civilize the West comes this museum, with a stagecoach, a two-pound gold nugget, plus photos and videos recalling 130 years of history. A **DASH** shuttle stops in front of the entrance. ♦ Free. M-F 9AM-5PM; weekends and evenings by appointment. 333 S. Grand Ave. 253.7166

RIK OLSON

23

**Pasqua** For downtown's working populace, Pasqua offers steaming Euro brew or local java to go for respite or rejuvenation. ♦ 330 S. Hope St. Also at: California Plaza; 300 S. Grand Ave; Civic Center Mall, 217 N. Hill St

**Stepps on the Court** ★★$$ An eclectic modern menu—including fresh shellfish, excellent pasta, and salads—is served in a cool, contem-

porary setting. It's a great resource for moderately priced lunches, drinks at one of the livelier downtown bars, and dinner before or after performances at the Music Center. Validated parking is available in the Wells Fargo Center. A free shuttle runs every 10 minutes, from 7PM to 10:30PM, to the Music Center. ♦ American ♦ M 11AM-3PM, 5-9:30PM; Tu-F 11AM-3PM, 5-11PM; Sa 4-11PM; Su 4-9:30PM. 626.0900

**Kachina** ★$ On a typical weekday, you'll find office workers lined up for lunch and a young crowd tossing back tequila shooters during happy hour. Designed by **David Kellen** with colorful sponge-painted walls, "concrete" tabletops, and high-tech lights, the space needs people to give it warmth. The enclosed patio looks to **Alexander Calder's** red stabile and the leafy plaza below. The Southwestern menu is devised by successful Orange County restaurateur **David Wilhelm.** Try the grilled salmon tucked in a corn husk, lamb chops with ranchera sauce and jalapeño jelly, and the stewed apple dessert crepe swathed in fresh caramel sauce. ♦ Southwestern ♦ M-Th 11AM-10PM; F 11AM-11PM; Sa 4-11PM. 625.0956

**Fountain Court** ★$ This calming courtyard cafe offers grilled sandwiches, cold poached salmon, and other light fare from Stepps' kitchen. ♦ American ♦ M-F 11:30AM-2PM. Dinner hours are usually reserved for banquets and receptions. 621.2155

**Taipan** ★$$ Their modern Mandarin cuisine includes orange-flavored beef and spicy Szechuan shredded pork. There's a full bar, too. **Taipan Express** is located in the Citadel shopping center in Commerce. ♦ Chinese ♦ Daily 11AM-9:30PM. 626.6688

**California Pizza Kitchen** ★$$ The friendly staff at this restaurant serves acclaimed designer pizza (topped with barbecued chicken or roasted garlic shrimp, for example), as well as the basic cheese and tomato. There's pasta, salad, and wine, too. Branches are located all over LA. ♦ California ♦ M-F 11AM-10PM; Sa noon-10PM; Su noon-9:30PM. 626.2616

**McDonald's** $ LAPD veteran **Don Bailey** has turned his franchise into a classy joint for the budget-conscious. There's no anguish here over who gets the power table, just telephone connections to every seat, fresh flowers, and a harpist or flutist to soothe executive stress at lunch on Thursday and Friday. Weight watchers can enjoy a chicken salad instead of the Big Mac and fries. Special events can be arranged. ♦ American ♦ M-F 5:30AM-10PM; Sa 7AM-7PM; Su 8AM-6PM. 626.0709

**7 Stuart M. Ketchum Downtown YMCA** This sleek coed facility features the latest equipment, an indoor lap pool, a running track, and squash and racquetball courts. Nonmembers pay a daily use fee. ♦ 401 S. Hope St. 624.2348

**8 World Trade Center** A pedestrian building is linked by bridges to the **Westin Bonaventure Hotel, Bunker Hill Towers,** and the **Sheraton Grande Hotel.** A passport office and currency exchange are located in its shopping arcade. ♦ 350 S. Figueroa St. 489.3337

**9 Sheraton Grande Hotel** $$$ This shiny luxury hotel offers an unusually refined level of service and interior design, including a lofty atrium lobby and duplex corner suites with huge windows. Complimentary limousine service to the Music Center and Beverly Hills is available. There is an informal restaurant, the **Back Porch,** as well as **Moody's,** a sophisticated bar. Next door is a cluster of four small **Laemmle** movie houses, showing the best new American and foreign films. ♦ 333 S. Figueroa St. 617.1133, 800/325.3535; fax 613.0291

Within the Sheraton Grande Hotel:

**Scarlatti** ★$$$ Complimentary limousine service to the Music Center is offered at this upscale Italian restaurant. Specialties include wine-braised fillet of beef and the sautéed rainbow trout with porcini and oyster mushrooms. ♦ Italian ♦ M-F 11:30AM-midnight; Sa-Su 3PM-midnight. 617.4546

**10 Original Sonora Cafe** ★★$$$ Located within the Union Bank building, this restaurant features stunning contemporary New Mexican decor with an exhibition kitchen. Chef **Felix Salcedo** prepares tasty Southwestern dishes (a lighter, more refined version of Mexican), which include goat cheese and leek quesadillas, duck tamales, and pasta with spicy shrimp. It's very busy at lunch and at the cocktail hour (order one of their nonslushy margaritas). ♦ Southwestern ♦ M 5:30-9PM; Tu-Sa 11AM-2:30PM, 5:30-10PM; F 11AM-2:30PM, 5:30PM-midnight; Su 5-9PM. 445 S. Figueroa St. 624.1800

The Los Angeles Philharmonic Orchestra was founded in 1919 by William Andrews Clark, Jr., who contributed $15 million to support the orchestra. The Los Angeles Philharmonic started out with 94 musicians, and ticket prices varied from 25¢ to $1.

On the television series "Superman," when Clark Kent was shown returning to the offices of the *Daily Planet* newspaper, he was actually entering LA's city hall.

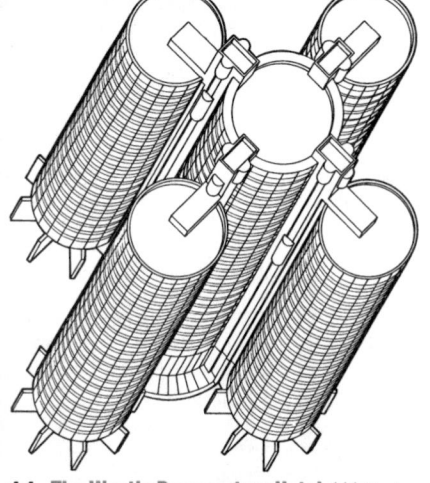

1990 by **Lawrence Halprin,** wrapped around the base of the First Interstate tower. Water cascades down from a fountain and restaurants open off terraces. The steps link Bunker Hill to Hope Street—the two vertically separated halves of the business district—and form part of a sequence of landscaped pedestrian areas that Halprin calls "choreography for the urban dance." To come are his **West Lawn of the Li-**

**brary** and **Hope Street Promenade** leading down to **Grand Hope Park.**

**11  The Westin Bonaventure Hotel** $$$ Buck Rogers beside the freeway best describes this 1976 **John Portman** design of five mirror-glass silos (pictured above) with glass-bubble elevators and a huge and fanciful atrium. The formula has exhausted its novelty. The hotel is thronged with conventioneers and business travelers who wander around trying to make sense of the eight levels of shops, fast food places, and restaurants. Among these, the revolving rooftop **Top of the Five** is notable for its 360-degree view. The lobby is located in the square base of the building, which can be entered from Flower or Figueroa streets. Guests receive complimentary membership in the adjoining **YMCA.** ♦ 404 S. Figueroa St. 624.1000, 800/228.3000; fax 612.4800

Within The Westin Bonaventure Hotel:

**Inagiku** ★★$$$ Dine in this elegant Japanese restaurant that specializes in tempura and has a teppan grill and handsome sushi bar as well. Tatami rooms are available by reservation. ♦ M-F 11:30AM-2PM; Sa-Su 5:30-10PM. Sixth floor. 614.0820

**12  444 S. Flower Building** This undistinguished corporate tower replaced the 1935 **Sunkist Building,** with its hanging gardens and statuary. Steps and escalators lead up from a palm-shaded plaza to an upper garden on Hope Street; along the way is a distinguished collection of modern art works by **Mark DiSuvero, Michael Heizer, Frank Stella, Bruce Nauman,** and **Robert Rauschenberg.** There's a pedestrian bridge over Flower Street to the **Bonaventure Hotel.** ♦ 444 S. Flower St

**13  First Interstate World Center** It's been called the tallest building in the West: a 1,017-foot, 73-story tower, designed in 1990 by **Pei, Cobb, Freed/Harold Fredenburg** and developed by **Maguire Thomas Partners.** The architects have achieved an interplay between orthogonal and circular geometries, which are revealed in the setbacks that lead up to a circular crown. ♦ 633 W. Fifth St

At First Interstate World Center:

**Bunker Hill Steps** Test your endurance by climbing this monumental stairway designed in

**14  Atlantic Richfield Plaza** To replace the 1929 **Richfield Building,** a flamboyant black-and-gold Art Deco tower, ARCO commissioned **A.C. Martin & Associates** in 1972 to design twin 52-story charcoal-gray shafts—the architectural equivalent of a sober business suit—to house its own expanded offices and the **Bank of America.**

Two 20-foot-high bronze doors from the old building are on display in the lobby of the south tower. On the plaza is a striking red helical sculpture, *Double Ascension,* by **Herbert Bayer,** who also designed the executive floors from the carpets on up. The escalators on Flower Street lead down to seven acres of subterranean shopping and eating, plus a church, fitness center, and post office. ♦ M-F 10AM-5:30PM; Sa 11AM-4PM. Flower St (between Fifth and Sixth Sts). 625.2132

Within the Atlantic Richfield Plaza:

**Chez François** ★★$$$ There's no view, but the contemporary cuisine is worth the descent into Atlantic Richfield Plaza. A standard like roast saddle of lamb with rosemary becomes a star when placed atop a fried-potato-and-watercress cake. A lunch menu for budget-conscious downtown workers is served at the bar. ♦ French ♦ M-F 7-10:30AM, 11:30AM-2:30PM. Level C. 680.2727

**15  The California Club** For years the city was effectively run by members of this private club. The Renaissance-style brick building, designed in 1930 by **Robert D. Farquar,** is still a bastion of power and old money. It's worth accepting an invitation; the food is surprisingly good. ♦ 538 S. Flower St. 622.1391

**16  Los Angeles Central Library** The building (pictured above), designed in 1930 by **Bertram Goodhue** and **Carleton Winslow, Sr.,** is one of the great landmarks of downtown. It was gutted by arson in April 1986 and is now being restored and extended. The design combines

Beaux Arts monumentality with touches of Byzantine, Egyptian, and Roman in the surface ornament and incised lettering. There's even a hint of Art Deco. Its interior murals, lawn, and multi-colored tiled pyramid peak enrich an increasingly bland neighborhood. Even before the fire, the library was threatened with destruction; it was saved by a transfer of air rights to neighboring plots, which permitted taller towers and a

$125-million contribution by the developer toward an expanded and improved library. **Hardy Holzman Pfeiffer** is currently designing new buildings that will double its capacity. Until their completion in fall 1993, the library is operating out of temporary premises at 433 S. Spring Street. ♦ 612.3200

**17 The Gas Company** Based on the plans of **Skidmore, Owings & Merrill/R. Keating, Designer,** and developed by **Maguire Thomas Partners,** this elegant dark gray and silver 62-story high rise of polished granite and tinted glass steps and tapers around a core of boat-shaped elliptical blue glass. The shape of the 1991 building is designed to resemble the blue gas flame that is now the official symbol of The Gas Company. The lobby, reached by an escalator on the steep site, faces a water garden and a 300-foot-high **Frank Stella** mural painted on the adjacent Pacific Bell/AT&T building. The colorful, abstract *Dusk* is part of Stella's *Moby Dick Series,* which explores motion and travel themes. ♦ 555 W. Fifth St

**17 One Bunker Hill** The former Southern California Edison building, built in 1931 by **Allison & Allison,** is a handsome Art Deco corner block with a lobby mural by **Hugo Ballin.** The building has been handsomely restored. ♦ S. Grand Ave at W. Fifth St

**18 Fountain Pen Shop** You'll find classic Waterman, Parker, and Mont Blanc models, plus gold and silver Montegrappas from Italy in this shop located on the eighth floor of the Metropolitan Building. ♦ M-F 8:30AM-12:30PM, 1:30-4PM. 315 W. Fifth St. 626.9387

**19 Caravan Book Store** This fine antiquarian bookseller specializes in California history and memorabilia. ♦ M-F 11AM-6PM; Sa 11AM-5PM. Also open by appointment. 550 S. Grand Ave. 626.9944

**19 Water Grill** ★★$$ This sophisticated fish house features 40 fresh fish or shellfish daily, not to mention that it's the only oyster bar downtown and it has the best crab cakes in LA. Chef **Matthew Stein** creates recipes according to the region where the fish is caught: trout fillets with Applewood smoked bacon, Southern pan-fried catfish, or seared rare big-eye tuna

with passion fruit broth. Located on the ground floor of the **Pacific Mutual Building,** the restaurant recalls urbane Art Deco with lots of warm-toned wood. Note the whimsical **Ann Field** murals and arty lighting by **Pam Morris.** ♦ Seafood ♦ M-Sa 11AM-10PM; Su 4:30-9PM. 544 S. Grand Ave. 891.0900

**20 Checkers Hotel** $$$$ This small, recently opened luxury hotel, a sister of the acclaimed **Campton Place** in San Francisco, was created within the shell of the **Mayflower**—itself a luxury hotel when it opened in 1927. The Checkers Hotel caters to those who want the best, need to stay downtown, but cannot stand the huge convention hostelries. The 190 guest rooms and suites are furnished in a traditional style with muted colors; niceties include a writing desk and marble bath. Every room has three telephones with multiline capability, and the hotel offers its guests a full range of electronic equipment, including personal fax machines, as well as 24-hour room service. There is a rooftop spa with a lap pool, several intimate meeting rooms, limousine service, and a multilingual staff to serve you. ♦ 535 S. Grand Ave. 624.0000, 800/628.4900; fax 626.9906

Within Checkers Hotel:

**Checkers Restaurant** ★★★★$$$$ The room is an oasis of elegance and calm, the service polished. Standout dishes include roast onion with pine-nut aioli, chanterelle soup, house-smoked salmon, and exceptional game and desserts. They have a fine California wine list. Chef **William Valentine's** breakfast menu is worth getting up early for. ♦ California ♦ Daily 6:30AM-10PM. 624.0000

**21 Casey's Bar** $$ This is the most popular after-work meeting place for young downtown office workers. Simple fare is served in a setting of white-tile floors, dark paneling, and tin ceilings ♦ American ♦ M-F 11AM-11PM. 613 S. Grand Ave. 629.2353

**22 Clifton's Silver Spoon Cafeteria** $ Occupying a turn-of-the-century building that once housed downtown's most prestigious jeweler, Clifton's is that rare thing: an elegant cafeteria. The **Meditation Room** in the basement offers food for thought. ♦ American ♦ M-Sa 7AM-3:30PM. 515 W. Seventh St. 485.1726

**23 The Broadway Plaza** The Broadway department store and 31 other shops are arranged around a skylit atrium. ♦ M-Th, Sa 10AM-6PM; F 10AM-7:30PM; Su noon-5PM. 700 W. Seventh St. The Broadway: 628.9311. Mall information: 624.2891

Within The Broadway Plaza:

**Hyatt Regency** $$$ This quality hotel is tastefully decorated. Ask for a room on the **Regency Floor**—it's well worth paying a little bit more. ♦ 711 S. Hope St. 683.1234, 800/223.1234; fax 629.3230

**23 Fowler Bros.** **Sieg Lindstrom** runs this century-old bookstore. Specialties include children's, travel, and foreign books, plus office supplies and stationery. ♦ M-F 9AM-5:30PM; Sa 9:30AM-5PM. 717 W. Seventh St. 627.7846

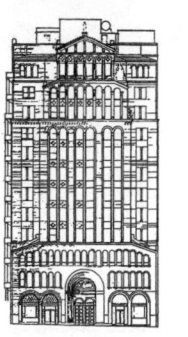

**24 Fine Arts Building** Designed by **Walker & Eisen** in 1925, this splendidly eclectic landmark (pictured above) was built as a complex of artists' studios enclosing an exhibition hall and was later converted to office space. Developers **Ratkovich and Bowers** commissioned **Brenda Levin & Associates** to restore the Romanesque facade and the high-ceilinged tiled lobby with its gargoyles, fountain, and fanciful murals, and to remodel its interiors. ♦ 811 W. Seventh St

**25 Sanwa Bank Plaza** Constructed in 1991 by **A.C. Martin & Associates,** the granite, glass, and bronze tower has the dull and dated look of a chunky block. But don't let this stop you from seeing where all the design time went. At its base, a 45-degree angled setback creates outdoor spaces that link the tower to the street. The interior screens flood two dramatic 80-foot-high lobbies with stripes of light, accenting granite and marble paving floors and walls. ♦ 601 S. Figueroa St

**26 Los Angeles Hilton and Towers** $$$ This huge hostelry is popular with business travelers. Amenities include three restaurants, a fitness center, and an outdoor pool. ♦ 930 Wilshire Blvd. 629.4321, 800/445.8667; fax 488.9869

Within the Los Angeles Hilton and Towers:

**City Grill** ★$$$ The Cobb salad is good at this very popular spot for business lunches. ♦ California ♦ M-F 11:30AM-2PM. 623.5971

**Cardini** ★★ $$$$ New York architects **Voorzanger and Mills** designed the stunning, beautifully lit postmodern interior in crisp tones of gray and blue. The space is divided by arches, columns, and open grilles to create a series of intimate enclosures. Standout dishes include an appetizer of thin slices of rare veal with an herb-laden sauce; black ravioli filled with shrimp, cream, and chives; and risotto with seafood and porcini mushrooms. ♦ Italian ♦ M-F 11:30AM-2PM, 5-10PM; Sa 5:30-10PM. 227.3464

**26 Engine Company No. 28** ★★$$$ This 1912 landmark firehouse has been reborn as a stylish traditional bar and grill. It's just the place to unwind with a cocktail and to enjoy comfort food at its best: Cobb salad, grilled fish, garlic chicken, and spicy french fries. The wine list is excellent. ♦ American ♦ M-F 11:15AM-9PM; Sa 5-9PM. 644 S. Figueroa St. 624.6996

**27 Los Angeles Visitor's Bureau** Maps, fliers, and advice on Southern California's attractions are available from a helpful and courteous staff who, at last count, were able to deliver it in English, Spanish, Japanese, French, German, Hungarian, and Portuguese. ♦ M-Sa 9AM-5PM. 685 S. Figueroa St. 689.8822

**28 Seventh Market Place** At the foot of **Citicorp Plaza,** three 42-story towers designed by **Skidmore, Owings & Merrill,** lies this urbane complex comprised of a sunken, palm-shaded

patio covered by **Peter Pearce's** 144-foot space-frame canopy, which is ringed with three levels of specialty stores, and **Bullock's** and **May Co.** department stores. Tenants include **Ann Taylor, Doubleday Books, Benetton,** and **Johnston and Murphy,** as well as services geared to local office workers. There's a choice of cafes and informal restaurants, or you can brown-bag it on a bench in the leafy, street-level plaza. **The Jerde Partnership** created this people-friendly space in a restrained neo-Victorian style. There's validated parking with a minimum purchase. ♦ M-F 10AM-7PM; Sa 10AM-6PM; Su noon-5PM (department stores and selected small shops). 735 S. Figueroa St. 955.7150

**29 777 Tower** Part of the Citicorp Plaza, this 53-story skyline standout (pictured at right), designed by **Cesar Pelli & Associates** in 1991 and developed by **Maguire Thomas Partners,** is a crisp profile of off-white metal luminous in sunlight. Indented corners, each with flared accents, emphasize its vertical height, curving form, and solidity. A three-story lobby is glass-walled on the east and south. A double-height colonnade faces the busy Seventh Market Place next door. ♦ 777 S. Figueroa St

**30 Metropolis** Due to civic controversy, the final construction date has not been scheduled for the $750 million, 6.5-acre "city within a city" mixed-use project that was proposed by **City Centre Development,** which calls for three 30-story towers, a cultural facility, a retail center, and a 500-room hotel. Architect **Michael Graves'** postmodern design shows colorful towers divided horizontally by bands of glazed ceramic tiles in shades of teal, ochre, and terra-cotta. Round three-story "party hats" cap the rectangular towers, octagonal pavilions overlook the Harbor Freeway, and the expansive terraces thrust out on the east and west from the 26th floor. ♦ Site located south of Eighth Street at Harbor Freeway

| Restaurants/Clubs: Red | Hotels: Blue |
| --- | --- |
| Shops/ 🌳 Outdoors: Green | Sights/Culture: Black |

# C. Downtown/Commercial and Exposition Park

This is an area of intriguing complexity. To the north are several shops and hotels; to the east commercial, wholesale, manufacturing, and distribution sites; and to the south, **Exposition Park** and the **University of Southern California (USC)** provide a green oasis amid treeless commercial streets and vintage but dilapidated housing. Most of the area around **Pershing Square**, which is the hub of the downtown business area, is active during regular business hours, but almost deserted at night. Near the **Coliseum** and the **Shrine Auditorium** (the site of such events as the Grammy Awards and the American Music Awards), nighttime traffic jams occur when football and concert fans collide. The streets of the wholesale distribution centers are quiet until after midnight, when hundreds of trucks fill the roadways. And in the early dawn hours, movie crews are likely to be anywhere downtown filming on the deserted streets.

**1 Oviatt Building** Designed in 1928 by **Walker & Eisen,** this was formerly an exclusive men's store, built for **James Oviatt,** who had fallen in love with Art Deco on buying trips to Paris. He commissioned the decorative glass from **Rene Lalique,** imported the furnishings from France, and lived in a marvelous zigzag penthouse. In 1976 the building was bought by developer **Wayne Ratkovich,** who hired architect **Brenda Levin** to restore its original glories and leased the upper floors as offices. You can rent the 13th-floor penthouse for catered parties of up to 50 and dance under the stars on the 1,500-square-foot rooftop. ♦ Olive St at Sixth St. 622.6096

Within the Oviatt Building:

**Rex-Il Ristorante** ★★★$$$$ Delicate portions of *nuova cucina* are served in owner Mauro Vincenti's imaginative re-creation of the 1930s luxury liner, the *Rex.* This is one of the most exquisite restaurants in the country. The original balconied room, with its dark polished wood and backlit Lalique glass, delights the eye, and chef **Odette Fada** dazzles the palate with marvelously full-flavored yet refined dishes that change with the season. The wine list is an education in Italian viniculture. And, for the price of a drink, you can sit in the stylish upstairs bar and dance on a tiny black marble floor as a pianist plays Cole Porter. ♦ Italian ♦ M-W, Sa 6-10PM; Th-F noon-2PM, 6-10PM. 617 S. Olive St. 627.2300

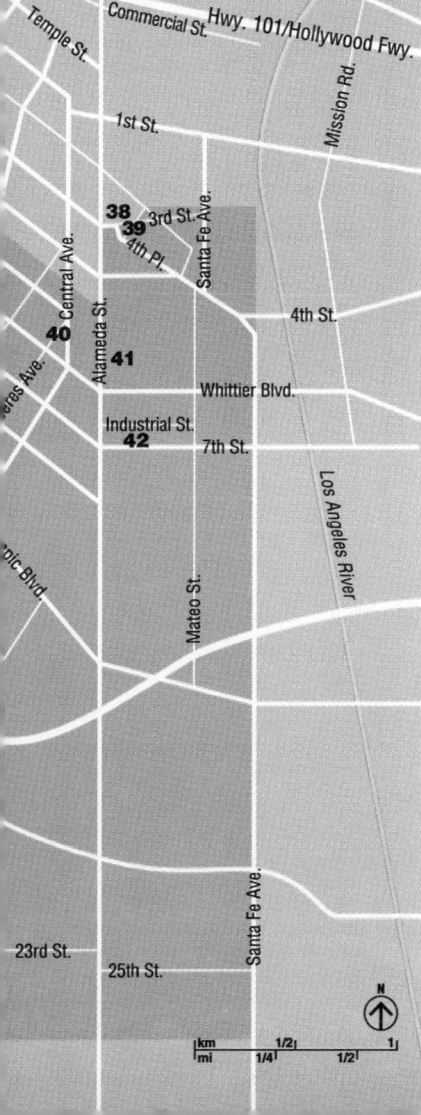

**2 The Biltmore Hotel** $$$ Recently restored at a cost of $40 million, this Italianate Beaux Arts structure (pictured above) was originally constructed in 1923 by **Schultze & Weaver.** It was long considered a social hub (movie industry leaders met here in 1927 to found the **Academy of Motion Picture Arts and Sciences**). The palatial decor of the public rooms has been refurbished and regilded by **A.T. Heinsbergen & Co**—which did the splendid Deco murals of the **Cognac Room** in the late 1930s. For the full effect, you should enter through the old portal on Olive Street, facing Pershing Square, and be dazzled by the soaring **Rendezvous Court** (which serves breakfast, tea, and cocktails accompanied by piano music). The new entrance turns its back on the square and is far less distinguished, and the recently added office tower is a postmodern horror. There are 700 traditionally furnished guest rooms and suites, all with **Jim Dine** prints. The **Presidential Suite** has a private elevator, the **Music Suite** a grand piano. Even those who hate health clubs should check out the music-free exercise rooms and sumptuous Roman bath. ♦ 506 S. Grand Ave. 624.1011, 800/245.8673 (CA); fax 612.1545

Within The Biltmore Hotel:

**Bernard's** ★★$$$$ Whether you come here for power lunches or romantic dinners, this is one of the loveliest restaurants in the city—a softly-lit, wood-paneled room with wide-spaced tables and 1920s silverware. The elegant modern menu makes inventive use of the freshest ingredients, especially fish. ♦ Continental ♦ M-F 11:30AM-2PM, 6-10PM; F 11:30AM-2PM, 6-10:30PM; Sa 6-10:30PM. 612.1580

**Grand Avenue Bar** ★$$$ Italian marble tables and plum-velvet **Mies van der Rohe** chairs, plus exotic plants and works of art that are changed seasonally, form an elegant setting for a delectable lunch buffet and for vintage wines that are served by the glass. There's evening jazz and a complimentary cocktail buffet, too. ♦ Eclectic ♦ M-F 11:30AM-10PM. 624.1011

## Downtown/Commercial and Expo Park

**Sai Sai** ★★★$$ Meals are served with artistry in this no-nonsense space frequented by Japanese businessmen and seekers of excellent, low-fat fare. Located in the basement of the hotel, this modern, spare restaurant has an elegant ambience. For private parties, there are five private dining rooms that are separated by opaque glass. Menu selections change weekly and seasonally to offer the freshest ingredients. Try the seafood salad, cold duck, or the *shabu shabu.* ♦ Japanese ♦ Daily 7AM-9AM, 11:30AM-2PM, 6-10PM. 624.1100

**3  Pershing Square SITE Projects,** the New York architects best known for their surreal Best Co. stores, won a 1986 competition with a proposal to transform Pershing Square into an undulating landscape, but the plan was rejected by neighboring property owners who said it lacked accessibility. Working with developer **Maguire Thomas Partners** and the **Community Redevelopment Agency,** the property owners instead hired Mexico City architect **Ricardo Legorreta,** chosen for his Hispanic roots, to design a new $14 million renovation plan with landscape architect **Hanna Olin.** The new design calls for a 125-foot sculpted campanile in a classic prismatic form flanked by two plazas: an amphitheater for public performances on the north, and a reflective pool (which will fill and empty like a tidal basin) on the south. Large shade trees and colorful kiosks are designed to bring pedestrians back to the park that was abandoned previously to drug dealers. The expected completion date is late this year. ♦ Bounded by Olive, Fifth, Hill, and Sixth Sts

**4  Jewelry Mart** This papery building does nothing for Pershing Square. More notable is a 1982 interactive neon art work, *Generators of the Cylinder,* by Canadian **Michael Hayden,** which runs the length of the facade. Pedestrians and passing vehicles determine the pattern of flashing lights. The old jewelry district, offering highly competitive prices, extends a block south on Hill Street between Sixth and Seventh streets. ♦ 550 S. Hill St

**5  Title Guarantee & Trust Building** John & Donald Parkinson's 1930 romanticized skyscraper with a Gothic crown and zigzag details on the facade and in the lobby is designated as a future entry for **Metro Rail.** ♦ 401 W. Fifth St

**6  Tuttopasta** ★$ **Jacques Jordan** operates this no-frills trattoria in an old subway building. The menu is a carbo junkie's fantasy, with stick-to-the-ribs pastas and several other options.

American breakfasts and Italian lunches are also served. The same owners recently opene **Bellapasta,** a promising upscale annex with refreshing outdoor seating at 865 S. Figueroa Street. ♦ Italian/American ♦ M-F 7AM-2:30PM 417 S. Hill St. 621.2625

**7  Kawada Hotel** $ Hidden on an undesirable stretch of downtown, the new 116-room hotel built in the shell of a once dilapidated 1920s brick building has the quaint exterior characte of original fire escapes and flower boxes. The interior is contemporary economy, with incred ibly reasonable room rates for downtown. ♦ 200 S. Hill St. 621.4455. 800/752.9232; fax 687.4455

Within the Kawada Hotel:

**Epicentre** ★$ This corner restaurant is a surprise hit with its trendy, eclectic interior de cor by **Janise Cooper & Associates.** The three level dining room with arty hanging lamps makes this busy lunch spot both spacious an intimate. Chef **Mike Olmeda,** formerly of **Sonora Cafe** and **Perinos,** offers everything from seafood quesadillas to New York steak. Try the pasta salad with grilled breast of free-range chicken ♦ California ♦ M-F 6:30AM-7:30PM; Sa 5-7:30PM. 625.0000

**8  Grand Central Public Market** Don't miss this indoor bazaar, frenzied and picturesque, extending from Broadway to Hill streets. **Ira Yellin**—a developer with the vision to see Broadway's potential—commissioned **Brenda Levin** to undertake a major restoration. The 4 stalls sell all types of food, and ready-made Mexican specialties are available for on-premises eating. Plastic wrap is unknown here—butchers use waxed paper—and fruit and veg etable vendors select your produce from beautiful piles (don't help yourself) and browr bag it. If you're hungry, try homemade *gordit* meat-and-bean-filled corn pockets, at **Ana Maria's.** Thirsty? **LA Hood's Juice Bar** serves more than 26 fresh-squeezed juices. Some stalls, such as **China Cafe** and **Leaders Foods** have been around since the 1930s. If you're re ally overwhelmed, have your blood pressure checked at the **Health Food** counter. ♦ M-Sa 9AM-6PM; Su 10AM-5PM. 317 S. Broadway. 624.2378

**9  Broadway** Considered the main shopping street for Los Angeles' Hispanic community, Broadway's crowded sidewalks, exotic sounds and smells give it an intensely urban quality—much like Upper Broadway in New York, or even Mexico City. But changing tastes, neglect and the crassest kind of speculative greed threaten the architectural legacy of the prewar years when this was LA's "Great White Way."

Facades have been covered in plastic signs, terrazzo sidewalk ornament is cracked and filthy, and, worst of all, the upper stories of several buildings have been lopped off to reduce tax assessments. A few of its monuments have been secured, but the rest of Broadway is in urgent need of enlightened intervention; enjoy its riches while you can.

**9 Bradbury Building** LA's most extraordinary interior (pictured above) is a Victorian treasure that was, in its time, futuristic. It was designed in 1893 by architectural draftsman **George Wyman**, who was inspired by a message from his dead brother, received via a Ouija board. Behind the plain brick facade is a skylit interior court that is a marvel of dark foliate grillwork, tiled stairs, polished wood, marble, and open-cage elevators. It was used to memorable effect in the movie *Blade Runner* (itself a vision of the future). Only the lobby level is open to the public. ♦ M-F 9AM-5PM. 304 S. Broadway. 626.1893

**10 Spring Street** What was once called the "Wall Street of the West" is slowly coming back from a long period of neglect. This **National Register Historical District** showcases a treasury of buildings from the first three decades of the century. Many have been imaginatively recycled; new structures, including the huge **Ronald Reagan State Office Building** between Third and Fourth streets, are being added. An **LA Conservancy** flier is a useful guide.

**10 Banco Popolar** A German immigrant commissioned this Beaux Arts tower in 1903, then considered the city's finest office building. Notice the fine ornament and marble lobby with a stained-glass dome. ♦ 354 S. Spring St

**11 Continental Building** At 175 feet high, this was LA's first skyscraper—an ornate pile designed by **John Parkinson** in 1904, who also designed 17 other surviving buildings on the street. ♦ 408 S. Spring St

**12 Central Library** Pending completion of its new home in 1993, the library has made a wide selection of books available to the public on six floors of the 1928 **Design Center**, with its wonderful zigzag lobby and facade. (The building also houses the offices of the **Los Angeles Conservancy** and the famed **Aman Folk Dance Ensemble**.) ♦ M-F 10AM-8PM; Sa 10AM-5:30PM. 433 S. Spring St

### Downtown/Commercial and Expo Park

**13 The Alexandria Hotel** $$ The best hotel in the city when it opened in 1906, the Alexandria has welcomed **Theodore Roosevelt, Enrico Caruso, Sarah Bernhardt,** and the first generation of moviemakers. The interior has been remodeled, and the stained-glass ceiling of the **Palm Court**, opening off the lobby, has been nicely restored. ♦ 501 S. Spring St. 626.7484; fax 624.5719

**13 Broadway Spring Arcade** An Australian company turned this enormous skylit space linking Broadway and Spring streets into a three-level shopping arcade. The 1923 Spanish Renaissance office block is being renovated. ♦ 542 S. Broadway

**14 Los Angeles Theatre Center** Originally a bank designed in 1916 by **John Parkinson,** this building was dramatically remodeled and expanded by **John Sergio Fisher and Associates** into a complex of four small, steeply raked theaters leading out of the original banking hall. The **Tom Bradley Theater** has an open stage; **Theater 2** has a proscenium; **Theater 3** has a thrust stage; and **Theater 4** is a black box with flexible seating. The center is a startling combination of classical and high-tech details. Failing to garner broader public following and patronage, the center has ceased presenting its own productions and now leases performance space to independent theater companies. ♦ 514 S. Spring St. 627.6500

**15 Finney's Cafeteria** Ernest Batchelder's Craftsman tiles ornament the interior of this 1914 building. ♦ 217 W. Sixth St

**16 Story Building & Garage** Morgan, Walls & Clements designed the 1916 Beaux Arts tower faced in white terra-cotta, with superb zigzag garage gates. The garage was designed by **Clement Stiles** in 1934. ♦ Broadway at Sixth St

**16 Clifton's Brookdale Cafeteria** $ You'll find a redwood forest interior with a waterfall and stuffed moose at this restaurant. On the sidewalk are early 1930s terrazzo roundels of city landmarks. ♦ American ♦ Daily 7AM-7PM. 648 S. Broadway. 627.1673

**17 Spring Street Towers** Schultze & Weaver's handsome 1924 Beaux Arts bank has been recycled as offices, though the exterior has changed little. ♦ 117 W. Seventh St

**18 Cole's Buffet** $ A bargain favorite of LA's work force for years, this local hangout serves corned beef, roast beef, pastrami, and French dip sandwiches. ♦ American ♦ Daily 9AM-midnight. 118 E. Sixth St. 622.4090

Restaurants/Clubs: Red    Hotels: Blue
Shops/ ♣ Outdoors: Green    Sights/Culture: Black

**19 Wholesale Flower Market** Like the Wholesale Produce Market (see page 34), the action here begins at 3AM. The **American Floral Exchange** at 766 Wall Street and the **Growers' Wholesale Terminal** at 766 Wall Street are huge halls of flowers reflecting the seasons that Southern California doesn't have. Wholesalers are willing to sell a box to anyone, and Wall Street is lined with smaller merchants who of-

Downtown/Commercial and Expo Park

fer potted plants to the public at substantial discounts. The best bargains are to be had after 9AM and on Saturday mornings, when traders are clearing their stocks for the weekend. ♦ M, W, F 2AM; Tu, Th 4AM; Sa 6AM. Wall St (between Seventh and Eighth Sts). 622.1966

**20 Gorky's** $ Help yourself to hearty Russian fare—borscht and blinis, chicken with kasha, and piroshki—and home-brewed beer, or come late for live jazz, folk music, and comedy at this lively artists' hangout. ♦ Russian ♦ M-Tu 6:30AM-10PM; W-Th 6:30AM-11PM; F-Sa 6:30AM-1AM; Su 9AM-9PM. 536 E. Eighth St. 627.4060

**21 Garment District** Los Angeles has been a major center for garment manufacturing since the 1930s. First gaining fame for women's sportswear (Cole of California, Catalina, and Rose Marie Reid transformed the nation's beaches), the current products fit everyone. Jobbers and discount stores offering bargains on everything from children's wear to leather coats line Los Angeles Street from Seventh Street down to Washington Boulevard. A good concentration of retail bargains in women's wear is to be found in the **Cooper Building** (860 S. Los Angeles Street, 622.1139). Located on the second floor is **Fantastic Sportswear** (627.4536) with great buys on Norma Kamali, Anne Klein, and other top labels. Across the street is **Academy Award Clothes** (811 S. Los Angeles Street, 622.9125), with good prices on a huge selection of quality men's suits and formal wear and courteous service. ♦ Bounded by Seventh St, Venice Blvd, Broadway, and San Pedro St

**22 Sam's Fine Foods** $ The good Greek salad and walnut cake will revive flagging energy. ♦ American/Deli ♦ M-Sa 6:30AM-4:30PM. 121 E. Ninth St. 627.5733

**23 The California Mart** The southwest corner of Ninth and Los Angeles streets houses apparel designers' manufacturers' showrooms and independent representatives, open to the trade only. It's open to the public one weekend of every month. Call ahead for the schedule. ♦ 110 E. Ninth St. 239.9512

**24 849** Formerly the **Eastern Columbia**, constructed in 1929 by **Claude Beelman**, this is downtown's finest Art Deco building since the Richfield Tower was razed. The 13-story tower faced in turquoise terra-cotta with dark-blue-and-gold trim and ornamented with oddly twisted zigzag moldings is now a wholesale

apparel center. The **International Food Court is** open weekdays for breakfast and lunch. ♦ 849 S. Broadway.

**25 Concrete Jungle. . .A Florist** Their unique and distinctive floral creations are delivered throughout Los Angeles. ♦ M-Sa 9AM-6PM. 740 S. Olive St. 689.9999; fax: 689.0123. Also at: Citicorp Plaza, 735 S. Figueroa. 955.7437

**26 Gill's Cuisine of India** ★$ The luncheon buffet includes good curries and Tandoori specialties. For dinner, don't miss the lamb *Biajia* (with onions) and *aloo gobhi masala,* a tasty vegetarian dish of spicy cauliflower and potatoes. ♦ Indian ♦ M-Th 11AM-2:30PM, 5:30-9:30PM; F-Sa 11:30AM-2:30PM, 6-10PM. 838 Grand Ave. 623.1050

**27 Embassy Auditorium** This concert hall with graceful balconies and stained-glass dome is available for rent. (The LA Chamber Orchestra now plays at the Japan-America Theater.) ♦ 851 S. Grand Ave. 891.2988

**28 Grand Hope Park** The two-acre park designed by **Lawrence Halprin** comprises a series of outdoor rooms created by trellises, a fountain, a clock tower, and trees, and enhanced by the work of leading local artists. It will be the hub of the planned South Park development, a residential/commercial/office neighborhood bounded by the Santa Monica and Harbor freeways, and Eighth and Main Streets. Soon to come is a landscaped promenade along S. Hope Street that will link the park with Bunker Hill Steps and the renovated library. ♦ Ninth St at Hope St

**28 Fashion Institute of Design and Merchandising** The **Jerde Partnership's** characteristically eclectic 1990 design comprises a four-story arcade and terrace overlooking Grand Hope Park. The complex (pictured above) houses a fashion museum and gallery, shops, video production facilities, classrooms, and offices. ♦ Ninth St at Hope St

**29 Country Life** ★$ Run by the Seventh Day Adventists, this vegetarian restaurant-cum-health food store is located in a cavernous but rather antiseptic basement. There's a lovely fruit and vegetable salad bar, but it's the creative, spicy dishes that shine. ♦ Vegetarian ♦ M-Th 11:30AM-3PM; F 11:30AM-2:30PM. 888 S. Figueroa St. 489.4118

**30 The Original Pantry** ★$ Steaks, coleslaw, sourdough bread, and the best hash browns in town are made here in this 1924 restaurant. They never close, not even to redecorate. Next

door is the Pantry's **Bake & Sandwich Shoppe,** which serves just what the name promises daily from 6AM to 8:30PM. ♦ American ♦ Daily 24 hours. 877 S. Figueroa St. 972.9279

**31 Figueroa Hotel** $$ This hotel has a superb location near the Los Angeles Convention Center. Amenities include an enormous swimming pool and a cafe, which is open from 6AM to 11PM. ♦ 939 S. Figueroa St. 627.8971, 800/421.9092; fax 689.0305

**32 Olympic Camera** A large stock of cameras, tripods, bags, and film issued at discount prices is sold. ♦ 828 W. Olympic Blvd. M-Sa 9:30AM-5:30PM. 746.0575

**33 Holiday Inn Los Angeles Convention Center** $$ This hotel is convenient to the commercial center of downtown and popular with business travelers. ♦ 1020 S. Figueroa St. 748.1291; fax 748.6028

**34 Los Angeles Convention Center** The municipal facility is being tripled in size, to 810,000 square feet, to lure major conventions, trade shows, and public events. Twin 155-foot-high glass-and-steel lobby pavilions will mark the $287 million project designed by **Gruen Associates/Pei Cobb Freed & Partners** on a 63-acre site. The addition will form a massive curve of light-refracting blue-green glass immediately north of the heavily traveled intersection of the Santa Monica and Harbor freeways. A four-acre open plaza named for late city councilman **Gilbert W. Lindsay** will front Figueroa Street. As part of the Art-in-Architecture program, more than 60,000 feet of artist **Alexis Smith's** terrazzo designs will pave floors, including a world map design featuring medallions derived from early Pacific Rim cultures. The center is expected to open in late 1993. ♦ Bounded by Venice Blvd and 11th and Figueroa Sts. 741.1151

**35 Transamerica Center** This 32-story commercial structure has an observation deck. ♦ Free. M-F 10AM-4PM. 1150 S. Olive St. 742.2111

Within the Transamerica Center:

**The Tower Restaurant** ★$$$$ If you're looking for a high-powered meal, this restaurant offers expense-account dining with good service and a stunning view. The chef, **Axel Dikkers,** is formerly of the **Regency Club** and **Camelions.** ♦ California ♦ M-Th 11:30AM-2:30PM, 5:30-10PM; F-Sa 5:30-11PM. 1150 S. Olive St. 746.1554

**36 Herald Examiner Building** **Julia Morgan,** the first woman trained at the Ecole des Beaux Arts in Paris and the designer of Hearst's San Simeon castle, created this Spanish Mission Revival design (illustrated above) in 1912, inspired by the California Building from the 1893 Chicago World's Fair. The newspaper is now defunct and the building faces an uncertain future. ♦ 1111 S. Broadway

**37 Mayan** An upscale nightclub now occupies what was once the **Mayan Theater,** built in 1927 by **Morgan, Walls & Clements.** The auditorium, which opened with a Gershwin revue and then was long relegated to porn, now contains a two-level dance floor and bar. The **Mayan Lounge** draws stars and top models. Warrior priests glare from the facade; inside is looming statuary and a riot of ornament inspired by a newly excavated Mayan tomb (much as King Tut's launched a fad for ancient Egypt in the early 1920s). Next door is another theater by the same architects, the **Belasco,** now available for rental. Across the street is **Tony's Burger,** a 1932 log cabin, and presiding over the parking lot is **Kent Twitchell's** 70-foot mural of **Ed Ruscha**—just a few of LA's surreal juxtapositions. ♦ Business hours: daily 9AM-5PM. Nightclub: daily 9PM-4AM. 1038 S. Hill St. 746.4287

**38 Cafe Vignes** ★$$ The stylish, industrial chic setting is for a menu of soups, salads, and steamed entrées. ♦ California ♦ M-F 11AM-7PM. 923 E. Third St. 687.9709

**38 Museum of Neon Art (MONA)** Neon artist and graphic designer **Lili Lakich** turned her loft into one of LA's most vibrant small museums, dedicated to the exhibition and preservation of neon, electric, and kinetic art. Vintage signs are exhibited alongside new work by artists and students. There are regular classes and special events for members, and gifts and publications for sale. Note: The MONA will be moving to Citywalk at Universal Studios sometime this year. Please call ahead for hours and location information. ♦ Admission fee for nonmembers over 16. 617.1580 (recording)

At Twentieth Century Fox, Rock Hudson's screen test was so bad it was shown to other aspiring actors as an example of how not to perform in front of the camera.

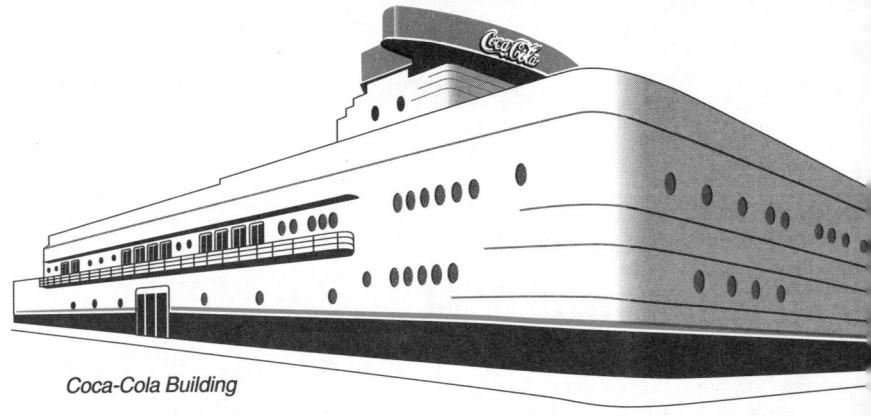

*Coca-Cola Building*

**39 Al's Bar** This crowded, smoky, and raw-edged Bohemian hangout specializes in underground music, performance art, and theater. ♦ M-F 6PM-2AM; Sa-Su 2PM-2AM. 305 S. Hewitt St. 687.3558; 625.9703

**40 American Fish & Seafood Company** Chefs shop this market, which sells to the public at wholesale prices. ♦ M-F 7AM-3PM; Sa 7-11AM. 550 Ceres St. 612.0350

**40 The Fisherman's Outlet** ★$ You can buy fish to take home at this retail and wholesale establishment, or eat at outdoor tables. There are a dozen varieties to choose from, in large portions at rock-bottom prices—broiled, deep-fried, or Cajun-style. ♦ Seafood ♦ M-Sa 10AM-3:30PM. 529 S. Central Ave. 627.7231

**41 Cirrus** Contemporary paintings and fine art prints by Southern Californian artists are showcased. ♦ Tu-Sa 11AM-5PM. 542 S. Alameda St. 680.3473

**42 Los Angeles Contemporary Exhibitions (LACE)** An annual St. Valentine's Day extravaganza was founded by this downtown art space, which provides diverse gallery and community art programs. Since 1977 LACE has presented significant video and audio pieces; performance, music, and installation pieces; and sculpture, drawings, and paintings by emerging and well-known regional and nonregional artists. This nonprofit interdisciplinary arts organization operates an art periodical bookstore for the public. ♦ W-F 11AM-5PM; Sa-Su noon-5PM. 1804 Industrial St (between Sixth and Seventh Sts). 624.5650; fax 624.6679

**43 Wholesale Produce Market** A cornucopia of produce, sold by the lug or the bushel only, is available every weekday from 3AM to noon. The market has two main sections: **Produce Court,** off Ninth Street just west of Central Avenue; and **Merchants Street,** off Eighth Street just west of Central Avenue. ♦ Off Eighth St

**43 Vickman's** $ This cafeteria-counter restaurant has been satisfying trenchermen's appetites at bargain prices since 1930. Baked goods are made fresh on the premises. ♦ American ♦ M-F 3AM-3PM; Sa 3AM-1PM; Su 7AM-1PM. 1228 E. Eighth St. 622.3852

**44 Coca-Cola Building** In 1937 **Robert V. Derra** designed five plain industrial buildings disguise as an ocean liner (pictured above). The streamlined forms, hatch covers, portholes, and flying bridge bring a little salt air to the land of asphal Inset at the corners are two enormous Coke bottles. ♦ 1334 S. Central Ave

**45 Second Baptist Church** Paul Williams' 192 Lombardian Romanesque church serves as a center for African-American community activiti ♦ 2412 Griffith Ave. 748.0318

**46 Stimson House** Originally designed in 1891 f prominent lumberman **Douglas Stimson,** the Queen Anne-style house has a tower and a num ber of medieval fortresslike details. It's now oc pied by the **Convent of the Infant of Prague** an not open to the public. ♦ 2421 S. Figueroa St

**46 The Inn at 657** $$ The 1930s apartment hou with bay windows was transplanted to this site near USC and renovated as a bed-and-breakfas inn. Like a middle-class home away from hom the inn has five suites with kitchens, stocked fridges, and a hodgepodge of residential furniture. Unfortunately, the surrounding area can g noisy. Amenities include made-to-order breakfasts, down comforters, and a lush fern garden with a hot tub. ♦ 657 W. 23rd St. 741.2200; 800.347.7512

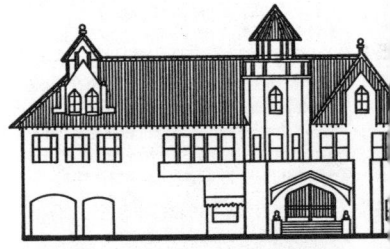

**47 Doheny Mansion and Chester Place** Thir teen grand and expensive houses were built he at the turn of the century on one block of a 15-acre residential park. The Doheny Mansion (pi tured above) is considered the finest structure the block. It was designed by **Theodore Eisen Sumner Hunt** for **Oliver Posey** in 1900. Short after its construction, oilman **Edward Doheny** bought the home. Few alterations have been made to the French Gothic château exterior. T

house and park are now owned by **Mount St. Mary's College.** ♦ 8 Chester Pl. 746.0450

**47 Chamber Music in Historic Sites** Another annual attraction that makes Los Angeles a mecca for music lovers is this series of concerts organized by **Dr. Mary Ann Bonino** for the **Da Camera Society of Mount St. Mary's College.** Many of the performances, by top groups and soloists, are held under the Tiffany glass dome of the Doheny Mansion, the society's home. But that's just for starters. The **Bartok String Quartet** has performed in **Frank Lloyd Wright's Ennis-Brown House;** Prague's **Music da Camera** in the **Grand Salon** of the *Queen Mary;* the **New World Basset Horn Trio** in a former **Masonic Lodge.** Churches, bookstores, a movie palace lobby, and the **Catalina Casino** have also matched architecture with music. ♦ 10 Chester Place. 747.9085

**48 St. Vincent de Paul Roman Catholic Church** Oilman **Edward Doheny** donated the funds for this church designed by **Albert C. Martin** in 1925 in the ornate Spanish style known as *Churrigueresque,* patterned after baroque scrolled silverwork. The interior is decorated in brightly colored tiles and contains ceiling decorations painted by **Giovanni Smeraldi.** ♦ 621 W. Adams Blvd.

**49 Automobile Club of Southern California** This handsome Mission-Revival building with a courtyard where early road signs are displayed was built in 1923. Services offered to members include insurance, towing, travel planning, and maps. Wall maps can be purchased by nonmembers. ♦ M-F 9AM-5PM. 2601 S. Figueroa. 741.3111

**50 North University Park** Feisty local preservation groups have protected a concentration of handsome late-Victorian houses, laid out after the 1880s population explosion as a prosperous residential neighborhood, linked by streetcar to downtown. The residents have restored several of the finest examples, including the **Bassett House** (2653 S. Hoover Street) and the **Miller and Herriott House** (1163 W. 27th Street). They are all private residences. ♦ S. Hoover St to Magnolia St (between W. Adams Blvd and 27th St)

**51 Hebrew Union College/Jewish Institute of Religion** This institute of Jewish higher learning opened in 1954. The **Frances-Henry Library of Judaica** contains a special collection of material on the American Jewish experience. **Skirball Museum** has a collection of archaeological and biblical Judaica, including textiles, coins, ritual objects, and marriage contracts. One gallery displays a biblical environment entitled *A Walk Through the Past* that is a delight for children. Changing temporary exhibitions are also offered. ♦ Free. Hebrew Union College: M-Th 8:30AM-5PM; F 8:30AM-4:30PM; Su 1-5PM. Skirball Museum: Tu-F 11AM-4PM; Su 10AM-5PM. 3077 University Ave. 749.3424

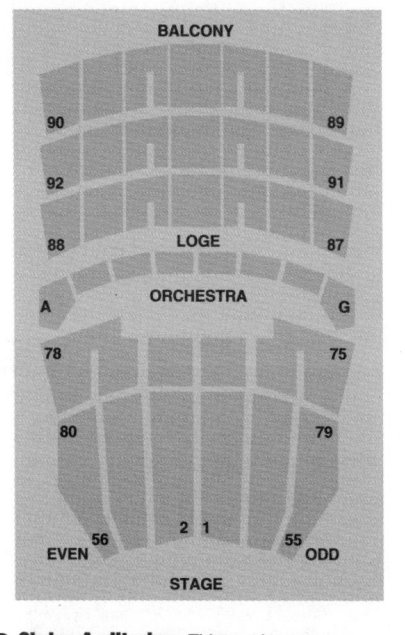

**52 Shrine Auditorium** This movie-set mosque, designed for and still used by the Shriners, was built in 1926. The cavernous auditorium (see the plan above) was neglected after the construction of the Music Center, but has been restored and is making a comeback. ♦ 665 W. Jefferson Blvd. 749.5123

# LA's Tallest

Earthquakes and a love affair with sunshine helped keep Los Angeles a horizontal city for more than 50 years. Only the 175-foot Continental Building, designed in 1904, and the 13-story city hall, designed in 1928, jutted skyward in this sprawling city until the late 1950s. Historians point to a 1904 law that limited building heights to 130 feet—all in a desire to prevent the construction of tall buildings that might keep LA's trademark sunshine from reaching the sidewalk (the dreaded "Manhattanization" of LA). Though the height limit was extended to 150 feet in 1911 (city hall was exempt by popular vote), it wasn't reversed until 1957, when new high-rise construction techniques satisfied earthquake protection requirements. Yet it wasn't until the 1970s that LA began to develop its distinct high-rise skyline. It now boasts the tallest skyscraper west of Chicago, along with some heady companions:

| | Feet |
| --- | --- |
| **First Interstate World Center** (1989) | 1,017 |
| **First Interstate Bank** (1973) | 858 |
| **Gas Company Tower** (1991) | 749 |
| **Security Pacific National Bank** (1973) | 738 |
| **Crocker Bank** (1982) | 723 |
| **777 Tower** (1991) | 717 |
| **Sanwa Bank Plaza** (1991) | 716 |
| **Atlantic Richfield Towers** (1971) | 699 |
| **Wells Fargo Bank** (1981) | 625 |
| **Citicorp Center** (1976) | 560 |

**53  The University Hilton** $$$ Located across the street from **USC's Davidson Conference Center**, this comfortable hotel offers a spa, swimming pool, restaurant, and cafe. ♦ 3540 S. Figueroa St. 748.4141, 800/244.7331 (CA), 800/872.1104 (US); fax 748.0043

**54  University of Southern California** Founded in 1880, USC is the oldest major independent coeducational nonsectarian university on the

West Coast. The student body has grown from 53 at the founding to the current 31,000. Numbered among the internationally known professional schools are: architecture, law, medicine, dentistry, social work, education, public administration, engineering, gerontology, cinema, performing arts, pharmacology, and international relations. The campus has 191 buildings on 152 acres, and is open daily year-round; specific buildings are open daily from 9AM to 5PM. Free hour-long walking tours of the campus are available. ♦ M-F 10AM-2PM. 743.2983. Bounded by Jefferson Blvd and Exposition, Figueroa, and Vermont Sts. 743.2311

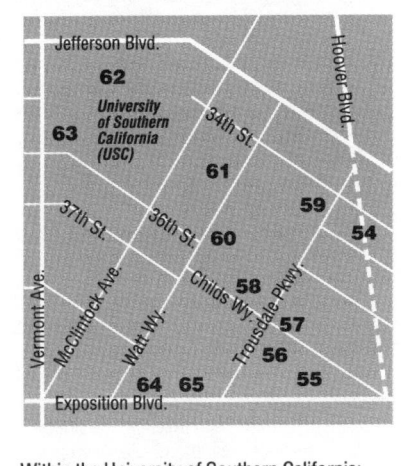

Within the University of Southern California:

**55  Widnezy Alumni House** Built in 1880, this two-story clapboard house is furnished in period style.

**56  Hancock Memorial Museum** Original furnishings from a now-demolished mansion are incorporated in historical rooms. ♦ Free. By appointment. M-F 10AM-4PM. 743.5213

**57  Doheny Memorial Library** This is the principal USC reference library, built in 1932.

**58  Bovard Administration Building** John & Donald Parkinson's 1921 Romanesque brick block contains the recently restored 1600-seat Norris Auditorium, which is used for a variety of cultural events.

**59  Bing Theater** Drama performances are given in this theater. ♦ 743.7923

**60  Norris Cinema Theater** Film programs in this luxurious theater are open to the public most evenings. ♦ 743.6089

**61  Arnold Schoenberg Institute** Adrian Wilson & Associates' complex, angular structure, built in 1978, houses the archive of the great 20th-century composer and a re-creation of the Brentwood studio in which he worked as an exile for the last 17 years of his life. Concerts of contemporary music are given in a small auditorium. ♦ Free. M-F 10AM-4PM. 743.5362

**62  McDonald's Olympic Swim Stadium** This is where USC hosts its swimming and diving events. ♦ 743.2222

**63  David X. Marks Tennis Stadium** USC tennis matches are held here. ♦ 743.2222

**64  Fisher Gallery** Temporary art exhibitions and selections from the **Armand Hammer Collection** of 18th- and 19th-century Dutch painting are showcased here. ♦ Tu-F noon-5PM; Sa noon-4PM; closed June-Aug. 743.2799

**65  Mudd Hall** Since its opening in 1930, this has been an important philosophy library. The building was modeled on a medieval Tuscan monastery.

**66  Exposition Park** In addition to the park, this is the location of the **Memorial Coliseum, Sports Arena,** and **Museums of Science, Industry, Space,** and **Natural History,** a community clubhouse, and several landscaped areas, including the rose garden. Exposition Park began as a casual open-air market, and in 1872 was formally deeded as an agricultural park for farmers to exhibit their products. Fairs and carnivals on the grounds were organized by the **Southern California Agricultural Society,** including occasional sponsorship of races on the lot to the rear of the park. The lot was used as a track for horse racing and, on a few occasions, was the site of camel races. Toward the turn of the century, it was home to bicycle and automobile competitions. During the park's decline in the early 1890s, it became a hangout for society's lower elements and home to three saloons. The transformation of the rowdy agricultural park into a major state, county, and city museum center was accomplished by **Judge William Miller Bowen.** The park's romantic attractions made truants of much of Judge Bowen's neighboring Sunday school classes. One Sunday he followed his class to discover their secret destination and utilized his shocking discovery to spearhead a drive to create a landmark of worthwhile cultural significance on the saloon site. By 1910 work on the County Museum of Natural History had begun. ♦ Exposition Blvd to Menlo St (between Figueroa St and Martin Luther King, Jr., Blvd)

**67  Exposition Park Rose Garden** The sunken garden contains more than 19,000 rose bushes representing more than 190 varieties. At the center are latticework gazebos. When the roses are in bloom, this is the most fragrant spot in town. ♦ Free. Daily 7AM-5PM. Exposition Blvd Wedding reservations: 310/548.7675

**68  California Afro-American Museum** This museum is dedicated to African-American achievements in politics, education, athletics, and the arts. The front part of the museum is a

13,000-square-foot sculpture court with a sloping space frame ceiling covered with tinted glass. Inside, there is space for changing exhibitions, a research library, a theater, and a gift shop. ♦ Free. Daily 10AM-5PM. 600 State Dr. 744.7432

**68 California Museum of Science and Industry Aerospace Hall** A blank-walled hangar, with echoes of radomes and space-assembly buildings, and an F-104 Starfighter pinned to the facade, seemingly frozen in flight, catch your eye when you first see this museum, designed by **Frank Gehry** in 1984. Inside, open walkways give you close-ups of suspended planes: a 1920 **Wright** glider, a 1927 *Mono Coupe*, a *T-38 Air Force Trainer*, and a *Gemini 11* space capsule. Eventually this building will become a lobby for a much expanded museum in the adjoining red brick armory, now closed for renovation. ♦ Free. Daily 10AM-5PM. 700 State Dr. 744.7400

**68 Mitsubishi Imax Theater** Next to the Aerospace Hall is **Gehry's** octagonal theater, showing different Imax films on a five-story-high by 70-foot-wide screen. ♦ Admission. Call for schedule. 700 State Dr. 744.2014

**69 California Museum of Science and Industry** This is a great place for kids of all ages. It's full of exciting new displays, including the **Mark Taper Hall of Economics and Finance** alongside old favorites like **Charles Eames' Mathematica,** talking computers, and the **Kinsey Hall of Health.** Innovative exhibitions allow you to check your health, understand electricity and earthquakes, and explore a DC3 and DC8 aircraft. There's a gift shop and a **McDonald's** cafeteria, too. ♦ Free. Daily 10AM-5PM. Exposition Blvd (at Figueroa St). 744.7400

**70 Los Angeles County Museum of Natural History** This handsome Spanish Renaissance building was restored for the museum's 75th anniversary in 1988. Some of the finest traveling exhibitions in LA, on topics as varied as Hollywood, nomads, volcanoes, and Indonesian court art, are presented here. But the image of the museum is indelibly set by its celebrated collections of reptile and mammal fossils (including several dinosaurs), its innovative

**Schreiber Hall of Birds,** and its minerals and pre-Columbian artifacts. The **Hall of American History** shows machinery and memorabilia. Native American and Folk Art festivals are presented every year and the annual **Dinosaur Ball** is a major social event. Children and adults will enjoy the **Discovery Center,** where they learn about nature by handling and working with artifacts. The new **Insect Zoo** features more than 25 live

insect exhibits, including giant beetles and hissing cockroaches. The museum has a bookstore, a fine gift shop, and a cafeteria serving low-priced meals. ♦ Admission. Tu-Su 10AM-5PM; free first Tuesday of every month. 900 Exposition Blvd. 744.3466, 744.3303 (recording)

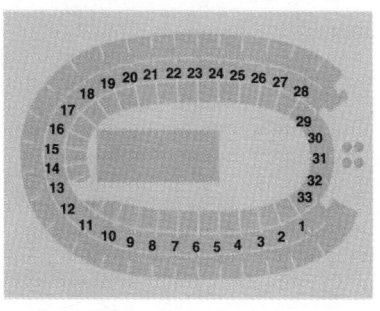

**71 Los Angeles Memorial Coliseum** Built in 1923, the Coliseum (see the plan above) was the major venue for the 1984 Olympics, as it was for the 1932 games. Other sports events (including USC football) and concerts are regularly scheduled. ♦ 3911 S. Figueroa St. 747.7111

**71 Olympic Arch** **Robert Graham's** massive sculpture in front of the coliseum is a permanent memento of the 1984 Summer Olympics. It is topped by two headless bronze nudes; water polo player **Terry Schroeder** was the model for the male figure. ♦ Figueroa St and Martin Luther King, Jr., Blvd

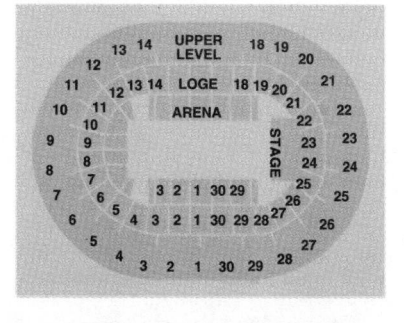

**72 Sports Arena** Built in 1958, this sister facility to the coliseum is used as a multipurpose indoor sports and entertainment facility. The main auditorium (see the plan above) is home to the LA Clipper and the USC basketball team, as well as host to ice shows, track meets, car shows, concerts, rodeos, wrestling, and conventions. ♦ 3939 S. Figueroa St. 748.6131

# Midtown

The area from downtown to the edge of Beverly Hills and the Westside is a geographical abstraction that includes many distinct neighborhoods. The easternmost section, from the **Harbor Freeway** to **Lafayette Park**, is home to thousands of new immigrants from Central America, Mexico, the Philippines, Southeast Asia, and Korea. West to **La Brea Avenue** is a transitional area, with new and landmark commercial buildings that date back to the 1920s. In the 1930s, **Wilshire Boulevard** from La Brea to **Fairfax Avenue** was developed into the prestigious business and shopping district known as Miracle Mile; following a long decline, this strip is being extensively rebuilt. The final section, west to **La Cienega** and **Robertson** boulevards, is a fashionable residential district, studded with design showrooms and art galleries.

Wilshire Boulevard, the spine of this corpulent entity, was originally a path followed by the **Yang-Na Indians** from their Elysian Hills settlement to the tar pits of **Hancock Park**, where they obtained pitch to waterproof their homes. Today's Wilshire runs 16 miles to the ocean, and was named after **H. Gaylord Wilshire** (1861-1927), a rascally entrepreneur from Ohio who made and lost fortunes in orange and walnut farming, gold mining, therapeutic electric belts, and real-estate development. The boulevard did not immediately achieve its present renown. Oil fever captured the city shortly after **Edward Doheny** struck oil near Second Street

nd Glendale Avenue. (Amazingly, Doheny discovered a small pool of oil with a shovel, 16 feet into the hillside.) By 1905 the neighborhood was dotted with oil wells, and fortunes were made—among them the Hancock family's, whose farm included the tar pits near Wilshire Boulevard and Fairfax Avenue. This field was soon exhausted, leaving only the tar pits and a few camouflaged wells as reminders of the boom years.

*Area code 213 unless otherwise noted.*

**1 Harbor Freeway Overpass** Between Figueroa Street and Beaudry Avenue, Wilshire Boulevard passes over the Harbor Freeway. A few blocks north is the stack interchange, where the Hollywood, Harbor/Pasadena, and San Bernardino freeways interlace to form the hub of the Southern California freeway system. Driving north gives you the closest view you will want of a pair of unusually inept buildings—pseudoclassical towers for **Coast Savings** and **Home Savings**—which provide two more good arguments for winding up the Savings and Loan industry.

**2 Bob Baker Marionette Theater** Since 1963 this has been one of LA's most delightful experiences—for children of all ages. Ticket prices include refreshments and a backstage tour to see how the puppets are made and operated. ♦ Performances Tu-F 10:30AM; Sa-Su 2:30PM. Reservations required. 1345 W. First St. 250.9995

**3 Pacific Stock Exchange** The Exchange was relocated here from its landmark building on Spring Street. ♦ Viewing gallery M-F 8:30AM-1PM. 233 S. Beaudry Ave. 977.4500

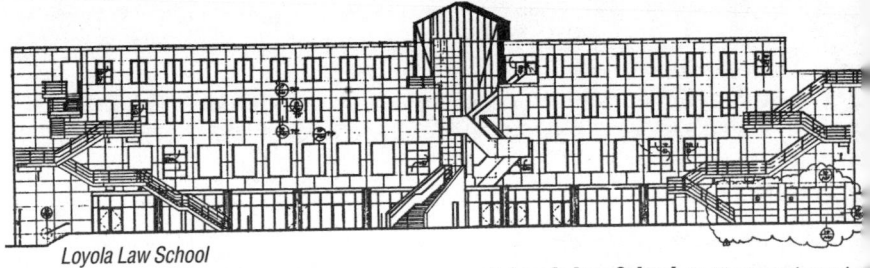

Loyola Law School

## Midtown

**4 Shangri-la Chinese Seafood** ★$$ Shark-fin soup, steamed *tilapia* (basslike fish), braised oysters, and meat-stuffed rice cake have been praised at this large Hong Kong-style restaurant. Dim sum are served at lunch. ◆ Chinese ◆ M-F 11AM-9:30PM; Sa-Su 10AM-9:30PM. 313 S. Boylston St. 250.2288

**4 Vertigo** Popular with the late-night dance crowd, this big, fashionable dance club has relocated here from Grand Avenue. Many are called, but only a few terminally hip people are chosen from the crowd on the sidewalk and allowed to enter. ◆ Cover. Club: F-Sa 10PM-4AM. Bistro: 9PM-4AM. 333 S. Boylston St. 747.4849

**5 Mary Andrews Clark Memorial Residence of the YWCA** This enormous French château was designed by **Arthur Benton** in 1913. ◆ 306 Loma Dr

**6 Pacific Dining Car** ★$$$$ Prime beef aged on the premises, a remarkable wine cellar, and a fine spinach salad are the draws here. The front dining room was once a railroad car. The breakfasts are good, too. ◆ American ◆ Daily 24 hours. 1310 W. Sixth St. 483.6000

**7 Mayfair Hotel** $$$ This vintage hostelry was newly restored, and is now a Best Western property, with a restaurant and lounge, and a free shuttle to downtown. ◆ 1256 W. Seventh St. 484.9614, 800/821.8682 (CA); fax 484.2769

**Some of Southern California's worst earthquakes:**

**28 June 1992** in Landers and Big Bear Lake: 7.4 and 6.5 magnitude (respectively), one death, 350 injuries, $92 million in damages

**28 February 1990** in Upland: 5.5 magnitude, no deaths, 38 injuries, $10.4 million in damages

**1 October 1987** in Whittier Narrows: 5.9 magnitude, eight deaths, more than 200 injuries, $358 million in damages

**8 July 1986** in North Palm Springs: 5.9 magnitude, no deaths or injuries, $5.3 million in damages

**9 February 1971** in Sylmar/San Fernando Valley: 6.4 magnitude, 58 deaths, 2,000 injuries, $511 million in damages

**21 July 1952** in Tehachapi: 7.7 magnitude, 12 deaths, 18 injuries, $50 million in damages

**10 March 1933** in Long Beach: 6.3 magnitude, 115 deaths, hundreds of injuries, $40 million in damages

**8 Loyola Law School** An idiosyncratic version of **Thomas Jefferson's** "Academical Village" has given a new spirit to what was formerly a drab commuter school. **Frank Gehry's** stylized versions of a classical temple and a Romanesque chapel are deployed on a tight-knit campus. Outside stairs create a forced perspective centerpiece on the administration building and encourage social intercourse. The school (illustrated above) has established a fine art collection that includes **Claes Oldenburg's** whimsical construction *Toppling Ladder*. Gehry's buildings were completed between 1981 and 1987. ◆ 1441 Olympic Blvd. 736.1000

**9 Paper Source** Owner **Rose Marie Dawes** loves paper, and she stocks the finest materials for artists, designers, and archivists. This is the place for handmade, marbleized, and gold-leaf sheets. They also have weekend workshops. ◆ M-F 9AM-5:30PM. 1506 W 12th St. 387.5820

**10 L'Adelita** ★$ This multipurpose Mexican and Central American emporium offers a wide range of baked goods, fresh tortillas, tamales, *pupusas* (Salvadoran cornmeal turnovers), sandwiches, and hot entrées. ◆ Mexican/Central American ◆ Daily 6AM-10PM. 1287 S. Union Ave. 487.0176. Also at: 5812 Santa Monica Blvd, Hollywood. 465.6526

**11 Alvarado Terrace** Laid out in the first decade of the century, this gently curving street is a fashionable suburb at the western boundary of the original pueblo of Los Angeles. It's a smorgasbord of eclectic architectural styles, including Queen Anne and Mission Revival, Shingle and English Tudor. **Juan Bautista Alvarado** was the Mexican governor of California from 1836 to 1842. ◆ Pico Blvd (between Alvarado and Hoover Sts)

**12 Vagabond Inn** $$ For the budget-minded traveler, this hotel offers inexpensive rates, Continental breakfast, and a pool. It's conveniently located between the LA Coliseum and USC's campus. ◆ 1904 Olympic Blvd. 380.9393, 800/522.1555; fax 487.2662. Also at: 3101 S. Figueroa St. 746.1531

**13 New Olympian Hotel** $$ The now-generic renovated lobby once housed an aviary of tropical foliage, statuary, and exotic birds, which were donated to the LA Zoo. There's a pool, too. ◆ 1903 W. Olympic Blvd. 385.7141; fax 385.5808

**Restaurants/Clubs:** Red
**Shops/ ◆ Outdoors:** Green
**Hotels:** Blue
**Sights/Culture:** Black

**14 South Bonnie Brae Street** Westlake (now MacArthur Park) was one of LA's first suburbs. Most of it has been rebuilt, but this street survives as a treasury of 1890s houses. Among the standouts are No. 818, a regal Queen Anne, with an immense veranda, elaborate woodwork, and several types of columns and piers; No. 824, the **Charles B. Boothe and Carriage House,** with its Islamic domed tower; and many on the 1000 block. ♦ Between Eighth St and Olympic Blvd

**15 Star 88** ★$ This bright addition to the Thai scene has a striking postmodern interior. The authentic menu includes such standards as *pad Thai* noodles and exotica like *nai voi* (organ meat soup); *tod mun* (fish cakes) are a must. The food is spiced to order. ♦ Thai ♦ M-Sa 11:30AM-9PM. 1901 W. Eighth St. 413.5510

**16 Langer's Delicatessen** ★$$ Langer's is one of the few places serving pastrami that a New Yorker would applaud. ♦ Deli ♦ Daily 6:30AM-11PM. 704 S. Alvarado St. 483.8050

**17 MacArthur Park** Laid out in 1890, the park was one of LA's first public gardens, and today it provides badly needed recreation space for local immigrant communities. It contains more than 80 species of rare plants and trees, a lake with paddleboats for rent, a small band shell for summer entertainment, snack bars, and some children's play areas. More than 11 site-specific artworks have been installed in the park as part of a program formerly supervised by **Adolfo Nodal,** now general manager of the city's Department of Cultural Affairs. They include **Judy Simonian's** *Pyramids* (two tiled ziggurats linked by a speaking tube), **Eric Orr's** *Water Spout* (which rises up to 500 feet from the lake), and **George Herm's** *Clock Tower* (constructed from discarded materials in the spirit of Watts Towers). The neon signs around the park and along Wilshire Boulevard have been relit to evoke the 1930s; especially notable is the marquee of the **Westlake Theatre,** a handsome 1926 movie palace overlooking the park. The area is currently threatened by drug-related violence, so be aware. ♦ Wilshire Blvd (between Alvarado and Park View Sts)

**17 Park Plaza Hotel** $$ Housed in the landmark 1925 **Elks Building,** this hotel is a near relation of the Central Library, with its grand arches, massive parapet sculptures, and interiors decorated by **Anthony Heinsbergen.** In addition to 140 rooms and 10 suites, the hotel features three ballrooms, a gym with an Olympic-size pool, squash courts, a cocktail lounge, and free parking. ♦ 607 S. Park View St. 384.5281; fax 480.1928

**18 Otis School of Art and Design** This is LA's oldest college of art and design, established in 1918. It offers undergraduate and masters degrees in fine and applied arts, public evening classes, and varied community outreach programs. **Kent Twitchell** has painted one of his best murals, a *Holy Trinity* of soap opera stars, on a wall overlooking Carondelet Street. The **Otis/Parsons Art Gallery** presents notable exhibitions. ♦ Free. Tu-Sa 10AM-5PM. 2401 Wilshire Blvd (at Sixth St). 251.0500

**18 La Fonda** ★$$ Los Camperos, one of the finest mariachi groups anywhere, entertains in this popular spot. The margaritas are especially good and the atmosphere is one of the most festive in town. ♦ Mexican ♦ M-F 11AM-2PM, 5PM-midnight; Sa 5PM-2AM; Su 5PM-midnight. 2501 Wilshire Blvd. 380.5055

**18 Vagabond Theater** The Vagabond is one of a fast-shrinking group of repertory revival houses that shows classic movies the way they were meant to be seen. Call for the film schedule. ♦ 2509 Wilshire Blvd. 387.2171

COURTESY OF CARLOS DINIZ ASSOCIATES

**19 Granada Building** Spanish Colonial architecture is combined with Mission-style arches and arcades in this 1927 building (pictured above), designed for architects and artists who wanted courtyard studio offices. ♦ 672 S. Lafayette Park Pl

**20 Lafayette Park** This park includes a recreation and senior citizens' center, tennis courts, a picnic area, and a scent garden with numerous fragrant flowers. ♦ 2800 Wilshire Blvd. Center: 625 S. Lafayette Park Pl. 387.9426

**20 CNA Building** The mirror glass slab of the 1972 CNA Building reflects the sky (actually disappearing at times) and the 1932 English Gothic First Congregational Church across the street. ♦ Sixth St at Commonwealth St

**20 Mi Guatemala** ★$ The storefront restaurant serves local specialties like *pepian* (a tasty pork stew) and *pan con chile relleno* (a delicious, spicy sandwich of shredded beef and pork with green peppers and diced vegetables). ♦ Guatemalan ♦ Daily 9AM-10PM. 695 S. Hoover St. 387.4296

**20 Al Fresco** $ Owner **Sumol Chomyong** makes this simple cafe a special place, and offers pizza, pasta, salads, and desserts at budget prices. ♦ Italian ♦ M-F 11:30AM-10PM. 524 S. Occidental Blvd. 382.8003

**21 Brooklyn Bagel Bakery** The bagels here will bring tears to the eyes of New York expatriates—the crisp, shiny crusts garnished with onion are great. ♦ M-Th 7AM-11:30PM; F 7AM-4AM; Sa 11:30AM- 4AM; Su 11:30AM-11:30PM. 2217 W. Beverly Blvd. 413.4114

**22 Tommy's** $ If you're craving chili burgers, many loyal fans say this street-side stand serves the best in LA. ♦ American ♦ Daily 24 hours. 2575 W. Beverly Blvd. 389.9060

**23 Shibucho** ★★$$ Sushi and sashimi of high quality are served in a traditional, woodsy interior with pebble floors. ♦ Japanese ♦ M-Sa 5:30PM-3AM. 3114 W. Beverly Blvd. 387.8498

**24 Lowenbrau Keller** ★$$ Huge helpings of German food are served at reasonable prices in an elaborate Bavarian setting. They have delicious sausages and sauerbraten, and a good choice of local wine and beer. ♦ German ♦ M-F 11:30AM-3PM, 6-10PM; Sa 5-10PM. 3211 W. Beverly Blvd. 382.5723

**25 Lotus Restaurant** ★★★$$ Improbably located in the **Midtown Hilton** overlooking the Hollywood Freeway, experts judge this to be one of the best places for Mandarin cuisine this side of Taipei. Specialties include crispy scal-

## Midtown

lops, Shanghai vegetarian goose, jellyfish with candied pine nuts, and pork filet in lotus leaves. ♦ Mandarin ♦ M-Th, Su 11:30AM-2:30PM, 5:30-9:45PM; F-Sa 5:30-10:45PM. 400 N. Vermont Ave. 661.8011

**26 Casa Carnitas** ★$ Kitsch decor, cutesy waitresses, Latino crowds, and Mexican music create an appropriate context for searingly soulful food. Rich Yucatecan specialties include excellent fish and shellfish, pork-and-black-bean stew, and fried plantains. ♦ Mexican ♦ M-Sa 11AM-midnight. 4067 W. Beverly Blvd. 667.9953

**27 Sheraton Town House** $$$ This luxury hotel in the middle of the city features tennis courts, a swimming pool, a sauna, and gardens. Lanai suites have private patios overlooking the pool and are a good value. ♦ 2961 Wilshire Blvd. 382.7171, 800/325.3535; fax 487.7148

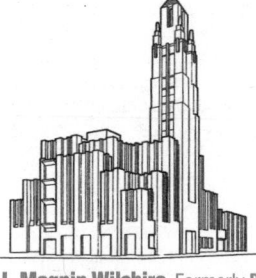

**28 I. Magnin Wilshire** Formerly **Bullock's Wilshire,** this is the grandest monument (illustrated above) of Art Deco in LA. Built in 1928 by **John & Donald Parkinson,** it was the city's first suburban department store, designed for the automobile rather than the pedestrian, entered from a rear porte-cochere facing over the parking lot. Its proximity to newly fashionable Hancock Park drew traffic away from Broadway, and it set a pattern that was imitated along Wilshire Boulevard to the ocean.

It's still LA's most handsome store, from its stepped profile to its soaring green-crowned tower, from **Herman Sachs'** portal mural of transportation to the miraculously preserved interior design. I. Magnin is known for its high-quality merchandise and old-fashioned service. The tearoom on the fifth floor features fashion shows at lunchtime. ♦ M-W, F-Sa 10AM-6PM; Th 10AM-8PM; Su noon-5PM. 3050 Wilshire Blvd. 382.6161

Within I. Magnin Wilshire:

**The Tea Room** $$ Located on the fifth floor, this genteel period piece also presents luncheon fashion shows and serves cocktails. ♦ American ♦ M-Sa 11:30AM-2:30PM; high tea 2:30-5PM. 382.6161 ext. 324

**29 Cassell's Patio Hamburgers** ★$ Homemade hamburgers, potato salad, and fresh-squeezed lemonade are served in a no-frills setting. ♦ American ♦ M-Sa 10AM-4PM. 3266 W. Sixth St. 480.8668

**30 Chapman Shopping Center** Originally designed in 1929 by **Morgan, Walls & Clements,** the indispensable **Wayne Ratkovich** rehabilitated this vintage shopping center (formerly called the Chapman Park Market), with its motor court and Churrigueresque facade. It boasts a quality market, florist, retail shops, and restaurants plus a Korean coffeehouse, the **Bohemian Cafe.** ♦ 3451 W. Sixth St. 487.6155

**31 Wilshire Plaza Hotel and Garden** $$$ This luxury hotel has a pool and use of a nearby health club, plus two restaurants (**Tulips Garden** and a sushi bar) and dancing on weekends. ♦ 3515 Wilshire Blvd. 381.7411, 800/382.7411; fax 386.7379

**31 St. Basil's Catholic Church** The massive, modernist church in reinforced concrete was designed by **A.C. Martin & Associates** in 1974. ♦ Daily 8:30AM-1PM, 2-6PM. 3611 Wilshire Blvd. 381.6191

**32 Ambassador Hotel** Built in the 1920s, this legendary hostelry was the home of the **Coconut Grove** nightclub. It was here that **Robert Kennedy** was shot while announcing his victory in the 1968 California primary. The hotel was purchased by **Donald Trump,** who wishes to convert it to an office building. ♦ 3400 Wilshire Blvd

**33 Hotel Chancellor** $$ An excellent budget-priced hotel, it's popular with European and Japanese visitors. Amenities include full breakfast and dinners and a pool. ♦ 3191 W. Seventh St. 383.1183, 800/446.5552 (CA); fax 385.6675

**34 Taylor's Prime Steaks** ★$$$ Taylor's is everything a good steak house should be: a clubby, wood-paneled space with the finest meat, generous portions, and very reasonable prices. The menu offers seafood and chops as well as steak. ♦ American ♦ M-F 11AM-10PM; Sa-Su 4-10PM. 3361 W. Eighth St. 382.8449

## Koreatown

Rambling, repainted old bungalows, storefronts provisioned with Korean foodstuffs, and distinctive angular calligraphy identify this dynamic ethnic neighborhood bounded roughly by Vermont, Pico, Eighth, and Western streets. It is the hub for Korean cultural, social, and business life, but only a third of the area's 160,000 Koreans (the largest Korean population in the United States) actually live here; it is now home to twice as many Latino immigrants, many from Central America. Korean-owned businesses

om here to South Central were hard hit during the 1992 riots. Simmering racial tensions—aggravated by he shooting death of a black customer by a Korean shopkeeper, who was later given a light sentence—erupted. Armed Koreans took to the roofs of their usinesses to protect their property from looters, rsonists, and drive-by gunmen. Hundreds of businesses were damaged or destroyed. Many burned-ut stores await rebuilding.

**34 Dong Il Jang** ★$$ A refined atmosphere of natural wood and subdued lighting is featured at this restaurant. Your order of beef or chicken is cooked on a grill hidden under the removable table top. ♦ Korean ♦ Daily 11AM-10PM. 3455 W. Eighth St. 383.5757

**34 Wilshire Towers Hotel-Apartments** $$ Rooms, suites, and apartments are located in a traditional residential neighborhood. Weekly rates are available, too. ♦ 3460 W. Seventh St. 385.7281; fax 382.1702

**35 Ham Hung** ★$ The food of the Ham Hung region of Korea, especially *naengmyon* (chilled buckwheat-and-potato-starch noodles with a spicy sauce) is the specialty. ♦ Korean ♦ Daily 11AM-10PM. 809 S. Ardmore Ave. 381.1865

**36 Chao Nue** ★★$$ Ask for a Thai menu (and its English translation) to enjoy the best northern regional dishes. These tend to be rich and well-seasoned—meat-and-vegetable chile, pork curry (*kaeng hung lae*), and catfish with basil steamed in banana leaves (*ap pla*). ♦ Thai ♦ Daily 10:30AM-10PM. 2810 W. Ninth St. 384.7049, 487.1927

**36 Arunee** ★★$ This is a family run restaurant with modest decor. The crab with cellophane noodles and the spicy seafood stew rate high as among the best Thai dishes in LA. ♦ Thai ♦ Daily 11AM-10PM. 401 S. Vermont Ave. 385.6653

**37 Korean Gardens** ★$$ You can be your own barbecue chef at this lively restaurant, but go prepared for spicy food and clouds of smoke. ♦ Korean ♦ Daily 11AM-11PM. 950 S. Vermont Ave. 388.3042

**37 La Plancha** ★$$ If you're looking for a gastronomic adventure, you've come to the right place. Specialties include meats and fish marinated in orange and lime, *empáñadas* (a ripe plantain that's stuffed with cotija cheese), and *nactamals* (delicious giant tamales). Beer, wine, refreshing *cacao* (a chocolate drink), and other drinks made with fruit and corn are also available. Owner **Milton Molina** is your effusive host. ♦ Nicaraguan ♦ M-F 11AM-9:30PM; Sa-Su 9AM-10PM. 2818 W. Ninth St. 383.1449

**38 El Colmao** ★$ One of the best Cuban restaurants in town, El Colmao serves excellent roast pork with black beans and Jerez chicken in a delicious sherry sauce with olives and onions. It's very crowded at lunchtime. ♦ Cuban ♦ M, W-F 10AM-9:30PM; Tu 11AM-6PM; Sa-Su noon-9:30PM. 2328 N. Pico Blvd. 386.6131

**39 The Salisbury House** $$ Proprietors **Sue** and **Jay German** have transformed a restored 1909 Craftsman-style house into a five-room bed-and-breakfast inn located in the historic West Adams district. The antique decor and stained-and leaded-glass ornamentation are the interior highlights. A full breakfast is served, too. ♦ 2273 W. 20th St. 737.7817; 800/373.1778

**40 Residence** Formerly a bed-and-breakfast inn, this impeccably restored 1913 Craftsman-style house has returned to private use. ♦ 1650 Westmoreland Blvd.

**41 El Cholo** $$ **Gable** and **Lombard** used to eat in this more than 50-year-old Mexican classic. Nostalgia and the atmosphere of a hacienda, plus the whopping margaritas, are the primary appeals today. ♦ Mexican ♦ M-Th 11AM-10PM; F-Sa 11AM-11PM; Su 11AM-9PM. 1121 S. Western Ave. 734.2773

**42 Hang Goo Seafood** ★$ This friendly seafood place features an exceptional young crab soup. The front doors are locked; enter from the back. ♦ Korean ♦ Daily (excluding the first Su of the month) 11:30AM-midnight. 1106 S. Western Ave. 733.2474

**43 The Wiltern Center**
Another Art Deco masterpiece, this one was designed by **Morgan, Walls & Clements** in 1931. **Wayne Ratkovich** rescued the building (pictured at right) at the eleventh hour from an insurance company that wanted to clear the site. His gamble proved sound, as it had on the Oviatt and Fine Arts buildings downtown. The corner tower and side wings are clad in green terracotta; closely spaced and lively moldings make the tower seem far more imposing than its 12 stories—in contrast to the banal bank towers all around. Architect **Brenda Levin** restored them for lease as offices, stores, and the **Upstage Cafe** (739.9913). Currently on hold is a plan to build a two-story retail courtyard behind the theater. ♦ 3790 Wilshire Blvd (at Western Ave). 388.1400

Within the Wiltern Center:

**Wiltern Theater** The theater has an imposing marquee and a patterned terrazzo forecourt that leads beneath the tower to a grand movie palace. Built in 1931 by **G. Albert Lansburgh,** it was severely vandalized but has been restored to its former glory by **Brenda Levin** and **Tony Heinsbergen,** son of the original interior designer, for use as a performing arts center. The theater is a fairyland of Art Deco ornament embellished in pink and green hues with gold trim. A masterly sequence of spaces guides the audience into an auditorium whose proscenium is crowned with a sunburst of low-relief

skyscrapers. There are frequent performances of music, opera, and dance. ♦ 380.5005/5030

**Atlas Bar & Grill** ★★$$ **Mario Tamayo** (who launched **Cha Cha Cha** and **Cafe Mambo**) is the ebullient host in this cavernous space, designed by **Ron Meyers** in 1989, with wrought-iron screens, splashes of gold, and glitzy lighting. The exotic menu matches the theatrical decor: Brazilian seafood stew, vegetable *tajine*, and black-pepper shrimp are signature dishes; the oysters and grills are for plainer tastes. The room is jumping but not deafening; there's live

## Midtown

entertainment most nights. ♦ Eclectic ♦ M-F 11:30AM-3PM, 6PM-midnight; Sa 6PM-1:45AM. 380.8400

**44 Ginza Sushi-ko** ★★★★$$$$ Hidden away in a mini mall is a branch of a Tokyo sushi bar that's famous for the perfection of its cuisine. Put yourself in the hands of the chef, and expect to pay at least $100 a person, for lunch or dinner. Even at these prices, it's packed every night, so reserve early for a memorable dining experience. ♦ Japanese ♦ M-Sa noon-2PM, 6-10PM. 3959 Wilshire Blvd, No. A 11. 487.2251

**45 Former Selig Store** This streamlined gem designed in black-and-gold glazed terra-cotta and glass brick dates back to 1931. ♦ Western Ave (at W. Third St)

**46 Kentucky Fried Chicken** The architecture, not the food, is the attraction here. **Grinstein-Daniels** created this superb piece of innovative design, with a curving facade and floating geometric masses, in 1990. ♦ 340 N. Western Ave

**46 Beverly Soon Tofu** ★$ "Soon" is the name and tofu's the game at this simple restaurant specializing in soft bean curd. It comes spiced to order, with clams, oysters, beef, pork, or seaweed. Don't miss the exotic iced tea made from roasted corn. ♦ Korean ♦ Daily 10AM-10PM. 4653 ½ Beverly Blvd. 856.0368

**47 Chan Dara Larchmont** ★$$ The slightly sleeker, fancier spin-off of the Thai favorite in Hollywood has been wowing the traditional crowd of Hancock Park. There is a bar as well as a patio that's open for dinner. Specialties include sausage with ginger and lime, stuffed chicken wings, and barbecued beef. The banana fritters are rolled in coconut and sesame seeds before being flamed in rum. ♦ Thai ♦ M-Th 11:30AM-11PM; F 11:30AM-midnight; Sa 5PM-midnight; Su 5-11PM. 310 N. Larchmont Blvd (at Beverly Blvd). 467.1052

**48 Larchmont Village** Don't miss this shopping street of small town charm and urban sophistication. Nearby is the **Wilton Historic District,** a modest area of California bungalows dating from 1907 to 1925. ♦ Larchmont Blvd (between First St and Beverly Blvd)

**48 Louise's Trattoria** $$ Large portions of acceptable Italian-American fare, served in a bleached-blond room, have made this family restaurant wildly popular with young pros all over town. ♦ Italian ♦ M-Th 11AM-10PM; F-Sa 11AM-11PM; Su noon-10PM. 232 N. Larchmont Blvd. 962.9510. Also at: 342 N. Beverly Dr. 274.4271; 10645 Pico Blvd. 475.6084; 100 Montana Ave. 394.8888

**48 Prado** ★$$ The picture-pretty setting (pale-blue walls, painted angels floating above the chandeliers) makes Prado ideal for dining on island food. The presiding chef is **Javier Prado** who is the brother of **Toribio,** who runs **Cha Cha Cha.** Prado has a similar menu of exotic dishes that are often over-spiced. No reservations are taken, and the tiny room is sometimes overwhelmed. ♦ Caribbean ♦ M-Sa 11AM-3PM 6-10:30PM; Su 5-10:30PM. 244 N. Larchmont Blvd. 467.3871

**49 Hancock Park/Windsor Square/Wilton Historic District** Capt. **G. Allan Hancock,** son of **Henry Hancock,** who bought Rancho La Brea in 1860, began this exclusive residential section in the 1910s. The palatial mansions have been owned by the **Doheny, Huntington, Van Nuys, Janss, Banning, Crocker,** and other notable California families. ♦ Bounded by Highland and Melrose Aves and Wilshire and Larchmont Blvds

**50 Getty House** This half-timbered English-style house, built in 1921, was donated to the city by the Getty Oil Company and used as the mayor's official home. It's now a private residence. ♦ 605 S. Irving Blvd

**51 Wilshire Ebell Theater and Club** Because of its Renaissance-style facade, this 1924 building is popular with movie and television companies. The theater is noted for its cultural and educational programs. ♦ 4401 W. Eighth St. 939.1128

**52 Fremont Place** The entry to the privately owned streets of this elegant residential neighborhood is through massive gates on the south side of the 4400 to 4500 blocks of Wilshire Boulevard. The area is not open to the public.

**53 La Cochinita** ★$ The specialty of this cheery Salvadoran restaurant is *pupusas,* the national dish. These ground corn-pancakes, made to order, are filled with cheese, pork rinds, or meat, and come with a spicy coleslaw. ♦ Salvadoran ♦ Daily noon-10PM. 4367 Pico Blvd. 937.1249

**54 La Brea Avenue** La Brea is a hot new location for art galleries, design-oriented stores, and restaurants, notably around the junction with Melrose Avenue, and south to Wilshire Boulevard, which are rehabilitating the long-neglected mix of Art Deco and Spanish 1930s buildings. Leading galleries of contemporary art and design include **Jan Baum** (170 S. La Brea, 932.0170), **Ovsey** (170 S. La Brea, 935.1883), **Fahey/Klein Photography** (148 N. La Brea, 934.2250), **Couturier Gallery** (166 N. La Brea, 933.5557), and **Iturralde Gallery** (154 N. La Brea, 937.4267).

Restaurants/Clubs: Red     Hotels: Blue
Shops/ ♣ Outdoors: Green     Sights/Culture: Black

**54 Louis XIV** ★★$$ Even jaded New Yorkers talk about this French country house-cum-dining club, with a beamed attic upstairs, a cozy room off the downstairs kitchen, a wine bar, frescoed burnished ochre walls, candelabras, and a handsome crowd. The honest bistro food includes vegetable soup, roasted peppers with anchovies, chicken with mustard sauce, steak *frite,* and lemon tart—as refreshing as the scene. ♦ French ♦ M-Sa 6PM-midnight. 606 N. La Brea Ave. 934.5102

**55 LinderDesign** Reproductions of classic early modern lamps and furnishings by designers **Desny, Josef Hoffmann,** and **Otto Wagner** are showcased here. ♦ Tu-F 10AM-7PM; Sa 10AM-5PM; Su noon-5PM. 440 N. La Brea Ave. 939.4020

**55 Rapport Co.** Imported contemporary furnishings are sold at affordable prices. ♦ Tu-Sa 9:30AM-5PM. 435 N. La Brea Ave. 930.1500

**56 East India Grill** ★$$ Original dishes, such as basil-coconut curries, tandoori ribs, and savory soups, are served in this friendly bistro. ♦ Indian ♦ Daily 11:30AM-3PM, 6-10:30PM. 345 N. La Brea Ave. 936.8844, 310/917.6644

**56 Modern Times** Classic American modern furniture and collectibles are sold here. ♦ Tu-Sa 11AM-5PM. 338 N. La Brea Ave. 930.1150

**57 Patina** Choose from custom-made hats in felt and straw trimmed with vintage lace, ribbons, and flowers—in period and contemporary styles. ♦ W-Sa noon-6PM. 119 N. La Brea Ave. 931.6931

**57 Farfalla** ★★$$ This larger version of the North Central LA trattoria on Hillhurst Avenue serves delicious pizzas, pastas, and desserts to a smartly dressed film industry crowd. Any dish with eggplant is worth a try. ♦ Italian ♦ M-Th 11:30AM-2:30PM, 6-10:30PM; F-Sa 11:30AM-2:30PM, 6-11PM; Su 6-10:30PM. 143 N. La Brea Ave. 938.2504

**58 The Living Room** If you enjoy elbow-to-elbow lounging, try this cozy coffeehouse. The adjacent billiards room gets packed, too. ♦ Coffeehouse ♦ M-Th 7AM-2AM; F-Su 7AM-4AM. 110 S. La Brea Ave. 933.2933

**58 Samy's Camera** A one-stop service station for professionals and novices, Samy's has good prices on film and processing, a wide choice of equipment for rent or purchase, and expert service. ♦ M-Sa 9AM-6PM; Su 11AM-4PM. 263 S. La Brea Ave. 938.2420. The location at 7122 Beverly Boulevard was destroyed during the April 1992 riots and is scheduled to reopen in late 1993.

**58 American Rag Company** Stop by this showroom of trendy recycled wearables at designer prices. Next door is a home-furnishing store for interior adornments and the **Maison et Cafe** (No.148) for a quick lunch or espresso. Steps away: **American Rag Cie Shoes** (No.144) and **American Rag Cie Youth** (No.136). ♦ M-Sa 10:30AM-10:30PM; Su noon-7PM. 150 S. La Brea Ave. 935.3154

**58 City Restaurant** ★★★$$$ French-trained chefs **Susan Feniger** and **Mary Sue Milliken** range the world in search of inspiration, and their eclectic, constantly changing menu makes this one of LA's most exciting restaurants. They also supervise the kitchen of the **Border Grill** on Melrose and in Santa Monica. Sample dishes include Thai duck curry soup, Chinese sausage salad and monkfish, and scallops in coconut broth. **David Kellen** and **Josh Schweitzer** designed this high-tech converted warehouse, which is—intentionally—noisy and upbeat. Only

snacks are served during the afternoon; brunch is served on weekends. ♦ Eclectic ♦ M-Th 11:45AM-11PM; F-Sa 11:45AM-11:45PM; Su 11AM-10PM. 180 S. La Brea Ave. 938.2155

**59 Ca' Brea** $$ **Antonio Tomasi,** co-owner/chef of **Locanda Veneta,** prepares Venetian specialties like *bigoletti* seafood pasta and osso buco, a veal shank, in this big, informal restaurant, which replaced the venerable **Robaire's.** ♦ Italian ♦ M-F 11:30AM-2:30PM, 5:30-10:30PM; Sa 5:30-11PM. 348 S. La Brea Ave. 938.2863

**60 Pikme-up** This local hangout is a showcase for undiscovered poets; it was one of the first of LA's bohemian coffeehouses. ♦ Coffeehouse ♦ M-Th, Su noon-2AM; F-Sa noon-3AM. 5437 W. Sixth St (at La Brea Ave). 939.9706

**61 Il Literature** An eclectic mix of books, frames, candles, cards, and unique gifts is stocked here. ♦ M-F 10AM-10PM; Sa 10AM-7PM; Su 10AM-6PM. 456 S. La Brea Ave. 937.3505

**61 Campanile** ★★★$$$ Old and new designs were combined to form a dramatic sequence of dining areas at this restaurant. Architect **Josh Schweitzer** inserted a glass roof and a concrete frame within the streetfront patio of a Spanish-style building, leaving the pretty tiled fountain and the signature tower, to create one of the most romantic settings in LA. The rustic cuisine, by **Spago** graduates **Mark Peel** and **Nancy Silverton,** draws enthusiastic crowds, sometimes overwhelming the kitchen. Quail is served with wild mushrooms on toasted penne, grilled whole bass on fresh herbs, and charred lamb on salad greens, and there's a scrumptious nougat tart with kumquat ice cream. Fans return for a mouth-watering selection of breads at the **La Brea Bakery,** located next door to the restaurant. ♦ California ♦ Restaurant: breakfast M-F 8AM-noon, Sa-Su 8AM-1:30PM; dinner M-Th 6-10PM, F-Sa 5:30-11PM. Bakery: M-Sa 8AM-6PM, Su 8AM-4PM. 624 S. La Brea Ave. 938.1447

**62 Miracle Mile** In 1920 visionary **A.W. Ross** bought 18 acres of empty land along Wilshire Boulevard, from La Brea to Fairfax, and in the late '20s and early '30s he developed it as a prestigious business and shopping district. A friend dubbed it "Miracle Mile." Ross closely supervised the designs of individual buildings, and a few relics survive ongoing redevelopment.

Along Miracle Mile:

**Security Pacific Bank** The black and gold miniature of the Richfield Tower was built in

1929 by **Morgan, Walls & Clements.** ♦ 5209 Wilshire Blvd

**Commercial Building** The imposing set-back tower was built in 1930 by **Meyer & Holter.** ♦ 5217-5231 Wilshire Blvd

**The Dark Room** The facade of **Marcus P. Miller's** 1935 building is a period camera in black vitrolite. ♦ 5370 Wilshire Blvd

**Dominguez-Wilshire Building** Another **Morgan, Walls & Clements** design, this is a finely detailed tower rising above a two-story retail base built in 1930. ♦ 5410 Wilshire Blvd

**Commercial Building** **Frank M. Tyler's** 1927 twin turrets look like towering Japanese origami. ♦ 5464 Wilshire Blvd

**Desmond's** Note the rounded corners on the low wings of **Gilbert Stanley Underwood's** handsome, eight-story tower, built in 1928. Housed in this building is the **Ace Gallery** (Tu-Sa 10AM-6PM, 935.4411). Owner **Doug Christmas** showcases such artists as **Roger Herman, Bob Zoeli,** and **Pauline Stella Sanchez.** ♦ 5514 Wilshire Blvd

**El Rey** This streamlined movie house, with the original marquee, was designed by **W. Clifford Balch** in 1936. Now abandoned, the remodeled theater was once home to the thriving **Wall Street** nightclub and restaurant. ♦ 5519 Wilshire Blvd

**62 Lew Mitchell's Orient Express** ★$$$ Copper and brass accents and modern rattan furniture are featured in this sleek setting for cuisine that runs the gamut from deep-fried calamari to grilled shark. ♦ Chinese ♦ M-Th 11:30AM-2PM, 5:30-9PM; F-Sa 5-10PM. 5400 Wilshire Blvd. 935.6000

**63 Miro** ★★$$ Owner **Dax** (who is also chef, photographer, designer, and artist) has successfully fused tradition and trend in his modern Korean restaurant. Wonderful dishes such as linguini with shrimps and scallops, delicately fried sea bass, and sweet and spicy beef ribs all come with an unusual beef soup, pungent dipping sauces, and of course, *kim chee*—the garlicky, spicy, fermented pickled cabbage that's a national staple. ♦ Korean ♦ Tu-Sa 6PM-2AM; Su 5-11PM. 809 S. La Brea Ave. 931.9315

The Lakers basketball team moved to LA from Minneapolis in 1960.

**64 Adray's** Discount electronics and appliances are sold here. For service, Circuit City is much better; for the biggest savings, order from 47th Street Photo in New York. ♦ M-F 10AM-8PM; Sa-Su 10AM-6PM. 5575 Wilshire Blvd. 935.8191. Also at: 11201 W. Pico Blvd. 479.0797

**65 Prudential Building** **Wurdeman & Becket's** 1948 design is a good example of the dated Gropius version of the International style. ♦ 5757 Wilshire Blvd

**66 Wilshire Courtyard** **McLarand & Vasquez's** sleek stepped-back commercial development, clad in brown marble and handsomely landscaped, is a welcome relief from the bland towers and fake-classical boxes that now dominate LA's most prestigious artery. The development was completed in 1988. ♦ 5750 Wilshire Blvd. 939.0300

**67 La Brea Tar Pits** La Brea is Spanish for tar, and the tar that seeps from these pits was used by Indians and early settlers to seal boats and roofs. In 1906, geologists discovered the pits had entrapped 200 varieties of mammals, plants, birds, reptiles, and insects from the Pleistocene Era, and preserved them as fossils. Disney-esque sculptures of doomed mammals add a surreal touch. ♦ Wilshire Blvd (at Curson Ave)

At the La Brea Tar Pits:

**George C. Page Museum of La Brea Discoveries** Established in 1977 within grassy berms topped by a steel-frame canopy, the museum offers exhibitions, films, and demonstrations that describe the evolution of the pits. Children will revel in the holographic displays that give flesh to the bones of a tiger and a woman excavated here, and a hands-on demonstration of how sticky tar is. Summer visitors can watch paleontologists at work in Pit 91. There's a gift shop, and free parking is available in back. ♦ Admission. Tu-Su 10AM-5PM. 5801 Wilshire Blvd. 936.2230

COURTESY OF HARDY HOLZMAN PFEIFFER ASSOCIATES

**67 Los Angeles County Museum of Art (LACMA)** When the Los Angeles County Museum (pictured above) opened in 1964, it became one of the finest, most varied art museums in America. The **Robert O. Anderson Building,** built in 1986 by **Hardy Holzman Pfeiffer,** comprises a vast wedge of limestone, glass brick, and green terra-cotta that pays homage to the streamline moderne **Coulter's Store** (a former highlight of Miracle Mile). An entry portal of Babylonian proportions frames the steps leading up to the original **Ahmanson,**

Hammer, and Bing pavilions and the courtyard, which is now roofed over. The sculpture garden has been restored and a Japanese garden added.

The **Japanese Pavilion,** overlooking the Tar Pits, was conceived by the late **Bruce Goff** in 1988, and was realized by his protégé, **Bart Prince.** Goff and Prince are true originals, though this gallery reminds some of **Eero Saarinen's** TWA Terminal at New York's Kennedy Airport, while others discover echoes of '50s googie-style coffeehouses. It was designed for **Joe D. Price,** an Oklahoma oil man, to house his collection of *Edo* scrolls and screens—which he donated to LACMA in 1982—and to display them in a traditionally Japanese manner. To avoid internal divisions, the building is suspended from a frame of concrete posts and beams and is lit from fiberglass wall panels that evoke shoji screens. Visitors take an elevator to the third floor and walk down a winding ramp through the east wing, past a series of wall niches that frame a constantly changing selection of 30 artworks. The west wing contains *netsuke* and other highlights from LACMA's rich collections, and a book/gift store.

LACMA originates superb temporary exhibitions. Its permanent collections offer comprehensive coverage of the history of Western Art, in addition to fine holdings of Oriental and Near-Eastern art, costumes, and textiles. The **Rifkin Collection of German Expressionism** is justly famous. Some of LA's best film series and concerts of contemporary music are regularly presented in the 500-seat auditorium of the **Bing Center,** and there is an outstanding museum shop. Jazz concerts are presented in the **Plaza** on Sunday afternoons, and with cocktails and hors d'oeuvres on Friday evenings. Members may rent artworks, and—if they decide to keep them—apply the charges to the purchase price. The new **Plaza Cafe,** with its painterly decor by **David Sheppard,** offers food of a quality far above most museum cafeterias, and is a favorite meeting place for young (art) lovers. ♦ Admission fee for nonmembers; free on second Tu of each month. Tu-Th 10AM-5PM; F 10AM-9PM; Sa-Su 11AM-6PM. 5905 Wilshire Blvd. 857.6000 (recording)

**68 May Co. Department Store** The immense gilded cylinder (illustrated above) set into the southwest corner of this rectangular block is a highlight of Miracle Mile. Designed in 1940 by **Albert C. Martin & S.A. Marx,** it is now threatened by redevelopment. ♦ Daily 10AM-9PM. 6067 Wilshire Blvd (at Fairfax Ave). 938.4211

Within the May Co. Department Store:

**Craft and Folk Art Museum** Changing exhibitions of crafts, folk art, and design are presented on the fourth floor of the May Co. store in a 10,000-square-foot gallery designed by **Charles Moore.** The art will remain here until the museum's new, greatly expanded quarters (by **Hodgetts** and **Fung**) are completed in late 1993. Books and fine crafts are available for sale. The museum-sponsored **International Festival of the Masks,** held annually in Hancock Park during the last week of October, is a

popular city event. ♦ Call ahead for specific hours and location. 937.5544

**69 Loehmann's** This discount clothing store is a woman's best friend, carrying an extensive selection of loungewear, suits, casual and formal wear, and accessories. The quality merchandise is discounted 30 percent and more. Haute couture is showcased in the **Backroom.** ♦ M-F 10AM-9PM; Sa 10AM-7PM; Su noon-6PM. 6220 W. Third St. 933.5675. Also at: 19389 Victory Blvd, Reseda. 818/345.7063

**70 Park La Brea Housing and Towers** Built in the 1940s, the large, Regency Moderne complex of low- and high-rise garden apartments is located in a 176-acre park. ♦ Bounded by Third, Cochran, Sixth, and Fairfax Sts

**71 The Tennis Place** There are sixteen lighted courts open to nonmembers, though most are reserved at peak hours. ♦ Daily 6:30AM-11PM. 5880 W. Third St. 931.1715

**72 The Whole** ★$ Don't miss the homemade blueberry coffee cake, Ping-Pong, and Parcheesi at this funky hangout that's popular among neighborhood teenagers and seniors. The place is more welcoming than hip, like a visit to a pal's playroom. Interesting insect sculptures made of found metal objects dangle overhead. ♦ Coffeehouse ♦ M-Th, Su 11AM-2:30AM; F-Sa 11AM-4AM. 5959 W. Third St. 965.8334

**73 Steve Turner Gallery** This gallery features American modernist paintings from the '30s and '40s, and international poster design from 1910 to 1950. ♦ W-F 11AM-5PM; Sa-Su noon-5PM. 7220 Beverly Blvd. 931.1185

**73 Fish Grill** ★$ A half-dozen varieties of fresh fish are simply grilled in this no-nonsense kosher cafe that serves a diverse crowd of value-seekers. ♦ Seafood ♦ M-Th, Sa-Su 11AM-9PM; F 11AM-2:30PM. 7226 Beverly Blvd. 937.7162

**73 Java** ★$ This stylish literary coffeehouse is run by UCLA graduates in a converted Art Deco building. Fresh breads, pastries, and light fare sustain those who are reading, playing chess, or listening to the Wednesday and Sunday night readings of poetry and fiction. ♦ American ♦ M-Th 9AM-2AM; F-Sa 9AM-3AM; Su 9AM-2AM. 7286 Beverly Blvd. 931.4943

| Restaurants/Clubs: Red | Hotels: Blue |
| --- | --- |
| Shops/ ❦ Outdoors: Green | Sights/Culture: Black |

**47**

**73 Tyler Trafficante** You'll find tailored suits and coats for men and women here, all designed by Australian expatriate **Richard Tyler,** with a winning blend of old-world elegance and very contemporary theatrics. The fashions are housed in a dramatic Art Deco corner building. ♦ M-F 11AM-7PM; Sa noon-6PM. 7290 Beverly Blvd. 931.9678

**73 Muse** ★$$$ A handsome skylit room, compelling modern art, and imaginative, sometimes even inspired, cooking draw a large crowd to this establishment. There's a nifty aquarium,

and a good bit of fishing, too, at the bar. ♦ California ♦ M-Th 6-10:30PM; F-Sa 6-11:30PM. 7360 Beverly Blvd. 934.4400

**74 Big & Tall** Philosopher **David Erickson** and former English teacher **Chris Song** opened this upbeat bookstore and cafe for those seeking cappuccino and culture, quite a contrast to the raucous **El Coyote Cafe** across the street. ♦ M-F 8AM-midnight; Sa-Su 10AM-2AM. 7311 Beverly Blvd. Books: 939.5022. Cafe: 939.1403

**74 Mexica Cafe** ★★$$ The casual atmosphere of this cafe draws both family diners and LA literati who haunt the coffeehouses along the boulevard. Delicious and creative Mexican nouveau fare is served. Ask the waiter about the good daily specials with fish and chicken. ♦ Mexican ♦ M-Th noon-3PM, 5-10PM; F-Sa noon-3PM, 5-11PM; Su 5-10PM. 7313 Beverly Blvd. 933.7385

**74 Skank World** It looks like a Goodwill store with punk overtones, but this is the place to find classic '50s furniture at affordable prices, including **Eames'** plywood chairs and the rare example of **Alvar Aalto.** It opens late so the owners can watch "All My Children." ♦ Tu-Sa 2-6PM; M by appointment. 7205 Beverly Blvd. 939.7858

**75 A.J. Heinsbergen Company** This tiny, 1925 medieval brick castle, with drawbridge and moat, is still occupied by the design company that built it. ♦ 7415 Beverly Blvd. 934.1134

**75 Mario's Cooking for Friends** ★$$ Chef **Mario Martinoli** serves good pasta, salads, and poultry dishes from a menu that changes daily in this light, bright dining room and terrace. Some dishes are available for takeout in the well-stocked deli that adjoins the restaurant. ♦ Italian ♦ Restaurant: M-F 11:30AM-2:30PM, 6-10:30PM; Sa 6-10:30PM. Deli: M-Sa 11AM-10PM. 7475 Beverly Blvd. 931.6342

**76 Authentic Cafe** ★★$$ Be prepared to stand in line, no matter when you go to this tiny and terminally trendy spot. Rest assured, the generous portions of ethnic fare are worth the wait, are reasonably priced, and are always served with a smile. They accept cash only. ♦ Eclectic ♦ M-Th 11AM-3:30PM, 5-11PM; F-Sa 11AM-3:30PM, 5PM-midnight. 7605 Beverly Blvd. 939.4626

**77 Sonrisa Art & Antiques** Folk and fine art of unusual quality from Mexico and Central America, and vintage accent pieces recalling early California are sold here. ♦ M-Sa 10AM-6PM. 7609 Beverly Blvd. 935.8438

**78 CBS Television City** Constructed in 1952 b **Pereira & Luckman** and renovated in 1976 by **Gin Wong Associates,** these high-tech boxes contain studios and offices for network execu tives. Free tickets to shows can be picked up a the information window; however, there are some age restrictions. For groups of 20 or more, call 852.2455. ♦ Daily 9AM-5PM. 7800 Beverly Blvd. 852.2624

**79 Farmers' Market** A favorite with locals and tourists, Farmers' Market (pictured below at right) was established in 1934 as a cooperative market where local farmers could sell their pro duce. Today there are more than 160 vendors, including 26 stands that offer hot and cold dishes from around the world. Browse, select an appetizer here, an entrée there, but save room for pastry, and find a seat beneath the umbrellas and awnings. The market section provides fine vegetables, cheeses, meats, pastries, baked goods, and exotic imported foodstuffs. **Mr. K's Gourmet Foods and Coffee** (stall 430) sells hard-to-obtain spices and teas try **Stone Farm Fresh Produce** (stall 816) for exotic fruits. Several of the fruit and nut stalls make up and ship gift boxes, as do some of the confectioneries, where you can watch candy being made. ♦ M-Sa 9AM-7PM; Su 10AM-6PM; closed major holidays. 6333 W. Third St. 933.9211

Within Farmers' Market:

**Kokomo** ★$ The New Age counter here offers the best in breakfasts, lunches, and fountain dishes. They make great granola, gumbo, and BLTs, too. ♦ American ♦ M-Sa 8AM-7PM; Su 10AM-6PM. 933.0773

**The Gumbo Pot** ★$ Spicy gumbo, fresh oysters, blackened fish, and meat loaf are the specialties; they have hearty weekend brunches, too. ♦ Cajun/Creole ♦ M-Sa 8:30AM-7PM; Su 10AM-6PM. 933.0358

**80 Fairfax Avenue** Since World War II, this has been the Main Street for the Jewish communit of Los Angeles. Although the majority of Los Angeles Jews currently reside on the Westside and in the San Fernando Valley, the Eastern Eu ropean Jewish tradition continues as a strong influence in this area. Elderly men congregate on street corners to discuss business and politics; Hassids and a large number of Orthodox Jews walk to the synagogue on Friday night and Saturday; other days, women carry their shopping bags to the local butcher, greengrocer, and bakery.

**80 Al's News** Newspapers and magazines in profusion line the racks here. ♦ M-Th 7AM-11PM; F 6:30AM-1AM; Sa 6AM-1AM; Su 6AM-10PM. Oakwood Ave. (at Fairfax Ave). 935.8525

**80 Canter's Fairfax Restaurant Delicatessen and Bakery** ★$$ This is the largest and liveliest of the delis on Fairfax. The interior has remained untouched since **Doris Day** was a girl,

---

and the neon sign on the facade is a classic. Waitresses not only bring your food, they also make sure you eat it. The pastrami is highly praised. ♦ Deli ♦ Daily 24 hours. 419 N. Fairfax Ave. 651.2030

**80 Cafe Largo** $$ **Anna Mariani** and **Jean Pierre Boccara,** who ran the late, lamented **Lhasa Club,** have created this restaurant/cabaret that presents nightly comedy, performance art, and rock, plus poetry readings on Tuesday. ♦ Eclectic ♦ M-Sa 7PM-closing; Su 6PM-closing. 432 N. Fairfax Ave. 852.1073

**81 Nowhere Cafe** ★$$ Chicken kabobs with ginger sauce, tofu with ginger-garlic sauce, and whole-wheat pasta with wild mushrooms make this cafe a consistent winner. ♦ Eclectic ♦ M-Sa noon-2:30PM, 6-10PM; Su 11AM-2:30PM, 6-10PM. 8009 Beverly Blvd. 655.8895

**82 Kings Road Cafe** ★$$ Purchase your favorite daily or magazine from the corner newsstand and grab a table as fast as you can at this popular cafe, for espresso, gourmet sandwiches, and plenty of wonderful baked goods. ♦ Coffeehouse ♦ Daily 8AM-midnight. 8361 Beverly Blvd (at Kings Rd). 655.9044

**83 I. Martin Imports** This is a mecca for those in training for the **Tour de France,** or for those who want to race up the side of **Mount Wilson** on the best bike money can buy. ♦ M 10AM-8PM; Tu-Sa 10AM-7PM; Su noon-6PM. 8330 Beverly Blvd. 653.6900

**83 Blueprint** High-end designer furniture and accessories are showcased in a concrete setting. The curtain-glass storefront reveals dramatic interior volume accentuated by a hangarlike ceiling. ♦ M-F 10AM-7PM; Sa 10AM-6PM; Su noon-5PM. 8366 Beverly Blvd. 653.2439

**83 Mandarette** ★$$ Ask your waiter's help in choosing from the eclectic selection of Chinese food from different regional traditions. The room is simple yet elegant, with high ceilings, white walls, and accents in black and a most calming shade of celadon. ♦ Chinese ♦ M-Th 11:30AM-3PM, 5-10:45PM; F 11:30AM-3PM, 5PM-midnight; Sa 5PM-midnight. 8386 Beverly Blvd. 655.6115

**83 Opera Shop of Los Angeles** Everything under the sun for opera, dance, and music can be purchased in this small shop. In addition to

memorabilia relating to the works of Mozart, Verdi, Puccini, and other great masters, the store is well-stocked with *Phantom of the Opera* merchandise. ♦ M-Sa 10AM-6PM. 8384 Beverly Blvd. 658.5811

**83 LaPaloma Designs** A trove of sturdy Southwestern furniture and bric-a-brac packs this shop. ♦ Tu-Sa 10AM-6PM; Su 11PM-5PM. 8408 Beverly Blvd. 655.2195

**84 Fun Furniture** Stop by this one-stop shop for whimsical architect-designed pieces for kids, including a skyscraper dresser, a taxi toy box, and a fire-engine bed. ♦ M-Sa 10AM-5PM; Su noon-5PM. 8451 Beverly Blvd. 655.2711

**84 Dale's Bistro** ★$ The food and the owner, **Dale Payne** (who worked with **Wolfgang Puck** during the **Ma Maison** days), are casual and unpretentious in this engaging cafe located along a fast-paced thoroughfare. Try the onion soup, a Caesar salad, or the daily specials. ♦ Continental ♦ M-F 11:30AM-2:30PM, 6-10:30PM; Sa-Su 6-10:30PM. 361 N. La Cienega Blvd. 310/659.3996

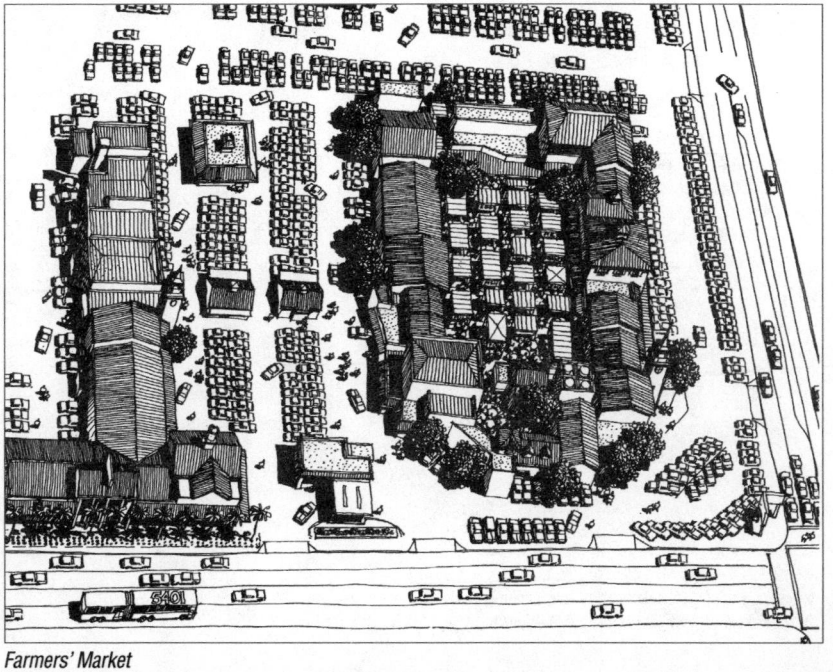

*Farmers' Market*

49

**84 Coronet Theater** This intimate movie house is set back in an almost hidden courtyard. ♦ 366 N. La Cienega Blvd. 310/652.9199

**84 Coronet Bar** Popular with actors, writers, and musicians, this small neighborhood spot is a comfortable, low-key place to drink. ♦ M, Sa 5PM-2AM; Tu-F 1PM-2AM. 370 N. La Cienega Blvd. 310/659.4583

**85 Trashy Lingerie** More than 8,000 items of very intimate apparel in a rainbow of colors are sold here. The window displays are a traffic stopper, and a membership fee is charged to

Midtown

discourage voyeurs. ♦ M-Sa 10AM-7PM. 402 N. La Cienega Blvd. 652.4543

**86 Tryst** $$$ Stylish show-biz people pack the noisy bar and dining room at this richly decorated new restaurant. Though advertised as a secret meeting place for lovers, this is no hideaway–it's a place to see and be seen. The menu offers hot and cold "bites," which can be combined for a meal, and exotic, foreign-flavored food prepared by chef **Ralf Marhencke,** formerly of **Noa Noa.** The quality of the food is uneven, but try the barbecued baby back ribs with smoked tomato sauce or the crispy Chinese air-dried duck entrée. ♦ Eclectic ♦ M-F 11:30AM-2:30PM, 6:30PM-1:30AM; Sa-Su 6:30PM-1:30AM. 401 N. La Cienega Blvd. 289.1600

**87 Ma Maison Sofitel Hotel** $$$ The exterior of this French chain hotel beats stiff competition to win the prize for the klutziest-looking building in LA; it even makes the **Beverly Center** seem tolerable. The interiors have a conventional rich look, but the rooms offer nice views north to the Hollywood Hills. Amenities include a health club, pool, and bargain weekend rates. ♦ 8555 Beverly Blvd. 310/278.5444, 800/763.4835; fax 310/657.2816

Within the Ma Maison Sofitel Hotel:

**Ma Maison Bistrot** ★★$$$ The original Ma Maison on Melrose, whose patio was furnished with plastic chairs and Astroturf, was the in place for food and celebrity glitter. This reincarnation, however, lacks charisma. But the room is much prettier, the menu is designed by **David Hockney,** and there are some nice surprises, including snails in a baked potato, fresh mozzarella on an eggplant puree, and cold asparagus with salmon caviar. Stars still come to be pampered and eat well-prepared duck and chicken salads, steak and fries, and chocolate sorbet. ♦ French ♦ M-F 11:30AM-2:30PM, 6-10:30PM; Sa 6-10:30PM. 310/655.1991

**88 Tail-o'-the-Pup** This hot-dog stand, built in 1946, is the most celebrated of LA's few remaining programmatic structures. Don't miss it. ♦ American ♦ Daily 6AM-8PM. 329 San Vicente Blvd. 310/652.4517

At the LA County Museum of Art, a gallery is named for donor Sidney Sheldon, the best-selling author of potboilers like *The Other Side of Midnight.*

**89 The Mysterious Bookshop** Spies and sleuths, gumshoes and hoods people this store. ♦ M-Sa 10AM-6PM; Su noon-5PM. 8763 Beverly Blvd. 310/659.2959

**90 Madeo** ★★$$$$ The chic, expense-account dining is worth the price. Superb veal chops, extraordinary risotto, and delicious desserts are just some of the specialties. Madeo is a favorite with the **ICM** (International Creative Management) agents and their celebrity clients. It helps to speak Italian. ♦ Italian ♦ M-F 11:30AM-3PM, 6:30-11:30PM; Sa-Su 6:30-11:30PM. 8897 Beverly Blvd. 859.0242. Also at: 295 Whaler's Walk, San Pedro. 831.1199

**90 Chasen's** $$$$ An institution dating from the time when good food was almost impossible to find in LA, Chasen's serves faithful regulars the world's most expensive chili and many other pedestrian dishes in a red-leather-booth-and-knotty-pine decor. To get good service, it helps to be a star. ♦ American ♦ Tu-Su 6PM-1AM. 9039 Beverly Blvd. 310/271.2168

**91 Palazzetti** Classic European and American modern furniture, from **Mackintosh** to **Mies,** is showcased. ♦ M-F 9AM-5:30PM; Sa 11AM-4PM. 9008 Beverly Blvd. 310/273.2225

**91 The Pace Collection** Artist-designed furniture is sold here. ♦ M-F 10AM-6PM. 8936 Beverly Blvd. 310/273.5901

**91 Pane Caldo Bistrot** ★$$ Agents from **ICM** across the street, and dealers, decorators, and shoppers from the surrounding designer's row continue to crowd this plain, second-story trattoria. It's hard to miss with a plate of pasta or risotto accompanied by fresh-baked Tuscan bread. ♦ Italian ♦ M-Sa 11:30AM-3PM, 6-10:30PM; Su 6-10:30PM. 8840 Beverly Blvd. 310/274.0916

**91 Kaleido** The unique stock of more than 300 kaleidoscopes is the work of about 90 artists. ♦ M-Sa 11AM-6PM. 8840 Beverly Blvd. 310/276.6844

**91 Diva** Offbeat contemporary lighting and furniture pack this showroom. ♦ M-F 9:30AM-6PM; Sa 11AM-5PM. 8818 Beverly Blvd. 274.0650

**91 Stylus** If you're looking for custom-upholstered California furniture in contemporary or traditional styling, you've come to the right place. Bring your own fabric or choose from more than 500 stock textiles. There are locations in West Los Angeles, Torrance, Pasadena, Sherman Oaks, Woodland Hills, Huntington Beach, and Laguna Hills. ♦ M-Sa 10AM-6PM; Su noon-6PM. 157 N. Robertson Blvd. 310/278.1135

**92 The Ivy** ★★$$$ This is one of the prettiest restaurants in town, and a favorite with industry types and the ladies who lunch. It's Southwestern in feeling, with adobe walls, open hearths, antiques, and an ivy-strewn terrace. Simple dishes are best; go for the corn chowder and mesquite-grilled shrimp. Save room for the desserts that made the Ivy's reputation, especially the lemon cake topped with white chocolate mousse. And carry some home from

**LA Desserts,** which shares space with the restaurant. ♦ American ♦ M-Th 11:30AM-3PM, 6-11PM; F 11:30AM-3PM, 6-11:30PM; Sa 11:30AM-3PM, 6-11PM; Su 11AM-3PM, 5:30-10:30PM. 113 N. Robertson Blvd. 310/274.8303

**92  Manhattan Coolers** $ If your American Express card is too maxed out to cover a meal at **The Ivy,** dash across the street to this popular hangout for a smoked chicken-pesto quesadilla or some fried Manhattan onions topped with parmesan cheese. ♦ Eclectic ♦ M-Th 11:30AM-midnight; F-Sa 11:30AM-2AM; Su 11:30AM-11PM. 120 N. Roberston Blvd. 310/652.4444. Also at: 309 Manhattan Beach Blvd, Manhattan Beach. 310/546.7344; 14649 Ventura Blvd, Sherman Oaks. 818/905.7221; 13490 Maxella Way, Marina del Rey. 310/305.1535

**93  Chaya Brasserie** ★★★$$$ The marvelous interior by **Elyse Grinstein** and **Jeff Daniels** combines a Japanese esthetic (skylit, pine-framed bamboo grove, and upturned parasol lampshades) with the friendly informality of a Parisian brasserie. Chefs **Goto Shingi** and **Shigefumi Tachibe** pull off the same East-meets-West magic in such innovative dishes as tuna tartare and seaweed salad, plus Japanese-accented French and Italian fare. There's a hot bar scene, too. ♦ Japanese/French/Italian ♦ M-Sa 11:30AM-2:30PM, 6PM-12:30AM; Su 6-10PM. 8741 Alden Dr. 310/859.8833. Also at: 110 Navy St, Venice. 310/396.1179

**93  Cedars Sinai Medical Center** Though inspiring for the philanthropy that made it possible, its uninspired gigantism makes it a fit companion for the Beverly Center. A bright spark, architecturally, is the outwardly inconspicuous cancer clinic designed by **Morphosis** in 1988. ♦ 8700 Beverly Blvd. 310/855.5000

**94  Beverly Center** This shopping center (pictured below) is comprised of three windowless levels of stores, restaurants, and movie theaters atop four open decks of parking. The best exterior features are the Beaubourg-inspired, glass-enclosed elevators and the tilted Cadillac of the **Hard Rock Cafe.** Boutiques on the upper floors include **By Design, Linea Uomo, Laura Ashley, Laise Adzer, Joan & David,** and **Traction Avenue,** plus **Warner Bros. Studio Store,** and the usual upscale department store chains, a **Bullock's,** and **The Broadway.** At the top of the pile are cafes, restaurants (including **La Rotisserie,** a dependable bistro), and the **Cineplex** movie theaters—13 shoeboxes and two comfortable balconied houses. ♦ M-Sa 10AM-9PM; Su 11AM-6PM. Between Beverly and La Cienega Blvds, and San Vicente Blvd and Third St

Within the Beverly Center (at street level):

**Irvine Ranch Farmers' Market** Chefs have acclaimed this as LA's best retail market for produce, fish, and meat. Come here to find the freshest and most exotic—at prices that may diminish your appetite. ♦ M-Sa 9AM-10PM; Su 9AM-8PM. 310/657.1931

**Conran's Habitat** This English emporium of well-designed, affordable furnishings for home and office is accessibly displayed and generously stocked. ♦ M-F 10AM-9PM; Sa 11AM-8PM; Su 11AM-6PM. 310/659.1444

## Midtown

**Hard Rock Cafe** ★$$ Owner **Peter Morton** has the Midas touch: from London to LA, these cafes are standing room only. Loud music, basic fare, rock 'n' roll memorabilia, and wall-to-wall crowds is the well-tested recipe. The Hard Rock is an obligatory stop for visiting teenagers, who cheerfully wait in line. ♦ American ♦ M-F 11:30AM-midnight; Sa-Su 11:30AM-12:30AM. 310/276.7605

**California Pizza Kitchen** ★$ Another branch of a fast expanding chain, this is the "Baskin-Robbins" of pizza parlors, whose 18 flavors include Cajun and Peking duck. The more conventional choices are a better bet. ♦ Pizza ♦ M-Sa 11:30AM-midnight; Su 11:30AM-11PM. 854.6555

**95  Beverly Connection** The behemoth Beverly Center overshadows this retail center, expanded from the popular sundries mecca, **Rexall Square Drug.** The architecture is undistinguished industrial chic but more pedestrian-friendly than its giant neighbor. Among the tenants are a consumer electronics store; a market; small restaurants; specialty shops including **Bookstar,** an upscale discount bookseller; **Sports Chalet,** an athlete's wonderland; **Strouds** for fine linen and bath supplies; and the **Daily Grill** for meat loaf, pasta, or Cobb salad. ♦ M-Th 11AM-11PM; F 11AM-midnight; Sa-Su 10AM-10PM. 100 N. La Cienega Blvd. 310/659.3100

**96  Katsu 3rd** ★★$$ The cool, minimalist room has hand-painted furniture and an atmosphere that might be described as hip zen. The short, innovative menu is a fusion of East and West. Fish is a specialty here, but the best bet at lunch is the *bento,* an array of delicious morsels in a lacquered box. More elaborate dishes include a terrine of scallops, halibut, and eel, and beef filet stuffed with monkfish mousse. ♦ California/Japanese ♦ M-F 11:30AM-2:30PM, 6-10PM; Sa 6-10PM. 8636 W. Third St. 310/273.3605

verly Center

**96 Locanda Veneta** ★★★$$ Host **Jean Louis de Mori** and chef **Antonio Tommasi** have created one of LA's most exciting and authentic trattorias, and the crowds have flocked in. Everything on the menu is a winner, but don't miss the handmade mozzarella, duck, and chicken dumplings with onion confit; rack of lamb in a mustard-peanut sauce; any of the pastas or risottos; and the vanilla ice cream with chocolate sauce. ♦ Italian ♦ M-F 11:30AM-2:30PM, 5:30-10:30PM; Sa 5:30-10:30PM. 8638 W. Third St. 310/274.1893

## Midtown

**96 Orso's** ★★$$$ The legendary showbiz hangout **Joe Allen's** has been transformed by the same owner into a great looking trattoria with the most seductive patio in town. The bread is fabulous, the hand-painted plates gorgeous, the service friendly, and the cosmopolitan clientele star-studded. The menu is ambitious and appealing, offering such delicacies as veal kidney, tripe, dandelion greens, and Italian cheeses, along with the pizzas, pastas, and grilled fish. However, some dishes are overpriced, and there is some strange house edict that prohibits waiters from pouring wine. ♦ Italian ♦ Daily 11:45AM-11:45PM. 8706 W. Third St. 310/274.7144

**96 Ma Be** ★★$$$ Light and dark wood, aged copper, natural stone, and floral prints are blended to great effect in this multilevel restaurant with its cozy bar and airy rooftop terrace. The California, French, and Italian cuisines are mixed with flair. Standouts include the sautéed wild mushrooms, salad of crayfish and *haricots verts,* sweetbreads with grapes, and pasta with squab. ♦ California ♦ M-Th, Su 11:30AM-3PM, 6-10PM; F-Sa 11:30AM-3PM, 6-11PM. 8722 -W. Third St. 310/276.6223

**97 Third Street** This less than half-mile corridor east of La Cienega and west of Sweetzer Street isn't as scintillating as Melrose Avenue or as indulgent as Rodeo Drive. Home to an array of small restaurants, antique shops, and lots of hair salons, Third Street is hip without the hype, more off the beaten path than offbeat. Third Street denizens, mainly apartment dwellers that reside north and south of the strip, can stroll around the corner and grab a sandwich at **Who's on Third;** walk in for a restyled coif at **Object Hair Salon;** purchase new threads at **Atlas Clothing Co.;** and launder clothes and possibly find romance at the **Washing Machine** self-serve laundry. ♦ Between La Cienega Blvd. and Sweetzer St

Early in the century, the fertile land of Southern California produced more walnuts, oranges, and avocados than any other part of the nation. This all changed with the post-World War II population boom, when land became more valuable for housing than for farming. In the late 1950s, orange trees were uprooted at the rate of one every 55 seconds. At the peak of this conversion frenzy, 3,000 acres of orange orchards were destroyed every day.

**98 New Stone Age** Off-the-wall, artist-designed objects are sold here. ♦ M-F 11AM-7PM; Sa 11AM-6PM; Su noon-5PM. 8407 W. Third St. 658.5969

**98 Freehand** Located steps away from New Stone Age, this shop features fine handcrafted goods–from colorful ceramics and jewelry to women's apparel and mantle pieces. Special craft shows and artists' receptions are held frequently. ♦ M-Sa 11AM-6PM. 8413 W. Third St. 655.2607

**98 Traveler's Bookcase** A wonderful collection of books for armchair travelers and serious adventurers fill the shelves. ♦ M-Sa 10AM-6PM. 8375 W. Third St. 655.0575

**98 The Cook's Library** Owner **Ellen Rose** turned her hobby into an occupation when she opened the only LA store that concentrates entirely on cookbooks—new, old, and out-of-print. ♦ M 1-5PM; Tu-Sa 11AM-6PM. 8373 W. Third St. 655.3141

**99 Cynthia's Restaurant** ★★★$ This intimate restaurant has an understated charm created by its proprietor, **Cynthia Hirsh.** Favorites on the menu include spaghettini with sautéed shrimp and asparagus in garlic butter or grilled lamb chops in a mint marinade. ♦ Eclectic ♦ M-F 11AM-3PM, 5:30-11PM; Sa 5:30-11PM; Su 10AM-3PM, 5-9PM. 8370 W. Third St. 658.7851

**99 Baby Motives** Discount clothes, toys, strollers, and furniture for the very young are sold here. ♦ M-F 10AM-5:30PM; Sa 10AM-5PM. 8362 W. Third St. 658.6015

**99 Beverly Plaza Hotel** $$$ This elegant small hotel is popular with solo travelers because of its in-house restaurant, exercise room, and complimentary limousine service. ♦ 8384 W. Third St. 658.6600, 800/624.6835; fax 653.3464

**99 Tazzina Coffeehouse** $ *Tazzina* is Italian slang for "little coffee cup," which aptly describes this friendly, intimately lit cafe. It's a convenient stop for a snack along the popular Third Street corridor. At press time, however, Tazzina's fate was uncertain, so please call ahead for location confirmation. 8334 W. Third St. 310/278.0989

**99 Katie's Dirty Dishes** The wacky, colorful, handmade crafts are as functional as they are frenetic. ♦ M by appointment; Tu-Sa 11AM-6PM. 141 Kings Rd. 653.1983

**100 Indigo** ★★$$ Breezy, whimsically decorated, and a little bit wild, Indigo has a patio, a small singles dining bar, and healthy portions of upscale pastas, pizzas, sandwiches, salads, and grilled meats, all with a Mediterranean or Southwest accent. Don't miss the great rosemary-flavored bread. ♦ California ♦ M-Th, Su 11:30AM-2:30PM, 5:30-10PM; F-Sa 11:30AM-2:30PM, 5:30-11PM. 8222½ W. Third St. 653.0140

The city's first escalator was installed in 1907 at Bullocks Department Store at 7th Street and Broadway downtown.

**01 Siamese Princess** ★★$$ The sedate, regal decor, serious service, a nice wine list, and refined, subtle cooking put this restaurant near the top of LA's ubiquitous Thai restaurants. A specialty is *mu sarong*—deep-fried, noodle-wrapped meatballs. ♦ Thai ♦ M-F noon-2:30PM, 5:30-11PM; Sa-Su 5:30-11:30PM. 8048 W. Third St. 653.2643

**01 Sofi Estiatorion** ★$$ This lively, family run restaurant serves excellent moussaka and daily specials. ♦ Greek ♦ M-Sa 11:30AM-3PM, 6-11PM; Su 6-11PM. 8030 3/4 W. Third St. 651.0346

**02 Mandarin Wilshire** ★★$$ Among the 143 offerings of chef **Tony Ngon** are wonderful dumplings, Peking duck, pan-fried noodles, tangerine beef, and flaming bananas. ♦ Chinese ♦ M-Th 11:30AM-10PM; F-Sa 11:30AM-11PM; Su 5-10PM. 8300 Wilshire Blvd. 658.6928

**03 Cafe Gale** ★$$$ Watching the bustling boulevard traffic in beautiful silence is enticement enough to dine in this glass-enclosed restaurant, which showcases an impressive collection of antique toy cars, trucks, and locomotives. Chef/co-owner **Shigaru Isuki** creates wonderful starters, such as pork dumplings in tangerine sauce and crab croquettes, for the pre-show crowd at nearby **Wilshire Theater**. ♦ Eclectic ♦ M-F 8AM-4:30PM, 5-10PM; Sa-Su 5-11PM. 8400 Wilshire Blvd. 655.2494

**04 Martyrs Memorial Museum of the Holocaust** Chambered in the **Jewish Federation Council** building, this archival storehouse honors the survivors and the six million victims of Nazi persecution and internment. The two-level gallery displays photo murals, documents, artifacts, and memorabilia recounting this tragic period in history. Names of the victims are inscribed on the walls of the Martyrs Memorial, designed to resemble the cattle car transports that carried millions to their deaths. In a wing dedicated to the children of the Holocaust is a scaled model of **Terezin**, a concentration camp which imprisoned 15,000 youth between 1942 and 1944. Also here is the **Jewish Community Library**, which contains literature on Jewish history and culture. ♦ Gallery: M-Th 9AM-5PM; F 9AM-3PM; Su 1-5PM. 6505 Wilshire Blvd. 852.1234 ext 3202

**05 Wilshire Crest** $$ This small hotel is reasonably priced and serves Continental breakfasts. ♦ 6301 Orange St. 936.5131; fax 936.2013

**06 Caffe Latte** ★$$ You'll find an interesting crowd at this friendly neighborhood place, with innovative, great-tasting fare, and artistic modern decor. They have home-baked breads and roasted-on-the-premises coffee beans, which can also be purchased. ♦ American ♦ M 7AM-5PM; Tu-F 7AM-5PM, 5:30-10:30PM; Sa 5:30-11:30PM. 6254 Wilshire Blvd. 936.5213

In the early 1900s oil was discovered in an area one mile square that was delineated by La Brea and Fairfax Avenue, and Wilshire and Beverly boulevards. Called the Salt Lake Oil Field by the main producer, it was the leading field in Southern California in 1905. Today it is the home of the Farmers' Market, which stands on the former site of the discovery well.

**106 SouperGreens** ★$ You'll find healthful fare in plain but pleasant minimall surroundings at this restaurant. They serve great vegetarian chili and a hearty burrito, but think twice about ordering the potato-heavy clam chowder and the too-rich quiche. ♦ American ♦ M-F 7AM-8PM; Sa 9AM-8PM. 6240 Wilshire Blvd. 933.9356

**107 South Carthay Circle** Don't miss this charming, leafy neighborhood of 1930s stucco cottages that mixes Spanish and Art Deco themes. Consistent in style and scale, this historic district is now threatened by predatory developers.

## Midtown

Long-gone is a legendary Mission Revival movie palace, the **Carthay Circle.** ♦ Located east and west of San Vicente Blvd, south of Wilshire Blvd

**108 Rosalind's West African** $$ Liberian-born **Rosalind** and her Peace Corps-veteran husband offer an adventurous selection of West African dishes, like ground-nut stew, yam balls, and plantains with ginger and cayenne. ♦ African ♦ Tu-Su 5-10PM. 1044 S. Fairfax Ave. 936.2486

**109 Versailles** ★★$ Built to accommodate loyal patrons from the Midtown area, this larger version of the original restaurant serves the same gutsy garlic chicken, pork with black beans, oxtail, and strong coffee. There's takeout, too. ♦ Cuban ♦ M-Th, Su 11AM-10PM; F-Sa 11AM-11PM. 1415 S. La Cienega Blvd (So of Pico Blvd). 310/289.0392. Also at: 10319 Venice Blvd, Culver City. 310/558.3168

**110 Carl's Bar-B-Q** ★★$ Those in the know come from miles around for what experts claim is LA's best East Texas-style barbecue, hickory-smoked and slathered with **Carl Adams'** magical sauce, medium or very hot. With only three tables, most of the business is to go. The ribs, chicken, hot links, greens, and dirty rice are probably the closest thing to heaven you will ever find in a yellow styrofoam takeout box. ♦ American ♦ M-F 11AM-10PM; Sa 11AM-11PM; Su 2-9PM. 5953 Pico Blvd. No credit cards. 934.0637

**111 Maurice's Snack 'n' Chat** ★$$ This popular soul food restaurant serves large platters of meat loaf, short ribs, and liver and onions, accompanied by yams, beets, or black-eyed peas. ♦ Soul food ♦ M-F noon-10PM; Sa 4-11PM; Su 4-9PM. 5549 Pico Blvd. 931.3877

**112 Fred's Bakery** Only in LA would bagels aspire to elegance, but these are good enough to lure movie stars. Other tempting treats to sample are the cakes, cookies, and fresh-baked bread. ♦ M-Sa 6AM-6PM; Su 7AM-3PM. 2831 S. Robertson Blvd. 310/838.1204

**113 St. Elmo's Village** Artist **Roderick Sykes** organized friends and neighbors to transform this derelict courtyard into a painted quilt of faces, figures, and inspirational messages whose verve would have delighted Picasso. ♦ Su noon-6PM. 4830 St. Elmo Dr (between La Brea Ave and Venice Blvd). 936.3595

# Hollywood/West Hollywood

Signs reading No Dogs, No Actors greeted the first movie pioneers to arrive in Hollywood, but the marriage of Midwestern farmers and Eastern entertainers overcame its rocky start. Hollywood soon became the symbol of glamour and excitement around the world, a mecca for established talent and unknown hopefuls.

Hollywood is divided economically and geographically into two communities: the flatlands and the hills. The flatlands contain the laboratories, stages, and studios in which movies are processed, television taped, and music recorded. Industrial zones are interspersed with bungalows and apartment buildings, many from the 1910s and 1920s. Some of them have been restored, others are much decayed. The **Community Redevelopment Agency's** Hollywood plan is a welcome response to the decline, but it has failed to answer the question: How can the area regain its vitality without losing its character? The old Hollywood had a strong sense of community and this was reflected in its architecture. Too many of the

dingbat apartments that have erupted on the side streets, as well as the new commercial structures along Hollywood, Sunset, and Santa Monica boulevards, are bland or overbearing.

**West Hollywood**—a pistol-shaped area of these flatlands, formerly administered by LA County—became an independent city in 1984, the 84th in the Greater Los Angeles area. In contrast to old Hollywood, its problem is not decay but excessive growth, and it has wisely applied the brakes. Design showrooms, fashionable shops, restaurants, and hotels abound, and there is a large gay community. Its spine is **Santa Monica Boulevard** from **La Brea Avenue** west to **Doheny Drive.** But its boundaries, from **Sunset Strip** to **Beverly Boulevard** in the west, narrowing to a few blocks in the east, are so ragged that it is more practical to describe its attractions together with those of the old Hollywood.

The hills span the rustic charms of **Nichols Canyon** and the raffish counterculture of **Laurel Canyon.** They feature a bizarre mixture of castles and cottages, Spanish haciendas and Moorish temples, and winding streets and wild areas of

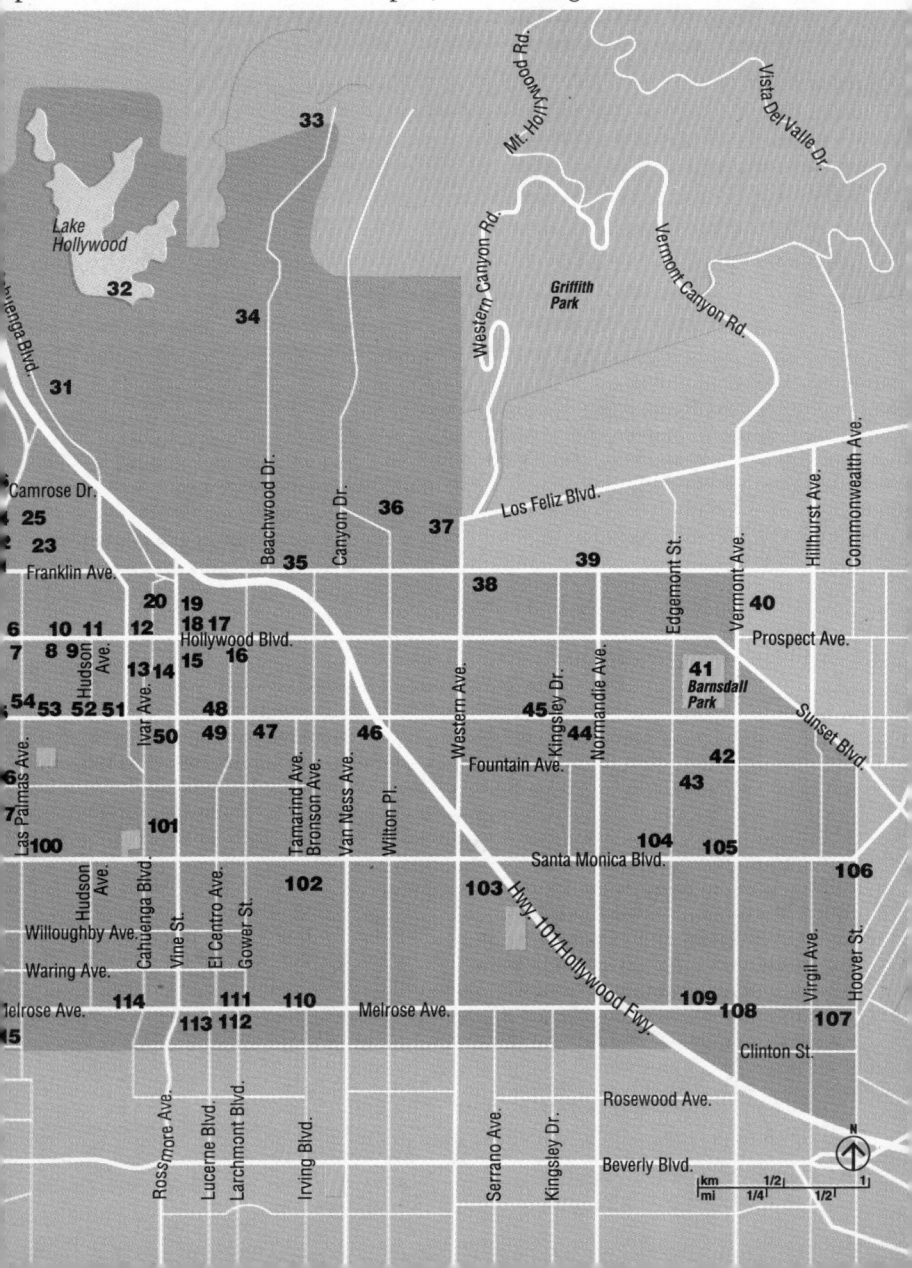

chaparral. The flatland residents of east and central Hollywood have an income that's half the LA average, and recent immigrants, especially from Southeast Asia, Latin America, and the Middle East, make up a high proportion of the population. The hills are more prosperous and settled, appealing to literary and artistic types.

Hollywood was a campground for the **Cahuenga Indians** and later (because of its proximity to the **Cahuenga Pass**) a way station on the Camino Real and a major stop on the Butterfield Stage route. When **Harvey Wilcox** registered the subdivision of Hollywood in 1887, it had few residents and only 165 voters participated in the 1903 vote to incorporate as a city of the sixth class. His wife, **Deaida Wilcox**, named the area after the Chicago summer home of a woman she met on the train, and she was its greatest supporter, giving land for churches and schools, keeping demon drink at bay, and welcoming French artist **Paul de Longpre**, whose garden became Hollywood's first tourist attraction. Hollywood surrendered its independence in 1910 to guarantee its access

to city water, but it remained a staid farming community of citrus orchards and sheep, with a scattering of houses along unpaved streets lined with pepper trees.

The moviemakers arrived like the Goths in Rome, taking over a saloon on Sunset as the first Hollywood studio, hiring cowboys who rode over front lawns in the excitement of the chase, and greasing intersections to film motorists' skids. The film industry soon became prosperous and respectable, and though most of the big companies moved out to Universal City, Burbank, and Culver City in search of cheaper land, their old lots and stages were taken over by independents and are still active. However seedy the reality, the myth endures.

*Area code 213 unless otherwise noted.*

**1 Hollywood Boulevard** Laid out as Prospect Avenue and lined with ornate mansions, Hollywood Boulevard was rebuilt in the '20s and '30s as the movie colony's Main Street. For a decade or so, it boasted fashionable stores, hotels, and restaurants, though the movie stars came out only at night—for gala premieres at Grauman's Chinese and other movie palaces. Forty years of decline have given the boulevard the reputation of a Times Square West, but the architecture has remained almost intact. **Hollywood Heritage,** a lively preservation organization, secured official recognition for the heart of the boulevard as a **National Historic District**—though this may not protect it from massive redevelopment. Look up to enjoy such treasures as the Gothic moderne tower of the **Security Pacific Bank** at Highland Avenue, the lively zigzag facades flanking **Frederick's of Hollywood's** purple tower, the streamlined drugstore on the corner of Cahuenga Boulevard, and the 1933 marquee of the **Hollywood Theater** (the interior is slated to become a

Guinness World of Records Museum). Look down for the 1,900-plus terrazzo stars of the **Walk of Fame,** commemorating more than a thousand entertainment celebrities. You may adopt your favorite star, if you are willing to polish it on the first Saturday of each month. There's a waiting list for **Marilyn Monroe,** but no lack of orphans. **Lupe Velez,** anyone? Call Michael Kellerman at 469.9880

**2 Hollywood Roosevelt Hotel** $$$ This restored 1927 landmark was the site of the first Academy Awards and the former social hub of the movie colony. **Errol Flynn** invented his recipe for gin in a back room of the barber's shop; **Scott Fitzgerald, Ernest Hemingway,** and **Salvador Dalí** patronized the **Cinegrill** upstairs. **Bill "Bojangles" Robinson** taught **Shirley Temple** to tap dance up the lobby staircase—or so the legends go. The two-story Spanish Colonial lobby with its painted ceiling is worth stopping in to see; **Theodore's** restaurant off the lobby and the Cinegrill (which offer live entertainment nightly) are both sleekly retro in feeling. The Olympic-size pool was painted by **David Hockney.** Memorabilia is displayed on the mezzanine level. ◆ 7000 Hollywood Blvd. 466.7000, 800/950.7667 (CA), 800/858.2244 (US); fax 462.8056

**2 LA Film Permit Office** Free daily listings of location filming are available here. ◆ M-F 7AM-6PM. 6922 Hollywood Blvd, Suite 602. 485.5324

The Academy Award trophy was called the Statuette until 1931, when the Academy librarian, Margaret Herrick, remarked that the trophy resembled her Uncle Oscar.

**Restaurants/Clubs:** Red
**Shops/ ◆ Outdoors:** Green
**Hotels:** Blue
**Sights/Culture:** Black

*Mann's Chinese Theatre*

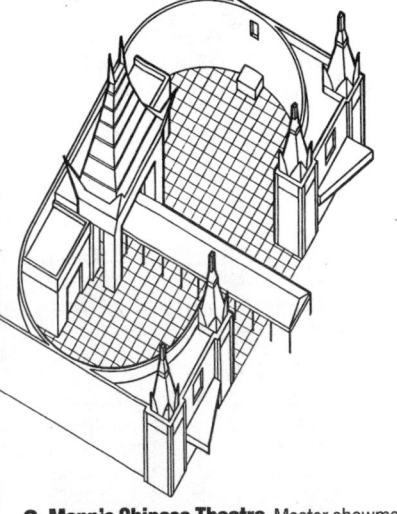

**3 Mann's Chinese Theatre** Master showman **Sid Grauman** commissioned **Meyer & Holler** to create this fanciful Chinese temple (pictured above) in 1927 so that he would have a new stage for his prologues—extravagant spectacles keyed to the movies they accompanied. Legend tells that **Norma Talmadge** accidentally stepped into the wet cement of the forecourt, inspiring Sid to round up **Mary Pickford** and **Douglas Fairbanks** to repeat the trick with their hands and feet, thus inaugurating the world's largest autograph album. He also created the first gala premiere, lining Hollywood Boulevard with klieg lights as the limousines arrived for **De Mille's** *King of Kings* on opening night, 18 May 1927. The cocoa palms have gone from the forecourt, but the theater is amazingly well preserved, inside and out. ♦ 6925 Hollywood Blvd. 464.8111

**3 Grave Line Tours** This tour is a treat for lovers of gallows humor. Ex-mortician **Greg Smith** organized the two-hour tour, in a converted Cadillac hearse, of the homes where stars (from **Sal Mineo** to **Mae West**) met their maker—an improvement on the conventional trips around the houses from which stars have long since moved. Tours depart daily at noon from outside Mann's Chinese. ♦ Reservations: 469.4149. Information: 469.3127

**4 El Capitan Theater** Fields & Devereaux Architects artfully restored this 1926 single-screen movie palace to its former glory, a magnificent blend of baroque, Moorish, East Indian, and churrigueresque ornamentation originally created by architects **Morgan, Walls and Clements** and theater designer **G. Albert Lansburgh.** A team of conservators re-created the stenciled ceiling coves, cornice moldings, and balcony boxes. Thanks to **Disney's Buena Vista Pictures** and **Pacific Theaters,** the preservation saved the elaborate interior from being partitioned into soulless multiscreen boxes. The theater reopened with a big, "old Hollywood" style premiere of Disney's *The Rocketeer.* ♦ Call for showings. 6838 Hollywood Blvd (at Highland Ave). 467.7674

**5 Max Factor Beauty Museum** S. Charles Lee, the master of '30s streamline movie theaters, created this 1931 Regency moderne shrine for the celebrated cosmetics company. Max Factor has vacated the office tower, but has turned its former studio into a fascinating display of how the stars were coiffed and made up. This is an authentic Hollywood shrine. Cosmetics are on sale at discounts of up to 70 percent next door. ♦ Free. M-Sa 10AM-4PM. 1666 N. Highland Ave. 463.6668

**6 B. Dalton Bookseller** The largest bookstore on the boulevard, Dalton's has discounted and remaindered books on the third floor. ♦ M-Th

10AM-9PM; F-Sa 9:30AM-11PM; Su noon-6PM. 6743 Hollywood Blvd. 469.8191

**6 Hollywood Wax Museum** This melancholy place is stuffed with unconvincing replicas of famous stars and assorted celebrities, plus a wax *Last Supper* at which visitors throw coins as though it were a fountain. ♦ Admission. M-Th, Su 10AM-midnight; F-Sa 10AM-2AM. 6767 Hollywood Blvd. 462.8860

**7 Guinness World of Records Museum** Oddities and world-record displays are featured in the refurbished Hollywood Theatre, Hollywood's first movie house. The most popular exhibit is the $30,000 tribute to singer **Michael Jackson's** "Thriller" album (which set a record when it sold 48 million copies). ♦ Admission. Daily 10AM-midnight. 6764 Hollywood Blvd. 463.6433

**7 Egyptian Theater** Sid Grauman's first Off-Broadway movie palace by **Meyer & Holler** was inspired by the newly discovered tomb of King Tut in 1922. Sphinxes, hieroglyphics, and winged cobras adorned the walls. At the big movie premieres, a spear carrier paced the ramparts and usherettes were dressed as Cleopatra's handmaidens. In the era of multiplex movie houses, owner United Artists shut down the theater in July 1992. LA preservationists hope private efforts that saved the nearby El Capitan will rescue what was once considered a national institution. ♦ 6712 Hollywood Blvd

**7 Universal News Agency** The newsstand is one of the best sources of hometown (whether Bangor or Bangkok) newspapers and international magazines. ♦ Daily 7AM-10PM. 1655 N. Las Palmas Ave. 467.3850

**8 Larry Edmunds** A longtime mecca for lovers of film and theater, they have a wide selection of books, posters, and stills, but it's not all it used to be. ♦ M-Sa 10AM-6PM. 6644 Hollywood Blvd. 463.3273

**8 Supply Sergeant** Survivalists, mercenaries, and bargain hunters can choose from such indispensables as boots, bugles, binoculars, and dummy grenades, plus military surplus clothing and camping gear. ♦ M-Th 10AM-7PM; F-Sa 10AM-9PM; Su 11AM-7PM. 6664 Hollywood Blvd. 463.4730

**9 Frederick's of Hollywood** Frank Falgien's and **Bruce Marteney's** 1935 purple-and-pink Art Deco tower is an appropriate symbol of the flamboyantly sexy apparel. There are outlets across America, but this is the original. During the April 1992 riots, an undergarment thief made off with **Madonna's** studded brassiere from the **Celebrity Lingerie Hall of Fame.** A 24-hour toll-free number for mail orders is also available. ♦ M-Th 10AM-6PM; F 10AM-9PM; Sa 10AM-6PM; Su noon-5PM. 6608 Hollywood Blvd. 466.8506, 800/323.9525

**9 Hollywood Toys and Costumes** LA's largest and best place for compulsive exhibitionists

COURTESY OF FRANK GEHRY

## Hollywood/West Hollywood

rents Halloween costumes year-round, plus masks, wigs, and all kinds of makeup. ♦ M-Sa 9:30AM-8PM; Su 11AM-7PM. 6562 Hollywood Blvd. 465.3119

**10 Musso and Frank Grill** ★$$ Hollywood's oldest restaurant, open since 1919, is reassuring in its paneled permanence and lack of change, with a comfortable counter for solitary diners. Waiters may be brusque unless they know you. Some rate this restaurant highly, especially for its martinis, grills, and sourdough bread. ♦ American ♦ Tu-Sa 11AM-11PM. 6667 Hollywood Blvd. 467.7788

**10 Book City** A huge selection of new and used books on all topics is stocked here. ♦ M-Sa 10AM-10PM; Su 10AM-8PM. 6627 Hollywood Blvd. 466.2525. Also at: 308 N. San Fernando Rd, Burbank. 818/848.4417

**11 Janes House** Constructed in 1903, this last survivor of the mansions that lined the boulevard until the 1920s was a family run school, and is now an official **Visitors Information Center.** ♦ M-Sa 9AM-5PM. 6541 Hollywood Blvd. 461.4213

**12 North Ivar Street** This block of North Ivar above Yucca Street still has a lot of '20s and '30s apartment buildings. The **Parva Sed** is where **Nathanael West** lived when he originally conceived the plan for his scathing Hollywood novella, *Day of the Locust.* He had befriended a lot of the local working girls and would drive them home. In return they sewed on his buttons. Farther up the block is the **El Nido,** which was the fictional home for the luckless screenwriter played by **William Holden** in the movie *Sunset Boulevard.*

**12 Joseph's Cafe** ★$ A long-established favorite, they serve fabulous gyros, lentil soup, and rice pudding throughout the day. The popular Irish rock group **U2** has eaten here. ♦ Greek/Mediterranean ♦ M-Sa 7AM-11PM. 1775 N. Ivar St. 462.8697

Amelia Earhart was a North Hollywood resident before she disappeared in 1937. Today a statue of the famed aviator stands in North Hollywood Park.

**Restaurants/Clubs:** Red  **Hotels:** Blue
**Shops/ 🌳 Outdoors:** Green  **Sights/Culture:** Black

**13 Frances Goldwyn Regional Branch Library** To replace the **Hollywood Library,** which was destroyed by arson, **Frank Gehry** created this cluster of luminous boxes (light bounces off water in shallow reflecting pools) in 1986. So outdoorsy is the feel that you hardly notice how well the building (pictured above) is protected ("tighter security than the American Embassy I designed for Damascus," says the architect). A surreal juxtaposition is the **Ivar Burlesque** next door. ♦ M-Th 10AM-8PM; F-Sa 10AM-5:30PM. 1623 Ivar St (at Sunset Blvd). 467.1821

**13 India Inn** ★★$ The proprietors here serve some of the best *naan,* tandooris, curries, and vegetarian dishes in town. ♦ Indian ♦ Daily noon-3PM, 5-10PM. 1638 N. Cahuenga Blvd. 461.3774

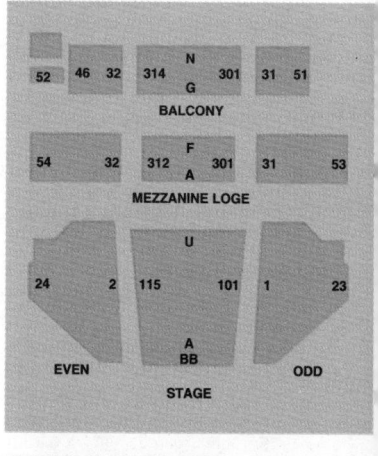

**14 James Doolittle Theater** The Doolittle (see the plan above) is one of the best places in LA to enjoy one-person shows and quality drama. ♦ 1615 N. Vine St. 462.6666

**15 Vine Street Bar & Grill** ★$$$ This stylish, intimate club books the best new and established jazz and blues artists. They have good Northern Italian food for pre- and post-theater dining. ♦ Italian ♦ Tu-Sa 11AM-3PM, 5PM-2AM; Su 5PM-2AM. 1610 N. Vine St. 463.4375

**16 Henry Fonda Theater** The conversion of the former **Music Box** is a brave attempt to bring quality drama to a depressed neighborhood. ♦ 6126 Hollywood Blvd. 468.1700

**17 Frolic Room** From the expressive neon lettering to the '40s decor, this bar is a hardy survivor. ♦ Daily 10AM-2AM. 6245 Hollywood Blvd. 462.5890

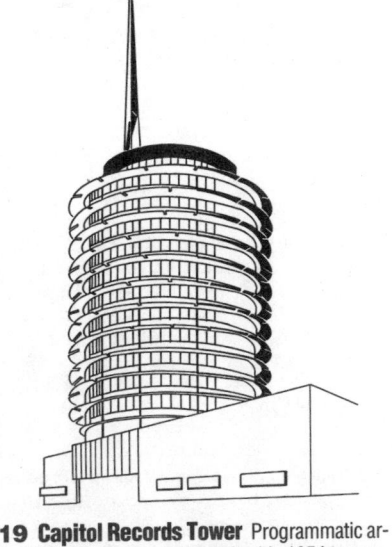

**20 Greens and Things** ★$ The rib-sticking, fingerlicking good food—short ribs, collard greens, cornbread, and peach pie—are served with lemonade in mason jars in a funky dive. ♦ Soul food ♦ Daily 11:30AM–10PM. 6357 Yucca St. 462.7555

**20 Chao Praya** ★$$ To underscore its proximity to the **Capitol Records** building, the menu is shaped like a record. Service is frequently slow, but the Thai dishes are good. Low lighting throughout the restaurant makes for a romantic late-night supper. ♦ Thai ♦ M-Th, Su 11:30AM–11:30PM; F-Sa 11:30AM–1AM. 6307 Yucca St. 466.6704

## Hollywood/West Hollywood

**21 Freeman House** The **Frank Lloyd Wright**-designed, Mayan-influenced residence located in the hills above the Hollywood Bowl is now being restored by USC. To help pay for the restoration of this 1924 concrete-block structure, reproductions of Wright's patterned blocks are being made available to donors of $250 or more. ♦ 1962 Glencoe Way (at Hillcrest Blvd). 740.2311

**22 Il Vittoriale** The 1929 **American Legion Headquarters** has been transformed into an Italian villa for the presentation of *Tamara,* a long-running living play about Italian poet/patriot **Gabriele d'Annunzio.** For a stiff fee, you can play voyeur and co-conspirator as the action unfolds in different parts of the house, and enjoy a champagne supper. ♦ Shows: Tu-F 8PM; Sa-Su 2:30PM, 8PM. 2035 Highland Ave. 851.9999, 480.3232

**23 Whitley Heights** Developed in the '20s and '30s by **Hobart J. Whitley,** these old Italian villa-styled houses are built into the hillside. **Marion Davies, Gloria Swanson,** and **Ethel Barrymore** are among those who once lived here. Many of the charming houses still have courtyards, fountains, crenelated balconies, and hidden gardens. They are private residences. ♦ Highland Ave (at Franklin Ave)

**24 The High Tower** This 1920 campanile, soaring sheer from the end of a cul de sac, is an elevator shaft that rises to the streamline villas on either side. Stepped streets reinforce the impression of San Gimignano in the Hollywood Hills. ♦ High Tower Rd

**25 Hollywood Studio Museum** **Cecil B. De Mille** rented this horse barn in December 1913, and used it as a set, offices, and changing rooms (alongside the horses) for *The Squaw Man,* the first feature-length movie shot in Hollywood. It stood at Selma and Vine streets, was trucked to what is now the Paramount lot, and was moved to its present site in 1985, where it was restored by **Hollywood Heritage** and furnished with stills and other exhibitions. ♦ Admission. Tu-F noon-4PM; Sa-Su 10AM-4PM. 2100 N. Highland Ave. 874.2276

**17 Pantages Theater** The movie palace turned showcase for Broadway musicals is a dazzling example of adaptive reuse. Originally designed by **B. Marcus Priteca** in 1929, the theater (see the plan above) rivals the Wiltern as an anthology of zigzag moderne, from the vaulted lobby guarded by statues of a movie director and an aviatrix, to the amazing fretted ceiling of the auditorium, designed by **Anthony Heinsbergen.** The Academy Awards were presented on this stage in the '50s. ♦ 6233 Hollywood Blvd. 310/410.1062

**18 Collector's Book Store** A treasure-trove of movie books, stills, and memorabilia is stocked here. ♦ Tu-F 10AM-5PM; Sa 10AM-5:30PM. 1708 N. Vine St. 467.3296

**19 Capitol Records Tower** Programmatic architecture on an epic scale, this 1954 tower (pictured above) by **Welton Becket** suggests a stack of records topped by a stylus. In December it is lit to create Hollywood's tallest Christmas tree. ♦ 1750 Vine St

"Hollywood is a great place if you're an orange."
**Fred Allen**

**26 Loft Towers** With a nod to neighboring High Tower, Australian architects **Koning & Eizenberg** created a pair of suburban lofts, each of which comprises three 20-foot-square rooms for working and living stacked on a double garage, with kitchen and service areas behind. The 1987 residences are private. ♦ 6949 Camrose Dr

**27 Yamashiro's Restaurant** $$ The oldest building in LA is a 600-year-old pagoda, imported by Oriental art dealers **Adolphe** and **Eugene Bernheimer** as an ornament for the Japanese palace and gardens they built in 1913. It rises high above another landmark, the **Magic**

## Hollywood/West Hollywood

Castle (1925), a French Renaissance château that is now a private club for magicians. The food at Yamashiro's is terrible, but the view at sunset is worth the climb and the price of a drink. Be sure to get a window seat. ♦ Japanese ♦ M-Th, Su 5:30-10PM; F-Sa 5:30-11PM. 1999 N. Sycamore Ave (at Franklin Ave). 466.5125

**28 Case Study Apartments** Adele Naude **Santos'** design for a villagelike cluster of low-income apartments was chosen by the **Museum of Contemporary Art** to be built as a homage to the Case Study House Program that *Arts+Architecture* magazine ran from 1945 to 1966. The construction broke ground in fall 1992, and the complex will serve as an incentive for better designed multiple-unit urban housing. ♦ Franklin Ave at La Brea Ave

**29 Wattles Mansion & Gardens** Hollywood Heritage has restored the 1905 house, built as the winter home of an Omaha businessman, and the formal gardens, which were a top tourist attraction in Hollywood's early years. Just beyond is a wilderness area that links up to **Runyon Canyon Park,** formerly the **Huntington Hartford Estate.** The Heritage (whose offices are here) gives quarterly tours of neighboring properties, plus walking tours of Hollywood Boulevard, departing from the Capitol Records Tower. ♦ M-F 10AM-4PM, or by appointment. 1824 N. Curson Ave. 874.4005 (or check at the Hollywood Studio Museum)

In 1978 the highest-paid Hollywood stars were Paul Newman, Robert Redford, and Steve McQueen. In 1990 the movie actors with the highest earning capacity were Jack Nicholson (who made $50 to $60 million for his role in *Batman*), Sylvester Stallone, Arnold Schwarzenegger, and Dustin Hoffman.

A few days after the 1992 LA riots, a guilt-plagued young man who had looted Frederick's of Hollywood handed a Hollywood parish priest a bag containing the pantaloons of late actress Ava Gardner and a bra belonging to actress Katey Sagal. The distraught youth said he was too afraid to return it to the lingerie museum. The thief who took Madonna's bustier is still at large.

Restaurants/Clubs: Red
Shops/ 🌳 Outdoors: Green

Hotels: Blue
**Sights/Culture:** Black

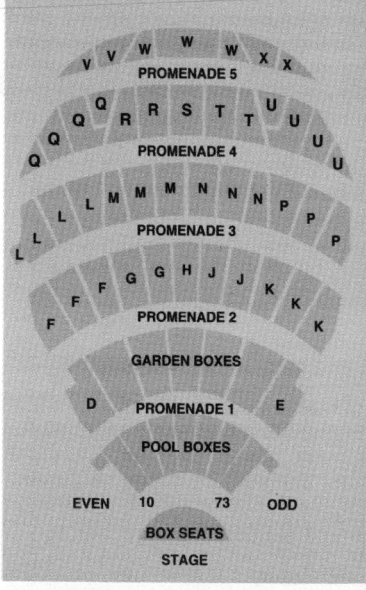

**30 Hollywood Bowl** The natural amphitheater, originally known as **Daisy Dell,** was developed in the 1920s as a concert shell, and now hosts the summer season of the **LA Philharmonic,** visiting musicians, and jazz and pop concerts. Popular perennials include the Easter sunrise service and the Fourth of July and closing night concerts with fireworks. The acoustics are spotty, and only subscribers in their box seats can hear the musicians without amplification, so you may as well sit high up in the cheaper seats and enjoy the view (see the plan above). Dress warmly, bring a cushion, and come early for a picnic—the sylvan glades around the Bowl fill up quickly. The **Patio Restaurant** serves moderately priced suppers alfresco on the patio. Parking, in lots along Highland Avenue, can be chaotic; a better bet are the 14 park-and-ride buses that serve different parts of LA. On your way in, note **George Stanley's** moderne statues of music, drama, and dance. For the Patio Restaurant and picnic baskets (to be ordered the previous day), call 851.3588. ♦ Grounds daily 9AM-dusk July-Sept. 2301 N. Highland Ave. 850.2000

At the Hollywood Bowl:

**Hollywood Bowl Museum** Exhibitions on the history of the Bowl include original drawings of concert shell prototypes by **Lloyd Wright** (the son of **Frank**). Visitors may also listen to tapes of memorable Bowl performances in several small listening booths. ♦ Tu-Sa 9:30AM-8:30PM. Adjacent to the Patio Restaurant. 850.2058

Although the growth of the film colony in Hollywood was once shunned by LA's high society, visiting foreign dignitaries considered Pickfair, the home of early movie idols Mary Pickford and Douglas Fairbanks, the home of royalty. Among their guests were the former King of Spain, Alfonso XIII, the King and Queen of Siam, and Crown Prince Hirohito, who later became Emperor of Japan.

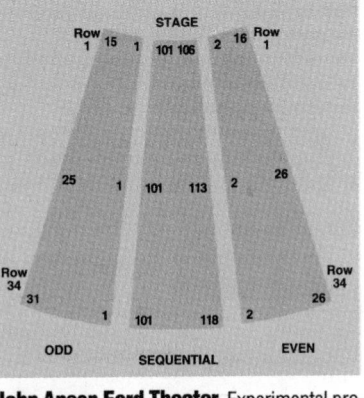

```
                STAGE
Row  15   1   101 105  2  16  Row
 1                          1

   25      1    101  113   2     26

Row                              Row
34   31                          34
                                   26
     1        101   118   2
ODD                          EVEN
        SEQUENTIAL
```

**31 John Anson Ford Theater** Experimental productions by the **Mark Taper Forum** (972.7211) are presented in the **Taper, Too**—underneath the main stage; and the annual **Shakespeare Festival LA** is held here every July (489.3232). The theater's seating plan is shown above. ♦ 2580 Cahuenga Blvd.

**32 Lake Hollywood** This reservoir up in the hills offers a splendid view of the Hollywood Sign, a rustic jogging trail, and a sense of what this place must have looked like a hundred years ago. Climb down to the base of the dam to admire the bear head sculptures. ♦ M-F 6:30-10AM, 2-7:30PM; Sa-Su 6:30AM-7:30PM. Drive north on Cahuenga Blvd across Franklin Ave, right on Dix St, left on Holly Dr, sharp right on Deep Dell Pl, left on Weidlake Dr to arrive at the lake entrance.

**33 Hollywood Sign** The 50-foot-high letters (pictured below) that sit near the summit of Mount Lee were first erected back in 1923 to advertise **Hollywoodland,** a residential development on the lower slopes. In 1949 the deteriorating sign and its acreage were deeded to the **Hollywood Chamber of Commerce,** who took down the -LAND to create a civic advertisement. A new sign costing $250,000 was erected in 1978. The sign has been a favorite target of stealthy typographers: from "Ollywood" (for Iran-Contra messenger Colonel Oliver North) and "Holly-weed," to a gigantic yellow ribbon for US troops in Desert Storm. In July 1992 a large cutout of cartoon femme fatale **Holli Would** perched her rump on the letter "D" as part of Paramount Studios' promotion for the animation flick *Cool World*. The **Rebuild LA** organization profited from a $27,000 use fee much to the ire of some locals who cried out prostitution of the movie capital's most beloved landmark. ♦ On Mt. Cahuenga above Hollywood

**34 Village Coffee Shop** ★$ The good food and warm atmosphere make the tables worth waiting for in this homey rendezvous for the area's actors, writers, and singers—the aspirants who live below the Hollywoodland gates and the more established who live in the hills above. ♦ American ♦ M-F 8AM-6:30PM; Sa 8AM-5PM. 2695 Beachwood Dr. 467.5398

**35 La Poubelle** ★★$$ How to resist a brasserie that calls itself the garbage pail? French waiters shout orders to the kitchen, **Edith Piaf** sings, and owner **Jacqueline Koster** won't let you order anything that doesn't satisfy her. Crepes, omelets, and coq au vin are staples. ♦ French/

## Hollywood/West Hollywood

Italian ♦ Daily 5:30PM-midnight. 5909 Franklin Ave. 465.0807

**36 Samuels-Navarro House** Designed for actor **Ramon Navarro** by architect **Lloyd Wright** in 1928, this house stretches horizontally along a natural ridge ending with a swimming pool (now enclosed) at one end and a private garden at the other. Pressed copper trims the white stucco surface. The private residence was recently remodeled by **Josh Schweitzer.** ♦ 5609 Valley Oak Dr

**37 American Film Institute** Offices of the American Film Institute (**AFI**) and its **Center for Advanced Film Studies** now occupy what was once the hillside campus of Immaculate Heart College. **The Louis B. Mayer Library,** open to serious film scholars, has the most extensive collection of movie scripts in the country. The AFI and its **Sony Video Center** present regular public screenings and classes, plus annual film and video festivals. ♦ 2021 N. Western Ave (at Franklin Ave). 856.7600

**38 5390 Franklin Avenue** The flamboyant apartment building, formerly the **Château Elysée,** is now owned by the **Church of Scientology.** ♦ Serrano Ave

**39 Sowden House** Another residence from **Frank Lloyd Wright's** son, **Lloyd,** this 1926 house fuses Mayan and Deco themes, is built around a courtyard, and is entered from within a cavelike opening framed with decorative concrete blocks. It's a private residence. ♦ 5121 Franklin Ave

**40 Onyx Sequel** $ This bohemian coffeehouse features the work of local artists. There's live music on Sunday afternoon. ♦ American ♦ M-Th, Su 9AM-1AM; F-Sa 9AM-2AM. 1802 N. Vermont Ave. 660.5820

# HOLLYWOOD

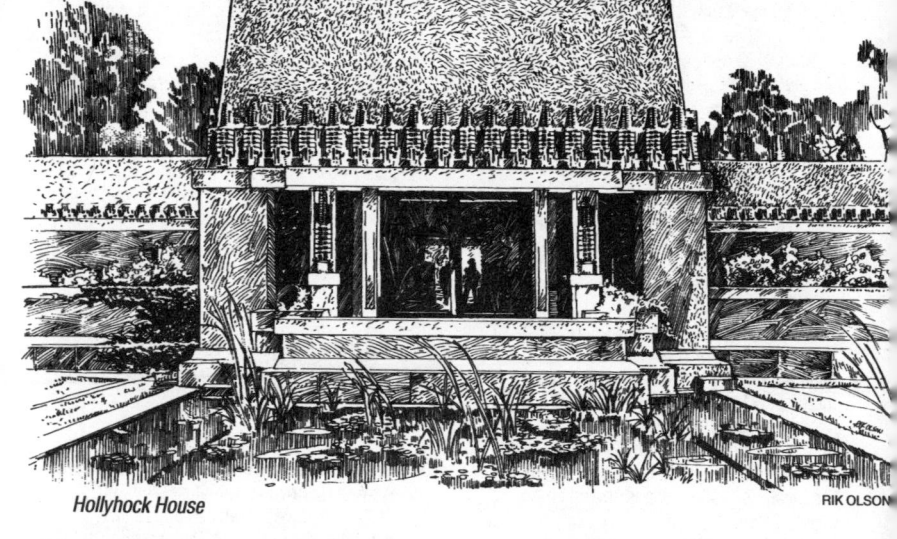

*Hollyhock House*

RIK OLSON

**41 Barnsdall Park** Located at the top of a hill and ringed by a thick grove of olive trees, this shady oasis and cultural center is in the flatlands of eastern Hollywood. The daily upkeep of the park is administered by the **City of Los Angeles Department of Cultural Affairs.** ♦ 4800 Hollywood Blvd

Within Barnsdall Park:

**Hollyhock House** Oil heiress **Aline Barnsdall** commissioned this house (illustrated above)—architect **Frank Lloyd Wright's** first in LA, built from 1917 to 1920—as part of a complex of cultural and residential structures. Named for an abstracted geometric motif based on the flower, it has been restored and includes many of the original Wright furnishings. An interesting guided tour is offered. ♦ Admission. Tours: Tu-Su noon, 1PM, 2PM, and 3PM. 485.4581

**Municipal Art Gallery** This exhibition space is a visual forum for the cutting edge of Southern California art. The theater presents a lively and varied bill of films and concerts. ♦ Gallery admission charge. Tu-Su 12:30-5PM. 4804 Hollywood Blvd. Group tours: 485.4581

**Junior Arts Center** The center offers an extensive program of sophisticated and innovative studio art classes for children and young people ages three to 18. The gallery has changing shows that are designed for a young audience emphasizing participation and activity. ♦ M-F 9AM-5:30PM. Gallery: Tu-Su 12:30-5PM. 485.4474

**Arts & Crafts Center** Arts and crafts classes for adults and older teenagers are offered for a small fee in this center designed by **Frank Lloyd Wright** in 1920. Class days and times vary, so call ahead for the schedule. ♦ 485.2116

**42 Brashov's** ★$$ For the adventurous gastronome, try this family-run Rumanian deli/restaurant. You'll find a few tables and plenty of folks from the old country who come to enjoy high-quality, honest food, including the good stuffed cabbage, schnitzel, fish borscht, kabobs, and a magnificent chocolate cake. ♦ Rumanian ♦ Daily 11AM-9PM. 1301 N. Vermont Ave. 660.0309

**43 California Patio Grill** $$ Check out this homey place with a patio that serves good, simple American meals with a health food emphasis. ♦ California ♦ Daily 7:30AM-9:30PM. 4854 Fountain Ave. 666.9100

**44 Paru's** ★$ Standouts of Paru's vegetarian menu include the *masala dosa* (a foot-long lentil flour crepe filled with potato curry), *samosas* (turnovers), *vada* (lentil donuts served with chutney), and *idli* (rice pancakes with lentil gravy). ♦ Southern Indian ♦ Tu-Su noon-9PM. 5140 Sunset Blvd. 661.7600. Also at: 9340 W. Pico Blvd, 273.8088; 9545 Reseda Blvd, Northridge. 818/349.3546

**45 Jitlada** ★★$$ This cozy little treasure, tucked away in a corner mall of no other apparent distinction, serves some of the most delicious Thai food in Los Angeles, and the price is right. Everything is good, especially the spicy squid salad. ♦ Thai ♦ Tu-Sa 11AM-3PM, 5-10PM. 5233 Sunset Blvd. 667.9809

**46 Starsteps** A 40,000-pound steel sculpture (illustrated above) by Chicago artist **John David Mooney** has been perched atop the **Metromedia TV** studio since 1981. Brightly illuminated at night, it seems to float above the freeway. ♦ Sunset Blvd (between Wilton Pl and Hollywood Fwy)

The 1922 opening season for the Hollywood Bowl (then known as the Daisy Dell) was saved by the Bowl Association's first secretary. Mrs. Artie Mason Carter solicited pledges door-to-door and even hocked her diamond ring to raise enough money.

"They've great respect for the dead in Hollywood, but none for the living."

**Errol Flynn**

**47 Columbia Bar & Grill** ★$$$ Part-owned by actor **Wayne Rogers,** this handsome, airy, brick-and-glass restaurant with a spacious patio is patronized by entertainment types from CBS and neighboring studios. Salads, crab cakes, and chili are typical of the straightforward menu. ♦ California ♦ M-Sa 11AM-3:30PM, 5:30-10:30PM. 1448 N. Gower St. 461.8800

**48 The Hollywood Palladium** Famous since 1940, the Palladium has swung to the sounds of the **Dorsey Brothers, Glen Miller, Stan Kenton,** and **Lawrence Welk.** Current attractions vary from dancing to conventions, but big names still make frequent appearances. A full bar and à la carte dinners are offered. ♦ 6215 Sunset Blvd. 962.7600

**49 Off Vine** ★$$ A shark juts through the roof of this frame house on a quiet side street, heralding such quirky dishes as New York steak with Jack Daniels sauce, turkeyburgers with three sauces, scallops in puff pastry, and blueberry-crumb cake. A show-biz clientele frequents this haunt. ♦ Eclectic ♦ M-F 11:30AM-2:30PM, 5:30-11PM; Sa 5:30-11PM. 6263 Leland Way. 962.1900

**50 Cinerama Dome** The impressive-looking cellular construction was originally built to accommodate the extra-wide screen of the Cinerama process. The acoustics and sightlines of the theater are remarkably good. ♦ 6360 Sunset Blvd. 466.3401

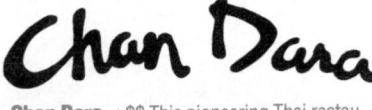

**51 Chan Dara** ★$$ This pioneering Thai restaurant has a large and loyal clientele, so you may have to wait to eat. There's a wide selection to choose from, including *mee krob* (sweet fried noodles), *sate,* squid with mint and chili, and several wonderfully spicy soups. ♦ Thai ♦ M-F 11AM-1AM; Sa 5PM-midnight; Su 5-11PM. 1511 N. Cahuenga Blvd. 464.8585

**51 Martoni's** $$ The bar and the hearty food are the main attractions at Martoni's. ♦ Italian ♦ M-F 11:30AM-3PM, 5PM-2AM; Sa 5PM-2AM. 1523 N. Cahuenga Blvd. 466.3441

**52 Club Lingerie** For after-hours fun, dance the night away at this New Wave club. There's a no-nonsense minimalist interior with a full bar and a spacious dance floor, plus live music every night. An aggressively imaginative booking policy features rockabilly, punk, R&B, and jazz greats, as well as good locally famous DJs. The admission charge varies, and you must be 21 with ID. ♦ Cover. M-Sa 9PM-2AM. 6507 W. Sunset Blvd. 466.8557

**52 Berwin Entertainment Center** Olympic gold medalist-turned-Tarzan **Buster Crabbe** was a swimming instructor in the former **Hollywood Athletic Club,** a handsome Spanish Deco-style tower. ♦ 6525 Sunset Blvd

The average Hollywood budget for a feature film in 1940 was $314,000. In 1990 the average was $18 million.

**53 Crossroads of the World** Here's an example of fantasy architecture in pristine condition: a liner (center building) sailing into a foreign port (surrounding English, French, Spanish, and Moorish shops) designed in 1936 by **Robert Derrah,** who did the Coca Cola Building downtown. ♦ 6671 Sunset Blvd. 463.5611

**54 Cafe des Artistes** ★★$$ You could easily imagine yourself on a back street of Cannes in **Michele Lamy's** idyllic French bistro: a leafy patio; a cool, undecorated dining room; friendly service; and a few delicious *plats du jour*—like the calamari salad, wild mushrooms baked in cream, and steak with *frites.* There's a very

good Sunday brunch, too. ♦ French ♦ Tu-F 11:30AM-2:30PM, 7-10:30PM; Sa 7-10:30PM; Su 11:30AM-3PM, 7-10:30PM. 1534 N. McCadden Pl. 461.6889

**54 Stages Trilingual Theater** Paul Verdier produces some of LA's most innovative theater—including plays by **Ionesco, Marguerite Duras, Ariane Mnouchkine,** and **René-Daniel DuBois**—in English, French, and Spanish. Seating is limited, so book well in advance. ♦ 1540 N. McCadden Pl. 463.5356. Box office: 465.1010

**55 Hollywood High School** Decorative reliefs and uplifting inscriptions embellish the surface of these 1935 streamline moderne buildings. Its students are a microcosm of Hollywood's ethnic diversity. ♦ Sunset Blvd at Highland Ave

**56 Hampton's** ★$$ Dine on great hamburgers made from beef that is ground daily and cooked to order, with exotic toppings and an outstanding salad bar. ♦ American ♦ M 7AM-3PM; Tu-F 7AM-10PM; Sa-Su 5-10PM. 1342 N. Highland Ave. 469.1090. Also at: 4301 Riverside Dr. 818/845.3009

**57 Little Red Schoolhouse** The building is just what it looks like—a little red schoolhouse. ♦ 1248 N. Highland Ave

**58 Arturo's Flowers** These people have a goofy genius for oddball promotion, and though the selection of flora is limited, their hours make this place a lifesaver for any occasion. ♦ Daily 8AM-9PM. 1261 N. La Brea Ave. 876.6482

**59 Samuel French** This bookshop stocks plays, from **Shakespeare** to **Stoppard,** as well as books on the theater. ♦ M-F 10AM-6PM; Sa 10AM-5PM. 7623 Sunset Blvd. 876.0570

## DAR MAGHREB

**59 Dar Maghreb** ★$$$ The Arabian Nights decor and good renditions of the standard dishes are popular with tour groups. ♦ Moroccan ♦ M-Sa 5:30-11PM; Su 5:30-10:30PM. 7651 Sunset Blvd. 876.7651

In 1941, actor James Stewart was the first film star to leave Hollywood to join the Army.

**60 Caioti Cafe** $$ The building that houses this quaint cafe and the **Canyon Country Store** was rebuilt in the late '20s after the original tavern—for many decades a favorite haunt of the intellectuals of Laurel Canyon—perished in a fire. The cafe is known for pizzas, pasta, and its catering service to reclusive dwellers of the most famous chasm of the Hollywood Hills. ♦ Continental ♦ M-W, Su 11AM-10:30PM; Th 11AM-11PM; F-Sa 11AM-11:30PM. 2100 Laurel Canyon Blvd. 650.2988

**61 Directors Guild of America** This overpowering curvilinear bronze glass tower, built in 1989, is out of scale and character with everything

around and is a textbook example of how not to build on Sunset. On the positive side, it has three excellent auditoriums, which are currently being used by the **American Cinematheque** for public programs (461.9622). ♦ 7920 Sunset Blvd. 310/289.2000

**61 Gaucho Grill** ★$$ The endangered species of meat eaters can indulge themselves at this paradise of the pampas. ♦ Argentine ♦ M-Th, Su 11AM-11PM; F-Sa 11AM-midnight. 7980 Sunset Blvd. 656.4152. Also at: 11838 Ventura Blvd, Studio City. 818/508.1030

**62 Villa d'Este Apartments** This 1928 structure is one of several lushly planted courtyard apartments in LA that evoke romantic Mediterranean villas. Other cherished examples are located within walking distance at 1400 and 1475 Havenhurst Drive, 8225 Fountain Avenue, and 1338 N. Harper Avenue. They are private residences. ♦ 1355 Laurel Ave

**63 Greenblatt's Delicatessen** ★$$ Service at this haven for expatriate New Yorkers became less brusque with the addition of the upstairs dining room. They have great pastrami, cheesecake, and wines; a full bar; and excellent take-out service. ♦ Deli ♦ Daily 9AM-2AM. 8017 Sunset Blvd. 656.0606

**63 Coconut Teaszer** This young, funky rock 'n' roll joint becomes a madhouse on weekends, with disco dancing, beer, and food included in the cover charge. ♦ Cover. M-Th, Su 8PM-2AM; F-Sa 8PM-4AM. 8121 Sunset Blvd. 654.4773

**63 La Toque** ★★★★$$$$ Chef/owner **Ken Frank** maintains a high level of inventive cuisine. The service and quiet, intimate atmosphere are attractive enough, but the kitchen is among the best in LA. Menus change daily, depending on what's available and fresh. The dishes are very French, very expensive, and very good, and the wine list is superb. The patio is a lovely spot on summer evenings. ♦ French ♦ M-F noon-2PM, 6:30-10PM; Sa 6-10PM. 8171 Sunset Blvd. 656.7515

**64 Château Marmont Hotel** $$$ This 1927 Norman castle once guarded the approach to the Sunset Strip. **Garbo** stayed here; **John Belushi** died here. Its faded elegance has been sensitively restored, and its privacy and charm lure movie and music celebrities. Accommodations include luxury suites with balconies and views, and cottages around the pool. ♦ 8221 Sunset Ln. 656.1010, 800/242.8328; fax 655.5311

**65 Roxbury** $$$ Chef **Dave Danhi's** popular requests are angel hair pasta with prawns and Southern fried chicken with lumpy mashed potatoes. After dinner enjoy a mellow evening with soothing jazz in the downstairs dining room/lounge or work off the meal on the upstairs dance floor to live music. ♦ American ♦ Dinner Tu-Sa 7-11PM. 8225 Sunset Blvd. 656.1750, 310/274.2213

**66 Carlos 'n' Charlie's** $$$ One of a chain of flashy restaurants that extends south to Acapulco, it's notable more for the singles scene than for the food on the whimsically worded menu. The action is even better upstairs at **El Privado** ♦ Mexican/Continental ♦ M-F 11AM-2AM; Sa-S 5PM-2AM. 8240 Sunset Blvd. 656.8830

**67 Mondrian** $$$ A standout (for all the wrong reasons), this hotel's exterior was painted by Israeli artist **Yaakov Agam** in a crude pastiche of the style of the Dutch modernist. The staff is multilingual. ♦ 8440 Sunset Blvd. 650.9999; fax 650.1212

COURTESY OF ST. JAMES'S CLUB

**67 St. James's Club** $$$$ The former Sunset Tower apartments, a long neglected 1931 Art Deco gem, have been lovingly restored as a glitzy English-owned residential club (pictured above). Members are entitled to special upgrades, when available; but if there are rooms, anyone can make a reservation. American Express Centurian Club members receive the same services as regular club members. The 12th-floor penthouse—where **John Wayne** once lived with, legend says, a cow on the balcony—now comprises two tiny but opulent suites with great views over the city and hills. The club is affiliated with clubs in Paris, London, and Antigua. ♦ 835 Sunset Blvd. 654.7100, 800/225.2637; fax 654.9287

**67 Butterfield's** ★★$$ The leafy patio screened from Sunset's heavy traffic is an idyllic place for lunch on all but the coldest days, and the salads, sandwiches, and daily specials are all excellent. They also have good wines by the glass here. ♦ American ♦ M-F 11:30AM-3PM, 6-10PM; Sa 10:30AM-3PM, 6-10:30PM; Su 10:30AM-3PM, 6-10PM. 8426 Sunset Blvd. 656.3055

**68 The Comedy Store** This is considered the most important showcase for comedians in the area. The **Main Room** presents established comics; the **Original Room** offers continuous shows of rising new comedians; and the **Belly Room** presents female talent. Call for hours. ♦ 8433 Sunset Blvd. 656.6225

**69 North Beach Leather** You need a model's figure not to split the seams of their skintight pants, fitted jackets, and miniskirts. An extrovert's color sensibility might also help. ♦ M-Sa 10AM-6PM; Su noon-5PM. 8500 Sunset Blvd. 310/652.3224

**69 Sunset Marquis** $$$$ What a find! This oasis hidden in the midst of Hollywood is *the* place to stay for show and music biz types. **Billy Joel, U2, Bruce Springsteen,** and the like come for such perks as 24-hour security and room service; multiline phones; a workout room with two trainers; and an MTV cable station. Accommodations consist of 106 suites and 12 palatial one- and two-bedroom villas that sit on parklike grounds along with two pools, a fish pond, and exotic birds in cages. The restaurants are for guests and "friends" of the hotel. There's complimentary stretch limousine service within seven miles of the hotel (including downtown LA and Beverly Hills). ♦ 1200 N. Alta Loma Rd. 310/657.1333, 800/858.9758; fax 310/652.5300

**70 Sunset Plaza** A strip mall may not have been what architect **Charles Selkirk** had in mind back in the 1930s, but **Honnold and Russell** have revamped his design and created a genteel, stageset piece of architecture along Sunset Boulevard that is the centerpiece of a cluster of exclusive stores and restaurants. Many of them have been restored to their original Colonial Revival, neoclassical, and Regency styles. Among the stylesetting establishments to shop in are **Oliver Peoples** (No. 8642, 310/657.2553) for optic wear; **Boulmiche** (No. 8641, 310/652.6446) and **Charles Gallay** (No. 8711, 310/858.8711) for women's fashions; and **Bloomer for Kids** (No. 8646, 310/854.6901) for the younger jet set. Also scheduled to open is **Armani A/X** at No. 8700. ♦ 8589-8720 Sunset Blvd (at La Cienega Blvd). 310/652.7137

**70 Chin Chin** $$ Dim sum, potstickers (pan-fried dumplings), noodles, *mu shu,* and roasted meats are served at a counter that borders a frantic open kitchen and at dining tables that spill out onto the Sunset Boulevard sidewalk. No alcohol is served. ♦ Chinese ♦ M-Th, Su 11AM-11PM; F-Sa 11AM-midnight. 8618 Sunset Blvd (at Sunset Plaza). 652.1818. Also at: 11740 San Vicente Blvd, Brentwood. 310/826.2525; 12215 Ventura Blvd, Studio City. 818/985.9090;13455 Maxella Ave, Marina del Rey. 310/823.9999

**70 Le Petit Four** ★$ Light meals and sumptuous patisserie are available to eat in or take out, along with delicacies from **Fauchon** in Paris. There's eclectic live music, too. ♦ French ♦ M-Sa 9AM-11PM; Su 9AM-6PM. 8654 Sunset Blvd. 310/652.3863

**71 Dressed to Kill** Evening gowns by **Ungaro, Givenchy, Dior,** and **Patrick Kelly** are for rent. ♦ Tu-F 11AM-7PM; Sa 10AM-6PM; by appointment only. 8762 Holloway Dr. 310/652.4334

**72 Le Dôme** ★★★$$$$ Elegant informality sets the stage for a great view and first-rate bistro food, including black sausage with apples, ham hocks and sauerkraut, roast chicken, and sal-

ads. Lots of movie producers and agents come here for power lunches; you can eat late, and there's a lively bar scene. ♦ French ♦ M-F noon-11:45PM; Sa 7PM-2AM. 8720 Sunset Blvd. 310/659.6919

**72 Nicky Blair's** $$$ This noisy, crowded, and glitzy singles bar, which also serves Italian food, is a great place for star-gazing. Ask the waiter about their nightly specials. ♦ Italian ♦ M-Sa 6PM-2AM. 8730 Sunset Blvd. 310/659.0929

**73 Spago** ★★★★$$$$ Chef **Wolfgang Puck** is as much a celebrity as any of his glamorous guests. He's often on hand to welcome you, but without neglecting his kitchen. And despite the noisy crowds that tend to jam the dining room and patio, he continues to turn out innovative and delicious pizzas and pastas, mouthwatering Chinese duck, roast salmon with Cabernet sauce, and terrific desserts. Nowhere can you eat so well while gazing at famous faces. ♦ California ♦ Daily 6-11PM. 1114 Horn Ave. Reservations are required in advance. 310/652.4025

**73 Tower Records** They bill themselves as the largest record store in the world. Across Sunset is an annex selling classical recordings (310/657.3910) and videos (310/657.3344). ♦ M-Th, Su 9AM-midnight; F-Sa 9AM-1AM. 8801 Sunset Blvd. 310/657.7300

**73 Pow Wow** $ If you're looking for an early start on the strip, this great little cafe may come in handy. The owners should extend their evening hours because of its convenient proximity to clubs such as **Whiskey A Go Go, The Roxy,** and **Gazzarri's.** ♦ American ♦ M-F 8AM-8PM; Sa noon-8PM; Su noon-6PM. 8868 Sunset Blvd. 310/852.0668

**74 El Chaya** ★★$ The Asian menu and Pacific Rim-inspired interiors by **Grinstein & Daniels** have been given a new, decidedly Southwestern flavor to complement Mexican-influenced dishes, including shrimp enchiladas, smoked chicken quesadillas, and vegetarian fajitas. ♦ Southwestern ♦ M-F 11:30AM-3PM, 5-11PM; Sa noon-11PM; Su noon-10PM. 8800 Sunset Blvd. 310/657.2083

**Restaurants/Clubs:** Red          **Hotels:** Blue
**Shops/ ♠ Outdoors:** Green          **Sights/Culture:** Black

**74  Book Soup**  This marvelous store, which has recently doubled its size and acquired parking in back, specializes in current and classic literature, books on the arts, and a rather remarkable choice of American and foreign magazines. ♦ Daily 9AM-midnight. 8818 Sunset Blvd. 310/659.3110

**75  Le Bel Age**  $$$$ The showcase of the **L'Ermitage Hotel Group** is plain on the outside but opulent and refined within. Amenities include a rooftop sports club complete with a sauna, pool, steambath, and knockout view. ♦ 1020 N. San Vicente Blvd. 854.1111. Reservations only: 800/424.4443; fax 854.0926

Within Le Bel Age:

**Diaghilev** ★★$$$$ Caviar (served with flavored vodkas), *koulibaca* of salmon, chicken Kiev, and quail stuffed with foie gras are among the specialties of this hotel restaurant of Czarist splendor. ♦ Russian ♦ Tu-Sa 6:30-10:30PM. 310/854.1111, ext 480

**76  Le Reve**  $$ This intimate 80-room hotel features split-level suites and a rooftop heated pool and spa. ♦ 8822 Cynthia St. 310/854.1114; fax 310/657.2623

**77  Le Montrose**  $$$ Formerly the Valadon Suite Hotel, the 110 charming suites are situated in a quiet residential area below the Sunset Strip. Suites feature kitchenettes, but you're within walking distance to many fine restaurants. ♦ 900 Hammond St. 310/855.1115; fax 310/637.9192

**78  Whisky A Go Go**  Live rock music is the specialty here, with a floor up front by the stage for dancing. This has been one of the most popular clubs on the Strip since its opening in 1964. Call for hours. ♦ Cover. 8901 Sunset Blvd. 310/652.4202

**78  Dukes**  ★$$ This is the most popular coffee shop in West Hollywood. The pace is fast, the food is good, and the feel is friendly. They seat you wherever they can, which is usually with strangers—but they won't be strangers for long. Customers come in all types, from punk bands to music execs to neighborhood cops. Expect a long wait for brunch on Sunday. ♦ Coffee shop ♦ M-F 8AM-9PM; Sa-Su 8AM-3:45PM. 8909 Sunset Blvd. No credit cards accepted. 310/652.9411

**79  The Roxy**  Decorated in Art Deco style, The Roxy is the foremost nightclub in town. Rock and jazz performers, already famous or on the right path, are the headliners here. The club is frequently booked by the local music industry to showcase hot new talent. Show times vary so call ahead for the schedule. ♦ Cover. 9009 Sunset Blvd. 310/276.2222

**79  Gazzarri's**  The oldest rock club on the Strip boasts two stages and dance floors. Local bands perform here. ♦ Cover. W-Su 8PM-2AM. 9039 Sunset Blvd. 310/273.6606

**79  Talesai**  ★★$$ Some of LA's most distinctive food is served in this chic, upscale Thai restaurant. Specialties include *hor mok* (shrimp and squid with lemon grass, basil, and coconut), squid sautéed with chile, barbecued chicken, and *masman* lamb (tender lamb cooked with chile-coconut sauce, curry style). ♦ Thai ♦ M-11:30AM-2:30PM, 6-10:30PM; Sa 6-10:30PM. 9043 Sunset Blvd. 310/275.9724

**80  Joss**  ★★$$$ East meets West in this stunning clean-lined interior with its innovative menu and a good, reasonably priced wine list. Owner **Cecile Tang,** formerly a film director in Hong Kong, has assembled a distinguished cast and offers innovative but often overpriced and modest-size dishes from her home territory. Best bets include sweet-and-sour soup, Mongolian lamb, paper-wrapped spare ribs, and Peking duck. There's a counter for late suppers and a terrace for a lunch of dim sum. The service can be erratic. ♦ Chinese ♦ Daily 11:30AM-11:30PM. 9255 Sunset Blvd. 310/276.1886

**81  Doug Weston's Troubador**  This long-established rock 'n' roll shrine now specializes in heavy metal bands. ♦ Cover. 9081 Santa Monica Blvd. 310/276.6168

**81  La Masia**  ★$$$ Celebrate a special occasion at this versatile restaurant with an upstairs tapas bar, and Latin jazz and salsa music downstairs from 9PM. They serve good paella and other standards. ♦ Spanish ♦ Tu-Th, Su 6PM-midnight; F-Sa 6PM-1AM. 9077 Santa Monica Blvd. 310/273.7066

**81  Dan Tana's**  ★$$$ Many frequent this old Hollywood favorite, with its Chianti-bottle decor, good steaks, and basics like veal, chicken, and linguine with clams. It's crowded and pricey, however, and service can be surly. ♦ Italian ♦ Daily 5PM-1AM. 9071 Santa Monica Blvd. 310/275.9444

**Palm**

**81  Palm Restaurant**  ★★★$$$$ The best steak and lobster in town—and also the most expensive—is served here. The dining room is always jammed, but the waiters are speedy. It's as harried as the New York original. ♦ American ♦ M-noon-10:30PM; Sa 5-10:30PM; Su 5-9:30PM. 9001 Santa Monica Blvd. 310/550.8811

Pete, the dog from the TV show "Our Gang," and Hopalong Cassidy's horse, Topper, are buried at the Los Angeles Pet Memorial Park.

**81  Greenhouse**  Located in front of the Pavilions market, this florist is aptly named and reputed for its fresh flowers. ♦ Daily 4AM-10PM. 8969 Santa Monica Blvd. 310/273.0977

**82  Studio One Backlot**  This popular nightclub, mostly for gay men, is jammed until late with a crowd that watches the shows on stage, then creates its own on the floor. There are also large-screen video projections and lighting extravaganzas, plus a disco and 10 bar stations throughout. ♦ Cover. Th-Su 9PM-2AM. 652 N. La Peer Dr. 310/659.0472

**82  Rose Tattoo**  ★$$$ Located behind Studio One disco, this pretty lounge/supper club/cabaret attracts a gay and straight crowd. Reasonable and usually excellent prix-fixe dinners here start with an overflowing basket of freshly made crudités and silken sauces for dipping. ♦ Continental ♦ Tu-Su 6:30PM-2AM; Su brunch 11:30AM-3PM. Cabaret: daily 5PM-2AM. 665 N. Robertson Blvd. 310/854.4455

**82  The Abbey**  ★$ The proprietors here serve possibly the best lemon squares in any LA coffeehouse, but the other delicious pies, cakes, and shortbreads should not go untried. Patio dining is available, too. ♦ M-Th 7AM-1:30AM; F 7AM-3AM; Sa 9AM-3AM; Su 9AM-1:30AM. 685 N. Robertson Blvd. 310/289.8410

**83  King's Cafe**  ★ This cozy cafe serves wonderful grilled brie and sundried tomato sandwiches, as well as generous Super Vegetarian sandwiches. The artist who lettered the menu board should be lauded for his scripting. ♦ California ♦ M-F 7AM-5PM; Sa-Su 8:30AM-5PM. 640 N. Robertson Blvd. 310/652.5445

**84  Revolver**  The hottest spot on the boulevard is a video/discotheque extravaganza, packed nightly with a young gay crowd who come to dance the night away. There's a small espresso bar upstairs. ♦ Cover F-Sa. M-Th 4PM-2AM; F-Sa 4PM-4AM; Su 2PM-2AM. 8851 Santa Monica Blvd. 550.8851

**84  Margo Leavin Gallery**  Claes Oldenburg, John Baldessari, and Alexis Smith strike again—with a blade slicing through the stucco facade, like a knife through pastry. It's just the thing to enliven a side street and win attention for serious offerings of contemporary art, including work by Dan Flavin and Donald Judd. ♦ Tu-Sa 11AM-5PM. 817 N. Hilldale Ave. Also at: 812 N. Robertson Blvd. 310/273.0603

**85  Koontz**  Russell Wilson offers one of the best selections of craftsman tools and housewares in the city. Notable items are lighting fixtures and German-made miniature toy trains. ♦ M-F 8:30AM-6PM; Sa 8:30AM-5:30PM; Su 10AM-4PM. 8914 Santa Monica Blvd. 310/652.0123

**86  Ramada West Hollywood**  $$ Dramatic white and pale gray stucco wings frame an entrance court that blooms with colorful metal flowers by designer Peter Shire. The bold facade, sleek lobby, and pleasant guest rooms are meant to entice designers visiting the neighboring showrooms. ♦ 8585 Santa Monica Blvd. 310/652.6400, 800/228.2828; fax 310/652.4207

**86  Red Car Grill**  ★★$$ Restaurant designer Pat Kuleto, the Northern California guru of haute diners, renders a classic Fog City ambience in this grill located in the Ramada West Hollywood hotel. Steaks, fish, hamburgers, and salads are among the many entrées. ♦ American ♦ M-F noon-2:30PM, 5:30-10PM; Sa-Su 5:30-11PM. 8571 Santa Monica Blvd. 310/652.9263

**86  EZTV**  This small upstairs space showcases independent video tapes. The quality is inconsistent, but some first-rate and often hilarious tapes show up with pleasing regularity. ♦ Admission. Call for hours. 8547 Santa Monica Blvd. 310/657.1532

## Hollywood/West Hollywood

**86  Little Frida's**  $$ Have a mocha in honor of Frida Kahlo, the late heroine of Mexican art and current champion of '90s arts feminism. Take a table outside in the pleasant courtyard if you're unable to occupy the crucifix table, the most interesting seat in the house. ♦ Coffeehouse ♦ M-Th, Su 9AM-12:30AM; F-Sa 9AM-3AM. 8545 Santa Monica Blvd. 310/854.0757

**86  Rosamund Felsen Gallery**  New and established LA artists, including Mike Kelley, Chris Burden, and Roy Dowell, are showcased here. ♦ Tu-Sa 10AM-5:30PM. 8525 Santa Monica Blvd. 310/652.9172

**86  Le Dufy**  $$$ The 103 suites make a wonderful quiet getaway within minutes of several upscale retail and dining establishments. ♦ 1000 Westmount Dr, south of Holloway Dr. 310/547.7400, 800/253.7997; fax 310/854.6744

**87  L'Orangerie**  ★★★★$$$$ This is the grandest, most formal of the French restaurants in LA, beautifully furnished and flatteringly lit. Under the exquisite hand of chef Jean-Claude Parachini (formerly of the three-star L'Ambrosie in Paris), there are high praises for the cassoulet of lobster with fennel, the sole with crayfish sauce, the roasted squab stuffed with wild rice, and the sinfully rich all-chocolate Dessert du Roy. ♦ French ♦ Daily 6:30-11PM. 903 N. La Cienega Blvd. 310/652.9770

**88  ESPRIT**  The San Francisco-based company's LA store is a stylish fashion palace of raw concrete and steel designed by Joe D'Urso. Inside are vibrant contemporary fashions in so many tempting colors and styles that management provides shopping carts for their customers. ♦ M-F 10AM-8PM; Sa 10AM-7PM; Su 11AM-6PM. 8491 Santa Monica Blvd (at La Cienega Blvd). 310/659.7575

The first moving picture ever filmed in Hollywood was a Western entitled *The Law of the Range*, which was shot by brothers William and David Horsley in 1911.

**89 Barney's Beanery** $$ Immortalized by sculptor **Ed Kienholz** in the '60s, Barney's still offers breakfast, lunch, and dinner selected from an enormous menu, a zillion labels of beer, and a friendly game of pool. ♦ American ♦ Daily 10AM-2AM. 8447 Santa Monica Blvd. 654.2287

**89 Globe Theater** The charming replica of Shakespeare's wooden "O" is host to the bard's plays and dramatic readings of his sonnets. ♦ 1107 N. Kings Rd. 654.5623

**90 Hugo's** ★$$$ A specialty butcher, deli, and restaurant are all packed into this establishment. They serve excellent pasta dishes, simple entrées, and salads to eat in or to go. Hugo's is

## Hollywood/West Hollywood

the place for power breakfasts, too. ♦ Italian ♦ Daily 6AM-11PM. 8401 Santa Monica Blvd. 654.3993

**90 Cafe La Boheme** ★★★$$$ The epitome of dining as theater, interior designer **Margaret O'Brien's** inviting and romantic setting combines the majesty of a Medieval castle's great hall with the atmosphere of a subterranean abode fit for the Phantom. Gauzed illumination and a reflecting pool help to offset the vastness of the two-level dining area. Impeccably attired and attentive waiters serve juicy filet mignons, range-free cooked chickens in cilantro and peppers, and a variety of deliciously prepared fish. ♦ International ♦ M-Th 11:30AM-2:30PM, 5:30-10:30PM; F 11:30AM-2:30PM, 5:30-11:30PM; Sa 11AM-2:30PM, 5:30-11:30PM; Su 11AM-2:30PM, 5:30-10:30PM. 8400 Santa Monica Blvd. 848.2360

**91 Marix Tex-Mex** ★$$ Their huge margaritas help pass the time while you are waiting for your table in this boisterous Tex-Mex restaurant. Fajitas and blue-corn tortillas are the specialties. ♦ Tex-Mex ♦ M-Th 11AM-11PM; F 11AM-midnight; Sa 8:30AM-midnight; Su 8:30AM-11PM. 1108 N. Flores. 656.8800

**92 Peanuts** Gay women predominate at this large and rambunctious dance club. There are theme nights and live entertainment. ♦ Cover. Daily 9PM-2AM. 7969 Santa Monica Blvd. 654.0280

**92 La Fabula** ★$$ This spacious and streamlined Mexican restaurant serves good Mazatlan-style dishes and is located within walking distance of many live-performance theaters in the Hollywood/West Hollywood area. ♦ Mexican ♦ M 6-10PM; Tu 11:30AM-3PM, 6-10PM; W-F 11:30AM-2:30PM, 6-10:30PM; Sa 6-10:30PM; Su 11:30AM-3PM, 6-10:30PM. 7953 Santa Monica Blvd. 650.8517

**93 Tuttobene** ★★$$ Owner **Silvio De Mori** hosts with assurance, and the kitchen staff is equally steady—from the complimentary *panzanella* (bread, tomato, and garlic salad) to the pastas and risottos to the sinful tiramisù. The crowd is always interesting and the service excellent. ♦ Italian ♦ M-F 11AM-2:30PM, 5:30-11PM; Sa 11AM-2:30PM; Su 5-10PM. 945 N. Fairfax Ave. 655.7051

**94 American-European Bookstore** Specialties include American literature and history, especially about the South and the Civil War and military and European affairs. More than 15,000 European books are catalogued here. ♦ Daily 10:30AM-6:30PM. 7781 Santa Monica Blvd. 654.1007

**94 The Pleasure Chest** The catalog of naughtiness is as prosaically displayed as produce in the supermarket. ♦ M-Th, Su 10AM-midnight; F-Sa 10AM-1AM. 7733 Santa Monica Blvd. 650.1022

**95 Plummer Park** A fragment of the ranch that operated as a truck farm and dairy from 1877 1943, this three-acre park now contains recreational facilities and the original Plummer home (876.1725). A farmers' market is held here every Monday from 10AM to 2PM. ♦ 7377 Santa Monica Blvd

**96 Port's** $$$ This dark and trendy bar attracts the creative community. The varied menu includes good salads and a long list of nightly specials. It's crowded on weekends. Food is served until 1AM. ♦ American ♦ Tu-Sa 7PM-1AM. 7205 Santa Monica Blvd (at Formosa St 874.6294

**97 Formosa Cafe** $ **Philip Marlowe** would have felt right at home in this classic Hollywood bar Stick to the Scotch and skip the Chinese food. ♦ American/Chinese ♦ M-Sa 10AM-2AM. 7156 Santa Monica Blvd. 850.9050

**98 Burnett Miller** Minimalist and conceptual American and European artworks and installations by **Charles Ray** and **Wolfgang Laib** are featured. ♦ Tu-Sa 10AM-5:30PM. 964 N. La Brea Ave. 874.4757

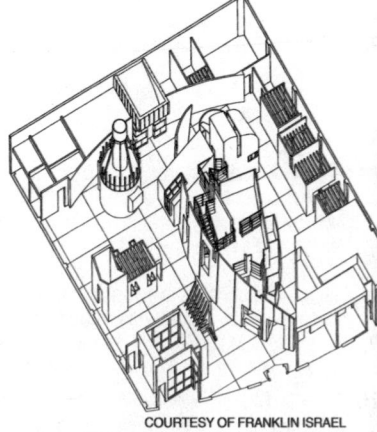

COURTESY OF FRANKLIN ISRAEL

**99 Propaganda Films** **Franklin Israel's** brilliant 1988 adaptation of an old warehouse (pictured above) features sculptural enclosures within a cavernous space. His design provides offices and meeting rooms for a progressive film production company. ♦ 940 N. Mansfield Ave. 462.6400

The "fluffer" has one of the most specialized jobs in the pornographic film industry. Her task—executed as she sits behind the camera—is to make male performers erect on cue.

**00 Maxine's Seafood Restaurant** ★$ Great fish at affordable prices is served with a smile. Clam chowder, fresh oysters on the half shell, steamed mussels and clams, and mesquite-grilled fish are among the specialties. ♦ Seafood ♦ M-Sa 11AM-10PM; Su 4-9PM. 6775 Santa Monica Blvd. 461.5644

**101 Mignon** ★★$ The ex-king of Rumania reportedly had to wait for a table, so you know this Balkan delight is authentic. Carp-roe pâté, white-bean soup, stuffed cabbage rolls, and sour-cherry crepes are all highly recommended. ♦ Rumanian ♦ Tu-F 11:30AM-9:30PM; Sa 5PM-12:30AM; Su 12:30PM-12:30AM. 1253 N. Vine St. 461.4192

**102 Hollywood Memorial Cemetery** A galaxy of top stars have found refuge from their fans in this 65-acre oasis. **Douglas Fairbanks** has the most elaborate memorial; **Valentino** is in wall crypt No.1205, but the lady in black who brought flowers on the anniversary of his death comes no more. Here, too, are **Jesse Lasky** and **Cecil B. De Mille** (who helped establish Paramount Studios, over the garden wall), **Tyrone Power, Peter Lorre,** and **Virginia Rappe,** whose unexplained death ruined the career of **Fatty Arbuckle.** Close by is **Beth Olam Cemetery,** where rests mobster **Bugsy Siegel,** a founding father of Las Vegas, who was shot down in his Beverly Hills home in 1947. ♦ M-F 8AM-5PM; Sa-Su 9AM-4PM. 6000 Santa Monica Blvd. 469.1181

**103 Don Felipe** ★$$ Pining for old Patagonia? Try Don Felipe. You'll find lots of Argentines and good, authentic food seasoned with gusto at a reasonable price. Try the mixed grill. ♦ Argentine ♦ Daily 11:30AM-10PM. 1050 N. Western Ave (at Santa Monica Blvd). 464.3474

**104 Marouch** ★$ This plain storefront serves delicious Middle Eastern appetizers and roast chicken with garlic. ♦ Lebanese ♦ Tu-Su 11AM-11PM. 4905 Santa Monica Blvd. 662.9325

**105 Bezjian's Grocery** Exotic spices and ingredients for Middle Eastern cooking, such as chutneys and authentic *basmati* rice, imported feta and olives, hummus, and flat breads, are sold here at very low prices. ♦ M-Sa 9AM-7PM; Su 10AM-4PM. 4725 Santa Monica Blvd. 663.1503

**106 Sompun** ★$$ Excellent noodles are served in this family style restaurant. Dine on the charming patio. ♦ Thai ♦ M, W-Su 11AM-10PM. 4156 Santa Monica Blvd. 669.9906

**107 Cha Cha Cha** ★★$$ This restaurant was a huge success from day one, despite its out-of-the-way location and cheerful disregard of production values. What draws the throng is an infectiously friendly spirit, spicy food, and wonderful daily specials. The corn tamale with golden caviar, the giant shrimp in black pepper sauce, and the chicken *poblana* are not to be missed. ♦ Latin/Caribbean ♦ M-F 11:30AM-3PM, 6-10:30PM; Sa-Su 11:30AM-3PM, 5-11:30PM. 656 N. Virgil Ave (at Melrose Ave). 664.7723

**108 Melrose Avenue** A cornucopia of adventurous restaurants, fast-food restaurants, radical fashions, vintage and used clothing, galleries, and design stores lures tourists, trendies, and punks to Melrose. On weekends sidewalks are thronged and parking is difficult; in compensation, it's the liveliest scene this side of the Venice boardwalk. Wear comfortable shoes; it's a three-mile stroll from Highland east to Doheny, though the choicest stretch lies between La Brea and Fairfax. New businesses are pioneering the lower-rent areas to the east, and Melrose's trendiness has spilled over onto Beverly Boulevard and Third to the south. Don't miss **Faux** (No. 7309, 931.3763) for jewelry;

**Rosso E Nero** (No. 7371, 658.6340) and **O'toto** (No. 7119, 937.5435) for fine eating; **Drake's** (No. 7566, 651.5600) for racy adult gifts; **Caffe Luna** (No. 7463, 655.8674) for espresso and dessert; **Aardvark's** (No. 7576, 655.6789) for vintage clothing; and **Emphasis** (No. 7361, 653.7174) for casual wear.

**108 Rincon Chileno** ★$$ Chile is a long coastal country and, understandably, much of its best cooking is seafood. Here is a warm, homey spot peopled largely by Chileans where you can sample some authentic dishes. Look for *paila de mariscos* (seafood stew), raw sea urchins, eel, and *pastel de choclo,* an unusual corn casserole. Order a bottle of strong Chilean wine with your meal. The place can be crowded on weekends and speaking a bit of Spanish to your waiter can be helpful. ♦ Chilean ♦ Tu-Th 11:30AM-10PM; F-Sa 11:30AM-11PM; Su 11AM-10PM. 4355 Melrose Ave. 666.6075

**109 Cafe Mambo** ★$$ **Mario Tamayo** has turned a Victorian house into a funky, colorful, Latin/Caribbean restaurant. Actors, artists, screenwriters, lawyers, poseurs, and just about anyone enjoy such spicy fare as *chilaquiles* (fried tortillas scrambled with eggs and salsa), lobster sandwich with garlic mayonnaise, and tropical chicken with black beans and rice. ♦ Latin/Caribbean ♦ Daily 9AM-3PM, 6-11PM. 707 Heliotrope Dr. 663.5800

**110 Paramount Studios** Paramount is the last of the major studios in Hollywood; the others departed in search of cheap land. The original entrance gate, through which **Gloria Swanson** was driven by **Erich von Stroheim** in *Sunset Boulevard,* is tucked away at the end of Bronson Avenue. There's a new double gate on Melrose. The stages along Gower Street were formerly part of the **RKO Studios;** the trademark globe can be seen at the corner. Paramount is closed to the public, but the site is full of atmosphere. Across the street is the **Raleigh** rental studio, which combines new stages with a wood-frame street that seems unchanged from 1915. And two blocks east is **Western Costume,** established in 1913, which rents stock clothes to the movies, stage, and Halloween revelers. ♦ 5555 Melrose Ave

---

Restaurants/Clubs: Red     Hotels: Blue
Shops/ 🌳 Outdoors: Green     Sights/Culture: Black

**110 Orza's** ★$$$ Tucked snugly in the shadow of Paramount Studios is this small neighborhood place. Combination appetizer plates and the mixed grill are suggested for the uninitiated. Stuffed cabbage and grilled sweetbreads are noteworthy. Portions are hearty and generously seasoned. Finish off the meal with a strong Turkish coffee. ♦ Rumanian ♦ M-Tu 11AM-3PM; W-F 11AM-3PM, 5-9PM; Sa 5-9PM. 708 N. Valentino Pl. 465.4884

**111 A-1 Record Finders** This is the best place for a disc nobody else has; if they don't have it, they'll send out a posse. It's open by appointment only. ♦ 5639 Melrose Ave. 732.6737

## Hollywood/West Hollywood

**112 Totah Design Inc.** Designer **Larry Totah** created this showcase for his furniture designs, displayed against a backdrop of Pompeian and steel columns. ♦ M-F 9AM-5PM. 654 N. Larchmont Blvd. 467.2927

**113 Zumaya** ★★$$ The fish tacos, special enchiladas, and chicken in spicy sauce are among the standouts in this cozy, upscale, family run restaurant that has pleasant service. ♦ Latin ♦ M-Th, Su 11AM-9:30PM; F 11AM-11PM; Sa 11AM-11:30PM. 5722 Melrose Ave. 464.0624

**113 Seafood Village** ★$ Fresh, reasonably priced seafood from the fish market next door is served in this popular neighborhood place. ♦ Seafood ♦ M-F 11AM-11PM; Sa 11:30AM-11PM; Su 11:30AM-10PM. 5730 Melrose Ave. 463.8090

**114 Patina** ★★★★$$$ With **Joaquim Splichal** in the kitchen and his wife, **Christine,** to welcome guests, this had to be a hit. The old **Le St. Germain** has been transformed by **Cheryl Brantner,** who has banished the red plush and created an invisible decor of wood, stone, and soft lighting in a succession of intimate dining rooms and a tiny bar. Highlights of the menu include corn blinis with marinated salmon, *mille feuille* of white fish with cabbage and lemon sauce, duck liver with beetroots, and John Dory with calf's feet and oysters—odd combinations that come off with effortless assurance. For lunch, the chicken salad redefines that clichéd dish. There's an exceptional wine list, too. ♦ Eclectic ♦ M-F 11:30AM-2:30PM, 6-10PM; F-Sa 6-10:30PM; Su 6-9:30PM. 5955 Melrose Ave. 467.1108

**115 Emilio's Ristorante** ★★$$$ With a central fountain, statuary, and more than its share of Chianti bottles perched on the backs of the red leather booths, Emilio's is more than a little theatrical. The food here reflects that same tendency for overabundance; there are a zillion dishes to choose from and lots appears on the plate. ♦ Italian ♦ M-W 11AM-3PM, 5-11:30PM; Th-F 11:30AM-2:30PM, 5-11:30PM; Sa-Su 5-11:30PM. 6602 Melrose Ave. 935.4922

Seats at the annual Academy Awards ceremony fetch some of the highest bootleg ticket prices—as much as $2,000.

**115 Il Piccolino** ★★$$ Emilio's wife, **Pauline,** and his son, **Dino Baglioni,** operate this attractive trattoria. Pizza *alla campagniolla* (lots of fresh vegetables on a thin crust) and *crespelle alla Valdostana* (baked pasta) are good choices, and there's a nice selection of fairly priced wines. ♦ Italian ♦ Tu-F 11:30AM-3PM, 5PM-midnight; Sa-Su 5PM-midnight. 641 N. Highland Ave. 936.2996

**115 Highland Grounds** LA Bohemians engage in esoteric discussions over generous bowls of lattes. Nightly entertainment ranges from acoustic blues and jazz to open-mike night every Wednesday. Breakfast and lunch menus are available. ♦ M-F 8AM-1AM; Sa-Su 8:30AM-2AM. 742 N. Highland Ave. 466.1507

**116 New Living** Furniture as artwork from the best local and European designers is found here. Competitively priced reproductions can be custom-made. ♦ M-F 10AM-7PM; Sa 11AM-6PM; Su by appointment only. 6812 Melrose Ave. 933.5553

**117 Citrus** ★★★★$$$$ An airy all-white shed with glass-brick walls enlivened with fresh flowers and colorful paintings is the setting for owner and chef **Michel Richard's** ambitious restaurant. A fashionable crowd fills every table for lunch and dinner (the leafy patio seems less cramped than the dining room), enjoying dishes that are pretty and tasty. Meltingly soft scallops with crisp-fried Maui onions, oyster custard, and shiitake mushrooms *en croute* are good starters; lamb with saffron ravioli, steak in Cabernet sauce, and soy-grilled tuna are fine, but leave room for the desserts. ♦ California ♦ M-Th noon-2:30PM, 6:30-10PM; F noon-2:30PM, 6:30-10:30PM; Sa 6-11PM. 6703 Melrose Ave. 857.0034

**117 The Rock Store** Elvis lives! Memorabilia of the King and the mortal stars who followed is sold here. ♦ M-F 11AM-8PM; Sa 11AM-6PM. 6817 Melrose Ave. 930.2980

**117 Intermezzo** $$ This charming, low-key espresso and pasta bar features a small front room with a bar built around an open kitchen; in the back is a breezy patio with blue and white umbrellas. Homemade pasta to eat in or to go, fresh seafood dishes, soups, sandwiches, and salads are among the popular choices. Beer and wine are available. ♦ Italian/Takeout ♦ M-Th 11AM-10PM; F 11AM-midnight; Sa-Su 5-11PM. 6919 Melrose Ave. 937.2875

**118 Every Picture Tells a Story** Original art and lithographs by illustrators of children's books are available in this gallery. The bookstore offers a wide selection of children's literature. ♦ Tu-Sa 10AM-5PM; Su noon-5PM. 836 N. La Brea Ave. 962.5420

**119 Pink's Famous Chili Dogs** ★$ You can choose from hot dogs, hamburgers, and tamales, but the chili dogs are what make this place world famous. ♦ American ♦ Daily 7AM-2AM. 711 N. La Brea Ave. 931.4223

**119 Danziger Studio** It was this minimalist house/studio built for designer **Lou Danziger** in 1965 that launched **Frank Gehry's** career. Three blank stucco boxes, adroitly positioned, transform LA's industrial vernacular into high art. It's a private residence. ♦ 7001 Melrose Ave

**120 George's Department Store** Larry Totah designed this loftlike space (formerly for **People**) with its wraparound mezzanine to display clothes that range from denim to Dior. ♦ Tu-Sa noon-8PM; Su noon-6PM. 7207 Melrose Ave. 938.1134

**120 Cottura** Shop here for Venetian glass, Florentine papers, and rustic hand-painted ceramics. ♦ M-Sa 11AM-6PM; Su noon-5PM. 7215 Melrose Ave. 933.1928. Also at: 10250 Santa Monica Blvd, 310/277.3828; 587 Newport Center Dr, 714/644.1151

**120 Chopstix** ★$ The high-tech setting (designed by **David Serrurier**) is the place for a quick lunch, snack, or late dinner located within a delightful Art Deco pavilion. Feast on dim sum, great barbecued ribs and chicken, and exotic noodle dishes at prices you won't believe. They deliver to your home or office—and it even tastes good when cold. ♦ Chinese ♦ M-Th, Su 11:30AM-11PM; F-Sa 11:30AM-midnight. 7229 Melrose Ave. 937.1111. Also at: 46 W. Colorado Blvd, Pasadena. 818/405.1111

**120 The Bakery on Melrose** Scrumptious pastries and, for your "best friend," whole-grain dog biscuits are baked here. ♦ Tu-Th 8:30AM-6PM; F 8:30AM-midnight; Sa 9AM-midnight; Su 10AM-5PM. 7261 Melrose Ave. 934.4493

**120 Nucleus Nuance** ★$$$ Late-night dining and dancing to live jazz and swing packs people in here. The food is pretty good, the clientele is colorful, and the music can be great. ♦ California ♦ Daily 7PM-2AM. 7267 Melrose Ave. 939.8666

**120 Unit 7301** Klaus Wille sells authorized reproductions of original Bauhaus furniture. ♦ Tu-Sa noon-6PM. 7301 Melrose Ave. 933.8391

**120 A Star is Worn** Celebrity wearables and collectibles, contemporary and period, are sold here. ♦ M-Sa 11AM-7PM; Su noon-5PM. 7303 Melrose Ave. 939.4922

**120 Groundlings Theatre** This resident company does sleight-of-mouth improvisation using suggestions from the audience. ♦ 7307 Melrose Ave. 934.9700

**121 Costumes for Kids** Big imaginations in small frames can realize their fantasies of being a fairy princess, a pirate, or a superhero. ♦ M-Sa 10AM-5PM. 7206 Melrose Ave. 936.5437

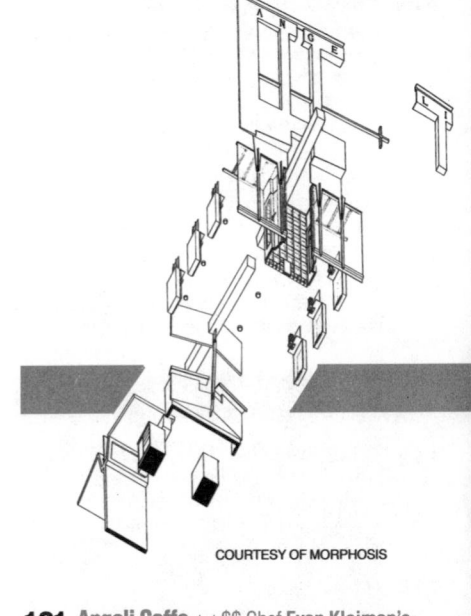

COURTESY OF MORPHOSIS

**121 Angeli Caffe** ★★$$ Chef **Evan Kleiman's** simple but delicious rustic Italian cooking combined with a well-selected wine list makes this a popular place to dine. The prices are reasonable, but Angeli is a victim of its own success; the two tiny dining rooms are often uncomfortably crowded and noisy. The restaurant is at its most relaxed in the late afternoon, when sandwiches and biscotti are served. Takeout is a specialty. **Morphosis**, a pace-setting architectural firm, has made the first room (illustrated above) a structuralist paraphrase of a baroque chapel, with wall niches and a pizza oven in place of the altar. The facade comprises a broken arch of rusted steel, glass brick to diffuse the light that floods inside, and a projecting beam (like a toothpick spearing a sandwich). ♦ Italian/Takeout ♦ M-Sa noon-10:30PM; Su 5-10PM. 7274 Melrose Ave. 936.9086. Also at: 11651 Santa Monica Blvd. 310/478.1191; 13455 Maxella Ave, Marina del Rey. 310/822.1984

**121 Condomania** Inventive safe sex is the message of this funky outlet of scented lubricants and candy-flavored contraceptives. The variety of erotic gift items includes kitty condoms for your tabbies. ♦ M-Th, Su 11AM-8PM; F-Sa 11AM-11PM. 7306 Melrose Ave. 933.7865

**122 Wound and Wound** Clockwork fanatics take note: this is where dreams come true. ♦ M-Th 11AM-10PM; F-Sa 11AM-midnight; Su 11AM-8PM. 7374 Melrose Ave. 653.6703

**122 Campo dei Fiori** Sensational flower arrangements fill the room in this sleek concrete frame with signature vases by **David Hertz**. ♦ M-Th 9AM-9PM; F-Sa 9AM-10PM; Su 10AM-8PM. 648 N. Martel Ave. 655.9966

"Hollywood is a place where they'll pay you $50,000 for a kiss and 50 cents for your soul."
                                                    **Marilyn Monroe**

The longest nonstop show of movies lasted 50 hours at the Variety Arts Center in Hollywood in 1983. Patrons brought sleeping bags to the "B Movie Marathon," and screened 37 films.

**122 La Luz de Jesus Gallery** With its array of colorful *Día de los Muertos* figurines, Mexican ceremonial masks, and other Indo-Hispanic folk art, the upstairs gallery/bookstore is a twisted manifestation of "Rod Sterling's Night Gallery." The entrance is on Martel Avenue. ♦ M-Th 11AM-9PM; F-Sa 11AM-midnight; Su noon-8PM. 7400 Melrose Ave. 651.4875

**122 Soap Plant/Zulu/Wacko** Three stores, under the same management, offer every wonderful little gift or knickknack that you didn't know you needed but suddenly can't live without. There are cards, makeup, funky clothes, fragrant soaps, beach balls that look like globes, plastic

dinosaurs, books, and a fine collection of wooden masks. It's the Melrose version of the old general store. ♦ Soap Plant and Zulu: M-W 10:30AM-11PM; Th-Sa 10:30AM-midnight; Su 11:30AM-8PM. Wacko: M-Th 10AM-11PM; F-Sa 10AM-midnight; Su noon-7PM. 7416 Melrose Ave. 651.3811

**123 LA Eyeworks** Eyeglasses are treated as art in this shop; the stark setting and inventive displays rival the best galleries. Both classic and outrageous frames of high quality are sold here at high prices. ♦ M-F 10AM-noon, 1-7PM; Sa 10AM-noon, 1-6PM. 7407 Melrose Ave. 653.8255

**123 Tommy Tang's** ★$$ Popular with a young, hip clientele, this restaurant serves good food in a fashionable pink-and-gray decor. Specialties include Thai toast, barbecued chicken, and Malaysian clams. Dine inside or on a pretty tiled patio. ♦ Thai ♦ M-Th 11:30AM-11:30PM; F-Sa 11:30AM-12:30AM; Su 5-10:30PM. 7473 Melrose Ave. 651.1810

**123 Chianti Cucina** ★★$$ Splendid pasta and the best breadsticks anywhere from the same kitchen as its parent, **Ristorante Chianti,** are served in a noisy, informal white-tiled room. The place is thronged with a young, attractive crowd, and is a good choice for a late-evening dessert and a cup of espresso. ♦ Italian ♦ Daily 11:30AM-11:30PM. 7383 Melrose Ave. 653.8333

**123 Ristorante Chianti** ★★$$$ This is one of the grande dames of Italian cuisine in LA, with etched glass and dark wood booths. The tradition of turning amaretto cookie wrappers into flying saucers began here. ♦ Italian ♦ Daily 5-11:30PM. 7383 Melrose Ave. 653.8333

**124 Johnny Rocket's** $ This spiffy '50s diner is a popular hangout for kids. On weeknights and weekends, fashionable bikers line their polished Harleys on the streetfront. There are branches all over LA. ♦ American ♦ M-Th, Su 11AM-midnight; F-Sa 11AM-2AM. 7507 Melrose Ave. 651.3361

**124 Leathers & Treasures** Bruce Springsteen and other rock stars have shopped here for vintage cowboy boots, bicycle jackets, and other gear. ♦ M noon-8PM; Tu-Sa 11AM-8PM; Su noon-7PM. 7511 Melrose Ave. 655.7541

**125 Grau** Gaudiesque columns frame an organic plywood cave, designed by **Ajax** in 1989. The clothing shop carries sophisticated casual wear for independent-minded women. Guatemalan weavings and Japanese kimonos inspire the richness of color and texture in **Claudia Grau's** designs. ♦ M-F 11AM-7PM; Sa 11AM-8PM; Su noon-6PM. 7520 Melrose Ave. 651.0487

**126 The Burger That Ate LA** $ This is what the city needs—a giant burger emerging hungrily from City Hall. It's vintage California Crazy. ♦ American ♦ M-Th, Su 11:30AM-midnight; F-Sa 11:30AM-1AM. 660 N. Stanley Ave. 653.2647

**126 California Beach Rock 'n' Sushi** $$ Godzilla meets the Beach Boys in this second-floor restaurant and sushi bar designed in 1989 by **Ted Tanaka.** The place looks like the demented vision of how a Japanese who had never left home might imagine Southern California. It's an improved version of an idea born in Newport Beach. ♦ Japanese ♦ M-Th, Su 5:30-11PM; F 5:30PM-midnight; Sa 4PM-midnight. 7656 Melrose Ave. 655.0123

**127 Matrix Theatre** Artistic Director **Joseph Stern** has presented LA previews of **Harold Pinter's** *Betrayal,* **Lyle Kessler's** *Orphans,* and **Simon Gray's** *The Common Pursuit* at this adventurous Equity-waiver playhouse, with time out to produce movies. ♦ 7657 Melrose Ave. 852.1445

**128 Genghis Cohen** ★$$$ Catering to a neighborhood crowd and a smattering of show biz types, this upscale Szechuan restaurant serves black-bean crab, crackerjack shrimp, and good *kung pau.* The place has a stylish New York feel. ♦ Chinese ♦ M-Sa noon-3PM, 5-11:30PM; Su noon-3PM, 5-9:45PM. 740 N. Fairfax Ave. 653.0640

**129 Gardel's** ★$$$ Terrific Argentinean food is served in this contemporary, bustling restaurant. There's roast garlic (make sure that everyone at your table eats it or that no one does), *boudin noir,* and a wonderful *parillada* (mixed grill), as well as pasta (Argentina was heavily settled by Italians). There's a good selection of Argentinean wines. Gardel was a movie idol and tango dancer *extraordinaire* in Argentina in the '30s. ♦ Argentinean ♦ M, Sa 6-11PM; Tu-F 11:30AM-2:30PM, 6-11PM. 7963 Melrose Ave. 655.0891

**Restaurants/Clubs:** Red    **Hotels:** Blue
**Shops/ 🌳 Outdoors:** Green    **Sights/Culture:** Black

**130 Rondo** ★★$$$ Wonderful Tuscan cooking and such specials as a rich *zuppa di pesce,* *tagliata all'erba aromatica* (herb-flavored grilled steak), and great risottos are served in a handsome contemporary dining room designed by **Kellen I. Schweitzer.** But the room can become overcrowded and noisy, like so many fashionable restaurants. ♦ Italian ♦ M-F noon-2:30PM, 6-11PM; Sa 6-11PM. 7966 Melrose Ave. 655.8158

**130 Silent Movie** Opened in 1942 by silent film collector **John Hampton,** this modest house was shuttered for 22 years when Hampton fell ill. His widow, 80-year-old **Dorothy** (who still collects tickets at the door), reopened the 250-seat venue in 1991. Classic silent films from Hampton's 3,000-odd collection, accompanied by live organ music, are screened here three nights a week. ♦ W, F-Sa 8PM. 611 Fairfax Ave. 653.2389

**131 Fantasies Come True** Animation cels and character figurines from Disney and the other great movie cartoon families are showcased here. ♦ Tu-Sa noon-4PM. 8012 Melrose Ave. 655.2636

**132 Modern Living** Philippe Starck, Massimo **Iosa Ghini, Ettore Sottsass,** and **Goodman/ Charlton** headline the list of talents whose work is found in this showroom of modern classics and contemporary furniture. ♦ M-F 10AM-7PM; Sa-Su noon-6PM. 8125 Melrose Ave. 655.3899

**133 Fred Segal** Check out this block-wide complex of youth-oriented stores specializing in nifty T-shirts and sweatshirts, lingerie, luggage, electronic gadgets, cards, kids' stuff, and stationery. In the main store, there is a huge selection of the latest (and more traditional) jeans, sportswear, shoes, and clothing that ranges from beach casual to 24-karat chic. Bargains can be found, and the late-September sale fills every parking spot for six blocks around. Compulsive buyers refuel on chocolate chip cookies and apple pie at the cafe. ♦ M-Sa 10AM-7PM; Su noon-6PM. 8100 Melrose Ave. 651.4129

**133 Improvisation** Locals and tourists can be found two or three deep at the bar on weekends. Catch the best and worst of stand-up comedy every night in the back room. Top names sometimes stop in to catch a show or try out new material. It's open nightly; call for performance times. ♦ Cover. 8162 Melrose Ave. 651.2583

**134 Cafe Mocha** $ Library shelves give this quaint and crowded coffeehouse a literary air. Savor the words of Proust, Rand, and Ginsberg with a cup of hot java. ♦ Coffeehouse ♦ M-F 8AM-3AM; Sa-Su 8AM-4AM. 8205 Melrose Ave. 653.6118

**135 Dailey Rare Books & Fine Prints** This shop carries art and illustrated books and literary first editions. ♦ Tu-F 10AM-6PM; Sa 11AM-5PM. 8216 Melrose Ave. 658.8515

**135 Le Chardonnay** ★$$$ You feel like you've dined in Paris after patronizing this Belle Epoque Parisian brasserie suffused with a warm glow, as if it was gaslit. Sinuous tendrils of teak meander around the mirrors that cover the walls. The spaces in between are covered with Art Nouveau tiles, and brass fixtures wink and glimmer. Unfortunately, the traditional cooking is uneven and the room is excessively noisy. They offer a superb California wine list. ♦ French ♦ M-F noon-2PM, 6-10PM; Sa 6-11PM. 8284 Melrose Ave. 655.8880

**136 Kiyo Higashi** This austerely handsome space shows the work of **Larry Bell, Penelope Krebs,**

Hollywood/West Hollywood

**Guy Williams,** and **Lies Kraal.** ♦ Tu, Th-Sa 11AM-6PM; W 11AM-8PM. 8332 Melrose Ave. 655.2482

**136 Tulipe** ★★★$$$ Roland Gilbert and **Maurice Peguet** are the chefs in this large, brightly lit bistro. Try the blue-cheese-and-pear *pithiviers,* braised veal shank with vegetables, scallops with caramelized shallots, and the grapefruit mousse and apple tart for dessert. ♦ French ♦ M-F 11:30AM-2PM, 6-10PM; Sa 6-11PM; Su 5:30-11PM. 8360 Melrose Ave. 655.7400

**137 Gemini G.E.L.** Fine art prints by such artists as **David Hockney, Jasper Johns, Robert Rauschenberg, Jonathan Borofsky,** and **Ellsworth Kelly** are spotlighted in this workshop/gallery designed by **Frank Gehry.** ♦ M-F 9:30AM-5:30PM. 8365 Melrose Ave. 651.0513

**137 Sculpture to Wear** Jan Ehrenworth sells unusually attractive contemporary jewelry. ♦ M-Sa 11AM-6PM. 8441 Melrose Ave. 651.2205

**138 Apartment Building** Come viz me to the Casbah! This 1925 building is a private residence. ♦ Sweetzer Ave at Waring Ave

**139 Schindler House** LA's most innovative house has been lovingly restored. **Rudolph Schindler** came from Vienna to work with **Frank Lloyd Wright,** and built this house/studio in 1921. He lived and worked here until his death in 1953. Inspired by a desert camp, the architect combined tilt-up concrete slab walls, canvas canopies, and open-air sleeping lofts—techniques and spatial treatments that were novel at the time. **Richard Neutra** lived here in the late '20s, and the house was a meeting place for the avant-garde. ♦ Admission. Sa-Su 1-4PM and by appointment. 835 N. Kings Rd. 651.1510

**140 Noura** $$ *Schwarma* (lamb and beef), chicken kebobs, and a fine choice of exotic salads, including *baba ghanooj,* a thick paste of eggplant, and *tahineh* lapped with pita bread, are some of the specialties. ♦ Greek/Mediterranean ♦ M-Th, Su 11AM-11PM; F-Sa 11AM-midnight. 8479 Melrose Ave. 651.4581

---

Sweden banned Hollywood's blockbuster film *E.T.* to children under 11 because it showed parents being hostile to their offspring.

Actor Douglas Fairbanks hosted the premiere Academy Awards show from the opulent Hollywood Roosevelt Hotel in 1929.

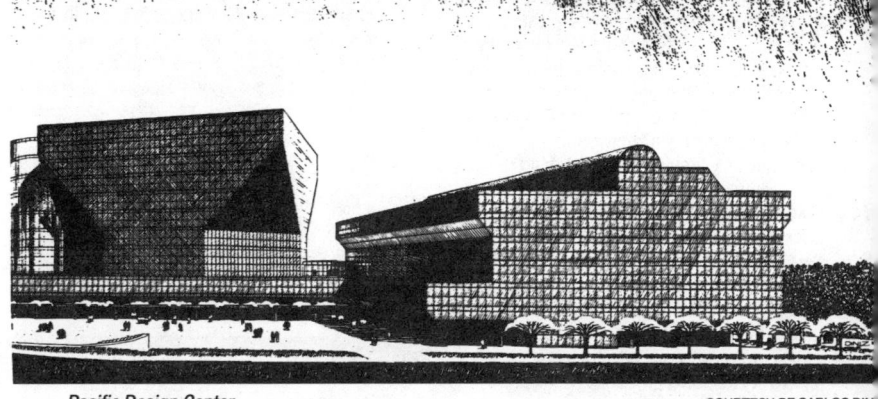

Pacific Design Center

**141 Cicada** $$ Chef **Jean Francois Meteigner,** formerly of **L'Orangerie,** calls up family recipes for this upscale bistro menu of French and Italian comfort food. Named for the French grasshopper, this noisy, tile-floored restaurant is like a Tuscan country villa, warmed by soft lighting and peach-colored wall murals reminiscent of faded Italian frescoes. Cicada is co-owned by the chef, songwriter **Bernie Taupin,** and former Le Dôme general manager **Stephanie Haymes.** Try the rotisserie chicken or the grilled lamb chops. ♦ European ♦ M-F noon-2:30PM, 6-10PM; Sa 6-11PM. 8478 Melrose Ave. 655.5559

**142 L'Ermitage** ★★★★$$$$ Opened in the '70s by chef **Jean Bertranou,** this treasure was given a lighter, brighter character in 1985 by **Dora Fourcade,** a young French-Tahitian entrepreneur. The look is soft and elegant; the cooking of chef **Michel Blanchet** is both refined and assured. Don't miss the house-smoked salmon, roast squab with foie gras and rosemary, lobster with scallions, mushrooms, and potato puree, and, of course, the celebrated cheese *chariot.* ♦ French ♦ M-Sa 6:30-10PM. 730 N. La Cienega Blvd. 652.5840

**143 Akuto** Exotic European fashions for men are shown in a dramatic concrete-and-steel set by **Faramaz Matloob.** ♦ M-Sa 10AM-8PM. 755 N. La Cienega Blvd. 657.0430

**143 Clacton & Frinton** English-made suits for trend-setting architects and designers, featuring easy cuts and good fabrics, are sold here. ♦ M-Sa 10AM-6PM. 731 N. La Cienega Blvd. 310/652.2957

**143 Paddington's Tea Room** Agatha Christie would have loved this cozy tea shop, which specializes in fresh scones with Devonshire cream and authentically strong tea. ♦ English ♦ M-Sa 10AM-7PM; Su noon-7PM. 729 N. La Cienega Blvd. 310/652.0624

**144 La Cage Aux Folles** $$$$ If you loved the movie, you may enjoy this restaurant/nightclub. Your evening comes complete with pink feathers, quasi-French food, and a drag-queen show. ♦ French cabaret ♦ Call for showtimes. 643 N. La Cienega Blvd. 310/657.1091

**144 Penny Feathers** $$ Just your basic sandwiches, simple entrées, and breakfast food are served here, plus beer and wine. ♦ American ♦ M-F 7AM-3AM; Sa-Su 24 hours. 631 N. La Cienega Blvd. 310/659.3545

**144 Le Parc** $$$ Formerly part of the defunct L'Ermitage Hotels group, this 154-suite hotel offers tennis courts, a swimming pool, a fitness facility, and a Westside sunset vista on the roof top. ♦ 733 West Knoll Dr. 310/855.8888, 800/424.4443; fax 310/659.7812

**145 Heritage Book Shop** Early manuscripts, 17th- to 20th-century first editions, fine bindings, and autographs are some of the treasure in this shop. ♦ M by appointment only; Tu-F 9:30AM-5:30PM; Sa 10AM-4:30PM. 8540 Melrose Ave. 310/659.3674

**145 Elliott Katt Bookseller** This is possibly the best bookshop in LA for old and new publications on film, radio, television, and theater. ♦ M-Sa 11AM-6PM. 8570½ Melrose Ave. 310/652.5178

**146 Bodhi Tree** Books on Eastern and Western philosophy, health, women's issues, astrology and religion stock the shelves, along with an array of herbs, soaps, and tarot cards. ♦ Daily 11AM-11PM. 8585 Melrose Ave. 310/659.173

**146 Details** Looking to update your wardrobe? Stop by this boutique for upscale architectural accessories by contemporary American and European designers. ♦ M-F 10AM-5PM. 8625½ Melrose Ave. 310/659.1550

**147 Du Vin Wine & Spirits** Ask owner René Averseng for current bargains in French wines and, while you're here, pick up some cheese and sandwiches. ♦ M-Sa 10AM-7PM. 540 N. San Vicente Blvd. 310/855.1161

---

In 1851 the city of El Monte became the first American town incorporated in Southern California outside the city of Los Angeles.

---

Rainer Werner Fassbinder's 15-hour *Berlin Alexanderplatz,* the longest commercially screened film, was shown at the Vista Cinema in Hollywood in 198

**48 Pacific Design Center** These mammoth glass-cladded geometric volumes (illustrated at left) by **Cesar Pelli** and **Gruen Associates** house more than 200 interior furnishings and accessories showrooms (1.2 million square feet of displays, from upscale traditional to the cutting edge). The public may visit **Center Blue** or **Center Green;** most showrooms allow you to browse on your own, but purchasing requires the services of an interior-design professional. Everyone is welcome to eat (or have a drink until 7PM) in the **Melrose Bar & Grill** on the fourth floor of Center Blue. It says a lot about the clientele that the two most popular dishes here are the chicken Caesar salad and Cobb salad.

On the handsome plaza that separates the center from San Vicente Boulevard is **Murray Feldman Gallery,** which is open to the public and presents high-quality architecture and design exhibitions (call for hours). Throughout the year, public exhibitions, including ongoing collections from the **LA County Museum of Art,** are held within both centers. ♦ Pacific Design Center: M-F 9AM-5PM. Restaurant: M-F 11:30AM-3PM. 8687 Melrose Ave (at San Vicente Blvd). 310/657.0800

**49 Kurland/Summers Gallery** Art-glass and clothes-as-art are shown side by side in this loft space. ♦ Tu-Sa 11AM-6PM. 8742A Melrose Ave. 310/659.7098

**49 Morton's** ★★$$$ The celebrities who pack this place every night from nine until late enjoy surprisingly good food and service. If you pass on people-watching and arrive early, you'll do even better, though you will miss the essential point of this stylish restaurant, which is so "in" it doesn't need a sign. The lime-grilled chicken and the moist rack of lamb are dependable; try to avoid the more complicated dishes. ♦ American ♦ M-Sa 6PM-midnight. 8800 Melrose Ave. 310/276.5205

**49 Ed's Coffee Shop** $ The decor may not pass the standards of the largely interior design patrons, but they keep coming back here for the house favorites such as the turkey quesadillas (oven-roasted, not processed poultry) and spaghetti, when it gets on the list of daily offerings. ♦ American ♦ M-F 7AM-3PM; Sa 7:30AM-12:30PM. 460 N. Robertson Blvd. 310/659.8625

**50 Jay Wolf** Designer **Waldo Fernandez** added his touch to this collection of sophisticated imported menswear. ♦ M-Sa 11AM-7PM. 517 N. Robertson Blvd. 310/273.9893

**50 Maxfield** Shop here for avant-garde couture at drop-dead prices in a spare concrete shell designed by **Larry Totah.** The window display is often worth a detour. ♦ M-Sa 11AM-7PM. 8825 Melrose Ave. 310/274.8800

**51 Asher/Faure** Contemporary American and European artists, including **David Reed, Jack Goldstein,** and **Llyn Foulkes,** are showcased here. ♦ M-F 10AM-5:30PM; Sa 11AM-5:30PM. 612 N. Almont Dr. 310/271.3665

The first television station west of the Mississippi, TLA, began broadcasting in LA in 1947.

**152 Jan Turner Gallery** Tony Delap, John Alexander, Guy Dill, and the late **Carlos Almarez** are on the eclectic list of artists shown here, where innovative landscapes are a specialty. The gallery shares its space with **Turner/Krull** (310/271.1536), which shows a variety of 19th- and 20th-century photography. ♦ M-F 10AM-5:30PM; Sa 11AM-5:30PM. 9006 Melrose Ave. 310/271.4453

**152 Cafe Figaro** $$ Namesake of the New York coffeehouse, this cafe serves delicious homemade wheat bread with butter. This dark and crowded place is popular for late-night snacks and long discussions about the meaning of life.

## Hollywood/West Hollywood

♦ American ♦ M-Th 11:30AM-11:30PM; F-Sa 11:30AM-12:30AM; Su 5:30-11:30PM. 9010 Melrose Ave. 310/274.7664

## Bests

### Albert Chiang
Art Director, *Islands Magazine*

Driving south on the elevated section of the **Hollywood Freeway** past the Capitol Records building. The hills and the Hollywood sign are to your left, the cityscape to your right. This is how George Jetson must feel when commuting to work.

Eating ginger catfish at **Chinois on Main** in Santa Monica. They bring the whole fish to your table, and it's a big one.

Dining in the outdoor cafe at the **J. Paul Getty Museum** in Pacific Palisades. It's like eating a good meal in a Roman villa by the sea. There is a spice garden just below the cafe, and if the breeze is just right, the air is cool and aromatic.

Watching classes at the **3rd Street Dance Academy.** You'll see the most elastic hard-bodies in LA here, and you can watch the future extras for a Michael Jackson video practice and drill through dance routines. (I only know this because my wife takes classes here every weekend....)

The best art supply store in LA is **H.G. Daniels.** Don't bother buying one of those heavy, expensive award-winning books or directories on creative types— browse through all of them here. There's a wonderful selection of artists' papers, too.

Get the best dining/architecture experience in LA at **Ben Frank's** diner on the Sunset Strip. It beats any of the Frank Gehry-esque trendy cafes in West LA or Santa Monica. Ask for a booth up front or sit at the counter.

The best people-watching in LA is at **Farmers Market.** Get a good table (preferably in the shade), have a beer, and watch the world go by. This place is popular with Japanese tour groups, elderly Jewish couples, and local Angelenos, who shop for Hollywood souvenirs and sample ethnic cuisine.

Cruising anywhere along the Pacific Coast, from **Redondo Beach** to **Zuma Beach.**

Reading a Raymond Chandler novel—who writes all about LA—on a rainy night.

Franklin Canyon Reservoir

Tower Grove Dr.

Beverly Dr.

Coldwater Canyon Dr.
Coldwater Canyon Dr.

Schuyler Rd.

Wallace Ridge

Loma Vista Dr.

Hillcrest Rd.

**60**

Doheny Rd.

San Ysidro Dr.

Summit Dr.

Beverly Dr.

Woodland Dr.

Doheny Rd.

Mountain Dr.

Sunset Blvd.

Cir.

Alta Dr.

Arden Dr.

Sierra Dr.

Benedict Cañon Dr.

Tower Rd.

Laurel Wy.

Maple Dr.

Palm Dr.

Hillcrest Rd.

Angelo Dr.

**61**

Lexington Rd.

Hartford Wy.

Oxford Wy.

Lomitas Ave.

Elm Dr.

Foothill Rd.

Elevado Ave.

Ladera Dr.

Roxbury Dr.

Rexford Dr.

Alpine Dr.

Carmelita Ave.

**62**

Crescent Dr.

Cañon Dr.

Beverly Dr.

Sunset Blvd

Rodeo Dr.

Whittier Dr.

Camden Dr.

Civic Center Dr.

Alden Dr.

Maple Dr.

**58**

**57**

Greenway Dr.

Bedford Dr.

Roxbury Dr.

Linden Dr.

Walden Dr.

3rd St.

**56**

For nos. 1-40,
see pg. 79

Santa Monica Blvd.
Little Santa Monica Blvd.

Foothill Rd.

Burton Wy.

Dayton Wy.

Trenton Dr.

**63**

Brighton Wy.

Dayton Wy.

Clifton Wy.

Wilshire Blvd.

**64**

Wilshire Blvd.

Comstock Ave.

Club View Dr.

Durant Dr.

Lasky Dr.

Moreno Dr.

**67**

**68**

Eastborne Ave.

**65**

Spalding Dr.

Linden Dr.

McCarty Dr.

Roxbury Dr.

Bedford Dr.

Peck Dr.

Camden Dr.

Rodeo Dr.

El Camino Dr.

Beverly Dr.

Reeves Dr.

Cañon Dr.

Crescent Dr.

Elm Dr.

Rexford Dr.

Maple Dr.

**83**

**82**

Century Park E.

**81**

**66**

Santa Monica Blvd.

Century Park W.

Fox Hills Dr.

Ave. of the Stars

**80**

Heath Ave.

Beverly Green Dr.

Beverly Dr.

Beverwil Dr.

Beverly Glen Blvd.

Constellation Blvd.

**79**

Galaxy Wy.

Hillgreen Dr.

Vidor Dr.

**77**

**76**

Holmby Ave.

Empyrean Wy.

Thayer Ave.

Olympic Blvd.

Cashio St.

Patricia Ave.

Tennessee Ave.

**78**

Motor Ave.

Beverwil Dr.

Reeves Dr.

Beverly Dr.

Rexford Dr.

Balsam Ave.

Pico Blvd.

Monte Mar Dr.

Century City

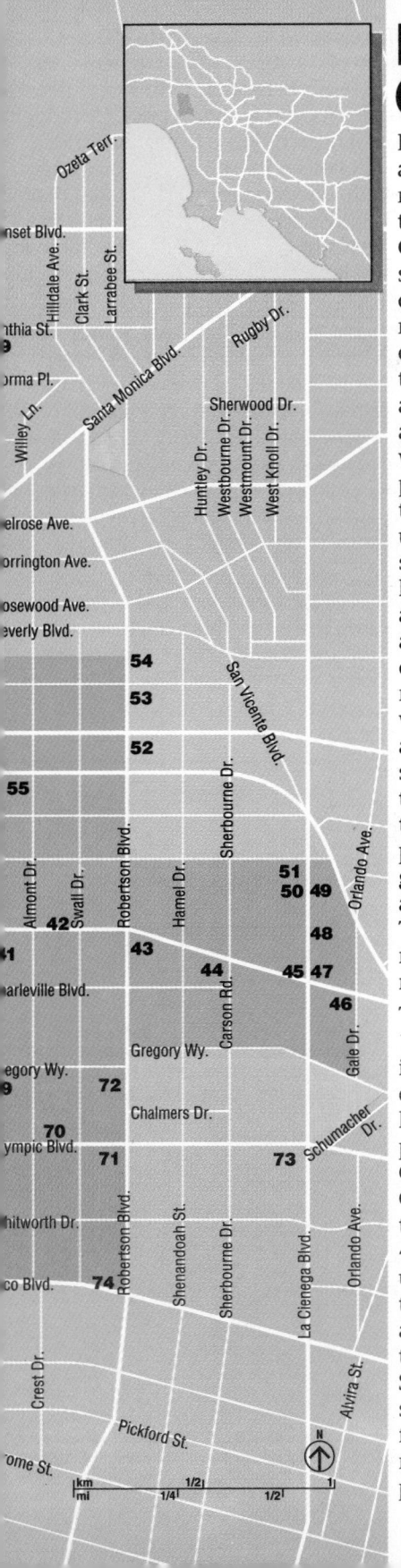

# Beverly Hills/ Century City

Beverly Hills is like Disneyland: a place apart from the real world, unnaturally neat and clean, full of expensive adult toy stores, and lined with trim rows of Old World buildings. It's the apotheosis of the American dream: a tree-lined city with low crime, nonpolluting commerce, pretty people, and two cars in every garage. The reality comes close to the myth created by journalists, movies, and television. The streets to the north and south of Sunset Boulevard are lined with opulent mansions with swimming pools, parklike lawns, and tennis courts, though there are simple cottages high up in the hills and modest apartments south of Wilshire Boulevard. Celebrities have lived here since **Mary Pickford** and **Douglas Fairbanks** set up home at **Pickfair** in 1920. Beverly Hills is narcissistic, and it flaunts its wealth in a manner that has gone out of style elsewhere. But—like Disneyland—it works, and families make sacrifices to live here so their children can attend some of the best public schools in LA. Most of the recent developments are bland—primarily cast-stone palazzi and blackglass boxes—and the house designers are still in love with Mount Vernon. To achieve this paradise, everything is regulated, from the size of signs to overnight parking.

The city got off to a late start; until the 1880s the area was chiefly noted for its fields of lima beans. An attempt to establish the town of Morocco in the land boom of 1887 soon fizzled. The present city was designed by **Wilbur Cook** for the **Rodeo Land and Water Company** in 1907. Cook laid out the triangular grid of business streets at a 45-degree angle to Wilshire, and the sinuously curving residential streets north to Sunset. The **Olmsted** brothers created the picturesque layout of streets that wind up through the hills above Sunset Boulevard as though in a landscaped park. According to local folklore, founder **Burton Green** picked the original name, **Beverly Farms**, from the place in Massachusetts where President

Taft was vacationing. One of the first buildings was **The Beverly Hills Hotel,** which was built in 1911 and 1912, but much of the surrounding area remained undeveloped until long after. As late as 1946, agent **Leland Hayward** was offered a snake-infested tract of hilly land in a prime location at a bargain price. He thought no one would ever want to live there; today it is the affluent **Trousdale Estates.** The residential streets are lushly planted with flowering and shade trees; look for the manicured palms on Benedict and Beverly canyons and the jacarandas that bloom in April and May along Palm and Whittier drives. The houses, when they are not obscured by bushes or high walls, display every known architectural style and many hybrids, mirroring the fantasies of immigrants from all over the world.

For the visitor, the main attractions are shopping, eating, and looking out for celebrities. The main shopping area—bounded by Wilshire Boulevard, Cañon Drive, and Little Santa Monica Boulevard—is known as the "golden triangle." **Rodeo Drive** is an upstart version of the luxury shopping streets in Europe's capitals. Publicity has made it as celebrated as London's Bond Street, Rome's Via Condotti, and the Rue du Faubourg St.-Honoré in

Paris. LA is too spread out and too new to be compared to the elegance and prestige of such European cities, but Rodeo Drive deserves a medal for trying. Many of the top designer labels are represented here and on the neighboring blocks of Wilshire Boulevard.

Century City is strategically placed between Beverly Hills and the booming Westside. It was once **Twentieth Century Fox's** back lot, which was sold in the late '50s and developed by the **Alcoa Corporation.** Unlike its glitzy neighbors, it's a sterile and unfriendly place, with no street life and little good architecture to redeem it. However, it is the site of the luxurious **Century Plaza Hotel,** the grand **Shubert Theater,** and the **Century City Shopping Center,** which covers an 18-acre stretch of land and is truly a shopper's mecca.

---

*Area code 310 unless otherwise noted.*

**1 Beverly Hills City Hall** The unique scroll ornament and colorful tile dome of **William Gage's** splendid 1932 baroque pile were scrubbed in the recent restoration. ♦ 455 N. Rexford Dr (at Santa Monica Blvd)

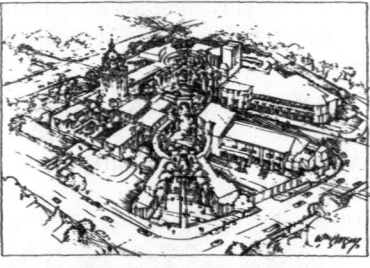

**1 Beverly Hills Civic Center** Architect **Charles Moore** won a competition with his romantic/historical design for a diagonal sequence of three landscaped courtyards that would link the library, fire and police stations, offices, and parking to the remodeled city hall. The grand vista toward the hills works well, and the human scale is pleasing, but the buildings (pictured above) have the insubstantial quality of a movie set—you wonder if they will still be there next week. Repetitive rusticated arches and tile inserts compete with the frilly decoration of the old building. And several of the best features were eliminated to cut costs. ♦ Rexford Dr at Santa Monica Blvd

**2 Union 76 Gas Station** The swooping cantilevered concrete canopy of the '50s is extraordinarily daring for this area. ♦ Rexford Dr at Little Santa Monica Blvd

**3 Litton Industries** Paul Williams' 1940 American Federal Revival office building has a grand portico. ♦ 360 N. Crescent Dr

**4 Kaktus** ★$ Refined south-of-the-border fare is served in a subdued setting. ♦ Mexican ♦ M-Th 11:30AM-3:30PM, 5:30-10PM; F-Sa 11:30AM-11PM. 400 N. Cañon Dr. 271.1856

**5 U.S. Post Office** Ralph Flewelling created this noble 1933 structure in the Italian Renaissance style with terra-cotta and brick and classically framed windows and doors. ♦ 9300 Santa Monica Blvd

**6 La Famiglia** ★★$$$ Modern, intimate, and friendly, this restaurant specializes in red and green pasta and low-cal *nuova cucina*. Next door, at No. 455, is **Piccola Cucina,** a patio restaurant, open weekdays from 11:30AM to 2PM and 5:30 to 10PM. ♦ Italian ♦ M-Sa 5:30-11PM 453 N. Cañon Dr. 276.6208

**7 Nate 'n' Al** ★$$ Big-name stars often come to this celebrated deli on weekends to read their Sunday newspapers and talk with friends. ♦ Deli ♦ M-F, Su 7:30AM-9PM; Sa 7:30AM-9:30PM. 414 N. Beverly Dr. 274.0101

**8 The Cheese Store** Shop here for an outstanding selection of imported cheeses. ♦ M-Sa 9:30AM-6PM. 419 N. Beverly Dr. 278.2855

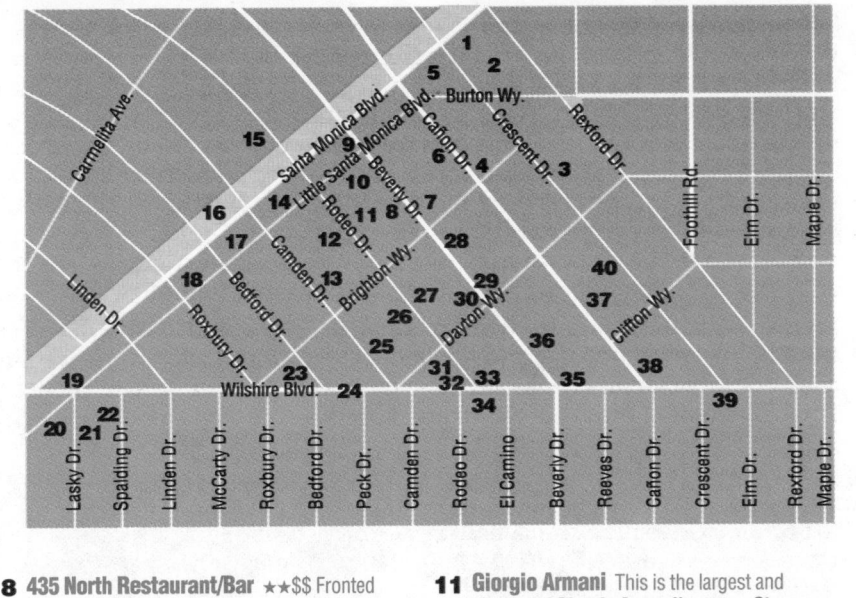

**8 435 North Restaurant/Bar** ★★$$ Fronted by a sleek, sweeping bar where people gather to see and be seen, this upscale, contemporary, and noisy night spot also has a more quiet enclosed patio with a retractable roof for open-air dining in the back. Many entertainment industry power brokers fill its roster of investors. Inventive chef **Joseph J. Choinard** mixes California, Asian, French, Italian, and Southwestern dishes in his "fusion" cuisine here. ♦ Eclectic ♦ M-Th 11:30AM-3PM, 6-10:30PM; F-Sa 6-11PM. 435 N. Beverly Dr. 273.2292

**9 The Corner Cafe, California Crisp** $ Small and bright with daylight streaming in from tall windows, this restaurant serves much the same fare found in the chain's shopping mall takeout delis, including Chinese chicken salad and meatloaf sandwiches. The expanded menu includes grilled steak and a popular grilled vegetable salad. ♦ American ♦ M-Th 7AM-10PM; F-Sa 7AM-11PM; Su 9AM-9PM. 475 N. Beverly Dr. 858.6690

**10 Rangoon Racquet Club** $$$ The name and much of the English decor are the same, but the Anglo/Indian cuisine is gone. The new owners are attracting a retro-dining crowd to the upscale international grill serving classic standards: steaks, chops, and seafood. ♦ American ♦ M-Th 11:30AM-11PM; F 11:30AM-midnight; Sa 5:30PM-midnight. 9474 Little Santa Monica Blvd. 274.8926

**11 Carroll & Co.** Men's clothes for the old guard, who have included such odd bedfellows as **Ronald Reagan, George McGovern,** and **Gregory Peck,** are sold here. ♦ M-Sa 9:30AM-6PM. 466 N. Rodeo Dr. 273.9060

**11 Polo/Ralph Lauren** No, you haven't strayed into an English country house—just the latest of Lauren's emporia for visiting squires and Anglophiles. If, by some curious mischance, you have no pedigree, Ralph will conceal the fact from your closest friends. ♦ M-W, F-Sa 10AM-6PM; Th 10AM-8PM. 444 N. Rodeo Dr. 281.7200

**11 Giorgio Armani** This is the largest and glitziest of **Giorgio Armani's** stores. **Steven Spielberg** and **Elton John** buy their suits here. ♦ M-Sa 10AM-6PM. 436 N. Rodeo Dr. 271.5555

**12 Rodeo Collection** Within this pink marble shopping mall (illustrated above) are designer boutiques, including **Gianni Versace, Sonia Rykiel, Fila,** and **Kenneth Jay Lane.** ♦ M-Sa 10AM-6PM. 421 N. Rodeo Dr. 859.8770

Within the Rodeo Collection:

**Burke & Burke** $ The gourmet deli from New York opened its first California offshoot here, serving 28 sandwich selections, including a "Caesar Sandwich," plus salads, pâtés, cheeses, and a full coffee bar. The pleasant patio has Roman umbrellas and a fountain that sounds like a waterfall. ♦ American ♦ M-Sa 8:30AM-5PM. 858.8095

**12 Frette** Exquisite Italian lingerie and table, bath, and bed linens are sold here. ♦ M-Sa 10AM-6PM. 449 N. Rodeo Dr. 273.8540

**12 Lina Lee** Many celebrities and locals shop here for casual, elegant sportswear. For men, there is suede and leather by **La Matta, Brecos,** and **Ginocchietti;** for women, a spectrum of 350 new and established designers. ♦ Daily 10AM-6PM. 459 N. Rodeo Dr. 275.2926

**13 La Scala** ★$$$ An institution that was once known for its celebrities, snooty service, and high prices, La Scala has changed its attitude as well as its location. It is now a kinder, gentler (and more affordable) neighborhood restaurant, serving so-so food with a smile. The wine list is excellent. ♦ Italian ♦ M-Sa 11AM-10:30PM. 410 N. Camden Dr. 275.0579. Also at: 3874 Cross Creek Rd, Malibu. 456.1979; 11740 San Vicente Blvd, Brentwood. 826.6100

# Rodeo Drive Shopping Map

## SANTA MONICA BOULEVARD

women's wear **Boulmiche Boutique**

## LITTLE SANTA MONICA BOULEVARD

young casuals **BB1** 465
**Baby Guess Georges Marciano** 461
casual children's wear
women's wear **Lina Lee** 459
handbags & accessories **Bottega Veneta** 457
women's wear **Theodore** 453
men's wear **Theodore Man** 451
linens **Frette** 449
women's wear **Jean Claude Jitrois** 447
decorative arts **Robert Zehil Gallery** 445
**Rodeo Collection** 421
Gianni Versace, Sonia Rykiel,
Kenneth Jay Lane, and other boutiques
**Bally of Switzerland** 409
women's shoes & accessories
beauty salon **Vidal Sassoon** 405
designer women's wear **Patricia Morange** 403
jewelry **Fred Joaillier** 401

**RODEO DRIVE**

466 **Carroll & Co.** traditional men's wear
460 **Celine** Parisian women's wear
458 **Zaiko Muraoka** women's wear
456 **Mila Schon** Milanese women's wear
444 **Polo/Ralph Lauren**
classic men's, women's & children's wear
442 **Michael Cromer** luggage
436 **Giorgio Armani**
designer men's & women's wear
430 **Galerie Michael** masterworks
428 **Pierre Deux** French home furnishings
420 **Bijan** men's wear
400 **Capital Bank of California**

## BRIGHTON WAY

jewelry **Harry Winston** 371
**Bang and Olufsen** 369
audio equipment & accessories
men's & women's shoes **A. Testoni** 365
women's shoes **Ferragamo** 357
**Gucci** 347
men's & women's fashions/accessories
women's fashions/accessories **Hermès** 343
art **Dyansen Gallery** 339
European men's wear **Bardelli** 335
leather goods **Gold Pfeil** 333
designer men's wear **Ted Lapidus** 329
perfume/gifts **Giorgio Beverly Hills** 327
art **Hanson Gallery** 323
women's wear **Adrienne Vittadini** 319
designer women's wear **Ungaro** 317
designer women's wear **Alaia Chez Gallay** 313
gadgets **Hammacher Schlemmer** 309
leather goods & luggage **Louis Vuitton** 307
women's wear **Chanel Boutique** 301

370 **Cartier** jewelry
366 **Andrea Carrano**
women's shoes & accessories
362 **Bernini** men's wear
360 **Beverly Rodeo Hotel & Cafe**
346 **Bernini II** European men's wear
340 **Bally of Switzerland**
men's shoes & accessories
338 **Villeroy & Boch** fine china
332 **Avi** men's wear
332 **Diamonds on Rodeo** jewelry
320 **David Orgell** jewelry & silver
314 **Bowles-Sorokko Galleries**
contemporary art
312 **Georgette Klinger** beauty salon
310 **Frances Klein Estate Jewels** rare antiques
308 **Sotheby's** auction house
306 **Battaglia** men's clothing & shoes
300 **Van Cleef & Arpels** jewelry

## DAYTON WAY

**Fred Hayman** 273
men's & women's fashion/fragrance
jewelry **Denmark Jewelers** 201
**Alfred Dunhill of London** 201
traditional men's wear

**Two Rodeo Drive** Cartier, Charles Jourdan,
Christian Dior, Valentino, Cole Haan,
Tiffany & Co., and other boutiques

## WILSHIRE BOULEVARD

**Beverly Wilshire Hotel** 9500
jewelry **Buccellati** 9500

**13 Mandarin** ★★$$$ Peking duck, braised lamb, and Beggar's Chicken are key dishes. The decor is light and bright. ♦ Chinese ♦ M-Th 11:30AM-10PM; F 11:30AM-11PM; Sa 5-11PM; Su 5-10PM. 430 N. Camden Dr. 272.0267

**14 Standard Cutlery** This shop has the world's largest selection of cutting implements. ♦ M-Sa 8:30AM-6PM. 9509 Little Santa Monica Blvd. 276.7898

**15 O'Neill House** Antonio Gaudí is alive and well in Beverly Hills! The Catalan architect would be proud of the writhing stucco on **Don Ramos'** 1989 Art Nouveau collector's house—and the still more whimsical guesthouse in the alley behind. It's a private residence. ♦ 507 N. Rodeo Dr

Restaurants/Clubs: Red
Shops/ ♣ Outdoors: Green

Hotels: Blue
Sights/Culture: Black

**16 Cactus Garden** Cacti and succulents from around the world occupy one section of the most handsome landscaping to be found on any city boulevard. Facing the garden, along the south side, are six block-long low-rise parking structures, an exemplary response to the influx of shoppers. ♦ Santa Monica Blvd (between Camden St and Bedford Dr)

**17 Camp Beverly Hills** T-shirts, sweats, and pants for the young California look are sold to trendy teens. ♦ M-Sa 10AM-6:30PM; Su noon-5PM. 9640 Little Santa Monica Blvd. 274.8317

**17 Banana Republic** The travel books have gone since this burgeoning chain fell into **The Gap,** but you can still find the *Out of Africa* look: safari jackets, khaki pants, skirts, and broad-brimmed hats displayed in a movie set interior. There are branches all over LA. ♦ M-Sa 10AM-6:30PM; Su noon-5PM. 9669 Little Santa Monica Blvd. 858.7900

**18 The Wine Merchant** Dennis Overstreet offers classes, tastings, and rental vaults as well as an outstanding selection of rare vintages. ♦ M-Sa 10AM-6PM. 9701 Little Santa Monica Blvd. 278.7322

**19 Creative Artists Associates** As the uncrowned king of the movie business, CAA president **Michael Ovitz** commissioned **Pei, Cobb, Freed** to design this appropriately sleek but understated palace, completed in 1989. Its curved marble, steel, and glass facade, circular glass lantern, and very precise detailing give an awkward intersection a big lift. ♦ Santa Monica Blvd at Wilshire Blvd

**20 The Peninsula Beverly Hills** $$$$ This new French Renaissance-style hotel has 200 rooms, including suites in five two-story villas. Built low-rise to fit in with nearby residences, the luxury hotel is decorated with fine antiques, tapestries, and tufted carpets. Part of the Hong Kong-based Peninsula Group international hotel chain, it is located near the busy intersection of Wilshire and Santa Monica boulevards, and offers courtesy chauffeured Rolls Royce service in Beverly Hills and Century City. Other amenities include a rooftop pool, health club, terrace dining, and full business center. ♦ 9882 Santa Monica Blvd. 273.4888; 800/462.7899; fax 858.6663

Within The Peninsula Beverly Hills hotel:

**The Belvedere** $$$ Classic gourmet cuisine—salmon smoked in-house with horseradish cream sauce and roasted rack of Colorado lamb, for example—is served in a dining room overlooking lush gardens. ♦ Continental ♦ 6:30AM-10:30PM. Jacket required. 273.4888

**21 Beverly House Hotel** $$ Located right on the edge of the shopping district, this modest, well-run hotel is full of old-fashioned charm. ♦ 140 S. Lasky Dr. 271.2145

**22 Beverly Crest Hotel** $$ This conveniently located 54-room hotel, with a pool and coffee shop, is a bargain for the area. Free parking, too. ♦ 125 S. Spaulding Dr. 274.6801; fax 273.6614

**23 Carroll O'Connor's Place** ★$$$ The daily specials at this noisy New York-style bar and restaurant are often above and beyond the call of duty. ♦ American ♦ M-Sa 11:30AM-11PM; Su 11:30AM-4PM. 369 N. Bedford Dr. 273.7585

**24 Wilshire Boulevard** Wilshire Boulevard between Roxbury and Crescent drives is home to some of LA's best department and specialty stores. Handsome older buildings, slick glass high-rises, and lofty palm trees, plus lively pedestrian traffic, give this stretch of LA's Main Street a great sense of style. This is one place smart New Yorkers can enjoy without a car.

Shopping highlights include:

**Neiman-Marcus** (9700 Wilshire Blvd. 550.5900)

**Jaeger** (9699 Wilshire Blvd. 276.1062)

**Saks Fifth Avenue** (9600 Wilshire Blvd. 275.4211)

**I. Magnin** (9634 Wilshire Blvd. 271.2131)

**Gump's** (9560 Wilshire Blvd. 449.7747)

**Buccellati** (9500 Wilshire Blvd. 276.7022)

**25 Mr. Chow's** ★$$$ A glossy black-and-white interior decorated with fine contemporary art is the setting for tame, expensive food that often looks better than it tastes. The chef comes out from the kitchen for a nightly noodle show. ♦ Chinese ♦ M-F noon-2:30PM, 6:30PM-11:15PM; Sa-Su 6:30PM-11:15PM. 344 N. Camden Dr. 278.9911

**25 Prego** ★$$ The chefs here serve tantalizing pizzas that are prepared in open wood-burning ovens, but they hardly upstage the carpaccio, gnocchi, pasta, and grilled entrées. Prego is an attractive, upbeat, bustling restaurant with a lively bar scene (separated from the dining area by a glass wall) and service that is very congenial, if a bit harried. ♦ Italian ♦ M-Sa 11:30AM-midnight; Su 5PM-midnight. 362 N. Camden Dr. 277.7346

**26 Giorgio Beverly Hills** The celebrated name sells its signature scents and designer casual wear here. ♦ M-Sa 10AM-6PM. 327 N. Rodeo Dr. 274.0200

**27 David Orgell** Superb jewelry and antique English silver are sold here. ♦ M-Sa 10AM-6PM. 320 N. Rodeo Dr. 273.6660

A 110-foot-tall Torrey pine in Beverly Hills' Beverly Gardens Park is the largest of its kind in the world.

**27 Anderton Court** This 1954 angular shopping complex with ramps and a jagged tower is one of **Frank Lloyd Wright's** last and least important works. ♦ 328 N. Rodeo Dr

**27 Beverly Rodeo Hotel** $$$ An intimate European air permeates this luxury hotel. Amenities include concierge and room service, a sundeck, and valet parking. The cafe serves delicious salads on a terrace overlooking Rodeo Drive. W-Th 7AM-10PM; F-Sa 7AM-10:30PM; Su 8AM-10PM. ♦ 360 N. Rodeo Dr. 273.0300; fax 859.8730

**28 The Jewish Quarter** One-of-a-kind Judaic artwork, ceremonial objects, and general gifts and crafts for any budget are sold in this upscale gift shop and art gallery. ♦ M-Th 10AM-6PM; F 10AM-5PM; Su 11AM-5PM. 365 N. Beverly Dr. 288.0364

## Beverly Hills/Century City

**29 The Carnegie Deli** ★$$ Woody Allen would choke on his pastrami sandwich, but there's magic in the name, and this designer version (by designer **Pat Kuleto**) of the scruffy original packs them in. The decor is a fantasy version of an Art Deco deli. There's valet parking and white bread, but the pastrami is original, the portions huge, and all the basic deli foods are here. ♦ Deli ♦ M-Th 7AM-10PM; F-Sa 7AM-midnight. 300 N. Beverly Dr. 275.DELI

**30 Il Fornaio** $ The bakery turns out wonderful breads and pizzas; the cafe serves pastas and salads. ♦ Italian ♦ M-Sa 6:30AM-9PM; Su 7:30AM-9PM. 301 N. Beverly Dr. 550.8330. Also at: 1627 Montana Ave, Santa Monica. 458.1562

**30 Graffeo Coffee Roasting Company** They offer just three coffee blends—light, dark, and decaf—but they may yield the best cup you've ever savored. ♦ M-Sa 9AM-5:30PM. 315 N. Beverly Dr. 273.4232

**31 The Grill** ★★★$$$ Chef **John Sola** has won applause for his assurance with corned beef hash, braised shortribs, and chunky Cobb salad, along with the oak-charcoal grilled fish and meats. This is a place with solid virtues: a warm, woodsy setting, professional waiters, and huge helpings at fair prices. ♦ American ♦ M-Sa 11:30AM-11:45PM. 9560 Dayton Way. 276.0615

**32 One Rodeo Drive** This whimsical pastiche of Palladio by **Johannes Van Tilburg** houses such boutiques as **Dunhill**, **Isis Unlimited**, and **Denmark Jeweler**. ♦ N. Rodeo Dr at Wilshire Blvd

**33 Two Rodeo Drive** Across the street from One Rodeo Drive is this even more ambitious retail development—an ersatz European village lane with a cobblestone street designed by **Kaplan/McLaughlin/Diaz** in 1990. The corner development houses the largest **Tiffany & Co.** store outside of New York, plus **Cole Haan**, **Bree** leather goods, **Jose Eber** hair design, **Cartier**, and **Charles Jourdan**. ♦ N. Rodeo Dr at Wilshire Blvd

Within Two Rodeo Drive:

# PIAZZA RODEO

**Piazza Rodeo** $ The quaint terrace restaurant mimics a Parisian sidewalk cafe and evokes some of the same charm. The food is very casual gourmet, with open-faced sandwiches, pasta, and fish. Try the hamburger with grilled onions or the fried cappelini with sun-dried tomatoes. ♦ Eclectic ♦ Daily 8AM-midnight. 208 N. Via Rodeo. 275.2428

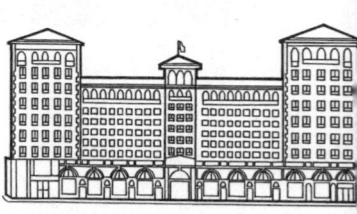

**34 Regent Beverly Wilshire Hotel** $$$$ Originally designed by **Walker & Eisen** in 1928, the **Regent Group,** which owns some of the finest properties around the Pacific, has spent $100 million to restore this grandest of luxury hotels (pictured above) to a level above its former excellence. From the columned gold, cream, and brown marble lobby to the guest rooms (many of which have been doubled in size), the improvements are immediately evident. Exemplary service includes 24-hour concierges and room stewards on every floor. On the ground floor of the Wilshire building is a handsome, clubby bar, a drugstore cafe, and the **Lobby Lounge,** which serves afternoon tea, light meals, and cocktails. ♦ 9500 Wilshire Blvd. 275.5200, 800/545.4000; fax 274.2851

Within the Regent Beverly Wilshire Hotel:

**Regent Beverly Wilshire Dining Room** ★★★$$$ Surprisingly bold California cuisine is served in this traditionally elegant setting of polished wood columns, colorful murals, and stunning flower arrangements. Ravioli of smoked chicken, grilled swordfish with sautéed sweet peppers, calf's liver with red wine and shallot sauce, and a garlicky roast chicken are a few of the standouts. The smoothly efficient service is equally remarkable, making this a preferred location for power breakfasts and lunches. ♦ California ♦ Daily 7-10:30AM, 11:30AM-3PM, 6-10:30PM. 9500 Wilshire Blvd. 274.8179

**35 Sterling Plaza** The stunning Art Deco office tower built by **Louis B. Mayer** in 1929 as the MGM Building has been beautifully refurbished. Ironically, the much diminished movie company has established its offices a block away behind the blandest of the bland white marble-and-black glass facade. Mayer would not have approved. ♦ Wilshire Blvd at Beverly Dr

**35 Israel Discount Bank** Odd symbolism: the mosque-like dome originally roofed a theater. ♦ 206 N. Beverly Dr (at Wilshire Blvd)

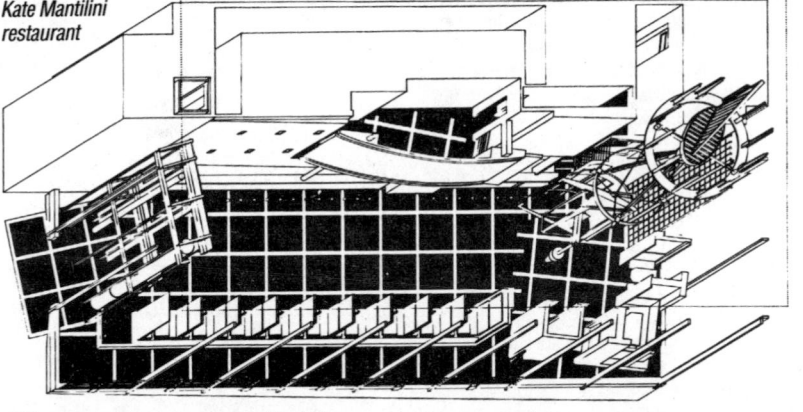

*Kate Mantilini restaurant*

COURTESY OF MORPHOSIS

**36 Tribeca** ★★$$ This handsome, Manhattan-cool, bi-level bar and restaurant offers tasteful business lunches, trendy dinners, and late-night suppers. The weekend bar crush can be intimidating, but push your way up the stairs to the dining room where the service is smooth and the food sublime. They have excellent wines by the glass. ♦ Seafood ♦ M-Th noon-4PM, 6PM-midnight; F noon-4PM, 6PM-1AM; Sa 6PM-1AM; Su 6PM-midnight. 242 N. Beverly Dr. 271.1595

**37 The Bistro** ★$$$$ This is a stellar spot for seeing and being seen. Stick to the simpler dishes on the menu. ♦ French ♦ M-Sa 6-11PM. 246 N. Cañon Dr. 273.5633

**38 Bistro Garden** ★$$$$ The restaurant has the prettiest garden—all flowers and white parasols—and one of the most romantic dining rooms in LA. Who cares about the food? Evidently the well-heeled regulars don't. ♦ French ♦ M-Sa 11:30AM-11PM. 176 N. Cañon Dr. 550.3900. Also at: 12950 Ventura Blvd, Studio City. 818/501.0202

**39 Beverly Pavilion Hotel** $$$ Decorated with a handsome rusticated stone facade and stylish interior, this sophisticated, small, European-style hotel offers complimentary limousine service, valet parking, a rooftop pool, a spectacular view of the city, and movie channels. ♦ 9360 Wilshire Blvd. 273.1400, 800/441.5050; fax 859.8551

Within the Beverly Pavilion Hotel:

**Colette** ★★$$$ Leading off the hotel lobby is an intimate and charming French restaurant designed with pleasing understatement by **Brent Saville.** Arched windows overlook Wilshire, but the mood is serene. Chef **Chris Blobaum,** following in the footsteps of **Patrick Healy** (now running **Champagne**), turns out consistently good modern French food and mouthwatering desserts. ♦ French ♦ M-F 7-11AM, 11:30AM-2:30PM, 5-10PM; Sa-Su 7AM-2:30PM, 5-10PM. 9360 Wilshire Blvd. 273.1400

**40 Mrs. Gooch's Natural Foods Market** Shop here for organic produce, naturally bred meats without hormones, humanely reared veal, and other goodies. ♦ Daily 9AM-9PM. 239 N. Crescent Dr. 274.3360. Also at: 3476 Centinela Ave, W. LA. 391.5209; 526 Pier Ave, Hermosa Beach. 376.6931

**41 Kate Mantilini** ★$$$ **Morphosis'** 1987 design is one of the most exciting interiors in LA, as expressive of its period as the Bradbury Building atrium was of the 1890s. Owner **Marilyn Lewis** requested a roadside cafe, named for a woman boxing promoter of the '40s. What the architects gave her was that and a lot more. Within the shell of a low-rise curtain-wall bank building (illustrated above) rises an extraordinarily complex layered space, indirectly lit, with a jagged steel sundial rising from the floor and up through the ceiling. Enclosed booths line the 100-foot-long outer wall. Above the open kitchen is a boxing mural by artist **John Wehrle.** The menu pays homage to **Musso and Frank,** offering hearty servings of meat loaf with crisp kale, roast chicken with mashed potatoes, and a score more of basics, plus a wonderful calf's brain omelet. The customers pay for the architecture. ♦ American ♦ M-Th 7:30AM-1:30AM; F 7:30AM-3AM; Sa noon-3AM; Su 10AM-midnight. 9109 Wilshire Blvd. 278.3699

**42 Academy of Motion Picture Arts & Sciences** LA's finest thousand-seat theater is the home of Oscar and a lively program of lobby exhibitions, plus occasional public screenings. ♦ 8949 Wilshire Blvd. 247.3000

**43 Wilshire-Robertson Plaza** This commercial block, designed by the provocative Miami-based firm **Arquitectonica** in 1990, stands out from the tedious succession of savings and loan offices. ♦ 8750 Wilshire Blvd

**44 Bombay Palace** ★$$$ Behind the klutzy pink-and-turquoise facade is a handsome, lofty interior ornamented with tiny gold deities. The Mughal cooking can be excellent, and the weekend brunch is a great bargain. ♦ Indian ♦ Daily 11:30AM-2:30PM, 5:30-10:30PM. 8690 Wilshire Blvd. 659.9944

The longest Academy Award ceremony took place in 1984 and lasted three hours and 40 minutes.

Restaurants/Clubs: Red          Hotels: Blue
Shops/ ♣ Outdoors: Green          Sights/Culture: Black

**45 Goethe Institute** This is a branch of a world-wide organization that promotes German language and culture. The language courses, screenings, exhibitions, and other events are often presented in cooperation with the local institutions. ◆ 8501 Wilshire Blvd, Suite 205. 854.0993

**46 Wilshire Theatre** The stylish zigzag movie house, designed by **S. Charles Lee** for Fox in 1929, has been restored for use as a stage for musicals and drama. ◆ 8440 Wilshire Blvd. 468.1700

**47 Benihana of Tokyo** ★$$ This is a branch of a popular Japanese teppan-grill chain. ◆ Japanese ◆ M-Th 11:30AM-2PM, 5:30-10PM; F 11:30AM-2PM, 5:30-11PM; Sa 5:30-11PM; Su 4:30-10PM. 38 N. La Cienega Blvd. 659.1511

## Beverly Hills/Century City

**47 Gaylord India Restaurant** ★★$$ Understated and beautiful, this local outpost of a high-class chain began in New Delhi in 1941. The food is consistently first-rate. ◆ North Indian ◆ Daily 11:30AM-2:30PM, 5:30-10:30PM. 50 N. La Cienega Blvd. 652.3838

**48 Lawry's Prime Rib** ★$$ The prime rib and 1940s decor are celebrated here; however, you might have to wait for a table. ◆ American ◆ M-F 5-11PM; Sa 4:30-11PM; Su 3-11PM. 55 N. La Cienega Blvd. 652.2827

**49 Ed Debevic's** $ Trendy retro coffee shops and diners open as fast as the originals (like **Ship's** in Westwood) close their doors. This is LA's most ambitious pastiche to date, from the streamlined facade to the '50s artifacts within. All it lacks is **Frankie, Annette,** and a gang of crew cut extras doing some soulful rocking. ◆ American ◆ M-Th, Su 11:30AM-11PM; F-Sa 11:30AM-1AM. 134 N. La Cienega Blvd. 659.1952

**50 Matsuhisa** ★★★$$$ Behind this storefront restaurant and innovative sushi bar is a sushi master with 20 years of experience in LA, Lima (Peru), and his native Tokyo. Put yourself in Matsuhisa's hands and prepare to be dazzled by the freshest fish and a poet's skill. ◆ Japanese ◆ M-F 11:45AM-2:30PM, 5:45-10:30PM; Sa-Su 5:45-10:30PM. 129 N. La Cienega Blvd. 659.9639

**51 Hotel Nikko at Beverly Hills** $$$$ The 304-room hotel targeted for business travelers resides on busy La Cienega Boulevard's restaurant row and could be mistaken for an office building. Part of Japan's largest international hotel chain, it offers both high-tech electronics and Japanese tradition: rooms have fax machines, computer hookups, and sophisticated remote control gadgetry, as well as deep Japanese soaking tubs. Other amenities includ a health club, an outdoor pool, and 24-hour room service. ◆ 465 S. La Cienega Blvd. 247.0400; fax 247.0315

Within the Hotel Nikko at Beverly Hills:

**Matrixx Restaurant** $ This is *the* place for noodles. Traditional pasta, mushroom papperdelle, sobas, and Thai fried noodles are topped with a choice of chicken, shrimp, sweetbreads, or a variety of fresh vegetables. ◆ California. ◆ Daily 6:30AM-2:30PM, 5:30-11PM. 246.2100

**52 Michel Richard** ★$$ Each dessert here is like a piece of artwork. There are tables for *petit déjeuner,* or salad and quiche lunches. A dinner menu is also served. ◆ French ◆ M-Sa 8AM-10PM; Su 9AM-3PM. 310 S. Robertson Blvd. 275.5707

**53 agnès b.** Shop here for classic French-style women's linen suits, cotton sweaters, and sna sweatshirts. ◆ M-Sa 11AM-7PM; Su noon-6PM. 100 N. Robertson Blvd. 271.9643

**54 Robata** ★★★$$$ Many regard this as the authoritative Tokyo restaurant, with a modern de cor of granite, glass, and wood. There is a discreet *robata* grill, but the emphasis is on pricey 12-course *kaiseki* dinners. Chief chef **Katsuo Koike** integrates sushi, country, and contemporary dishes. ◆ Japanese ◆ M-Sa 11:30AM-2PM, 6-11PM; Su 6-11PM. 250 N. Robertson Blvd. 274.5533

**55 Il Cielo** ★★$$$ Choose from alfresco dining in two charming courtyards or a white-walled room with a trompe l'oeil sky. Baked scamorza cheese with eggplant and whole baked snappe filleted at your table are standout dishes. ◆ Italian ◆ M-F 11:30AM-2:30PM, 6:30-10PM; Sa 6-11PM. 9018 Burton Way. 276.9990

**55 Pratesi** Hand-embroidered silk sheets, cashmere blankets, and huge fluffy towels for sybaritic millionaires can be found here. ◆ M-Sa 10AM-6PM. 9024 Burton Way. 274.7661

**56 L'Ermitage Hotel** $$$$ Intimate and luxurious, this 112-suite hotel attempts to capture the fine European spirit with traditional furnishings, original artworks, and exemplary service. Amenities include a rooftop garden, pool, and spa, and free chauffeured Rolls' for excursions within Beverly Hills. The **Club California** cuisin is exclusively for guests. More reasonably priced is the 14-suite **Le Petit Ermitage** hotel next door. ◆ 9291 Burton Way. 278.3344, 800/424.4443; fax 278.8247

Greystone Park

RIK OLSON

**57 Il Giardino** ★★$$$$ In a trellised, garden-like dining room with small tables set close together, you may feast on a wonderful and varied menu of Tuscan delights, including pasta, risotto, perfectly grilled fish, and herb steak. The food is cooked to order using the freshest ingredients. The only drawback is the service, which is leisurely at best. ♦ Italian ♦ M-Sa noon-2:30PM, 6-10:30PM. 9235 W. Third St. 275.5444

**58 Maple Drive** ★$$$ The same team that created **72 Market Street** in Venice—**Tony Bill, Dudley Moore, Julie Stone,** and chef **Leonard Schwartz**—have assembled this large, loud, and fashionable restaurant and nightclub. The interior design is by **Anthony Greenberg.** There's an oyster bar, basic food like rotisserie chicken and Caesar salad, and live entertainment. ♦ Eclectic ♦ M-Th 11:30AM-2:30PM, 6-10PM; F 11:30AM-2:30PM, 6-11PM; Sa 6-11PM. 345 N. Maple Dr. 274.9800

**59 858 N. Doheny Drive** Lloyd Wright's 1928 concrete-block house with a dramatic two-story living room is located on a tiny corner lot. The side patio surrounds a spreading tree. It's a private residence. ♦ Vista Grande St

**60 Greystone Park** Oil millionaire **Edward L. Doheny** built this 55-room English Tudor mansion (illustrated above) for his son in 1928. Long abandoned, it was used as a set for *The Loved One* and later leased by the **American Film Institute.** The city authorities seem unable to decide what to do with the house, which remains closed. The 16-acre garden, with its balustraded terraces and grassy slopes, is one of LA's loveliest public parks. ♦ Daily 10AM-6PM. 905 Loma Vista Dr. Concert and event information: 550.4654

**61 Virginia Robinson Gardens** Forget touring the walled-off homes of the stars; by calling a week in advance, you can tour the oldest residence in Beverly Hills, plus six acres of lush gardens, groves of king palms, azaleas, and camellias in the spring. It's a treasury of rarities and specimen trees, including the largest monkey hand tree in California. ♦ Admission. Tours Tu-Th 10AM, 1PM; F 10AM. 1008 Elden Way. 276.4823

---

There are about 30 earthquakes every day in Southern California, and most are a magnitude of less than 2.0.

---

In 1991, more than 6,370,000 vehicles are registered in LA County, one for every 1.4 people.

---

In a 1992 survey measuring how well cities are managed, Los Angeles ranked 22nd out of America's 30 largest cities.

**Restaurants/Clubs:** Red    **Hotels:** Blue
**Shops/ ♦ Outdoors:** Green    **Sights/Culture:** Black

# The Beverly Hills Hotel and Bungalows

**62 The Beverly Hills Hotel** $$$$ Nicknamed "the pink palace," this sprawling Mission Revival hotel (which opened in 1912) has become an unofficial symbol of the city and its hedonistic lifestyle. Sheltered from traffic and prying eyes by dense planting, the hotel has the grace of an earlier era. Embowered in 12 acres of lush tropical gardens are the legendary pool and the 21 luxurious bungalows where such luminaries as **Chaplin, Garbo, Gable,** and **Lombard** stayed. **Howard Hughes,** obsessive about pri-

vacy, lived in his bungalow 24 hours a day, leaving messages in a tree outside his room. There's a formal dining room and a highly acclaimed breakfast counter. Service is the hotel's greatest strength: head concierge **Robert Duncan** claims he got one guest an audience with the Pope, and for another, a game of Scrabble in Russian. The hotel will close 2 January 1993 for a renovation that may take as long as two years. Parking, utilities—such as heating—and bathrooms will be modernized, and some rooms will be refurbished, but the overall look of the hotel will remain the same. ♦ 9641 Sunset Blvd. 276.2251, 800/283.8885; fax 281.2919

Within The Beverly Hills Hotel:

**Polo Lounge** $$$ Power meetings are held over breakfast and lunch here; deals are made on phones at the tables. Not since the fall of Byzantium has the hierarchy of who sits where (or whether) been as solemnly enforced. Don't come unless your status—or self-esteem—is impregnable. The Cobb or chicken salad with a glass of Chardonnay in the leafy patio is an affordable treat. ♦ American ♦ Daily 7AM-2AM. 276.2251

**63 Spadena House** Hansel and Gretel would have lived here if they had made it big with their screenplay. The thatched-roof residence was designed by **Henry Oliver** in 1921 as a combined movie set and office. It was moved here from Culver City and may eventually be moved back. It's a private residence. ♦ Walden Dr at Carmelita Ave

**64 Beverly Hilton** $$$ Balconied rooms surround the large pool, giving this Hilton the feeling of a resort. Guest and public rooms and the restaurants (among them **Mr. H,** which serves generous buffet) are decorated in light, soft colors. A well-equipped fitness center is available for guests. ♦ 9876 Wilshire Blvd. 274.7777, 800/HILTONS; fax 285.1313

Within the Beverly Hilton:

**L'Escoffier** ★★$$$$ This is the only restaurant in LA with haute cuisine, dancing, and a great view. Designer **Robert Barry** gave this dowager an elegant new dress, though there was nothing he could do about the low ceiling. It's a favorite place for anniversary celebrations. ♦ French ♦ Tu-Th 6:30PM-midnight; F-Sa 6:30PM-1AM. 285.1333

**Trader Vic's** ★$$$$ Silly rum drinks with little umbrellas and the South Seas setting are the main draws here, though the kitchen can produce good appetizers. ♦ Polynesian ♦ M-Th, S 5PM-1AM; F-Sa 5PM-2AM. 9876 Wilshire Blvd 276.6345

**65 Jimmy's** ★★$$$$ Yet another haunt of the rich and famous, Jimmy's has leisurely service and a rich menu with prices to match. Surprisingly, the food can be quite good and the veal chop is a classic. There is a lively piano bar, which is a nice place for a late-night drink. ♦ French/Seafood ♦ M-F 11:30AM-3PM, 5:30PM-midnight; Sa 5:30PM-midnight. 201 Moreno Dr. 213/879.2394

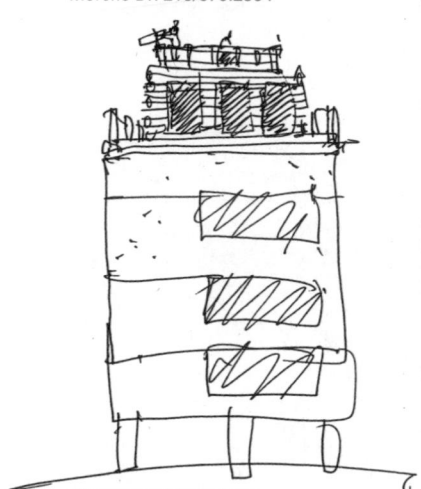

COURTESY OF FRANK GEHRY

**66 Wosk Apartment** **Frank Gehry** and **Miriam Wosk's** 1983 surreal penthouse (illustrated above)—gold ziggurat, blue dome, black marble arch, and turquoise-tiled walls clustered atop a pink apartment building—juices up an otherwise bland street. Admire it from the tennis courts across the street. It's a private residence. ♦ 440 S. Roxbury Dr

**67 Chez Helene** ★$$ The brick-walled patio in this charming, homespun bistro offers a delightful place to dine. Specialties here include salmon mousse, buttery roast chicken, bouillabaisse, great *pommes frites,* and rich raspberry cake topped with thick cream. ♦ French ♦ Tu-Th 11:30AM-3PM, 6-10PM; F-Sa 11:30AM-3PM, 6-10:30PM; Su 6-10PM. 267 S. Beverly Dr. 276.1558

**68 Ruth's Chris Steak House** ★★$$$ Some say this acclaimed restaurant serves the best steaks in town. Order your favorite cut from their traditional menu. ♦ M-Th 5-10PM; F-Sa 5-10:30PM; Su 5-9:30PM. 224 S. Beverly Dr. 859.8744

**68 Celestino** ★★★$$$ Chef **Antonio Zizo** and co-owner **Celestino Drago** serve delicious, light dishes in a cool, elegant setting designed by **Brent Saville.** The antipasti, pastas, and seafood are wonderful. Specialties include spaghetti baked in a bag and roast rabbit with olive sauce. ♦ Italian ♦ M-F 11:30AM-3PM, 5:30-11PM; Sa 5:30-11PM; Su 5:30-10PM. 236 S. Beverly Dr. 859.8601

**68 Savories** ★$ Many find this place a useful resource for salads, sandwiches, and desserts—to eat in or to go. Order their picnic baskets a day ahead. ♦ California ♦ M-F 8AM-7PM; Sa 9AM-6PM. 240 S. Beverly Dr. 276.9481

**69 Four Seasons** $$$$ The 179 rooms and 106 suites in this European-style luxury hotel are furnished with antiques. The public areas have marble floors and quality fine art (including a **Picasso** in the lobby), and fresh flowers are everywhere. There's also a charming garden, a terrace pool with a cafe, an exercise facility, a Jacuzzi, and complimentary limo service to Rodeo Drive. ♦ 300 S. Doheny Dr. 273.2222, 800/332.3442; fax 859.3874

Within the Four Seasons:

**Garden's** ★★$$$ Lovely meals are served in this pretty setting. The service and fine wine list are as good as ever. ♦ California ♦ Daily 7AM-2:30PM, 6-10:30PM. 273.2222 ext. 2171

**70 Dolores Drive-In** $ This original 1950s coffee shop is still in mint condition. Burgers, cherrylime rookies, and Suzy-Q fries are standouts on the vintage menu. ♦ American ♦ M-Th, Su 6AM-midnight; F-Sa 24 hours. 8925 W. Olympic Blvd. 657.7455. Also at: 11407 Santa Monica Blvd. 447.1061

**71 Christopher Hansen** Kirkpatrick Associates designed this museumlike setting for custom audio installations and home entertainment centers in 1990. Their classy conversion of a former Rolls-Royce dealership was sensitive. ♦ M-Sa 10AM-6PM. 8822 W. Olympic Blvd (at Robertson Blvd). 858.8112

**72 Rosebud** Elin Katz is an artist in icing, creating Memphis-inspired white-chocolate cakes and other delectable confections. ♦ Tu-Sa 10AM-5PM. 311 S. Robertson Blvd. 657.6207

**73 Center for Motion Picture Study** Fran Offenhauser and Michael J. Mekeel did the imaginative conversion of this 1928 landmark building, which was inspired by Seville's **La Giralda,** but actually housed a water treatment station. The project was a triumph for local preservationists—to offset the loss of the zigzag Beverly Theater on Wilshire. The **Margaret Herrick Library,** with one of the country's finest collections of film books, magazines, and archival treasures, is open without charge to serious students of cinema. The center also houses the **Academy Film Archives,** an offshoot of the **Academy of Motion Picture Arts & Sciences** foundation. ♦ M-Tu, Th-F 9AM-4:30PM. Tours on first of the month at 10AM, by reservation only. 333 S. La Cienega Blvd (at Olympic Blvd). 247.3000

## Beverly Hills/Century City

**74 Raja** ★$$ Kashmiri specialties, tandoori shrimp and chicken, and vegetable dishes are served here at very reasonable prices. An all-you-can-eat lunch buffet is available, too. ♦ Indian ♦ M-Th 11:30AM-2:30PM, 5:30-10:30PM; F-Sa 11:30AM-2:30PM, 5:30-11PM; Su 11:30AM-2:30PM, 5-10PM. 8875 W. Pico Blvd. 550.9176

**75 Hymie's Fish Market** ★$$$ Top show-biz types come to this no-nonsense place for the excellent lobster bouillabaisse, clams, oysters, etc. It has an excellent fresh fish market, too. ♦ Seafood ♦ Restaurant: M-Th, Su 11:30AM-2:30PM, 5:30-10PM; F 11:30AM-2:30PM, 5:30-10:30PM; Sa 5-10:30PM. Fish market: M-F 10AM-10PM; Sa-Su 3-10:30PM. 9228 W. Pico Blvd. 550.0377

**75 Beverlywood Bakery** Some of the best pumpernickel and rye this side of Central Europe is baked here. ♦ M-Sa 6AM-6:30PM; Su 6AM-5:30PM. 9128 W. Pico Blvd. 550.9842

**75 Gordon's Fresh Pacific & Eastern Fish Market** Whole fish at very reasonable prices is sold here, and it's open on Saturday morning when **Hymie's** is not. ♦ M-Sa 8:30AM-6PM; Su 9-10AM pick-ups only. 9116 W. Pico Blvd. 276.6603

**76 Delmonico's** ★★$$ When the fad for Cajun-Creole faded, this restaurant switched to seafood. The large, airy dining area, with ceiling fans and tables crowded in the center of the room, is reminiscent of an old Parisian brasserie and filled with the same fearsome din; to avoid it, try for one of the wooden booths that hug the walls. The long, lively bar in front serves fresh oysters and makes great Bloody Marys. ♦ Seafood ♦ M-Th 11:30AM-10PM; F 11:30AM-11PM; Sa 5-11PM; Su 5-10PM. 9320 W. Pico Blvd. 550.7737

"Thank heavens we can escape to Beverly Hills on the weekends. No one in Sacramento can do hair."

**Nancy Reagan** during Ronald Reagan's term as Governor of California

**Restaurants/Clubs:** Red    **Hotels:** Blue
**Shops/ 🌳 Outdoors:** Green    **Sights/Culture:** Black

**77 Osteria Romana Orsini** ★★$$$ Perhaps it's the lunching execs from nearby Twentieth Century Fox who give this place such a clubby feel. The kitchen serves well-prepared Italian food, including Roman specialties. The desserts are fine and the bountiful lunchtime antipasto buffet is memorable. There's a nightclub upstairs that persists in such amusingly antediluvian behavior as charging women less for admission than they charge men. ♦ Italian ♦ Restaurant: M-F noon-3PM, 6-9PM; Sa 6-9PM. Club: W-Sa 10PM-2AM. 9575 W. Pico Blvd. 277.6050

**78 Twentieth Century Fox Film Corp.** There are no tours offered here, but you can drive up to the gate and take a glimpse at the *Hello Dolly* street, a re-creation of turn-of-the-century New

York, with false facades and painted stages. This was Hollywood's first studio planned for sound, created by pioneer **William Fox,** who then lost control of the company he had established. **Darryl Zanuck** ruled here over such eminent subjects as **Shirley Temple, Carmen Miranda,** and director **John Ford.** It was also the home to **Marilyn Monroe,** *Cleopatra,* and *M★A★S★H.* Fox has survived more predators than the maiden in a melodrama; currently it's flourishing. ♦ 10201 Pico Blvd. 277.2211

**79 JW Marriott Hotel at Century City** $$$$ This is another chain luxury hotel, but at least it's warmer and more welcoming than the Century Plaza. It's housed in a peach pyramid, and peach is a favorite tone within. There's a Roman-style spa and outdoor pool and a limo to drive you in style the half-mile up the street to the Shubert Theater. **JW's Restaurant** ($$) within the hotel serves eclectic cuisine. ♦ 2151 Avenue of the Stars. 277.2777, 800/228.9290; fax 785.9240

**80 Century Plaza Hotel** $$$$ If you are not the president of the United States or a mere CEO arriving by helicopter, you may feel intimidated. The scale, from the forecourt to the 8,000-square-foot **Plaza Suite** that occupies the 30th floor of the tower, is vast. The original hotel, an elliptical block designed by **Minoru Yamasaki,** opened in 1966 and contains 750 rooms and huge banquet facilities. In back is a 14-acre garden with a large pool.

The 30-story 320-room **Tower,** inaugurated by **President Ronald Reagan** in 1984, is more intimate and exclusive; it's handsomely furnished and full of museum-quality artworks. Afternoon tea is served in the **Living Room,** off the lobby. There's also a health club. Restaurants include the informal **Water's Edge Seafood Bar & Grill, Cafe Plaza,** and **Terrace.** ♦ 2025 Avenue of the Stars. 277.2000, 800/228.3000; fax 551.3355

Within the Century Plaza Hotel:

**La Chaumière** ★★$$$$ Such dishes as duck liver piccata, seafood with lobster saffron sauce and calf livers with a sauce of black currants and dry vermouth are served in a clublike room paneled in alderwood, with 18th-century French pastoral paintings. Twenty-three wines are served by the glass. ♦ Eclectic ♦ M-F 11:30-2:30PM, 5:30-10PM; Sa-Su 5:30-10PM. 551.3360

**80 Fox Plaza** Johnson, Fain & Pereira Associates' 1987 design represents the most dramatic addition to Century City since the original twin towers. This handsome 34-story office tower is faceted like a crystal, banded in salmon granite and gray-tinted glass, and positioned to dominate the sweep of Olympic Boulevard and the midtown skyline. ♦ 2121 Avenue of the Stars

**81 The ABC Entertainment Center and Century Plaza Towers** Minoru Yamasaki's silvery triangular towers, built in 1975, are an improvement on his World Trade Center in New York. The low-rise offices and theaters, by another architect, are pedestrian. Ramps and escalators lead to an underpass that links the center to the Century Plaza Hotel. The street, plaza and concourse levels include a shopping mall, theaters, and restaurants. ♦ Avenue of the Stars at Constellation Blvd

At The ABC Entertainment Center and Century Plaza Towers:

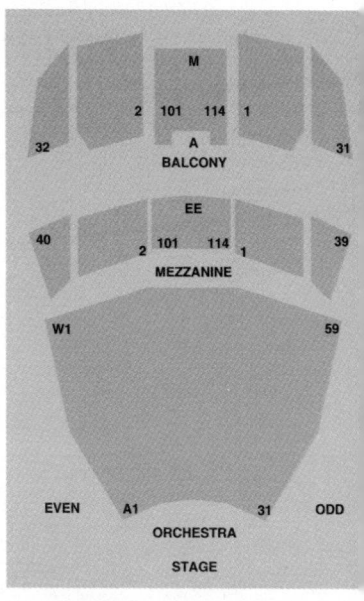

**Shubert Theatre** This cavernous playhouse (see the plan above) hosts long runs of Broadway spectaculars. ♦ Box office: 201.1500, 800/233.3123

---

The first issue of the *Los Angeles Times,* which was published in 1881, was delivered by horse-drawn wagons and carriages.

Actor Douglas Fairbanks built the "Pickfair" mansion for young bride Mary Pickford in the Beverly Hills foothills in 1920. It is now owned by singer Pia Zadora and her husband.

## Cineplex Odeon Century Plaza Theaters

The 600-seat **Theater Two,** with its big screen and luxurious rocking chairs, is one of the best places in LA to enjoy a first-run movie. But, be warned: the theater does not validate, and parking charges before 5PM on weekdays are exorbitant unless you sneak over from the **Century City Shopping Center. ♦** 553.4291

**Harper's Bar & Grill** $$ The New York-style bar has an excellent view. ♦ American ♦ M-F 11:30AM-3PM, 5:30-10:30PM; Sa 5:30-10:30PM. Open Sunday when the Shubert is open: 5:30-10:30PM. 553.1855

**Harry's Bar & American Grill** ★★$$$ Modeled after **Harry's Bar** in Florence, this restaurant resembles an oasis in the desert. Harry's sponsors an annual Hemingway write-alike contest. Carpaccio, veal scalloppine, tortellini, and hamburgers with crisp onion rings are standouts. It's crowded at lunch. ♦ Italian ♦ M-F 11:30AM-3PM, 5:30-10:30PM; Sa 5:30-10:30PM. 277.2333

**Sports Deli** $ Three 25-inch televisions satisfy the sports fans; salt-water aquariums are for others. ♦ Deli ♦ M-F 7:30AM-9PM; Sa-Su 10:30AM-9PM. 553.5800

**82 Tripp's** ★★$$ This is a well-regarded steakhouse that also serves grilled fish, chicken, and fine potato pancakes. ♦ American ♦ M-F 11:30AM-2:30PM, 5:30-11PM; Sa 5:30-11PM. 10131 Constellation Blvd. 553.6000

**83 Century City Shopping Center** One of the earliest of LA's malls, this shopper's mecca has been upgraded, with the addition of lively graphics, the **Marketplace** (by **BTA Associates** of Boston), and the **AMC** theaters, a superior multiplex in which the quality of sound, projection, and sightlines are far above average. The center comprises a hundred stores on an 18-acre site, with ample free parking below. A major attraction is **Gelson's,** one of LA's top markets (277.4288). The anchor department stores are **Bullock's** and **The Broadway.** Other stores in the mall include **Crate & Barrel** (well-designed housewares), **Brentano's** (an exemplary general bookstore), **Laise Adzer** (hand-dyed exotic women's wear), **Politix** (contemporary Italian men's wear), **Godiva Chocolatier,** and a well-stocked newsstand. New York's **Metropolitan Museum of Art** also has a gift shop here. The youngsters will enjoy the **Imaginarium,** a hands-on toy store. ♦ Free parking with validation. M-F 10AM-9PM; Sa 10AM-6PM; Su 11AM-6PM. 10250 Little Santa Monica Blvd. 277.3898

At Century City Shopping Center:

**Cabo Cabo Cabo** $ This lively bar features 250 brands of spirits, 50 beers, and 50 tequilas. Typical Mexican fare is served, too. ♦ Mexican ♦ M-Th, Su 11:30AM-10PM; F-Sa 11:30AM-11PM. 552.2226

**Stage Deli of New York** ★$ Oversized sandwiches and egg creams are served in this big, brightly lit place with an authentic New York feel. ♦ M-Th 7:30AM-10PM; F-Sa 7:30AM-midnight; Su 7:30AM-11PM. Century City Marketplace. 553.3354

### Sara Campbell

Chief Curator, Norton Simon Museum

The all-day Christmas Music Program at the **Music Center's Dorothy Chandler Pavilion.** It's a wonderful way to get into the holiday mood and glory in the cultural variety of the LA community. You can come and go all day, but if you can't make your way into downtown, watch it on **KCET** (Channel 28).

Decorating the **Tournament of Roses** floats for the New Year's Day parade. It's a great activity for everyone with a volunteer spirit (and those who don't mind freezing and getting covered with glue). The Rose Parade floats are awesome, ephemeral, and phantasmic sculptures.

## Beverly Hills/Century City

In May don't miss the jacaranda trees all over the city, particularly those in the UCLA gardens, where the lavender blankets of blossoms on the ground mirror the trees.

The **USC plaza** next to *Tommy Trojan*—the new design, fountains, and trees make it one of the best public spaces in LA.

Degas' small painting of the *Laundress;* Picasso's 1923 *Bust of a Woman;* the ninth-century Thai Buddha; and Zurbaran's *Still Life* at the **Norton Simon Museum.**

The **Huntington Library and Gardens** in San Marino, where you see Reynold's *Mrs. Siddons as the Trojan Muse,* as well as the rose and cactus gardens.

For food: spicy garlic fries at **Engine Company No. 28** in downtown, lamb chops and sourdough at **Musso and Frank Grill** on Hollywood Boulevard, anything at the **Plum Tree Inn** in Chinatown. In Pasadena: rosemary bread from the **Old Town Bakery,** grilled eggplant and breadsticks from the **Market City Cafe,** potstickers at **Roxxi,** Diane Salad at **Green Street,** and cheese bagels at **Goldstein's.**

For books: **Vroman's** in Pasadena, the **USC student store,** and the **Norton Simon Museum** gift shop.

For shopping: **Jacob Maarse** on Green Street in Pasadena, which is not just a florist; and **Left Bank Fabrics** on West Third, which is like a candy shop for fabric freaks, and the buttons are great, too.

### John Walsh

Director, J. Paul Getty Museum

**Dutton's** bookstore in Brentwood, for New York titles and LA courtesy.

Dinner at **Röckenwagner** in Venice.

Sunset at **Griffith Park Observatory**—a '30s movie fantasy.

The hike to **Sandstone Peak** from Circle X Ranch Ranger Station in Point Mugu State Park, Malibu, and a swim in the surf afterward.

A Saturday stroll on **Melrose Avenue,** with nothing at all in mind.

Watching weekend cricket in **Will Rogers Memorial Park** in Watts, then visiting **Watts Towers** nearby.

# Westside

In Los Angeles, wealth and fashion have moved steadily to the Westside over the past century. Space, greenery, and hills are obvious attractions, and proximity to the ocean brings cleaner air and evening breezes that make air-conditioning unnecessary, even at the height of summer. The entire area is primarily residential, but there's a sharp contrast between the modest houses and apartments that predominate south of **Wilshire Boulevard** and the lushly planted estates of **Bel Air**, **Brentwood**, and **Pacific Palisades** to the north of that axis. In this affluent section, private tennis courts, pools, Porsches, and Mercedes are almost commonplace, and there are five major country clubs—the **Los Angeles**, **Hillcrest**, **Brentwood**, **Bel Air**, and **Riviera**. But in contrast to **Beverly Hills**, which flaunts its wealth, the golden ghettoes of the Westside are outwardly restrained, the homes hidden by trees and high walls, the preferred stores villagelike in their apparent simplicity.

**Westwood** attracts property speculators as a stray dog collects fleas, and they have trashed what may once have been LA's most charming village. Banal apartment and office towers have turned Wilshire Boulevard into a traffic-clogged canyon. The Mediterranean-style shopping village, created by a single visionary developer 60 years ago, has been cheapened by a proliferation of undistinguished banks, shacks, and fast-food chains. Modestly scaled houses on leafy side streets are

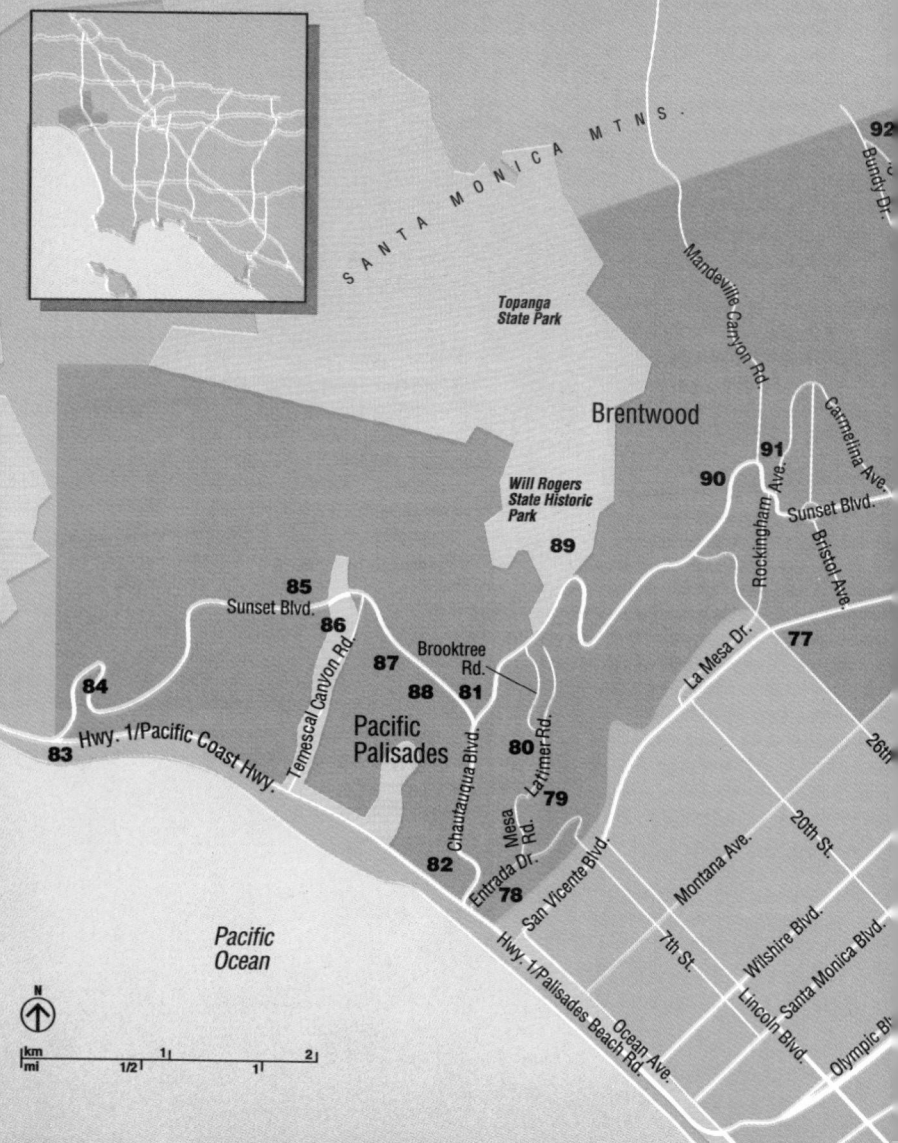

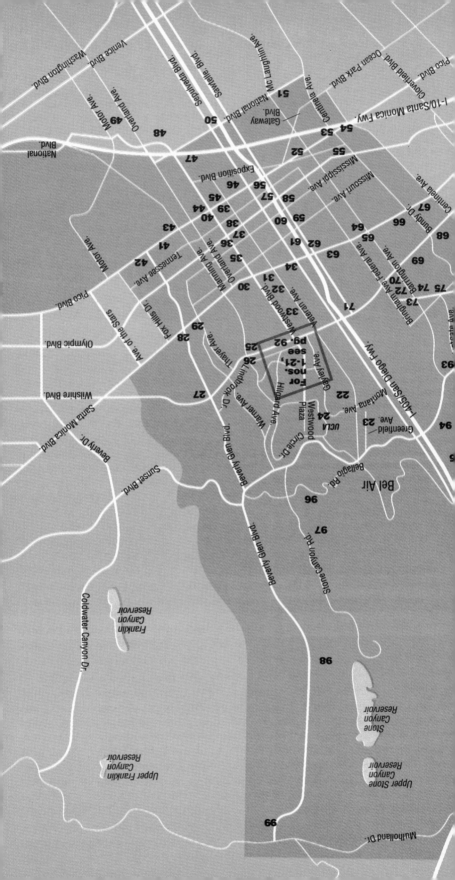

giving way to filing cabinets of stunning mediocrity. **The University of California at Los Angeles (UCLA)**, which might have set a good example, has been among the worst offenders.

The area was originally part of the 1843 land grant of **Rancho San Jose de Buenos Ayres**. The property changed hands numerous times, becoming the **John Wolfskill** Ranch after 1884. In 1919 **Arthur Letts**, founder of **The Broadway** and **Bullock's** department stores, bought the farmland and turned a neat profit by selling it to the **Janss Company**. In 1926 Westwood was annexed to Los Angeles in a civic enlargement that included a large portion of the **Santa Monica Mountains**, the Pacific Palisades, and Brentwood. In 1929, when UCLA opened its Westwood campus, the Janss Company had already built 2,000 houses and a bustling master-planned shopping village. The Westside boom had begun.

**Westwood Village** was designed for promenades, not cruising, and by the 1960s it was clogged with traffic, a problem that worsened as it succeeded Hollywood as the moviegoing center of LA, with what may be the greatest concentration of first-run theaters in the world. The intersection of Wilshire and Westwood boulevards is one of the city's busiest. High rents have driven out many quality stores, and some controversial movie premieres have led to rioting among unruly elements. Westwood Village has also lost some of its older weekend audience to the revitalized Third Street Promenade in Santa Monica. But if you are young, there is no better place to gather, and the sidewalks are still jammed on the weekends. Fast noshing is the dominant element today. There seems to be a croissant or cookie store on every block, a score of pizza places and ice cream and frozen yogurt parlors, plus hamburgers and falafel. You'll also find clothes, from preppy to pop, but mostly athletic; video outlets; **Tower Records;** several bookstores, including **B. Dalton** and **Crown;** and a **Bullock's** department store. Parking lots fill quickly, and on Friday and Saturday nights it makes sense to leave your car in the large free parking lot behind the **Federal Building** (11000 Wilshire Boulevard and Veteran Avenue) and take the shuttle into the village. A **DASH** minibus runs a loop past all the major theaters every 10 to 15 minutes on Friday from 6:30PM to 1:30AM and on Saturday from 11AM to 1:30AM.

*Area code 310 unless otherwise noted.*

**1 Mann's Village Theatre** This marvelous 1931 Spanish moderne tower still dominates the village. Architect **P.O. Lewis** designed the gleaming white-stucco moldings, porte-cochere with free-standing box office, and golden flourishes within to enhance the street and the pleasure of moviegoing. **Fox Studios** built a chain of Spanish theaters along the West Coast before the Depression put them out of business; the Deco "FOX" sign that crowns the tower has been refurbished and relit. ♦ 961 Broxton Ave. 208.5576

**2 Bruin Theatre** This 1937 streamlined bijou, with a sensuously curved and neon-lit marquee, carries the design signature of architect **S. Charles Lee**. Traffic between the Bruin and Mann's Village theaters and neighboring stores makes this the liveliest pedestrian crossing in the city. ♦ 948 Broxton Ave. 208.8998

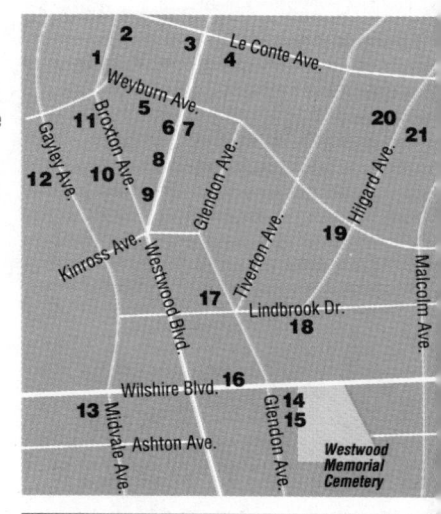

| Restaurants/Clubs: Red | Hotels: Blue |
|---|---|
| Shops/ ☂ Outdoors: Green | Sights/Culture: Black |

According to the Vampire Research Center in Elmhurst, New York, Los Angeles is the nation's vampire capital, with 20 confirmed bloodsuckers.

**3 Butler/Gabriel Books** The selection and personal service make this the kind of store that rekindles the joy of reading. ◆ M 10AM-9PM; Tu-Sa 10AM-10PM; Su 10AM-6PM. 919 Westwood Blvd. 208.4424

**4 Contempo-Westwood Center** Restored and refurbished in the 1960s by **A. Quincy Jones** and named for the fine Danish furniture store that occupies the center, this is a pleasant compound that houses a theater and a second-floor photographic exhibit chronicling the history of Westwood Village. The current owners are negotiating with UCLA to incorporate the site as part of the campus across the street. ◆ Exhibit hours: M-Sa 10AM-close; Su noon-close. 10886 Le Conte Ave. 208.4108

Within the Contempo-Westwood Center:

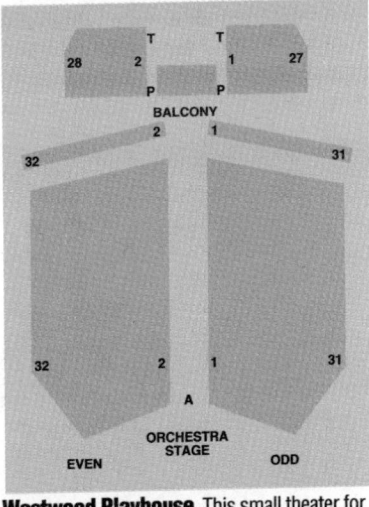

**Westwood Playhouse** This small theater for revues and musicals (see the plan above) has good sightlines and a thrust stage. Chicago's **Annoyance Theater** group presents the campy stage versions of "The Brady Bunch" episodes here, reviving popular interest in the 1970s family sitcom. ◆ Call ahead for show times. 208.6500

**5 Wilger Co.** Traditional men's clothes by **Canali** and some sharper Italian styles are sold here. ◆ M-W, F-Sa 10AM-6PM; Th 10AM-7:30PM. 10924 Weyburn Ave. 208.4321

**6 Bel Air Camera** The wide range of camera, audio, and video equipment, plus competitive prices and expert service, make this the place to come for your recording needs. ◆ M-F 9AM-6PM; Sa 9:30AM-6PM. 1025 Westwood Blvd. 208.5150

**7 Campbell-Tolstad Stationers** A survivor of a more gracious age, they sell fine pens and writing papers alongside more prosaic needs. Enjoy the good, old-fashioned service. ◆ M-Th 9AM-6PM; F-Sa 9AM-8PM; Su noon-6PM. 1002 Westwood Blvd. 208.4322

**8 Alice's Restaurant** $ A favorite with students and moviegoers, Alice's serves dependable fare in a friendly and informal setting. ◆ American ◆ Daily 10AM-midnight. 1043 N. Westwood Blvd. 208.3171

**9 Contempo Casuals** The first of the village's Spanish landmarks, this handsome domed structure (pictured above) with its portico and

arched windows anchors a major street intersection. Originally designed by **Allison & Allison** in 1929, the building was transformed by **Morphosis** into a trendy women's clothing store. ◆ M-Sa 10AM-9PM; Su noon-6PM. 1099 Westwood Blvd. 208.8503

**10 Stratton's Grill** ★$$ This unpretentious, moderately priced saloon/grill has splendid period decor—polished tile, gleaming mahogany, a huge oval bar, and animal heads on the walls. Chili, mesquite-grilled chicken and fish, and sausages with apples are dependable; desserts, from sundaes to apple and pecan pies, are the real homemade article. The service by clean-cut students is exemplary. The bar scene downstairs is noisy; ask for an upstairs booth if you want to converse. ◆ American ◆ M-F 11AM-2PM, 5-11PM; Sa-Su 11AM-2AM. 1037 Broxton Ave. 208.0488

**11 Mario's** $$ Students jam this cheerful, unsophisticated Southern Italian restaurant and pizzeria. ◆ Italian ◆ M-F 11:30AM-11PM; Sa-Su noon-midnight. 1001 Broxton Ave. 208.7077. Also at: 1444 Third Street Promenade, Santa Monica. 576.7799

**12 Breadstiks** Astonishingly, a full-service independent supermarket, with fresh take-out dishes, has taken on the convenience stores. ◆ M-F 8AM-11PM; Sa-Su 9AM-11PM. 1057 Gayley Ave. 209.1111

**12 Videotheque** A good stock and knowledgeable staff are the big pluses at this video store. Ask about their mid-week two-for-one special. ◆ M-Th, Su 10AM-10PM; F-Sa 10AM-midnight. 1035 Gayley Ave. 824.9922. Also at: 8800 Sunset Blvd, W. Hollywood. 657.8800; 330 N. Beverly Dr, Beverly Hills. 858.7600

**13 The Tower** This striped marble concoction was designed by Chicago's *meister* of slick, **Helmut Jahn**, in 1988. Its pretentiousness is all the more obvious amid the mediocrity of Westwood's high rises. ◆ 10940 Wilshire Blvd

**14 Westwood Inn Motor Hotel** $$ If you want convenience and you're on a budget, this motel may be one of your best bets in the area. ♦ 10820 Wilshire Blvd. 474.3118

**15 Westwood Memorial Cemetery** The graves of **Marilyn Monroe, Natalie Wood,** and **Peter Lorre** are tucked away behind the Avco Center movie houses. ♦ M-F 8AM-7:30PM; Sa-Su 8AM-5PM. 1218 Glendon Ave. 474.1579

**16 Armand Hammer Museum of Art and Cultural Center** The late, jet-setting chairman of Occidental Petroleum broke a pledge to donate his art to LACMA in order to build this monument, which squats, shiny and windowless, like a footstool beneath his corporate tower. Designed by **Edward Larabee Barnes,** the museum opened in 1990 shortly after Hammer's death. As architecture, it's another nail in the coffin of the village; as an art repository, it has been derided by professionals for planning to

put profit ahead of curatorial expertise. As a showcase for Hammer's masterpieces and visiting shows—such as the premiere exhibition of Russian Supremastist **Malevich** and the 1991 to 1992 "Treasures of Imperial Russia"—it may surmount these handicaps. ♦ Admission. Daily 10AM-6PM. 10889 Wilshire Blvd. 443.7000

**17 Hamlet Gardens** ★★$$$ **Marilyn Lewis** of **Hamburger Hamlet** fame opened this crisp and savvy restaurant in a Spanish-style brick rotunda. The salmon tartare, pizzas, salads, and grills justify the high prices. The guacamole is ground at your table with mortar and pestle. ♦ California ♦ M-Th, Su 11:30AM-3PM (pizza and light-fare menu until 5:30PM), 6-10PM; F-Sa 11:30AM-11:30PM. 1139 Glendon Ave. 824.1818

**18 Flax Art Supplies** An eye-catching red sculpture by **Franco Assetto** wraps around the front of this shop, with its two floors of brushes, paints, papers, and drafting equipment. The store is a valuable resource. ♦ M-F 8AM-5:30PM; Sa 9AM-5:30PM. 10852 Lindbrook Dr. 208.3529

**19 International Student Center** $ This multilingual restaurant is operated by UCLA. ♦ American ♦ Daily 11AM-2PM. 1023 Hilgard Ave. 825.3384

**20 Hilgard House Hotel** $$$ The small, elegant hotel is located a few minutes from the village and UCLA. ♦ 927 Hilgard Ave. 208.3945, 800/826.3934 (US); fax 208.1972

**21 Westwood Marquis** $$$$ Civility and luxury permeate this medium-size 258 suite hotel located across the street from UCLA and just a short walk from the village. Managing director **Jonathan Q. Loeb** continues to maintain the high standards of service refined by the retired general manager **Jacques P. Camus.** The rooms are spacious and well-furnished, and there's a leafy garden, a pool, and two restaurants. The **Dynasty Room** offers classic French cuisine in an elegant, romantic setting and a

special 600-calorie *cuisine minceur* dinner. Formal teas are served in a handsome lounge. There is a concierge, complimentary limousine service, and a spa for men and women. ♦ 930 Hilgard Ave. 208.8765, 800/421.2317; fax 824.0355

**22 Strathmore Apartments** When this modern bungalow court by **Richard Neutra** rose from a then-empty hillside in 1937, its stark lines attracted such tenants as **Orson Welles, Charles** and **Ray Eames** (who experimented with laminated plywood in the bathtub), **Clifford Odets,** and **Luise Rainer.** It remains one of the best preserved of several Neutra apartment buildings in and around the village. It's a private residence. ♦ 11005 Strathmore Dr

**23 Tischler House** This geometrically sculptured house was designed by **Rudolph Schindler** in 1949; the private residence was one of the architect's last and best works. ♦ 175 Greenfield Ave

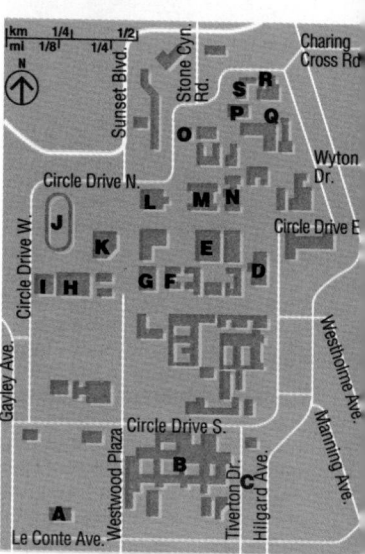

*UCLA Campus*

**24 University of California at Los Angeles (UCLA)** This university is celebrated worldwide, and it has grown to be a city within the city. It was established in May of 1919 as the University of California's "Southern Branch," a small two-year college located on the site of the former Los Angeles State Normal School. The fledgling institution grew rapidly, and in 1929 moved to Westwood. Today UCLA has the largest enrollment (35,200 students) of the nine University of California campuses. The first four buildings—Italian Romanesque brick palazzos laid out around a grassy quadrangle (known as the **Royal Quad**)—remain the best. Most of the 85-plus that followed, such as the **Doris Stein Eye Research Center** and the **Ueberroth Building,** are architecturally insignificant. Happily, the gardeners' talents make up for the lack of building aesthetics. The 419-acre campus is beautifully landscaped with superb trees and exotic plants, and with wonderful paths and spots for walking, jogging, or

quiet reverie. Perhaps the moral is that if you are asked for a donation, make it for a tree or a scholarship, not a building. Many of the academic departments and professional schools have exceptional national and international reputations, including chemistry; earth and space sciences; philosophy; linguistics; history; theater, film, and television; the schools of medicine and law; and the **John E. Anderson Graduate School of Management.** Library holdings total more than 6.1 million volumes, making them among the world's largest.

The best way to get to the campus is by bicycle or shuttle bus; cars are restricted to a few ring roads. Local authorities have covered the area with meters or restricted or permit parking ordinances. RTD, Santa Monica, and Culver City bus lines have direct routes to UCLA. Limited parking is available in campus parking structures; access tokens are sold at the information kiosks located at the main entrances on Westwood and Sunset boulevards and Hilgard Avenue. ♦ 405 Hilgard Ave. 825.4321

At the University of California at Los Angeles (the letters preceding the following entries refer to the map at left):

**A Visitor's Center** Walking tours depart from the **Visitor's Center** in Room 1417 of the **Ueberroth Building** on weekdays at 10:30AM and 1:30PM. Free maps in English, Japanese, Spanish, and French are available in the center, which is open weekdays from 8AM to 5PM. For information about group tours, call 206.8147. The free **Campus Express** buses circulate from Westwood Village through the campus every five minutes on weekdays from 7:15AM to 6PM. ♦ 10945 Le Conte Ave. 825.4321

**B Center for Health Sciences** The entire southern end of the campus, from Tiverton to Gayley fronting on Le Conte, is occupied by one of the largest medical complexes in the nation. The schools of Medicine, Dentistry, Nursing, and Public Health are located here, as well as an ambulatory care complex and numerous research institutions, including the world-famous **Neuropsychiatric Institute and Hospital** and the **Jules Stein Eye Institute.** The **UCLA Hospital and Clinics,** also located in the center, operates a 24-hour emergency room, which is reached via an entrance at Tiverton and Le Conte. ♦ Emergency: 825.2111. Physicians referral: 825.0881, 800/825.2631

**C Mathias Botanical Gardens** This eight-acre shaded canyon, on the southeast end of campus off Hilgard and Le Conte, was planted to create a peaceful, woodsy retreat with mature specimens of unusual size. There are no restroom facilities. ♦ Free. M-F 8AM-5PM; Sa-Su 8AM-4PM. Garden information: 825.3620

A telephone "surf line" gives more than wave information. It includes a bacteria level count for the water at Los Angeles' surfing hot spots.

Though LA has the dirtiest air in the nation, it was 50 percent cleaner in 1992 than it was in 1982, according to the State Air Resources Control Board. Two-thirds of LA's air pollution comes from automotive exhaust.

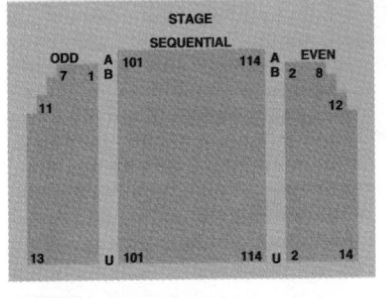

**D Schoenberg Hall** The hall (see the plan above) is named for the Austrian composer **Arnold Schoenberg,** who lived in Los Angeles between 1933 and 1951 and was a professor of music at UCLA from 1936 to 1951. The departments of music, musicology, ethnomusicology, and systematic musicology are located here, as well as the **Schoenberg Auditorium** and the **Jan**

**Popper Theater.** ♦ UCLA Central Ticket Office: 825.9261

**E Powell Library** Originally the main library of the campus, it now houses the undergraduate collection. The rotunda and grand staircase of the 1928 building are notable. ♦ Closed until 1994 for seismic upgrading; holdings have been transferred to a high-tech temporary structure located between the Men's Gym and the Dance Building. Reference desk: 825.1938

**F Kerckhoff Hall** Student activity offices and a moderately priced coffeehouse are located here. ♦ Coffeehouse hours: M-F 7:30AM-midnight; Sa-Su 9AM-midnight. 206.0740

**G Ackerman Student Union** A bustling center of campus activity, the Student Union houses the **Student's Store** and the **Treehouse Restaurant.** Actually several restaurants in one, the Treehouse has fresh fruit and salads and a full meal section, all at very low prices. The Student's Store on the first floor has a fine selection of academic books, and the "Bearwear" department carries a full range of UCLA insignia merchandise. ♦ Open daily. For hours, call 825.7711

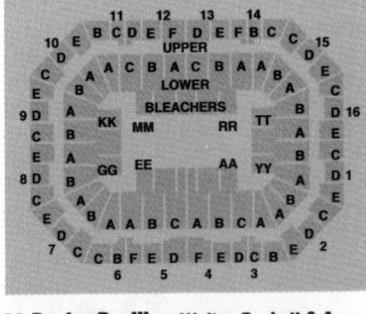

**H Pauley Pavilion** Welton Beckett & Associates designed this 1965 home of the UCLA Bruins (see the plan above) women's and

men's basketball teams. Concerts, cultural events, gymnastic meets, and volleyball games are also held in the arena. ♦ UCLA Central Ticket Office: 825.2101

**I LA Tennis Center** Built for the 1984 Olympics, the center is the current home of the annual **Volvo Tennis/Los Angeles Men's Tournament.** ♦ Event information: 825.4546

**J Drake Stadium** The track and field stadium seats 11,000. ♦ Event information: 825.4546

**K UCLA Athletics Hall of Fame** A two-story display of trophies, photos, and memorabilia relating to the UCLA athletic tradition is located in the **J.D. Morgan Intercollegiate Athletics Center.** ♦ M-F 8AM-5PM. 825.8699

**L Fowler Museum of Cultural History** The three-story museum houses one of the nation's leading collections of African, Oceanic, and American Indian art and material culture,

## Westside

with more than 750,000 artifacts in all. There are also four exhibition galleries, as well as an amphitheater, an auditorium, a central courtyard, a museum store, a conservation laboratory, and a library. ♦ Free. W-Su noon-5PM; Th noon-8PM. 825.4361

*Royce Hall*

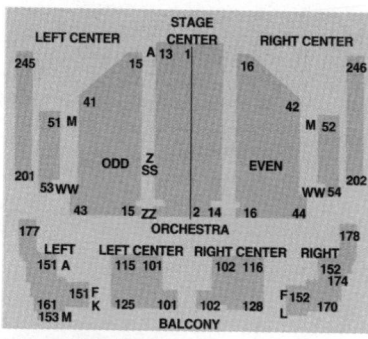

*Royce Hall Auditorium*

**M Royce Hall** Designed by **Allison & Allison** in 1919, this is one of the buildings of the original quadrangle (see the plan and the illustration above), with classrooms, offices, and an auditorium that is a year-round venue for internationally known visiting artists and professional music, dance, and theatrical presentations. ♦ UCLA Central Ticket Office: 825.2101

**N Haines Hall** This 1928 building was one of the original buildings on the quadrangle. It used to contain collections from the **Museum of Cultural History,** but they have been moved to the new **Fowler** building, and the hall now houses classrooms.

**O North Campus Student Center** This popular campus dining spot offers the same low prices as all UCLA restaurant facilities. ♦ M-Th 7AM-10PM; F 7AM-8PM; Sa 9:30AM-6PM; Su 11AM-6PM. 206.0720

**P University Research Library** This 1964 building designed by **A. Quincy Jones** houses a superb reference collection. It's open to the public for reading; loans are available to the university's community and library card purchasers. Exhibitions of literary material from the **Department of Special Collections** are displayed on the first floor. A guide to all of UCLA's specialized libraries is available. For hours, call 825.8301. ♦ Reference desk: 825.1323

**Q Franklin Murphy Sculpture Garden** This idyllic five-acre greensward looks its best when the jacaranda trees bloom in April. Major works by **Jean Arp, Henri Matisse, Joan Miró, Henry Moore, Auguste Rodin, David Smith,** and others are here.

**R UCLA Film and Television Archive** Screenings of more than 500 films a year are a major activity in the former **Melnitz Hall,** dedicated to the preservation, study, and exhibition of the moving image. In addition, the archive presents a wide range of programs, including major retrospectives, festivals, tributes, and documentaries. The **Archive Research and Study Center,** located in Powell Library, makes available to the UCLA community and general public in-site viewing of archival material for research purposes (206.5388). ♦ Information about public screenings: 206.8013

**S UCLA Wight Art Gallery** A vital, innovative force within the Southern California art community, the gallery is located within the **Dickson Art Center.** It encompasses exhibition galleries, as well as the **Grunwald Center for the Graphic Arts** and the **Franklin D. Murphy Sculpture Garden.** Exhibitions are complemented by a wide range of programs, including lectures, tours, educational workshops, and publications. The museum shop sells books, posters, jewelry, and crafts. ♦ The Grunwald Center is open free to the public by appointment. Wight Art Gallery: Free. Tu 11AM-7PM; W-F 11AM-5PM; Sa-Su 1-5PM. Docent tours Sa-Su 1:30PM or by appointment. 825.9345

**25 Century Wilshire Hotel** $$ The mid-size hotel features a garden patio and fully equipped kitchen units. ♦ 10776 Wilshire Blvd. 474.4506, 800/421.7223 (US); fax 474.2535

**26 Del Capri Hotel** $$ Though most units have kitchens, the hotel serves a Continental breakfast every morning. ♦ 10587 Wilshire Blvd. 474.3511, 800/444.6835; fax 470.9999

**27 The Beverly Hills Ritz Hotel** $$$ This low-key, reliable hotel in a converted apartment building has a homey feeling that makes it popular with those guests on extended visits. Each of the 116 suites has a living room, dining area, kitchen, and one or more bedrooms. There's also a courtyard with a swimming pool. ♦ 10300 Wilshire Blvd. 275.5575, 800/800.1234; fax 278.3325

**28 Lunaria** ★★★$$$ Bernard Jacoupy left Le Meridien in Newport Beach and brought Antoine's chef, Dominique Chavanon, to his new restaurant. It's a treasure: a cool, spacious dining room, caring service, good acoustics, and a reasonably priced menu. Standout dishes include seared scallops with green lentils, smoked duck with onion tart, gratin of sea bass with pesto, and mouth-watering desserts. ♦ French ♦ Tu-F 11AM-2PM, 6-11PM; Sa-Su 6-11PM. 10351 Santa Monica Blvd. 282.8870

**29 Bel Air Wine Merchant** They have a broad selection of European and California wines, including many small labels. ♦ M-Sa 10:30AM-7PM. 10421 Santa Monica Blvd. 474.9518

**30 Mormon Temple** The 257-foot tower crowned with a 15-foot gold-leaf statue of the angel Moroni makes this a familiar landmark on the LA skyline. Seen from Santa Monica Boulevard, it looks like a gigantic '40s cocktail cabinet. Designed by Edward Anderson in 1955, this is the largest temple of the Church of Jesus Christ of Latter Day Saints outside of Salt Lake City, and it's open only to church members. Visitors may tour the grounds or the Visitor Information Center. Daily 9AM-9PM. ♦ 10777 Santa Monica Blvd. 474.1549

**31 Ramayani** ★$ For the hungry and penurious, the *rijstaffel* (multicourse rice feast) promises a pleasurable orgy of eating. ♦ Indonesian ♦ Tu-Su 11:30AM-9PM. 1777 Westwood Blvd. 477.3315

**32 La Bruschetta** ★★★$$$ The elegant service and decor are as savory as the excellent Northern Italian cuisine. The portions are homestyle hearty, and there's a very good wine list. Recommended are the osso buco (veal shank), roasted squab, and any of the pasta dishes. ♦ Italian ♦ M-F noon-2PM, 6-10:30PM; Sa 6-10:30PM. 1621 Westwood Blvd. 477.1052

**33 Sisterhood Bookstore** Books of every kind by and about women are in stock, plus music and cards. They have frequent humanist and feminist readings. ♦ Daily 10AM-8PM. 1351 Westwood Blvd. 477.7300

**34 The Spanish Bookstore** A variety of Spanish and Latin American titles are sold here. ♦ M-Sa 10AM-5:30PM. 10977 Santa Monica Blvd. 475.0453

**34 Jasmine Tree** ★★$$ The Taiwanese chef prepares excellent mushroom-and-duck soup, pan-fried dumplings, Peking duck, and fiery *kung pao* squid in this upscale Mandarin restaurant, which is located on the second level of a mini-mall. ♦ Chinese ♦ M-F 11:30AM-10PM; Sa-Su noon-10PM. 11057 Santa Monica Blvd. 444.7171

**35 Shamshiry** ★$ This popular family restaurant serves huge portions of shish kebab, chicken *faisanjan* (braised in pomegranate sauce), and pilaf in a bare-bones setting at modest prices. This stretch of Westwood has been dubbed "Teherangeles" for its high concentration of Iranian bakeries and restaurants. ♦ Persian ♦ M-Th, Su 11:30AM-10PM; F 11:30AM-11PM; Sa 11:45AM-11PM. 1916 Westwood Blvd. 474.1410

**35 Technical Book Company** This is one of several small, specialized bookstores along Westwood Boulevard between Santa Monica and Pico boulevards. The specialties here are professional and scientific books. ♦ M-Sa 9:30AM-5:30PM. 2056 Westwood Blvd. 475.5711

**36 Koutoubia** ★★$$$ Named for a famous mosque in Marrakesh, this desert tent, with its hassocks and low brass tables, is a showcase of the customs and cuisine of the Magreb. Chef/owner Michael Ohayon is a master of couscous and *tajines* (well-done lamb cooked with onion, parsley, cilantro, honey, raisins, and other fruits), but will prepare special treats if

you call ahead—fresh brains with coriander sauce, *b'stilla* (flaky pastry stuffed with chicken, cinnamon, and spices) with squab, and sea bass with red chiles, all with delicious anise bread. ♦ Moroccan ♦ Tu-Su 6-10PM, sometimes later on weekends. 2116 Westwood Blvd. 475.0729

**37 Wally's Liquor and Gourmet Foods** Within this California redwood and high-tech store is the best in food and wine, including boutique vineyard labels unavailable elsewhere, and a cheese department that includes buffalo mozzarella, California goat cheese, pizzas, and chili dogs. The ever-present owner, Steve Wallace, knows everything about California wines. ♦ M-Sa 10AM-8PM; Su 10AM-6PM. 2107 Westwood Blvd. 475.0606

**38 Barry Levin** Science fiction and fantasy books are sold by appointment only. ♦ 2253 Westwood Blvd. 458.6111

**39 Nizam** ★★$ A lovely couple runs one of LA's nicest Indian restaurants. Exemplary renditions of standards and such unusual dishes as *dai papri* (fried lentil wafer chips tossed with potatoes, onion, cilantro, and yogurt) are among the highlights. ♦ Indian ♦ M-Sa 11:30AM-3PM, 5:30-11PM. 10871 W. Pico Blvd. 470.1441

**39 Anna's** $$ Stop in for Sicilian-style thick-crusted or crispy thin-crusted pizza with good sauce and lots of cheese. ♦ Pizza ♦ M-Th 11:30AM-11PM; F 11:30AM-midnight; Sa 4PM-midnight; Su 4-11PM. 10929 W. Pico Blvd. 474.0102

"The city of Philip Marlowe and Charlie Chaplin, of Mickey Mouse and Frank Lloyd Wright, of weirdos, professors, gangsters, gurus, millionaires and nice ordinary people, a failed Jerusalem, a low-density Babylon."

**Mark Girouard** in *Cities and People*, 1985

| | |
|---|---|
| **Restaurants/Clubs:** Red | **Hotels:** Blue |
| **Shops/ ❀ Outdoors:** Green | **Sights/Culture:** Black |

**39 Matteo's** $$$$ This celebrity hangout caters to the older generation, especially on Sunday nights. People go to see and be seen more than to eat. ♦ Italian ♦ Tu-Su 5-11PM. 2321 Westwood Blvd. 475.4521

**40 The Apple Pan** $ Midwestern basics draw crowds at all hours of day and night to this homely clapboard cottage. ♦ American ♦ M-Th, Su 11AM-midnight; F-Sa 11AM-1AM. 10801 W. Pico Blvd. 475.3585

**40 Compact Disc-Count** This shop is filled wall-to-wall with new, vintage, and used CDs. You can review your choices on a CD player before you purchase them. There's a wide selection of rock, classical, and international editions of pop hits. ♦ Daily 10AM-10PM. 10741 W. Pico Blvd. 475.4122

**40 La Cite des Livres** Books, magazines, maps, and tapes from France, as well as a comprehensive international selection, are stocked

here. ♦ Tu-Sa 10AM-6PM. 2306 Westwood Blvd. 475.0658

**41 Primi Plus** ★★★$$$ **Piero Selvaggio** of **Valentino** opened Primi for anyone who likes to make a meal from first courses. In fact, the portions are as generous as main courses in more pretentious restaurants. Pastas are the forte; risotto *nero* (cooked in black squid's ink) is one of the stars. The choices range from bread and salami with extra-virgin olive oil to grilled quail and hearty traditional fare. There's a choice of ambience between the shiny, high-style dining room and a covered patio. Takeout is available, too. ♦ Italian ♦ M-Th 11:30AM-2:30PM, 5:30-10:30PM; F 11:30AM-2:30PM, 5:30-11PM; Sa 5:30-11PM. 10543 Pico Blvd. 474.0632

**42 C.G. Jung Library, Archive & Bookstore** Everything you ever wanted to know about analytical psychology is available here. ♦ M-Sa noon-5PM. 10349 W. Pico Blvd. 556.1196

**43 John O'Groats** ★$ Great breakfasts and lunches with tartan touches—like biscuits, fish and chips, and shortbread—are the specialties here. ♦ Scottish ♦ M-F 7AM-3PM; Sa-Su 7AM-2PM. 10628 W. Pico Blvd. 204.0692

**44 Westside Pavilion** Architect **Jon Jerde** (of San Diego's Horton Plaza fame) makes retail whimsical in this 1987 indoor shopping mall, centered around an elongated glass-vaulted atrium and accentuated with trendy paste-on postmodern design. In form it borrows from 19th-century arcades, but the colors and

details are overdone, and the labyrinthine free parking structure can be a shopper's nightmare. **Nordstrom** (see description below) and **May Co.** (475.4911) department stores anchor three levels of retail establishments, including clothing stores and gift shops, fast food restaurants, and places such as a **GTE Phone Mart.** The **Samuel Goldwyn Cinemas** fourplex (474.0202) often has exclusive runs of the better independent releases. In mid-1991 an unremarkable expansion, with carbon copy detailing, was completed and connected to the mall by a skybridge above Westwood Boulevard. Within, the sodahoppish **Boogies Diner** (446.8800) and **Disney Store** (474.7022) are appropriate tenants, given the mall's theatricality. ♦ M-F 10AM-9:30PM; Sa 10AM-7PM; Su 11AM-6PM. 10800 W. Pico Blvd (at Westwood Blvd). 470.6155

Within Westside Pavilion:

**Nordstrom** The stock and service are exemplary at this Seattle-based chain. Most remarkably, they give the customer the benefit of the doubt. By example, they are forcing improvements on competing stores. Shoes and stylish American clothes are specialties. ♦ M-10AM-9:30PM; Sa 10AM-7PM; Su 11AM-6PM. 470.6155

**Sisley** ★$$ Dependable pizzas and homemade pastas energize exhausted shoppers. ♦ Italian ♦ M-Th, Su 11:30AM-10PM; F-Sa 11:30AM-10:30PM. 446.3030

**Brentanos** Located in the **Westside Pavilion** expansion, this upscale bookseller stocks unique, noncommercial titles for the serious fiction and non-fiction reader. ♦ M-F 10AM-9:30PM; Sa 10AM-7PM; Su 11AM-6PM. 10850 W. Pico Blvd. 470.4830

**45 Bryan's Country Saloon** ★$ Finger-licking sliced beef in a spicy sauce, beef hot links, beans, cornbread, and peach cobbler are served here in a woodsy Western interior. ♦ American ♦ M-Th 4-10PM; F-Sa 11AM-11PM; Su 10:30AM-9PM. 10916 W. Pico Blvd. 474.4263

**46 Disc Connection** Original-cast and soundtrack albums are a specialty of this eclectic used record store. ♦ M-Th, Sa 11AM-7PM; F 11AM-9PM. 10970 W. Pico Blvd. 208.7211

**47 Petal House** Architect **Eric Moss** has taken modest suburban house and, using the simplest materials, opened it up like a flower. The private residence is pictured above. ♦ 2828 Midvale Ave

**48 Trader Joe's** Come here for great deals on wine, cheese, coffee, and nuts, plus exotica that are wittily described in the monthly catalog. There are branches all over town. ◆ Daily 9AM-9PM. 10850 National Blvd. 470.1917

**49 Hu's Szechwan Restaurant** ★$ Bring your own bear to this bare-bones joint, which is packed with locals digging their chopsticks into the spicy Szechuan specialties. ◆ Chinese ◆ Tu-Sa noon-2:30PM, 5-9:30PM. 10450 National Blvd. 837.0252

**50 Circuit City** This store is part of a national chain that offers electronics and appliances at competitive prices *and* caring service—a rare combo. ◆ M-F 10AM-9PM; Sa 10AM-7PM; Su 11AM-6PM. 3115 Sepulveda Blvd. 391.3144

**51 Orleans** ★★$$$ The Cajun-Creole craze has passed as quickly as it came, but this exuberant shoot from the **Paul Prudhomme** tree is still flowering. Owner **Mary Atkinson** offers hard-to-resist gumbo, zesty shrimp creole, blackened prime rib and redfish, and jambalaya. Save room for the bread pudding with Bourbon sauce. ◆ Cajun/Creole ◆ M-Th 11:30AM-2PM, 6-9:30PM; F 11:30AM-2PM, 6-10:30PM; Sa 6-10:30PM; Su 6-9:30PM. 11705 National Blvd. 479.4187

**52 From Spain** ★$ Chef **Juan Rodriguez** prepares such Catalan dishes as grilled fresh sardines with garlic, sautéed *chorizo*, and grilled pork chops with red-pepper sauce. Bread with serrano ham is always a good bet, and don't miss the suckling pig if it's available. ◆ Spanish ◆ Tu-F 11AM-2:30PM, 5-10PM; Sa 3-10PM. 11510 W. Pico Blvd. 479.6740

**53 Chan Dara** ★★$$ This is the third in a family that began in Hollywood and Larchmont Village. **Don Carsten's** neon-accented interior glows with rich lacquers, and the kitchen also sparkles. The vegetable soup (crammed with goodies), huge and flavorful naked shrimp, broad noodles with chicken, and beef *panang* are standouts. ◆ Thai ◆ M-F noon-11PM; Sa 5PM-midnight; Su 5-11PM. 11940 W. Pico Blvd. 479.4461

**54 Bellini's Trattoria** ★$ Innovative pasta dishes in this modern neighborhood place include *farfalle* with artichoke hearts and walnuts, and saffron linguini with fresh tomato *coulis*. ◆ Italian ◆ M-F 11:30AM-3PM, 5:30-11:30PM; Sa-Su 5:30-11:30PM. 12021 W. Pico Blvd. 477.4057

**54 Music Machine** Leading rock, blues, and reggae groups perform through the week. There's a large dance floor and two bars. ◆ Cover. Tu-Su. Call for showtimes. 12220 W. Pico Blvd. 820.5150

**54 Rent-a-Wreck** Owner **Dave Schwartz** has successfully franchised his idea country-wide, but still manages this original facility. Don't say anything rude about the poster that hangs over the counter or you may be turned away. If you pass the test, you can choose from hundreds of cars with personality. Vintage Mustang convertibles are a specialty here. The scruffy surfaces are deceptive; the cars rarely let you down and

will dramatize your disdain of conventional status symbols. In the land of Mercedes, a battered Chevy is king. ◆ M-F 8AM-6PM; Sa 8AM-4PM; Su 10AM-4PM. 12333 W. Pico Blvd. 478.0676, 478.4393

**55 Kirk Paper** If you need paper, you can't beat this paper supermarket. Wheel your basket down the aisles and pick up reams of the stuff, plus every kind of office supply, at budget prices. The service is indifferent. ◆ M-F 7:30AM-5PM; Sa 8AM-4PM. 11800 Olympic Blvd. 478.4026

**56 The Wine House** Their huge and eclectic stock of wines, beers, and spirits is competitively priced. ◆ M-Sa 10AM-7PM; Su noon-6PM. 2311 Cotner Ave. 479.3731

**57 LAX Luggage** One of a row of discount stores, LAX has good prices on name-brand bags. ◆ M-Sa 10AM-6PM; Su 11AM-5PM. 2233 Sepulveda Blvd. 478.2661

**58 Sawtelle Boulevard** Named for a subdivision that didn't take, Sawtelle is now a thriving Japanese/Mexican community of restaurants and small businesses, most related to the gardening trade. ◆ Between Santa Monica and Olympic Blvds

**58 Cafe Katsu** ★★$$ Owned by **Katsu Michite**, whose **Los Feliz** restaurant is a sushi shrine, this one offers Japanese-influenced French cooking in a tiny, spare space. ◆ French ◆ M-Sa 11:30AM-2:30PM, 5:30PM-10PM. 2117 Sawtelle Blvd. 477.5444

**58 Hide Sushi** ★★$$ The counter chefs never seem to get a moments rest in this perpetually crowded cafe, but they seem to relish the attention and praise for the excellent sushi delicacies and finger appetizers. ◆ Japanese ◆ Tu-Th 11:30AM-9:30PM; F-Sa 9:30AM-11:30PM. 2040 Sawtelle Blvd. 477.7242

**59 Yamaguchi Bonsai Nursery** Buy a 100-year-old miniature tree or lotus stock, or leave your bonsai here while you vacation. ◆ M-Sa 7AM-5PM; Su 8:30AM-4:30PM. 1905 Sawtelle Blvd. 473.5444

**59 Lulu's Alibi** $$ Around the corner from the arty movie house **Nuart**, this Westside coffeehouse offers a more relaxed atmosphere than many of its Midtown counterparts. In addition to espresso, they serve a Brazilian menu. ◆ Coffeehouse ◆ M-Tu 10AM-2AM; W-Th 10AM-3AM; F-Sa 10AM-4AM; Su 10AM-1:30AM. 1638 Sawtelle Blvd. 479.6007

**60 Odyssey Theatre** Artistic Director **Ron Sossi** heads this three-stage avant-garde theater offering plays and performances. ◆ 2055 S. Sepulveda Blvd. 477.2055

**61 The Sports Club LA** In earlier times we built temples to God or Mammon; now it's the body beautiful that's enshrined, and this is St. Peter's. There are 100,000 square feet, marble-paved or carpeted, where subscribers can exercise, work off steam, and save a trip to the

singles bar. The club is for members only. ♦ M-F 5:30AM-11PM, Sa-Su 7AM-8PM. 1835 Sepulveda Blvd. 473.1447

**62 Nuart Theater** One of LA's last surviving movie repertory houses, the Nuart shows adventurous new work, theme series, classics, and camp favorites. Notice the fine streamline neon marquee. ♦ 11272 Santa Monica Blvd. 478.6379

**63 The Isle of California** The much-faded classic mural, done in the late '60s by the **LA Fine Arts Squad,** shows the rugged Arizona coastline after the "Big One" has sent California off into the Pacific. ♦ Santa Monica Blvd at Butler Ave

**63 Gianfranco** ★$ Stop for a bite at this deli/restaurant before or after an art film at the neighboring Nuart or Royal theaters. At this spot it's best to stick to the antipasti and homemade pastas. Try the pasta with cabbage, potatoes,

and fresh sage. ♦ Italian ♦ M-Sa 11AM-3PM, 5:30-11PM. 11363 Santa Monica Blvd. 477.7777

**64 Javan** ★$ This Persian restaurant has a crisp black-and-white interior, delicious off-beat dishes, and a full license. Specials have included *zereshk polo* (chicken with rice pilaf flavored with dried barberries), *gheymeh* (lamb shank with split yellow peas), and steamed spinach with tart yogurt. ♦ Persian ♦ Daily 11:30AM-11PM. 11628 Santa Monica Blvd. 207.5555

**65 Toledo** ★$$$ Authentic Castilian cuisine is served in two dark, cozy rooms. It helps to love garlic. This is one of the few places to go for real paella. ♦ Spanish ♦ Tu-Th 11:30AM-2PM, 5:30-10:30PM; F 11:30AM-2PM, 5:30-11PM; Sa 5:30-11PM; Su 4:30-10PM. 11613 Santa Monica Blvd. 477.2400

**65 Trattoria Angeli** ★★★$$$ The trattoria is an ambitious version of the **Angeli Caffe** on Melrose by the same team. Architect **Michele Saee** (formerly with **Morphosis**) has created a dramatic, high-ceilinged, wood-and-steel structure within an old warehouse, preserving its original bow trusses. Chef **Kathy St. Hilare** gives full rein to her passion for rustic regional fare, complemented by an impressive cellar of native and Italian wines. The room can get crowded and noisy, but never like Melrose. There's a private dining room upstairs. ♦ Italian ♦ M-F 11:30AM-2:30PM, 6PM-close; Sa-Su 5PM-close. 11651 Santa Monica Blvd. 478.1191

**66 U-zen** $$ Sit at the sushi bar or order traditional-style Japanese dishes. ♦ Japanese ♦ Tu-Th 11:30AM-2PM, 5-10:30PM; F-Sa 11AM-11PM; Su 5:30-11PM. 11951 Santa Monica Blvd. 477.1390

**67 Bombay Cafe** ★$ Tandoori chicken, samosas, *sev puri* (bread layered with vegetables and chutney), and homemade mango and ginger ice cream are good choices in this simple, second-floor mall restaurant. ♦ Indian ♦ Tu-Th 11AM-10PM; F 11AM-11PM; Sa 4-11PM; Su 4-10PM. 12113 Santa Monica Blvd. 820.2070

## Brentwood

West of Bel Air, this exclusive residential area is chic, casual, and countrified. Stucco and clapboard cottages and substantial houses sit well back from leafy streets. You can imagine yourself in a small town, but this is high-rent territory, and the condo builders are moving in. The roads that wind up into the hills have an even more rustic feel. Brentwood's main street is **San Vicente Boulevard,** whose green median is lined with huge coral trees, making it a shady trail for joggers. The activities center around the sleek, multistory **Brentwood Gardens** complex for high-end fashion, and patio dining at the **California Pizza Kitchen** (826.3573). Across the street is the more rustic **Brentwood Town & Country,** home to **Flowers with Love** (207.3075), a petite but colorful floral stand, and **Salutations, Ltd.** (820.6127) for home adornments that can transform your residence into the cover story for *Metropolitan Home.*

**68 Bicycle Shop Cafe** $$ This bistro-type cafe offers crepes, salads, and light dinners amid antique and modern cycling regalia. ♦ Continental ♦ M-Sa 11AM-midnight; Su 11AM-11PM. 12217 Wilshire Blvd. 826.7831

**68 Castel Bistro** $$ Chef **Jean-Pierre Bosc** plans daily pasta and seafood specialties in this pleasant cafe that spices up the corner of its bland corporate tower location. ♦ California ♦ Tu-F 11:30AM-2:30PM, 6-10PM; Sa 6-10PM 12100 Wilshire Blvd. 207.4273

**69 Fragrant Vegetable** ★$$ Refined vegetarian dishes are served amid elegant decor at this Chinese restaurant. ♦ Chinese ♦ M-Th, Su 11:30AM-10PM; F-Sa 11:30AM-11PM. 11859 Wilshire Blvd. 312.1442

**70 India's Oven** ★★$$ Great tandoori chicken and curries are served in an elegant second-floor restaurant. ♦ Indian ♦ Daily 10:30AM-10:30PM. 11645 Wilshire Blvd. 207.5522

**71 Sawtelle Veterans' Chapel** This picturesque white gingerbread chapel was designed by **J. Lee Burton** at the turn-of-the-century. It's part of the **Sawtelle Veterans' Hospital** complex, one of the nation's first veterans' facilities opened after the Civil War. ♦ 11000 Wilshire Blvd

Los Angeles' official flower is the Bird of Paradise.

**Restaurants/Clubs:** Red    **Hotels:** Blue
**Shops/ ⚘ Outdoors:** Green    **Sights/Culture:** Black

**71 Wadsworth Theater** Located near the Veterans' Chapel, the auditorium is used by UCLA for chamber music, plays, and special film screenings. Free jazz concerts have been offered on the first Sunday of the month. Call for details. ♦ Ticket information: 825.9261, evenings 478.7578. Corner San Vicente and Wilshire Blvds

**72 Stoney's** $$ Sumatran shrimp linguini, Tiga Tikka chicken (grilled and marinated in yogurt, ground cilantro, garlic, and onion), and scallop and cashew nut salad give an Oriental twist to California cuisine. ♦ California ♦ M-Th 11:30AM-2:30PM, 5:30-10PM; F 11:30AM-2:30PM, 5:30-11:30PM; Sa 5:30-11:30PM. 11604 San Vicente Blvd. 447.6488

**72 Pasta Maria** ★★$$$ **Maria Giordano** maintains a cheerfully casual restaurant where the carpaccio and Caesar salad, gnocchi and pasta, and grilled prawns and veal chop are excellent though pricey. ♦ Italian ♦ M-Sa 9AM-11PM. 11620 San Vicente Blvd. 207.2833

**72 Petit Casino de France** $ This reliable cafe/bakery serves steam moo, frothy hot milk with almond and honey, the perfect early riser's chaser with an apricot croissant. ♦ Patisserie ♦ M-F 6:30AM-7PM; Sa 8AM-7PM; Su 8AM-5PM. In Brentwood Town & Country: 11640 San Vicente Blvd. 207.0848. Also at: 1767 S. Elena, Redondo Beach. 543.5585; 4709 Admiralty Way, Marina del Rey. 306.6988

**72 The New York Bagel Company** $ Ex-New Yorker **Dave Rosen** came West to the glee of his friends and bagel aficionados. Slap everything from cream cheese and lox to fruit jams on 11 varieties of the ringed rolls, including cinnamon raisin, pumpernickel, garlic, and sesame. Rosen's old friend, master architect **Frank Gehry,** created a design that reminds patrons that the best bagels come from the Big Apple: a 33-foot-long replica of the Chrysler building floats over this high-ceilinged deli and diner like an armored zeppelin in a Buck Rogers movie. ♦ Deli ♦ Daily 7AM-6PM. In Brentwood Town & Country, 11640 San Vicente Blvd. 820.1050

**72 Paris Pastry** The cheerful owner and staff serve delicious baked treasures, and the shelves and freezers are stocked with fine French gourmet foods. ♦ M-Sa 7:30AM-5:30PM. 11650 San Vicente Blvd. 826.2131. Also at: 1448 Westwood Blvd. 474.8888

**73 Toscana** ★★★$$$ Splendid rustic food is served in a bright, modern restaurant that hums with a crowd of satisfied diners at lunch and dinner. Standouts from an unchanging menu include the grilled vegetables, pizzas, and perfect risottos, plus sautéed sea bass, a variety of grilled meats (including an authentic *bistecca Fiorentina*), and the tiramisù. ♦ Italian ♦ M-Sa 11:30AM-3PM, 5:30-11:30PM; Su 5-10:30PM. 11633 San Vicente Blvd. 820.2448

**73 Brentwood Bar & Grill** ★★$$$ This is the very model of a modern million-dollar restaurant: a handsome room, an even more handsome clientele, an active bar, an exposed kitchen, and an exemplary wine cellar Don't miss the grilled duck or steak. The pacific oysters, potato-and-onion tart, and decadent desserts are good, too, and the service is excellent. ♦ California ♦ M-Th 11:30AM-2:30PM, 6-10:30PM; F 11:30AM-2:30PM, 6-11PM; Sa 6-11PM. 11647 San Vicente Blvd. 820.2121

**73 Daily Grill** ★$$ Sibling of **The Grill** in Beverly Hills, this one is located upstairs in an upmarket mall. The setting is masculine, the mood fun, and the food dependable. Chicken potpie, Cobb salad, great onion rings, french fries, and rice-pudding pie are favorite choices. ♦ American ♦ M-Th 11:30AM-11PM; F-Sa 11AM-midnight; Su 11AM-11PM. 11677 San Vicente Blvd. 442.0044

**74 Berty's** ★$$$ Try the blue-crab ravioli and a grilled veal chop before moving on to a tempting dessert in this casual restaurant with a cool, tranquil environment. ♦ California ♦ M-F

11:30AM-2:30PM, 6-10PM; Sa 6-10PM. 11712 San Vicente Blvd. 207.6169

**74 Chin Chin** $ **Brent Saville** designed this offshoot of the popular cafe on Sunset Strip. Dim sum and other light Chinese dishes are served in a bright tiled room and on a handsome roof terrace with large white umbrellas. ♦ Chinese ♦ M-Th, Su 11AM-11PM; F-Sa 11AM-midnight. 11740 San Vicente Blvd. 826.2525

**74 Kelly's Café & Bakery** $ Located below **Chin Chin,** this immaculate coffee bar and bakery offers a fine choice of roasted beans to go. ♦ M-Th 7AM-10PM; F 7AM-11PM; Sa 8AM-11PM. 11740 San Vicente Blvd. 826.5282

**74 La Scala Presto** $$ The stylish junior version of the Beverly Hills original is popular with the young for its pastas, pizzas, and antipasti at reasonable prices. ♦ Italian ♦ M-Th 11:30AM-10PM; F-Sa 11:30AM-11PM. 11740 San Vicente Blvd. 213/826.6100. Also at: 3821 Riverside Dr, Toluca Lake. 818/846.6800; 3874 Cross Creek Rd, Malibu. 456.1979; 410 N. Cañon Dr, Beverly Hills. 275.0579

**75 Mezzaluna** ★$$ Fancy Italian dishes with fancy names (grilled chicken breast is called *Battuta Di Pollo Alle Erbe e Aceto Balsamico*) are served in a high-ceilinged space generously

appointed with windows and encompassed by outdoor seating. The tiramisù and *Torta Alle Pere Caramelizzate* (or pear tart) are killer desserts. ♦ Italian ♦ Daily 11:30AM-10:30PM. 11750 San Vicente Blvd. 447.8667. Also at: 9428 Brighton Way, Beverly Hills. 275.6703

**75 Gaucho Grill** ★$$ This meat-eaters' haven in waistline-conscious Brentwood is similar to its Hollywood sister. The great take-out menu features Argentinian-style ribs designed for two or 10. ♦ Argentinian ♦ Daily 11:30AM-11PM. 11754 San Vicente Blvd. 447.7898

**76 Dutton's** This may be the finest bookstore in the city. Three separate rooms are grouped around a courtyard, making it easier to locate your chosen theme. Music and the humanities are Dutton's strong suits, but there's a good choice of new and used books in every major field, plus discs and tapes, readings, and book signings. The service is expert and friendly.

♦ M-F 9:30AM-9PM; Sa 9:30AM-6PM; Su 11AM-5PM. 11975 San Vicente Blvd. 476.6263. Also at: 3806 W. Magnolia Blvd. Burbank. 818/840.8003; 5146 Laurel Canyon Dr, N. Hollywood. 818/769.3866

**77 Brentwood Country Mart** This red barn houses more than 26 village shops, including an espresso bar, a fresh juice bar, a deli, and a grocery. Standouts here include the **Brentwood Camera Shop** (394.0256), the **Book Nook** (393.7903), and **Country Mart's Meat** (394.5279), which also sells fish and barbecued chicken. When the Westside was a refuge for émigrés fleeing from Hitler, **Arnold Schoenberg** and **Marta Feuchtwanger** shopped here. There's outdoor dining and a post office. ♦ 26th St (at San Vicente Blvd). 395.6714

# Pacific Palisades

The community was founded as a new Chautauqua in 1922 by the Southern Conference of the Methodist Episcopal Church. Made famous by its western border of oceanfront bluffs that frequently crumble down onto Pacific Coast Highway, the Palisades are an upper-class neighborhood with the highest median income of any area in the city of Los Angeles—twice that of most other areas. Many of the streets in the Palisades are named for bishops of the Methodist Church.

**78 Marix Tex Mex Playa** ★$$ This is a branch of the rambunctious West Hollywood restaurant. ♦ Mexican ♦ M-Th, Su 11AM-11PM; F-Sa 11AM-midnight. 118 Entrada Dr. 459.8596

**79 Uplifters Club Cabins** In the early 1920s an offshoot group of the **Los Angeles Athletic Club** (L. Frank Baum, author of the *Wizard of Oz* books, was one member of this splinter group) built cottages in the rustic hills of the Pacific Palisades. Many of the residences were log cabins, but some were stage sets. They are private residences. ♦ Nos. 1, 3, 18 Latimer Rd; nos. 31, 32, 34, 38 Haldeman Rd

**80 Rustic Canyon Recreation Center** The quiet sylvan glade is perfect for picnics and barbecues. For groups of more than 20, call 454.5734. ♦ 601 Latimer Rd

**80 Kappe House** The founder of **SCI-ARC, Raymond Kappe,** built this expansively scaled concrete-and-wood home for himself. It's a private residence. ♦ 715 Brooktree Rd

**81 Bridges House** In 1989 **Robert Bridges** designed and engineered this woodsy three-level house/office atop concrete piers. It rises from a precipitous site, 70 feet above the traffic on Sunset Boulevard. It's a private residence. ♦ 820 Chautauqua Blvd

# LA's Firsts

**1881** First issue of the *Los Angeles Times* newspaper is published

**1888** First LA swimming pool—the Los Angeles Natatorium, an indoor swimming pool, is built

**1897** First LA golf course—nine holes (tin cups) at Pico Boulevard and Alvarado Street

**1901** First discovery of La Brea fossils by Union Oil

**1902** First movie house in the world—the Electric Theatre

**1903** First Pacific Coast baseball league formed—featuring two LA teams, the Los Angeles Angels and the Hollywood Stars

**1905** First directional traffic signs in LA—erected by the Southern California Automobile Club

**1906** First Rose Bowl football game (which was declared too dangerous to repeat by the Tournament Committee)

**1906** First LA escalator—installed at Bullock's department store

**1912** First LA gas station—located at Grand Avenue and Washington Boulevard, selling gasoline eight cents per gallon

**1917** First million-dollar movie contract—signed by Mary Pickford

**1922** First LA shopping center—A.W. Ross buys 18 acres of bean fields on Wilshire Boulevard; begins the "Miracle Mile"

**1922** First LA radio stations—KFI and KHJ

**1927** First footprints at Grauman's Chinese Theatre—Norma Talmadge

**1927** First LA supermarket—Ralph's

**1928** First Mickey Mouse is born

**1932** First Olympic Games are hosted in LA

**1940** First LA freeway—Arroyo Seco Parkway

**1944** First use of the word "smog"

**1945** First LA Baskin Robbins ice cream shop

**1948** First Rolls-Royce car dealer in the United States—Peter Satori

**1949** First Emmy awards

**1959** First Barbie Doll manufactured—by Mattel in Los Angeles

**1973** First black LA Mayor—Thomas Bradley

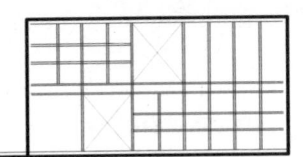

*Case Study House by Charles and Ray Eames*

**82 Case Study Houses** Some of LA's most innovative houses were commissioned or brokered by **John Entenza,** owner and editor of the pace-setting *Arts+Architecture Magazine* from 1938 to 1962. He launched the **Case Study House Program** in January 1945 to encourage locally based progressive architects to create affordable prototypes for the postwar house using the latest materials, techniques, and furnishings. Over the next 20 years, 24 of the 36 houses and apartment buildings published in the magazine were built, all over Southern California. Two of the most famous are located here, on a meadow overlooking the ocean: the classic steel-and-glass house/studio that **Charles** and **Ray Eames** built for themselves (illustrated above), and a more conventional house that Eames designed with **Eero Saarinen** for Entenza, both in 1949. Also on the site is a small house by **Richard Neutra.** None are visible from the street, and they are all private residences. ♦ Chautauqua Blvd (South of Corona del Mar)

**83 Gladstones 4 Fish** $$$ Close-up views of the ocean and the sun sinking over Malibu attract romantic couples and rowdy beachcombers, especially on weekends. As for food and service, you'd do better for less with a cold lobster and a bottle of Chardonnay on the beach. ♦ Seafood ♦ M-F 7AM-11PM; Sa-Su 7AM-midnight. 17300 Pacific Coast Hwy. 478.6738

**84 Self-Realization Fellowship Lake Shrine** Once a movie set, the open-air temple was founded in 1950 by followers of **Paramahansa Yogananda.** The ponds, lakes, waterfalls, windmills, and gazebos make this a pleasant place for walking or meditation. ♦ Tu-Su 9AM-4:45PM. 17190 Sunset Blvd. 454.4114

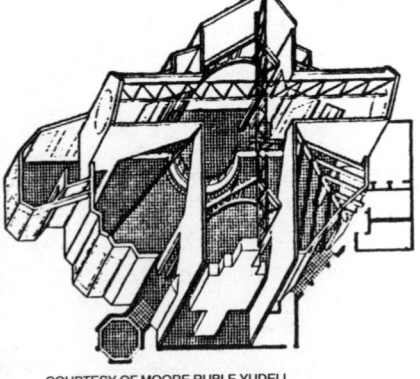

COURTESY OF MOORE RUBLE YUDELL

**85 St. Matthew's Episcopal Church Charles Moore** of **Moore Ruble Yudell** worked closely with the parishioners when designing this replacement (pictured above) for a church destroyed by fire. The result is indisputably modern, but the subtle use of historic design elements, from Renaissance to California Craftsman, ground the building in tradition. Of note in the 1983 design are the exposed wooden rafters under a lofty ceiling, inset windows that capture the landscape, and Moore's sensitivity to natural light. ♦ 1030 Bienveneda Ave. 454.1358

**86 Moss House** Architect **Eric Moss** transformed this '40s house for his family in 1979, adding a flying buttress, super graphics, and

other witty touches. It's a private residence. ♦ 708 El Medio Ave

**87 Gelson's Market** A cornucopia of fresh produce, specialty meat cuts, and exotica lines the shelves. ♦ Daily 8AM-10PM. 15424 Sunset Blvd. 459.4483

**88 Orï Olá** ★★★$$$ If anything could be described as both rustic and sophisticated, it would be this fine addition to **Kathie** and **Michael Gordon's** small but winning stable of fine restaurants (Brentwood's **Toscana** and the take-out **Rosti**). Unlike the packed Brentwood trattoria, the Gordon's newest eatery is a quiet ristorante where tables have breathing room for privacy. Chef **Agostino Sciandri,** who also guided Toscana's and Rosti's kitchen direction, culls his recipes from the different regions of Italy; meaty rabbit-and-tomato pasta, ravioli with spinach and mushrooms, and breaded sweetbreads are the choicest entrées. ♦ Italian ♦ M-Sa 11:30AM-2PM, 5:30-9:30PM; Su 5:30-9:30PM. 152000 Sunset Blvd. 459.9214

**88 Tivoli Cafe** ★$$ An upscale neighborhood spot, it specializes in designer pizzas, sandwiches, and tiramisù, plus daily specials. ♦ Italian ♦ M-Th 11:30AM-11PM; F-Sa 11:30AM-3PM, 5-10PM; Su 11:30AM-10PM. 15306 Sunset Blvd. 459.7685

**89 Will Rogers State Historic Park** This 187-acre park was the home of cowboy/humorist/writer/performer Will Rogers between 1924 and 1935. Inside the house are possessions and memorabilia from his busy career. A nearby **Visitor Center** shows a 10-minute film on Rogers' life, narrated by his friends and family, and sells Rogersiana. An avid polo player, Rogers' 900-by-300-foot polo field is the site of polo matches on Saturday from 2PM to 4PM and Sunday from 10AM to noon, year-round, weather permitting. (Rogers, who was once mayor of Beverly Hills, gave the **Polo Lounge** its name when he and his pals repaired there after a game.) The extensive grounds and the chaparral-covered hills invite hiking and

picnicking. This is a fire-hazard area, so no fires are allowed. ✦ Park: daily 8AM-7PM. House: daily 10:30AM-4:30PM. 14253 Sunset Blvd. 454.8212

**90 Cliff May Office** The renowned master of the California ranch-style house, **Cliff May,** designed this wood-paneled studio in 1952, which is tucked in a corner lot on Sunset Boulevard and near a generous selection of his celebrated residences on the 13000 blocks of Rivera Ranch and Old Oak streets. Immediately recognized by their broad shingle roofs and stucco walls, the homes are partially visible through the cradle of dense foliage, with exception to May's former residence "Mandalay" (220 Old Ranch Road), which is gated and totally hidden by trees and plants. ✦ 13151 Sunset Blvd

**91 Temple House** As a child, actress **Shirley Temple** lived with her parents in this delightful small-scale European farmhouse designed by

## Westside

John Byers and Edla Muir in 1936. It's a private residence. ✦ 231 N. Rockingham Ave

**92 Mount Saint Mary's College** The small, private liberal arts college sits atop one of the most beautiful view sites in the city. The **J. Paul Getty Center,** to be designed by **Richard Meier** as a showcase for all but the Greek and Roman art now displayed in Malibu, will rise from a neighboring eminence in 1995. ✦ 12001 Chalon Rd. 476.2237

**93 Maria's Italian Kitchen** $ Standout pizza with a delightful crust and a variety of toppings is the highlight of this mostly take-out place. ✦ Pizza ✦ Daily 10AM-10PM. 11723 Barrington Ct. 476.6112

# Bel Air

The posh hillside community, developed by **Alphonzo E. Bell** in the early '20s, rapidly became a preferred location for stars and other celebrities who valued the privacy and the views. There's not much for the outsider to see along the winding roads with their Mediterranean names since the best houses are hidden from the street.

**94 Bel Air Sands Hotel** $$$ A Radisson property, this peaceful, exotic hideaway, with rattan furniture and jungle prints in the lobby, is within a stone's throw of the San Diego Freeway. ✦ 11461 Sunset Blvd. 476.6571; fax 471.6310

**95 The Getty Center** **Richard Meier** designed the $360 million, six-building project now under construction on a dramatic 110-acre hilltop site in the Santa Monica Mountains of Brentwood. Slated to open in 1996, the 24-acre center will house a second museum with five two-story pavilions, each devoted to a particular period in the history of art, and unite the J. Paul Getty Trust's five other programs, including art education and conservation. (The original museum near Malibu will house the trust's Greek and Roman art.) Meier's early plan to model the

project on spired Tuscan hill towns was killed by neighbors who fought to restrict heights. The result is a series of low-scale geometric-shaped buildings in a campus-like design. Natural ridges were bulldozed to create a mesa for the project. Density is somewhat masked because nearly half the project is underground where all the buildings are connected. Plans call for crisp detailing and rough travertine marble cladding alternated with porcelain steel panels with a metallic finish. Bridges, pergolas, and formal gardens will link the buildings. Viewed from the San Diego Freeway below, which passes east of the hill, drivers will see mostly blank fortress-like walls. ✦ At Getty Center Dr

**96 UCLA Hannah Carter Japanese Garden** The enchanted garden, designed by **Nagao Sakurai** in 1961, is a tranquil retreat amid private estates, with rocks and wooden structures imported from Japan and Japanese trees and plants. Behind the teahouse is a Hawaiian garden. Reservations are required. ✦ Tu 10AM-1PM; W noon-3PM. 10619 Bellagio Rd. UCLA Visitor's Center: 825.4574

**97 Hotel Bel-Air** $$$$ The most exclusive and sybaritic hotel in LA features 92 exquisitely appointed rooms and suites in rambling Mission-style buildings. Even the setting induces a sense of tranquillity: a wooded canyon five minutes north of Sunset Boulevard but a world away in spirit. Like the Mansion on Turtle Creek in Dallas, the Hotel Bel-Air was lovingly made over by **Caroline Hunt Schoellkopf** after her **Rosewood Hotels** group purchased the hotel in 1982. Five designers brought their personal style to the guest and public rooms, which are further enhanced by wood-burning fireplaces, natural stone, and masses of fresh flowers. The 11-acre gardens, with their waterfall and swan lake, were further improved. Under current co-management by the **Bel-Air Hotel Company** and **Sazale,** the emphasis, as always, is on seclusion: it is possible to imagine that you are the only guest in residence.

The restaurants are under the direction of executive chef **George Mahassey.** There's a choice between a wood-paneled bar, an open-air terrace, and **The Restaurant** (★★★$$$$), which imaginatively combines the best of French and new California cuisines. ✦ 701 Stone Canyon Rd. 472.1211, 800/648.4097; fax 476.5890

Los Angeles places 11th, right behind Newark, New Jersey, for the largest number of residents in a metropolitan area who subscribe to gourmet magazines; San Francisco is first. LA comes in 55th for the largest percentage of city dwellers who subscribe to science magazines; Omaha ranks first.

**98  Cafe Four Oaks** ★★★$$$ This has always been one of the most charming hideaways in town, but the kitchen has seesawed. Currently, it's in the talented hands of chef **Peter Roelant,** who is putting his emphasis on vegetarian dishes, including terrine of eggplant, tomatoes, and fresh basil, and fresh soups and vegetable salads. ♦ California ♦ M, Su 6:30-9PM; Tu-Sa 11AM-2PM, 6:30-9PM. 2181 N. Beverly Glen Blvd. 470.2265

**99  Adriano's Restaurant** ★★$$$$ The food, the hilltop, and the personal attention will transport you to Italy. This elegant spot offers such authentic treats as Genovese minestrone and wonderful risotto and gnocchi, as well as simple grills. ♦ Italian ♦ Tu-Th 11:30AM-3PM, 6-10:30PM; F 11:30AM-3PM, 6-11PM; Sa 6-11PM; Su 5-10:30PM. 2930 Beverly Glen Circle. 475.9807

**99  Shane (Hidden on the Glen)** ★★$$ Barbara Lazaroff helped transform this tiny shopping center storefront into a colorful southwestern cave—apt decor for a restaurant that marries Santa Fe to Spago. Spicy chicken soup, fried calamari with aioli, pizzas, and pastas are all good bets. ♦ Southwestern ♦ M-F 11:30AM-2:30PM, 6-10PM; Sa 6-11PM; Su 5:30-9:30PM. 2932 Beverly Glen Circle. 470.6223

**99  Santo Pietro's Pizza** $$ Stop by this casual sidewalk cafe and espresso bar for daily Italian specialties as well as pizza spun in the air by a champion Frisbee thrower. ♦ Italian ♦ Daily 11AM-11PM. 2954 Beverly Glen Circle. 474.4349. Also at: Santo West, 1000 Gayley, Westwood Village. 208.5688; 12001 Ventura Pl, Studio City. 818/508.1177

## Bests

### Aaron Betsky
Designer/Architecture Critic/Author

Driving around LA on Christmas morning, when the air is as clear as the road, and every form is etched against the mountains.

The **Schindler House** (835 North Kings Road)—a romantic oasis in the city that reminds you that architects should build a better world.

The **Village Green Housing Project** and the **Eames House,** for the same reason.

Landing at **LAX** on a clear night—the city looks like it goes on forever—followed by driving down either La Cienega or La Brea boulevards from Baldwin Hills.

**Watts Towers,** the assemblage that puts all of LA together.

Hiking **Mount San Jacinto**—an Alpine Shangri-la you reach by aerial tram.

Anything designed by Frank Gehry because he understands this city and gives it shape.

### Ken Frank
Owner/Chef, LaToque

My favorite thing to do is eat, and I make a point of spoiling myself as much as possible right in my own kitchen. If I want a great meal, I'll usually head straight over to **Citrus** to see my friend Michel Richard. For great sushi, I go to **Hirozen** on Beverly Boulevard near the Beverly Center. When I'm not in the mood to deal with restaurants and waiters, I head over to **Jay's Jayburgers** at Virgil and Santa Monica with my son. Jay has been making hamburgers for a good 50 years now, and a Double Jayburger, with a slice of fresh tomato, a tiny spoonful of chili, and mustard thinned with the pickle juice, is a real treat for someone who cooks foie gras every day.

In winter, right after a good storm, I like to sneak off to ski at **Mount Waterman.** You might not think we have great skiing here, but Waterman has world-class snow from time to time and it's only 54 miles from the Sunset Strip! During the week, when there is nobody there, you can ski 'til you drop and be back in town before dinner.

### Henry T. Hopkins
Director, Wight Art Gallery, UCLA;
Chair, Department of Art, UCLA

Los Angeles is the future with a charm-filled past.

Since the age of three, an annual balmy evening visit to **Olvera Street** has been a must, usually after a day at the **Santa Anita Racetrack** (beer and rare roast beef on rye never tasted so good).

A weekend breakfast at **West Beach** or **Rose Cafe,** and then a walk from **Venice Beach** to the end of **Santa Monica Pier.**

Watching movies at West LA's **Royal** and **Nuart** theaters.

An evening at the **Hollywood Bowl** on a starry night, and a late dinner at **Musso and Frank Grill.**

A Beefeater Gibson straight-up (stirred not shaken) at the **Beverly Wilshire Bar.**

A little theater and dinner at **Citrus.**

An early trip on Sunday to the **Rose Bowl Flea Market,** and then escape from the heat and crowds at the **Huntington Library** (*Pinkie, Blue Boy,* and the gardens speak of our LA art beginnings).

Cocktails and dinner at the **Hotel Bel-Air** sets up any elegant late-evening adventure.

Spending the day at the **J. Paul Getty Museum** and the **Santa Monica Galleries,** followed by a dinner at **The Ivy** and, when it's in town, the spectacular **Cirque du Soleil** show.

Having my daily morning coffee at Westwood's **Gypsy Cafe** and my once-a-week favorite cheeseburger behind the bar at **Hamlet Garden,** followed by a five-minute walk to the lounge at the **Westwood Marquis** for a warmed Remy-Martin.

### Dr. Jerry Buss
Owner, Los Angeles Lakers

**Nicky Blair's,** for the *capelli di Angelo alla checca.*

**Dan Tana's,** for the fettuccine Alfredo.

**Chasen's,** for the Hobo steak.

The **Regency Club,** for every one of the delightful items they serve, especially the soufflé.

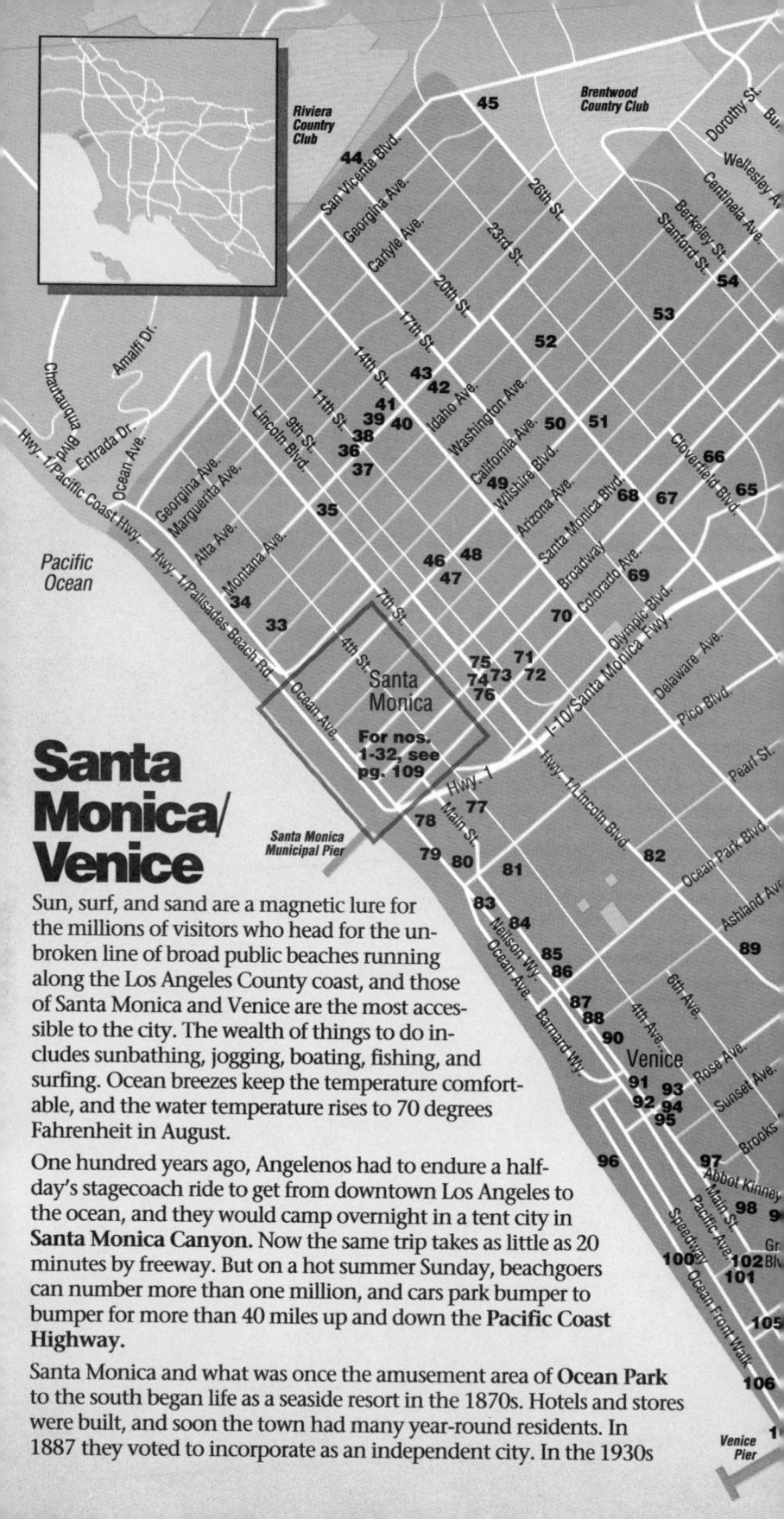

# Santa Monica/ Venice

Sun, surf, and sand are a magnetic lure for the millions of visitors who head for the unbroken line of broad public beaches running along the Los Angeles County coast, and those of Santa Monica and Venice are the most accessible to the city. The wealth of things to do includes sunbathing, jogging, boating, fishing, and surfing. Ocean breezes keep the temperature comfortable, and the water temperature rises to 70 degrees Fahrenheit in August.

One hundred years ago, Angelenos had to endure a half-day's stagecoach ride to get from downtown Los Angeles to the ocean, and they would camp overnight in a tent city in **Santa Monica Canyon.** Now the same trip takes as little as 20 minutes by freeway. But on a hot summer Sunday, beachgoers can number more than one million, and cars park bumper to bumper for more than 40 miles up and down the **Pacific Coast Highway.**

Santa Monica and what was once the amusement area of **Ocean Park** to the south began life as a seaside resort in the 1870s. Hotels and stores were built, and soon the town had many year-round residents. In 1887 they voted to incorporate as an independent city. In the 1930s

For nos. 1-32, see pg. 109

SANTA MONICA
YACHT HARBOR
SPORT FISHING BOATING
Cafes

Santa Monica led a dual life as a quiet residential suburb and a haven for offshore gambling ships. It appears in **Raymond Chandler's** novels as *Bay City*. The opening of the **Santa Monica Freeway** in 1966 permanently altered the town's sleepy tempo.

The northern sector of Santa Monica is wealthy and family oriented, while the central and southern parts of the city have attracted an influx of professionals and young singles, drawn to the many apartments and condominiums, the short commute downtown, the temperate weather, the clean air, and the abundant outdoor recreational facilities. In recent elections, these middle-class tenants rebelled against escalating rents and threats of redevelopment and voted in a city council that was dubbed the "People's Republic of Santa Monica" by those for whom rent control and curbs on building herald a communist takeover. Passions have since cooled, and the city seems to be sharing in the Westside's building frenzy.

Venice—complete with a network of canals—was built to mimic its namesake on the Adriatic. Founder **Abbot Kinney** imported Italian gondolas and planned to ignite an American Renaissance by transforming marshland into a vibrant community. Nearly a century later, surviving waterways are being refurbished along gentrified streets, and art and architecture studios thrive in the diverse coastal enclave best known for its real-life tourist attraction: the **Venice Beach boardwalk**.

*Area code 310 unless otherwise noted.*

**1 Santa Monica Pier** The smells of popcorn, cotton candy, and corn dogs, the soft resonance of the boardwalk underfoot, the calliope of the merry-go-round, and the metallic din of the penny arcade make the pier a spot for fun and nostalgia. Two piers were built side by side between 1909 and 1921, were threatened with demolition in 1973, and were badly damaged by storms in 1983. Many citizens rallied to save them, and the city now backs the **Pier Restoration Corporation's** ambitious development plan that will add to and upgrade what has survived. Coming attractions include a parking garage for the cars that now clutter the pier, a museum and a library on the pier's history, and a 13-ride fun zone with a Ferris wheel and roller coaster at the far end. Presently, food services, amusement arcades, and souvenir stores line the pier. Children will love the 70-year-old carousel with its 56 prancing horses, familiar for its supporting role in *The Sting*. Free concerts with dancing under the stars are presented on Thursday night in the summer. At night the long strand of white lights strung along the pier's edge creates a poetic landmark for those coming down the coast highway from the north. Architects **Moore Ruble Yudell** created **Carousel Park** to the south as a stepped gateway to the pier, an open theater for beach sports, and a children's park—with a dragon of river-washed granite boulders (the entrance is at Colorado and Ocean avenues). To the south, the same architects have landscaped a section of **Ocean Park Beach,** and the entire three-mile stretch of beach is being turned into the **Natural Elements Sculpture Park.** Already installed across from Pico is **Douglas Hollis'** "Wind Harp" (singing beach chairs). **Carl Cheng's** "Santa Monica Art Tool" is a concrete roller that is towed by a tractor to imprint a miniature metropolis on the sand. ◆ Carousel: Sa-Su 10AM-5PM. Party rentals: 394.7554

There is one police officer for every 432 people in Los Angeles.

Restaurants/Clubs: Red     Hotels: Blue
Shops/ 🌳 Outdoors: Green     Sights/Culture: Black

**1 South Bay Bicycle Trail** This beachside trail runs from the pier 22 miles south to the city of Torrance. ♦ At Santa Monica pier

**2 Santa Monica Freeway** Known as the "Christopher Columbus Transcontinental Highway," this highway sweeps through a curved tunnel from the Pacific Coast Highway, setting you on a dramatic new course. It's as exciting a way to begin a cross-country journey as on the long-lamented Super Chief train.

**3 Coral Reef Restaurant & Bar** $ A casual restaurant that welcomes beachgoers has replaced the respected **Opera** at this strategic location kitty-corner from the pier. The wide-ranging menu of pasta, sandwiches, and 40-ounce porterhouse steak for two, plus an oyster bar, is offered in an amateur, slapdash, California/Italian decor. ♦ Eclectic ♦ Daily 11AM-2AM. 1551 Ocean Ave. 393.9224

**3 Ivy at the Shore** ★★$$$ This informal oceanfront version of the more stylish Ivy in West Hollywood is spacious and airy, with big rattan chairs and an outdoor terrace. The menu includes crab cakes, grilled fresh fish, steaks, pasta, and salads. It's a good place to show to out-of-town visitors looking for the elusive "LA lifestyle." ♦ California ♦ M-F 11:30AM-11PM; Sa 11AM-11PM; Su 11AM-10PM. 1541 Ocean Ave. 393.3113

**4 i. Cugini** $ Owned by the same successful restaurateurs who opened **Water Grill** downtown and **Ocean Ave. Seafood** down the street, this restaurant has two personalities. Inside it's noisy and clanging at night, while an outdoor patio—facing Palisades Park and the Pacific—is quiet and candlelit. The veal chops, sea bass, and spaghetti with seafood are popular. The decor is turn-of-the-century Northern Italian, with mahogany wainscoting, marble accents, and cove ceilings. A lobby bakery sells fresh rosemary breadsticks, spinach bread, and an olive puree that diners lather onto their bread. ♦ Italian ♦ M-Th 11:30AM-10:30PM; F-Sa 11:30AM-11:30PM; Su 11AM-10:30PM. 1501 Ocean Ave. 451.4595

**5 Santa Monica Place** Architect **Frank Gehry's** 1979 to 1981 design of this huge white skylit galleria features three levels of shops. The cutaway facade with its balcony views of the ocean, the mesh screen on the parking garage, and the asymmetrical plan show that an architectural intelligence rather than a cookie cutter was involved. **Robinson's** and **The Broadway** anchor the complex, which includes **Eddie Bauer, Compagnie BX** (**Michael Glasser's** boutique), **Natural Wonders, Cotton Kids,** more than a dozen specialty carts selling everything from candles to jewelry, and 150 other stores. The **USC School of Fine Arts** shows innovative Southern California artists in its **Atelier.** ♦ M-Sa 10AM-9PM; Su 11AM-9PM. Bounded by Broadway, Colorado Ave, and Second and Fourth Sts. 394.5451

**6 Carmel Hotel** $ This well-kept economy hotel is close to Santa Monica Place. ♦ 201 Broadway. 451.2469

**7 Ye Olde King's Head** $ You'll find this bar to be a convincing facsimile of an English pub, complete with darts, fish and chips, and warm beer. It's popular with the local British colony. ♦ English ♦ M-Th 11AM-11PM, bar until 1AM; F-Sa 11AM-midnight; Su noon-11:30PM. 116 Santa Monica Blvd. 451.1402

**7 Ye Olde King's Head Shoppe** Homesick Brits know to come here for English candies, bangers, marmalades, and biscuits, and teapot collectors will find a fabulous selection to choose from. British men's toiletries, dart supplies, and, of course, teas can be found in this quaint corner shop. ♦ M-Sa 10AM-6PM; Su noon-5PM. 132 Santa Monica Blvd. 394.8765

**8 Ocean Ave. Seafood** ★★$$ Superlative fresh fish, raw oysters, and genuine New England clam chowder are served in a yuppified Las Vegas setting. Patio dining overlooks Palisades Park. ♦ Seafood ♦ M-Th 11:30AM-4PM, 5:30-10PM; F 11:30AM-4PM, 5:30-11PM; Sa 5:30-11PM; Su 11AM-3PM, 5-10PM. 1401 Ocean Ave. 394.5669

## Santa Monica/Venice

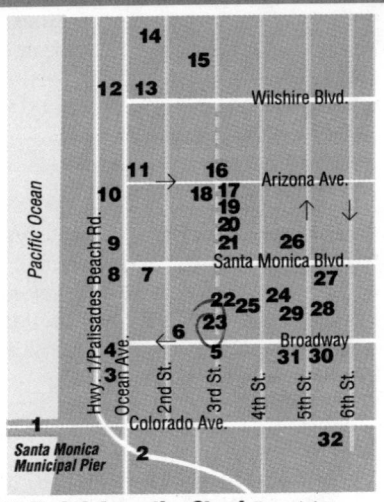

**9 Visitor's Information Stand** Free sightseeing maps and bus and tour information are available here. ♦ Daily 10AM-4PM. Ocean Ave at Santa Monica Blvd. 393.7593

**10 Art Safaris Lorel Cornman** organizes tours of the best of LA's contemporary art scene. Small groups are escorted by knowledgeable guides in a limo or minivan to selected galleries and studios. Join an existing tour or call in advance for one that is tailored to your special interests. ♦ 1341 Ocean Ave. 458.8028

**10 Shangri-la Hotel** $$$ Like the monastery in the classic 1937 movie, this is a streamline moderne gem, and—with its view over **Palisades Park** and the ocean—it's almost as idyllic. There's no lounge or bar, just a quiet, unassuming lobby. Rooms and suites have been remodeled with a clean-edged '30s look, including Deco posters, grays and pinks, and frosted glass. Most have ocean views; many

have sundecks. Prices are very reasonable and it's within walking distance of shops and the beach. ♦ 1301 Ocean Ave. 394.2791

**11 Camera Obscura** Nearby the visitors information stand in the **Senior Recreation Center** is a quiet upstairs room where startling projections of the outside world appear on a circular white surface. ♦ Daily 10AM-4PM. 1450 Ocean Ave. 394.1227

**12 Palisades Park** The steep, crumbly cliffs along the edge of the ocean are called the Palisades. It's a traditional spot for Angelenos to watch the sunset fade over the ocean; the park is one of the oldest and best maintained in the city. Its towering palms and semitropical trees form beautiful bowers for strolling or jogging, as well as a haven for the elderly—who gossip and play chess—and for the homeless. Steps lead down to the beach. ♦ Ocean Ave from Colorado Blvd to Adelaide Dr

Within Palisades Park:

**Palisades Park Gates** The Craftsman-style field stone gates, made in 1912 and decorated

with tiles by **Ernest Batchelder** of Pasadena, are worth a visit. ♦ Ocean Ave at Wilshire Blvd

**13 Miramar Sheraton Hotel** $$$ This luxury resort hotel is popular with Japanese and European tourists. The enormous Moreton Bay fig tree in the center courtyard was planted in the 19th century. **Garbo, Bogart,** and others have stayed in the bungalows. ♦ 101 Wilshire Blvd. 394.3731, 800/325.3535; fax 458.7912

**14 Radisson Huntley Hotel** $$$ This 18-story hotel has an upstairs restaurant and great ocean views. ♦ 1111 Second St. 394.5454, 800/333.3333; fax 458.9776

Within the Radisson Huntley Hotel:

**Toppers** ★$ Located atop the hotel, this Mexican restaurant and bar has a lively happy hour crowd and a wide array of hors d'oeuvres. There's nightly musical entertainment in the bar. ♦ Mexican ♦ Daily 11:30AM-10PM. Music: 7PM-1AM. Happy hour: 4:30-7:30PM. 393.8080

**15 Michael's** ★★★★$$$ **Michael McCarty's** white-on-white restaurant pioneered the new California cuisine; now it has settled down to being an institution. The prices have been lowered and you will probably be seduced by the inventive dishes (such as grilled quail with a confit of Maui onions) made from the freshest ingredients in season—locally or from around the world. The flowery patio with its big white umbrellas (heaven for Sunday brunch) and the dining room that doubles as one of LA's better contemporary art galleries (works by **David Hockney** and **Jasper Johns** have graced these walls) are a matchless setting for the rich and beautiful in fashionably casual attire. A meal here is a magical experience. ♦ California ♦ Tu 6:30-10PM; W-F noon-2PM, 6:30-10PM; Sa 6:30-10PM. 1147 Third St. 451.0843

**16 Third Street Promenade** This three-block pedestrian street with its faded stucco facades has been landscaped (with topiary dinosaur fountains) and given a major facelift, revealing such architectural gems as the **Keller Building** restored by **Frank Dimster** (at Third and Broadway), the **Europa** (at Third and Wilshire), and the **W.T. Grant Building** (1300 block of Third). Architect **Johannes Van Tilburg** designed the block at Third and Arizona streets in the style of the Viennese Werkstatte. The promenade is home to the best specialty bookstores west of New York's SoHo, including **Arcana Books on the Arts** (No. 1229, 458.1499), as well as two rare bookdealers, **Kenneth Karmiole** (No. 1225, 451.4342) and **Krown & Spellman** (No. 1243, 395.0300). The outdoor walking mall used to roll up after dark. But a bustling nightlife now thrives, due to the opening of 22 movie screens as well as several new restaurants and bars—many with sidewalk patios. Currently the shops are a mixed bag of everything from **W.F. Woolworth** to optical boutiques and New Age-crystal shops. Most are open late. On Wednesday the area is animated by a farmer's market on the 200 to 400 blocks of Arizona. ♦ Third St (between Broadway and Wilshire Blvd)

**16 Congo Square** A funky, hip, and casual coffeehouse popular with chess players, readers, the politically correct, and browsers from the nearby art and architectural bookstore, Congo Square offers open poetry readings Monday night and live music weekend nights. ♦ M-Th, Su 8AM-2AM; F-Sa 8AM-3AM. 1238 Third St Promenade. 395.5606

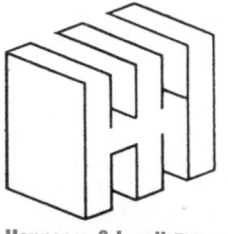

**16 Hennessy & Ingall** This is LA's best resource for books and magazines on art, architecture, and design, with a spiky Constructivist facade designed by **Morphosis**. ♦ M-W 10AM-6PM; Th-F 10AM-7PM; Sa 10AM-5PM; Su noon-4PM. 1254 Third St Promenade. 458.9074

**16 Krown & Spellman** Shop here for classic, medieval, and Renaissance books. ♦ M-Sa 10AM-5PM. 1243 Third St Promenade. 395.0300

Legend has it that Santa Monica was named by Father Juan Crespi. The area's spring waters reminded him of the tears shed by St. Monica when her son, later known as St. Augustine, turned to Christianity.

**17 Pyramid Music**  This offbeat record shop offers hard-to-find new and used compact discs, cassettes, and albums, as well as popular hits. ♦ M-Th 11AM-11PM; F-Sa 11AM-midnight; Su noon-10PM. 1340 Third St Promenade. 393.5877

**18 Legends Sports Bar and Restaurant**  $ An offshoot of the popular Long Beach sports bar founded by former rugby player **John Morris** and Rams All Pro **Dennis Harrah,** this spot has sidewalk dining and the same menu (basic American fare and party-animal drinks), but fewer rowdy drinkers and television screens. ♦ American ♦ M-W, Su 11:30AM-10PM; Th 11:30AM-11PM; F-Sa 11:30AM-midnight. Bar until 2AM. 1311 Third St Promenade. 451.2332

**19 Nature's Own Jeffrey** and **Leslie Marshall** moved their shop from Main Street to the currently booming Third Street Promenade. They still sell fossils, minerals, and crystals in jewelry and in large-size samples, but the merchandise has been downgraded, with fewer high-quality, high-priced items and a much lower inventory. ♦ M-Th, Su 11:30AM-11PM; F-Sa noon-midnight. 1334 Third St Promenade. 576.0883

**20 Midnight Special Bookstore**  The specialties are politics, sociology, and literature. Call for information on readings. ♦ M-Th 10:30AM-9PM; F-Sa 10:30AM-11PM; Su 1-10PM. 1318 Third St Promenade. 393.2923

**21 African Arts Etc.**  The trend in African Kente cloth is even showing up on tuxedo cummerbunds, and business is booming at this shop, which sells more traditional versions of Central and West African arts and crafts. Textiles, jewelry, and a wide selection of masks are all sold to benefit **The Pygmy Fund.** ♦ M-Th 10AM-10PM; F 10AM-11PM; Sa 10AM-1AM; Su noon-11PM. 1344 Third St Promenade. 393.3212

**22 Yankee Doodles**  $ Adults like the billiards parlor, restaurant, and bar, but the place is wholesome enough for kids, who while away the time at the Foosball and golfing machine. Music blares in the two-level space offering 29 pool tables, TV screens, and a menu of tostada salad, pork chops, pasta, and barbecued ribs. ♦ American ♦ M-Sa 11AM-2AM; Su 10AM-2AM. 1410 Third St Promenade. 394.4632

**23 Gallery Gourmet**  $ A dozen take-out kiosks, sidewalk seating, and cuisine that ranges from burgers to sushi are found in this indoor alleyway. French-fry lovers travel great distances to munch on **Benita's Frites,** where crisp, twice-fried Belgian potatoes are served in big paper cones with a choice of 22 dips—from fresh dill sour cream to honey mustard. ♦ Eclectic ♦ M 11:30AM-8PM; Tu-Th 11:30AM-10PM; F-Sa 11:30AM-midnight; Su 11:30AM-9PM. 1437 Third St Promenade. 458.2889

**23 Broadway Deli ★$$ Steven Erlich** designed this stripped Deco interior of stylish simplicity that links the restaurant with the bar and the shopping area (bakery, grocery, and wine shop). They serve sandwiches, salads, grills, and deli basics, and there's a good choice of beers and wines by the glass. ♦ American ♦ Restaurant: M-Th 7AM-midnight; F 7AM-1AM; Sa 8AM-1AM; Su 8AM-midnight. Stores: M-F 10AM-10PM; Sa 8AM-10PM; Su 8AM-9PM. 1457 Third St Promenade. 451.0616

**23 Remi ★★★$$$** The cool, sophisticated interior in this restaurant was designed by **Adam Tihany** in 1990. Chef **Francesco Antonucci** offers the most authentic Venetian food in LA, served by an unusually civilized staff. *Bigoli* (whole-wheat linguine with red onions and anchovies), squid in its ink with polenta, and sweet-and-sour duck have been acclaimed. ♦ Italian ♦ M-Th, Su 11:30AM-10:30PM; F-Sa 11:30AM-11PM. 1451 Third St Promenade. 393.6545

### Santa Monica/Venice

**23 Broadway Bar & Grill ★★$$** Those who left their heart in San Francisco can reclaim it here. The food, service, and decor are delightfully old-fashioned at this bar and grill. ♦ American ♦ M-Th, Su 11:30AM-11PM; F-Sa 11AM-2AM. 1460 Third St (at Broadway). 393.4211

**24 Fama ★★$$ Hans** and **Mary (Fama) Röckenwanger** opened this spin-off from their Venice original, and it's a big success. **David Kellen** has opened up the restaurant to the street through a big picture window, creating a stylized forest—a blond plywood version of the Expressionist set for *The Cabinet of Dr. Caligari.* The menu includes such delights as broad noodles with duck confit and shiitake mushrooms, roasted pork loin with toasted ricotta ravioli, and walnut plum tart. ♦ California ♦ M-F 11:30AM-2:30PM, 6-10PM; Sa-Su 5:30-11PM. 1416 Fourth St. 458.6704

---

The first public defender in the United States, Walton J. Wood, began his practice in LA on 13 June 1913.

---

The nation's first chinchilla farms opened in Los Angeles in 1923.

**25 Border Grill** ★★$$ The decor is half Mexican cantina, half punk nightclub; and the place vibrates with sound and color. Designed by **Josh Schweitzer** in 1990, this is a showcase for the inventive cuisine of chefs **Mary Sue Miliken** and **Susan Fenniger**. Shrimp ceviche, bread soup, braised duck, and lamb tacos are standouts here. There are communal tables for single diners and those without reservations. ♦ Mexican ♦ M-Th 11:30AM-2:30PM, 5:30-10:30PM; F 11:30AM-3PM, 5:30PM-midnight; Sa 11:30AM-3PM, 5PM-midnight; Su 11:30AM-3PM, 5-10PM. 1445 Fourth St. 451.1655

**26 James Corcoran Gallery** Contemporary Southern California artists, including **Ed Ruscha, Joe Goode,** and **Ken Price,** are showcased here. ♦ Tu-F 10AM-6PM; Sa 11AM-5PM. 1327 Fifth St. 451.4666

**27 The British Raaj** ★$$$ Traditional Indian food such as lamb Bombay and chicken Madras is served in charming surroundings. ♦ Indian ♦ M-F 11:30AM-1:45PM, 5:30-10PM; Sa-Su 5:30-10PM. 504 Santa Monica Blvd. 393.9472

## Santa Monica/Venice

**27 Axe Cafe** ★★$ A small cafe arranged like a hip coffeehouse, Axe offers great homemade food for sit down and takeout. Plate-size nine-grain pancakes served with genuine maple syrup and excellent coffees make it a popular breakfast spot, and fresh breads, desserts, soups, vegetable pie, and gourmet sandwiches (try the grilled spinach and goat cheese) are served all day. ♦ California ♦ M-Th 8AM-9PM; F 8AM-11PM; Sa 9AM-11PM; Su 9AM-midnight. 510 Santa Monica Blvd. 458.4414

**28 Shoshana Wayne Gallery** American and international contemporary art is shown here. Artists represented include **Fay Jones** and **Michael Schulze** (Germany), and **Kiki Smith** and **Rachel Lachowicz** (US). ♦ Tu-F 10AM-5:30PM; Sa 10AM-5PM. 1454 Fifth St. 451.3733

**29 Bikini** ★★★$$$ **John Sedlar**, executive chef of **St. Estephe,** has moved to this handsome space where he combines French technique and Latin ingredients in such light and colorful dishes as crab-stuffed chiles, shrimp with vanilla, plus the most unusual fortune cookies you've ever seen. The modern, spare, sensually detailed and subdued interior was designed by **Cheryl Brantner.** ♦ Eclectic ♦ M-F 11AM-2PM, 6-10PM; Sa 6-10PM; Su 5:30-9:30PM. 1413 Fifth St. 395.8611

**30 Fred Segal** A spin-off of its Melrose parent, this cluster of specialty stores is like a tiny contemporary village under one roof, with gourmet Italian takeout and espresso; youthful, hip, and classy upscale goods; and a DJ spinning oldies and Top-40 hits. Hats, jewelry, clothing, and scents for women, a pricey kids' shop with handmade quilts, men's clothing and gifts, and the latest eyewear are all available. ♦ M-Sa 10AM-7PM; Su noon-6PM. 500 Broadway. 393.2322

**31 Fred Segal for a Better Ecology** The burgers are turkey; the bedsheets, clothing, face products, and paints are bleach- and chemical free; and ecology and energy information is displayed alongside products, but don't confuse this complex with earthier, more bohemian stores. It is still upscale fare for environmentalists who drive Range Rovers. ♦ M-Sa 10AM-7PM; Su noon-6PM. 420 Broadway. 394.6448

Within Fred Segal for a Better Ecology:

**Phoenix Bookstore** Relocated from Santa Monica Boulevard to this open and airy space, the Phoenix Bookstore still offers a wide selection of books on Western and Eastern philosophy, metaphysics, and psychology. ♦ M-Sa 10AM-9PM; Su 10AM-6PM. 395.9516

**32 Angels Attic Museum** Miniatures, toys, and dolls are on display in this restored Victorian-style house. Tea and cookies are served from 12:30PM to 3:30PM on the porch. ♦ Admission. Th-Su 12:30-4:30PM. 516 Colorado Ave. 394.8331

**33 The Sovereign Hotel** $$ Designed by **Julia Morgan,** the architect of the Hearst Castle in San Simeon, this small Mediterranean-style hotel is a pleasant mixture of old-world charm and modern convenience. ♦ 205 Washington Ave. 395.9921, 800/331.0163; fax 458.3085

**34 Montana Avenue** If the 10 blocks from Seventh to 16th streets were to be covered in lava, future archeologists could construe the tastes of the local inhabitants from the evidence they would find. The natives were fond of personal adornment (26 women's clothing stores, 21 hair and beauty shops), cleanliness (nine laundries and cleaners), and eating (22 restaurants and gourmet takeouts). They were a generous people (19 gift boutiques), but worried about their health (12 doctors and 10 dentists). They worshipped children (six specialty stores), dogs, and cats (one each). These were probably brought to the **Aero,** a neighborhood shrine in which rows of seats face a blank white screen. Judging from the contents of the eight design stores, this region may have been settled by the English. Back to the present, the chance of seeing movie stars is highest along this strip of upscale stores. It's close to home for many of them.

**35 Marmalade** ★$ The fancy takeout food in this cozy and bustling European-style deli includes pastries, cheeses, and smoked salmon as well as homestyle treats such as cookies and chicken pot pie. There's limited cafe seating. ♦ Deli ♦ Daily 6AM-8PM. 710 Montana Ave. 395.9196

**35 Le Petit Moulin** ★$$$ Homemade pâté, roast rack of lamb, and crisp duck are served in a traditional setting. ♦ French ♦ Daily 5:30-10PM. 714 Montana Ave. 395.6619

**36 Imagine** Imported toys and gifts for children inhabit this shop. ♦ M-Sa 10AM-6PM; Su noon-5PM. 1001 Montana Ave. 395.9553

**37  Babalu** ★$ Many come here for the tropical decor, folk art on the walls, and tasty light dishes like crab cakes and shrimp quesadillas. ◆ Caribbean/Mexican ◆ Tu-Th, Su 8AM-10PM; F-Sa 8AM-11PM. 1002 Montana Ave. 395.2500

**37  Louise's Trattoria** $$ This is a favorite with the young crowd, which comes for the pizzas, calzone, *focaccia* with roasted garlic, and homemade pastas. ◆ Italian ◆ M-Sa 11AM-11PM; Su 10AM-10PM. 1008 Montana Ave. 394.8888

**37  My Father's Office** More than 20 esoteric brews are on tap in this friendly neighborhood tavern. ◆ M-F 11:30AM-2AM; Sa-Su 10AM-2AM. 1018 Montana Ave. 393.2337

**37  Palmetto** The skin, hair, and bath products are natural, homeopathic, and therapeutic, but this store is upscale, not earthy. The healthful and handsomely packaged soaps and scents attract celebrity customers such as **Demi Moore, Annette Bening, Lauren Bacall,** and **Angela Lansbury.** ◆ M-F 10AM-6PM; Sa 10AM-5:30PM. 1034 Montana Ave. 395.6687

**38  Cinzia** European country collectibles are found in this quaint shop with a rear patio displaying garden accessories. You might bump into actress **Julia Roberts** browsing through the picture frames and hand-painted tableware. ◆ M-Sa 10AM-6PM; Su noon-5PM. 1129 Montana Ave. 393.7751

**39  Weathervane** Sophisticated dressers are high on the women's sportswear by **Matsuda** and others. For the guys, there's **Weathervane for Men** at 1132 Montana Avenue (395.0397). ◆ M-Sa 10AM-6PM; Su 11AM-5PM. 1209 Montana Ave. 393.5344

**40  Nonesuch Fine Art** American paintings between World Wars, WPA Regional Art, and Social Realism are on display here. ◆ Tu-F 11AM-5:30PM; Sa 11AM-5PM. 1210C Montana Ave. 393.1245

**41  Le Marmiton** ★$ For the most elegant of picnics, or when you would love to eat in a very fine French restaurant but can't afford it, Le Marmiton is the answer. ◆ Takeout ◆ Daily 10AM-7PM. 1327 Montana Ave. 393.7716

**42  Hemisphere** Shoppers in search of the frontier look (for a price) will find tribal dhurries, textiles, jewelry, and California ranch furniture here. ◆ M-Sa 10AM-6PM. 1426 Montana Ave. 458.6853

**42  Montana Mercantile** Shelves of great kitchen equipment can be found in this stark white and glass-brick building. Cooking classes are given in back. ◆ M-F 10AM-6:30PM; Sa 10AM-6PM. 1500 Montana Ave. 451.1418

**42  Federico** Native American and Mexican textiles, antiques, and jewelry are sold here. ◆ M-Sa 10AM-6PM. 1522 Montana Ave. 458.4134

**42  Cafe Montana** ★$ This local favorite, which moved a block to larger, spiffier premises, is flooded with natural light and has a contemporary interior design by **Eddie Silkaitis.** But they've kept the same pleasing menu of soups, salads, and grilled fresh fish. Breakfasts and desserts are excellent. ◆ California ◆ Tu-Th 8AM-3PM, 5:30-9:30PM; F-Sa 8AM-3PM, 5:30-10PM; Su 8AM-3PM, 3:30-9PM. 1534 Montana Ave. 829.3990

**42  17th St. Cafe** $ This cafe took over **Cafe Montana's** old space, added pink accents, and was quickly dubbed the "Pink Shoebox" because of its rectangular dining room. The pleasant room has whitewashed brick walls and hardwood floors, and the menu offers great tortilla soup, cioppino, roasted lamb loin, and homemade desserts. Sunday brunch is also notable. Be careful of the tricky name, however: the restaurant isn't located on 17th Street, it's just east of that cross street. ◆ California ◆ M-Th 8AM-3PM, 5:30-9PM; F-Sa 8AM-3PM, 5:30-10PM; Su 9AM-3PM, 5:30-9PM. 1610 Montana Ave. 453.2771

**43  a.b.s. California** Casual and career womenswear and costume jewelry are sold here. ◆ M-Sa 10AM-7PM; Su 11AM-5PM. 1533 Montana Ave. 393.8770

# SOHO
## ON MONTANA

**43  Soho on Montana** There's no need to scour thrift and vintage clothing shops for retro-style dresses; beautiful reproductions of 1930s and '40s styles are found here. ◆ M-Sa 10AM-6PM. 1609-A Montana Ave. 451.8050

**43  Brenda Cain** Vintage clothes for men and women, including a stash of Hawaiian shirts, are available here. Their other shop at 1211 Montana Avenue specializes in vintage textile furnishings and draperies (Tu-Sa 11AM-6PM; 395.1559). ◆ M-Sa 11AM-6PM; Su noon-4:30PM. 1617 Montana Ave. 393.3298

**43  Il Fornaio** Partygivers do their shopping at this one-stop shop for seductive country breads, pastries, and pizza to go. Within the store is **Tanaka's,** for quality produce, **Ashford Flowers,** and the **LA Gourmet.** ◆ M-F 6:30AM-6:30PM; Sa 7AM-6:30PM; Su 7:30AM-4PM. 1627 Montana Ave. 458.1562

**44  La Mesa Drive** Huge Moreton Bay fig trees canopy this lovely street, which is lined with fine Spanish-Colonial style '20s houses by **John Byers.** Examples are at Nos. 1923, 2102, and 2153. Byers' own home at No. 1034 is a Monterey Colonial variant with a second-story balcony. They are all private residences.

**45  Camelions** ★★$$$ Another **John Byers** house has been converted to one of the most enchanting restaurants in LA. Small rooms are ranged around a courtyard fronting a quiet street. Chef **Steve Gonberg** prepares a mixture of old favorites and innovative fare, with a nod to French tradition. ◆ California ◆ Tu-Sa 11:30AM-2:30PM, 6-10PM; Su 11AM-2PM, 6-10PM. 246 26th St. 395.0746

**113**

**46 Tampico Tilly's** $ This restaurant is a pleasant hybrid of old Mexico and young California. ♦ Mexican ♦ M-Th, Su 11:30AM-10PM; F-Sa 11:30AM-11PM. 1025 Wilshire Blvd. 451.1769

**47 At My Place** The eclectic nightclub with a restaurant offers jazz and rhythm and blues. Call for hours and nightly performances. ♦ Cover. 1026 Wilshire Blvd. 451.8596, 451.8597

**47 Anastasia's Asylum** $ Located next door to **At My Place,** this dark, bohemian space offers an entertainment venue of a more alternative nature. Specially priced coffee and espresso are served to early morning risers and during happy hour. ♦ Coffeehouse ♦ M-Th 7AM-2AM; F-Sa 8AM-3AM; Su 8AM-1PM. 1028 Wilshire Blvd. 394.7113

**48 The Address** Make a splash without going broke at this boutique that sells slightly worn designer-label clothes. ♦ M-Sa 10AM-6PM; Su noon-5PM. 1116 Wilshire Blvd. 394.1406

**49 Verdi** ★★★$$$ **Bernard** and **Sheila Segal's** *ristorante di musica* combines sophisticated Tuscan food with excerpts from operas, operettas, and Broadway musicals sung by some of the finest young artists in the Los Angeles area. **Morphosis** converted a historic building whose exterior resembles a toy opera house, creating a marvelous fusion of theater and dining room, and a bar with excellent sight lines where you can enjoy the music for the price of a drink or a dessert. The opera murals are by **David Schorr**. You can receive their monthly newsletter or check the program when you make your reservation. ♦ Italian ♦ F-Sa 6:30PM-2AM; Su 6:30-11PM. 1519 Wilshire Blvd. 393.0706

**50 Chartreuse** ★$$ Owner/chef **Bruno Moeckli** serves such signature dishes as Roquefort soufflé and roast duck with gooseberries in a casual French setting. They have a good California wine list. ♦ Eclectic ♦ M-F 11AM-2PM, 5:30-9:30PM; Sa 5:30-9:30PM. 1909 Wilshire Blvd. 453.3333

**51 Carlos & Pepe's** $$ A favorite after-work meeting spot for the young of the Westside, this central bar serves great nachos. ♦ Mexican ♦ Daily 11:30AM-10PM. Bar: M-Th, Su until midnight, F-Sa until 1:30AM. 2020 Wilshire Blvd. 828.8903

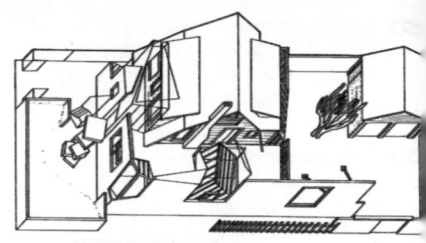

COURTESY OF FRANK GEHRY

**52 Gehry House** Renovated by the master architect himself, **Frank Gehry,** this is a mecca for students of architecture but an outrage to the neighbors. Gehry described the original Dutch-gabled cottage as "a dumb little house with charm." In 1978 he built a carapace of corrugated metal, plywood, chain link, and glass around the house (illustrated above), creating a design statement that might have been concocted by a Russian Constructivist of the early '20s. Expect some changes—Gehry has something up his sleeve. It's a private residence. ♦ 22nd St (at Washington Ave)

**53 McGinty's Irish Pub** $ Ale, music, dancing, and darts make this a cozy haven for traditionalists. Spicy curries and other Indian foods are served at long tables. ♦ Irish/Indian ♦ Daily 10:30AM-11:30PM. The bar is open until 2AM. 2615 Wilshire Blvd. 828.9839

**54 Wilshire Books** A diverse collection of new and used books can be found here. ♦ M-Sa noon-7PM; Su noon-5PM. 3018 Wilshire Blvd. 828.3115

**55 Marquis West** ★$$$ This traditional, rather formal restaurant serves consistent Southern Italian food. Some say the fried calamari is the best in LA. ♦ Italian ♦ M-F 11:30AM-2:30PM, 5:30-10:30PM; Sa 5-10:30PM; Su 4:30-9:45PM. 3110 Santa Monica Blvd. 828.4567

**56 LA Farm** ★★★$$ A wooden gate with a steer's head leads to this noisy, hip, and citified version of the rural and rustic, with stone and pine and a lovely patio surprisingly situated in an office building. **Jean-Pierre Peiny,** former chef of the genteel **La Serre,** offers braised corned beef and cabbage, but the menu is primarily cosmopolitan and worldly. Try the fresh salmon marinated in aquavit or the zucchini tempura. ♦ Eclectic ♦ M-F 11:30AM-2:30PM, 5:30-10:30PM; Sa 5:30-10:30PM. 3000 W. Olympic Blvd. 829.0600

**57 Valentino** ★★★★$$$$ Sicilian-born owner **Piero Selvaggio** is a magician, pulling truffles from his hat and surprising his devoted clientele with unfamiliar dishes from all over Italy. These have included fried squid and ricotta fritters, lobster cannelloni, and loin of beef in balsamic vinegar. He will be happy to compose a menu for a special dinner, given a week's notice. The wine list is one of the best in America, the service is warm and professional, and the decor combines elegance, comfort, and striking contemporary style. ♦ Italian ♦ M-Th, Sa, Su 5-11PM; F noon-2:30PM, 5-11PM. 3115 W. Pico Blvd. 829.4313

**57 McCabe's Guitar Shop** On weekends, there's live performances by well-known musicians. Call for show times. ♦ M-Th 10AM-10PM; F-Sa 10AM-6PM; Su 1-5PM. 3101 W. Pico Blvd. 828.4497, 828.4403 (recording)

**58 California Map Center** Owner **Sheldon Mars** has LA's best stock of maps, both local and international. ♦ M-F 8:30AM-6PM; Sa 9AM-5PM; Su noon-5PM. 3211 Pico Blvd. 829.6277

**59 Denim and Diamonds** Caught on the wings of the retro Urban Cowboy trend fueled by crossover megastar **Garth Brooks,** this nightclub is a hot dance spot for DJ-spun country-western music *and* rock 'n' roll. The basic barbecued pork, beef, and chicken is almost an afterthought—dancing the Double D Shuffle is what packs them in. The club is incongruously located in an office park. Free dancing lessons are offered nightly. ♦ M-F 11AM-2AM; Sa-Su 5PM-2AM. 3200 Ocean Park Blvd. 452.3446

**60 Il Forno** ★$$ Wonderful pizza and pasta is served in a noisy, crowded room. ♦ Italian ♦ M-Sa 11:30AM-3PM, 5:30-11PM. 2901 Ocean Park Blvd. 450.1241

**61 Typhoon** $$ The dramatic two-level space in the airport terminal, across the tarmac from **DC3** restaurant, was designed by **Grinstein-Daniels** in 1991. The eclectic, moderately priced menu is served in a cherry-paneled dining room with a mirror-glass map of the world, and on an observation terrace shaded by pierced metal silhouettes of vintage planes. ♦ Asian ♦ M-F 11:30AM-10:30PM; Sa 4:30-10:30PM; Su 11AM-10:30PM. 3221 Donald Douglas Loop South (at Bundy Dr)

**62 Museum of Flying** Aeronautical enthusiasts will enjoy the close-up views of vintage planes, including a 1924 **Douglas World Cruiser** and a **DC3** that were built on this site before Douglas Aircraft merged with McDonnell and moved to Long Beach. Also on display here are **Spitfires** and **Mustangs,** the workhorse fighters of the Second World War. There's a theater, store, and views out over Santa Monica Airport, from which these veterans still fly. ♦ Admission. W-Su 10AM-5PM. 2772 Donald Douglas Loop. 392.8822

**62 DC3** ★$$$ The stunning interior of this restaurant, which adjoins the **Museum of Flying** and overlooks the airport, was designed by **Charles Arnoldi** in 1989. The sun-filled room is a delightful setting for lunch, though executive planes taking off are better glimpsed through glass than from the terrace. At night it becomes a singles scene with a lively bar and a lot of table-hopping, which distracts from the long waits and erratic food. There's disco dancing Wednesday to Saturday. ♦ California ♦ Restaurant: Tu-F 11:30AM-10PM; Sa 6-10PM. Disco: W-Sa 10PM-2AM. 2800 Donald Douglas Loop North. 399.2323

---

**staurants/Clubs:** Red    **Hotels:** Blue
**ops/ ♣ Outdoors:** Green    **Sights/Culture:** Black

**63 Sun Tech Town Houses** **Urban Forms** designed this striking high-tech terrace of condominiums in 1981. A similarly scaled group, with a false classical facade, is located at 2332 28th Street. These are private residences. ♦ 2433 Pearl St

**64 Maryland Crab House** ★★$$ Fresh seafood from the East is the specialty, including spicy steamed crabs (which you crack with a hammer, protected by a bib), bluefish, scrod, oysters, and shad roe in season. ♦ Seafood ♦ Tu-Th noon-2:30PM, 5-9PM; F noon-2:30PM, 5-10PM; Sa noon-10PM; Su noon-9PM. 2424 Pico Blvd. 450.5555

## Santa Monica/Venice

**65 Opus** ★★★$$$ Chef **Eberhard Muller** of New York's famed **La Bernardin** has come to LA to open this quiet, expensive, grown-up restaurant. Extraordinary fish and seafood dishes—such as the trout soup with Riesling and spring vegetables, or the hand-pounded carpaccio of tuna—are served in a luxurious room covered in curving wood, like an elegant yacht. It is located in a new, spiritless office complex where lunch diners can glimpse a man-made lake. ♦ Seafood/French ♦ M-F 11:45AM-2:15PM, 6-10:30PM; Sa 6-10:30PM. 2425 W. Olympic Blvd. 829.2112

**66 Cutter's** $$$ This stylish hangout occupies a corner of the **Colorado Place** atrium and offers an eclectic range of grills, grazing fare (such as pizzas and pastas), and vintage wine by the glass. Colorado Place has been expanded by **Maguire Thomas Partners** and may soon fulfill its long neglected potential. ♦ California ♦ M-Th 11:15AM-10PM; F 11:15AM-11PM; Sa 5-10PM; Su 5-9:30PM. 2425 Colorado Ave. 453.3588

**67 Daniel Weinberg Gallery** Paintings, drawings, and sculpture by young and established New York artists such as **Sol Lewitt** and **Jeff Koons** are exhibited here. ♦ Tu-Sa 11AM-5PM. 2032 Broadway. 453.0180

**68 Santa Monica Gateway Hotel** $$ The new 125-room, four-story hotel, centrally located at a busy intersection, is a modern version of the familiar Best Western. Suites are available, too. ♦ 1920 Santa Monica Blvd. 829.9100, 800/528.1234; fax 829.9211 .

**69 Richard Kuhlenschmidt** Conceptual and post-conceptual American artists, including **Cindy Bernard, Douglas Huebler,** and **Matt Mullican,** are shown here. ♦ Tu-Sa 11AM-5:30PM. 1630 17th St. 450.2010

**70 Santa Monica Seafood** Shop here for the largest, freshest selections of fish outside of downtown. ♦ M-F 9:30AM-7PM; Sa 9:30AM-6PM. 1205 Colorado Blvd. 393.5244

**71 Roy Boyd Gallery** Art dealer Boyd exhibits mixed media by emerging Los Angeles and New York artists. ♦ Tu-Sa 10AM-5PM. 1547 10th St. 394.1210

**72 G. Ray Hawkins Gallery** Hawkins opened the first LA gallery exclusively devoted to photography 17 years ago, long before collecting the medium as an art investment was a trend. He offers rare, vintage, and contemporary artworks, including photographs by **Paul Outerbridge, Edward Steichen, Edward S. Curtis,** and **Robert Mapplethorpe.** ♦ Tu-Sa 10AM-5:30PM. 908 Colorado Ave. 394.5558

**72 Fred Hoffman Gallery** Sophie Calle, John McCracken, Manuel Ocampo, and Vernon Fisher are among the American and European artists shown here. ♦ Tu-F 9:30AM-5:30PM; Sa 10AM-5PM. 912 Colorado Ave. 394.4199

## Santa Monica/Venice

**72 Linda Cathcart** The former director of Houston's Contemporary Art Museum shows the work of **Cindy Sherman, Robert Longo,** and **Louise Bourgeois.** ♦ Tu-Sa 11AM-5PM. 924 Colorado Blvd. 451.1121

**73 Dorothy Goldeen Gallery** Contemporary painting, sculpture, and works on paper by emerging and mature artists, including **Nam June Paik, Ed Paschke,** and **Robert Arneson,** are exhibited here. ♦ Tu-Sa 10:30AM-5:30PM. 1547 Ninth St. 395.0222

**74 Zipangu** $ With nearly invisible signage and a spare, minimal interior, this restaurant comes off as serene to some, stark to others. Set on an unlikely corner, Zipangu (which means "Italian" in Japanese) offers even more unlikely cuisine. The chefs combine the dishes of both countries to create an unusual menu that includes spaghetti *pescatore* and impeccably fresh sushi. ♦ Italian/Japanese ♦ M-Th 11:30AM-2PM, 5:30-10:30PM; F 11:30AM-2PM, 5:30PM-12:30AM; Sa 5:30PM-12:30AM. 802 Broadway. 395.3082

**75 Warszawa** ★★$$ Borscht, hunter's stew, and cheesecake are just some of the hearty, homemade peasant dishes served in these warm, friendly surroundings. ♦ Polish ♦ Daily 5:30-10:30PM. 1414 Lincoln Blvd. 393.8831

**76 Bay Cities Importing** Mediterranean foods, a deli counter, sandwiches, pastas, cheeses, wines, and extra-virgin olive oils make this a one-stop shop for creating your favorite meal. ♦ M-Sa 8AM-7PM; Su 8AM-6PM. 1517 Lincoln Blvd. 395.8279

**77 Guest Quarters** $$$ Sweeping views, a terrace restaurant, an outdoor pool, and fitness facilities are some of the amenities offered at this new all-suite hotel. It's a great buy for families, since the suites sleep four. ♦ 1707 Fourth St. 395.3332, 800/424.2900; fax 458.6493

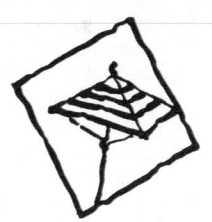

**78 Loew's Santa Monica Beach Hotel** $$$$ This new luxury hotel high above the beach and looking far out to sea is located near the Santa Monica Pier. There are 350 rooms and suites flanking a lofty glass-roofed atrium, Victorian inspiration, out of which flow the restaurants and a half-covered pool. There's a fitness center run by trainer-to-the-stars **Jackson Sousa,** and an array of business facilities and meeting spaces. The **Coast Cafe** (★$$) has an ocean view and offers lighter fare all day. **Riva** (★$$) features California/Italian cuisine in a stylish decor. ♦ 1700 Ocean Ave. 458.6700, 800/223.0888; fax 458.0020

**79 Pacific Shores Hotel** $$$ The rooms on the top three floors of this eight-story hotel have ocean views. ♦ 1819 Ocean Ave. 451.8711, 800/622.8711; fax 394.6657

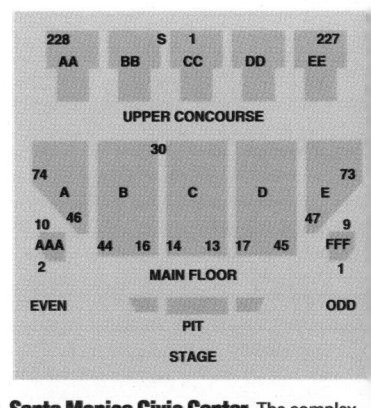

**80 Santa Monica Civic Center** The complex includes the **Santa Monica Civic Auditorium** (see the plan above), which presents big-name rock and jazz concerts, exhibitions, and trade shows. ♦ 1855 Main St (box office on Main St at Pico Blvd) 393.9961

**81 Vidiots** Independent, foreign, and cult movies are for rent and sale. ♦ M-Th, Su 11AM-11PM; F-Sa 11AM-midnight. 302 Pico Blvd. 392.8504

**82 Marlow's Books** New and used books of all kinds, plus sheet music and magazines are sold here. ♦ M-F 10AM-8PM; Sa 10AM-6PM; Su noon-6PM. 2314 Lincoln Blvd. 392.9161

**83 Main Street** Slightly south of Santa Monica proper is **Ocean Park,** once a seaside resort with thousands of tiny beach cottages and a large Coney Island-style amusement park. The neighborhood now includes an active shopping and trendy dining area for several blocks of Main Street—a pleasant place for walking and window-shopping. There is a high concentration of restaurants, many with rear patios or sidewalk seating.

**84 Pioneer Boulangerie and Restaurant** $$
There's a casual sit-down restaurant serving Continental fare; a take-out gourmet deli with hot Basque roasted chickens; a cafeteria buffet on a patio; and a European-style candy, wine, and coffee-bean shop, all surrounding a busy (take a number) bakery. ♦ International ♦ Restaurant: Tu-Su 11AM-3PM, 4:30-9PM. Cafeteria/deli: daily 7AM-7PM. Bakery: M-Th 7AM-8PM; F-Su 7AM-9PM. 2012 Main St. 399.1405

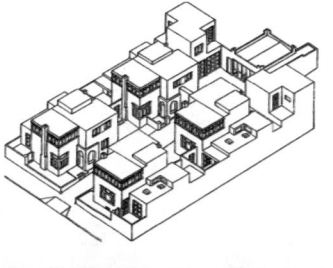

**85 Horatio West Court** Located one block off Ocean Park Boulevard near Neilson Avenue, these impressively modern two-story apartments (illustrated above), designed by **Irving Gill** in 1919, were far ahead of their time. They are private residences. ♦ 140 Hollister Ave

**85 Gilliland's** ★★$$ The restaurant is very popular for its unexpected menu, which ranges from samosas to yellowtail in tomatillo sauce to potato pancakes and Irish stew. ♦ Eclectic ♦ M-F 11:30AM-2:30PM, 5:30-10:30PM; Sa-Su 5:30-10:30PM. 2424 Main St. 392.3901

**86 Edgemar** Developer **Abby Sher** commissioned **Frank Gehry** to design this urban village in 1989. The mixed-use development points up the numbing mediocrity of the minimalls elsewhere in the city. Gehry has created not a facade with a car park in front, but a cluster of unique sculptural forms (high-tech, streamline, and minimalist) that relate well to neighboring buildings and define a series of pedestrian spaces. An eclectic mix of businesses occupies the development, including an art museum, an upscale restaurant, and retail stores offering functional art, pricey retro children's wear, business services, records, and **Ben & Jerry's** ice cream. ♦ 2435 Main St

Within Edgemar:

**Röckenwagner** ★★★$$$ Moved from Venice Beach to this more upscale location, Röckenwagner offers the same wonderfully subtle yet simple cooking. **Hans** and **Mary Röckenwagner** are personally involved, and it shows. Hans and **David Kellen** designed the unique space that combines both modern and homey elements with sleek blonde wood and brick and log accents. The design echoes the larger villagelike complex. Specialties have included herb-crusted tuna in rice paper and roast veal sirloin. A takeout deli offers breads by a German master baker and excellent plum streusel. ♦ California ♦ M-Th 8-11AM, 11:30AM-2:30PM, 6-10PM; F 8-11AM, 11:30AM-2:30PM, 6-10:30PM; Sa 9AM-2:30PM, 5:30-10:30PM; Su 9AM-2:30PM, 5:30-10PM. 399.6504

**Gallery of Contemporary Photography** Owner and photographer **Rose Shoshana** exhibits works for their visual and emotional appeal, and stages both group and solo exhibitions. New and established photographers, including **Antonin Kratochvil** and **MacDuff Everton**, have shown here. ♦ Tu-Su 11AM-7PM. 2431 B Main St. 399.4282

**Harriet Dorn Children** Expensive and arty children's clothes and furniture—including the one-of-a-kind hats, shirts, sweaters, and quilts—are sold in this whimsical shop named for a stylish grandmother. ♦ M-Sa 11AM-6PM; Su noon-5PM. 2439A Main St. 392.6889

**Piece of Mind** The tiny, funky shop offers a vast selection of domestic and imported music—everything from new jazz to industrial rock, ethnic folk, and world music—in all formats (CDs, cassettes, vinyl, and video). ♦ Tu-Th 2-10PM; F-Sa noon-10PM; Su noon-8PM. 2431C Main St. 399.8297

**Santa Monica Museum of Art** Designers **Paul Lubowicki** and **Susan Lanier** transformed this egg-processing plant in 1989 into a sympathetic showcase for a diversity of contemporary art shows and events. Director **Thomas Rhoads** alternates between LA and European artists, photographers, and performers. ♦ Admission. W-Th, Su 11AM-6PM; F-Sa 11AM-10PM. 2437 Main St. 399.2801

**86 Gallery of Functional Art** Artist- and architect-designed objects, lighting, and environments are showcased here. ♦ Tu-Sa 11AM-7PM; Su noon-6PM. 2429 Main St. 450.2827

**86 Highlights** Owners **Ron Rezek** and **Lori Thomsen** have displayed their choice of the "50 best lights in the world"—and can order up many more. Call ahead if you plan to come at lunchtime. ♦ M-F 10AM-6PM. 2447 Main St. 450.5886

**86 Art Options** Designer **Brian Murphy** created a tropical industrial interior for this contemporary crafts store. ♦ Tu-Sa 10AM-6PM; Su noon-6PM. 2507 Main St. 392.9099

**87 Heritage Square Museum** Period rooms, local archives, and photographs are housed in this restored 19th-century house designed in 1984 by **Sumner P. Hunt** for **Roy Jones**, a son of one of the city's founders. ♦ Free. Th-Su 11AM-4PM; Su noon-4PM. 2612 Main St. 392.8537

**Restaurants/Clubs:** Red  **Hotels:** Blue
**Shops/ 🌳 Outdoors:** Green  **Sights/Culture:** Black

**87 Monica's on Main** $ Casual, homestyle cooking is served in this restored 1906 house that was built for a former mayor of Santa Monica. ◆ American ◆ Daily 11AM-11PM. 2640 Main St. 392.4956

**87 Bootz** Urban cowboys shop here for exotic boots in any skin you can think of. ◆ M-W, Su 10AM-7PM; Th-Sa 10AM-11PM. 2654 Main St. 396.2466

**87 Starbucks Coffee Company** Taking its name from the coffee-loving first mate in **Herman Melville's** *Moby Dick,* this Seattle-based company sold coffee beans long before doing so was trendy. The finest arabica beans from

## Santa Monica/Venice

around the world are sold in this coffee bar visited at all hours by devotees who want the best fresh ground. ◆ M-Th, Su 6AM-11PM; F-Sa 6AM-midnight. 2671 Main St. 392.3559

**88 Merlin McFly's Magical Bar and Grill** Magic acts every night but Monday enliven this bar. ◆ American ◆ M-F 5PM-1:30AM; Sa-Su 11:30AM-1:30AM. 2702 Main St. 392.8468

**88 Max Studio** Trendy 20-year-olds shop here for **Leon Max's** casuals, suits, and special dresses. ◆ M-Sa 11AM-7PM; Su 11AM-5PM. 2712 Main St. 396.3963

**88 Paris 1900** This shop sells museum-quality antique clothing, by appointment only. ◆ 2703 Main St. 396.0405

**88 Chinois on Main** ★★★★$$$$ **Wolfgang Puck's** noisy, crowded, and expensive restaurant is not to be missed by anyone who loves inventive cuisine in the most stylish of settings. Puck's creations fuse East and West: try the warm curried oysters, Mongolian lamb, or ginger-stuffed whole sizzling catfish with sweet pepper sauce. Desserts are special here, the standout being an assortment of three *petits crème brûlées.* **Barbara Lazaroff** (Puck's wife) did the wonderful decor, which incorporates a fine screen by **Miriam Wosk.** Try for a table away from the open kitchen. ◆ French/Chinese ◆ M-Tu, Sa 6-10:30PM; W-F 11:30AM-2PM, 6-10:30PM; Su 5:30-10PM. 2709 Main St. 392.9025, 392.3037

**88 Main Street Gallery** Shop here for Japanese antiques, folk art, and **Issey Miyake's Plantation** clothes for women. ◆ Daily 11AM-6PM. 208 Pier Ave. 399.4161

**88 Wildflour Boston Pizza** $$ They have whole wheat crust as well as white, and a huge spinach salad loaded with avocado and artichoke hearts. ◆ Pizza ◆ M-Th 11AM-10:30PM; F-Sa 11AM-11:30PM; Su noon-10PM. 2807 Main St. 392.3300. Also at: 2616 Lincoln Blvd. 392.8551; 13723 Fiji Way, Marina del Rey. 821.3666

**89 Galaxy Cafe** $ The huge portions of hearty, healthful food, including chicken stir-fry, pepper garlic prawns, and salads, are served in a streamlined '50s coffee shop. ◆ Eclectic ◆ M-Th 11:30AM-2:30PM, 5-10:30PM; F 11:30AM-2:30PM, 5-11:30PM; Sa 5-11:30PM; Su 5-10:30PM. 2920 Lincoln Blvd. 392.9436

**90 The Fish Company** ★★$$ This fish eater's haven captures the seafaring ambience of the Chesapeake Bay and the Pacific Northwest. A big bucket of steamed mussels, chunky clam chowder, and fried calamari are great openers for swordfish, mahimahi (Hawaiian tuna), orange roughy, and fresh Pacific salmon that are broiled on an open mesquite grill. It's a popular destination for hungry Japanese tourists who arrive by the busloads. ◆ Seafood ◆ M-Th, Su 11:30AM-10PM; F-Sa 11:30AM-11PM. 174 Kinney St (at Main St). 392.8366

**90 The Buttery** Stop by this bakery for croissants and coffee, muffins, chocolate chip cookies, and La Brea bread. ◆ M 7AM-3:30PM; Tu-Su 7AM-5PM. 2906 Main St. 399.3000

**90 Homeworks** Novel gifts and housewares are sold here. ◆ M-Sa 10AM-7PM; Su 11AM-6PM. 2923 Main St. 396.0101

**90 The Oar House** $ A popular haunt among local beer addicts and rambunctious collegiates, this watering hole lives up to its uproarious reputation. Music is programmed by DJs, but live bands perform most Wednesday evenings. ◆ M-Sa 11:30AM-2AM; Su 11:30AM-midnight. 2941 Main St. 296.4725

**91 Schatzi on Main** $$ **Arnold Schwarzenegger** and **Maria Shriver's** new restaurant/bar is casual, comfortable, and cheery, with colorfully upholstered banquettes, brick cove ceilings, and a garden patio. The menu features lots of homey food, and veers from his contributions (bratwurst on a pretzel roll) to hers (chicken pot pie) to crab blintzes with tomato salsa. The food doesn't match the celebrity draw, but try the excellent homemade corned-beef hash for breakfast or the linguine with shrimp, mussels, and calamari for dinner. ◆ Eclectic ◆ M-F 8AM-2:30PM, 6-10PM; Sa-Su 9AM-3PM, 6-10PM. 3110 Main St. 399.4800

# Venice

At the turn of the century, tobacco magnate **Abbot Kinney** tried to create a model community fashioned after Venice, Italy, that would spur Americans to achieve their own cultural renaissance. A network of canals drained the marshy land and fed into the Grand Lagoon, and a three-day opening celebration, beginning on 4 July 1905, featured gondola and camel rides. The community was briefly self-governing, but the developers concentrated on oil exploitation and honky-tonk entertainment. In 1925 residents voted for annexation by the city of LA, which soon paved over all but three of the original 16 miles of canals and closed the speakeasies and gambling houses that thrived during Prohibition. The arcades along Windward Avenue and a few beleaguered waterways to the south are all that survive of Kinney's grand design.

But Venice and neighboring **Ocean Park** continued to flourish as "Coney Island West," defying the bluenoses and devastation by storm and fire. Flanking the boardwalks and several piers were Arabian bathhouses and Egyptian bazaars, roller coasters, and freak shows. As the area became more raffish and run-down, it lured those who couldn't afford to live—or didn't feel at home—elsewhere. Beats gave way to hippies, Hell's Angels to drug gangs; the elderly, artists, urban pioneers, and the adventurous all settled here in a crazy quilt of humanity. The diversity is symbolized in the weekend circus on **Ocean Front Walk**, during which jocks, executives, panhandlers, hipsters, families, bikini-clad girls, and cops in shorts promenade or roll along the boardwalk on every imaginable wheeled device. It has become a compulsory stop for tourists from Tokyo to Topeka. You can rent skates or bikes and join the scene.

Away from this colorful craziness are the studios and galleries of leading artists—many of which can be explored on the annual **Art Walk** (for more information, call 392.8630)—and a ferment of cultural activity. Some of LA's most adventurous new architecture and restaurants are slotted in amid the peeling stucco and clapboard cottages. The greatest threats today are from crime and gentrification, not physical deterioration. When there's no room at the beach parking lots, you can leave your car in the city lot at Washington and Venice boulevards and take the Dash shuttle to the beach, which runs every 15 minutes on Saturday and Sunday from 9AM to 9PM.

**92 Venice Renaissance Building** Johannes Van Tilburg's design for this building was lauded for its mixed-use concept when completed in 1990, and the 34-foot-high ballerina clown sculpture mounted at its southeast prow has become a landmark. The bizarre kinetic work unites the contrasting images of a classical performer and a low-brow comedian. Artist **Jonathan Borofsky** designed the vulgar, kitschy image to echo Venice and to contrast the upscale site. ♦ Corner of Rose Ave and Main St

Within the Venice Renaissance Building:

**Chaya Venice** ★★$$ This stunning restaurant was designed by **Grinstein/Daniels,** who created the interior for **Chaya Brasserie** in West Hollywood and the **Chaya Diner** (now **El Chaya**) in Hollywood. Bronze and copper, natural woods and stone, and a Japanese ceiling

mural achieve a pleasing harmony. Chef **Kondo** serves great curried-crab soup, tuna spring rolls, spicy swordfish, and saffron paella. Late supper is offered nightly until 12:30AM.
♦ Eclectic ♦ M-Th, Su 11:30AM-2:30PM, 6-10:30PM; F 11:30AM-2:30PM, 6-11PM; Sa 6-11PM. 296.1179

weller

**93 Robin Rose Ice Cream** A life without chocolate raspberry truffle or white-chocolate ice cream is a life not lived to its fullest. The other irresistible flavors are listed on a multicolored neon signboard; don't miss their ice cream cakes. There are branches in downtown LA and Brentwood. ♦ M-Th, Su 11AM-11PM; F-Sa 11AM-midnight. 215 Rose Ave. 399.1774

**94 The Rose Cafe and Market** ★$$ Eclectic modern dishes are served in the dining area; lighter fare, including breakfasts and great pastries, can be ordered at the counter, to go or to eat on the patio. ♦ Eclectic ♦ M-Sa 9AM-11PM; Su 9AM-3PM. 220 Rose Ave. 399.0711

**94 Gold's Gym** This is the original home of the unbelievable well-oiled and rippling bod. There are free weights and Universal and Nautilus equipment for men and women. Intermediate bodybuilders work out here, as well as pros like **Samir Bannut, Mr. Olympia, Barry Demey, Gary Strydom,** and **David** and **Peter Paul**, aka the "Barbarian Brothers." There are 80 individually-owned gyms throughout Southern California. ♦ M-F 4AM-midnight; Sa-Su 5AM-midnight. 360 Hampton Dr. 392.6004

Median household income in Los Angeles (in 1990): $34,965
Median cost of a home: $226,400
Median rent: $626

The city of Santa Monica collects about $5 million in parking fees every year.

The first Jewish religious services took place in predominantly Catholic LA in 1854, and the first Protestant church was built 10 years later.

The five-county area of LA—Riverside, Ventura, Orange, and San Bernardino—measures 34,149 square miles and is home to 14.5 million people.

**95 Chiat-Day-Mojo Building** Serendipity placed a four-story pair of binoculars at the entrance to this advertising agency headquarters designed by **Frank Gehry.** Two sections flanking the entry—a boat-shaped white office wing on the north and an innovative abstract tree form made of copper-clad steel on the south—were already designed when **Jay Chiat** pushed for an entry solution. Gehry grabbed a nearby Claes Oldenburg maquette of a pair of binoculars and placed it on the model as an example. Chiat liked it. The result is an unusual building (completed in 1991) designed to create a three-part streetscape on scale with the neighborhood. The structure still appears massive because it reaches the edge of the site (to compensate for coastal height limits). The treelike form creates a sunscreen for the west-facing building, and the binoculars contain two small meeting rooms. ♦ 340 Main St

**96 Venice Bistro** ★$$ Mexican-American dishes, including pasta and a variety of salads, are served at this popular patio restaurant.

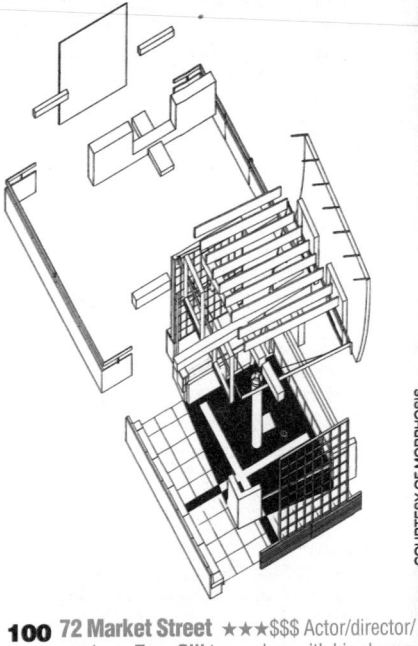

## Santa Monica/Venice

There's live music Wednesday through Sunday evenings. ♦ Mexican/American ♦ Daily 11AM-10PM. 323 Ocean Front Walk. 392.3997

**96 The Fig Tree** $$ Grilled fish and flavorful vegetarian dishes are served both indoors and on a peaceful patio just off the boardwalk. ♦ California ♦ Daily 8AM-10PM. 429 Ocean Front Walk. 392.4937

**97 World Gym** **Joe Gold** left his first gym to establish this indoor and outdoor workout space. World Gym has produced a long list of champions, among them current gym owner **Arnold Schwarzenegger.** There are more than 175 locations internationally. ♦ Daily 6AM-10PM. 812 Main St. 399.9888. Also at: 39 S. Altadena Dr, Pasadena. 818/304.1133; 2010 N. Hollywood Way, Burbank. 818/563.4203

**98 Caplin House** This quirky, idea-packed house by **Frederick Fisher** built in 1979 for the editor of *Wet* magazine was a statement of style for both the architect and the client. It's a private residence. ♦ 229 San Juan Ave

**99 Hal's Bar & Grill** ★$$ A favorite with local artists, this place with a casual interior offers salads, pasta, and other basic fare. ♦ California ♦ M-F 11:30AM-3PM, 6PM-closing; Sa-Su 10AM-3PM, 6PM-closing. 1349 Abbot Kinney Ave. 396.3105

**100 Sidewalk Cafe** $ Many come to this bustling spot for seeing and being seen. ♦ American ♦ M-Th, Su 8AM-midnight; F-Sa 8AM-1AM. 1401 Ocean Front Walk. 399.5547

**100 Spiller House** In 1980 **Frank Gehry** designed a pair of houses, each with two parking spaces and a garden, shoehorned onto a very tiny plot. They combine a corrugated steel exterior with a woodsy interior, thus creating an archetypal low-cost Venice landmark. This is a private residence. ♦ 39 Horizon Ave

**100 72 Market Street** ★★★$$$ Actor/director/producer **Tony Bill** teamed up with his chums **Dudley Moore** and **Liza Minnelli** to create this hot spot. The classy modern art and the prospect of Moore tickling the ivories draws the show biz and art crowds. **Morphosis** brilliantly remodeled the lofty interior (illustrated above), formerly used as a studio by **Frank Gehry** and **Robert Irwin,** as an airy, skylit space, with shutters opening into the street arcade, a semi enclosed bar, and a glass-brick wall to enclose the back dining room. Chef **Leonard Schwartz** transformed the most basic dishes, such as chili, black-bean soup, meat loaf, and catfish, into irresistible treats, and is just as successful with more innovative dishes. Though now a consultant, Schwartz has gone on to create the same culinary magic at another Tony Bill-led enterprise, **Maple Drive,** in Beverly Hills. ♦ American ♦ M-Th 11:30AM-2:30PM, 6-10PM; F 11:30AM-2:30PM, 6-11PM; Sa 6-11PM; Su 10AM-2:30PM, 6-10PM. 72 Market St. 392.8720

**101 Venice Mural** **Terry Schoonhoven's** large, much-faded mural shows a mirror image of the city on a very clear day with the distant mountains in view. Venice is full of murals—French filmmaker **Agnes Varda,** a local resident, did a poetic documentary about them called *Murs Murs.* One of the best, **Jon Werhle's** *The Fall of Icarus* is located a block north, facing the Pacific Ocean across a parking lot. Another, recently renewed, is **Wallace Cronk's** *Venice on the Half-Shell.* A local agency, **SPARC,** is commissioning more murals to be created with city funds. ♦ Windward Ave at the Speedway

**102 Windward Circle** From 1905 to 1929, this was known as the **Grand Lagoon.** Architect **Steven Erlich** has tried to awaken its ghosts with three complementary buildings that use concrete-filled culvert pipes to suggest Venetian porticoes. The giant **Race Through the**

**Clouds** roller coaster finds an echo in the neon loop of a retail block; a food market is flanked by metal frames that recall the steam-driven dredgers that excavated the canals. A residential block occupies the site of the **Antlers Hotel,** which was demolished in 1960. To the south is a post office containing **Edward Biberman's** mural of the history of Venice. ◆ Main St at Windward Ave

**102 Hama Sushi** ★$$$ This is a favorite neighborhood sushi bar. ◆ Japanese ◆ M-Th 11:30AM-2:30PM, 6-11PM; F 11:30AM-2:30PM, 5:30-11:30PM; Sa 5:30-11:30PM; Su 5-10PM. 213 Windward Ave. 396.8783

**102 St. Mark's** ★★$$$ Though the service is hurried and occasionally obnoxious at this loud, hip jazz club, the food is sometimes outstanding. The dramatic granite, stainless-steel, and cobalt blue suede interior was designed by architect **Osvaldo Maiozzi.** ◆ French/Italian ◆ Cover W-Su. Daily 6PM-2AM. Dinner: Tu-Th 6-11:30PM; F-Sa 6PM-12:30AM. 23 Windward Ave. 452.2222

**103 Capri** ★★$$$ Owner **Alana Hamilton Cooke** offers superb food in a minimalist setting. Chef **John Beriker,** formerly of **Spago,** conjures up some excellent pasta, poultry (don't miss the quail), and seafood creations. Cooke boasts an impressive but reasonably priced Italian wine list, and she took the initiative in introducing some wonderful desserts, from tiramisù to flourless chocolate cake. ◆ Italian ◆ M-Th, Su 6-10:30PM; F-Sa 6-11:30PM. 1616 W. Abbot Kinney Blvd. 392.8777

**104 Dandelion Cafe** $ This alfresco sandwich and salad bar is a peaceful retreat from beach madness. ◆ American ◆ Tu-Su 7AM-3PM. 636 Venice Blvd. 821.4890

**104 Beyond Baroque Literary/Arts Center** Don't miss the adventurous readings, lectures, and performances in the old City Hall that sustain the bohemian tradition of Venice. **Abbot Kinney** would have approved. Call ahead for program information. ◆ 681 Venice Blvd. 822.3006

**105 West Beach Cafe** ★★★$$$ The chefs in this sleek white skylit box helped to pioneer the new California cuisine and the practice of exhibiting serious artworks on the walls. The bar and restaurant remain favorite hangouts for the local art scene, despite (or perhaps because of) the noise and erratic service. Shrimp and sausage salad, napoleon of salmon, and roasted lamb with sage are typical dishes. There's an excellent wine list. Pizza is served until late. ◆ California ◆ Tu-F 8AM-2:30PM, 6-10:30PM; Sa-Su 10:30AM-2:30PM, 6-10:30PM. 60 N. Venice Blvd. 823.5396

**105 Rebecca's** ★$$$ The interior of this restaurant, designed by **Frank Gehry** in 1987, features a forest of rough wood that's juxtaposed with sleek back-lit onyx panels. Metal-scaled crocodiles hang from the ceiling, and there's a chandelier in the form of a glass octopus. Few consider the food worth the high prices, but owner **Bruce Marder** has the magic touch and the place is fashionably jammed (and noisy)

every night of the week. If you want to hear yourself talk, ask for a booth. Best bets here include the chicken *fajitas,* lamb-tongue tacos, grilled shrimp, and meltingly tender leg of lamb *adobada.* The bar is a flourishing singles scene. ◆ Mexican ◆ Daily 6-11PM. 2005 Pacific Ave (entrance on Venice Blvd). 306.6266

**105 L.A. Louver Gallery** Works by important LA artists, including **David Hockney, Ed Moses, Tony Berlant,** and **Michael McMillen,** are showcased here. ◆ Tu-Sa noon-5PM. 55 N. Venice Blvd. 822.4955. Also at: 77 Market St. 822.4955

**105 Venice Canals** A frail remnant of **Abbot Kinney's** vision can be found along this succession of side canals and Venetian bridges. The city would like to fill them in, so catch them while they are still here. ◆ SE of Venice Blvd and Pacific Ave

**106 Norton House** **Frank Gehry** created this 1984 family house for a Japanese-American artist (notice the log *torii* over the gate) and her screenwriter husband (who works at a life-

guard shelter that overlooks the beach ). His design provides privacy and complexity on a minuscule site. This is a private residence. ◆ 2509 Ocean Front Walk

**107 The Venice Beach House** $$ Just off the oceanfront, this charming bed-and-breakfast is located in a quieter part of Venice. Each of the eight rooms is individually decorated. ◆ 15 30th Ave. 823.1966

**Bests**

**Glenn Goldman**
Bookseller, Book Soup

A ride on the **Goodyear Blimp.**

Go to the parking lot of **Beachwood Market** after 2AM to see the coyotes come out of the hills.

Don't miss the cedar-smoked salmon and chef Nancy's sticky buns at **Campanile.**

Drive the full length of **Sunset Boulevard,** preferably in a convertible, starting downtown and heading west to the Pacific Coast Highway; then turn right, and follow the sun.

**Restaurants/Clubs:** Red   **Hotels:** Blue
**Shops/ 🌴 Outdoors:** Green   **Sights/Culture:** Black

# Malibu/The Canyons

The chaparral-covered Santa Monica and San Gabriel mountain ranges form an arc around the northern and eastern reaches of LA. Their canyon-marked hills trap the smog in the flatlands of the city they define but deliver urban dwellers with a rim of rural wilderness. Hikers find respite here, and affluent homeowners, who have carved a place of their own in the hills and canyons, have some of the best king-of-the-castle views anywhere.

Mountains and ocean meet at Malibu, a world-renowned place where reality and image sometimes collide. Everything you've heard about its laid-back hedonism is true. But the celebrated beaches, with bikini-clad sunbathers and die-hard surfers, are largely walled off from public view along the **Pacific Coast Highway.** Million-dollar estates reveal a usually scruffy backside along the coastal drive or hide

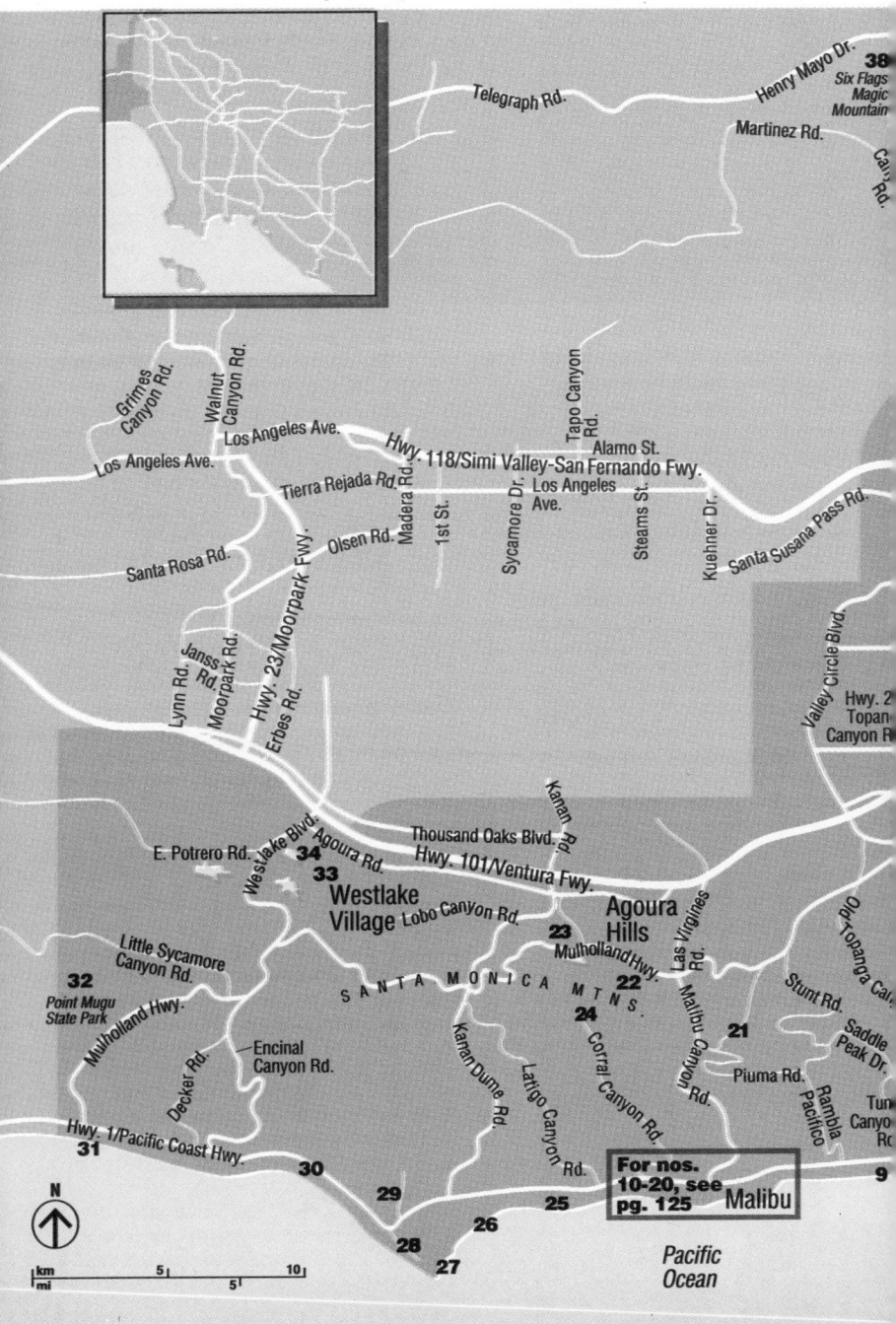

For nos. 10-20, see pg. 125

ehind anonymous gates, and Malibu's scattershot commercial strip is as ordinary nd undistinguished as anywhere, leaving tourists to wonder where Malibu actu- lly *is*. The Malibu of legend must be stalked. Rural, coastal, and hilly, it is isolated rom the city and about the same size as the rancho it replaced. Chumash Indians vere the first to settle in the area. In 1887 wealthy easterner **Frederic H. Rindge** ought the Topanga-Malibu-Sequit rancho, an expanse that had been granted o **Jose Tapia** and included more than 22 miles of pristine Pacific oceanfront. Rindge built a private railroad and pier, planted alfalfa, and spent the rest of his ife trying to shut out newcomers, carrying the protest to the Supreme Court. The government eventually won, and in 1929 the Pacific Coast Highway (then alled Roosevelt Highway) officially opened, paving the way for more develop- ment. The first film star to settle in Malibu Beach was **Anna Q. Nilsson**, who built a house on a deserted beach just north of Malibu Creek in 1928. **Clara Bow, Gloria Swanson, Ronald Coleman,** and **Frank Capra** soon followed, and by 1930 it was dubbed the **Malibu Motion Picture Colony.** Now simply "The Colony," it is still home to celebrities such as **Larry Hagman, Johnny Carson,** and **Shirley MacLaine.** Many other stars own houses and estates along the beaches or in the canyons. In 1990, voters, again working to limit growth, wrenched the area from county control and, in 1991, realized a hard-won dream and became an independent city.

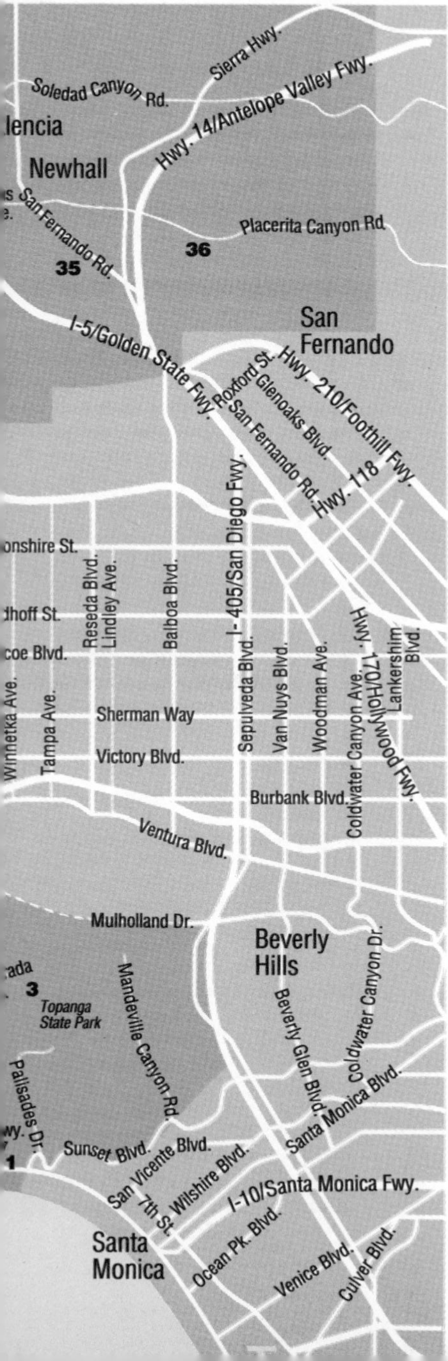

*Area code 310 unless otherwise noted.*

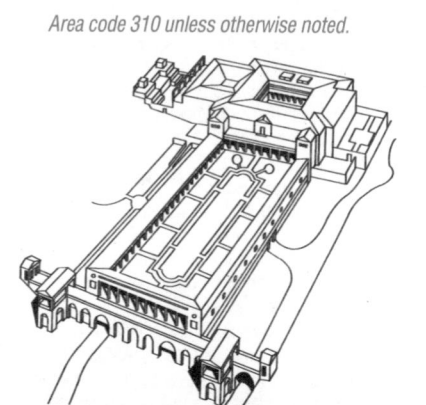

**1 J. Paul Getty Museum** Located in a wooded canyon just off the Pacific Coast Highway, the museum (pictured above) re-creates the **Villa dei Papiri,** a large Roman seaside villa at Herculaneum that was buried in AD 79 by the eruption of **Mount Vesuvius** and has yet to be fully excavated. When it opened in 1974, some critics compared this brightly colored facsimile to Disneyland. Since then, architectural fashions have changed, and the building and its immaculate formal gardens seem almost mainstream. It was J. Paul Getty who conceived this new home for his extensive collections of Roman and Greek antiquities, European paintings, and French decorative arts. He endowed the

**123**

## J. Paul Getty Museum

*Plan of Main Level Galleries (Antiquities)*

museum with a trust that is now worth $3 billion—of which 4.2 percent must be spent each year on the trust's seven operating programs, including the museum—making the Getty the richest institution of its kind in the world.

Among the antiquities is an outstanding collection of classical Greek vases. Paintings range from a magical **Vittore Carpaccio** panel of a hunt on the Venetian Lagoon, through the Renaissance masters (splendid works by **Pontormo** and **Mantegna** have recently been

added), to **Manet, Renoir,** and **van Gogh** (including his *Irises*). French furniture, porcelain, and silver of dazzling quality are shown in period rooms (see the plan above).

Since Getty's death in 1976, the museum has made important acquisitions, including three new collections. There is a small but exquisite selection of Old Master drawings with works by **Raphael, Veronese, Dürer,** and the elder **Cranach**. Also on display are changing groups of extraordinary illuminated manuscripts and classic photographs from collections that feature work by **Nadar, August Sander, Lazlo Moholy-Nagy,** and **Man Ray**. When the **J. Paul Getty Center**, designed by **Richard Meier** and currently under construction on a 110-acre hilltop site in Brentwood, opens in 1996, the antiquities will inherit the entire villa, and a larger selection of the other collections will be exhibited in the new galleries. The study center and other Getty programs and offices will also be housed here amid terraced gardens in a complex of new buildings designed to preserve the natural beauty of the site and to enhance its sweeping vistas of mountains, ocean, and city.

The museum's well-stocked bookstore sells cards and reproductions. The **Garden Tea Room** serves lunches and afternoon snacks (no picnicking is allowed on the grounds). Orientation talks and gallery lectures are given daily. You can also teach yourself about the Greek vases and medieval manuscripts by using the interactive video discs developed for these exhibitions. For information on Friday afternoon and evening concerts, lectures, and other educational programs, call 458.2003. Parking is limited, so advance reservations are required for all visitors arriving by car, van, or charter bus. Visitors may also come by bicycle,

taxi, or RTD bus No. 434 (request a museum pass from the bus driver), or they may be dropped off at the gatehouse by car without advance museum reservations. Parking at the museum is limited, therefore you must call ahead to reserve a space. The museum is accessible to the handicapped. ◆ Free. Tu-Su 10AM-5PM. 17985 Pacific Coast Hwy. Reservations recommended. 458.2003

**2 Sassafras Nursery** This nursery stocks miniature vegetables and everything you need to create a grand garden with an emphasis on the English country look. ◆ Daily 9AM-5PM. 275 N Topanga Canyon Blvd. 455.1933

**3 Topanga State Park** With 9,000 untouched acres to explore and enjoy, Topanga State Park offers a perfect respite from civilization. The high peaks offer superb views of the ocean and San Fernando Valley, and the grassy meadows and woodlands are perfect for picnics and long walks. A self-guided trail explains the ecology. Water and sanitary facilities are available in the park, but overnight camping is not allowed. ◆ There is a parking fee. Daily 8AM-7PM. 20825 Entrada Rd. (Entrada Rd leads off Topanga Canyon Blvd. There are no park signs on Topanga Canyon Blvd, so watch carefully.) 455.2465

**4 Topanga Canyon** Before anyone ever hand-painted a VW bus, before anyone other than a Mexican wore *huaraches,* Topanga was an alternative community. Its bucolic homes are sheltered on the hillsides under large groves of sycamores or scattered along the creek running through the base of the canyon. Indian settlements in the area have been dated back to at least 5,000 years ago. The name Topanga means "mountains that run into the sea." ◆ North of Pacific Coast Hwy on Topanga Canyon Blvd

**5 Will Geer's Theatricum Botanicum** This outdoor theater, established by the late Will Geer, presents Shakespeare and new and classic modern plays from June to September. ◆ 1419 N. Topanga Canyon Blvd. 455.3723

**6 Inn of the Seventh Ray** ★$$ Four miles from the Coast Highway is this bucolic New Wave restaurant, with tables set up beside a stream where you can absorb the benign vibrations and recorded harpist while enjoying a salad, grilled fish, and a glass of Chardonnay. ◆ California ◆ M-F 11:30AM-11:30PM; Sa 10:30AM-midnight; Su 9:30AM-midnight. 128 Old Topanga Canyon Rd. 455.1311

**7 Reel Inn Restaurant and Fresh Fish Market** ★$ Fresh fish is cut in the kitchen daily, prepared grilled or pan-blackened Cajun style, and served alongside a hearty meal with homestyle potatoes, Cajun rice, and coleslaw. The setting is casual rustic boathouse, with long wooden picnic-style tables and a patio. Celebrities like to slip in here unnoticed. ◆ Seafood ◆ M-Th, Su 11AM-10:30PM; F-Sa 11AM-11PM. 18661 Pacific Coast Hwy. 456.8221. Also at: 1220 Third St, Santa Monica. 395.553

# Santa Monica Mountains

In 1978 the Santa Monicas were designated a national recreation area and administered by the National Park Service. They offer numerous breathtaking views of the Los Angeles basin and the San Fernando Valley from their summits, while retaining a wild environment within their ridges and valleys. The mountains are part of a chain that rises from the floor of the Pacific, forming the Channel Islands, the beach plateau, and the series of peaks that extend into the city center at heights averaging one to two thousand feet. Slopes are covered with a collection of evergreen shrubs and scrubby trees known as chaparral. This plant life includes chamise and sage on the lower, drier hills, and denser cover of scrub oak, sumac, wild lilac, and manzanita along the stream beds. The wild plants that you can see everywhere were introduced only 200 years ago by the Franciscan *padres*. Fire is a major hazard in this region. Plant life is bone-dry in the summer, and the smallest spark or flame can ignite a raging brush fire that will quickly spread over thousands of acres.

For a fast look at the wilderness and the housing that imperils it, you can drive the length of **Mulholland Drive,** a narrow country road that snakes 50 miles along the crest of the Santa Monicas, from the Hollywood Freeway to Leo Carillo State Beach. It was named for the self-taught Irish engineer who developed the first major aqueduct in the city, thus spurring its rapid growth.

**8  Las Tunas State Beach** The name does not refer to canned fish, but is Spanish for the fruit of the prickly pear cactus. ♦ Between Tuna Canyon Rd and Big Rock Dr

**9  Moonshadows** $$$ Bountiful salads, steaks, and the piped-in sounds of the surf—plus the view of the breakers—are the attractions here. ♦ American ♦ M-Th 5-11PM; F 5PM-midnight; Sa 10:30AM-2:30PM, 3PM-midnight; Su 10:30AM-2:30PM, 3-10:30PM. 20356 Pacific Coast Hwy. 456.3010

**10  Ackerburg Residence** Designed by **Richard Meier & Partners,** this 1991 beachfront house translates Meier's white rational design into Southern California courtyard living. On the same strip of beach are the contrasting styles of three renowned architects. **John Lautner's** 1979 **Segal Residence,** a heavily landscaped curving wood and concrete home, is located at 22426, and a **Gwathmey, Siegel & Associates** wood and glass house is located at 22350. They are all private residences. ♦ 22466 Pacific Coast Hwy

**11  La Salsa** ★$ A huge rooftop figure marks the site of this popular takeout place overlooking the ocean. The fresh vegetables, grilled chicken, fish, and meat tacos have won acclaim. ♦ Mexican ♦ M-Th 8AM-10PM; F-Sa 8AM-11:30PM; Su 8AM-10:30PM. 22800 Pacific Coast Hwy. 456.6299

**12  Malibu Beach Inn** $$$ This beachfront Spanish-style hotel offers romantic vistas of the Pacific sunset. Every room in the low pink stucco range has a balcony looking onto the sand. The hotel prices match the privileged location. ♦ 22878 Pacific Coast Hwy. 465.6444, 800/462.5428

**12  Saint Honoré French Bakery** Homemade loaves, brioches, fresh juices, and sandwiches attract a steady stream of enthusiasts. ♦ M-Th 6:30AM-7PM; F 6:30AM-10PM; Sa 7:30AM-10PM; Su 7:30AM-7PM. 22943 Pacific Coast Hwy. 456.2651

**13  Malibu Surfrider State Beach** Affectionately known as "the Bu" by surfers, the beach has a world-famous right reef point break. The surfing here is best in August and September when south swells are in evidence. A good lo-

cation to watch surfers in action is from the adjacent Malibu Pier. ♦ Off the Pacific Coast Hwy

**13  Malibu Pier** Built in 1903 as a landing point for ranch supplies and for **Frederick Rindge's** private railroad, the pier was reconstructed in 1946 and is now owned by the state. Fishing is permitted. ♦ 23000 Pacific Coast Hwy

On Malibu Pier:

**Alice's** ★$$ Long noted for its view of the surf and sunsets, Alice's now has a good chef, **André Guerrero,** and is worth more than a drink at the bar. Unlike most other beachfront restaurants, the menu is light and healthy, with an emphasis on salads and mesquite-grilled chicken and fish, though some of the more elaborate dishes are worth a try. ♦ California ♦ M-Sa 11:30AM-10PM; Su 10AM-9:30PM. 456.6646

**Malibu Pier Sportfishing** They offer regular day and half-day surface fishing cruises. The bait and tackle shop rents equipment for pier or boat use. Fishing licenses are sold for boat fishing; no license is necessary for pier fishing. ♦ Daily 6AM-6PM. 456.8030

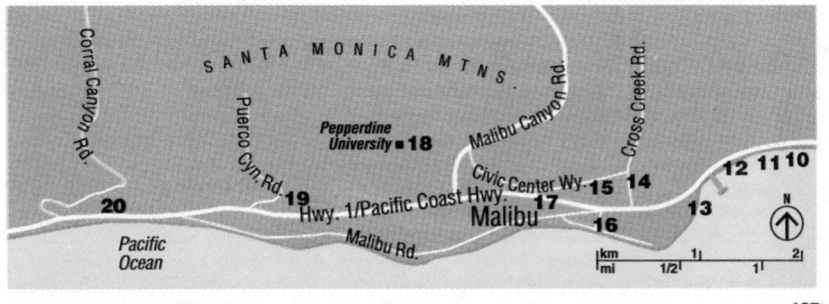

**13 Adamson House** This romantic Spanish Colonial house designed by **Stiles O. Clements** in 1929 is preserved the way its owner, **Rhoda Rindge Adamson,** left it at her death in 1962. It is a showcase of colorful Malibu tiles and a reminder of the imperious family that once owned 17,000 acres in and around Malibu. The house and adjoining **Malibu Lagoon Museum** are open for frequent 45-minute tours. ♦ Admission. Tours W-Sa 10AM-3PM. 23200 Pacific Coast Hwy. 456.8432

**14 La Scala Malibu** ★$$$$ The flower-filled patio overlooking Malibu Creek is a lovely place for lunch, and for dinner there's a cozy interior. Smoked salmon and pasta with eggplant, risotto, calamari salad, and herbed roast chicken have all been praised. ♦ Italian ♦ Tu-F 11:30AM-2:30PM, 5:30-10:30PM; Sa 5:30-11PM; Su 5:30-10PM. 3874 Cross Creek Rd. 456.1979

**14 Malibu Deli** Cravings for authentic deli treats, from lox to corned beef to egg creams, can be satisfied here. ♦ M-Sa 7AM-10PM; Su 7AM-8PM. 3894 Cross Creek Rd. 456.2444

**15 Godmother of Malibu** ★★$$ There are a few tables, but this is primarily a catering service and takeout—for which it is praised above

all the restaurants in Malibu. A young, enthusiastic staff prepares such specialties as vegetable lasagna, truffled chicken breast, and stuffed veal. ♦ Italian ♦ Tu-F 9:30AM-7:30PM; Sa 9:30AM-6PM; Su 9:30AM-4PM. 23410 Civic Center Way. 456.5203

**15 Malibu Books** This bookstore offers food for the mind and is an invaluable resource for resident writers (and compulsive readers). The stock is rich and varied. ♦ M-Sa 10AM-6PM; Su 11AM-5PM. 23410 Civic Center Way. 456.1375

**15 Malibu Adobe** ★$$ **Ali McGraw** designed this Southwestern-style celebrity hangout. Salads, grills, and pasta with smoked chicken are some favorites. ♦ Southwestern ♦ M-Th, Su 11:30AM-3PM, 5-10PM; F-Sa 11:30AM-3PM, 5-11PM. 23410 Civic Center Way. 456.2021

**15 Tops Malibu** Folkloric furniture, jewelry, and accessories are all sold here. ♦ M-Sa 11AM-6PM; Su noon-5PM. 23410 Civic Center Way. 456.6002

**15 Tra Di Noi Ristorante** $$ Family style (owner **Claudio Borin's** mama **Rosa** is in the kitchen) Northern Italian cuisine is served in this small, quiet restaurant offering patio dining on a parklike courtyard. The name means "between us," and the setting is intimate and often movie-star studded. ♦ Italian ♦ M-Th noon-2PM, 5:45-10PM; F-Sa noon-2PM, 5:45-10:30PM; Su noon-2PM, 4-10PM. 3835 Cross Creek Rd #8A (Malibu Country Mart). 456.0169

**15 Malibu Shaman** Instrumental New Age music, including meditation hypnosis, and subliminal programming tapes, doesn't get much airplay, so owner **Scott Sutphen** lets customers don headsets to hear any of the more than 300

titles. **Shirley MacLaine** and other Malibu actors shop at this book and music store pungent with incense. Psychics give individual readings on weekends. ♦ M-F 11AM-6PM; Sa-Su 10AM-6PM. 3835 Cross Creek Rd #19 (Malibu Country Mart). 456.5617

**16 Malibu Beach Colony** At last, a listing about where the movie stars *do* live. "The Colony," as insiders call it, has been an exclusive and very private beach community for the famous and wealthy since 1926, when silent movie queen **Anna Q. Nilsson** moved here. Many of the beach cottages have bedrooms sufficient to sleep the staff of the *Tonight Show* and hot tubs big enough to soak the Olympic swim team. The drives and beach here are private, but the dramatic **Stevens House** by **John Lautner** can be seen from the Pacific Coast Highway as a double-height concrete quarter-circle rising into the sky. ♦ Webb Way off Pacific Coast Hwy

**17 Granita** ★★★$$$ **Wolfgang Puck** and **Barbara Lazaroff,** owners of **Spago** and **Chinois on Main,** opened their latest restaurant in Malibu, where grateful local celebrities eat as often as three times a week. Full of artisan-crafted details and undulating curves, the oceanic interior with seaform ceramic glazes and handblown glass is an original contemporary/neoclassic design. Signature dishes include the Mediterranean fish soup with half lobster and couscous, and *fritto misto* with shrimp. Puck also serves his classics, such as lamb sausage pizza. ♦ California/Mediterranean ♦ M-Tu 5:30-11PM; W-F 11:30AM-2:30PM, 5:30-11PM; Sa-Su 11AM-2:30PM (brunch), 5:30-11PM. 23725 West Malibu Rd (at the Malibu Colony Plaza). 456.0488

**17 The Foxes' Trot** The contemporary general store offering arty domestic and personal items has moved to a new, larger location at the Malibu Colony Plaza shopping center. ♦ M-Sa 10AM-6PM; Su noon-5PM. 23733 West Malibu Rd. 456.1776

**18 Pepperdine University** Popularly known as "Surfers U" for its oceanfront site, this is actually a respected four-year college that offers bachelor's and master's degrees in 50 major subject areas. It has a law school, four satellite centers in Southern California, and a year-in-Europe program at Heidelberg University. ♦ 24255 Pacific Coast Hwy. 456.4000

**19 24955 Pacific Coast Highway** The crisp low-rise commercial development designed by **Goldman Firth Architects** in 1989 lifts the spirits of motorists speeding by. ♦ North of Malibu Canyon Rd

**20 Beau Rivage** ★$$$ This warm and cozy roadhouse with a piano indoors and a patio in back has a rich, steeply priced menu that has drawn mixed reviews, but locals still throng in. ♦ Mediterranean ♦ M-Sa 5-11PM; Su 11AM-4PM (brunch), 5-11PM. 26025 Pacific Coast Hwy. 456.5733

LA is home to 250,000 surfers, 35 square-dance callers, and 9 skywriters.

**21 Saddle Peak Lodge** ★★★$$$$ Wonderful hearty food is served in a romantic mountain lodge with a roaring fire and stags' heads on the walls. Seasonal game is the specialty; the roast venison is especially good, but so are the vodka-cured salmon and the carpetbagger steak. It's well worth a long drive, but don't go without a reservation. ♦ American ♦ W-Sa 6-11PM; Su 5-11PM. 419 Cold Canyon Rd, Calabasas. Reservations recommended. 818/222.3888

**22 Malibu Creek State Park** Four thousand acres of park including **Malibu Creek**, two-acre **Century Lake**, ageless oaks, chapparal, and volcanic rock are found here. There is excellent day hiking on almost 15 miles of trails. Movie companies sometimes film on location in this secluded park. Camping is allowed here. Enter the park from Las Virgenes/Malibu Canyon Road. ♦ Parking fee. 28754 Mulholland Hwy, Agoura. 818/706.8809

**23 Paramount Ranch** Since the early 1920s on, Westerns have been shot on the standing set and what was formerly a 4,000-acre expanse of hills. Ranger-guided hikes over the ranch and movie set are offered once a month, and 436 acres of wooded countryside are open daily for riding, walking, and picnicking. Silent films are shown under the stars from July to August. ♦ Daily dawn to dusk. 2813 Cornell Rd, Agoura (Kanan exit off the Ventura Fwy). 818/597.9192, 213/874.2276

**24 Sunset Viewing** For a 360-degree panorama of ocean, mountains, and the San Fernando Valley, drive up into the hills to the end of Corral Canyon Road, beyond Malibu Canyon, and climb to the boulders on the crest of the hill. ♦ Corral Canyon Rd off Pacific Coast Hwy

**25 Geoffrey's** ★$$$$ Go for the fabulous cliff-edge terrace with its sweeping ocean view, or the handsome **Richard Neutra** interior, ribbed like the interior of a boat hull. The health-conscious menu includes grilled fresh fish, pastas, salads, and some hearty dishes such as stuffed lambchops. There's live piano music nightly. ♦ California ♦ M-Th noon-4PM, 5-11PM; F-Sa noon-4PM, 5PM-midnight; Su 10AM-4PM, 5-11PM. 27400 Pacific Coast Hwy. 457.1519

**26 Paradise Cove** This private beach is full of nooks and crannies for walking and exploring. The **Sandcastle**, a staid, inexplicably popular restaurant, overlooks the ocean. ♦ Admission. Paradise Cove Rd off 28100 block of Pacific Coast Hwy

**27 Point Dume** This residential area with a hard-to-get-to beach was named in 1782 by **George Vancouver**, the English explorer, for **Father Dumetz**, a Jesuit at the Ventura Mission. Until the 20th century, Point Dume was high and peaked, but the top has been shaved off to build a housing development. ♦ Off the Pacific Coast Hwy

**28 Monroe's Restaurant** ★$$$ Intimate, elegant rooms facing the ocean and a rich, innovative menu are the draws. ♦ Continental ♦ Daily 5PM-midnight. 6800 Westward Beach Rd. 457.5521

**29 Zuma Canyon Orchids** Prize-winning plants bred here are sent all over the world. ♦ Daily 10AM-4PM. 5949 Bonsall Dr. 457.9771

**30 Zooma Sushi** ★$ College students and casual celebrities such as **Emilio Estevez** and **Nick Nolte** frequent this 25-seat sushi bar and restaurant located in architect **Ed Niles'** woodsy office building. The most popular is the Vegas Roll—five kinds of fish rolled in seaweed, deep fried and wrapped in spicy crab—but more traditional fare is also available. ♦ Japanese ♦ M-Th 5-10:30PM; F-Sa 5-11PM; Su 4-10:30PM. 29350 Pacific Coast Hwy. 457.4131

**31 Leo Carrillo State Beach** This broad, clean sandy beach was named for the Los Angeles-born actor **Leo Carrillo** (1880-1961). A descendant of one of California's oldest families and son of the first mayor of Santa Monica, Carrillo became famous as *Pancho*, the sidekick to TV's *Cisco Kid*. There is surfing at the northern end of the beach. ♦ North of Nicholas Beach Rd to Ventura County Line

**32 Point Mugu State Park** The secluded and idyllic park, with 70 miles of trails, a tall-grass prairie preserve, beautiful sycamores, and lovely canyons, is excellent for day hikes and

picnics. Advance camping reservations are required. ♦ 9000 W. Pacific Coast Hwy, five miles north of the Los Angeles and Ventura county line. 818/880.0350

**33 Boccaccio's** $$$ Despite its location in the midst of a housing development, this dependable standby offers some degree of sophisticated service and a truly marvelous oak tree and lakeside view. ♦ Italian/French ♦ M-Th 11:30AM-2:30PM, 6-10PM; F 11:30AM-2:30PM, 6-10:30PM; Sa 6-10:30PM; Su 5:30-9PM. 32123 W. Lindero Canyon Rd, Westlake Village. 818/889.8300

**34 Tuscany** ★★$$ Come here for serious eating in a remote location. Try the herb-flavored veal chops, cheese-stuffed chicken breast, and inventive antipasti. **Tommaso Barletta** runs a tight ship. ♦ Italian ♦ M-F 11AM-2PM, 5-10PM; Sa 5-10PM. 968 #4 Westlake Blvd Westlake Village. 818/880.5642

**35 William S. Hart Park** "While I was making pictures, the people gave me their nickels, dimes, and quarters. When I am gone, I want them to have my home." With this testament, silent film cowboy star **William S. Hart** bequeathed his 253-acre ranch for use as a public park. One-hundred-and-ten acres have been preserved as a wilderness area. The developed portion of the property includes an animal compound stocked with domestic beasts and a herd of buffalo, picnic sites, and Hart's ranch-style home, **La Loma de los Vientos**, which contains paintings and sculpture by **Charles M. Russell**. ♦ Park: daily 10AM-dusk. Museum: W-Su 11AM-4PM, mid-June to mid-Oct; W-F 10AM-1PM, Sa-Su 11AM-4PM, mid-Oct to mid-June. 24151 San Fernando Rd, Newhall. 805/254.4584

*Six Flags Magic Mountain*

**36 Placerita Canyon Park and Nature Trail**
This 314-acre native chaparral park is located in a picturesque canyon amid stands of California live oak. The nature center and self-guided tour are designed to illustrate the relationships of the plants and animals in the area. ♦ Free. Nature Center: Tu-F 9AM-5PM; Sa-Su 10AM-5PM. 19152 Placerita Canyon Rd, Newhall. 805/259.7721

**37 California Institute of the Arts** Founded with an endowment from **Walt Disney** in 1970, Cal-Arts is an elite, cutting-edge college with schools of film, dance, theater, art, and music. Graduates here (including **David Salle** and **Eric Fischl**) have invigorated the fine arts world on both coasts. ♦ 24700 McBean Pkwy, Valencia. 805/255.1050

**38 Six Flags Magic Mountain** If the kids want thrills and fun, but you want a day in the country, the one hundred rides and attractions of Magic Mountain are the answer. The amusement park (illustrated above) is set on 260 beautifully landscaped acres atop the rolling hills of **Valencia**, with grassy knolls, trees, and shrubbery, creating a spacious and sylvan feeling quite different from the crowded hurly-burly of the conventional entertainment park.

Rides at Magic Mountain are guaranteed to be fast and scary. There are eight roller coasters to test your mettle. The **Colossus** is billed as the largest, fastest, highest, and steepest wooden roller coaster ever built. After 9,200 feet at speeds of up to 65 miles per hour, who could argue? The **Revolution** offers a 360-degree vertical loop at 60 miles per hour; the **Shock Wave** gives thrill seekers the opportunity to loop the loop while standing up; the **Gold Rusher** is a theme roller coaster on which you become a passenger aboard a runaway mine train; the **Viper** has several loops and an 18-story drop; and the latest, **Flashback,** is the world's only hairpin drop roller coaster, with six spiral dives.

Magic Mountain has some memorable rides for those who like to get soaking wet as part of the fun. Similar in concept and course, the rides differ in modes of conveyance: the **Tidal Wave** takes you by boat over a 50-foot waterfall; the **Log Jammer** features hollowed-out logs; the **Jet Stream,** speed boats; and the **Roaring Rapids,** white-water rafts.

For panoramic views of the surrounding territory, try the **Eagle's Flight Tramway,** a 40-degree inclined funicular railroad to the top of Magic Mountain, or the **Sky Tower,** a ride to the observation deck of a 384-foot space needle structure.

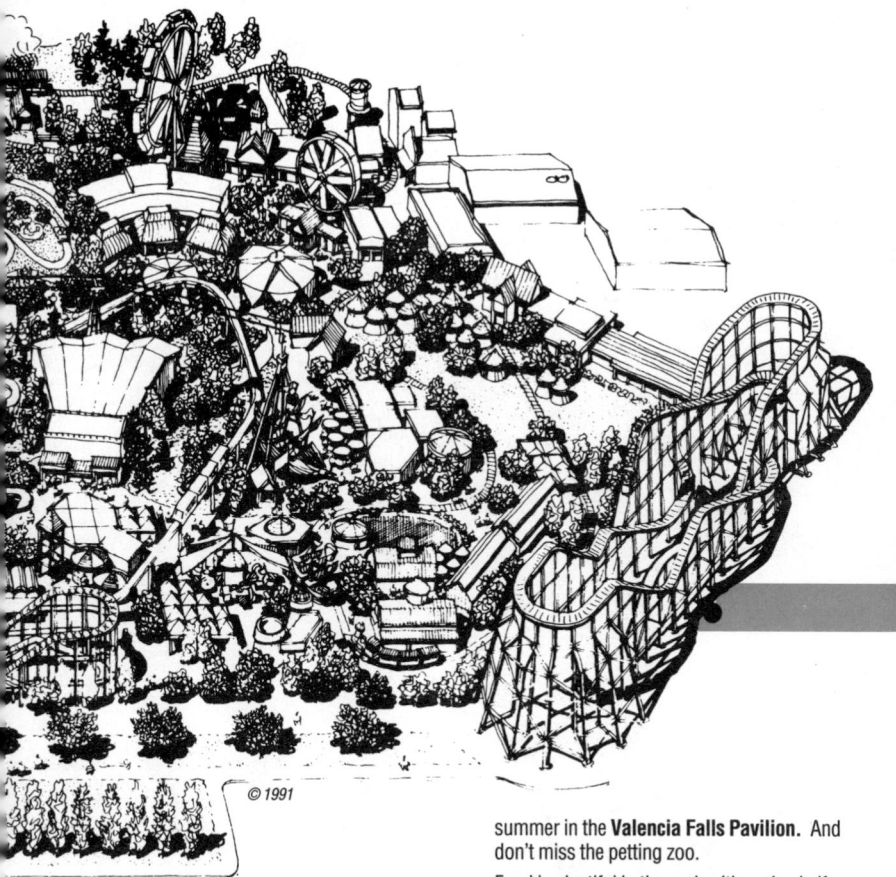

© 1991

Fast fun on the level is featured at **Sand Blasters,** where dune buggies are powered by electric motors, or **Grand Prix,** where visitors can play at being **Mario Andretti.**

The past is not forgotten at Magic Mountain. The **Grand Carousel** is an exquisitely restored 1912 merry-go-round. At **Spillikin Handcrafters Junction** traditional American crafts such as glassblowing and blacksmithing are demonstrated, and the goods are sold in quaint shops.

Nighttime attractions for teenagers include **Back Street,** a high-energy city block, and **After Hours,** a high-tech dance club. The **Magic Moments Theater** presents *California Dreamin';* and there's plenty of rocking at the **Contempo Pavilion.** Divers and dolphins are the stars at the **Aqua Theater,** and exotic animals take center stage at the **Greenwillow Theater.** A fireworks extravaganza explodes over **Mystic Lake** nightly through the summer.

**Bugs Bunny, Daffy Duck, Wile E. Coyote,** and other Warner Brothers' cartoon characters welcome youngsters to the six-acre **Bugs Bunny World** with its 15 pint-size rides, and they can enjoy a magic show through the

summer in the **Valencia Falls Pavilion.** And don't miss the petting zoo.

Food is plentiful in the park, although a half-hour wait after meals before hitting the larger rides is recommended. The **Four Winds,** at the summit of Magic Mountain, offers a delicious salad buffet at lunchtime and hot meals in the evening. The **Timbermill** serves hearty American-style food. **Food Etc.** is a fast-food restaurant with a surprisingly sophisticated Mondrian-influenced decor by **Shari Canepa.** Other spots include **Valencia Terrace, La Cantina,** and **Suzette's Bakery.** Naturally, hot dogs, soda pop, and the like, are abundant everywhere.

One admission fee at Magic Mountain conveniently covers all rides and attractions. There are height and weight restrictions on some rides. ◆ M-Th, Su 10AM-10PM; F-Sa 10AM-midnight Memorial Day-Labor Day. Rest of year weekends and school holidays only, from 10AM; call for closing times. Magic Mountain Pkwy off Interstate 5, Valencia. 818/367.5965, 818/992.0884, 805/255.4100

The first LA population count was taken in September 1781. There were 44 residents.

**Restaurants/Clubs:** Red     **Hotels:** Blue
**Shops/ ◈ Outdoors:** Green     **Sights/Culture:** Black

# San Fernando Valley

To truly grasp the scope of the San Fernando Valley, drive out of the LA basin and look down from the crest of the hills. As far as the eye can see is a vast, sprawling city, surpassing in scale anything you might have imagined. At night it's spectacular: colorful and glittering with millions of lights, its mountain-ringed boundaries disappearing into the sky. Although it is separated from the city proper by a full-blown mountain range, the **Santa Monicas**, most of the San Fernando Valley (known to residents as **"The Valley"**) is part and parcel of the city of Los Angeles. Some things distinguish it, however: space —a lot, and predominantly flat; heat—more, since the valley is usually 10 to 20 degrees warmer than the LA basin; people—more than

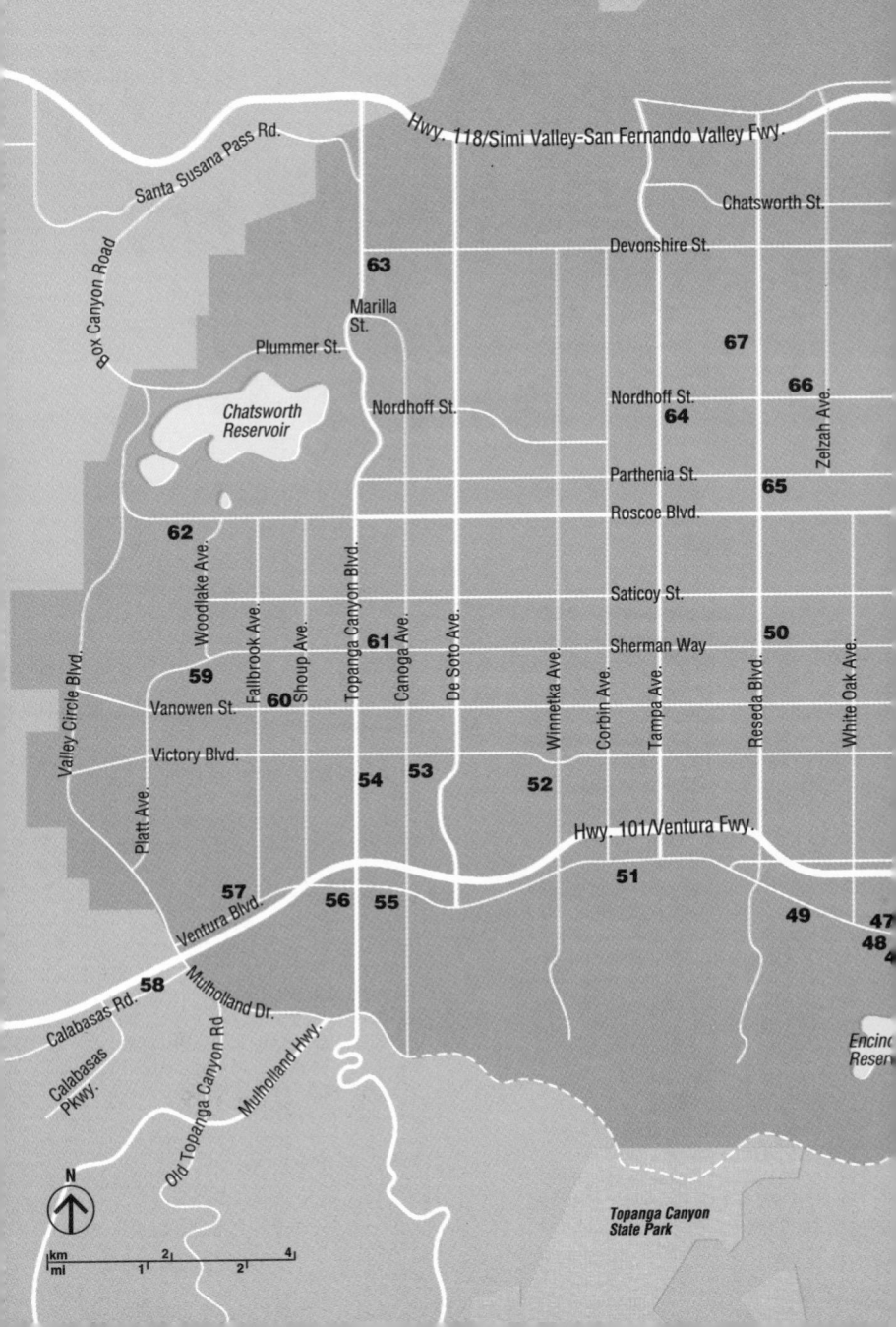

one million, a third of the population of the city of Los Angeles and nearly as many as the city of Dallas; and traffic—an extended grid of seemingly endless boulevards and streets crossing the length and breadth of the valley, reinforcing its dominant car culture. Hopelessly inadequate public transit makes an automobile a necessity here. For anyone accustomed to eastern American or European cities, the sprawl of the valley is unimaginable. When the City of Los Angeles originally annexed the San Fernando Valley on 22 May 1915, it effected a land grab that added 177 square miles to its existing 108 square miles.

Until the early 1900s, land use in the valley was limited to ranching and non-irrigated agriculture. But then speculators, anticipating the arrival of the **Owens River Aqueduct** in 1913, began to buy up thousands of acres of valley property. To share in the water brought by the aqueduct, ranchers voted to join the municipality of Los Angeles. Property values boomed, and one group of investors profited on their investment at a ratio of about eight to one. Boom succeeded boom, and hundreds of thousands moved into the valley, encouraged by jobs in the nearby aviation, electronics, and entertainment industries. Several decades of accelerated development made the area famous for rapid-start tract-house neighborhoods and instant shopping centers. The vast spaces quickly filled up due to a low-density development pattern: only 7.2 people per acre here compared to the Wilshire district's 38.9 persons per acre. The valley is predominantly residential and almost 80 percent white, remarkably homogeneous for such a large population. The west and south sides are more affluent than the east, and heavy industry is almost exclusively concentrated in the northern area around **San Fernando, Sylmar,** and **Pacoima.** With these few exceptions, the valley is basically all of one fabric, very middle class, and extremely mobile. Until recently, single-family ranch-style homes outnumbered multiple dwellings two to one, leaving this a place where it's still possible to maintain a semblance of the American dream: to own a home with a spacious yard and a two-car garage.

**San Fernando Valley**

---

*Area code 818 unless otherwise noted.*

**1 The Palomino** $$ The primo country-western club in the city also features R&B and blues and is a favorite of **Jerry Lee Lewis.** The long tables and rustic decor add atmosphere. Arrive early for a good seat and a generous helping of barbecue. ♦ American ♦ Cover. M-Sa 7:30PM-2AM. 6907 Lankershim Blvd, N. Hollywood. 764.4010

**2 Norah's Place** ★$ Quinoa, the sacred grain of the Incas, is a key ingredient in the distinctive cuisine of Bolivia. So are a few of that country's hundred-plus kinds of potatoes. Other dishes are more familiar—empanadas, *lomo saltado* (sirloin tips). Enjoy live folk music and dancing on weekends. ♦ Bolivian ♦ Tu-Th 5-11PM; F-Su 10AM-10PM. 5667 Lankershim Blvd, N. Hollywood. 980.6900

**3 Erawan** ★$$ Good Thai cooking in a non-descript setting is served here. The beef curry and the special seafood dish, which includes shrimp, squid, and clams in a delicious spicy sauce, are highly recommended. ♦ Thai ♦ Tu-F 11AM-2:30PM, 5-10PM; Sa noon-10PM; Su noon-9PM. 5145 Colfax Ave, N. Hollywood. 760.1283

**4 Salomi** ★$$ The exceedingly hot curries are of high quality. ♦ Indian ♦ M-Th noon-2:30PM, 5-9:45PM; F noon-2:30PM, 5-10:30PM; Sa 5-10:30PM; Su 5-9:45PM. 5225 Lankershim Blvd, N. Hollywood. 506.0130

**5 Arte de Mexico** Create your own hacienda from the items in seven warehouses crammed with crafts from Mexico and the southwest. ♦ M-Sa 9:30AM-5:30PM; Su 10AM-5:30PM. 5356 Riverton Ave, N. Hollywood. 769.5090

**6 Beograd** ★$ Hearty Serbo-Croatian food, wine, and songs enliven this friendly home-away-from-home for expatriates. The music and celebration can be infectious on weekends ♦ Yugoslavian ♦ W-Th, Su 5-10PM; F-Sa 5PM-2AM. 10580 Magnolia Blvd, N. Hollywood. 766.8689

**7 China Chef Wang** ★$$ The lighting isn't romantic and the flowers may be plastic, but it's got some of the best Chinese food in the valley, mostly Szechuan and Mandarin. There may be a wait on weekends. ♦Szechuan/Mandarin ♦ M-Th, Su 11AM-10PM; F-Sa 11AM-11PM. 5049 Lankershim Blvd, N. Hollywood. 509.9999

**8 La Maida House** $$$ This 1920s Mediterranean villa surrounded by lush gardens offers bed, breakfast, and, if you order in advance, delicious dinners. The pretty rooms and suites

---

**Restaurants/Clubs:** Red   **Hotels:** Blue
**Shops/ 🌳 Outdoors:** Green   **Sights/Culture:** Black

offer a civilized alternative to the chain hotels. ♦ 11159 La Maida St (at Lankershim Blvd), N. Hollywood. 769.3857

**9 Barsac Brasserie** ★★$$ Delicious bistro food complements the cool setting. Duck-and-mushroom salad, penne with olives and tomatoes, and choucroute with veal sausage have been praised. ♦ French ♦ M-Th 11:30AM-2:30PM, 5:30-10PM; F 11:30AM-2:30PM, 5:30-10:30PM; Sa 5:30-10:30PM. 4212 Lankershim Blvd, N. Hollywood. 760.7081

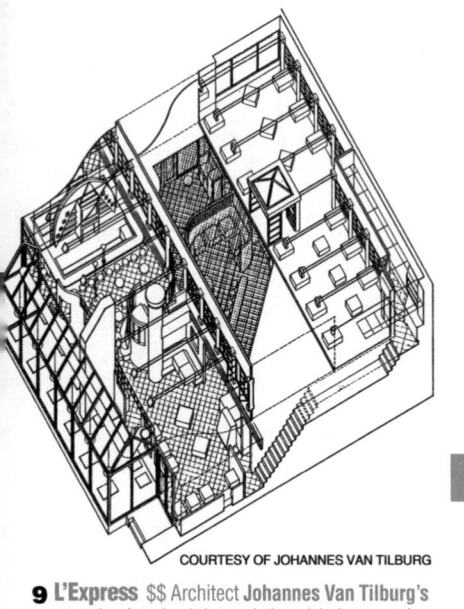

COURTESY OF JOHANNES VAN TILBURG

**9 L'Express** $$ Architect **Johannes Van Tilburg's** stunning interior (pictured above) helps sustain the popularity of this cafe/restaurant frequented by different age groups at different times of day—for a business lunch, a quiet dinner in the enclosed room upstairs, or action at the stand-up bar. It's located in the base of a large brick-and-glass wedge designed to catch the attention of motorists speeding by Universal City on the freeway. ♦ California ♦ M-F 7AM-1AM; Sa-Su 8AM-1AM. 3575 Cahuenga Blvd, Universal City. 763.5518

**9 Thai Barbecue** $$ This slick, reliable Thai restaurant offers the usual Thai egg rolls and *mee krob* (sweet fried noodles), plus deep-fried squid and sautéed baby clams. ♦ Thai ♦ M-Th 11:30AM-3PM, 5-10:30PM; F 11:30AM-3PM, 5-11PM; Sa 5-11PM; Su 5-10:30PM. 3737 Cahuenga Blvd, N. Hollywood. 760.9691

**9 The Baked Potato** $$ The guitar gods **Lee Ritenour** and **Larry Carlton** got their start here at one of LA's best established clubs for contemporary jazz. It's loud and intimate. Shrimp-and-cheese stuffed potatoes are a specialty. ♦ Cover. Daily 7AM-2AM. 3787 Cahuenga Blvd, N. Hollywood. 980.1615

**10 Mary's Lamb** ★$ Everything in this cozy restaurant and takeout is homemade, from the meat loaf and fried chicken to the pies and baked goods. ♦ American ♦ Tu-F 7AM-3PM, 5:30-10PM; Sa-Su 9AM-3PM, 5:30-10PM. 10820 Ventura Blvd, Studio City. 505.6120

**11 The Racquet Center** For a small annual fee, you can reserve any one of the 20 lighted tennis courts and 10 racquetball courts and use the well-appointed locker room. ♦ M-F 6AM-midnight; Sa-Su 7AM-midnight. 10933 Ventura Blvd, Studio City. 760.2303

**12 Hortobagy** ★$$ Since it's named for the plains region of Hungary, home of the fabled Hungarian horsemen, it's no surprise that the food here is solid, spicy, unpretentious stuff. There are stews, rich soups, and grilled and breaded meats, as well as amazing homemade sausages, plus a small deli case and a selection of Hungarian wines. ♦ Hungarian ♦ Tu-Su 11AM-10PM. 11138 Ventura Blvd, Studio City. 980.2273

**12 Sushi Nozawa** ★★$$ Victorian table manners are observed at this splendidly old-fashioned restaurant. But the stern warnings on what not to do or eat are worth it: chef Nozawa serves some of the best and freshest sushi in town. ♦ Japanese ♦ M-F noon-2PM, 5-10PM; Sa 5-10PM. 11288 Ventura Blvd, Unit C, Studio City. 508.7017

**13 Jitlada** ★★$$ One of the best Thai restaurants in LA, Jitlada specializes in shellfish. Among the stars: crunchy fried squid, barbecued chicken, Thai sausage salad, and Bangkok duck. ♦ Thai ♦ M-Th 11:30AM-10PM; F-Sa

11:30AM-11PM; Su 11:30AM-10PM. 11622 Ventura Blvd, Studio City. 506.9355

**13 St. Moritz** ★$$ The longtime area favorite draws an older crowd of people with its reliable Central European cuisine—notably the Wiener schnitzel—served in generous portions. There is a lovely patio. ♦ Swiss ♦ M-Th 11:30AM-2:30PM, 5-9PM; F 11:30AM-2:30PM, 5-10PM; Sa 5-10PM. 11720 Ventura Blvd, Studio City. 980.1122

**14 La Loggia** ★★$$ Movie moguls and power brokers keep this modern trattoria jumping. Its popularity hasn't waned since the day it opened—locals describe it as the valley's answer to Spago. Pasta and risotto are standouts. ♦ Northern Italian ♦ M-F noon-2PM, 5:30-10PM; Sa 5:30-10PM; Su 5-10PM. 11814 Ventura Blvd, Studio City. 985.9222

**14 Teru Sushi** ★$$ This hugely popular sushi bar launched what is now LA's favorite grazing fare. The theatrical presentation by the chefs also adds flair to the service of other Japanese specialties. ♦ Japanese ♦ M-Th, Su noon-2:30PM, 5-11PM; F-Sa noon-2:30PM, 5:30-11:30PM. 11940 Ventura Blvd, Studio City. 763.6201

**133**

**15 Il Mito** $$ This busy trattoria, with unique lanterns, a long concrete bar, and shiny parquetry walls in a remodeled 1920s Art Deco tile factory, is simple and cosmopolitan. Chef **Michael Fekr,** who honed his craft at such restaurants as **Locanda Veneta** and **Chianti Cucina,** offers a small menu with excellent grilled and oven-roasted meats and linguini with seafood. Il Mito means "the myth." ◆ Italian ◆ M-Th 11:30AM-2:30PM, 6-10PM; F 11:30AM-2:30PM, 6-10:30PM; Sa 6-10:30PM. 11801 Ventura Blvd, Studio City. 762.1818

**15 Wine Bistro** ★$$ Wine and pretty good bistro fare are served in a warm and woodsy setting. ◆ French ◆ M-F 11AM-10PM; Sa 5:30-10PM. 11915 Ventura Blvd, Studio City. 766.6233

**15 San Pietro Bar & Grill** ★★$$ Prawns with rice-wine sauce, pasta with salmon and cucumber, and grilled meats and vegetables are good bets at this improved version of the Bel Air pizza place. ◆ Italian ◆ M-Sa 11:30AM-2AM; Su 11:30AM-1AM. 12001 Ventura Pl, Studio City. 508.1177

**16 Dutton's Bookstore** This is a well-stocked branch of the store in Brentwood. ◆ M-F 9:30AM-9PM; Sa 9:30AM-6PM; Su 11AM-6PM. 5146 Laurel Canyon Blvd, Studio City. 769.3866. Also at: 11975 San Vicente, Brentwood. 310/476.6263

## San Fernando Valley

**17 Le Pavillon** ★$$ Cafe food with an organic bent is served here, including crepes, omelets, and more than generous salads. ◆ French ◆ M-Th 11AM-10PM; F-Sa 11AM-11PM. 12161 Ventura Blvd, Studio City. 980.0225

**18 Art's Deli** $$ The full-service deli is a favorite among valley tennis players. Pastrami is a house specialty. ◆ Deli ◆ Daily 7:30AM-9:30PM. 12224 Ventura Blvd, Studio City. 762.1221

**19 Oyster House Saloon and Restaurant** ★$$ The oyster bar and the pasta with seafood are the main attractions in this popular watering hole. ◆ Seafood ◆ M-Sa 11:30AM-11:30PM; Su 4-10PM. 12446 Moorpark St, Studio City. 761.8686

**20 Sportsmen's Lodge and Sportsmen's Lodge Restaurant** ★$$$ The moderately priced hotel ($$) is located in a verdant setting. Inside, the glass-walled dining room looks out onto ponds, a stream, and a waterfall. Along with all this beauty is good food, too. ◆ American ◆ Tu-Sa 5:30-10PM; Su 4:30-10PM. Hotel: 12825 Ventura Blvd, Studio City. 769.4700. Restaurant: 12833 Ventura Blvd, Studio City. 984.0202

**21 Tujunga Wash Mural** The world's longest mural (a half-mile and still unfinished) occupies the west wall of a concrete flood control channel and tells the history of California from the age of the dinosaurs to the present. Anger brings history to life, as in the revolutionary murals of Mexico City, and though this collaborative effort is no artistic masterpiece, it's a provocative learning experience for participants and visitors. **Judy Baca** has directed the project over the past dozen or so years for **SPARC,** a nonprofit Venice arts group. ◆ Coldwater Canyon Blvd (between Burbank Blvd and Oxnard St), N. Hollywood

**22 Iroha Sushi** ★★$$ Excellent sushi is served in a quiet, caring bar that's well hidden from the street. ◆ Japanese ◆ M-Th noon-2:30PM, 5-10:30PM; F noon-2:30PM, 5:30-11PM; Sa 5:30-11PM. 12953 Ventura Blvd, Studio City. 990.9559

**22 Pinot** $$ At press time, this new restaurant had not yet opened its doors, but master chef **Joachim Splichal** of **Patina** fame is expected to bring his culinary expertise to this inviting and predictably busy bistro. As with his Melrose Avenue restaurant, Splichal enlisted the design expertise of **Cheryl Brantner,** whose designs for the interior complement the flavors of good French cooking with a setting that echoes simple but very elegant country French dining. ◆ French ◆ M-Th 11:30AM-2:30PM, 6-10PM; F 11:30AM-2:30PM, 5:30-10:30PM; Sa 5:30-10:30PM. 12969 Ventura Blvd, Studio City. 990.0500

**23 Bistro Garden** ★$$$ The light, airy room with traditional decor is an indoor version of the Beverly Hills favorite of the ladies who lunch. The service is good and the menu long, but stick to the simplest dishes. ◆ Eclectic ◆ M-F 11AM-10:30PM; Sa-Su 5:30-11PM. 12950 Ventura Blvd, Studio City. 501.0202

**23 Marrakesh** ★★$$ Couscous with lamb, chicken with olives, and *b'stilla* (chicken with spices, nuts, and fruit beneath a flaky pastry crust) are served amid authentic decor. ◆ Moroccan ◆ M-Th, Su 5-10PM; F-Sa 5-11PM. 13003 Ventura Blvd, Studio City. 788.6354

**24 The Great Greek** ★$$$ Greek food is served in an exuberant atmosphere, but the appetizers are a better bet than the entrées. The 14-course banquet, intended to serve one, is enough for any three people we know. Music and dancing are featured nightly. ◆ Greek ◆ M-Th, Su 11:30AM-11PM; F-Sa 11:30AM-12:30AM. 13362 Ventura Blvd, Sherman Oaks. 905.5250

**24 Mistral** ★$$ This generally good French bistro offers a warm atmosphere and a touch of Provence in the generous use of herbs to enliven the baked mussels and grilled steak. ◆ French ◆ M-Th 11:30AM-3PM, 5:30-10:15PM; F-Sa 11:30AM-3PM, 5:30-11:30PM. 13422 Ventura Blvd, Sherman Oaks. 981.6650

**25 Prezzo** ★$$$ The food is surprisingly good in this favorite meeting place of the valley's *jeunesse dorée*. Scallops in red pepper sauce, pasta with smoked chicken, and grilled swordfish are highly recommended. ♦ Italian ♦ M-F 11:30AM-midnight; Sa-Su 5PM-1AM. 13625 Ventura Blvd, Sherman Oaks. 905.8400

**26 Moonlight Tango Cafe** ★$$ A band in white suits plays rhumbas on white instruments in a '40s setting; all it needs is **Carmen Miranda** to sashay on stage and lead a conga line. The food here can be quite good—seafood gumbo, juicy lamb, fettucine with wild mushrooms, and spicy homemade sausages. ♦ Eclectic ♦ M-Th, Su 5PM-midnight; F-Sa 5PM-2AM. 13730 Ventura Blvd, Sherman Oaks. 788.2000

**27 Sherman Oaks Fashion Square** Bullock's and **The Broadway** anchor one of the first large shopping plazas in the area. The brick-paved outdoor promenades are lined with quality shops. ♦ M-F 10AM-9PM; Sa 10AM-6PM; Su noon-5PM. 14006 Riverside Dr (at Hazeltine Ave), Sherman Oaks. 783.0550

**27 Sunkist Headquarters Building** The striking concrete crate was designed in 1969 by **A.C. Martin & Associates**. Sunkist is the trademark of a citrus-growing collective of ranches all over the Southland. ♦ 14130 Riverside Dr, Sherman Oaks

**28 Cevicheria El Silencio** ★$ South American seafood of rare authenticity is served here. The standouts include *ceviche* of scallops, deep-fried stuffed potatoes, and fried rice with seafood. ♦ Peruvian ♦ M, W-Su noon-10PM. 14111 Burbank Blvd, Van Nuys. 997.9412

**29 Fab's Italian Kitchen** ★$$ This friendly restaurant and storehouse of imported specialties from the "Old Country" offers hearty pizzas and traditional pasta favorites. ♦ Italian ♦ M-Th 11AM-10PM; F-Sa 11AM-11PM; Su noon-10PM. 4336 Van Nuys Blvd, Sherman Oaks. 995.2933

**29 Gen Mai-Sushi** ★$$ Peace, love, and sushi are dished out at this spot run by disciples of **Masahisa Goi**. They serve both vegetarian and macrobiotic dishes as well as sushi made with brown rice. ♦ Japanese ♦ Tu-F noon-2:30PM, 5:30PM-midnight; Sa noon-2:30PM, 5:30-11PM. 4454 Van Nuys Blvd. Suite M, Sherman Oaks. 986.7060

**30 Lannathai** ★$$ Diners sit around what was once a swimming pool, now full of koi. The menu boasts 86 Thai specialties. ♦ Thai ♦ M-Th, Su 11:30AM-10:30PM; F-Sa 11:30AM-11PM. 4457 Van Nuys Blvd, Sherman Oaks. 995.0808

**30 Forbidden Planet** This is the place for contemporary pop culture—American and European adult comics, fantasy, and science fiction—and art works and collectibles. ♦ Daily 11AM-9PM. 14513 Ventura Blvd, Sherman Oaks. 995.0151

**30 Le Cafe** $$$ Simple dishes are served in a strikingly modern setting. The **Room Upstairs** features top-flight jazz talent nightly. ♦ American ♦ Daily 8:30AM-2AM. 14633 Ventura Blvd, Sherman Oaks. 986.2662

**31 The Scene of the Crime** This bookstore features **Raymond Chandler** along with 15,000 other mystery and detective titles, including many that are out of print. ♦ M-Sa 10AM-6PM. 14450 Ventura Blvd, Sherman Oaks. 981.2583

**31 L'Express** ★$$$ Unfortunately, the view from this cafe is of Ventura Boulevard, but nevertheless; L'Express tries to be a lively French bistro. It's *the* place in the valley for steak and *pommes frites* and pâté with cornichons. ♦ French ♦ M-F 7AM-1:30AM; Sa-Su 8AM-1AM. 14910 Ventura Blvd, Sherman Oaks. 990.8683

**31 Posto** $$ Sicilian-born owner/chef **Piero Selvaggio** has brought the flavors of **Valentino** and **Primi un Ristorante** to the valley. The menu carries Italian favorites that have made his two

Westside establishments excel. The wine cellar, featuring some choice selections, is also used as a private banquet room with a 40 person capacity. ♦ Italian ♦ M-F 11:30AM-2:30PM, 5:30-10:30PM; Sa 5:30-10:30PM; Su 5-10:30PM. 14928 Ventura Blvd, Sherman Oaks. 784.4400

**32 La Frite** $$ Crepes, omelets, and quiche are all nicely prepared and served until late. ♦ French ♦ M-Th 11AM-11PM; F-Sa 11AM-midnight; Su 11AM-11PM. 15013 Ventura Blvd, Sherman Oaks. 990.1791. Also at: 22616 Ventura Blvd, Woodland Hills. 347.6711

**33 Kenny's Kitchen** ★$ A friendly couple from Bombay offers good home-cooking smack in the middle of a minimall. The vegetable dishes are outstanding, as are the chicken in garlic sauce and lamb *korma*. ♦ Indian ♦ Tu-Su 11:30AM-9:30PM. 14126 Sherman Way, Van Nuys. 786.4868

**34 Western Bagel** Jalapeño and blueberry are among the 18 varieties, freshly baked and sold 24 hours a day. ♦ Daily 24 hours. 7814 Sepulveda Blvd, Van Nuys. 786.5847. Also at: 11628 Santa Monica Blvd, W. Los Angeles. 310/826.0570

**35 Dr. Hogly-Wogly's Tyler Texas BBQ** ★★$ This is the real thing, good enough to bring tears to the eyes of a Lone Star exile. People line up to eat down-home ribs, links, chicken, and beans, despite the lack of amenities. ♦ Barbecue ♦ Daily noon-10PM. 8136 Sepulveda Blvd, Van Nuys. 780.6701

In 1838 an LA ordinance was passed prohibiting the serenading of women without a license.

**36 94th Aero Squadron Headquarters Restaurant** ★$$ Located near the Van Nuys Airport, this 1973 version of a French farmhouse is complete with bales of hay in the front yard. American standards—from burgers to prime rib to fried chicken—are served. It's a fun place to take the kids. ♦ American ♦ M-F, Su 11AM-3PM, 5-10PM; Sa 5-11PM. 16320 Raymer St, Van Nuys. 994.7437

**37 Sepulveda Basin Recreation Area** The 2,000-acre basin is leased by the City of Los Angeles from the **US Army Corps of Engineers.** Within the park are three 18-hole golf courses, a 20-acre picnic area, a cricket field, a model airplane field, an archery range, and plenty of bicycle and roller skating paths. ♦ Daily sunrise to sunset. 17017 Burbank Blvd, Encino. 989.8188. Golf information: 213/485.5566

**38 India Palace** ★$$ Chicken *tikka* and lamb *vindaloo* are standouts at this serious restaurant. ♦ Indian ♦ M-Sa 11:45AM-2:15PM, 5:30-10PM; Su 5:30-10PM. 4523 Sepulveda Blvd, Sherman Oaks. 986.8555

**39 Shihoya** ★★$$ This is another strict sushi bar, where (as at **Nozawa's** in Studio City) you obey the rules and enjoy outstandingly fresh and beautiful sashimi and sushi. ♦ Japanese ♦ M, W-Sa 5:30-9:45PM; Su 5:30-9:30PM. 15489 Ventura Blvd, Sherman Oaks. 986.4461

## San Fernando Valley

**40 Angkor** ★$ Steamed sole in a yellow-bean sauce, charbroiled pork, and poached salmon in lemon-grass sauce are standouts in this simple but satisfying storefront. ♦ Cambodian ♦ M-Sa 11AM-2:30PM, 5-9:30PM; Su 5-9:30PM. 16161 Ventura Blvd, Suite B, Encino. 990.8491

**41 Benihana of Tokyo** ★$$$ The Teppan-grill tradition of Japan is raised to the level of theater by a chef trained to handle a knife like a samurai. ♦ Japanese ♦ M-Th 11:30AM-2:30PM, 5:30-10:30PM; F 11:30AM-2:30PM, 5:30-11PM; Sa 5-11PM; Su 5-10PM. 16226 Ventura Blvd, Encino. 788.7121

**42 Tempo** $ A taste of the Middle East is welcome for its unfamiliarity. Try the falafel, hummus, or even the shish kebab. ♦ Middle Eastern ♦ Daily 11AM-midnight. 16610 Ventura Blvd, Encino. 905.5855

**43 Rancho de los Encinos State Historical Park** Visitors can leave the traffic behind and recall the stagecoach era, when dusty travelers stopped off here to refresh themselves. Among the five acres of expansive lawns, duck ponds, and tall eucalyptus are a nine-room adobe built in 1849 by **Don Vicente de la Osa** and a two-story limestone French-style home that was designed in 1870 by **Eugene Garnier.** ♦ Admission. Grounds: W-Su 10AM-5PM. Home tours: W-Su 1-4PM. 16756 Moorpark St, Encino. 784.4849

**44 Stratton's** ★$$$ This branch of the cozy restaurant in Westwood Village has drawn praise for its veal chops, braised ribs, and steaks. ♦ American ♦ Daily 11:30AM-3PM, 5-9:30PM. 16925 Ventura Blvd, Encino. 986.2400

**44 Akbar** ★★$$ Superb Mogul cooking, with excellent tandoori dishes, is the draw here. This is a branch of the original in Marina del Rey. ♦ Indian ♦ M-F, Su 11:30AM-2:15PM, 5:30-10:30PM; Sa 5:30-10:30PM. 17049 Ventura Blvd, Encino. 905.5129

**45 Town and Country Shopping Center and Plaza de Oro** The two plazas are open and rambling multilevel complexes with handsome landscaping. Unusual for the absence of large department stores, shopping here has a relaxed, almost villagelike quality. ♦ M-F 10AM-9PM; Sa 10AM-6PM; Su noon-5PM. 17200 Ventura Blvd, Encino. 788.6100

Within the Town and Country Shopping Center and Plaza de Oro:

**Oak Tree** The astonishing oak tree is estimated to be more than a thousand years old. The branches spread 150 feet and the trunk is more than eight feet in diameter. ♦ Louise Ave, just south of Ventura Blvd

**Bao Wow** ★$ Dim sum, salads, and noodle dishes are served in a high-tech dining room or on the patio. ♦ Chinese ♦ M-Sa 11:30AM-9:30PM; Su 11:30AM-9PM. 17209 Ventura Blvd. 789.9010

**Silver Grille** ★$$ This health-conscious restaurant serves such dishes as tortilla soup laden with fresh herbs, grilled tuna with an orange-ginger sauce, chicken quesadillas, and a great *tarte tatin.* ♦ California ♦ M-Tu 11:30AM-3PM, 5-10PM; F 11:30AM-3PM, 5:30-10:30PM; Sa 5:30-10:30PM; Su 5-10PM. 17239 Ventura Blvd. 784.4745

**The LA Cabaret Comedy Club** $$ Lively talent draws enthusiastic regulars to this restaurant and separate bar. Call for showtimes. ♦ Cover. Restaurant: daily 5:30PM-closing. 17271 Ventura Blvd. 501.3737

**46 Juel Park** **Edwina Skaff** creates lingerie for perfectionists, continuing the tradition of her mother, **Sue Drake,** who joined the firm (long in Beverly Hills) a year after its founding in 1929. She created form-fitting, bias-cut silk gowns for **Jean Harlow, Carole Lombard,** and **Norma Shearer.** Custom-made negligees and teddies come in satin, lace, and organdy. ♦ By appointment only. 17940 Rancho St, Encino. 609.7342, 310/276.3292

**47 Cha Cha Cha** $$ A spin-off of owner **Mario Tamayo's** first valley restaurant, this one is larger than the original, but the spicy Caribbean-Latin fare is still familiar. Chef **Toribio Prado** cooks chicken, pastas, and pizzas with a tropical treatment (notables are the spicy corn chowder and the ferocious *camarones negros,* which is shrimp in a dark and challenging chili

sauce). Brightly colored high back chairs in aqua, green, and orange and animal objects give a playroomlike sensitivity to the expansive white-washed dining room. ♦ Caribbean/Latin ♦ M-Th 10:30AM-3PM, 5-10PM; F-Sa 11:30AM-3PM, 5-11PM. 17499 Ventura Blvd, Encino. 789.3600

**48 Adam's** $$$ One of the most popular and lively places in the valley, Adam's packs 'em in for ribs broiled over oak and mesquite, a 55-foot salad bar, and an authentic soda fountain. There's also an extensive historical photo collection of the San Fernando Valley and 350 potted plants. ♦ American ♦ M-Th 11:30AM-2:30PM, 5-10:30PM; F-Sa 11:30AM-2:30PM, 4-11PM; Su 4-10PM. 17500 Ventura Blvd, Encino. 990.7427

**48 Domingo's** The well-stocked family run Italian grocery also has a deli. ♦ Tu-Sa 9AM-6PM; Su 10AM-4PM. 17548 Ventura Blvd, Encino. 981.4466

**49 Mon Grenier** ★★$$$ If you had an attic with French cooking like this, your house would be jammed, too. Reliable standbys include salmon *en croûte* and pheasant with wild mushrooms. Service can be surly. ♦ French ♦ M-Th 6-9PM; F-Sa 6-9:30PM. 18040 Ventura Blvd, Encino. 344.8060

**50 The Country Club** $$ Top country-western, rock, New Wave, R&B, etc., are played in a concert setting, live most nights. The restaurant serves soft drinks only. Free parking is available. Days and showtimes vary. ♦ Cover. 18415 Sherman Way, Reseda. 881.5601

**51 Silver Chopsticks** ★$ Bold Szechuan dishes, including noodles with chicken and sesame paste, wonderful *siu mai* (pork-filled noodle dumplings), and wontons in peanut chili sauce, are the specialty here. ♦ Chinese ♦ M-Sa 11:30AM-9:30PM; Su 4-9PM. 19538 Ventura Blvd, Tarzana. 344.6112

**52 Los Angeles Pierce College** This branch of the Los Angeles Community College system specializes in agriculture, horticulture, landscape architecture, and animal husbandry. ♦ 6201 Winnetka Ave, Woodland Hills. 347.0551

**53 La Paz** ★$ Oscar Iturralde has made his Yucatán eatery a culinary adventure, with pork baked with annato seeds in banana leaves, barbecued goat, and garlicky octopus, plus whole baked fish and paella. ♦ Mexican ♦ M-Th, Su 11AM-9PM; F-Sa 11AM-10PM. 21040 Victory Blvd, Woodland Hills. 883.4761

**53 Gaetano's Bistro** ★★$$ Among the delicious standouts at this *simpatica* trattoria located in the **Trillium Building** are shrimp with green beans, fusilli with smoked duck, and grilled whole bass with a sauce of wild mushrooms. ♦ Italian ♦ M-F 11:30AM-2:30PM, 5-10:30PM; Sa 5-10:30PM. 6336 Canoga Ave, Woodland Hills. 596.5900

**54 Woodland Hills Promenade** One of the poshest of the indoor malls, the anchors include **Saks Fifth Avenue, Robinson's,** and **I. Magnin,** and the tiled corridors are lined with luxury mercantiles. Lighting, fountains, and indoor landscaping add to the cool elegance of the place. ♦ M-F 10AM-9PM; Sa 10AM-6PM; Su 11AM-5PM. Topanga Canyon Blvd (between Oxnard and Erwin Sts), Woodland Hills. 884.7090

**55 Brother's Sushi** ★★$$ The sushi is wonderful, but don't miss the ultrafresh oysters, deep-fried soft-shell crabs in season, or the crackly salmon skin. ♦ Japanese ♦ Tu-F 11:30AM-2PM, 5:30-10PM; Sa 5:30-10:30PM; Su 5:30-10PM. 21418 Ventura Blvd, Canoga Park. 992.1284

**55 Cobalt Cafe** $ LA counterculture is alive and well in the valley. The friendly but noisy environment is filled with second-hand and vintage furnishings. There's nightly entertainment plus open mike night on Monday and poetry readings every Tuesday. ♦ Coffeehouse ♦ M-Th, Su 5PM-1AM; F-Sa 5PM-2AM. 21622 Ventura Blvd, Woodland Hills. 348.3789

**56 Lautrec** ★$$ Lamb and seafood are the specialties of this stylish restaurant. ♦ Eclectic ♦ M-Th 11AM-3PM, 5-10PM; F-Sa 11AM-3PM, 5-11PM; Su noon-3PM, 5-9PM. 22160 Ventura Blvd, Woodland Hills. 704.1185

## San Fernando Valley

**57 Adagio** ★★$$ Pastas, fish, and meat dishes all excel, and the *penne all'amatriciana* and fried calamari have won applause. ♦ Italian ♦ Tu-F 11:30AM-2:30PM, 5:30-10PM; Sa-Su 5:30-10PM. 22841 Ventura Blvd, Woodland Hills. 346.5279

**58 Calabasas Inn** $$$ The expansive garden setting is the ideal site for weddings and banquets, now the sole function of this former restaurant. ♦ 23500 Park Sorrento, Calabasas. 222.8870

**58 Sagebrush Cantina** $ This movie-set Old West saloon and patio houses a lively singles bar and a popular restaurant serving mostly Mexican standards. ♦ Mexican ♦ M-Th, Su 11AM-10PM; F-Sa 11AM-11PM. 23527 Calabasas Rd, Calabasas. 888.6062

**58 Leonis Adobe** The home-improvement tendencies of the San Fernando Valley may be traced back to 1879, when **Miguel Leonis** decided to upgrade an 1844 adobe he owned. A second level and balcony in the modish style of Monterey, then the capital, were added to the simple rectangular structure, thus making it the first chic home in the area. ♦ Free. W-Su 1-4PM. 23537 Calabasas Rd, Calabasas. 712.0734

**59 Canoga Mission Gallery** In 1936 early film star **Francis Lederer** designed and built this as a mission-style stable. Later, she remodeled it for use as a gallery and gift shop of Californian and Mexican arts. ♦ W-Su 11AM-5PM. 23130 Sherman Way, West Hills. 883.1085

---

A County measures 4,083 square miles and contains 8 incorporated cities.

**Restaurants/Clubs:** Red
**Shops/ 🌲 Outdoors:** Green
**Hotels:** Blue
**Sights/Culture:** Black

**60  Shadow Ranch**  This restored 1870 ranch house built by LA pioneer **Albert Workman** is located on nine acres that were at one time part of a 60,000-acre wheat ranch. The stands of eucalyptus trees on the property, planted in the late 19th century, are purported to be the parent stand of the trees that are now one of the most prominent features of Southern California botany. The ranch is presently used as a community center. ◆ Free. Tu-Th 9AM-9PM; Sa 9AM-5PM; Su 12:30-5:30PM. 22633 Vanowen St, Canoga Park. 883.3637

**61  Antique Row**  More than 28 shops here specialize in Americana, ranging from memorabilia to publications, with an emphasis on golden-oak Victorian furniture, bric-a-brac, and collectibles. A good place to start is the **Antique Company.** ◆ M-Sa 11AM-5PM; Su noon-5PM. 21513 Sherman Way, Canoga Park. 347.8778

**62  Orcutt Ranch Horticultural Center**  Originally part of a 200-acre estate belonging to **William** and **Mary Orcutt,** the extensive gardens, lush landscaping, and venerable trees accented by statuary are relaxing and lovely. There are spots for picnics, hiking trails, and horticultural demonstrations. Tours of the 1920 house designed by **C.G. Knipe** are given the last Sunday of each month from 2 to 5PM

## San Fernando Valley

between September and June. ◆ Free. Ranch: daily 8AM-5PM. 23600 Roscoe Blvd, West Hills. 883.6641

**63  Les Sisters Southern Kitchen**  ★$ Authentic down-home fare is served in this restaurant, including shrimp jambalaya, potent gumbo, the best fried chicken, and hush puppies. BYOB. ◆ Southern ◆ Tu-F 11AM-2:30PM, 5-9PM; Sa-Su 5-10PM. 21818 Devonshire St, Chatsworth. 998.0755

**64  Alexis**  $ This exceptional deli/market has sandwiches, salads, Greek specialties, and imported groceries. ◆ Greek ◆ M-Th 11:30AM-3PM, 5-9PM; F-Sa 11:30AM-3PM, 5-10PM. 9034 Tampa Ave, Northridge. 349.9689

**65  Thai Gourmet**  ★$ Their great northern Thai/Laotian food is absolutely the spiciest in town, so don't be a tough guy and ask them to make it hot. Cartoon smoke will pour out of your ears and you won't be able to taste the rest of your dinner. Not for everyone, but certainly interesting, is a jackfruit ice cream with garbanzo beans in it. ◆ Thai ◆ M-F 11:30AM-3PM, 5-9:30PM; Sa-Su 5-10PM. 8650 Reseda Blvd, Reseda. 701.5712

**65  Common Grounds**  $ Close to Cal State University at Northridge (CSUN), this spacious and inviting coffeehouse is popular with both students and locals. If you're not in the mood for some great, hearty coffees (try Hawaiian hazelnut, Vienna cinnamon, or chocolate raspberry), then try the cool fruit shakes. ◆ Coffeehouse ◆ M-F 7AM-midnight; Sa 9AM-1AM; Su 10AM-midnight. 9250 Reseda Blvd (at Prairie St), Northridge. 882.3666

**66  California State University at Northridge**  CSUN is one of the most popular branches of the California State University system, offering both undergraduate and graduate courses in a number of liberal arts and science disciplines. Recent government cutbacks have forced the university to curtail programs and classes, making the traditional four-year baccalaureate pursuit more difficult. **Richard Neutra** was made architect of the campus in 1960, but designed only the 1961 **Fine Arts Building.** ◆ 18100 Nordhoff St, Northridge. 885.1200

**67  Paru's**  ★$ Delicious vegetarian dishes—curries, pilafs, *samosas,* and crunchy pancakes—are served in a tiny white storefront. ◆ Indian ◆ Tu-Sa 11:30AM-9PM; Su 11:30AM-5PM. 9545 Reseda Blvd, Northridge. 349.3546. Also at: 5140 W. Sunset Blvd, Hollywood. 213/661.7600

**68  Andreas Pico Adobe**  This is the second oldest home in Los Angeles (circa 1834), built by Mission San Fernando Indians. **Andreas Pico,** brother of the one-time governor, bought it in 1853 and with his son, **Romulo,** added a second story in 1873. By the early 1900s it had fallen into disuse, but in 1930 the curator of the **Southwest Museum** purchased and restored it. It was bought by the City of Los Angeles in 1967. The **San Fernando Historical Society** has its headquarters here. ◆ W-Su 1-4PM; weekdays by appointment. 10940 Sepulveda Blvd, Mission Hills. 365.7810

**69  Mission San Fernando Rey de España**  Until the dissolution of the missions in the mid-1830s, San Fernando was an essential part of the economic life of Los Angeles, supplying a great portion of the foodstuff for the fledgling community.

Founded in 1797 by **Friar Fermin Lasuen,** the mission was completed in 1806, but was subsequently destroyed by an earthquake and replaced in 1818. History repeated itself in the 1971 Sylmar/San Fernando earthquake, when the church again sustained damage so grave that it had to be reconstructed in 1974. The adobe construction of the early period had a simple yet monumental quality that achieved richness through the repetition of structural elements. This quality is best observed in the 243-foot-long convento, where 19 semicircular arches supported by massive square pillars form a loggia over time-hollowed tiles. Tours of the mission include working, sleeping, and reception areas, giving visitors a sense of day-to-day life during the early days of the complex. ◆ Admission. Daily 9AM-4PM. Gift shop: 9AM-5PM. 15151 San Fernando Mission Blvd, Mission Hills. 361.0186

**70  Merle Norman Museum**  This treasure-rich storehouse features vast assortments of classic cars, nickelodeons, and 19th-century musical instruments, including the **Emperor Franz Joseph's** piano, which are played on the two daily tours, Tuesday to Saturday at 10AM and 1:30PM. Reservations must be made six weeks in advance. ◆ 15180 Bledsoe St, Sylmar. 367.2251

## Piero Selvaggio

Owner, Valentino

A Mexican Restaurant: **El Cholo**—on Sunday evening, for margaritas, mariachis. Latin folklore, and people of all races, groups, and looks. A real piece of floating life...with salsa!

An Amphitheater: the **Hollywood Bowl**—the most extravagant picnics, the pops, and the stars.

A Charity Event: **Meals on Wheels at Universal Studios**—the greatest chefs of America, the best wineries, a great setting, and a great cause (feeding the hungry poor).

A Special Occasion: **Citrus**—the Temple of Michel Richard for incredible food and super desserts.

A Road: **Pacific Coast Highway**—driving back and forth to Malibu for the sea breeze, the beach settings, pacing, and thinking.

A Memory: **Rex, Il Ristorante**—because of my wedding, because of Mauro Vincenti, and because it's one-of-a-kind and keeps sailing along!

A Free Show: **Venice Beach** on the weekend—maybe the single, most eccentric mixture of show and attractions, with people, pets, bikes, waves, and freedom. A sketch in the life of a bohemian community.

A Market: **Gelson's** in Pacific Palisades—it is the state-of-the-art supermarket.

With Kids: the **LA Zoo** at Griffith Park—a place for my children, with so many activities, animals, people, and space.

Favorite Food Notes: pizza at **Madeo's**, ice cream at **Pazzia**, fun and food at **Emilio's**, plum duck at **Chinois on Main**, steak and fries at **Michael's** in the garden, pasta at **Primi**, fish at **Spago**, and something else at **Patina**.

## Willette and Manny Klausner

Founding Members, American Institute of Wine & Food

No Los Angeles chefs are more creative than Michel Richard at **Citrus** and Joachim Splichal at **Patina**. These two artists always deliver a dazzling and exciting food experience.

**Katsu** is one of our favorite neighborhood restaurants. The sushi is fresh, delicious, and spectacularly presented. This is great "diet" food.

Piero Selvaggio makes everyone feel right at home in his smartly redecorated **Valentino**. Let Piero select your menu and recommend an interesting wine from his award-winning cellar.

It's always a special treat for us to dine at **Rex**, with its romantic and elegant setting and chef Odette Fada's creative dishes. For Umberto Bombana's equally inspired Italian dishes in a smart, casual setting—with the best gelati in town—**Pazzia** is the place. Both restaurants are creations of the visionary restaurateur Mauro Vicenti.

Entertaining a group of friends is always a delight at **Fujean Kang's** in Pasadena. They serve innovative Chinese dishes (with spectacular dim sum), and an unusually wide range of wines are specially selected to accompany the eclectic cuisine.

We go to **Barragan's** in Echo Park (on Sunset Boulevard) for tasty, country-style enchiladas, beef tacos, and *costillas de puerco en salsa chipotle*.

Vegetarian pizza and *scamorza* (warm mozzarella with chopped tomatoes and basil) at **Angeli** on Melrose are our personal favorites. We also like the pesto pizza at **Pazzia** and the special pizzas served at **Spago**.

**Chinois on Main** in Santa Monica is a high-energy and exciting restaurant, and always a special experience for out-of-town foodies. We love Mako's extraordinary eel and lobster rolls and the cabbage stuffed with squab and foie gras.

For an unusual and exhilarating progressive dinner in the South Bay, try the **Depot** for appetizers (call the peripatetic Michael Franks to arrange a very special evening), **Fino** for main course, and **Chez Melange** for dessert.

For breakfast meetings, we like **Campanile** (for the best granola) and **Victor's** (on Franklin and Bronson).

For downtown lunch spots, try the **Sonora Grill** (superb Southwest cuisine) and **Uncle Moustache's Falafel** (at the Bonaventure Hotel) for chicken kabobs and fresh watermelon juice.

Other current favorites include **Bikini** (for John Sedlar's dazzling creations) and **Opus** (for Eberhard Mueller's spectacular seafood dishes).

## San Fernando Valley

Our favorite Valley places are **Pinot Bistro, Posto,** and the **Great Greek**.

Other longtime favorites: Ken Frank's **La Toque**; **Harriet's Cheesecakes** (the best in LA); **Tulips**, order the "Roland Burger"; **L'Orangerie**, for an elegant dining experience; **Fennel**, for the best goat cheese and potato salad; **Border Grill**, for exciting Mexican cuisine; **Joss**, for creative Chinese delicacies; **Michael's**, to dine in Santa Monica's loveliest outdoor setting; **Langer's**, for the best pastrami sandwich; and **Yuca's**, for some delectable Yucatán street food.

## Richard Meier

Architect

Checking in at the **Bel-Air Hotel,** surrounded by what appears to be the world in bloom, particularly after departing New York on a bleak winter's day.

Having dinner at **Spago**, a unique restaurant that catches the rhythm of Los Angeles' most interesting inhabitants.

A Sunday stroll on the **Venice Boardwalk,** for the other half of LA's interesting inhabitants.

A visit to the **Museum of Contemporary Art (MOCA),** the most beautifully designed museum, with a stop in **Little Tokyo** for sushi.

The **Huntington Library and Botanical Gardens** are another must-see for visitors, and certainly more than an annual excursion for locals.

Patio dining at **Michael's** in Santa Monica on a warm summer evening.

A drive up the coast through **Malibu,** with a stop at a seaside restaurant for drinks and an ocean view.

# Griffith Park/ North Central

Northeast of Hollywood, in the foothills of the Santa Monica Mountains, are two of LA's most attractive neighborhoods and its grandest park. Griffith Park covers more than 4,000 acres, making it one of the largest urban green spaces in America. It is named for **Colonel Griffith J. Griffith.** Immensely rich, he bought the land in 1882 and donated it to the city in 1896.

South of the park are the residential communities of **Los Feliz** and **Silver Lake.** Begun in the 1920s before the advent of pad construction, the homes here conform to the picturesque undulations of the land. The winding roads and tiled roofs massed on the slopes around the 1907 **Silver Lake Reservoir** resemble a

Mediterranean hill town; there are stunning views of the city and a road around the lake for biking and jogging. This area also has LA's highest concentration of modern architectural masterpieces, notably by **Richard Neutra, Rudolph Schindler, Gregory Ain**, and **John Lautner**.

Tucked into two pockets of steep hills and bordered by freeways at the northern end of downtown, North Central is predominately a blue-collar Hispanic-American district. The small frame houses perched high on the tightly woven streets give the appearance of a rural setting, and huge stands of eucalyptus trees run across the hillsides and into the canyons. Trails form a network through the overgrown wild areas across slopes and ravines leading up to **Mount Washington.** A mix of romance and economy makes this residential area attractive to creative young people.

The first residents of the neighborhood were the **Yang-Na Indians,** who camped in the **Elysian Park Hills** and hunted for small game with bows and arrows. Several hillside springs fed by the Los Angeles River supplied the Indians with water. When the pueblo's first settlers arrived, they continued to use these water sites and added a waterwheel and rope system to bring the water down to the settlement from the hills. Around 1910 moviemakers came to the neighborhood, among them **Mack Sennett,** who built his first studio near Glendale Boulevard.

*Area code 213 unless otherwise noted.*

 **1 Griffith Park** The park is divided into two main areas: the flatlands, with their lush golf courses, picnic areas, pony and train rides, tennis courts, **Merry-Go-Round, Zoo, Travel Town, Observatory,** and the **Greek Theatre;** and the mountainous central and western areas, which have been left undeveloped except for numerous hiking and horse trails. There are four main entrances to the park: Western Canyon Road, off Western Avenue north of Los Feliz Boulevard, leading to Ferndell; Vermont Avenue and Hillhurst Avenue, north of Los Feliz Boulevard, leading to the Greek Theatre and the **Bird Sanctuary;** Crystal Springs Drive, off Riverside Drive, leading to the Ranger Station, merry-go-round, and golf courses; and the junction of the Golden State (Interstate 5) and Ventura (California 134) freeways, leading to the zoo and Travel Town. Rangers lead a hike on the first Saturday of the month at 9AM from the merry-go-round parking lot. **Sierra Club** tours include evening outings during full

moons. Call 665.5188 for the schedule. There are no specific bike paths, but regular paved roads are open to cyclists. Bikes are not permitted on the fire roads or horse trails. Eighteen picnic areas are located in the park, and some have benches and tables; those in Ferndell and Vermont Canyon have barbecues and water. **Park Center** and **Mineral Wells** have some areas with cooking facilities. Visitors may also picnic on the grass. ♦ Daily 5:30AM-10:30PM; mountain roads close at sunset. Visitors Center: 4730 Crystal Springs Dr. 665.5188

Within Griffith Park:

**Ranger Station** Stop here for information and free road and hiking trail maps. ♦ Daily 6AM-10PM. 4730 Crystal Springs Dr. 665.5188

**2 Merry-Go-Round** The well-preserved merry-go-round on the green was constructed in 1926 and moved to the park in 1936. ♦ Admission. Daily 10AM-4:30PM mid-June to mid-Sept; Sa-Su and LA public school holidays 10AM-4:30PM mid-Sept to mid-June. Park Center Picnic Area, off Griffith Park Dr. 665.3051

**3 Baseball** A baseball diamond in the **Crystal Springs Picnic Area** is open by permit. It is used by city college teams for their league games. ♦ Along Crystal Spring Dr

**4 Golf** There are two 18-hole courses and two nine-hole courses in Griffith Park that are open to the public. City-registered golfers may make reservations. Others will be allowed on the green

as space becomes available. ♦ The 18-hole courses are: **Harding** and **Wilson,** 4730 Crystal Springs Drive, 663.2555. The 9-hole courses are: **Roosevelt,** 2650 N. Vermont Avenue, 665.2011, and **Los Feliz 3-Par,** 3207 Los Feliz Boulevard, 663.7758

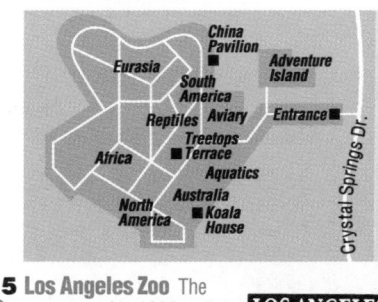

**5 Los Angeles Zoo** The zoo opened in 1966 and has more than 2,000 animals grouped according to continent of origin on 75 landscaped acres (see the plan above). Many of the animals are in environments that simulate their natural habitats with surrounding moats, thus allowing visitors to see them without bars. The

zoo preserves 78 endangered species. Explore the **Koala House** and the **Aviary;** go for a camel or elephant ride; and take in a bird show. Children may mingle with gentle beasts and explore the American Southwest on **Adventure Island.** The **Animal Nursery** proudly displays the newest arrivals. Baby stroller and wheelchair rentals are available. There are also picnic tables, a snack bar, and a tram tour. ♦ Admission. Daily 10AM-5PM (animals are taken in at 4:30PM). 5333 Zoo Dr, near the junction of the Golden State and Ventura Fwys. 666.4090 (recorded information), 666.4650

**6 Gene Autry Western Heritage Museum** The singing cowboy of movies, radio, and television opened this wonderful tribute to the spirit of the West in 1988. **Walt Disney Imagineering** has brought the memorabilia, art works, and the movie clips to life so that you can get a visceral sense of what it was like to be a settler, a

cowboy, or a sheriff. Scholarship and show biz are fruitfully combined, and the museum presents regular exhibitions along with the permanent collection. The museum was designed by **Widom Wein Cohen**. ♦ Admission. Tu-Su 10AM-5PM. 4700 Zoo Dr. 667.2000

**7 Travel Town** The romance of the rails lives on at this open-air museum of transportation, displaying many antique railroad and trolley cars, locomotives, planes, and automobiles. An enclosed structure houses several fire trucks and a circus animal wagon. Many of the exhibitions are open for children to climb on board. Members of a model train club work on an enormous train layout on Saturday. ♦ Free. M-F 10AM-5PM; Sa-Su 10AM-6PM. 5200 Zoo Dr, near Forest Lawn exit from Ventura Fwy. 662.9678

**7 Live Steamers** The **Los Angeles Live Steamers Club** brings its tiny steam locomotives to an area just northeast of **Travel Town** each Sunday. The trains run on tracks only seven inches apart, but they are authentic in every detail and powerful enough to pull several fully loaded cars. Children are given free rides and a chance to examine the miniatures. ♦ Su 11AM-2:30PM. One mile west of the LA Zoo in Griffith Park, east of Travel Town. 669.9729

**8 Equestrian Center and Cricket Fields** Two fields are located in the center of the equestrian track near Riverside Drive. The track functions as a practice area that leads to all trails. There are 43 miles of horse trails within the park. While the Department of Parks and Recreation does not maintain stables, several commercial stables on the outskirts of the park rent horses by the hour. All accept cash only and require a security deposit. ♦ M-F 8AM-7PM; Sa-Su 8AM-4PM. Riverside Dr and Main St. 818/840.8401

**9 Circle 'K' Stables** Couples and families can enjoy day rides on horseback through the picturesque trails of Griffith Park. Group rides can be arranged in advance. ♦ Daily 7:30AM-5PM. 914 S. Mariposa St, Burbank. 818/843.9890

**10 Bar 'S' Stables** Adults and children over the age of seven can ride any of the more than 45 horses. Group rides with guides are available. Riding lessons are offered to adults and children by appointment only (818/547.0203). ♦ Daily 8AM-4PM. 1850 Riverside Dr, Glendale. 818/242.8443

**11 Sunset Ranch** The Old West flourishes in the heart of the city at this ranch, with photogenic stables and moonlit rides to the top of the mountains, where you'll have stupendous views over LA. Night rides every Friday at 5PM are on a "first come first served" basis; groups must make appointments on other nights. ♦ Daily 9AM-5PM. 3400 N. Beachwood Dr. 469.5450

**12 The Ferndell**  This natural glade along a spring-fed stream is planted with native and exotic ferns. Paths and picnic tables make this an outstanding place to retreat from the world for an alfresco meal. ♦ Daily 6AM-5PM. Fern Dell Dr bounded by Black Oak and Red Oak Drs (off Los Feliz Blvd near Western Ave)

**13 Observatory and Planetarium** The restored 1935 copper-domed moderne structure (pictured below) by **John C. Austin** and **F.M. Ashley** dominates the Hollywood Hills and commands a view over the city and—on rare clear days—to Catalina. Get a closeup of the heavens through the observatory's twin refracting telescope, on clear nights only from 7PM to

## Griffith Park/North Central

10PM. For a weather update, call Sky Report at 663.8171. Displays in the **Hall of Science** explain astronomy and physical sciences in participatory exhibitions. When you enter the observatory, the **Foucault Pendulum** in the center of the rotunda hypnotizes visitors with its constant gentle swing. A fascinating show in the **Planetarium Theatre** re-creates eclipses, northern lights, and cycles of the stars through the use of a huge Zeiss projector. For sci-fi lovers, a show in the **Laserium** surrounds the audience with laser light, laser rock, and starship-sound. For more information on this popular show, call 818/997.3624.
♦ Admission. Hall of Science: Free. Daily 12:30-10PM June-Sept; Tu-F 2-10PM, Sa-Su 12:30-10PM, Oct-May. Planetarium: Admission. Shows in the afternoons and evenings. Closed Monday in winter. Northern end of Vermont Ave. 664.1191

Observatory and Planetarium

GRIFFITH OBSERVATORY

RIK OLSON

# LA's Neon: What a Gas....

Motorists lined up to see the first neon signs in America glowing at a Los Angeles car showroom in 1923. Car salesman **Earle Anthony** had brought the Packard signs from Paris, where the **Claude Neon Company** had a worldwide monopoly. But soon the techniques were franchised, and by the 1930s the flickering gas-filled tubes were everywhere in America. In neon's heyday, 5,000 glass-bending crafters were churning out complex designs. Today, LA preserves some of the best vintage neon, especially the movie theater marquees on Broadway in downtown. And along Melrose Avenue and the San Fernando Valley's Ventura Boulevard, neon has made a comeback with contemporary designs.

LA's **Museum of Neon Art (MONA)**—the only such museum in the world—was forced to vacate a 10-year location near Little Tokyo downtown when the LA riots and the temporary closure of the nearby Temporary Contemporary museum caused attendance to plummet. The MONA (see page 33) reopened as a small shop and gallery in **Universal Studios'** new **Citywalk** in late 1992. Several large vintage signs

from its collection are on permanent display at the popular tourist site (a four-block pastiche of shops and restaurants), including the 47-foot-tall, **1957 Gas Company flame;** the **1923 Melrose Theatre marquee;** and the animated **1934 Steele's Motel sign,** portraying a diver hitting the water with a splash. MONA also gives night tours of LA neon, which includes these highlights:

**Canter's Fairfax Restaurant Delicatessen Bakery** (1951) 419 North Fairfax Avenue

**El Capitan Theatre** (building 1920s; sign 1991) 6838 Hollywood Boulevard

**Generators of the Cylinder** (1982) 550 Hill Street

**Golden Pagoda** (1938) 950 Mei Ling Way, Chinatown

**L.A. Angel** (1992) Olive Street at Fourth Street

**Leonardo's Nightclub** (1930) 831 South La Brea Boulevard

**Mann's Chinese Theatre** (1928) 6925 Hollywood Boulevard

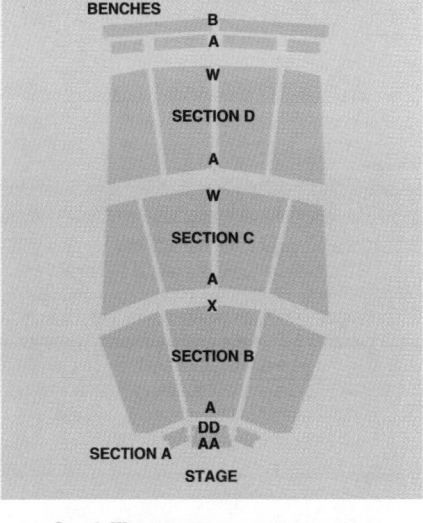

BENCHES

B
A
W
SECTION D
A
W
SECTION C
A
X
SECTION B
A
DD
AA
SECTION A
STAGE

**14 Greek Theatre** The amphitheater (see the plan above) presents mostly popular music from June through the first week in October. It is ringed by picnic tables; box suppers may be purchased from concessionaires inside. Beer and wine are available. Bring a sweater. ♦ Admission. 2700 N. Vermont Ave. Tickets and schedules: 410.1062. Subscription information 468.1767

**15 Bird Sanctuary** Birds are encouraged to nest in this wooded canyon with ponds and a stream. There are picnic tables. ♦ Daily dawn-dusk. Vermont Canyon Rd, just north of the Greek Theatre

**16 Griffith-Vermont Canyon Tennis Courts** Free play is available at the 12 day-use only courts before 4PM. No reservations are taken. ♦ Fee. Courts daily 7AM-7PM. Vermont Ave at Vista del Valle Dr. 664.3521

**17 Griffith-Riverside Tennis Courts** Twelve day- and evening-use courts are available to city-registered players through reservations. Others will be allowed to play as courts become available. Refreshments are sold. ♦ Fee. Courts daily 7AM-9PM. Corner of Riverside Dr and Los Feliz Blvd. 661.5318, 520.1010

**17 Train Ride** Another tiny train, this one runs daily. Adults as well as children may ride. ♦ Fee. M-F 10AM-5PM; Sa-Su 10AM-6PM. 4400 Crystal Springs Dr. 664.6788

**17 Pony Rides** This is a safe, small track with ponies for children. ♦ Tu-Su 10AM-4:30PM. Crystal Springs Dr (near the Los Feliz-Riverside Dr. entrance of Griffith Park). 664.3266

**18 Swimming Pool** An Olympic-size pool is open during the summer at the **Griffith Recreation Center.** ♦ M-F 11AM-3PM, 4-7PM; Sa-Su noon-3PM, 4-7PM mid June-mid Sept. 665.4372

**19 Tam O'Shanter Inn** $$ **Lawry's** runs this haven for expatriate Scots. Prime rib is the best choice from the straightforward menu. For true believers, haggis is served on **Robert Burn's** birthday. If you don't know what haggis is, don't ask. The restaurant claims to have been the first LA restaurant to introduce valet parking. ♦ Scottish ♦ M-Th 11AM-3PM, 5-10PM; F 11AM-3PM 5-11PM; Sa 5-11PM; Su 10:30AM-2:30PM, 4-10PM. 2980 Los Feliz Blvd. 664.0228

**19 La Strada** $$ The attraction here is opera, sung tableside by professionals. The atmosphere sometimes gets zany, with singers singing, waiters serving, and patrons coming and going. ♦ Italian ♦ Tu-Su 8PM-2AM. Show: Sa 8:30PM. 3000 Los Feliz Blvd. 664.2955

**19 Woody's Bicycle World** Griffith Park is full of bike trails, and this is the place to rent your wheels. ♦ Tu-Sa 9AM-6PM; Su 9AM-4PM. 3157 Los Feliz Blvd. 661.6665

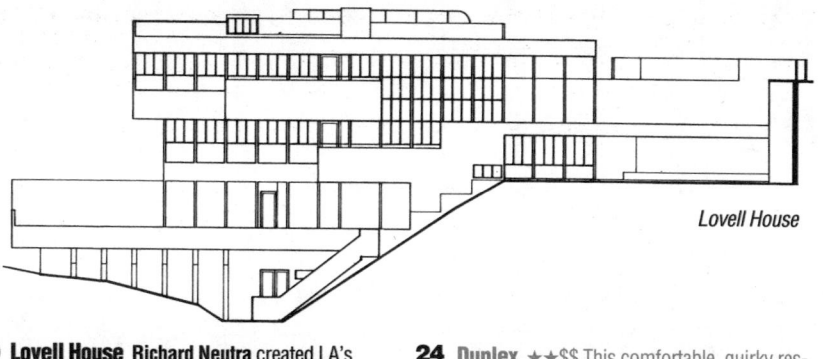

*Lovell House*

**20 Lovell House** **Richard Neutra** created LA's finest example of International Style architecture (pictured above): a steel-framed, stucco-clad composition of stacked planes flowing out from a hillside. Built in 1929, the design launched Neutra's 40-year career as the most productive and prestigious of LA's modern architects. This is a private residence. ♦ 4616 Dundee Dr

**21 Ennis-Brown House** **Frank Lloyd Wright** built this home resembling a Mayan temple on a hill overlooking the city in 1924. This is the most impressive and best-sited of Wright's concrete block houses. It is a private residence; however tours of the interior, which has been sensitively restored to its original appearance, are given on the second Saturday of each odd-numbered month from noon on. ♦ Admission. 2655 Glendower Ave. Tour reservations: 660.0607

**22 La Conversation** One of the two or three best French bakeries in LA, it has tables for those who can't wait to carry the goodies home. Croissants with lox and cream cheese are a specialty. ♦ M-Th 7:30AM-7PM; F 7:30AM-8PM; Sa 8AM-8PM; Su 8:30AM-2:30PM. 2118 Hillhurst Ave. 666.9000

**22 Mise en Place** Kitchen gadgets, pots, pans, tableware, and linens are available in profusion. ♦ M-Sa 10AM-6PM; Su 10AM-3PM. 2120 Hillhurst Ave. 662.1334

**22 Pierre's Los Feliz Inn** ★$$$ For those who want to eat in a formal atmosphere as respectable Angelenos did 50 years ago, this fills the bill. It was once a **Brown Derby**, and it still serves the signature Cobb salad. ♦ Continental ♦ M-Th 11:30AM-10:30PM; F-Sa 11:30AM-11:30PM; Su 5-10:30PM. 2138 Hillhurst Ave. 663.8001

**23 SanSui** ★$ "Healthy food in a peaceful room" is the goal of owner-chef **Shinichi Kishi**, and he delivers on both promises. The Shojin dinner includes 10 small vegetarian courses, and the music that wafts through sounds like wind on a mountaintop. ♦ Japanese ♦ Tu-Sa noon-2PM, 5:30-9:30PM; Su 5:30-10PM. 2040 Hillhurst Ave. 660.3868

**23 Yuca's Hut** ★$ People come from miles to eat the *carnitas, carne asada* tacos, and burritos made by **Dora** and her family at this little stand. Grab a beer and join the gang. ♦ Mexican ♦ M-Sa 11AM-6PM. 2056 N. Hillhurst Ave. 662.1214

**24 Duplex** ★★$$ This comfortable, quirky restaurant run by a hip neighborhood couple has a small but interesting menu (spinach and oyster soup, noodle pancakes, and tea-smoked chicken). The desserts really shine. ♦ Eclectic ♦ Tu-F 11:30AM-2:30PM, 6-10PM; Sa-Su 6-10PM. 1930 Hillhurst Ave. 663.2430

**24 The Pasta Shoppe** Buy pasta in every shape and flavor—from squid to spinach. ♦ M-F 10:30AM-6:30PM; Sa 9:30AM-5:30PM. 1964 Hillhurst Ave. 668.0458

**24 Katsu** ★★★★$$$ One of the city's most popular Japanese restaurants is perhaps one of the best restaurants in the United States. If we were giving five stars, Katsu would deserve the extra one. The stunning, black-and-white interior features a collection of **Mineo Mizuno** ceramics on the walls and tables, and dramatic paintings by

contemporary California artists. Chef **Katsu Michite** is a magician with the knife, using the freshest seafood to create exquisite dishes that display an unerring sense of culinary and esthetic harmony. Reservations, needless to say, are a must. ♦ Japanese ♦ M-F noon-2PM, 6-10PM; Sa 6-10PM. 1972 Hillhurst Ave. 665.1891. Also: **Cafe Katsu,** 2117 Sawtelle Blvd. 310/477.3359; **Katsu III,** 8636 W. Third St. 310/273.3605

**24 Trattoria Farfalla** ★$ Delicious pizzas and pastas are served in this hole in the wall, and the desserts are worth the wait. ♦ Italian ♦ M-F 11:30AM-2:30PM, 6-11PM; Sa-Su 6-11PM. 1978 Hillhurst Ave. 661.7365. Also at: 143 N. La Brea Ave. 938.2504

**25 Chatterton's Bookshop** This high-ceilinged, airy white-barrel bookstore is brimming with books, and it has one of the best selections of American and foreign literature, contemporary poetry, and literary periodicals in the city. Music plays in the background, and there are seats for reading. ♦ M-Sa 10AM-10PM; Su noon-9PM. 1818 N. Vermont Ave. 664.3882

**25 Palermo** $ Stop by for a bite at this popular pizza place. ♦ Pizza ♦ M, W-Su 11AM-10:30PM. 1858 N. Vermont Ave. 663.1430

**26 Amok Bookstore** An eclectic range of literature, from the macabre to the philosophical, fills the shelves. ♦ Tu-Su noon-8PM. 1763 N. Vermont Ave. 665.0956

**27 Mercedes Designer Resale** Slightly worn designer labels at a discount are sold. ♦ M, F-Su 11AM-6PM; Tu-Th 11AM-8PM. 1775 Hillhurst Ave. 665.8737

**28 El Chavo** $$ The menu features *rinones fritos* (sautéed kidneys with chopped vegetables), tongue in Spanish sauce and mole, and a wonderful, tender poached chicken, plus excellent grilled steaks. The softly lit atmosphere is quite pleasant and the music is thankfully unobtrusive. ♦ Mexican ♦ M-Th, Su 11:30AM-10:30PM; F-Sa 11AM-11:30PM. 4441 Sunset Blvd. 664.0871

**29 Uncle Jer's** Peace and love live on in this selection of floral, gauze, and tie-died clothing. A share of the profits is donated to environmentally conscious groups. ♦ Tu-F 11AM-7PM; Sa 10AM-6PM; Su noon-5PM. 4459 Sunset Blvd. 662.6710

**30 El Cid** $$ The food in this Spanish Colonial cabaret is only run-of-the-mill, but the flamenco guitar and flamenco dancing are remarkable. It's located on the site of **D.W. Griffith's** studio, where the 150-foot-high set of *Babylon* rose in 1916. ♦ Mexican/Spanish ♦ W 6:30-10PM; Th 6:30-11:30PM; F-Sa 6:30PM-1:45AM; Su 11AM-3PM, 6:30-11:30PM. 4212 Sunset Blvd. 668.0318

**31 Say Cheese** This shop is a great neighborhood resource for fresh cheeses, teas, coffees, and imported delicacies. ♦ Daily 10AM-6:30PM. 2800 Hyperion Ave. 665.0545

## Griffith Park/North Central

**32 Red Lion Tavern** ★$$ Not a place for nibbling, this unpretentious, inexpensive neighborhood place is the real home-cooked German article, with delicious food and lots of it: schnitzel, bratwurst, smoked pork loin, veal loaf, sauerkraut, potato salad, etc. There's also *weiss* beer and *dortmunder ritter* on tap and a fine selection of after dinner liqueurs, such as *kirschwasser, slivovitz,* and apple schnapps. ♦ German ♦ M-Th, Su 11AM-midnight; W-Sa 11AM-2AM. 2366 Glendale Blvd, Silver Lake. 662.5337

**33 Neutra House** Richard Neutra built this daringly experimental house for himself in his first decade of work in 1933, and when it was destroyed by fire in 1963, he created a more romantic version, completed one year later. This is a private residence.

On the 2200 block of Silver Lake is a concentration of Neutra houses dating from 1948 to 1961. They are at Nos. 2250, 2242, 2240, 2238, 2226, 2218, 2210, and 2200, and are all private residences. ♦ 2300 E. Silver Lake Blvd

**34 Olive House** This wonderfully complex house was designed by **Rudolf Schindler, Neutra's** compatriot and rival, who was more innovative and less successful in his LA career. This street has a uniquely rich concentration of classic modern houses. They are all private residences. ♦ 2236 Micheltorena St

**35 Casita Del Campo** $$ Come here for pleasant eating in an outdoor patio. ♦ Mexican ♦ M Th 11AM-11PM; F-Su 11AM-midnight. 1920 Hyperion Ave. 662.4255

**36 Seafood Bay** $$ Some of the cheapest fresh seafood dinners in town can be found here. There's little atmosphere, but the enthusiasm of the customers makes up for it. It doubles as a fish market. ♦ Seafood ♦ M-Th 11:30AM-9:30PM; F 11:30AM-10PM; Sa-Su 4-10PM. 3916 Sunset Blvd. 664.3902

**37 Millie's** $ Traditionally hearty breakfasts are served amidst authentic Depression-era decor (with a portrait of **FDR** on the wall). ♦ American ♦ M-Th 7AM-midnight; F 7AM-1AM; Sa 8AM-1AM; Su 8AM-11PM. 3524 Sunset Blvd. 661.5292

**38 Longest Staircase** The earliest moviemaker built studios in Silver Lake and filmed on its streets. **Laurel and Hardy** tried to carry a grand piano up these steps in *The Music Box* (1932). ♦ 927 Vendome St, Silver Lake

**38 Tropical Bakery** Guava cream cheese pie and good coffee are specialties. ♦ Daily 6AM-10PM. 2900 Sunset Blvd. 661.8391

**39 Netty's** $ Soups, pasta, grilled chicken, and dishes of the day, to go or to eat at a few small tables, are the mainstays of the menu. ♦ American ♦ M-Sa noon-9PM. 1700 Silver Lake Blvd. 662.8655

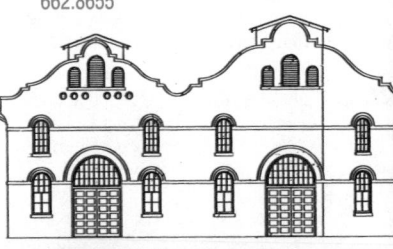

**40 Olive Substation** Restored by the **Jerde Partnership,** this 1907 structure (pictured above) was originally one of several Mission-style stations in the city taken over by the Pacific Electric Railway Company in 1911. It now houses a private office. ♦ 2798 Sunset Blvd

**41 Los Arrieros** ★$ You'd be delighted to find a place like this in Bogotá, Colombia. The good news is that you don't have to risk your life in this friendly neighborhood restaurant to enjoy boudin, chicken, and black beans. ♦ Colombia ♦ M, W-Su noon-10PM. 2619 Sunset Blvd. 483.0074

**42 Minnette's Antiques Etcetera** Americana, vintage silver and jewelry, and much more are crammed into this tiny store. ♦ M-Sa noon-6PM. 2209 Sunset Blvd. 413.5595

**42 Managua** ★$ Tasty dishes include the *nacatamal* (sweet, pork-filled tamales made with cornmeal and raisins) and *picadillo* (spicy ground meat with chopped onions, peppers, tomatoes, olives, raisins, and garlic). Try the nonalcoholic *cacao* or *tamarindo*, and save room for the flan. ♦ Nicaraguan ♦ Daily 10AM-10PM. 1007 N. Alvarado St. 413.9622

**42 Burrito King** $ This take-out stand offers wonderful burritos at low prices. ◆ Mexican ◆ Daily 7:30AM-3AM. 2109 Sunset Blvd (at Alvarado St). 413.9444

**43 Les Freres Taix** $$ The largest and oldest of LA's French restaurants, they offer wholesome, budget-priced dishes and reasonably priced wines, served family style at long tables. ◆ French ◆ M-Sa 11:30AM-10PM; Su 4-9PM. 1911 Sunset Blvd. 484.1265

**44 Angelus Temple** In the '20s and '30s **Aimee Semple McPherson** preached her Foursquare Gospel within this circular structure. The large domed classical building was based on the design of the Mormon Tabernacle in Salt Lake City. ◆ M-F 9AM-5PM. Services: Su 10:45AM, 6PM; W 7:30PM. 1100 Glendale Blvd. 484.1100

**45 Echo Park** During the 1870s **Echo Park Lake** provided water for nearby farms. In 1891 the land was donated to the city for use as a public park. **Joseph Henry Tomlinson** designed the layout utilizing the plan of a garden in Derbyshire, England. The 26-acre park is attractively landscaped with semitropical plants and a handsome lotus pond. The lake has paddle boats available for hourly rental. Special events include an annual celebration by the local Samoan community. ◆ Daily 5AM-10:30PM. Glendale Blvd at Park Ave

**46 Barragan Cafe** ★$$ This neighborhood favorite for Mexican food serves up honestly prepared platters of the usual dishes and old favorites. There's nightly entertainment in the bar. ◆ Mexican ◆ Daily 7AM-10:30PM. 1538 Sunset Blvd. 250.4256

**47 Angelino Heights** LA's first commuter suburb, Angelino Heights was begun in the land boom of 1886 to 1887, when it was linked by cable car along Temple Street to the stores and offices downtown, just over a mile away. The hilltop site offered impressive views and a cool refuge (with three tennis courts) from the noise and dust of Spring Street. Professionals moved into handsome Queen Anne and Eastlake houses, but the boom soon fizzled. The 1300 block of **Carroll Avenue** is a time capsule of the period, and it has been lovingly restored by its residents, who organize an annual house tour to raise money for improvements, including the installation of period street lamps and the burying of overhead wires. It's a favorite location for film and television crews, but it has kept an authentic neighborhood atmosphere, especially on the adjoining streets, where Craftsman bungalows are interspersed with the Victorians. Highlights on Carroll Avenue include No. 1316, a treasury of virtuoso Eastlake carpentry work with a restored carriage barn in back; No. 1330, a Moorish design with fine spindle work designed by **Joseph Cather Newsom** (pictured below at left); and No. 1334, a delicate Gay Nineties house with a witch's hat corner turret. Eleven other houses have been designated as LA's cultural historical monuments. For a detailed flier, information on the May house tour, and other events, call the **Carroll Avenue Restoration Foundation,** 626.9968. The homes are private residences. ◆ Off Carroll Ave

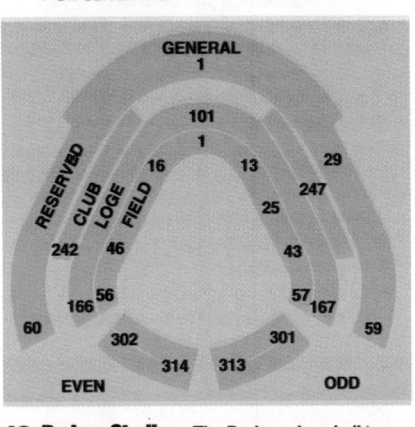

**48 Dodger Stadium** The Dodgers baseball team fled Brooklyn in 1958, but it wasn't until 1962 that the stadium designed by **Emil Prager** was completed. The home of the "blue-and-white" (see the plan above) is located at the heart of Chavez Ravine, and is surrounded by one of the world's largest parking lots. The unique cantilevered construction eliminates view-blocking pillars within the stadium. Boxes are usually in short supply because they are generally sold to season ticket holders. All levels of the stadium are well supplied with food stands selling the famous Dodger Dogs; you might ask for the unadvertised spicy dog, a Polish sausage on an onion roll. And this is one of the only fields in America that sells sushi. Numerous kiosks sell such Dodger-imprinted merchandise as T-shirts, baseball equipment, stuffed animals, and team pennants. A giant color screen in the outfield flashes instant replay, baseball quizzes, batting averages, and the scores of other games around the country. The screen also acts as an electronic cheerleader, signaling when it's time to bellow the Dodger cheer, "Charge!" The screen can't be seen from the bleachers. The ticket office is in the parking lot. ◆ Ticket office: M-Sa 8:30AM-5:30PM. 1000 Elysian Park Ave. 224.1400

**49 Elysian Park** The second largest park in the Los Angeles area (more than 600 acres), Elysian Park occupies several hills and valleys. The parkland was set aside for public use at the

founding of the city in 1781. The main part of the park has been left in its natural state, its slopes covered with the shrubs and low trees known as chaparral. These areas are criss-crossed with hiking trails. **Chavez Ravine Arboretum,** the area in Stadium Way, from Scott Avenue to Academy Road, was planted with rare trees at the end of the 19th century; many mature and beautiful specimens remain. The center of the park along Stadium Way has picnic areas, some with cooking facilities. A scenic plaza with a small man-made lake is located a quarter-mile north of the end of Stadium Way. There's also a small children's play area. A small cafe at the **Police Academy** is open to the public weekdays from 6AM to 3PM, serving hearty, reasonably priced meals. ♦ 1880 Academy Dr. 222.9136

**50 Lawry's California Center** Lawry's restaurant and gift shop has closed, and the building is now home to Lawry's corporate offices. Note the distinctive Spanish-style architecture. ♦ 570 West Ave 26 (at San Fernando Rd)

**51 Lummis House** This unique owner-built residence was conceived and executed between 1898 and 1910 by **Charles Fletcher Lummis,** founder of the Southwest Museum and the first city librarian. Constructed of granite boulders from the nearby arroyo, hand-hewn timbers, and telephone poles, the structure is a romantic combination of styles. Most of the original furniture is gone, but the home and gardens re-

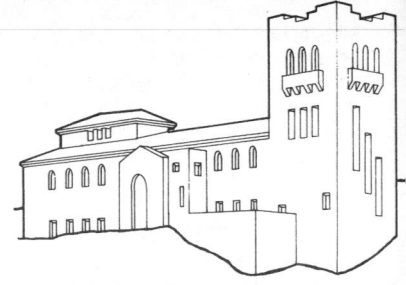

## Griffith Park/North Central

main as a monument to a most extraordinary man. ♦ Sa-Su 1-4PM. 200 East Ave 43. 222.0546

**52 Heritage Square Museum** The president of the National Trust described this as an "architectural petting zoo," and certainly these vintage houses had a greater impact on the city when they occupied their original sites. But just as zoos preserve endangered species, so the **LA Cultural Heritage Board** has rescued these eight historic buildings, built between 1865 and 1920, from the insatiate greed of developers. They include the **Hale House,** the **Palms Railroad Depot,** and the **Lincoln Avenue Methodist Church.** Ask about tours and special events. There's also a gift shop. ♦ Admission. Sa-Su noon-4PM 10 June to mid-Sept; Su 11AM-4PM mid-Sept to May. 3800 N. Homer St (Ave 43 exit off Pasadena Fwy). 818/449.0193

The word "smog" was coined to describe the combination of smoke and fog, first noticed in LA in 1943. Ironically, LA's severe smog problem is exacerbated by two of its greatest assets: the mountains, which hold the pollutants in place instead of allowing them to be dispersed; and the sunshine, which burns the pollutants into a visible hazy layer. An atmospheric phenomenon known as an "inversion layer" holds automobile and industrial pollutants trapped by warm air currents from above in a low, poorly ventilated layer.

**53 Southwest Museum** One of the city's sleepers, this museum (pictured above) houses a magnificent collection of Native American art, from Alaska to South America, in a Mission-style building on Mount Washington overlooking the Pasadena Freeway. The permanent displays of art and artifacts from the Southwest, Great Plains, Northwest coast, and California have been dramatically improved. Notable among the holdings are the **Poole Collections** of American Indian basketry, Navajo blankets, pottery, and a full-size Blackfoot tepee. Loan exhibitions, lectures, and workshops for the entire family are held throughout the year. **The Festival of Native American Arts,** with food, music, and dance, is held every October. There is also a well-stocked gift and book store and the important **Braun Research Library** for scholarly reference. Controversy visited the museum in 1992, when a former director of the museum was sued for allegedly removing 127 items (valued at about $3 million) from the collection and selling or trading them for personal gain. ♦ Admission. Tu-Su 11AM-5PM. 234 Museum Dr (Ave 43 exit from Pasadena Fwy). Recorded information: 221.2163, offices: 221.2164

**54 Judson Studios** This studio has been well known for its stained-glass work since 1897. The Moorish and Craftsman-style building is owned by a fourth-generation Judson descendant. ♦ Lobby M-F 8AM-4:30PM. 200 S. Ave 66. 255.0131

**55 San Encino Abbey** The hybrid of California Mission and European Gothic styles was created by **Clyde Brown** between 1909 and 1925. Brown imported parts of old European castles and monasteries to create his own medieval environment. It's a private residence. ♦ 6211 Arroyo Glen

**56 Sparklett Drinking Water Corporation** LA is full of Islamic pastiches, and this 1929 mosque is one of the finest. The minarets were shaken down in the 1971 earthquake. ♦ 4500 Lincoln Ave

**57 Occidental College** This small liberal arts college, founded in 1887, was formerly affiliated with the Presbyterian Church. It is currently broadening its enrollment and undertaking a major building program. The campus core was designed by **Myron Hunt** after the college's move to the Eagle Rock area in 1914. Occidental figures as Tarzana College in **Aldous Huxley's** *After Many a Summer Dies the Swan.* The inventively designed **Keck Theatre** presents a wide range of plays and visiting dance companies throughout the year. ♦ 1600 Campus Rd. 259.2500. Box office. 259.2737

**58  Eagle Rock**  The massive sandstone rock, 150 feet high and imprinted with a natural formation, resembles an eagle in flight on its southwest side. It was described by **Dr. Carl Dentzel,** the late director of the Southwest Museum, as the most distinctive natural landmark in the city. The rock is visible from the 134 Freeway traveling east from Glendale to Pasadena. ♦ Northern end of Figueroa St

**59  Eagle Rock Playground Clubhouse**  **Richard Neutra** designed this significant building with a magnificent view in 1953. ♦ 1100 Eagle Vista Dr

## Bests

### Gary Schneider

Concierge, St. James's Club & Hotel

Three-on-three basketball at sunset at the **Venice Beach Recreation Center.**

Trying to stare down people from their seats so I can take their place just to order steak burgers at the **Apple Pan.**

LA Dodger game announcer, Vin Scully.

Any movie at the **Crest.**

The **Sorrento Market** in Culver City.

The view from the pool at the **St. James's Club.**

### Susan Feninger and Mary Sue Milliken

Chefs/Owners, CITY Restaurant and Border Grill, Santa Monica

**Itacho** (at the corner of Santa Monica Boulevard and Highland Avenue) has to be the very best for superb, relaxed, Japanese-pub food. They're only open for dinner, they don't serve sushi, and reservations are required. Ask about their daily specials, and be sure to try the special dry sake.

**Arunee** is located in a sparkling new shopping center at 401 South Vermont Avenue, at the corner of Fourth Street and Vermont Avenue (their original location was burned down during the Los Angeles riots). They serve the best spicy Thai food, which is great for takeout, too.

**C&K Importing** (2771 West Pico Boulevard, at Normandie Avenue) is a great Greek market, and the best place to find a variety of Middle Eastern products.

### Kenneth Turan

Film Critic, *Los Angeles Times*

**Bradbury Building**—One of the great interior spaces of the nineteenth century. It was designed by a man who never felt the need to do another.

**Art's Deli**—All the heavy-hitting Manhattan delis, from Carnegie to the Stage, have opened branches here, but this remains the best in town, effortlessly living up to its neon motto, "Every Sandwich is a Work of Art."

**Amok**—The strangest bookstore in this strangest of cities, maybe even the strangest anywhere. If it is bizarre or over the line you're looking for, you can find it here.

**J. Paul Getty Museum**—Breathtakingly designed to duplicate an expansive Roman villa, this is a true monument to "only in LA." Once seen, it's never forgotten.

Tennis at **Palisades Park** in Pacific Palisades—Quiet, shaded by enormous trees, this is as lovely a group of public tennis courts as you can imagine.

**Academy of Motion Picture Arts and Sciences Library**—The folks who bring you the Oscars have amassed an extraordinary collection of movie material and they have housed it in a renovated water department building that is a model of intelligent, imaginative reuse.

**Aero Theater** in Santa Monica—An old-fashioned neighborhood theater—one of the last of a breed—where they still believe in double features, and the trendy crowd gets to relive its misspent youth.

The transition from the Santa Monica Freeway going west to the San Diego Freeway going south. If you live in LA you both love and hate its freeways, and this particular stretch really soars.

**Dutton's** bookstore in Brentwood—Sprawling, comprehensive, with the most knowledgeable of staffs and a charming air of casual bonhomie.

**Society of Architectural Historians Southern California Chapter (SAH/SCC)** tours—This group gives thorough and eclectic architectural tours, touching all the bases from Neutra and Schindler to Wright and Geary.

Driving from the Malibu Colony to Trancas Beach on the Pacific Coast Highway, with a stop for brunch at

## Griffith Park/North Central

**Geoffrey's.** One of the few times Southern California looks and feels the way you imagined it would when you lived somewhere else.

**Venice Beach's** canals—Forget the crowded boardwalk scene and search out these enclaves of tranquility, where ducks very definitely have the right of way.

**Samson Tyre and Rubber Company** factory (renamed and redeveloped as the **Citadel**)—Though its tire-making days are long in the past, seeing this enormous, mock-Babylonian building from a car window remains the choicest of freeway sightings.

**KCRW-FM**—At 89.9 on the dial, this is the best and most popular public radio station in the city, featuring a model mix of eclectic music, news, and spoken word. Keep your car radio dial here and don't even think about moving it.

Los Angeles' population is exceeded by only four other states (not including California).

Kentucky fur-trapper William Wolfskill came to Los Angeles in the early 1830s and planted the area's first orange grove.

The community of Tarzana in the west San Fernando Valley can trace its name back to Tarzan, the character created by Edgar Rice Burroughs, who lived in the area.

After World War II, tourists flocked to sunny California, where the sight of acres of orange trees was a popular attraction.

# Burbank/Glendale

They seem like the Siamese twins of the eastern San Fernando Valley, but the two stubbornly independent cities of Glendale and Burbank are as unlike each other as border mates can be. Although they share a common boundary at the base of the **Verdugo Mountains**, Glendale is a conservative bedroom community, while Burbank is a land of papier-mâché bricks, styrofoam trees, rubber boulders, and breakaway walls.

Both cities were originally part of **Mission San Fernando** and were deeded in 1794 to **José Maria Verdugo,** the captain of the guards at the **San Gabriel Mission.** The 433-square-mile **Rancho San Rafael** remained in the Verdugo family until a financial crisis forced foreclosure in 1869. By 1883, 13 Americans had arrived and were working on farm plots in a townsite they chose to call Glendale, the name coming from the title of a painting one of them had seen. In 1887 five speculators filed plans for the town of Glendale.

Within the year a small town was founded nearby by real-estate promoters on the site of the Rancho La Providencia, which had been owned by a physician/sheep rancher, **Dr. David Burbank.** The two cities grew slowly until the 1904 extension of the **Pacific Electric Railway** brought hundreds of new citizens. In 1906, Glendale incorporated, followed by Burbank in 1911. **Tropico,** a competing city, sprang up south of Glendale in 1911 (it was also the site of photographer **Edward Weston's** first studio). The town's main economic activity was strawberry farming. Glendale annexed Tropico in 1918.

Many of Glendale's homes date from the 1920s, when it flourished as a suburban haven for transplanted midwesterners. Glendale still retains a Main Street USA image on some of the older downtown streets. Its southern portion is predominantly commercial, while the northern side has the original residential array of small, pastel-colored stucco homes. A series of newer, more affluent subdivisions has recently been constructed on the steep hillsides of the Verdugo Mountains.

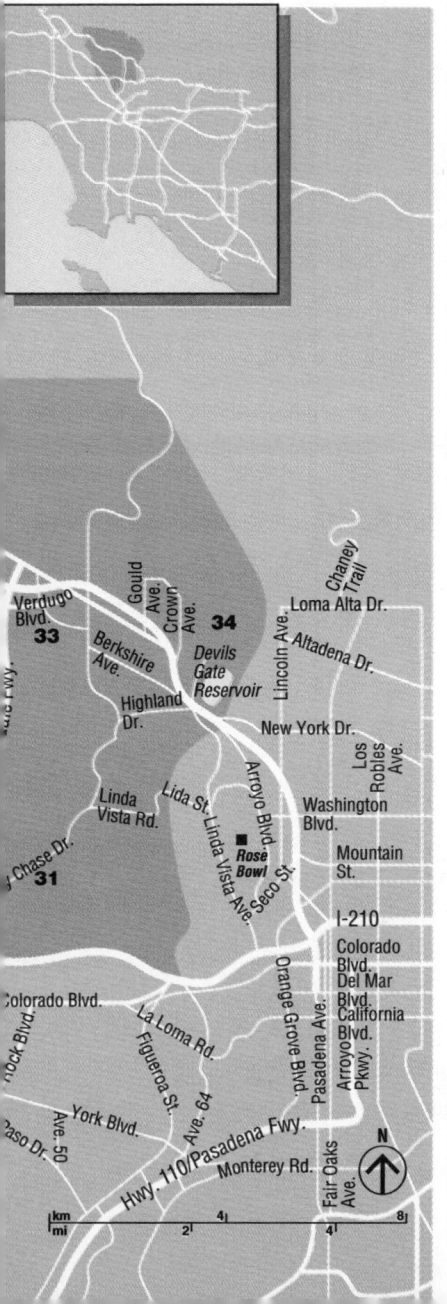

Much of Burbank's growth is attributed to the opening in 1928 of a small airplane manufacturing site near the Burbank airfield. **Alan Loughead's** (he later changed the spelling to **Lockheed**) prototype industrial plant spawned a huge aerospace and electronics industry employing thousands, centering on the **Burbank-Glendale-Pasadena Airport.** To visitors, Burbank's fame and fortune is not in fuselages, but in its four major television and film studios (**NBC, Universal, Burbank,** and **Disney**). With the exception of the closed Disney lot, guided tours are available to show you what the stars do when they go to work.

*Area code 818 unless otherwise noted.*

**1 Burbank-Glendale-Pasadena Airport**
Six airlines serve a variety of domestic destinations, making this a convenient alternative to LAX for those living on the north side of LA. The airport is located between three freeways, No. 170 (Hollywood), No. 134 (Ventura), and No. 5 (Golden State). Adjoining the terminal are expensive short- and long-term parking lots, which can be entered from Empire Avenue. A free shuttle runs to a 24-hour economy lot located north of the airport on Hollywood Way. Ground transportation to and from the airport is available by **SuperShuttle** (244.2700).
♦ 2627 Hollywood Way, Burbank. 840.8847

**2 Barron's Cafe** $ Hearty food is dished out by friendly waitresses in this traditional coffee shop. ♦ American ♦ M-F 7AM-7:30PM; Sa 8AM-1PM. 4130 W. Burbank Blvd. 846.0043

**3 Cafe Mediterranean** ★$ Middle Eastern standards are served in an informal, all-pink setting. ♦ Lebanese ♦ Daily 11AM-11PM. 10151 ½ Riverside Dr, Toluca Lake. 769.0865

A contest to rename the San Fernando Valley was staged by the *Los Angeles Times* after surrounding neighborhoods began adopting fancy nicknames to improve their image. The winning name in the tongue-in-cheek competition: Twenty-nine Malls. Some runners-up: Beige-Air, Minimallia, McValley, Valle de Nada, and West Emphysema.

**4 Universal Studios Hollywood** Movie mogul **Carl Laemmle** moved his studio (illustrated below) from Hollywood to the undeveloped hills of Universal City in 1915, anticipating the need for a huge backlot. This visionary augmented revenue with the first studio tour: for a quarter, visitors could watch films being shot and buy eggs from "Uncle" Carl's hatchery as they left. The tour was discontinued when it proved too distracting to moviemakers, but in 1963 a tram ride was inaugurated, and the tour has now drawn more than 70 million visitors, making it the most popular manmade attraction in the US after the two Disney parks.

Compulsively humorous guides escort visitors on a 45-minute tram ride around the lot, which brings you face to face with a 30-foot-high **King Kong** (smell the bananas on his breath!) and the giant mechanical shark from *Jaws*. You will barely survive an avalanche, a collapsing bridge, and the parting of the Red Sea. **Earthquake—the Big One** is a simulation of what most Angelenos expect to experience without paying for the privilege. Visitors are invited to participate in demonstrations on the **Special Effects Stage** that reveal the astounding developments in movie magic, from the early years to the fantasies of director **Steven Spielberg.** In the latest attraction, visitors can experience 10,000 degrees of excitement in **Backdraft,** based on **Ron Howard's** film of firefighting heroism.

From the tram you can glimpse over 500 outdoor sets, ranging from the Bates mansion for *Psycho* to the facades for *Back to the Future* and *Kojak.* Artificially aged streets are redressed for every new movie and TV series: here are the New England village; Six Points, TX; and Old Mexico that you've seen a hundred times in different guises on the screen. After the tour, visitors can wander at will in the **Entertainment Center,** with its array of exciting live shows, including the **Miami Vice Spectacular, The Wild, Wild West Stunt Show, The Animal Actors Stage,** and two new attractions: **The Beetlejuice Graveyard Revue** and **The Rocky & Bullwinkle Show.** Old favorites are **The Adventures of Conan,** a $4.4-million sword and sorcery extravaganza, featuring lasers, flashing sword fights, and a fire-breathing dragon; and the **Star Trek Adventure,** where selected guests have the opportunity to don Federation garb and do battle against the Klingons from the command deck of the *U.S.S. Enterprise.*

Star lookalikes from **Charlie Chaplin** and **Marilyn Monroe** to the *Phantom of the Opera* will pose with you for photos, and special celebrations are held in the Center throughout the year. In 1991 the studios expanded with the addition of the new multimillion dollar **Studio Center** facility, which features the futuristic **Universal Starway** people mover and the famed **E.T. Adventure,** plus **Lucy: A Tribute, Backdraft,** open-to-the-public video production stages, and the **Studio C** commissary. Food stands and gift stores abound, and there are 50 acres of free parking. Call for hours and tours. ♦ Admission. 100 Universal City Plaza, Universal City. 508.9600

Within Universal Studios Hollywood:

**Universal Amphitheatre** The theater presents a full range of entertainment year-round. ♦ 980.9421. Ticket charge line: 213/480.3232

Burbank/Glendale

*Universal Studios Hollywood*

© 1991

152

## Cineplex Odeon Universal City Cinemas

The latest motion picture spectacle is not a movie but a multiplex: the world's largest, comprising 18 theaters with 5,600 seats and a 1,400-car garage all under one roof. This is the latest venture from the Canadian company that has become the fastest-expanding exhibitor in the US. ♦ 508.0588

**4 Victoria Station** $$ This family oriented steak house is one of many re-creations of London's famous train station. ♦ American ♦ M-Th, Su 11:30AM-10PM; F-Sa 11:30AM-11PM. 100 Universal Terrace Pkwy, Universal City. 777.8180

**4 Universal Citywalk** This retail complex is a combination of Rodeo Drive, Melrose Avenue, Venice Beach, and Hollywood Boulevard manifested in the form of shake-and-bake architecture by the **Jerde Partnership**. Jon Jerde (of Westside Pavilion and San Diego's Horton Plaza fame) designed a four-block, open-air retail promenade with 27 individual facades, each dedicated to one of the popular architectural styles that have molded the cityscape of Southern California. Signature animated graphics, abundant foliage, and a mosaic of postmodern ornaments were also thrown into the design. A colorful array of awnings, trellises, and canopies provides visual accents.

Urban critics have condemned this mixed-use development as artificial, contrived, and lacking soul; they argue that the reason for the popularity of Melrose Avenue and Venice Beach has more to do with history and geography, something even the $100 million **Music Corporation of America (MCA)** spent on Citywalk can never emulate. Nevertheless, the spot is a winner with local residents and visitors from neighboring **Universal Studios**, as well as with the movie crowd from the cinema complex, and it's bustling with pre- and post-concert activity overflowing from the **Universal Amphitheatre**. Dining is anchored around **Gladstone's 4 Fish**, the inland version of the popular Santa Monica establishment, and **Camacho's Cantina**, an authentic Mexican restaurant decorated in the charming style of LA's historic Olvera Street. Attracting the Cantina was a coup for Citywalk (Santa Monica's Third Street Promenade has one, too). ♦ 100 Universal City Plaza, Universal City. No phone

**5 Campo de Cahuenga** The treaty ending the war between Mexico and America was signed here on 13 January 1847 by **Lt. Col. John C. Fremont** and **Gen. Andreas Pico**. The historic meeting opened the way for California's entry into the Union. The declaration was known as the Treaty of Cahuenga, after this building constructed by **Thomas Feliz** in 1845. The existing structure is a 1923 replica of the original, which was demolished in 1900. ♦ Free. M-F 8AM-4PM by reservation, or ask the caretaker. 3919 Lankershim Blvd, Universal City. 763.7651

**6 Sheraton Universal** $$$ Solid comfort and attractive weekend packages, along with free tickets to the Universal Studios Tour, are offered at this more than 25-year-old tower block.

Within the hotel are **Californias** ($$$), offering contemporary California cuisine in a patio atmosphere, and **Telly's Sport Bar,** named after one of the hotel's most famous guests, **Telly Savalas.** ♦ 333 Universal Terrace Pkwy, Universal City. 980.1212, 800/325.3535; fax 985.4980

**6 Universal City Hilton and Towers** $$$$ The handsome, 24-story, steel-and-glass tower features elegant and spacious rooms, plus three fine restaurants: **Cafe Sierra** ($$) for California cuisine, the **Mandarin Room** ($$$) for Cantonese-style Chinese dishes, and **Hiro** ($$) for sushi. In former lives, this was the **Sheraton Premiere** and the **New Registry Hotel**. Now, as a Hilton, it remains the best place to stay in the area. ♦ 555 Universal Terrace Pkwy, Universal City. 506.2500, 800/727.7110; fax 509.2058

**7 Smoke House** ★$$ This good, long-established steak house takes care with the thing that really matters—meat. They age their own and grill it over hickory. ♦ American ♦ M-Th, Su 11:30AM-10:30PM; F-Sa 11:30AM-11PM. 4420 Lakeside Dr, Burbank. 845.3731

**8 Warner Bros. Studios** Begun in 1925 for **First National** and long occupied by **Warner Bros.**, the lot is now shared with independent companies, which produce television shows and feature films in comfortable cohabitation. Tours are limited to 12 adults per group and involve a lot of walking, so wear comfortable, casual clothes. Unlike the tour at Universal Studios, tours here are designed as an introduction to the actual behind-the-scenes technical workings of the motion picture crafts. At the end of the tour, guests may dine, at extra charge and

subject to space availability, in the **Blue Room,** the studio commissary, where a number of actors and technicians take their meals. No cameras are allowed on the tours. And additional reservations must be made for the Blue Room. ♦ Admission. Tours M-F 10AM, 2PM. Reservations required. Hollywood Way and Olive St, Burbank. 954.1744

**9 La Scala Presto** $$ This branch of the Beverly Hills **La Scala** serves antipasti, pizzas, and pastas. ♦ Italian ♦ M-Th 11:30AM-9:45PM; F-Sa 5-9:45PM. 3821 Riverside Dr, Burbank. 846.6800

**9 Bob's Big Boy** $ This is the nation's oldest in the acclaimed coffee shop chain, built in 1949 by owner **Bob Wian** and architect **Wayne McAlister.** Originally one of the first six, it currently survives demolition (fate of the others) through preservation efforts. ♦ American ♦ M-Sa 6AM-1AM; Su 6AM-midnight. 4211 Riverside Dr, Burbank. 843.9334

In the 1920s the sermons of Los Angeles evangelist Aimee Semple McPherson were broadcast over radio station KFSG. The call letters were borrowed from her church: Kalling Foursquare Gospel.

The intersection of Adams and Palmer streets was the site of the first Baskin-Robbins ice cream store in 1948.

**10 NBC Television Studios** Famous as the home of "The Tonight Show," NBC Television Studios are the largest color facilities in the United States. Things don't seem the same with the retirement of late-night icon **Johnny Carson**, but **Jay Leno** has comfortably settled into the long-time king's special spot. Only time will tell. Tickets to attend tapings of NBC shows are available. A number of seats are on a stand-by basis. Out-of-state visitors should write to: Tickets, NBC Television, 3000 W. Alameda, Burbank, California 91523. No tickets will be sent out of state, but a letter of priority will be returned, which gives the holder first chance at the Burbank ticket line. Because of frequent changes in availability, it is recommended that would-be taping attendees call the studio for current information. Don't miss the 75-minute tour through a number of sound stages, a studio (home of "The Tonight Show"), the prop warehouse, and the wardrobe department. ♦ Show tickets free. Tour: Admission. M-F 9AM-3PM. 3000 W. Alameda Ave, Burbank. 840.3537 (recording), 840.3538

**10 Chadney's** $$ The friendly, hospitable steak house is a favorite hangout for people from across the street at NBC. ♦ American ♦ M-F 11:30AM-1:45AM; Sa-Su 5PM-1:45AM. 3000 W. Olive Ave, Burbank. 843.5333

**11 Pickwick Five Horsemen Inn Restaurant** $ The undiluted American coffee shop decor includes red leather booths, cheap-looking Tiffany lamps, and kitschy valances. Patrons ignore the Western overkill and enjoy the wholesome club sandwiches, hefty hamburg-

ers, crunchy fried chicken, and king-size banana splits. ♦ American ♦ Daily 7AM-11PM. 1001 Riverside Dr, Burbank. 846.2668

**12 Safari Inn** $$ A '50s period piece, this inn is conveniently close to the Burbank studios, and has a restaurant and pool. ♦ 1911 W. Olive Ave, Burbank. 845.8586, 800/782.4373; fax 845.0054

**13 Genio's** $$ Their upbeat Italian menu changes constantly but it achieves consistent quality. ♦ Italian ♦ M-Th 11AM-10PM; F 11AM-11PM; Sa 4-11PM. 1420 W. Olive Ave, Burbank. 848.0079

**14 Burbank City Hall** This 1941 WPA moderne classic is distinguished by its tall fretted screen, fountain, and jazzy lobby. ♦ Olive Ave at Third St

**14 The Golden Mall** The tree-lined pedestrian street features two excellent bookstores: **Book City** (848.4417) and **Book Castle** (845.1563). Nine blocks away is **Dutton's,** another first-class bookstore (3806 W. Magnolia Boulevard. 840.8003). ♦ San Fernando Rd (between San Jose and Tujunga Aves), Burbank

**15 Boulder Bungalows** Boulders were once a favorite building material in the foothills; these circa 1929 bungalows are fine examples of the style. They are private residences. ♦ Olive Ave at Ninth St, Burbank

**16 Castaways** $$ The spectacular nighttime view of the LA basin is the highlight of this hilltop restaurant. There are banquet facilities for large receptions. ♦ Polynesian ♦ M-Th 11:30AM-11PM; F-Sa 11:30AM-midnight; Su 9AM-10PM. 1250 Harvard Rd, Burbank. 848.6691

**17 Theodore Payne Foundation** Preserving and propagating native California flora are the goals of this organization, named for the pioneer California botanist. The foundation maintains a nature trail up the hillside and a nursery where seeds and plants are sold at very reasonable prices. The book room offers informative literature. ♦ Free. W-Sa 8:30AM-4:30PM. 10459 Tuxford St, Sun Valley. 768.1802

**18 McGroarty Cultural Arts Center** This historic house is the former home of **John Steven McGroarty,** a congressman, poet, and historian. It's now maintained by the City of Los Angeles as a showcase for mementos and as a community arts center. ♦ M-Sa 9AM-5PM. 7570 McGroarty Terrace, Tujunga. 352.5285

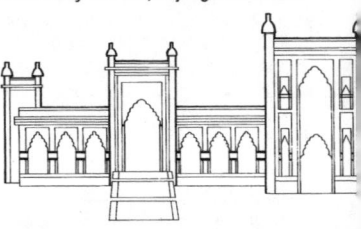

**19 Brand Library** The exotic *El Miradero* was inspired by the East Indian Pavilion at the 1893 Chicago World's Fair. The white-domed Saracenic-style home with minarets (pictured above) was built in 1904 for **Leslie C. Brand,** who donated it to the city of Glendale with the stipulation that the property be used as a public library and park. In 1956 it was opened as an art gallery for contemporary Southern California art, a lecture and concert auditorium, and arts and craft studios. The extensive, beautifully landscaped grounds are lovely for picnicking. The Queen Anne-style **Doctor's House** has been moved onto the grounds and restored. ♦ Free. Tu, Th 12:30-9PM; W, F-Sa 12:30-6PM. Tours Su 2-4PM. 1601 W. Mountain St at Grandview Ave, Glendale. 548.2051

**20 Casa Adobe de San Rafael** Thomas A. Sanchez, one-time sheriff of Los Angeles County, lived on Rancho San Rafael. His one-story hacienda is surrounded by huge eucalyptus trees planted by **Phineas Banning,** founder of the Los Angeles Harbor. The historic house was restored in 1932 by the city of Glendale. ♦ W, Su 1-4PM. 1330 Dorothy Dr, Glendale

Johnny Carson's old jokes about "beautiful downtown Burbank" are enjoying a new lease on life as an odd assortment of colorful postmodern towers enlivens the skyline. Burbank lost its venerable icon (and free publicity) in 1992 when the "King of Late Night" relinquished his crown, prompting the chamber of commerce to allocate $230,000 to keep Burbank in the spotlight.

**Restaurants/Clubs:** Red    **Hotels:** Blue
**Shops/ 🌳 Outdoors:** Green    **Sights/Culture:** Black

**21 First Church of Christ, Scientist** **Moore Ruble Yudell** designed this new, beautifully lit church in the arts and crafts tradition in 1989. ♦ 1320 N. Brand Blvd, Glendale

**22 Gennaro's** ★$$$ Discreet decor, honest food—including clam soup, Caesar salad, and osso buco—and a good wine list, are the elements at work here. ♦ Italian ♦ M-F 11:30AM-2:30PM, 5:30-9:30PM; Sa 5:30-10PM. 1109 N. Brand Blvd, Glendale. 243.6231

**22 Red Lion Hotel** $$$ At the eastern door to the San Fernando Valley, the 18-story glass-sheathed luxury hotel perfectly matches Glendale's contemporary skyline and affords panoramic views of the San Gabriel Mountains and downtown Los Angeles. Within is **Maxi's** ($$$), a gourmet restaurant offering a wide selection of Continental cuisine, plus three bar/lounges and a three-meal-a-day restaurant. They have convention facilities, too. ♦ 100 W. Glenoaks Blvd, Glendale. 956.5466

**23 Kix** ★★$$ Owner **Ara Kalsayan** has transformed his former establishment, **Phoenicia,** into a warm restaurant, where chef **Michael Levin,** previously with **La Serre,** prepares a masterful lamb with lentils and mango sauce, duck with polenta and cranberry sauce, and crackling salmon. ♦ California ♦ M-Sa 11AM-11PM. 343 N. Central Ave, Glendale. 956.7800

**24 Glendale Galleria** The complex of more than 150 shops, boutiques, and restaurants is anchored by **The Broadway, Nordstrom,** and **J.C. Penney.** There's ample parking. ♦ M-F 10AM-9PM; Sa 10AM-7PM; Su 11AM-6PM. Central Ave at Colorado St, just off Ventura and Glendale Fwys

**25 Red Lobster** $$ The decor is slightly fast-food, but the fish is fresh and quickly cooked over charcoal, and the prices are reasonable. ♦ American ♦ Daily 11AM-10PM. 919 S. Central Ave, Glendale. 243.1195

**26 Osteria Nonni** ★★$$ The high-tech setting accentuates the sharply focused menu, inspired by the **Trattoria Angeli** in West LA. Tiny clams in a white wine and prosciutto sauce, designer pizza, lightly fried baby salmon, and breaded calamari are all good choices. ♦ Italian ♦ M 5:30-10:30PM; Tu-Th 11:30AM-2:30PM, 5:30-10:30PM; F 11:30AM-2:30PM, 5:30-11PM; Sa 5:30-11PM; Su 5:30-10PM. 3219 Glendale Blvd, Atwater. 213/666.7133

**27 Forest Lawn** This is perhaps the best-known resting place, next to Valhalla or the Elysian Fields. Founder **Hubert Eaton** envisioned "the greenest, most enchanting park that you ever saw in your life...vistas of sparkling lawns, with shaded arborways and garden retreats and beautiful, noble statuary." Forest Lawn contains reproductions of **The Church of the Recessional,** modeled after a 10th-century English church; **Wee Kirk o' the Heather,** a copy of a 14th-century church in Glencairn, Scotland; and the English church in **Thomas Gray's** *Elegy in a*

*County Churchyard.* All three may be visited when they are not being used for services; each contains a room of historical memorabilia. The **Memorial Court of Honor** in the **Great Mausoleum** contains a stained-glass interpretation of **da Vinci's** *The Last Supper,* as well as reproductions of famous Italian statuary. The world's largest religious painting, entitled *The Crucifixion,* by **Jan Stykam,** measuring 195 feet by 45 feet, is displayed every hour on the hour in the **Hall of Crucifixion-Resurrection.** A companion behemoth, *The Resurrection,* by **Robert Clark,** is revealed every hour on the half-hour in the same hall. The **Court of Freedom** displays objects from American history, as well as a 20-by-30-foot mosaic copy of **Turnbull's** *The Signing of the Declaration of Independence.* Additional attractions are the collection of originals of every coin mentioned in the Bible; the **Court of David,** containing a reproduction of **Michelangelo's** famous work; and the chance to pay your respects to the earthly remains of a number of Hollywood luminaries, such as **Clark Gable, W.C. Fields, Nat King Cole,** and **Jean Harlow.** The exact whereabouts of graves are never disclosed by the Forest Lawn staff. A replica of Boston's **Old North Church,** made famous by **Paul Revere's** ride, stands on the rise of Forest Lawn's Hollywood Hills property, located off the Ventura Freeway at 6300 Forest Lawn Drive. ♦ Free. Daily 8AM-6PM. 1712 S. Glendale Ave, Glendale. 241.4151

**28 Gourmet 88** ★$$ Fresh seafood is delicately prepared with spicy sauces to add punch. Rock cod comes steamed with ginger and scallions;

scallops are served with garlic or lemon sauce. ♦ Chinese ♦ M-Th 11:30AM-10PM; F-Sa 11:30AM-10:30PM. 315 S. Brand Blvd, Glendale. 547.9488

**29 The Exchange** A unique collection of upscale shops and boutiques, plus fine restaurants and movie theaters, encompass an open-air plaza. ♦ Bounded by Brand Blvd, Wilson Ave, Maryland Ave, and Broadway, Glendale

Within The Exchange:

**Fenderbenders Diner** $ Gum-chewing servers theatrically deliver good ol' American fare in this nostalgic 1950s diner decorated with memorabilia of the Sputnik and Eisenhower era. Karaoke on Friday and Saturday from 6PM to 1AM. ♦ American ♦ M-Th 8AM-11PM; F-Sa 8AM-1AM; Su 8AM-10PM. 108 N. Brand Blvd. 246.8408

**Louise's Trattoria** $$ Hearty Italian food made with fresh, natural ingredients is served in a casual, contemporary setting. The restaurant also offers fresh breads by **Old Town Bakery.** ♦ Italian ♦ M-Th 11AM-11PM; F-Sa 11AM-midnight; Su noon-10PM. 130 N. Maryland Ave. 241.8860

**Hana Sushi** $$ As the name suggests, Japanese cuisine served here includes fresh sushi. ♦ Japanese ♦ M-Th, Su 11:30AM-2:30PM,

5:30-10PM; F-Sa 11:30AM-2:30PM, 5-11PM. 139 N. Maryland Ave. 507.4819

**Beaches** $$ Flying fish and a giant replica of a wave at high tide abound in this animated tropical environment. Exotic dishes include blackened ahi salad, soy ginger lime chicken, blackened New York steak with Cajun seasonings, and highly acclaimed cioppino. Weekend entertainment includes a piano bar or a classical guitarist. ♦ Eclectic ♦ M-Th 11:30AM-3PM, 5-10PM; F 11:30AM-3PM, 5-11PM; Sa noon-11PM; Su noon-10PM. 137 N. Maryland Ave. 409.9228

**29 Mann's Alex Theatre** The fluted pylon of this dramatic 1939 streamline moderne movie house once dominated the cityscape along Glendale's Brand Boulevard. Today it is closed, a victim of the rise of multiplex movie theaters nearby, but plans have been approved to build a new performing arts center in its place. ♦ 216 N. Brand Blvd, Glendale

**29 Far Niente** ★$$ The rich menu draws crowds, though the results are uneven. Pasta with peas, prosciutto, and cream; veal chops with a meaty sauce; and the chocolate soufflé are good bets—and should take care of your calorie intake for the week. ♦ Italian ♦ M-Th 11:30AM-2:30PM, 5:30-10PM; F 11:30AM-2:30PM, 5:30-10:30PM; Sa 5:30-10:30PM; Su 5-9PM. 204½ Brand Blvd, Glendale. 242.3835

**29 Panda Inn** ★$$ This is the place for dependable contemporary Chinese food. ♦ Chinese ♦ Daily 11:30AM-10:30PM. 111 E. Wilson Ave (at Brand Blvd), Glendale. 502.1234

## Burbank/Glendale

**29 Aoba** ★★$$ Excellent food is served in a simple setting. ♦ Japanese ♦ M-F 11:30AM-3PM, 5:30-9:30PM; Sa 5:30-9:30PM. 303½ N. Brand Blvd, Glendale. 242.7676

**30 Scarantino** ★$ Home-cooked minestrone, chicken *roletine,* baked zucchini, and spaghetti Napoletana are good choices here. Come here with an appetite—the portions are generous. ♦ Italian ♦ Daily 4:30PM-10PM. 1524 E. Colorado St, Glendale. 247.9777

**31 Derby House** This 1926 house by **Frank Lloyd Wright's** son, **Lloyd,** is a superb example of the architect's precast concrete block house patterned after pre-Columbian designs. Also in the neighborhood are Lloyd Wright's **Calori House,** a free interpretation of the Spanish Colonial Revival style (3021 E. Chevy Chase Drive), and his **Lewis House** (2948 Graceland Way). They are all private residences. ♦ 2535 Chevy Chase Dr, Glendale

**32 Catalina Verdugo Adobe** The Catalina Verdugo Adobe was built in 1875 for **José Maria Verdugo's** blind daughter, **Dona Catalina,** on part of the original Rancho San Rafael. The single-story adobe is now a private residence. ♦ 2211 Bonita Dr, Glendale

**33 Descanso Gardens** The 165-acre gardens  are famous for their collection of camellias, with more than 100,000 plants representing 600 varieties. The landscaping also includes extensive displays of azaleas, roses, deciduous trees and shrubs, and bulb flowers, all located in a mature California live-oak grove. The variety of plants ensures that something is almost always blooming. The camellias perform from late December through early March. The serene tea house is nestled in a Japanese-style garden featuring a flowing stream that forms waterfalls and pools. Tea and cookies are served daily from 11AM to 4PM. **Hospitality House** sells books and gifts and offers exhibitions of flower arrangements and art. Concerts and plays are presented outdoors in the summer. ♦ Nominal admission. Daily 9AM-5PM. Tram tours on the hour Tu-F 1-3PM; Sa-Su 11AM-3PM. 1418 Descanso Dr, La Cañada-Flintridge. 952.4400

**34 Jet Propulsion Laboratory** Fifty years ago, a group of Cal Tech graduates performed what one described as rather odd experiments in rocketry. Today, the **JPL,** as the lab is known, covers 175 acres of the Verdugo foothills, has 200 buildings, and employs 5,000. From the 1958 *Explorer 1,* America's first satellite, to the *Voyager* missions that blazed a trail to the edge of the solar system, it has brought the sights and sounds of space to scientists and into our living rooms. ♦ Occasional tours; call for schedule. 4800 Oak Grove Dr, La Cañada-Flintridge. 354.8594

## Bests

**Gordon Davidson**
Director, Mark Taper Forum

The framed view of the Pacific Ocean through the tunnel at the end of the **Santa Monica Freeway.**

Walking through the back trails of the **Santa Monica Canyon.**

**Chaya Brasserie** in West LA.

**Siamese Princess** restaurant, for Thai food.

Skipping lunch and taking in the **Museum of Contemporary Art (MOCA)** or the **Los Angeles County Museum of Art (LACMA).**

**The Huntington Library.**

Viewing the fountain through the Robert Graham Door at the **Music Center.**

**Trader Joe's** in West LA.

The **Golden Legend Bookshop.**

**Victor Benes** pastries.

**Dutton's Bookstore** in Brentwood.

**Stepps** restaurant.

**Indigo** restaurant.

The bar at **Ma Maison** in the **Sofitel Hotel.**

**72 Market Street,** for brunch.

**Franklin Murphy Sculpture Garden** at UCLA, for peace and quiet.

## Carol Soucek King

*Vice President/Editor-in-Chief, Designers West Magazine*

Have a picnic along the **Arroyo Seco's** banks; try the archery targets; cast a line in the pond south of the **Colorado Street Bridge;** rent a horse at **Arroyo Stables** and ride north past **Brookside Park,** the **Rose Bowl, Devil's Gate Dam,** and even the **Jet Propulsion Laboratory;** or just swim in **Brookside Park's** two Olympic-size pools.

Have tea at the **Huntington Library and Gardens,** and tour the Huntington's fine collections of art, books, and research materials, as well as the gardens. Don't miss the library's gift shop.

Tour the **Norton Simon Museum,** the **Southwest Museum,** the **California Institute of Technology,** the **Art Center College of Design,** and, in particular, the **Gamble House,** which was designed by the architects Greene and Greene.

Walk around the restaurants and shops in **Old Town,** the city's oldest area, located north and south of Colorado Boulevard between Union and Fair Oaks. While here, try dinner at **Pappagallo, Tra Fiore, Mi Piace,** or **Yujean Kang's** (where you'll get the best Chinese food in the country).

For '50s-style diner selections morning, noon, and night, eat at **Rosey's.**

## William Devane

*Actor (also known as Gregory Sumner on CBS' TV show, "Knots Landing")*

One colorful spectator sport is visiting the **Venice Beach** boardwalk, where bodybuilders mold their physiques at Muscle Beach, sidewalk performers entertain, vendors hawk their wares, and scantily clad women rollerblade at high speeds. Venice Beach's carnival-like atmosphere is the best place to see the city's eccentrics.

**Fabs** in the San Fernando Valley is a good place to go for New York-style Italian food. Located at 4336 Van Nuys Boulevard (one block south of Ventura Boulevard), the menu offers an array of delicious and filling meals.

Gawk at the homes in **Bel Air.** Drive through the east gate of Bel Air, past the 50 to 60 homes that many people could never afford in two lifetimes, and then exit through the west gate, which will put you at the eastern border of Westwood and the UCLA campus.

Watch polo at **Will Rogers State Park** on a Sunday afternoon. Located in Pacific Palisades off Sunset Boulevard, the park offers a welcome retreat from the bustle of LA sight-seeing. This park represents a part of LA's history—polo has been played here since the 1930s on the field built in front of Will Rogers' home. Take a picnic lunch and enjoy the weekend games, which are played on Saturday from 2PM to 4PM and Sunday from 10AM to 1PM. Call 310/459.8770 for more information.

Horse enthusiasts will enjoy the horseback riding in **Griffith Park,** located off the Golden State Freeway north of downtown (near the LA Zoo). Also located in Griffith Park is singing cowboy **Gene Autry Western Heritage Museum.** This tribute to Gene Autry's past features a colorful and varied collection.

Anyone feeling the need to slow down and escape the frenetic LA scene should seek refuge at **Catalina Island,** located 26 miles off the coast. The Catalina Express shuttles visitors daily from San Pedro or Long Beach. Chewing-gum magnate Wrigley developed Catalina in the early part of this century as a playground for the wealthy. Approximately 20 miles long and only a few miles wide, this island getaway offers secluded beaches, snorkeling, bicycling, the charming port town of Avalon, and trips to see the wild bison in the hills. Catalina is definitely a place for a battle-weary traveler to rest.

If it's summertime and you're in the mood for music, the **Hollywood Bowl's** serene setting (located off Cahuenga and Highland) offers a variety of concerts, from classical to jazz to rock. In June the annual **Playboy Jazz Festival** kicks off the summer season in grand style. Hosted for the last several years by Bill Cosby, the day-long fest showcases spectacular jazz legends. Jazz enthusiasts can listen to the local talents at the **Baked Potato** in North Hollywood.

Finally, for a nostalgic look at old Hollywood, the **Musso & Frank Grill** at 6667 Hollywood Boulevard serves basic Continental fare à la carte.

## Rodger Voorhees

*President, Whisler Patri, Architectural and Interior Design Firm*

Dancing at **Dana Point Resort**—The only place my wife and I have found that has a great band, spacious dance floor, and no deafness after the experience.

Breadsticks at the **Market City Cafe** in Pasadena— The best breadsticks plus great food that's casual and moderately priced.

Sailing to **Avalon, Catalina Island**—Anchor in Avalon Bay and try every bar in town (on a Saturday night it will take at least three hours). Don't miss the Marlin Bar if you're a power boater (beware if you're a sailboater).

Spending a Christmas Day afternoon at the flicks at **Cineplex Odeon** in Universal City—Unwind from Christmas anxiety by seeing two or three holiday features, followed by a gourmet Chinese dinner at **Fung Lum.**

Having a power breakfast at the **Pacific Dining Car** in downtown—You'll find the best breakfast menu in downtown here, with an impressive clientele for aggressive networkers. The steaks (at dinner) will fall off your plate. Come hungry.

Sushi *hara kiri* style at **Masa Sushi** in Glendale— Don't miss the absolutely great sushi. Owner Yasu Masa is the only sushi chef known to wield his razor sharp knives all night, while drinking every beer offered by his adoring customers. (And he still has all ten fingers.) Try the Rainbow sushi.

A swim and a stroll at the **Biltmore Hotel's** health club in downtown—The Art Deco design and the availability of equipment make an aerobic workout, swim, and a steam a truly aesthetic event. Cool off with a cocktail at the **Grand Avenue Bar** (located within the hotel), which usually features a live jazz band and complimentary hors d'oeuvres.

**157**

# Pasadena

The international fame of Pasadena rests on a single day's activity: the annual New Year's Day **Tournament of Roses Parade** and the post-parade **Rose Bowl** football game. Parade festivities have been held yearly since 1890, when a "Battle of the Flowers" was first fought. Citizens draped garlands of fresh flowers over horse-and-buggy teams and carts in a celebration of the Southland's mild winter climate and climaxed the event with a gala Roman chariot race. The races were thought to be too dangerous, so a substitute event, the national football college championship game known as the Rose Bowl, has been held since 1916.

Those who feel overwhelmed by the epic scale and relentlessly wholesome quality of the Rose Parade may enjoy a rival venture, the November **Doo Dah Parade**, which is fast becoming an institution. The Doo Dah has no floats, no queens (except, perhaps, in drag), and, best of all, no television celebrities. Its stars are the precision briefcase drill team and assorted zanies with lawnmowers, supermarket carts, and odd musical instruments.

Pasadena had a false start in 1873, when midwestern pioneers established a farming community here, giving it a name that means "Crown of the Valley" in the Chippewa Indian language. The tiny settlement exploded during the real-estate boom of 1886. In that year, Pasadena had 53 active real-estate agencies for a population of less than 4,500. Promoters arranged five daily trains to Los Angeles and a special theater express for the downtown area three nights a week. Salespeople advertised the region's sunny, healthful climate, hotels were quickly erected, and get-rich-quick schemes proliferated. The city incorporated in 1886, but the boom

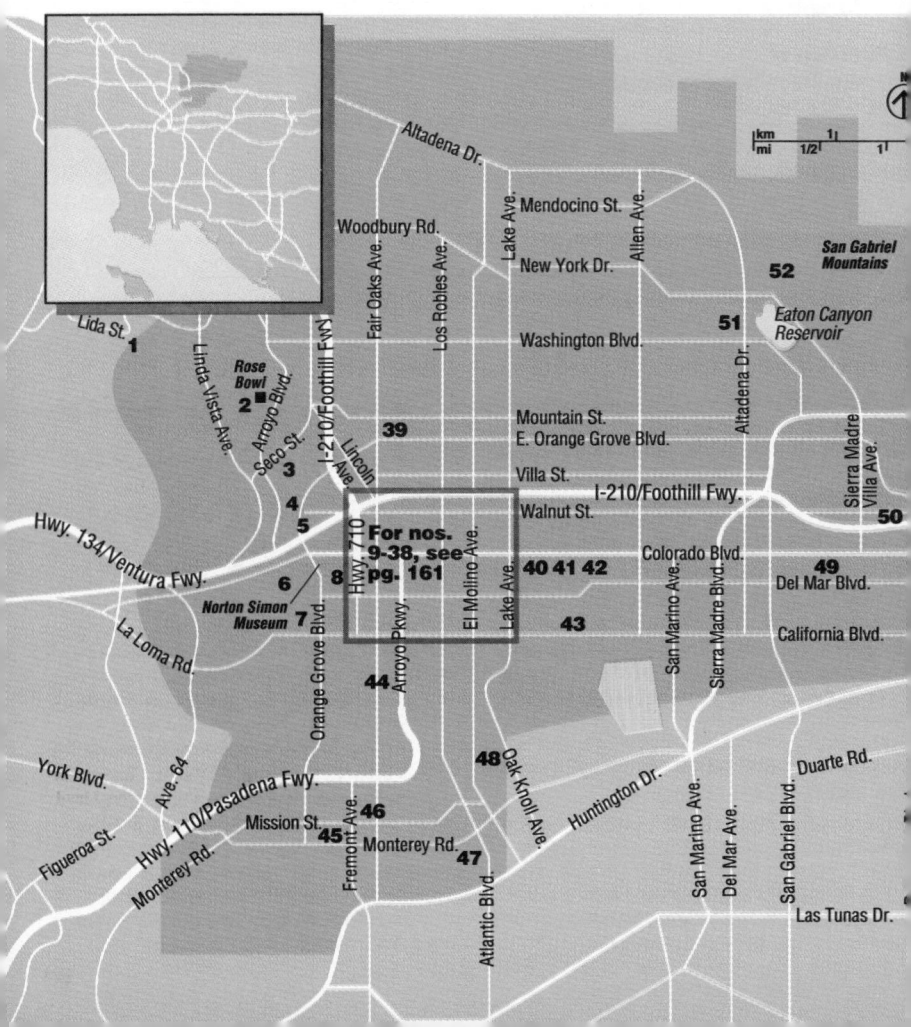

For nos. 9-38, see pg. 161

ollapsed, the population dwindled, and town lots, once clamored for, grew weeds. But the clear air, citrus blooms, and mountain views (now but a memory) drew a steady stream of affluent Easterners. The **Ritz-Carlton Huntington Hotel** and the **Hotel Green** (now converted to apartments) are reminders of an era when this was a fashionable winter resort. And the Craftsman bungalows, designed by architects **Charles** and **Henry Greene**, recall how some travelers stayed on.

Pasadena's population increased through several small booms in the 1920s, and it soon became the most important suburb of Los Angeles. LA's first freeway—the 1942 **Arroyo Seco Parkway**—stimulated commuter traffic. Today Pasadena has 100,000 residents, a mixture of old money to the north and low income to the south, opulent homes, lush gardens, and outstanding scientific and cultural resources.

*Art Center College of Design*

Area code 818 unless otherwise noted.

**1 Art Center College of Design** The college (pictured above) is housed in a Miesian steel-framed bridge that spans a ravine. It was designed by **Craig Ellwood** and opened in 1976. The center, established in 1930, has an international reputation as a school of industrial design, photography, graphics, illustration, film, and fine arts. The hilly 175-acre campus is an idyllic setting for artworks. Changing exhibitions of work by students and established artists and designers are held in the center's gallery. ◆ Campus and gallery: W, F-Su noon-5PM; Th noon-9PM. 1700 Lida St. 584.5000

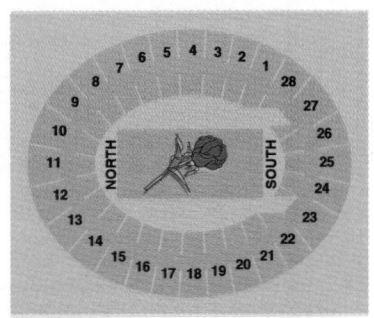

**2 The Rose Bowl** Since 1902 the Midwest has met the West here in the most famous college football match of all, and **UCLA** plays its home games here (see the plan above). Special events are held throughout the year. The **1993 Super Bowl** and the **1994 World Cup** soccer finals will be held here. ◆ 1001 Rose Bowl Dr. 577.3106

### Los Angeles' Wins in The Rose Bowl

| 1923 | USC over Penn State | 14-3 |
| 1932 | USC over Tulane | 21-12 |
| 1933 | USC over Pittsburgh | 35-0 |
| 1939 | USC over Duke | 7-3 |
| 1940 | USC over Tennessee | 14-0 |
| 1944 | USC over Washington | 25-0 |
| 1945 | USC over Tennessee | 25-0 |
| 1953 | USC over Wisconsin | 7-0 |
| 1963 | USC over Wisconsin | 42-37 |
| 1966 | UCLA over Michigan | 14-12 |
| 1968 | USC over Indiana | 14-3 |
| 1970 | USC over Michigan | 10-3 |
| 1973 | USC over Ohio State | 42-17 |
| 1975 | USC over Ohio State | 18-17 |
| 1976 | UCLA over Ohio State | 23-10 |
| 1977 | USC over Michigan | 14-6 |
| 1979 | USC over Michigan | 17-10 |
| 1980 | USC over Ohio State | 17-16 |
| 1983 | UCLA over Michigan | 24-14 |
| 1984 | UCLA over Illinois | 45-9 |
| 1985 | USC over Ohio State | 20-17 |
| 1986 | UCLA over Iowa | 45-28 |
| 1990 | USC over Michigan | 17-10 |

At the Rose Bowl:

**Rose Bowl Flea Market** Held on the second Sunday of each month, this bargain-picker's paradise offers everything from junk to antiques. ◆ Admission. Second Sunday of every month 9AM-3PM. 213/588.4411

**3 Prospect Boulevard and Prospect Crescent** The stone entrance gates at Orange Grove and Prospect boulevards were designed by **Charles** and **Henry Greene** in the 1910s. Along this boulevard that's lined with camphor trees is the Greenes' 1906 **Bentz House** at 657 Prospect Boulevard. At No. 781 is **Alfred** and **Arthur Heineman's Hindry House,** half hidden behind shrubbery. A narrow street entered from the southwest side of the boulevard is Prospect Crescent. This leads to **Frank Lloyd Wright's** 1923 **Millard House** at No. 645, which resembles a small pre-Columbian tower, giving it the name of **La Miniatura**. (The studio house near the pond was designed by Wright's son, **Lloyd Wright,** in 1926.) The house is set in a ravine, and there's a better view from below on Rosemont Street. All are private residences. ◆ Along Prospect Blvd (between Orange Grove Blvd and Seco St)

*Gamble House*

**4 Gamble House** This 1908 house (pictured above) designed by **Charles** and **Henry Greene** is a masterpiece of craftsmanship and planning, from the polished teak and original furnishings to the cross ventilation that provides natural air-conditioning. The best known of the Craftsman-style bungalows was commissioned by the **Gamble** family (of **Proctor & Gamble**) in Cincinnati, who, like other affluent sun-starved Easterners, wintered here at the turn of the century. It is now maintained by the **USC School of Architecture** as a study center and retreat for visiting scholars. Docents lead public tours, explaining the Japanese influences on the home's deep overhanging roofs and crafted woodwork. The house is furnished with tables, chairs, and Tiffany glassworks designed by the architects. (Next door is the **Cole House** at 2 Westmoreland Place. This 1906 Greene and Greene house is now part of the **Neighborhood Church**.) ♦ Admission. Tours offered Th-Su, from noon-3PM. 4 Westmoreland Pl. 793.3334

**4 Arroyo Terrace** Behind Westmoreland Place is the loop of Arroyo Terrace, with its colony of **Greene and Greene** bungalows. All are worth noting, although some are in better condition

than others. They are: **Charles Sumner Greene House** (1906) at No. 368; **White Sisters House** (1903) at No. 370, home of Charles Greene's sisters-in-law; **Van Rossen-Neill House** (1903, 1906) at No. 400, which has a wall of burnt clinker brick and Arroyo boulders; **Hawkes House** (1906) at No. 408, which resembles a Swiss chalet; **Willet House** (1905) at No. 424, a remodeled bungalow; and at No. 440, the **Ranney House** (1907). Also notable is the Greenes' **Duncan-Irwin House** (1900, 1906), which is close by at 240 N. Grand Avenue. They are all private residences.

**5 Pasadena Historical Museum** Designed by **Robert Farquhar** in 1905, the neoclassical residence, also known as the **Fenyes Mansion** and formerly the home of the **Finnish Consul**, is now occupied by the **Pasadena Historical Society Museum**. The main floor retains its original furnishings, including antiques and paintings. The basement houses a display of memorabilia, paintings, and photographs chronicling Pasadena's history. The adjacent library is open to researchers only. The four-acre grounds are beautifully landscaped and contain a wandering stream with several pools as well as the **Sauna**

**House,** a replica of a 16th-century Finnish farmhouse with a display of Finnish folk art. ♦ Admission. Tu-Su 1-4PM. 470 W. Walnut St (at Orange Grove Blvd). 577.1660

**6 The Colorado Street Bridge** Pasadena's 1913 *Pont du Gard* has graceful, high concrete arches that span across the Arroyo Seco. The dilapidated bridge was closed in 1987, but this local and national landmark is now undergoing a $27.4 million restoration. Dubbed "suicide bridge" because of the approximately one hundred people who have jumped to their deaths 160 feet below, it will reopen in 1994 with a spiked suicide-prevention fence and replicas of the original ornamental balustrade and lampposts. ♦ Colorado Blvd

**7 The Tournament House and Wrigley Gardens** The Italian Renaissance-style home, once owned by the chewing-gum magnate, **William Wrigley, Jr.,** is surrounded by a rolling lawn and well-kept gardens. It is an example of the grand mansions found on the boulevard in the first decades of the century. This is now the headquarters of the **Tournament of Roses Association.** ♦ Garden: daily sunrise-sunset. Tours: W 2PM, Feb-Aug. 391 S. Orange Grove Blvd. 449.4100

**8 Ambassador Foundation** The campus that once housed **Ambassador College** (and is still the headquarters for the **Worldwide Church of God** and the Ambassador Foundation) includes four fully restored mansions, several newer buildings, and award-winning gardens. It is located on a strip that was once part of Pasadena's millionaire's row. ♦ Free tours M-F 10AM, noon, and 2PM; Su noon, 2PM. 300 Green St. 304.6123

**8 Ambassador Auditorium** Conductor **Herbert von Karajan** chose to lead the **Berlin Philharmonic** here; other top artists have included **Vladimir Horowitz, Leontyne Price,** and the **Juilliard Quartet.** Extraordinary acoustics, excellent sightlines, and sumptuous decor make this LA's top hall for serious concerts. ♦ 300 W. Green St. Schedule and tickets: 304.6161

**9 Norton Simon Museum** One of America's greatest collections of European, East Indian, and Southeast Asian art is housed in this 1969 **Ladd and Kelsey** building. Norton Simon installed his holdings here after the failure of the Pasadena Museum of Modern Art (a good idea later reborn as MOCA). The spacious galleries are hung with works according to school or century, and include seven centuries worth of

European and Asian art spanning more than 2,000 years. Old Master paintings and drawings, including works by **Rubens, Rembrandt, Raphael, Botticelli,** and **Zurbaran; Goya** etchings; tapestries; 17th-century botanical watercolors; Impressionist paintings and sculpture, including works by **Cézanne, Toulouse-Lautrec, Renoir,** and **Van Gogh;** a large selection of work by **Degas,** including an exquisite series of small bronze dancers; **Picasso; Matisse;** and work by the German Expressionists are among the notable holdings. So rich is the permanent collection that outstanding exhibitions can be generated in-house without recourse to outside loans. The museum shop has one of the finest selections of art books in the city and also offers prints and cards. ♦ Admission. Th-Su noon-6PM. 411 W. Colorado Blvd (at Orange Blvd). 449.6840

**10 Market City Caffe** ★★$$ The chef at this handsomely designed cafe prepares flavorful cuisine reminiscent of Naples, Italy. Savor the grilled seafood, poultry, and meat dishes accompanied by the fresh-from-the-oven focaccia bread. For waist-watchers, the Market City salad or colorful antipasto bar are irresistible alternatives to the rich pasta and pizzas. ♦ Italian ♦ M-Th 11:30AM-3PM, 5-11PM; F 11:30AM-3PM, 5PM-midnight; Sa 11:30AM-midnight; Su 11:30AM-10PM. 33 S. Fair Oaks Ave. 568.0203

**10 Tanner Market** This quaint, rehabilitated retail complex features more than 25 boutiques and restaurants that anchor the west end of Pasadena's Old Town. Mixed with various men's and women's apparel stores are **Roseberry's** for fancy stationery (795.8296), **The Pavilion** for home accessories (792.2956), and **Bellini** for children's designer furniture (449.8113). ♦ Corner of Colorado Blvd and Pasadena Ave

Within Tanner Market:

**Old Town Bakery** ★$ Many Southland restaurants and coffeehouses purchase their mouth-watering sweets from this popular bakery, such as peanut-buttercup cheesecake, three-layer chocolate-raspberry cake, and double-crusted Snickerdoodle. Breakfast, lunch, and dinner are also served. ♦ American ♦ M-Th, Su 8:30AM-11PM; F-Sa 7:30AM-midnight. 166 W. Colorado Blvd. 792.7943

**Ritz Grill** $$ The courtyard ambience of this Old Town restaurant is more appealing than its cuisine. ♦ California ♦ M-Th 11:30AM-2:30PM, 5-10PM; F 11:30AM-2:30PM, 5-11PM; Sa 5-11PM; Su 10:30AM-3PM, 5-9PM. 168 W. Colorado Blvd. 405.0806

**Pappagallo** ★★$$ Wonderful patio dining, award-winning Sicilian veal chili, and a manicotti pasta stuffed with crab and shrimp are the highlights of this ristorante. Work off the meal at the **Premiere** nightclub next door. ♦ Italian ♦ Tu-Th 5-10:30PM; F-Sa 5-11:30PM; Su 5-9:30PM. 168 W. Colorado Blvd. 578.0224

**10 Chicago Ribs** $ Generous portions of everything and anything barbecued are served in this classic rib joint. ♦ American ♦ M-Th, Su 11:30AM-10PM; F-Sa 11:30AM-11PM. 90 W. Colorado Blvd. 405.8138

CIAO YIE

**10 Ciao Yie** $$ Though the blending of Occidental and Oriental spices and flavors isn't novel in this town, you'll find some refreshing tastes in Ciao Yie's *kung pao* chicken pizza, Shanghai ravioli, and *mooshi* duck calzone. ♦ International ♦ M-Th, Su 11AM-11PM; F-Sa 11AM-1AM. 54 W. Colorado Blvd. 578.1231

**10 Z Gallerie** An affordable designer collection of gifts and home accessories, and a wide selection of poster art are sold here. ♦ M-Th 10AM-10PM; F-Sa 10AM-11PM; Su 10AM-8:30PM. 42 W. Colorado Blvd. 578.1538

**10 Aux Delices** $ Old Town residents get an early start with a variety of croissants and pastries at this French-style bakery and cafe. ♦ French ♦ M 7AM-7:30PM; Tu-Th 7AM-9:30PM; F-Sa 7AM-11:30PM; Su 8AM-8PM. 16 W. Colorado Blvd. 796.1630

## Pasadena

**10 Penny Lane** Shop here for new, used, and cut-out CDs, tapes, and LPs. ♦ M-Th, Su 11AM-11PM; F-Sa 11AM-midnight. 12 W. Colorado Blvd. 564.0161

**11 Pasadena Heritage** This energetic preservation society offers walking tours and seminars, rescues historic buildings, and raises public awareness. ♦ 80 W. Dayton St. 793.0617

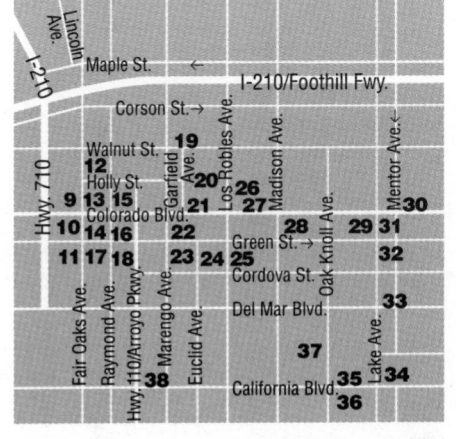

**11** **The Folk Tree** Folk art, fine art, and books, mostly from Latin America, are sold here. Don't miss the seasonal theme exhibitions. Down the street is the **Folk Tree Collection** (217 S. Fair Oaks Ave, 795.8733), specializing in ethnic-inspired beads, clothing, and textiles, and rustic crafts and furniture. ♦ M-Sa 11AM-6PM; Su noon-5PM. 199 S. Fair Oaks Ave. 793.4828

**12** **Armory Center for the Arts** Contemporary art shows are held at the center, which also has workshops offering kids hands-on experience of the arts. ♦ Free. Tu-Su noon-5PM. 145 N. Raymond Ave. 792.5101

**13** **Patakan** ★$ Because of its obscure location on a one-way street, many customers stumble into this Thai restaurant by accident. Winning entrées include *kang ka-lee*, a yellow curry with chicken, coconut milk, and vegetables, and any of the three ways they prepare pompano fish. ♦ Thai ♦ M-Th 10:30AM-3PM, 5-10PM; F-Sa 10:30AM-3PM, 5-10:30PM. 43 E. Union St. 449.4418

**13** **Xiomara** ★★$$ Chef and owner **Xiomara Ardolina,** who gave us **Epicurean,** donates her culinary talents to this establishment, with original dishes that capture a Caribbean flair. Abalone is a popular choice, as is lamb with couscous. The crab cake with black beans appetizer is heavenly. ♦ California/French ♦ M-F 11:30AM-2:30PM, 5:30-10:30PM; Sa-Su 5:30-10:30PM. 69 N. Raymond Ave. 796.2520

*Yujean Kang's*

**13** **Yujean Kang's** ★$$ Dine on a variety of gourmet Chinese dishes that are sparse but

## Pasadena

very elegant, much like the setting. ♦ Chinese ♦ M-Th, Su 11:30AM-2:30PM, 5:30-9:30PM; F-Sa 11:30AM-2:30PM, 5:30-10PM. 67 N. Raymond Ave. 585.0855

**13** **Mi Piace** ★★$$ This restaurant is always busy—and with good reason. The excellent and well-priced Italian fare is served in a cheerful, bright, high-ceilinged interior with glass curtain frontage. It's a popular spot for the jet set of Pasadena. ♦ Italian ♦ M-Th, Su 11AM-11:30PM; F-Sa 11AM-1PM. 25 E. Colorado Blvd. 795.3131

**13** **Pasadena Baking Co.** If you just want a snack or dessert, this spot has a fine selection of baked goods in the patisserie tradition. ♦ M-F 7AM-midnight; Sa 8AM-midnight; Su 8AM-11PM. 29 E. Colorado Blvd. 796.9966

**14** **Merida** $ The distinctive cooking of Yucatán is featured in an intimate dining room and a pretty outdoor patio. Specialties include *cochinita pibil* (pork steamed with spices in banana leaves), good seafood, and tortillas with chicken and black beans. ♦ Mexican ♦ Daily 9AM-10PM. 20 E. Colorado Blvd. 792.7371

**14** **Birdie's Cafe** $ Delicious salads and hot muffins and pasta are served in a pseudo-contemporary classic decor. ♦ American ♦ M-Th, Su 7:30AM-9PM; F-Sa 7:30AM-10PM. 17 S. Raymond Ave. 449.5884

**15** **Cafe Sixty North** $ Crowds gather here after sunrise for special breakfasts, which includes a create-your-own-omelet menu. ♦ American ♦ M-Th 7AM-9PM; F 7AM-11PM; Sa 8AM-11PM; Su 8AM-2PM. 60 N. Raymond Ave. 793.9000

**15** **The Talking Room** $ Amiable owner **Jeff Martin** brews steaming cups of cappuccino and makes great sandwiches on focaccia bread in this very mellow-yellow interior setting. ♦ Coffeehouse ♦ M-Th 10AM-11PM; F 10AM-1AM; Sa 8AM-1AM; Su 8AM-11PM. 58 E. Colorado Blvd. 449.9390

**16** **Old Town** Who would have expected to see the kind of action usually reserved for Melrose Avenue or Westwood Village in this bastion of Old Money? Though more tempered than its Westside counterparts, the streets of Old Town are bustling around the small scale, vintage, recycled buildings. Several new cinema complexes and a number of interesting gift and antique shops share the spotlight. Both sides of **Colorado Boulevard** are lined with small shops and boutique-type eateries. Along **Holly Street** are a number of shops selling antiques and memorabilia. Within Old Town is another attractive group of restored buildings, the **Pasadena Marketplace.** ♦ Bounded by Delacey Ave, Arroyo Pkwy, Holly and Green Sts

**16** **Espresso Bar** $ This funky, crowded coffeehouse serves fine desserts until late. There's live music on Tuesday nights. ♦ Coffeehouse ♦ M-Th noon-1AM; F-Sa noon-2AM; Su noon-midnight. 34 S. Raymond Ave. 356.9095

**16** **Distant Lands** Run by **Adrian Kalvinskas,** this traveler's bookstore offers maps, videos, and more than 7,000 book titles. ♦ Tu-Th 10:30AM-7PM; F-Sa 10:30AM-9PM; Su 11AM-6PM. 62 Raymond Ave. 449.3220

A 450-foot-long, 90-foot-high medieval castle was erected in Pasadena in 1922 for Douglas Fairbanks' version of *Robin Hood;* it was the largest single structure ever built as a movie set.

**17 Hotel Green Apartments** This is one of the two remaining examples of Pasadena's grand hotel era (the other is the **Ritz-Carlton Huntington Hotel**). Architect **Frederick Roehrig's** grand Moorish and Spanish Colonial design is an immense extension to the older Hotel Green structure, originally known as the **Webster Hotel**, and built in 1890 for promoter **E.C. Webster** and patent medicine manufacturer **Colonel G.G. Green.** In the 1920s Roehrig more than tripled the hotel's size with elaborate bridged and arched additions, including the domed and turreted **Castle Green Apartments** built in 1897 across the street at 99 S. Raymond Avenue, and the **Green Hotel Apartments** at 50 E. Green Street, newly renovated and modernized as a senior citizen's home. ♦ 50 E. Green St

**18 Santa Fe (AMTRAK) Railroad Station** In the '30s, before the completion of Union Station in downtown LA, movie stars made splashy departures on the *Super Chief* to Chicago, and on to New York aboard the *Twentieth Century Limited.* Now there's one train a day—the *South West Chief*—and a connecting bus to Bakersfield. The waiting room at this colorful 1935 Spanish Colonial depot is lined with **Batchelder.** ♦ 222 S. Raymond Ave. Amtrak information: 800/872.7245

**19 Pasadena Public Library** The Renaissance-style building at the north end of the Civic Center axis was designed by **Hunt and Chambers** in 1927. ♦ M-Th noon-9PM; Sa 9AM-6PM; Su 1-5PM. 285 E. Walnut St. 405.4066

**20 Plaza Las Fuentes** The $200-million, six-acre development (pictured below) by **Maguire Thomas Partners,** comprising a hotel, offices, retail, and restaurants to the east of City Hall, was designed by **Moore, Ruble, Yudell** in 1989. **Lawrence Halprin** designed the landscape. In a break with the concrete boxes that have proliferated in recent years, the architects integrated buildings and gardens, drawing on the Beaux Arts spirit of the Civic Center and the Hispanic tradition. They created a sequence of pedestrian spaces enlivened by fountains, with low buildings and plantings to soften the impact of major blocks. ♦ Bounded by Colorado and Los Robles Blvds, Walnut and Euclid Aves

Within Plaza Las Fuentes:

**Doubletree Hotel** $$$ The 360 rooms and suites at this luxury hotel offer low weekend rates. Within the hotel is **The Oaks on the Plaza** restaurant, which serves California specialties in a grand space. The bar offers tapas from 4PM to 7PM and light dining until midnight. ♦ 191 N. Los Robles Ave. 792.2727, 800/528.0444; fax 795.7669

**21 Pasadena City Hall** **John Bakewell, Jr.,** and **Arthur Brown, Jr.,** designed this handsome domed baroque structure located at the junction of two broad avenues in 1925. (The same firm designed San Francisco's City Hall.) As notable as the architecture are the formal courtyard garden and fountain. ♦ 100 N. Garfield Ave. 405.4222

**22 Plaza Pasadena** Artist **Terry Schoonhoven's** trompe l'oeil mural enlivens the 60-foot vault of this otherwise conventional shopping mall. ♦ M-F 10AM-9PM; Sa 10AM-7PM; Su 11AM-6PM. Colorado Blvd (between Marengo and Los Robles Aves). 795.8891

**23 Civic Auditorium** Built in 1932, this is the attractive home of the **Pasadena Symphony Orchestra** and varied music, dance, and theater events. Don't miss a concert that showcases the mighty 1920s Moeller, the largest theater organ west of the Mississippi. The Italian Renaissance auditorium is the centerpiece of a convention center built of concrete in a disagreeably brutal style in 1974. ♦ 300 E. Green St. 449.7360

**24 Miyako** ★$$ The house specialty is sukiyaki, a mixture of meat and vegetables cooked in a seasoned sauce, prepared at your table by a kimono-clad waitress. Traditional Japanese decor enhances the meal. ♦ Japanese ♦ M-Th 11:30AM-2PM, 5:30-9:30PM; F 11:30AM-2PM, 5:30-10PM; Sa 5:30-10PM; Su 4-9PM. 139 S. Los Robles Ave. 795.7005

**Pasadena**

**25 Pasadena Hilton** $$$ This 13-story, 291-room hotel was recently refurbished. It is conveniently located within walking distance to Old Town, the convention center, and the business district. **Trevos** ($), a new Italian restaurant located inside the hotel, is open daily from 6:30AM to 11PM and serves a good Sunday brunch. ♦ 150 S. Los Robles Ave. 577.1000, 800/445.8667; fax 584.3148

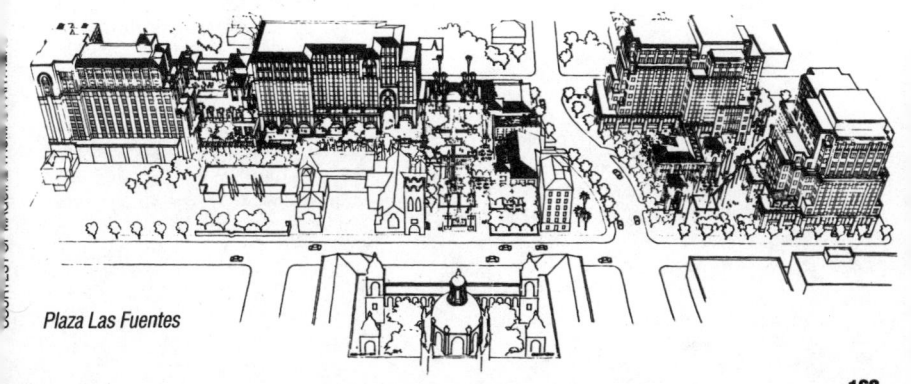

*Plaza Las Fuentes*

**26 Pacific-Asia Museum** Grace Nicholson commissioned the firm of **Mayberry, Marston, and Van Pelt** in 1924 to design a traditional Northern Chinese building to house her extensive collection of Far Eastern art. The building (illustrated above) is an imaginative amalgam of rare beauty and serenity, and features changing exhibitions on the arts of the Far East and Pacific Basin. ♦ Admission. W-Su noon-5PM. 46 N. Los Robles Ave. 449.2742

**27 Warner Building** Don't miss the sensational Art Deco frieze of seashells on this 1927 building. ♦ 481 Colorado Blvd

**28 Pasadena Playhouse** Founded in 1917, the Pasadena Playhouse flourished for 50 years,

## Pasadena

nurturing the careers of **Gene Hackman, Kim Stanley, William Holden,** and other leading actors. The 1925 building closed in 1969 and stayed dark for nearly 20 years. It was elaborately restored and reopened in 1986 with **Shaw's** *Arms and the Man* in the proscenium-arch auditorium. There is also an Equity waiver performance space. Both are flourishing under artistic director **Paul Lazarus.** Behind-the-scenes tours are led by theater alumni. ♦ 39 S. El Molino Ave. Tickets: 356.7529. Information: 763.4597

**29 Lake Avenue** One of Pasadena's main shopping streets, Lake Avenue has numerous specialty shops clustered around **Bullock's** and **I. Magnin.** Three arcades are notable: **The Commons** (quality food stores); **The Colonnade and Burlington Arcade** (elegant imports); and **Haskett Court** (flowers, toys, and curios from "merrie England"). ♦ Between California and Colorado Blvds

**29 Beadle's Cafeteria** $ You'll find plain American food freshly prepared here. The prime rib and leg of lamb are favorites with the regulars who line up daily. ♦ American ♦ Daily 11AM-7:45PM. 825 E. Green St. 796.3618

**30 The Ice House** Lily Tomlin, Robin Williams and **Steve Martin** got their start here, and you may catch tomorrow's top talent at this friendly night spot. Blues musicians perform live at a small club. ♦ Shows: Tu-F 8:30PM; Sa 8PM, 10PM, 11:45PM; Su 7PM, 9PM. Club: Th-Sa 9PM-2AM. 24 N. Mentor Ave. 577.1894

**31 Bistro 45** ★★$$ Ensconced in a 1939 Art Deco building, this unpretentious and elegant California-style French bistro (formerly the home of **Marianne's**) is light and airy by day and romantic by night. Food served with artistry fits the bistro mold: pan-roasted sweetbreads, roasted lamb, and a hearty cassoulet with fresh sausage, duck, rabbit, and white beans. ♦ California/French ♦ Tu-Th 11:30AM-2:30PM, 6-10PM; F 11:30AM-2:30PM, 6-11PM; Sa 5:30-11PM; Su 5-9:30PM. 45 S. Mentor Ave. 795.2478

**32 Crocodile Cafe** $ A junior version of the **Parkway Grill,** this cafe serves eclectic, trendy cuisine, including barbecued chicken, pizza, and spicy chicken salad, in a noisy, popular room. ♦ California ♦ M, Su 11AM-10PM; Tu-T 11AM-11PM; F-Sa 11AM-midnight. 140 S. Lake Ave. 449.9900

**33 Konditori** $ Open-face Danish sandwiches served on freshly baked bread are the specialty of the house. Breakfast offers popular Swedish pancakes, smoked salmon, and eggs. The umbrella-shaded patio is a lovely spot to relax with pastry and coffee. ♦ Scandinavian ♦ M-Sa 7:30AM-5PM; Su 8AM-4PM. 230 S. Lake Ave. 792.8044

**34 The Chronicle** ★★$$$$ This lovingly restored Victorian house reminiscent of San Francisco serves competent classic cuisine, including oysters Rockefeller, poached salmon and broiled swordfish. The front room is lace-curtained; the back is draped in elegance. The wine list emphasizes California vintages and is one of the best in the city. ♦ Continental ♦ M-Th 11:30AM-2:30PM, 5-10PM; F-Sa 11:30AM-2:30PM, 5-11PM; Su 5-9PM. 897 Granite Dr (at S. Lake Ave). 792.1179

**34 Pie 'n Burger** ★★$ Stop here for possibly the best burgers in town; they taste like you grilled them in your own backyard. Remember to ask the waitress for a generous supply of napkins for the juices and dressing that drip with every bite. Top your meal off with a slice of old-fashioned peach-apple pie. ◆ American ◆ M-F 6AM-10PM; Sa 7AM-10PM; Su 7AM-8PM. 913 E. California Blvd. 795.1123. Also at: 9537 E. Las Tunas Blvd, Temple City. 287.5797

**35 Burger Continental** ★$ Gourmet hamburgers in native or exotic dress are offered at the self-serve counter or in the sit-down restaurant. Middle Eastern specialties are one of the surprises on Burger Continental's menu, and belly dancers perform on weekends. The rear patio is tree-shaded by day and lit with Christmas bulbs in the evening. ◆ American/Middle Eastern ◆ M-Th, Su 6:30AM-10:30PM; F-Sa 6:30AM-midnight. 535 S. Lake Ave. 792.6634

**36 Rose Tree Cottage** ★$ Book a day early for an authentic English tea complete with fresh scones, Devonshire cream, and strawberry jam. It's a pretty place set in a British gift shop. ◆ English ◆ Daily 10AM-5:30PM. 824 E. California Blvd. 793.3337

**37 Kidspace** Children from about age two to 12 will enjoy the interactive exhibitions at this museum, which include **Critter Caverns** (a nature exhibit), a fire station, a TV studio, grown-up tools, and even a live ant colony. There are special events throughout the year; large groups and birthday parties can be arranged by calling in advance. ◆ Admission. W 2-5PM, Sa-Su 12:30-5PM, Oct-May; Tu-F 1-5PM, Sa-Su 12:30-5PM, June-Sept. 390 S. El Molino Ave. 449.9144

**38 Parkway Grill** ★★$$$ Chef **Hugo Molina** serves outstanding contemporary California cuisine in the aggressively creative tradition of **Spago**. Eating here is a delicious lesson in topsy-turvy geography: gumbo, applewood-smoked chicken with chutney, oysters with corncakes, sausage and a tomatillo sauce, pasta, and, of course, the ubiquitous pizza straight from the wood-burning oven. The obligatory bustling open kitchen is the centerpiece of the warm and attractive high-beamed brick room. ◆ California ◆ M-F 11:30AM-2:30PM, 5:30-10PM; Sa-Su 5-10PM. 510 S. Arroyo Pkwy. 795.1001

The Pasadena City Council outlawed tortilla tossing at the annual Doo Dah Parade after spectators pelted the marchers.

**39 James/Randell** Cabinetmaker **James Ipekjian** and architect/historian **Randell Makison** sell handcrafted reproductions of **Greene and Greene** furniture. Call ahead for an appointment to visit their showroom. ◆ 768 N. Fair Oaks Ave. 792.5025

**40 Roxxi** ★$$ This popular California grill with Southwestern decor offers pizza with wild boar sausage, chicken pot-sticker salad, and crisp roasted duck with Zinfandel and plum sauce. ◆ California ◆ M 11:30AM-2:30PM, 5:30-9PM; Tu-Th 11:30AM-2:30PM, 5:30-10PM; F 11:30AM-2:30PM, 5:30-11PM; Sa 5-11PM; Su 5-9PM. 1065 E. Green St. 449.4519

**40 Pasadena Post Office** **Oscar Wenderoth** designed this Italian Renaissance building in 1913. ◆ 1022 E. Colorado Blvd

**41 Maldonado's** ★$$$ One of the city's most successful combinations of food and entertainment, Maldonado's offers well-prepared and handsomely presented food that's accompanied by light opera and musical comedy. ◆ French/Continental ◆ Tu-F 11:30AM-2:30PM, 6PM-midnight; Sa 6PM-midnight; Su 5:30PM-midnight. 1202 E. Green St. 796.1126

**42 Pasadena City College** The two-year accredited college is part of the Pasadena Area Community District. ◆ 1570 E. Colorado Blvd. 585.7123

**43 California Institute of Technology** World-famous for physics, engineering, and astronomy, the school's faculty and alumni have won 21 Nobel prizes, and it has spawned a plethora of high-technology firms in the area. **Albert Einstein** once taught here. It is a far cry from **Throop University,** its forerunner, founded in 1891 to "foster higher appreciation of the value and dignity of intelligent manual labor." Archi-

tect **Bertram Goodhue** laid out the plan of the institute in 1930, which was inspired by a medieval scholastic cloister. Other buildings of that era were designed by **Gordon Kauffman,** notably the Spanish Renaissance **Atheneum Faculty Club** nearby at 551 South Hill Avenue. ◆ Campus tours M, Th, F 3PM; Tu-W 11AM. Architectural tours fourth Th of every month 11AM (reservations required). No tours in July, August, and December. 1201 E. California Blvd. 356.6228

At the California Institute of Technology:

**Beckman Auditorium** This auditorium hosts lectures, concerts, films, plays, and dance performances. ◆ 332 S. Michigan Ave (at Constance St). Schedule and tickets: 356.4652

On 30 December 1940 a six-mile stretch of the new Arroyo Seco Parkway, known today as the Pasadena Freeway, was opened as the first commuter freeway of LA. It was followed by the Hollywood Freeway, completed in 1947, linking LA with the San Fernando Valley.

**Restaurants/Clubs:** Red  **Hotels:** Blue
**Shops/ 🌳 Outdoors:** Green  **Sights/Culture:** Black

**165**

**44 The Raymond** ★★★$$$ Carefully prepared and refreshingly homespun food is served in this charming turn-of-the-century California bungalow that was once home to the Raymond Hotel caretakers. The menu changes weekly but usually includes veal, chicken, and beef dishes; fresh, steamed vegetables; and delicious, old-fashioned desserts. Colorfully landscaped patios offer quiet, bucolic dining. ♦ American ♦ Tu-Th 11:30AM-2:30PM, 6-9PM; F 11:30AM-2:30PM, 5:45-10PM; Sa 5:45-10PM; Su 10AM-2:30PM, 4:30-8PM. 1250 S. Fair Oaks Rd. 441.3136

**44 Bristol Farms** You'll find the freshest produce and fish, a dazzling array of wines and groceries, and exemplary service at this four-star market. ♦ Daily 8AM-9PM. 606 S. Fair Oaks Ave. 441.5450. Also at: 837 Silver Spur Rd, Rolling Hills Estates. 310/541.9157

ice cream & coffee stop

**45 Buster's Ice Cream & Coffee Stop** $ From blended yogurts to frosted mocha drinks, Buster's offers a variety of delicious beverages to enjoy with the mellow live music that's featured five nights a week. Just right off the railroad tracks, it's worth a visit even with the occasional rattling as a locomotive rumbles by. ♦ Coffeehouse ♦ M-Th 7AM-11PM; F 7AM-midnight; Sa 8:30AM-midnight; Su 8:30AM-11PM. 1006 Mission St, South Pasadena. 441.0744

## Pasadena

**46 Restaurant Shiro** ★★★$$ Chef **Hideo Yamashiro** left **Cafe Jacoulet** to open this delectable storefront restaurant, bringing joy to the neighborhood. The freshness of the fish and the delicacy of the sauces have won acclaim. Standouts have included seafood salad, ravioli stuffed with shrimp and salmon mousse, and whole sizzling catfish. ♦ French/Japanese ♦ Tu-Su 6-10PM. 1505 Mission St, South Pasadena. 799.4774

**47 Miltimore House** This purified Mission Revival house designed by **Irving Gill** in 1911 is a private residence. ♦ 1301 Chelten Way, South Pasadena

**48 Ritz-Carlton Huntington Hotel** $$$$ Formerly the **Huntington-Sheraton Hotel,** this resort hotel from Pasadena's golden age was closed after a 1985 earthquake. Rehabilitated and reopened in 1991 as the Ritz-Carlton Huntington Hotel, the 383-room, tile-roofed hotel—home to the state's first Olympic-size pool—offers six cottages in a turn-of-the-century country club/estate setting. The original gardens were designed by **William Hetrich,** and a covered picture bridge was re-created on the 23-acre site at the base of the San Gabriel

Mountains. Highlights include luncheon garden tours that are led by a gardener, a traditional club-like grill that offers nightly entertainment, and old-fashioned tea dancing, which takes place on Sunday afternoons in the lobby lounge. ♦ 1401 S. Oak Knoll Rd. 568.3900; fax 792.6613

**49 Acapulco** ★$ The crab enchilada is famous at this casual family restaurant that offers imaginative interpretations of Mexican favorites. ♦ Mexican ♦ M-Th 11AM-10PM; F-Sa 11AM-11PM; Su 10AM-10PM. 2936 E. Colorado Blvd 795.4248

**50 Panda Inn** $$ This is one of a dependable group of Pandas that serves spicy food in a cool postmodern room. ♦ Chinese ♦ Daily 11:30AM-10:30PM. 3488 E. Foothill Blvd. 793.7300

**51 Domenico's** ★$$ A family run pizzeria for more than 30 years, Domenico's offers good pizza with fresh toppings. ♦ Pizza ♦ Tu-F 3-11PM; Sa noon-11PM; Su noon-10PM. 2411 E. Washington Blvd. 797.6459

**52 Eaton Canyon County Park and Nature Center** Visitors can see native California plants at this 184-acre park just east of central Pasadena. The small museum contains displays of the ecology of the area and gives leaflets for self-guided tours through the canyon. The Naturalist's Room houses live animals and natural history objects. There are docent-led nature walks on Saturday at 9AM. ♦ Museum: Tu-F 9:30AM-5PM; Sa 9:30AM-4PM; Su 1-4PM. Park: dawn-dusk. Naturalist's Room: Sa 9:30AM-3PM. 1750 N. Altadena Dr. 398.5420

**52 San Gabriel Mountains** True wilderness is found in the San Gabriel Mountains, which were inaccessible to anyone but a seasoned outdoorsman until 1935, when the **Angeles Crest Highway** (State 2) was opened. It was the first of an interlacing network of mountain highways that brought travelers to secluded destinations. Route 2 begins in **La Canada** and leads to the 691,000-acre **Angeles National Forest,** of which the San Gabriels are only a part.

Some of the more remote sections of the region have colorful histories. The discovery of placer gold deposits triggered a small gold rush as early as 1843 near the east and west forks of the **San Gabriel River.** At the end of the decade, a town named **Eldoradoville** sprang up and soon rivaled northern Gold Rush towns as a den of iniquity. The town was later destroyed by heavy floods. Gold fever revived during the Depression, when jobless Southern Californians improvised a camp and panned for hard-scrabble gold with kitchen utensils.

During the boom of the 1880s, Angelenos made the horse trail up **Mount Wilson** a favorite vacation spot. Professor **T.S.C. Lowe** opened up the **Mount Lowe Railroad** in 1893 to bring delighted tourists 3,000 feet up the steep incline to the mock-alpine hamlet near **Echo Mountain's** peak. The railway was destroyed by fire, but another famous landmark, the **Mount**

Wilson Observatory, still stands near the peak of 5,710-foot Mount Wilson. The observatory grounds and an astronomical photo exhibition are open Saturday through Sunday from 10AM to 4PM. For more information, call 818/440.1136.

The San Gabriels are popular for hiking, bicycling, fishing, birdwatching, and in winter, a variety of snow sports. The quiet trails are seldom crowded—the only groups you might see are Boy Scout troops. There are great contrasts in vegetation and terrain; water makes all the difference (Crystal Lake is one of the most spectacular sights). One moment you may be walking in a fern dell, the next taking in an arid chaparral landscape. Wildflowers abound, including poppies, Indian paintbrush, lupines, and wild tiger lilies. Skunk cabbage grows near springs, and at altitudes of more than 5,000 feet, pine trees flourish.

Three levels of ranges add variety to hiking pleasure. The front slopes near Altadena are good for day hikes, with well-maintained trails leading through waterfalls and pools and near cliffs and ravines. Vegetation here is primarily alders, oaks, and cedars. In places such as Bear Canyon, the middle ranges take you to the last reserves of mountain lions and bighorn sheep in Southern California. At the top of the range, many of the slopes are stark and are a rugged rock climber's paradise. One of the most challenging of the higher areas is Mount San Antonio, or "Old Baldy," at 10,080 feet the county's highest peak. Sight-seeing drives will provide only a sample of the wealth that the San Gabriels contain. Getting out and walking around is the best way to experience this area. Much is virgin territory, and the thrill of trailblazing is still available. It is recommended that visitors stop at the Red Box Ranger Station for trail and road information, brochures, and books. ◆ Route 2 at Mt. Wilson junction. To phone ahead, dial 0 for the operator and ask for red box No. 2 station.

## Bests

### Michael Woo
A Councilman, 13th District

The City of the Angels offers many delights for the intrepid urban explorer.

Spectacular architecture accessible to the public: Hollyhock House (Frank Lloyd Wright) in Barnsdall Park; Gamble House (Greene and Greene) in Pasadena; Schindler House in Pasadena; the Bradbury Building (George Wyman) on Broadway in downtown; the Aerospace Museum (Frank Gehry) in Exposition Park; Loyola Law School (Gehry); the Japanese Pavilion (Bruce Goff/Bart Prince) at the LA County Museum of Art; the Biltmore Hotel (Schultze and Weaver) on Pershing Square; the El Capitan Theater on Hollywood Boulevard; the Wiltern Theater (Morgan, Walls, and Clements) in midtown on Wilshire Boulevard; and Union Station (Parkinson). Or sign up for one of the irregularly scheduled tours showcasing private residences in the Silver Lake area (my neighborhood, incidentally), which high-

light trailblazing work by Richard Neutra, Rudolph Schindler, Gregory Ain, John Lautner, and others.

Varieties of pedestrian experiences: A walk around the Lake Hollywood reservoir on a clear morning. Strolling through the Farmers Market on Sunday mornings. Watching the world go by at World Book and News in Hollywood, the city's best all-night newsstand. And prepare to be astonished at the Museum of Neon Art.

Favorite nighttime driving routes: A slow cruise along Melrose Avenue to see the exotic storefront signs from La Brea to Robertson, or along the Sunset Strip to take in the one-of-a-kind billboards.

Cultural treasure-hunting: Used books at Wilshire Books in Santa Monica, Book City and Aldine Books in Hollywood, or Vagabond Books in Westwood. Used CDs and records at Eastside Records in East Hollywood, Rhino Records in Westwood, or Aron's Records in Hollywood. Best independent booksellers: Book Soup on the Sunset Strip, Chatterton's Books in East Hollywood, Dutton's Books in North Hollywood and Brentwood, Hennessy and Ingalls Books (for art and architecture) in Santa Monica.

LA is a good town for citrus desserts. Try the premium lemon meringue pie from Junior's Delicatessen, or its sibling, the lemon meringue tart from Michel Richard, or its close relative, the key lime pie from The Ivy or Hampton's.

Best Armenian restaurant fronting as a hamburger joint: Burger Continental in Pasadena.

Best restaurants for ordering low-cholesterol breakfasts without egg yolks: Kate Mantilini, Checkers Hotel, and Pacific Dining Car.

Best place for cha-shu (Chinese-style barbecued pork) and rice for breakfast at 3AM: Paul's Cafe on San Julian Street.

Best dim sum in Chinatown: Empress Pavilion and Ocean Seafood.

Best restaurant bread: Campanile, Maison et Cafe (next to American Rag on La Brea), Louise's Trattoria, Daily Grill for the sourdough, Musso and Frank Grill for the sourdough, Nizam for the Indian garlic naan, Aunt Kizzy's Back Porch for the cornbread, and Mary's Lamb for the homemade biscuits.

Best roast chicken takeout: Zankou Chicken (Armenian—East Hollywood and Glendale) and El Pollo Loco (Mexican—ubiquitous).

For aural delights, try live jazz at Catalina Bar and Grill in Hollywood, the best place in town to hear those who have already "made it"; or World Stage, a stark but comfortable storefront in Leimert Park founded by drummer Billy Higgins to provide a forum for up-and-coming talent.

LA has nurtured public radio as a humane alternative to the crass noise emitted by commercial radio stations. I especially enjoy eclectic KCRW (89.9 FM) and KLON (88.1 FM), the jazz station.

| Restaurants/Clubs: Red | Hotels: Blue |
| Shops/ 🌲 Outdoors: Green | Sights/Culture: Black |

# San Gabriel Valley

In the 1920s and 1930s, the San Gabriel Valley was a near paradise of dense orange, lemon, and walnut groves, with such exotic attractions as lion, ostrich, and reptile farms in between. Over the past 15 years the Anglo population has sharply declined as Latinos and, most recently, Asians have flocked to the area. The small communities of the valley, nearly all independent cities, have sprawled one into another, creating a large suburban region of small stucco homes extending some 30 miles.

The first settlement of the Los Angeles region was made here in 1771, when 2 priests, 14 soldiers, and 4 mule drivers chose a spot near the banks of the San Gabriel and Rio Hondo rivers to found the **Mission San Gabriel Archangel**.

While life at San Gabriel was relatively peaceful, revolution was brewing in Mexico. Colonials in California and Mexico resented Spain's civil and economic restrictions, and the revolt of 1821 successfully created a new government. Church and state were split asunder when Mexican authorities declared a secularization of the mission regime. The Indians who were to have shared in ownership of mission properties lost out to counter claims by settlers of

uropean descent. By the time California became part of the Union, the San
ïabriel Valley area was a well-known stopping place on the traveler's route into
.os Angeles. Several small towns popped up in the San Gabriel region as the
ranchos" began to be broken up into small farm tracts. One of the first was **El
Monte**, which started as a trading post for Americans arriving overland from the
ast. For many years thereafter, El Monte was the region's hog-ranching center.
he site of **Alhambra** is part of the former **Rancho San Pascual** and was later ac-
uired by **J.D. Shorb** and **Benjamin D. Wilson**. Shorb and Wilson laid out a sub-
ivision in 1874 and named it Alhambra, after **Washington Irving's** novel *The
lhambra*. Irving's "stern, melancholy country" reminded them of the landscape
round the tract.

he next big spurt of development in this eastern valley came in 1903, when
rcadia and **San Marino** were founded by two of the wealthiest men of the
mes. **E.J. "Lucky" Baldwin** named his subdivision Arcadia after the district in
ïreece whose poetic name meant "a place of rural simplicity," while **Henry E.
Iuntington** named his palatial estate after the Republic of San Marino and
reated a small, independent city of luxurious homes.

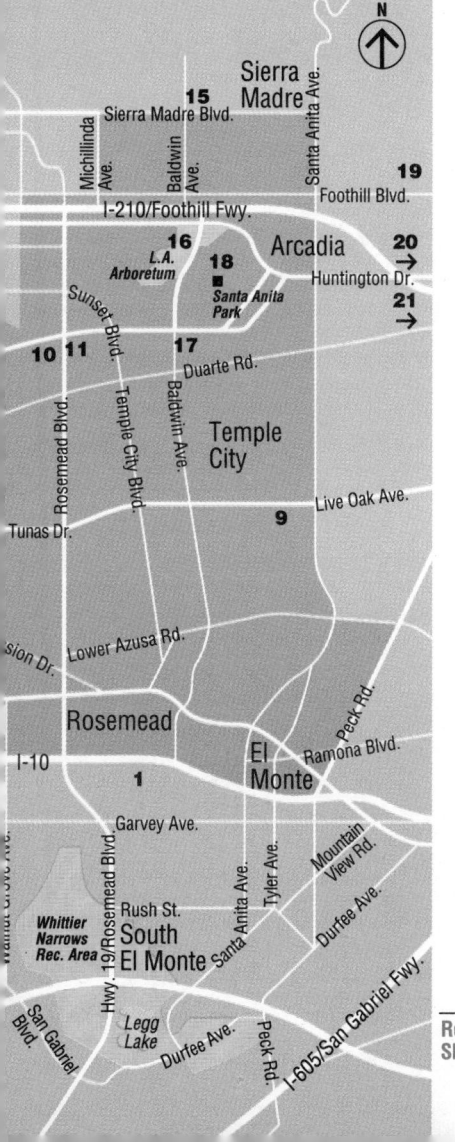

*Area code 818 unless otherwise noted.*

**1 Edward's Steak House** $$ You can count
on nicely grilled steaks and chops, a surprise
or two (like lamb shanks), and at least one
fresh fish each day. The sawdust-on-the-floor
informality makes Edward's a good place for
kids. ◆ American ◆ M-F 11:15AM-10:15PM;
Sa 3-11PM; Su 1-9PM. 9600 E. Flair Dr, El
Monte. 442.2400

**2 El Emperador Maya** ★$ The specialties of
this local treasure include Yucatán seafood
dishes, turkey tostadas, and mild mole
sauces. ◆ Mexican ◆ Tu-Th 11AM-2:30PM,
5-9PM; F-Sa 11AM-2:30PM, 4-10PM; Su
11AM-9PM. 1823 S. San Gabriel Blvd, San
Gabriel. 288.7265

**3 Pine Garden** ★$$ Fine-tune your chopsticks skills for some excellent sushi, delicate
tempura, clams steamed in sake, and *bentos*
(lunch boxes) to go. After dinner, there's
dancing to live bands. ◆ Japanese ◆ Daily
5:30PM-midnight. 323 W. Valley Blvd, San
Gabriel. 282.6101

**4 Middle East** ★$ Food is a bargain in this
tiny shack. Two Druze from Lebanon prepare
aromatic stews, couscous, stuffed chicken
and lamb with yogurt, and all the traditional
starters and desserts. No alcohol is served in
this treasure of a restaurant. ◆ Lebanese
◆ Daily 8AM-10PM. 910 E. Main St,
Alhambra. 576.1048

**5 Panchito's** ★$$ Everything from the salsa
to the building itself has been made by the
owner, and the personal involvement shows.
The 18-ingredient marinade, a secret family
recipe, soaks flavor into steaks and seafood.
The grapevine that shelters the patio comes
from rootstock at the **San Gabriel Mission**.
◆ Mexican ◆ M-Th, Su 11:30AM-2PM, 5-
9PM; F-Sa 11:30AM-2PM, 5-10:30PM. 261
S. Mission Dr, San Gabriel. 289.9201

**Restaurants/Clubs:** Red        **Hotels:** Blue
Shops/ 🌳 **Outdoors:** Green    **Sights/Culture:** Black

**6 San Gabriel Civic Auditorium** Designed especially for **John Steven Groarty's** *Mission Play,* a favorite tourist attraction during the 1920s, **Arthur Benton's** authentic Mission-style playhouse was modeled after the **Mission San Antonio de Padua** in Monterey County. Heraldic shields of the Spanish provinces, donated by Spanish **King Alfonso XIII** on the auditorium's opening in 1927, adorn the immense interior. The fine theater organ is used for concerts and to accompany silent movies. ♦ 320 S. Mission Dr, San Gabriel. 308.2865

**6 Museum of the San Gabriel Historical Association** Visitors can obtain a walking tour brochure from the headquarters of this society dedicated to the preservation of local history. A major exhibit is the Victorian **Hayes House** (circa 1887), located next door and undergoing restoration supervised by the museum. ♦ W, Sa, Su 1-4PM. 546 W. Broadway. 308.3223

**7 Mission San Gabriel Archangel** Founded in September 1771 by fathers **Pedro Cambon** and **Angel Somera,** the present mission church (pictured below) consists of the remains and renovation of the one built by Indian workers from 1791 to 1805. Constructed of stone, mortar, and brick, the mission has an unusual design because the north side is the major facade. Its capped buttresses and narrow windows were influenced by the style of the **Cathedral of Cordova** in Spain. The church originally had a vaulted roof, but it was damaged in the earthquake of 1803. In 1812 the church tower on the facade was toppled by another earthquake. When the church was completely restored in 1828, a new bell tower was constructed on the north wall of the altar end. The bell-tower wall, with its three rows of arched openings, creates the characteristic image of the mission. The interior is still closed

San Gabriel Valley

for repairs from earthquake damage. ♦ Gardens, cemetery, gift shop: daily 9:30AM-4:15PM. 537 W. Mission Dr, San Gabriel. 282.5191

**8 Tokyo Lobby** $$ Decorated with folk art, this Japanese restaurant features generous entrées that appeal to Americans. ♦ Japanese ♦ Daily 11:30AM-2:30PM, 5-9:30PM. 927 Las Tunas Dr, San Gabriel. 287.9972

**9 Alex's** ★$$ Good pizza, good lasagna, and good value keep the regulars *molto contenti.* ♦ Italian ♦ Tu-Su 4-11PM. 140 Las Tunas Dr, Arcadia. 445.0544

**10 Clearman's Northwoods Inn** $$ Kitschy log cabin architecture says it all—the Yukon in the heart of San Gabriel. The floors of the dark but hospitable interiors are covered with sawdust and peanut shells, which customers are encouraged to freely toss by waitresses in frilly, plaid cocktail dresses. Generous entrées are accompanied by delicious cheese breads and two salads. If you can't decide, try the hearty sampler—a steak, scallop, and chicken combination. ♦ American ♦ Daily 11:30AM-9PM. 7247 N. Rosemead Ave, San Gabriel. 286.8284. Also located at: 540 N. Azusa Ave, Covina. 331.7444; 14305 Firestone Blvd, La Mirada. 714/994.4590

**10 Steak 'n Stein** $$ If you're in the mood for reliable American standards but not the Klondike environs of **Clearman's Northwoods,** the same owners offer similar dishes next door at this cozy, sawdustless restaurant. ♦ American ♦ M-Sa 5-10PM; Su 3-9PM. 7269 N. Rosemead Blvd, San Gabriel. 287.1424. Also at: 9545 E. Whittier Blvd, Pico Rivera. 310/699.4716

**11 Peony** ★★$$ **Michael Chang,** formerly of **Joss** in West Hollywood, has created a sophisticated decor and menu. Standouts include *Pin pei* chicken (crispy-skinned and served like Peking duck), fish broth with ginger and cilantro, diced fish with pine nuts, and clams with satay sauce. ♦ Chinese ♦ Daily 11AM-10PM. 7232 N. Rosemead Blvd, San Gabriel. 286.3374

**12 El Molino Viejo** Erected in 1816, the first water-powered gristmill in Southern California is maintained by the **California Historical Society.** ♦ Admission. Tu-Su 1-4PM. 1120 Old Mill Rd, San Marino. 449.5450

**13 Julienne** ★$ Great homemade bread, delicious salads, roast chicken, and daily specials are served at this charming cafe. ♦ French ♦ M-Th 7AM-6PM; F-Sa 8AM-5PM. 2649 Mission St, San Marino. 441.2299

*Mission San Gabriel Archangel*

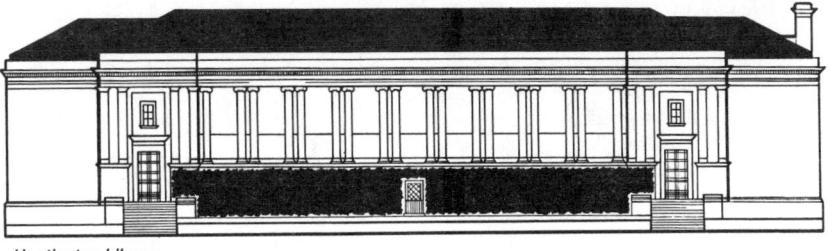

*Huntington Library*

**14 Huntington Library, Art Collections, and Botanical Gardens** This 207-acre estate (illustrated below), formerly the home of pioneer railroad tycoon and philanthropist **Henry E. Huntington** (1850-1927), is one of the greatest attractions in Southern California. Designed by **Myron Hunt** and **Elmer Grey** in 1910, the Huntington residence now houses the art gallery. The collection emphasizes English and French painting of the 18th century. Among the famous works displayed are **Gainsborough's** *Blue Boy,* **Lawrence's** *Pinkie,* **Reynold's** *Sarah Siddons as the Tragic Muse,* and **Romney's** *Lady Hamilton.* The gallery also exhibits an impressive collection of English and French porcelains, tapestries, graphics, drawings, and furniture. Acquisitions include a full-length **Van Dyck** portrait, *Mrs. Kirke,* and a late **Turner** canvas, *Neapolitan Fishergirls Surprised Bathing by Moonlight.*

The Huntington Library (pictured above), designed by Myron Hunt and **H.C. Chambers** in 1920, houses extensive holdings of English and American first editions, manuscripts, maps, letters, and incunabulum. Displayed are a number of the most famous objects in the collection, including a **Gutenberg Bible,** the **Ellesmere** manuscript of **Chaucer's** *Canterbury Tales,* the double elephant folio edition of **Audubon's** *Birds of America,* and an unsurpassed collection of the early editions of **Shakespeare's** works. In the west wing of the

*Huntington Library, Art Collections, and Botanical Gardens*

library is the **Arabella Huntington Memorial Collection** of French porcelain, furniture, sculpture, and Renaissance paintings.

With the 1984 opening of the **Virginia Steele Scott Gallery of American Art,** designed by **Warner and Gray,** the Huntington added another dimension to its collections. Works range in date from the 1730s to the 1930s, and include paintings by **Mary Cassatt** (*Breakfast in Bed*), **Gilbert Stuart, Winslow Homer, John Singleton Copley, Edward Hopper,** and **Robert Henri.** American artifacts and furniture, including pieces by **Gustav Stickley,** are distributed throughout the gallery and matched with paintings from the appropriate period. A new permanent exhibition in the Scott Gallery features furniture and decorative arts designed by **Charles** and **Henry Greene.**

The beautiful and lush gardens were designed and developed by **William Hertrich** beginning in 1904. In addition to expansive lawns and formal planting arrangements that incorporate 17th-century Italian sculpture, they contain extensive rose and camellia gardens, a Shakespearean garden of plants mentioned by the bard, and a number of annual beds. The Japanese garden is entered through a gate overlooking a half-moon-shaped bridge spanning a koi pond. It features an authentically furnished 18th-century-style house, specimens of bonsai, and a Zen rock garden. The astonishing 12-acre desert garden has one of the largest and most unique varieties of cacti and succulents in the world. ♦ Admission. Galleries and gardens: Tu-F 1-4:30PM; Sa-Su 10:30AM-4:30PM. Huntington Patio Restaurant: Tu-F 1-4PM; Sa-Su 10:30AM-4:30PM. English tea: Tu-F 1-3:30PM; Sa-Su noon-3:30PM. Tea room reservations: 584.9337. 1151 Oxford Rd, San Marino. Information: 405.2100. Directions: 405.2274

## San Gabriel Valley

**15 Restaurant Lozano** ★$$ The folksy setting provides a backdrop for healthy, flavorful food. Black bean soup, stuffed peppers, and AHA-approved burgers are specialties here. ♦ Southwestern ♦ M-Th 11AM-3PM, 5-9PM; F-Sa 11AM-3PM, 5-10PM; Su 11AM-9PM. 44 N. Baldwin Ave, Sierra Madre. 355.5945

**16 LA Arboretum** There is no need to go to Africa or Brazil to visit a jungle—a trip to the arboretum and the lake where **Humphrey Bogart** once pulled the *African Queen* through the slimy muck, leeches and all, is certainly more economical. Located on a 127-acre portion of the former **Rancho Santa Anita,** the arboretum houses plant specimens from all over the world, arranged by continent of origin. The lake in the middle of the property is spring fed, a result of natural waters seeping up along the Raymond fault, which runs across the property. The **Gabrieleno Indians** used this as a water source for hundreds of years before **E.J. "Lucky" Baldwin** bought the ranch in 1875. The Baldwin ranch was not only a working ranch but one of the earliest botanical collections in the Southland. Witness several exceedingly tall *Washingtonia robusta* palm trees; at 121 feet they might set a world record. Peacocks and guinea fowl roam among the lush plantings, delighting with their vivid promenades and startling with their raucous cries. Demonstration gardens show California domestic horticulture at its best. A snack bar offers refreshments; a shop sells books and gifts. ♦ Admission. Daily 9AM-6PM. Gift Shop: 10AM-5PM. 301 N. Baldwin Ave, Arcadia. 821.3222

Within the LA Arboretum:

**Lucky Baldwin Queen Anne Guest Cottage** Baldwin, a high-living and often outrageous silver-mining magnate, owned the rancho between 1875 and 1909. This Queen Anne-style building (pictured below) was created in 1881 as a lavish guesthouse for

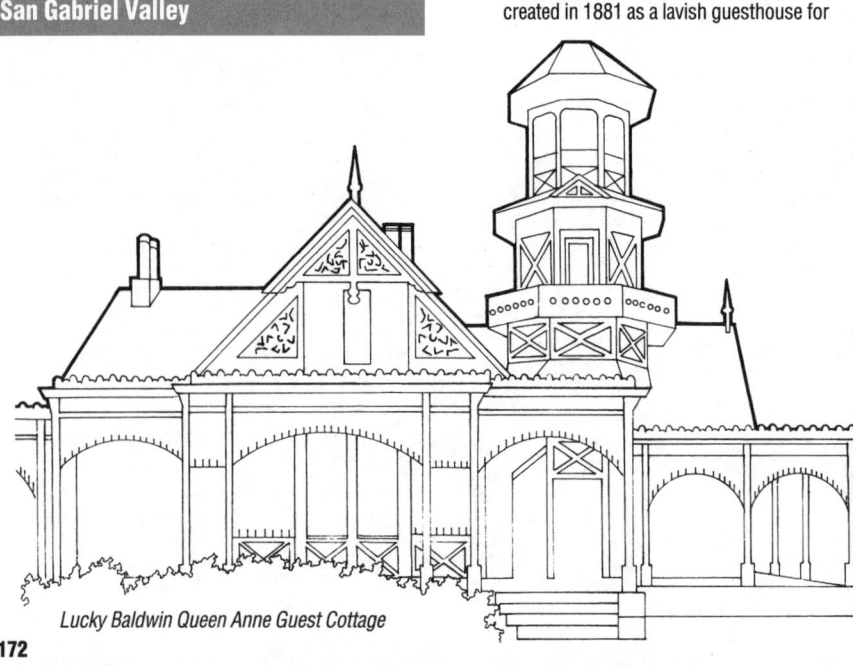

*Lucky Baldwin Queen Anne Guest Cottage*

visitors. The red-and-white gingerbread cottage, with its delicately scrolled woodwork, is a favorite location for film and television crews. Close by, and in the same style, are stables, a doghouse, and an 1890 railroad station.

**Hugh Reid Adobe** A reconstruction of Reid's original 1839 structure, it is built of more than 15,000 handmade adobe blocks. Reid owned the 13,319-acre **Rancho Santa Anita** between 1841 and 1847.

**17 Chez Sateau** ★★★$$$ This oasis in the culinary desert is conveniently close to Santa Anita and the LA Arboretum. Japanese chef **Ryo Sato** combines his own traditions with inventive French cooking, delighting diners with such unusual dishes as grapefruit consommé and oyster-veal mousse. Nice service makes up for the plain decor. Sumptuous picnics to go can be purchased here and next door at **Chez Sateau Pâtisserie.** ♦ French ♦ Tu-F 11:30AM-2:30PM, 5:30-9:30PM; Sa 5:30-9:30PM; Su 10:30AM-2:30PM, 5:30-9:30PM. 850 S. Baldwin Ave, Arcadia. 446.8806

**18 Santa Anita Race Track** Thoroughbred horses race against the backdrop of the San Gabriel Mountains on one of the most beautiful racetracks in the country. The park features a lushly landscaped infield, a children's playground, and numerous eating places that run the gamut from hot dogs to haute cuisine. Weekdays, the public is invited to watch morning workouts (a Continental breakfast is served at **Clocker's Corner**); on Saturday and Sunday, a free tram tour of the grounds is offered. The action in the saddling enclosure and walking ring may be viewed immediately prior to post time. In addition to the regular season, the **Oak Tree Racing Association** sponsors thoroughbred racing from October through mid-November. ♦ Admission. Season: 26 Dec-late April. Post time: 1PM. Morning workouts: 5-9:30AM. Tram tours: Sa-Su 8:30AM. 285 W. Huntington Dr, Arcadia. 574.7223

**19 Aztec Hotel** This wonderfully eccentric, freshly restored stucco facade was built in 1925 and designed by **Robert Stacy-Judd,** an enthusiastic advocate of the pre-Columbian Revival style. ♦ 311 W. Foothill Blvd (at Magnolia Ave), Monrovia. 358.3231

**20 La Parisienne** ★★$$$ A venerable yet unpretentious restaurant, La Parisienne offers highly professional service and traditional French cooking. The portions are generous and the pastries win raves. ♦ French ♦ M-F 11:30AM-2PM, 5:30-9PM; Sa 5:30-9PM. 1101 E. Huntington Dr, Monrovia. 357.3359

**20 Monrovia Historical Museum** This Spanish Colonial-Revival structure built in the early '20s and once the offices and changing rooms for the municipal pool was saved from demolition to safeguard Monrovia memorabilia. Though the collections may not have mass appeal, the museum is a walk back in history, especially for those who enjoy discovering long-lost treasures in an attic. Among the highlights are items chronicling the life of the city's founder, **William Monroe,** and relics from the San Marino estate of **General George Patton.** ♦ W-Th 1-5PM; third Sunday of each month. 742 E. Lemmon Ave, Monrovia. 357.9537

**21 Raging Waters** Families flock to this 44-acre water park extravaganza, where waves and a sandy beach offer welcome relief from scorching days. A popular summer attraction is **Dive-in Movies,** where you can watch everything from *Splash* to *Creature from the Black Lagoon* while floating in an inner tube. New to the park is **Thunder Rapids,** a five-person rafting adventure that culminates in a six-story drop. ♦ Admission. Daily 10AM-6PM, April-May; daily 10AM-7PM, late May-mid June; M-F 10AM-6PM, Sa-Su 9AM-10PM, mid June-mid Sept; Sa-Su 10AM-6PM, mid Sept-mid Oct. 111 Via Verde, San Dimas (take Via Verde exit from Foothill Fwy, I-210). 714/592.6453

## Bests

### om Schnabel
roducer of the music program "Evening Becomes clectic," KCRW 89.9 FM, National Public Radio

enjoy driving up to the **Griffith Park Observatory,** ot because it was the site of a fabled rumble in *Reb- Without a Cause,* but because it offers a fantastic iew of Los Angeles, from the downtown skyscrapers the Pacific Ocean. Riding so high above the city, it *quiet* up there. The architecture is both classic and 1oderne, and the grounds are spacious.

he observatory pays homage to the incredible inds—Galileo, Copernicus, Kepler, and others— iat contemplated the vastness of the cosmos, pon-ered its mysteries, and gave us priceless informa-on, thanks to their scientific rigor and genius. It's ee to walk around the grounds, but if you want to ok through the telescopes, there's a modest admis-ion charge. To get to the observatory, take Vermont venue and head north until you arrive at the end.

### Richard Koshalek
Director, Museum of Contemporary Art

A weekend visit to the **Museum of Contemporary Art,** which occupies buildings designed by architects Arata Isozaki and Frank Gehry.

An evening at the **Mark Taper Forum** to watch contemporary theater presentations directed over the last 20 years by Gordon Davidson.

Unexpected views, as you travel the freeways of Los Angeles, of the monumental **Hollywood sign** propped up on the side of Mount Lee.

Lunch or dinner with artists, architects, collectors, and museum curators at **Locanda Veneta, Opera, Indigo,** or **Fennel.**

Visits with my daughter to study the design of private homes by such architects as Greene and Greene, Irving Gill, Richard Neutra, Frank Lloyd Wright, Charles Eames, and Frank Gehry.

# South and East Central

This is the true Los Angeles basin, edged by mountains and water and scored by railroad tracks, freeways, and rivers. Industry provides the economic base of the area, and a main attraction of this part of the city is the flat geography, which offers no obstacles to the construction of factories and roads. Development was largely dependent on the **Southern Pacific Railroad** and the **Pacific Electric Inter-Urban Railroad.** Buying up huge tracts of land as they built their lines, the transportation giants later subdivided their holdings into a series of communities for workers and their families.

The flat expanses, right-angled streets, and unimpeded vistas seemed familiar to newcomers from the Midwest and the South who had responded to the boosterism and land fever of the 1880s and 1920s. Many of these communities

ave remained unincorporated; like the jigsaw patterns of the other parts of Los
ngeles County, the boundaries between city and county hop and skip around
ch other.

**ulver City** was formerly the home to three major motion picture studios:
**Ietro-Goldwyn-Mayer, Selznick International Studios,** and **Hal Roach Stu-
ios.** At one time, this small town outstripped Hollywood and was the producer
f half of the films made in the United States.

ast LA is overwhelmingly Hispanic; it has the largest concentration of Latinos
n the United States—from the homesites of **Boyle Heights** to the ranch homes
f **Whittier Hills. Monterey Park** is the preferred destination for Chinese immi-
rants, and rivals Chinatown for good Chinese cuisine. South-Central—from
aldwin Hills to the plains area that includes **Watts, Willowbrook,** and

**Compton**—is home to the country's largest concentration of black residents, and a burgeoning Latino population. This area, hit hard by the 1992 riots, ranges from affluent hillside homes on the west to inner-city neighborhoods that have both neatly trimmed older homes and rundown and dilapidated streets. A number of commercial strips, especially the businesses between the 405 and 710 freeways, were ravaged by arson and looting during the riots. Many goods and services in the central area—from gasoline to groceries—became scarce. The rebuilding is planned, but for now, burned-out buildings are part of the landscape.

*Area code 310 unless otherwise noted.*

**1 Artemide** The best in contemporary lighting, from European and American designers, is offered in this showroom. ♦ M-F 9AM-5PM. 4200 Sepulveda Blvd. 837.0179

**1 Allied Model Trains** One of America's largest stores for model train buffs of all ages has relocated to these larger premises designed as a miniature of Union Station. ♦ M-Sa 10AM-6PM. 4411 Sepulveda Blvd. 313.9353

**2 Columbia Pictures Studios** How the mighty have fallen! **Metro-Goldwyn-Mayer,** once an empire, with five lots, theaters and studios around the world, and "more stars than there are in heaven," surrendered its last piece of turf to the producer of TV's "Dallas" and "Falcon Crest" and is now located in a bland Beverly Hills office building. The sequel is even more ironic. Columbia Pictures, born on Gower Street's **Poverty Row** in the same year as MGM, has relocated here from Burbank—a poor-boy-makes-good story worthy of the movies. Meanwhile, you can see the exteriors of the two major buildings on the lot: the 1916 **Triangle Company** office, with its classical colonnades, which MGM took over in 1924; and the monumental moderne **Thalberg Building** of 1939, named for MGM's legendary head of production. And, of course, there are the echoes—of **Lillian Gish** and **Greta Garbo, Clark Gable** and **Joan Crawford, Judy Garland** and

## South and East Central

Gene Kelly. ♦ Not open to the public. 10202 W. Washington Blvd. 818/954.6000

**3 Versailles** ★★$ Roast pork with black beans, chicken with garlic, and paella are delicious in this modest, budget-priced restaurant. ♦ Cuban ♦ Daily 11AM-10PM. 10319 Venice Blvd. 558.3168

**4 The Beaded Bird** This is a treasure house of depression-era glass, bakelite jewelry, porcelain, and other pre-1940 collectibles. ♦ M-W, F 10AM-5PM; Th 12:30-5PM; Sa 11AM-5PM. 9416 Venice Blvd. 204.3594

**4 Sacks Fashion Outlet** Popular unisex sportswear is deeply discounted here. ♦ M-Tu 10AM-6PM; W-F 10AM-8PM; Sa 10AM-7PM; Su 11AM-6PM. 9608 Venice Blvd. 559.5448

"Visit LA. It's a Riot."

Message on a Los Angeles T-shirt

**5 Culver City Studios** King Kong roared, Atlanta burned, and boy wonder **Orson Welles** directed *Citizen Kane* on this lot. Its southern plantation offices were built by pioneer producer **Thomas Ince,** later housed **RKO,** and were the trademark of **David O. Selznick's** company long before he built *Tara* on the land cleared by torching the surviving sets of **Cecil B. De Mille's** *King of Kings.* All of this history has gone with the wind, leaving only the facade and a cluster of vintage rental stages. ♦ Not open to the public. 9336 W. Washington Blvd

**5 Warehouse Conversions** Expressive remodelings of the old **Paramount Laundry,** across from the **Culver City Studios,** and another '20s industrial facility were accomplished by architect **Eric Moss** in 1988. ♦ 3958-60 Ince Blvd, 8522 National Blvd

**6 The Antique Guild** The block-long 1930 moderne building, formerly the home of **Helms Bakeries,** now houses a collection of stores specializing in antiques and period reproductions. A small tearoom is located among the departments devoted to furniture, jewelry, books, plants, and gifts. ♦ M-F 10AM-7PM; Sa 10AM-6PM; Su 11AM-6PM. 8800 Venice Blvd. 838.3131

**7 Harry** "Too much of a good thing can be wonderful," said **Mae West,** and designer **Harry Segil** thinks so, too. Here is a dazzling collection of original and re-created '50s furniture, curved and spiked, and patterned in lime green and puce, and leopard-skin and luminescent vinyl, all refurbished and even jazzier than when they were new. ♦ M-F 9:30AM-5:30PM. 8639 Venice Blvd. 559.7863

**8 Baldwin Hills Village** Here is a rare model of planned housing that became a tight-knit community. Completed on the eve of America's entry into World War II, Baldwin Hills Village was considered a progressive urban experiment, combining occupant-friendly affordable rental housing with features that characterized single-family residences and neighborhoods. Situated within 80 acres, dwellings varied in one- and two-story volumes, from studios to three-bedroom units. Though many units had private walled gardens, the complex was well integrated, with its generous landscape of spacious green lawns and giant sycamores and oaks. It was renamed **Village Green** in the mid-1970s when it became condominiums. They are all private residences. ♦ 5300 Rodeo Rd

**9 Kenneth Hahn State Recreational Area**
Once a former oil reservoir, the grassy 315-acre park (named after the long-time LA County supervisor) represents a sound, public-oriented, adaptive reuse solution for an otherwise bleak landscape of unimproved oil wells nodding away like mechanical storks. An Olympic Forest was planted with 140 trees and shrubs from around the world, representing every nation that competed in the 1984 Summer Olympics. The park has hiking trails and two lakes for fishing. ♦ Weekdays 6AM-sunset; weekends 5:30AM-sunset. 4100 La Cienega Blvd (between Rodeo Rd and Stocker St). 213/291.0199

**10 Fox Hills Mall** The Broadway, May Co., and J.C. Penney anchor this large, popular shopping mall, and 137 other stores on three floors sell everything from fresh-roasted nuts to bolts of cloth to clothing for all ages. The electronic game center is a popular spot with youngsters. ♦ M-F 10AM-9PM; Sa 10AM-7PM; Su 11AM-6PM. Sepulveda Blvd at Slauson Blvd, Fox Hills. 390.7833

**11 Centinela Ranch House** Built in 1834 for **Ignacio Machado,** this well-preserved house is made of adobe with a wood-shingle roof, and is furnished with 19th-century antiques. Some of the original planting is maintained. Within the site are a research library and the office once used by **Daniel Freeman,** whose 22,000 acres became the city of Inglewood ♦ Free. W, Su 2-4PM. 7634 Midfield Ave. 649.6272. Tours: 677.1154

**12 Harriet's Cheesecakes Unlimited** $
Choose from fifty flavors of cheesecake to go or by the slice. Try the chocolate amaretto, apple 'n' spice, or coffee flavors if the exquisite French vanilla is too tame for you. ♦ Bakery ♦ Tu-Sa noon-8PM; Su noon-5PM. 1515 Centinela Ave, Inglewood. 419.2259

**13 JB's Little Bali** ★$$ Multidish *rijstaffel* (which starts off with a salad and moves on to a variety of spicy meat and poultry dishes) is the only meal, but you may think you've eaten your way through an entire menu. ♦ Indonesian ♦ Th-Su 6-10PM. 217 E. Nutwood St, Inglewood. 674.9835

**14 Hollywood Park** Thoroughbred racing occurs April through July and mid-November through December on a track landscaped with lagoons and tropical trees. A computer-operated screen offers patrons a view of the back stretch, as well as stop-action replays of photo finishes and racing statistics. Refreshments are available at the elegant **Turf Club Terrace, International Food Fair, Paddock Club,** and **Hollywood Bar.** The children's play area, designated **North Park,** now features a carousel. ♦ Admission. Call for post times. 1050 S. Prairie Ave, Inglewood. 419.1500

reater Los Angeles encompasses more than 40,000 quare miles.

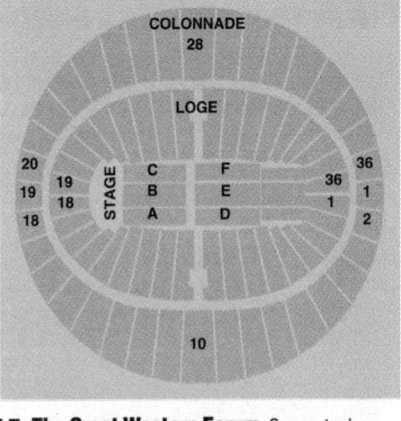

**15 The Great Western Forum** Concerts, ice hockey, basketball, tennis, boxing, and other sports and public events are held here. From October through April, the Forum (see the plan above) is home to the **Los Angeles Lakers** basketball team and the **Los Angeles Kings** hockey team. ♦ Admission varies with event. Box office: daily 10AM-6PM. 3900 Manchester Blvd (at Prairie Ave), Inglewood. 673.1300

**16 Academy Theatre** This 1939 streamline moderne landmark, designed by **S. Charles Lee,** is notable for its spiral-finned tower. The building is now used as a church. ♦ 3100 Manchester Blvd (at Crenshaw Blvd), Inglewood

**17 Museum in Black** Part museum/part store, they feature more than one thousand pieces of traditional African art and African-American memorabilia. ♦ Free. Tu-Sa noon-6PM. 4331 Degnan Blvd. 292.9528

**18 Harold & Belle's** ★★$$ Generous helpings of fabulous gumbo, jambalaya, hot sausage, shrimp creole, and barbecued ribs draw enthusiastic crowds to these pleasant surroundings. ♦ Cajun/Creole ♦ Tu-Th noon-10PM; F-Sa noon-1AM; Su noon-10PM. 2920 W. Jefferson Blvd. 735.9023

## South and East Central

**19 William Grant Still Community Arts Center** The center is named for the famous late black composer and long-time resident of LA. It offers exhibitions, festivals, and workshops. ♦ Free. M-Sa 9AM-5PM. 2520 West View St. 734.1164

**20 Clark Memorial Library** English literature and music of the 17th and 18th centuries are well-represented in this research library, bequeathed to UCLA in 1934 by **William Andrews Clark, Jr.,** in memory of his father, **Senator William A. Clark.** The Italian Renaissance building is decorated with murals and ceiling paintings by **Allyn Cox,** and is furnished with period antiques. The underground vaults are covered with formal gardens. Tours can be arranged by appointment only. ♦ Open to researchers weekdays 9AM-5PM. 2520 Cimarron St (W. Adams Blvd). 731.8529

# Tinseltown—Take One

Early moviemakers shot their scenes primarily in the streets, making everyday life a part of the action. The **Keystone Kops** comedies (1913), **Harold Lloyd's** *Safety Last* (1923), and **Laurel and Hardy's** *Big Business* (1926) document Los Angeles as it was in those times. Some of the best films featuring the City of Angels that were produced in later years include the following:

**Annie Hall** (1977) For **Woody Allen,** the only cultural advantage of LA is turning right on a red light—and he can't even drive.

**Blade Runner** (1982) **Ridley Scott's** fantasy of LA in the year 2019 as a megalopolis of 90 million people choking on smog makes inspired use of the Bradbury Building and Wright's Ennis-Brown House.

**Boyz N the Hood** (1991) The *hood* means neighborhood in this realistic drama about college-bound teenagers and gang members growing up in South Central LA. It was written and directed by South Central-native **John Singleton,** who was nominated for an Oscar as best director.

**Bugsy** (1991) Based on the true story of **Benjamin "Bugsy" Siegal,** the playboy mobster (played by **Warren Beatty**) who dreams of Hollywood stardom and the creation of Las Vegas.

**Chinatown** (1974) **Robert Towne's** script and the white-and-burnt-ochre images capture the true look and feeling of LA in the '30s.

**Colors** (1988) A violence-choked East LA is the setting for this hard-hitting police drama starring **Robert Duvall** and **Sean Penn,** but much of it was filmed in Venice, where director **Dennis Hopper** lives.

**Die Hard** (1988) The action- and violence-packed blockbuster—starring **Bruce Willis** as an ex-cop fighting off terrorists—was filmed in Century City's Fox Tower, which was then under construction.

**The Doors** (1991) The **Oliver Stone** film biography starring **Val Kilmer** as legendary rock star **Jim Morrison** follows the musician from Venice Beach to the Sunset Strip and the Château Marmont.

## South and East Central

**Down and Out in Beverly Hills** (1984) Feature-length version of the caricature of Beverly Hills in **Woody Allen's** *Annie Hall.*

**E.T. The Extra Terrestrial** (1982) TV-perfect suburbia, as exemplified by the San Fernando Valley, is the setting of this (and many other) **Steven Spielberg** movies.

**Earthquake** (1974) The Big One hits LA in this drama heavy on special effects. It has become pure camp. **Charlton Heston** and **Genevieve Bujold** star.

**Encino Man** (1992) A San Fernando Valley high-school dude unearths a Cro-Magnon man while digging a backyard swimming pool in this comedy starring MTV veejay **Pauly Shore.**

**Grand Canyon** (1991) Chance encounters change lives from Brentwood to Inglewood, and a dad teaches his son one of LA's most difficult lessons—how to make a left turn against LA traffic—in **Lawrence Kasdan's** redemption film starring **Danny Glover** and **Kevin Kline.**

**Into the Night** (1985) More than a dozen directors make guest appearances in this bizarre adventure filled with cinematic in-jokes and set in contemporary late-night LA. **Jeff Goldblum** and **Michelle Pfeiffer** star in this film.

**Kiss Me Deadly** (1955) LA's mean streets, Malibu, and a decaying Bunker Hill are expressive backdrops for **Micky Spillane's** thriller.

**L.A. Story** (1991) **Steve Martin's** valentine to the city where he met his wife, **Victoria Tennant,** stars both in this movie. Martin dates a Venice Beach valley girl and roller-skates through the Museum of Contemporary Art in the comedy that embraces LA and satirizes its lifestyles.

**The Loved One** (1965) **Liberace** plays a funeral director in this uneven adaptation of **Evelyn Waugh's** satire of Forest Lawn.

**Mildred Pearce** (1945) In this adaptation of **James M. Cain's** novel, Glendale, Pasadena, and Malibu chart **Joan Crawford's** social ascent.

**The Morning After** (1986) New York director **Sidney Lumet** captures the texture of LA's commercial strip and apartment buildings, an aspect of the city that is rarely filmed.

**The Player** (1992) **Robert Altman's** insider's view of today's movie business stars **Tim Robbins** as a studio dealmaker who kills a screenwriter. More than a dozen stars make cameo appearances in this ironic, funny, and accurate portrait of the industry.

**Rebel Without a Cause** (1955) The Griffith Park Observatory and a deserted house in the hills are sets for angst-ridden **James Dean.**

**Ruthless People** (1986) Designer **Lilly Kilvert** exploits the surreal juxtapositions of LA architecture to comic effect.

**Save the Tiger** (1973) **Jack Lemmon's** finest performance as a man at the end of his tether, set in LA's garment district.

**Shampoo** (1975) Beverly Hills as seen by hip hairdresser **Warren Beatty,** and designed by **Richard Sylbert** as a study in narcissism.

**Smog** (1962) LA through the eyes of a visiting Italian lawyer: an alienating city of cracked stucco, empty vistas, nodding oil wells, and Pierre Koenig's Stahl House in the Hollywood Hills.

**Sunset Boulevard** (1950) **Gloria Swanson's** *Norma Desmond* holds court in her crumbling mansion, and **William Holden's** screenwriter escapes his creditors to end face-down in her pool.

**Tequila Sunrise** (1989) Seductive images of life in the fast lane in South Bay beach communities enhance **Robert Towne's** thriller.

**To Live and Die in L.A.** (1985) A US Secret Service agent tracks his partner's killer through the underbelly of LA in this violent, bleak film starring **Willem Dafoe.**

**Touch of Evil** (1958) **Orson Welles** uses the arcades and crumbling canals of Venice at night to conjure up feelings of fear and corruption within a Mexican border town.

**Valley Girl** (1983) A teenage morality drama that contrasts the white-bread Valley lifestyle with the sleazy energy of Hollywood Boulevard at night.

**20 Amateur Athletic Foundation of LA** The **Paul Ziffren Sports Resource Center** was built with proceeds from the 1984 Olympics, and named for the chairman of the LAOOC. It houses a state-of-the-art sports library and archive that's open to the public by appointment. ♦ 2141 W. Adams Blvd. 730.9696

**21 Janet's Original Jerk Chicken** $ Pork, ribs, chicken, and Jamaican roast beef are the tasty treats in this storefront restaurant. ♦ Jamaican ♦ M-Sa noon-9PM; Su 1-8PM. 1541 Martin Luther King, Jr. Blvd. 296.4621

**22 El Sol** ★$ **Don Julio,** the Chinese/Peruvian owner/chef, serves delicious ceviche and tripe, lamb with cilantro sauce, and fried red snapper at very reasonable prices—as he did at the previous location in Hollywood. There's live music on weekends. ♦ Peruvian ♦ Tu-Th 11AM-10:30PM; F-Sa 11AM-midnight; Su 11AM-9PM. 15651 Hawthorne Blvd, Lawndale. 973.2486

**23 El Pollo Inka** ★$ Marinated spit-roasted chicken is the signature dish, but just as delicious are the braised lamb in cilantro sauce and potato slices with a walnut-chile sauce. ♦ Peruvian ♦ Daily 11:30AM-9PM. 15400-D Hawthorne Blvd, Lawndale. 676.6665

**24 Kampachi** $$ While many sushi bars offer tempura and other batter-dipped dishes, this Japanese eatery concentrates solely on the raw and makes exceptional presentations of fresh seafood. ♦ Japanese ♦ M-F 11:30AM-2PM, 5:30-10PM; Sa 5:30-10PM. 1425 W. Artesia Blvd, Gardena. 515.1391

**25 Pacific Supermarket** Foods of the Pacific Rim line the shelves in mind-numbing variety. Begin browsing and you may decide to change your diet. ♦ M-Sa 8AM-9PM; Su 8AM-8PM. 1620 W. Redondo Beach Blvd, Gardena. 323.7696

**26 Goodyear Blimp** The best-known, best-loved corporate symbol in the United States is 192 feet long, 59 feet high, 50 feet in diameter, and 202,700 cubic feet in volume. Deflated, the dirigible weighs 12,000 pounds; filled with helium, an inert lighter-than-air gas, her weight drops to 150 pounds. Her cruising speed is 35 miles per hour; her top speed 53 miles per hour. The normal cruising altitude of 1,000 to 1,500 feet gives the blimp and its logo maximum recognition from the ground. The blimp is used for a number of purposes besides advertising. It acts as a camera platform for TV coverage of sports and public events; it assists the American Cetacean Society with the annual count of the California gray whales during their winter migration; and it has carried instruments aloft for a number of scientific experiments. The *Columbia* travels six months out of the year, but you are most likely to see her on the ground in the early morning or at twilight from the intersection of the Harbor and San Diego freeways. Flights are not available to the public (it's invitation only from the Goodyear Sales Division), but you can view the blimp Monday and Tuesday when it's not in flight. ♦ 19200 S. Main St, Carson. 213/770.0456

**27 Dominguez Ranch Adobe** A relic of the Spanish settlement of California, the adobe (pictured below) sits on the property owned by **Juan José Dominguez,** a soldier who accompanied Father Serra on the original expedition from Mexico to found the California missions. In 1782 he was rewarded for his service with a land grant covering the harbor area south of the Pueblo de Los Angeles, more than 75,000 acres. His nephew built an adobe in 1826, and its interior has been restored as a historical museum, displaying many of the original furnishings. Also shown are photographs and displays

Dominguez Ranch Adobe

chronicling the First International Air Meet held at Dominguez Field in 1913. The adobe is now part of the **Dominguez Memorial Seminary,** operated by the Claretian Order. Groups of more than 15 must make advance reservations. ◆ Free. Tu-W 1-4PM; second and third Su of every month 1-4PM. 18127 S. Alameda St, Compton. 636.6030, 631.5981

**28 Watts Towers** Paris has the Eiffel Tower, Barcelona has the Sagrada Familia cathedral and LA has the Watts Towers, created by **Sam Rodia** and one of the world's greatest works of folk art. Between 1921 and 1954, an unlettered plasterer created these masterpieces (illustrated below), framing them from salvaged steel rods, dismantled pipe structures, bed frames, and cement. He worked alone. "How could I have been helped?" asked Rodia. "I couldn't tell anyone what to do...most of the time I didn't know myself." Building without a conscious plan—though he may have been inspired by childhood memories of similar structures used in an annual fiesta held near Naples—and scaling the heights of his work using a window-washer's belt and bucket, Rodia's glistening fretwork grew slowly over the years until the central tower topped out at 99½ feet tall. Glass bottle fragments, ceramic tiles, china plates, and more than 25,000 seashells embellish his creation, encrusting the surface so thickly that they seem to be the primary building material, forming skin that has the calcified delicacy of coral. When the towers were completed, Rodia deeded his property to a neighbor and left LA forever. He died in 1965 in Martinez, CA, unwilling to the end to talk about his life's work. Vandals disfigured the spires, and they were threatened with demolition. But citizens rallied and saved them. Extensive renovation commenced in 1978 and is ongoing under the direction of the **LA Cultural Affairs Department**. Recently, the towers have been named a National Historic Landmark. Public access to the interior is limited to most weekends from noon to 4PM. Cultural events, such as the **Day of the Drum,** an ethnic foods and music festival celebrated in late September, are held here. Be aware of the high crime rate in the area. ◆ 1765 E 107th St, Watts. 213/485.2433

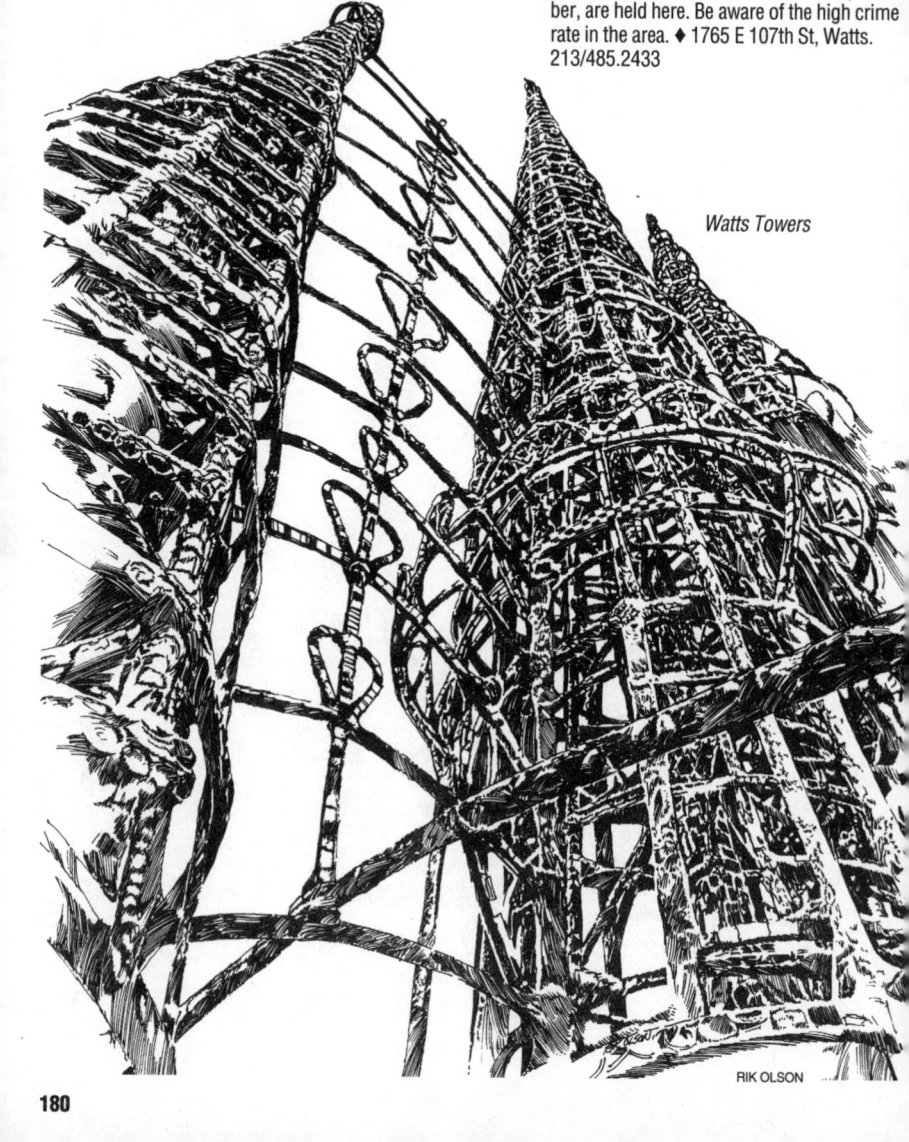

*Watts Towers*

RIK OLSON

**28 The Watts Towers Art Center** This community art center hosts exhibitions, art classes, and special programs of music, dance, and poetry reading. ♦ Tu-Sa 9AM-4PM. 1727 E 107th St, Watts. 213/569.8181

**28 Watts Train Station** The 1904 depot was restored as a railroad museum and office for the **Department of Water and Power.** It is meant as a symbol of the CRA's efforts to revitalize Watts. The **Metro Rail Red Line** from Long Beach to downtown LA stops close by—much as the Big Red Cars used to. ♦ 103rd St (at Grandee Ave), Watts

**29 Main Post Office** LA's main mail distribution center is the nation's largest single-level post office, and processes 5.5 million pieces of mail per day. The mail-processing facility is as large as 10 football fields. ♦ Tours: 586.1705. Window service: M-F 7AM-7PM; Sa 7AM-3PM. (213/586.1724). 7001 S. Central Ave at Florence. 586.1723

**30 Dunbar Hotel** The Dunbar was the first hotel in America built specifically for blacks—when white-owned hotels refused to take them in. It opened in 1928, and during its heyday in the 1930s, almost every prominent black who visited LA stayed here. It has been restored and converted to affordable housing for seniors. ♦ 4225 S. Central Ave. 213/231.0333. Tours: 213/234.7882

**31 Street Clock** A vintage free-standing clock is the centerpiece of a delightful row of Art Deco storefronts in a section that has retained its original flavor. ♦ 2423 Broadway, Lincoln Heights

**32 Winnie and Sutch Company Building** Since the 1989 torching of the Pan Pacific Auditorium by vandals, these structures, designed by **William E. Myer** in 1939, represent the best examples of streamline moderne architecture in LA. The landscaped grounds with flowers and shrubs were designed to draw attention away from the building's industrial purpose. ♦ 5610 S. Soto St, Huntington Park

**33 Farmer John's Pig Mural** Little pigs romp and play in a painted, life-size farm landscape that becomes a part of the real building. Real trees become inseparable from painted ones, and pigs peer into windows, real and painted. The murals, begun in 1957, were done by **Leslie A. Grimes,** a scenic artist who usually worked for movie studios. When he fell to his death from a scaffold in 1968, the **Arco Sign Company** assumed responsibility for maintaining and extending the murals. ♦ 3049 E. Vernon Ave, Vernon

During Mexican rule (1821-1848), LA alternated with Monterey as the capital of *Alta California.*

In 1904, the first Buddhist temple in the nation opened in Los Angeles.

Restaurants/Clubs: Red          Hotels: Blue

Shops/ 🌳 Outdoors: Green       Sights/Culture: Black

**34 Hollenbeck Park** This 21-acre park was donated to the city in 1892. There are a number of old trees, including a lovely stand of jacaranda. The clubhouse sponsors recreation programs. ♦ M-F 8AM-10PM; Sa 9AM-5PM; Su 10AM-3PM. 415 S. St. Louis St. 261.0113

**35 El Mercado** For Mexican flavor without leaving LA County, try El Mercado, a bustling combination of food markets, shops, and restaurants moving to the music of mariachis on the mezzanine and Latin records in the basement. The main floor is a market full of stalls selling the ingredients for Mexican cooking; along the walls on this level are a *tortillaria,* a bakery, snack bars with food to go, and delicatessens. The mezzanine has a series of cafeteria-style restaurants where a large variety of dishes are available. Mariachis play from noon until midnight on this level; they'll take special requests for a small donation. In the basement are shops selling everything from furniture to Mexican crafts to utilitarian domestic goods. ♦ Shops: M-F 10AM-8PM; Sa-Su 9AM-9PM. Restaurants: daily 9AM-midnight. 3425 E. First St. 213/268.3451

**36 La Parilla** ★★$ Authentic Mexican cuisine is found here in the heart of the barrio, where little English is spoken, but the welcome is just as friendly as it is south of the border. Handmade tortillas, fresh and feisty salsa, deep-fried snapper, and well-garlicked shrimp are some of the specialties. ♦ Mexican ♦ Daily 8AM-11:30PM. 2126 Brooklyn Ave. 213/262.3434

**37 Los Angeles County USC Medical Center** The highly visible 20-story moderne structure, completed in 1934, covers 89 acres and is one of the nation's largest general acute-care hospitals in the country. The **University of Southern California Health Sciences Campus,** located seven miles northeast of the main campus, serves USC's schools of Medicine and Pharmacy, the University Hospital, the Doheny Eye Institute, and the Kenneth Norris Jr. Comprehensive Cancer Center. The hospital is a training

ground for future physicians from the USC School of Medicine. ♦ Medical Center: 1975 Zonal Ave. 213/342.2000. Hospital: 1200 N. State St (at Marengo St). 213/226.2622

**38 Lincoln Park** One of the oldest parks in the city, the 46 acres were purchased in 1874. More than 300 varieties of trees grace the grounds; a number of them are rare and enormous, dating back to the beginning of the park. ♦ M-F 9AM-9PM; Sa 9AM-5:30PM; Su 10AM-6PM. N. Mission Rd at Valley Blvd, Lincoln Heights. 213/237.1726

Within Lincoln Park:

**Plaza de la Raza** Fronting on the park's small lake is a complex with a theater, a classroom, and office space serving as a cultural and educational center. It is the main forum for activities of interest to LA's Spanish-speaking community. Activities include musical performances,

dance, drama, and seasonal festivals based on themes related to Mexican holidays and family life. ♦ Nominal admission. 3540 N. Mission Rd. 213/223.2475

**39 California State University, Los Angeles** This is a branch of the popular California State University system. ♦ 5151 State University Dr (at Eastern Ave). 213/343.3000

**40 St. Honoré** $$ This Hong Kong-style cafe caters to lunch crowds and late-night owls. Spaghetti and chow mein are side-by-side on the menu. ♦ Chinese/American ♦ Daily 24 hours. 141 N. Atlantic Blvd, Monterey Park. 818/281.3281

**41 Diamond Bakery** $ In addition to the wide array of pastries and cakes, there are a variety of *bao*, which are Chinese versions of croissants with a meat filling. ♦ Bakery ♦ Daily 8:30AM-8:30PM. 744-46 W. Garvey Ave, Monterey Park. 818/289.5171

**42 Ocean Star Seafood** ★★$$ The chefs here create no-frills authentic Cantonese seafood, which includes steamed live shrimp and scallops, baked lobster, and fish prepared in several distinctive ways. Duck soup with citrus peel and beef hot pot are also recommended. The owners have also opened a much larger version of the restaurant, serving a variety of seafood delicacies in a palatial dining room with private banquet rooms. ♦ Chinese ♦ M-Th, Su 5PM-3AM; F-Sa 5PM-4AM. 112 N. Chandler Ave (at Garvey Ave), Monterey Park. 818/300.8446. Also at: 145 S. Atlantic Blvd. 818/308.2128

**42 Dragon Regency** ★★$$ Their extraordinary preparations of shrimp, crab, and sole put most Western seafood restaurants to shame. It's crowded at lunchtime. ♦ Chinese ♦ Daily 11AM-10PM. 120 S. Atlantic Blvd, Monterey Park. 818/282.1089

**43 Fragrant Vegetable** ★★$$ One of the best Chinese vegetarian restaurants in LA, Fragrant Vegetable convincingly simulates forbidden meats with tofu; elsewhere on the menu, real vegetables play starring roles. The restaurant is located in the Garfield Lincoln Center. ♦ Chinese ♦ Daily 11AM-10PM. 108-110 N. Garfield Ave, Monterey Park. 818/280.4215

**43 Cocary** ★$ This frantic and fun Mongolian barbecue lets you select (from refrigerated

cases down one wall) such delicacies as tiger prawns, baby clams, and fish dumplings to gr or simmer in a pot at your table. Bring a crowd of friends and a good appetite. ♦ Chinese ♦ Daily 11:30AM-1AM. 112 N. Garfield Ave, Monterey Park. 818/573.0691

**44 Sushi Ichiban** ★★$$ Set back from the street, this sushi bar is one of the Eastside's truly hidden treasures. Be prepared to try sushi in nontraditional garb, such as tempura wrapped in seaweed and California roll in hollowed cucumber slices. Even usually gamey fish such as mackerel gets wonderful treatment. ♦ Japanese ♦ M-Tu, Th-F 11:30AM-2:30PM, 5-9:30PM; Sa-Su 5-9:30PM. 2201 S. Garfield Ave. 213/721.3242

**45 NBC Seafood** ★★$$ Like its sibling, **ABC** in Chinatown, NBC specializes in Cantonese seafood, fresh from the tank. Perch steamed with ginger, catfish with garlic, and live crab prepared to order are highly recommended. Dim sum are served for breakfast and lunch. ♦ Chinese ♦ Daily 8AM-10PM. 404 S. Atlantic Blvd, Monterey Park. 818/282.2323

**45 Thai Heaven** ★$ It's nice to know that outstanding Thai food can survive in a city known for great Chinese food. Specialties here include barbecued chicken, steamed crab, and Thai Pan, a seafood potpourri blended with fresh herbs and chili. Come hungry. ♦ Thai ♦ M-Th, Su 11AM-10PM; F-Sa 11AM-10:30PM. 410-M S. Atlantic Blvd, Monterey Park. 818/284.0702 Also at: 2 S. Garfield Ave, Unit 16, Alhambra. 818/300.9266

**46 Yi-Mei Deli** ★$ This small, crowded deli and bakery features a wide selection of Chinese fast foods and sweets, including a popular soy bean soup that's served with *yu jow gwui*, a tasty deep-fried bread. ♦ Chinese ♦ Daily 7AM-8PM. 736 S. Atlantic Blvd, Monterey Park. 818/284.9306. Also at: 18414 Colima Rd, Row land Heights. 818/854.9246

**47 East Los Angeles College** The free, public two-year community college offers a variety of undergraduate courses and occupational programs. It was one of the first colleges to offer free, noncredit courses to anyone in the community. ♦ 1301 Brooklyn Ave, Monterey Park. 213/265.8650

**48 Tamayo** $$ Named for Mexican muralist **Rufino Tamayo,** whose artworks adorn this handsome, restored 1927 building with its painted wood ceilings, this ambitious restaurant is a delightful oasis, except for the food, which has drawn mixed reviews at best. ♦ Mexican ♦ M-W 11AM-10PM; Th-F 11AM-11:30PM; Sa 5-11PM. 5300 E. Olympic Blvd. 213/260.4700

"There is nothing to match...Los Angeles by night. A sort of luminous, geometric, incandescent immensity, stretching as far as the eye can see...the muted fluorescence of all the diagonals: Wilshire, Lincoln, Sunset, Santa Monica...you come upon the horizontal infinite in every direction."

**Jean Baudrillar,** French sociologist, philosopher, and postmodern theorist

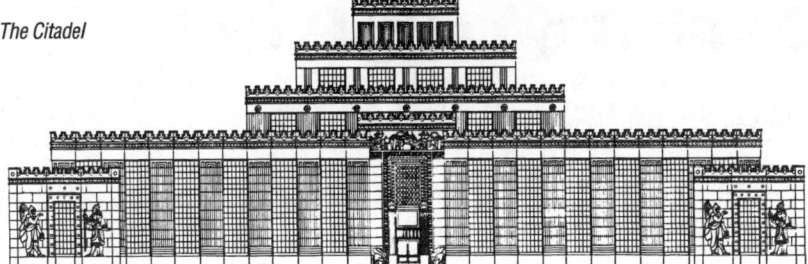

*The Citadel*

COURTESY OF SUSSMAN-PREJZA & COMPANY, INC.

**49 The Citadel** Sound the trumpets! The Assyrian fortress (pictured above), designed by **Morgan, Walls & Clements** in 1929 as an impressive facade for the **Samson Tire and Rubber Factory,** has been restored. Long a forlorn landmark glimpsed from the freeway by tourists who wondered if they had misread the map and arrived early at Disneyland, it has been remodeled and redeveloped by the **Trammell Crow Company** and is now a 130,000-square-foot manufacturer's outlet center with new vitality in the architecture, thanks to the sharp graphics, colors, and shopper-friendly geometry created by **Sussman-Prejza & Co.** Visitors can find contemporary fashions at **Benetton** and **The Gap,** shoes from **Joan & David** and **Perry Ellis,** outdoor wear from **Eddie Bauer,** and cookware from **Corning Revere.** After loading up on gifts, rest at the **Castle Garden Cafes,** which features an array of fast food in a stylish food court canopied by existing trusses and skylights. ♦ M-Sa 9AM-8PM; Su 10AM-6PM. 5675 Telegraph Rd (at Santa Ana Fwy), City of Commerce. 888.1220

**50 All American Home Center** This family owned home-improvement store is comprised of 21 departments on four acres and another six acres of parking. It claims to be the best-stocked store in the US and—more importantly it motivates its staff through profit sharing. So, if you want to build your dream house.... ♦ M-Sa 8AM-9PM; Su 8AM-7PM. 7201 E. Firestone Blvd, Downey. 927.8666

**51 Heritage Park** The restored 1880s ranch and history museum is located in six acres of gardens. Close by is the 1919 **Clarke Estate,** one of the best-preserved works by landmark architect **Irving Gill.** ♦ 12100 Mora Dr, Santa Fe Springs. 213/946.6476

**52 Pio Pico State Historic Park/Casa de Pio Pico** Don Pio Pico, former governor of California, built this hacienda on his 9,000-acre El Ranchito in 1850. The U-shaped house is a 13-room, two-story adobe mansion with two-to three-foot-thick walls. Covered porches link the side wings to the central portion of the house; a well is located in the courtyard. The house is closed for restoration through 1994. ♦ Park: W-Su 9AM-5PM. 6003 Pioneer Blvd, Whittier. 695.1217

---

LA County measures 4,083 square miles and contains 88 incorporated cities.

---

Restaurants/Clubs: Red    Hotels: Blue
Shops/ 🌳 Outdoors: Green    Sights/Culture: Black

**53 Whittier Narrows Nature Center** An enormous variety of birds, plants, and animals find sanctuary in this 127-acre nature center, located along the San Gabriel River. The small museum has exhibitions that describe the aquatic environment. ♦ Free. Daily 9AM-5PM. 1000 N. Durfee Ave, El Monte. 818/444.1872

**54 El Monte Historical Museum** Located in a 1936 WPA building, the museum contains archives of pioneer diaries, books, maps, photographs, and other printed material chronicling the history of the first American town incorporated in Southern California (1851), formerly called Willow Grove. Construction of an interior reproduction of an El Monte home, circa 1870 to 1890, located in nearby Pioneer Park, has been slowed as a result of shrinking government support. ♦ Free. Tu-F 10AM-4PM. 3150 N. Tyler Ave, El Monte. 818/444.3813

**55 Do-Nut Hole** This 1958 structure is one of the city's great pop monuments. You can drive through the two giant donuts and pick up one, or a bag to go, at any hour of the day or night. ♦ Daily 24 hours. Elliott Ave at Amar Rd (at Hacienda Blvd), La Puente. 818/968.2912

**56 Workman & Temple Homestead** Relive the colorful history of Los Angeles, from the first American settlers of the 1840s (when California was still under Mexican rule) through the booms of the 1870s and 1920s. Each of these formative decades is dramatically evoked by historic buildings on a six-acre site and re-

## South and East Central

stored by the **City of Industry** as an educational showpiece. The major attraction is a 26-room Spanish Revival house built in the '20s with the profits from an oil strike and furnished in period style, complete with a wind-up Victrola and a bearskin rug in the hall. The original mid-19th-century adobe, an English-style manor house, a lacy gazebo, and a private cemetery are also featured. The Homestead has become an important cultural resource, scheduling art fairs, concerts, lectures, and seasonal activities. ♦ Guided tours on the hour Tu-F 1-4PM; Sa-Su 10AM-4PM; closed fourth weekend of every month. 15415 E. Don Julian Rd, City of Industry. 818/968.8492

**57 China Pavilion** Once a restaurant, the China Pavilion was transformed into a nightclub featuring live performances of Chinese pop and rock 'n' roll bands. Disco dancing nightly. ♦ Daily 9PM-2AM. 2140 S. Hacienda Blvd, Hacienda Heights. 818/330.5388

**183**

# South Bay/Long Beach

A string of beach towns dots the coast from **Venice** to **Naples**, each with its own distinct character and attractions as well as ideal spots for bathing, surfing, sailing, and fishing. The sandy expanses are interrupted by man-made **Marina del Rey**, the rocky outcrop of the **Palos Verdes** peninsula, and by the industrial enclave around the **Los Angeles Harbor, San Pedro**, and **Long Beach**. Inland is LA's most prominent harbor: the **Los Angeles International Airport (LAX)**, the third busiest airport in the world.

*Area code 310 unless otherwise noted.*

**1 Los Angeles International Airport (LAX)**
The hub of the LA regional airport system also includes **Ontario International Airport** to the east, **Burbank/Glendale/Pasadena Airport** to the north, and **Long Beach Municipal Airport**

Santa Monica

Hwy. 1/Lincoln Blvd.

Main St.

Pacific Ave.

Venice Blvd.

Washington Blvd.

Culver Blvd.

Venice City Beach

For nos. 10-20, see pg. 186

Marina del Rey

Hwy. 90

Jefferson Blvd.

Centinela Ave.

Dockweiler State Beach

Pershing Dr.

Vista Del Mar

Hwy. 42/Manchester Ave.

Inglewood

La Cienega Blvd.

M.L. King Jr. Blvd.

Exposition Park

Los Angeles

Slauson Ave.

Crenshaw Blvd.

Western Ave.

Vermont Ave.

San Pedro St.

Santa Fe Ave.

Pacific Blvd.

Hwy. 42/Firestone B.

La Brea Ave.

Century Blvd.

Los Angeles International Airport

Imperial Hwy.

Avalon Blvd.

Central Ave.

Alameda St.

El Segundo

Sepulveda Blvd.

I-405

Hwy. 107/Hawthorne Blvd.

Rosecrans Ave.

Manhattan State Beach

Highland Ave.

Manhattan Beach Blvd.

Redondo Beach Blvd.

I-110/Harbor Fwy.

Manhattan Beach

Hwy. 91/Artesia Blvd.

Hwy. 91/Redondo Beach F.

Hermosa Beach

Pacific Coast Hwy.

Torrance

I-405/San Diego Fwy.

Redondo Beach

Crenshaw Blvd.

Western Ave.

Vermont Ave.

Avalon Blvd.

Redondo State Beach

Sepulveda Blvd.

Sepulveda Blvd.

Alameda St.

Pacific Ocean

Palos Verdes Blvd.

Lomita

Hwy. 1/Pacific Coast Hwy.

Hwy. 103

Anaheim St.

Rocky Point

Palos Verdes

Hawthorne Blvd.

Palos Verdes Dr. North

B St.

Gaffey St.

Rancho Palos Verdes

Rolling Hills

Ocean Bl.

Pt. Vicente Lighthouse

Palos Verdes Dr. South

Hwy. 47

Pacific Ave.

Point Vicente

9th St.

25th St.

For nos. 43-55, see pg. 191

N

km
mi
1/8    1/4    1/4    1/2

and **John Wayne Orange County Airport** to the south. A general flying field in the early '20s, LAX was known as the Municipal Airport of Los Angeles. The post-war building boom and the westward migration prompted city planners to greatly expand the airport between 1959 and 1962, masterplanned by **William Pereira and Associates.** In 1991 it handled 657,436 landings and takeoffs, and 45,668,204 passengers (up from seven million when jet service began in 1962). There are four east-west runways on a 3,500-acre site, and the buildings are constantly being improved. For detailed information on airlines, airport transportation, and parking, see "Airport" in the Orientation chapter on page 6.

**2 Quality Inn** $$ This moderately priced hotel features an outdoor pool, exercise room, two restaurants, room service, a ballroom, conference rooms, and a complimentary 24-hour airport shuttle. ◆ 5249 W. Century Blvd. 645.2200, 800/228.5151; fax 641.8214

**3 Los Angeles Airport Hilton & Towers** $$$ The Los Angeles Airport Hilton has 1,280 rooms and a full family fitness center, plus executive towers. ◆ 5711 W. Century Blvd. 410.4000, 800/445.8667; fax 410.6250

**3 LA Airport Marriott Hotel** $$$ Another caravansary for families and business travelers, the Marriott offers a health club with a Jacuzzi and sauna, a children's game room, a beauty salon, three restaurants, a 24-hour airport shuttle, 24-hour room service, and concierge service. ◆ 5855 W. Century Blvd. 641.5700, 800/228.9290; fax 337.5358

**4 Sheraton Los Angeles Airport Hotel** $$$ This 807-room hotel has the only sushi bar in the airport area, plus free shuttles to nearby beaches and Manhattan Beach shopping, and 24-hour room service. ◆ 6101 W. Century Blvd. 642.1111, 800/325.3535; fax 410.1267

**4 Hyatt at Los Angeles Airport** $$$ A cut above the other airport hotels, this Hyatt offers four Gold Passport floors, a Regency Club with a private lounge, and general amenities, including a health spa, pool, and a 24-hour airport shuttle. ◆ 6225 W. Century Blvd. 670.9000, 800/233.1234; fax 641.6924

**5 Loyola Theater** Once a luxurious preview theater for **20th Century-Fox,** this 1946 building was gutted and turned into offices. The swan's-neck facade survived. ◆ Sepulveda Blvd at Manchester Ave

**6 Airport Marina Hotel** $$ Close to LAX but not on hotel row, this 770-room hostelry is located across from a city park with a golf course, and next door to a bowling alley. Free shuttles to LAX and to Marina del Rey and Culver City shopping malls are available. ◆ 8601 Lincoln Blvd. 670.8111, 800/225.8126; fax 337.1883

**7 Loyola Marymount University** The successor to **St. Vincent's,** the first college in Los Angeles, founded in 1865, Loyola Marymount is now a coeducational private Catholic university. ◆ Loyola Blvd at W 80th St. 642.2700

**8 Southern California Institute of Architecture (SCI-ARC)** This creative design laboratory was established by **Ray Kappe** in 1972 and is currently headed by **Michael Rotondi,** one of the first graduates. Rotondi (formerly a principle with **Morphosis**) also heads his own firm, **Roto.** Four hundred students from 50 countries study with a talented and aggressive faculty in the nondescript two-story commercial and warehouse space. Exhibitions and lectures by the world's leading architects are open to the public without charge. ◆ 5454 Beethoven St. 574.1123, 574.3801

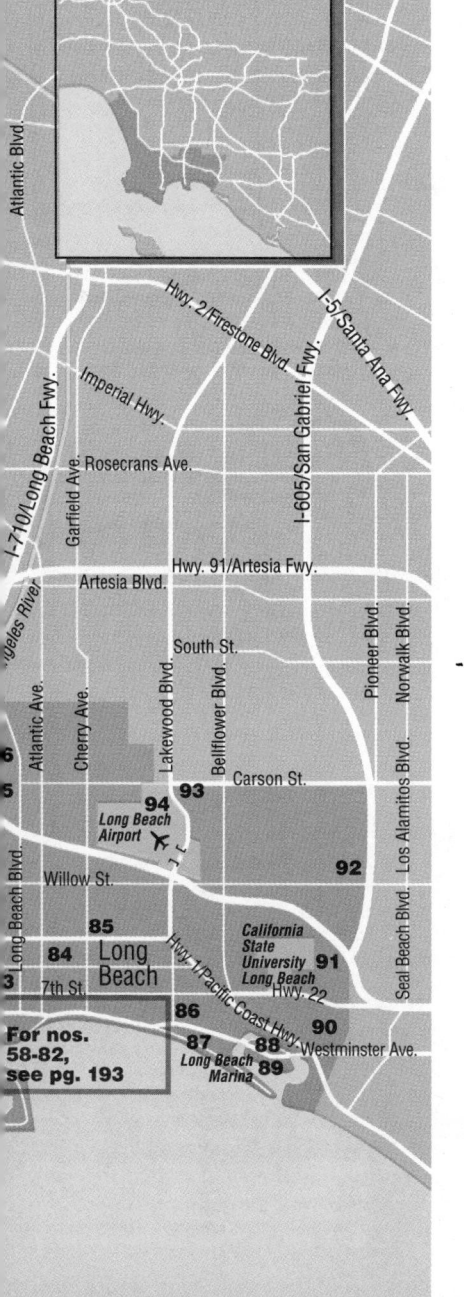

For nos. 58-82, see pg. 193

**9 Lannan Foundation** Admire the changing art exhibitions that are presented in the galleries of this adventurous philanthropic venture. A serene garden designed by artist **Siah Armajani** is also open to the public. Amid the new Puritanism, Lannan's support for controversial art and literature is of key importance. ♦ Tu-Sa 11AM-5PM. 5401 McConnell Ave. 306.1004

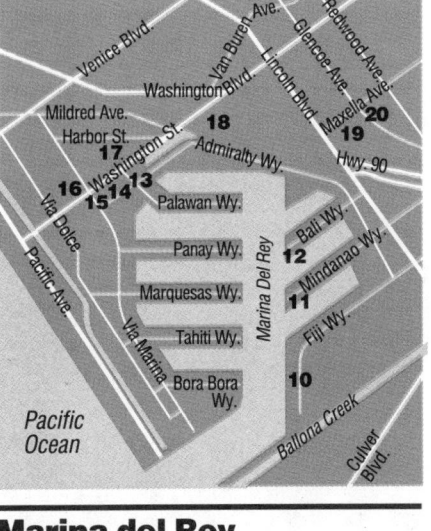

## Marina del Rey

Home to the world's highest concentration of blond singles, this waterfront community was laid out in the '60s on marshy land between Venice Beach and the LAX airport. It is also the world's largest man-made small-boat harbor, with moorings for 10,000 private pleasure craft. The adjoining open space of **Playa Vista,** bought by **Howard Hughes** for aircraft testing in the '40s, is being redeveloped as a planned community by a talented group of designers working for **Maguire Thomas Partners.**

**10 Fisherman's Village** Sunday afternoon jazz concerts enliven this tourist attraction of quaint restaurants (with marginal food) and shops. A great spot for yacht watching along the Marina

**South Bay/Long Beach**

channel, it also offers harbor cruises. ♦ 13755 Fiji Way. 823.5411

**10 Marina del Rey Sportfishing** Charter fishing boats go offshore for half- and three-quarter-day cruises. Dock fishing, boats, and tackle are also available. ♦ Daily 6AM-5PM. 13759 Fiji Way. 822.3625

**11 Burton Chace Park** This park is perfect for yacht watching, fishing, kite flying, or moon gazing from the watchtower. Picnic facilities and restrooms make this a good place for a family outing. ♦ End of Mindanao Way past Admiralty Way

**12 Marina del Rey Hotel** $$$ An ideal base for sailors, this nautical-style, low-scale, 160-room luxury hotel is surrounded by water on three sides. The **Crystal Seahorse** ($$) restaurant

overlooks the marina's main channel. ♦ 13534 Bali Way. 301.1000, 800/862.7462 (CA), 800/882.4000 (US); fax 301.8167

**13 Marina International Hotel and Bungalows** $$$ Commanding views of the marina are one of the attractions of this luxury hotel, offering 25 European-style bungalows with private patios and balconies. A free airport shuttle is available to hotel guests. ♦ 4200 Admiralty Way 301.2000, 800/862.7462 (CA), 800/882.4000 (US); fax 301.8867

**13 Jamaica Bay Inn** $$ Best Western's pleasant motel has 42 units of which 12 have kitchenettes. Rates vary for the bayside and cityside rooms. There's also a cafe. ♦ 4175 Admiralty Way. 823.5333; fax 823.1325

**14 Cafe Del Rey** $$$ Here is a restaurant with all the trendy Westside accoutrements (sleek interiors and beautiful people), but the view of the picturesque marina gives it an advantage over its landlocked counterparts. Seafood and pasta dishes are prepared in interesting ways. ♦ California ♦ M-Th 11:30AM-2:30PM, 5:30-10PM; F-Sa 11:30AM-2:30PM, 5:30-11PM; Su 10AM-2:30PM, 5-10PM. 4451 Admiralty Way, Marina Del Rey. 823.6395

**14 Marina City Towers** Designed by **Anthony Lumsden** for **DMJM** in 1971, the towers' rounded shapes resemble enormous horseshoe magnets tugging at each other. ♦ 4333 Admiralty Way

**15 The Cheesecake Factory** $$ Specialty drinks include the Flying Gorilla and the Strawberry Creamsicle at this popular restaurant overlooking boat slips. Combine one of these with the 35 house cheesecakes and kiss your diet good-bye. Or you can choose something less calorific from the vast menu. ♦ American ♦ M-Th 11:30AM-11:30PM; F-Sa 11:30AM-midnight; Su 10AM-11PM. 4142 Via Marina. 306.3344

**16 Siamese Garden** ★★$$ The specialties served in this friendly and delightful little place include the barbecued chicken, grilled shrimp, steamed crab claws, and fine *pad thai* noodles. The courtyard is delightful, too. ♦ Thai ♦ M-Th 11:30AM-3PM, 5-10PM; F-Sa 11:30AM-3PM, 5-11PM; Su noon-10PM. 301 Washington Blvd. 821.0098

**17 Akbar** ★★$$ Mughal cooking of unusual quality, with excellent tandoori and vegetarian dishes, is served here. ♦ Indian ♦ M-F, Su 11:30AM-2:30PM, 5:30-10:30PM; Sa 5:30-10:30PM. 590 Washington Blvd. 822.4116

**18 Touche** $ This is a hot spot after nine, when live bands play world beat, jazz, R&B, and swing music in a supper club with fake French windows, video screens, and reasonably priced eclectic food. ♦ Eclectic ♦ Daily 6PM-2AM. 822 Washington Blvd. 822.7221

**19 Villa Marina Marketplace** A newer 1989 complex and a 20-year-old center are oddly combined in this shopping area that straddles both sides of the street. **Gelson's** gourmet supermarket and **Maximillian,** which has upscale resort and evening wear for men and women, are in the newer complex, as are several new restaurants and movie screens. Across the street are more mainstream retailers, including **The Gap, Clothestime,** and **Tower Records,** plus six movie screens and an old Southern restaurant. ♦ 13450 Maxella Ave. 827.0253

Within the Villa Marina Marketplace:

**Souplantation** ★★$ A healthful version of the all-you-can-eat smorgasbord, this salad and soup bar offers a wide array of fresh vegetables, fruits, and breads. Unlike most shopping center restaurants, this one is airy and light. ♦ American ♦ M-Th, Su 11AM-9PM; F-Sa 11AM-10PM. 305.7669

**Angeli Mare** ★★★$$ Architect **Michele Saee** designed this ribbed, wavelike space that is sharp-edged and sensual, woodsy and watery. Entrées such as pizza and roast chicken are carried over from the other Angeli restaurants, but it's the seafood that wins this place its extra star. The fish soup and pastas, plus the daily specials, are outstanding. ♦ Seafood ♦ M-F 11:30AM-11:30PM; Sa-Su 11AM-11:30PM. 822.1984

**20 Aunt Kizzy's Back Porch** ★★$ Catfish, fried chicken, short ribs, and smothered pork chops, just like down-home in the old South, are served in this country cabin-style restaurant. ♦ Southern ♦ M-Th, Su 11AM-10PM; F-Sa 11AM-midnight. 4325 Glencoe Ave. 578.1005

# Beach Cities of El Segundo, Manhattan, Hermosa, and Redondo

A jumble of pastel cottages squeezed along a stretch of beachfront marks a series of former summer resorts, now prospering as permanent communities. El Segundo has the least developed waterfront and is hemmed in by the airport and a huge oil refinery. Manhattan Beach is part family neighborhood and part singles capital of the beach party circuit. South of Manhattan Beach is Hermosa Beach, the prototypical beach town with its concentration of suntanned surfers. At the south end is Redondo Beach, a mixture of affluent new and slightly seedy old, with an interesting and well-kept pier and marina complex.

**21 Radisson Plaza Hotel** $$$ The luxurious Radisson has its own golf course, complimentary airport shuttle, shuttle service to the beach, and concierge service. Other amenities include Continental breakfast, a full-service health club, and a pool. ♦ 1400 Parkview Ave, Manhattan Beach. 546.7511, 800/333.3333; fax 546.7520

Within the Radisson Plaza Hotel:

**Califia** ★★$$$ Dine on inventive California cuisine with a French twist in this pretty gray-and-pink room. ♦ California ♦ M 11:30AM-2PM; Tu-F 11:30AM-2PM, 6-10PM; Sa 6-10PM. 546.1668

**22 Barnaby's** $$$ Though this Victorian fantasy hotel seems like a combination of **Charles Dickens** and **Disneyland,** somehow the leaded glass, deep carpets, marble statuary, and thousands of dollars worth of antiques come together in a charming, elegant whole, helped along by the high-quality service. Rooms have old books and four-poster beds, plus well-disguised modern conveniences. There's a pool, and a garden that's so pretty you may have to share it with a string of wedding receptions. Call for special weekend rates. The intimate Victorian restaurant (**Barnaby's** $$) serves traditional cuisine daily. **Rosie's Pub** is popular with locals and guests; it offers nightly entertainment and dancing on weekends. ♦ 3501 Sepulveda Blvd, Manhattan Beach. 545.8466, 800/552.5285; fax 545.8621

**23 Sloopy's Beach Cafe** $ Sandwiches, hamburgers, and salads are served before the hearth in winter, or at sidewalk tables when the weather cooperates, at this popular lunch spot. ♦ American ♦ Tu-Su 11AM-8:30PM. 3416 Highland Ave, Manhattan Beach. 545.1373

**24 Café Pierre** $$ Franco-California cuisine (regional herbs melded with French-style cooking) visits the beach cities in this rustic and comfortable setting, ideally located within walking distance to **The Strand** nightclub and Manhattan Beach pier for an after-dinner stroll. ♦ French/California ♦ M-F 11:30AM-2:30PM, 5:30-11PM; Sa 5:30-11PM; Su 5:30-10:30PM. 317 Manhattan Beach Blvd, Manhattan Beach. 545.5252

**24 The Hungry Mind** $$ This wonderful haven for beach bohemians is a cafe, bakery, and bookstore in one. ♦ Coffeehouse ♦ M-W, Su 6AM-11PM; Th-Sa 6AM-1AM. 916 Manhattan Ave, Manhattan Beach. 318.9029

**25 Manhattan Beach State Pier** This 900-foot municipal facility, without tackle or snack shops, is located at the end of Manhattan Beach Boulevard. ♦ At The Strand

**26 Hermosa Beach Fishing Pier** The tackle shop along this 1,320-foot municipal pier rents equipment and sells bait. There's a snack bar, too. ♦ Pier: daily 24 hours. Bait shop: daily 7AM-

midnight. End of Pier Ave, Hermosa Beach. 372.2124

**26 The Lighthouse** In the block next to the pier is one of the best and oldest jazz clubs in Los Angeles. The fine music and top-flight performers rather than fancy decor have kept its doors open since the '50s. Weekend brunches are accompanied by jazz. ♦ Cover. M-F 4PM-1:30AM; Sa-Su 10AM-1:30AM. 30 Pier Ave, Hermosa Beach. 372.6911, ~~372.8653~~ *310/N.C.*

**27 The Either/Or Bookstore** Writer **Thomas Pynchon** used to come in here to pick up the latest in fiction when he lived nearby. ♦ Daily 10AM-11PM. 124 Pier Ave, Hermosa Beach. 374.2060

| Restaurants/Clubs: Red | Hotels: Blue |
|---|---|
| Shops/ 🌳 Outdoors: Green | Sights/Culture: Black |

**187**

**27 Ajeti** $ Owner **Din Ajeti** gives you a warm welcome and heaping platters of roast lamb and other native Albanian specialties. ◆ Albanian ◆ Tu-Sa 5-10PM; Su 5-9PM. 425 Pier Ave, Hermosa Beach. 379.9012

**27 Comedy & Magic Club** Good food, Art Deco decor, and eclectic humor are abundant in this friendly club. ◆ Cover. Hours vary; call ahead for show times. 1018 Hermosa Ave, Hermosa Beach. Reservations required. 372.1193

**27 Pedone's** $ The thin-crusted pizza served here is very good. ◆ Pizza ◆ Daily 11AM-10PM. 1501 Hermosa Ave, Hermosa Beach. 376.0949

**28 Habash Cafe** ★$ Homemade Arab specialties by the owner include barbecued lamb, hummus, *baba ghanouj*, and *tabouleh*. ◆ Middle Eastern ◆ M-Sa 10AM-9:30PM. 233 Pacific Coast Hwy, Hermosa Beach. 376.6620

**28 Monstad Pier** This two hundred-foot privately owned pier has a tackle shop that rents and sells equipment and bait. ◆ Admission. Pier: daily 24 hours. **Tony's Fish Market Restaurant:** M-Th, Su 11:30AM-11PM; F-Sa 11AM-12:30AM. 376.6223. **Redondo Coffee Shop Bait and Tackle:** M-Th 7AM-10PM; F-Sa 7AM-midnight; Su 7AM-11PM. 318.1044. Coral Way, Redondo Beach

**29 Fisherman's Wharf** Many unusual shops, as well as places to buy and eat fresh fish and the ubiquitous souvenir shops, line the narrow path leading to the end of the pier. This is a popular place on summer nights, when many restaurants are open late. ◆ At Redondo Beach

**29 The Cheesecake Factory** $$ Cheesecake connoisseurs will be in dessert heaven here. There are 40 different cheesecakes, from lemon and cookies and cream, to white chocolate raspberry. The novella-thick menu lists a variety of pastas, salads, sandwiches, and seafood as preludes to the baked delights. ◆ Eclectic ◆ M-Th, Su 11:30AM-11PM; F-Sa 11:30AM-11:30PM. 605 N. Harbor Dr, Redondo Beach. 376.0466. Also at: 364 N. Beverly Dr, Beverly Hills. 278.7270; 4142 Via Marina, Marina del Rey. 306.3344; 6324 Canoga, Warner Center, Woodland Hills. 818/883.9900

**29 Portofino Inn** $$$ Every room has a balcony and a view overlooking picturesque King's Harbor in this middle-size oceanfront hotel. Amenities include a complimentary shuttle to and from the airport, a health club, and a hospitality bar in every room. ◆ 260 Portofino Way, Redondo Beach. 379.8481, 800/468.4292 (CA), 800/338.2993 (US); fax 372.7329

**29 Redondo Sport Fishing** Choices from this charter service include a 45-minute harbor cruise, local offshore fishing, or deep-sea cruises to Catalina and Santa Barbara islands. An exciting seasonal whale watch allows you to observe the migration of the California gray whale from breathtakingly close range. ◆ 233 N. Harbor Dr. A 24-hour reservation is required. 372.3566

**29 Redondo Sportfishing Pier** The tackle shop at this 250-foot-long, privately owned pier rents and sells equipment and bait. There's a snack bar, too. ◆ Pier: daily 24 hours. Tackle shop: daily 4:30AM-9PM. End of Harbor Dr and Portofino Way, Redondo Beach. 372.2111

**30 Redondo Beach Historical Museum** Artifacts, photographs, and memorabilia reflect the one-hundred-year history of this seaside community that was a thriving commercial port in the late-19th century. Among the other treasured documents are photographs of **Henry Huntington's** trolley line (Red Cars), which brought thousands to the beach resorts, and the famed **Lightning Racer** roller coaster, one of three claimed by Pacific storms. ◆ Tours arranged by appointment. W, F, Su 1-4PM. 320 Knob Hill Ave. 318.0160, ext. 2252

**30 Palos Verdes Inn** $$$ This medium-size hotel is located two blocks from the beach. ◆ 1700 S. Pacific Coast Hwy, Redondo Beach. 316.4211, 800/352.0385 (CA), 800/421.9241 (US); fax 316.4863

Within the Palos Verdes Inn:

**Chez Melange** ★★$$ There's a sushi bar, a wine counter, and a dining room serving contemporary international cuisine in chef **Robert Bell's** exciting restaurant. Warm lamb salad with mixed greens, seafood specials, and fresh fruit tarts are among the standouts. The wine-tasting dinners are celebrated citywide. ◆ Eclectic ◆ M-Th 7-11AM, 11:30AM-4PM, 5-11PM; F-Sa 7-11AM, 11:30AM-4PM, 5-11:30PM; Su 8AM-2:30PM, 5-10:30PM. 540.1222

# Palos Verdes Peninsula

In 1913 New York banker **Frank Vanderlip** bought most of this hilly peninsula and planned to turn it into millionaires' colony. Slightly less ambitious developments began in the 1920s, creating a series of exclusive, often gated residential enclaves and modest commercial centers—all in very conservative taste. Ranch houses alternate with Spanish haciendas, horse trails, and countless lovely hiking paths leading through the forests of eucalyptus. The hills are a succession of 13 marine uplift terraces created by Palos Verdes' slow rise from the ocean floor.

**31 Malaga Cove Plaza** In their 1922 plan for Palos Verdes, **Charles H. Cheney** and the **Olmsted** brothers envisioned four area community centers. This was the only one built. Designed by **Webber, Staunton & Spaulding** in 1924, it is a Spanish Revival design of two-story shops in an arcade. The plaza has a picturesque brick bridge over Via Chico and a fountain inspired by the *Fountain of Neptune* in Bologna, Italy. ◆ 200 Palos Verdes Dr (at Via Corta), Palos Verdes

**31 La Rive Gauche** ★★$$$ Classic French cuisine is served in this rustic but chic French-country setting. The veal chop with wild mushroom sauce is a standout. ◆ French ◆ M 5:30-10PM; Tu-Su 11AM-3PM, 5:30-10PM. 320 Tejon Place, Palos Verdes. 378.0267

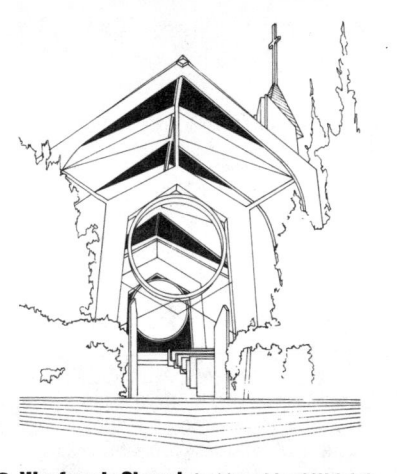

**32 Wayfarer's Chapel** Architect **Lloyd Wright's** most visited building occupies a prominent hillside location overlooking the ocean. The 1946 chapel (pictured above) is the national monument to **Emmanuel Swedenborg,** Swedish theologian and mystic. The glass structure, supported by a redwood frame, is transparent and blends with the surrounding redwood grove. ♦ Daily 9AM-5PM. Services: Su 11AM. 5755 Palos Verdes Dr. South, Rancho Palos Verdes. 377.1650

**33 Borrelli's** ★$$ This long-established restaurant, with lovely Mediterranean decor, has particularly solicitous service and good veal zingara with wild mushrooms. ♦ Italian ♦ M-F 11:30AM-2:30PM, 5-10PM; Sa-Su 5-10PM. 672 Silver Spur Rd, Rolling Hills Estates. 541.2632

**34 South Coast Botanic Gardens** Until 1956 this site was a diatomaceous earth mine. When mining activity ceased, the trash dumping began—3,500,000 tons were poured in. Starting in 1960, the **Los Angeles Department of Arboreta and Botanic Gardens** initiated a planting program. Now beautifully landscaped, the 87-acre gardens are a model experiment in land reclamation. They contain mature specimens from all continents except Antarctica. Plants are grouped according to botanical family. The gardens also offer horticultural and botanical displays, a gift shop, gardening demonstrations every Sunday at 2PM, and a picnic area. ♦ Admission. Daily 9AM-5PM. 26300 S. Crenshaw Blvd, Rolling Hills Estates. 544.6815

**35 Fino** ★★$$ Hearty, aromatic Mediterranean cuisine is served in this rustic bistro. From the imported olives and cured meats to the tapas and mushroom risotto, this is the spot to make anyone start dreaming about ancient, faraway places. ♦ Mediterranean ♦ M-Th 5-10PM; F-Sa 5-10:30PM; Su 5-9PM. 24530 Hawthorne Blvd, Torrance. 373.1952

**36 Big Wok** ★$ The Golden Horde never had it so good. They had to eat as they galloped over the steppes; you can serve yourself from a buffet in an opulent room and add sauces to taste at your table. ♦ Mongolian ♦ Tu-Sa 11:30AM-3PM, 4:30-10PM; Su 4:30-9:30PM. 24012 Vista Montana (between Anza Ave and Pacific Coast Hwy), Torrance. 375.1513

**37 Fabio** $$ The former **Symphonie**—built around chef **Susumu Fukui**—closed with his departure, but the owners have reopened this new place with contemporary Milanese decor, a Florentine chef, and traditional Northern Italian cuisine. Homemade *tagliatelle* with aromatic chicken sauce, pan-fried veal chop, and *caciucco* seafood stew are popular. ♦ Northern Italian ♦ M-F 11:30AM-2PM, 5:30-10PM; Sa 5:30-10PM. 23863 Hawthorne Blvd, Torrance. 373.8187

**38 Del Amo Fashion Center** With more than 350 stores in 2.6-million-square-feet of space, this is one of the largest retail centers of its kind. Department stores include **The Broadway, Sears, JC Penney, Robinson's, Bullock's, I. Magnin,** and **Montgomery Ward.** Aside from the major department stores, there are several independent fashion stores, more than 55 restaurants, and dramatic interior spaces. ♦ M-F 10AM-9:30PM; Sa 10AM-7:30PM; Su 11AM-6PM. Bounded by Hawthorne, Sepulveda, and Torrance Blvds, and Madrona Ave, Torrance. 542.8525

**39 Lomita Railroad Museum** Housed in a replica of the 19th-century Greenwood Station in Wakefield, MA, the museum displays memorabilia from the steam era of railroading. The station is flanked by an impeccably restored 1902 steam locomotive and an old 1910 wooden caboose, both of which may be toured. The annex across the street has picnic benches, a fountain, and a 1913 boxcar. There's a gift shop, too. ♦ Admission. W-Su 10AM-5PM. 250th St at Woodward Ave, Lomita. 326.6255

**40 Depot** ★★$$ The latest venture by **Robert Bell** and **Michael Franks** of **Chez Melange** is packing in South Bay diners. Set in a 1912 Red Car electric railway station with whitewashed brick walls, dark wood, classic tilework, and moderne-style sconces, the Depot is aptly named and decorated, but the food is offbeat and adventurous. Though there are traditional American dishes, Asian, Latin, and Mediterranean influences make for exciting fare. There is Thai-dyed chicken; mélanges that might include a lamb chop, filet, and chicken sausage;

## South Bay/Long Beach

and a Mexican hominy stew with lamb. ♦ Eclectic ♦ M 11:30AM-2:30PM; Tu-Th 11:30AM-2:30PM, 5:30-10:30PM; F 11:30AM-2:30PM, 5:30-11PM; Sa 5-11PM; Su 5-9PM. 1250 Cabrillo Ave, Torrance. 787.7501

---

The Beach Boys attended Hawthorne High in the South Bay area, where Brian Wilson flunked a music class when he turned in the song that later became "Surfin' Safari."

In 1929 Graf Zeppelin completed the first transpacific flight from Japan to Los Angeles. He landed at the site of Los Angeles International Airport, then a dirt strip called Mines Field.

---

More than 45.5 million airline passengers passed through Los Angeles International Airport in 1991.

**41 Alpine Village** You can quaff a stein and down huge portions of German-Swiss food while listening to the band in the beer garden at this replica of an Alpine Village with a restaurant and 24 shops offering an array of goods. ♦ Shops: daily 11AM-7PM. Restaurant: daily 11AM-10PM; dancing until midnight. 833 Torrance Blvd (west of Harbor Fwy), Torrance. 327.4384

**42 Paradise** ★$$ Designer **Scott Johnson** created the contemporary Polynesian interior for this welcome oasis at the junction of the Harb and San Diego freeways. The menu features a potpourri of exotic drinks and contemporary favorites like goat-cheese salad, pizza, and tur niçoise. ♦ Eclectic ♦ M-F 11AM-2:30PM, 5-10PM; Sa 5-10PM; Su 9AM-2PM, 5-9PM. 889 W 190th St, Gardena. 324.4800

# LA Story

Much has been written about the City of Angels, everything from fiction by the likes of **F. Scott Fitzgerald** to telltale historical accounts of Hollywood's rich and famous. Here is a guide to the most compelling and informative works on LA; you may want to read through some of them before embarking on your journey into the city.

## Non-Fiction:

*Architecture in Los Angeles* by **David Gebhard** and **Robert Winter** (1985, Peregrine Smith Books). Future editions of this architectural guide will cover all of Southern California.

*Bargain Hunting in Los Angeles* by **Barbara Partridge** (1987, Peregrine Smith Books).

*California Crazy: Roadside Vernacular Architecture* by **Jim Heimann** and **Rip George** (1980, Chronicle Books). An amazing collection of architectural follies, nearly all of which have been demolished.

*California Festivals* by **Carl** and **Katie Landau** with **Kathy Kincade** (1989, Landau Communications, San Francisco).

*California People* by **Carol Dunlap** (1982, Peregrine Smith Books). Short biographies of men and women who made LA and the rest of the state what it is, from Earl C. Anthony to Frank Zappa.

*The City Observed: Los Angeles, A Guide to its Architecture and Landscapes* by **Charles Moore, Peter Becker,** and **Regula Campbell** (1984, Vintage Books).

*City of Quartz* by **Mike Davis** (1990, Vintage Books). A social history of LA creatively researched and written with wit and irony.

*East Los Angeles* by **Ricardo Romo** (1983, Texas). A history of the barrio from 1900 to 1930.

*Ethnic LA* by **Zena Pearlstone** (1990, Hillcrest Press). Short histories of many of the city's ethnic groups with statistical data from the 1980 census.

*Happy Birthday, Hollywood* by **Michael Webb** (1987, Motion Picture and Television Fund, LA). A hundred years of movie history, and the town that became a symbol of the industry.

*Hollywood: The Pioneers* by **Kevin Brownlow** and **John Kobal** (1979, Knopf). A fascinating anthology of the silent movies.

*Inventing the Dream: California Through the Progressive Era* by **Kevin Starr** (1985, Oxford University Press). Chapters on the growth of Southern California, Pasadena, and the movie industry, plus an excellent bibliography.

*LA Freeway: An Appreciative Essay* by **David Brodsky** (1981, University of California).

*LA Lost and Found* by **Sam Hall Kaplan** (1987, Crown). Outstanding photographs taken by **Julius** Schulman accompany an architectural history of Los Angeles.

*Los Angeles: The Architecture of Four Ecologies* by **Reyner Banham** (1971, Penguin Books). An approv ing look at LA, years before it became fashionable, by a maverick English architectural historian.

*Los Angeles: Biography of a City* edited by **John** and **LaRess Caughey** (1977, University of California). Brilliant anthology of writings on LA, grouped by topic.

*The Magic of Neon* by **Michael Webb** (1987, Peregrine Smith Books). Follies that have survived and the renaissance of neon on Melrose Avenue.

*The Movielover's Guide to Hollywood* by **Richard Alleman** (1989, Harper & Row). Historic sites and lore of Tinseltown.

*Raymond Chandler's Los Angeles* by **Elizabeth War** and **Alain Silver** (1988, Overlook). Quotations from LA's acerbic scribe juxtaposed with photos of real-life locations.

*Southern California: An Island on the Land* by **Carey McWilliams** (1973, Peregrine Smith Books). An impassioned exposé of the dark side of the dream.

*Trails of the Angeles: One Hundred Hikes in the San Gabriels* by **John W. Robinson** (1984, Wilderness Press, Berkeley).

## Fiction:

Writers and journalists flocked to Hollywood with th coming of the talkies and then bit the hand that fed them. The classic put-down is **Nathanael West's** *Da of the Locust* (1939, Penguin Books).

**Budd Schulberg's** *What Makes Sammy Run?* (1941 Random House) is a devastating portrait of greed and chicanery by a movie-industry insider.

**F. Scott Fitzgerald's** *The Last Tycoon* (published posthumously in 1941) is a romanticized portrait of **Irving Thalberg,** MGM's boy wonder.

**Evelyn Waugh** was invited by MGM to discuss a movie version of *Brideshead Revisited;* the visit yielded the funniest-ever poison-pen letter to LA, *The Loved One.*

**F. Scott Fitzgerald, Henry Miller,** and **Raymond Chandler** are just a few of several famed writers featured in **John Miller's** *Los Angeles Stories.*

## Periodicals:

*LA Style* carries some of the city's sharpest restaurant reviews, as well as stories on cutting-edge music and fashion, architecture, and design.

*LA Weekly* seems torn between compulsive consum erism and outspoken radicalism but is valuable for its comprehensive listings of movies, concerts, and theater.

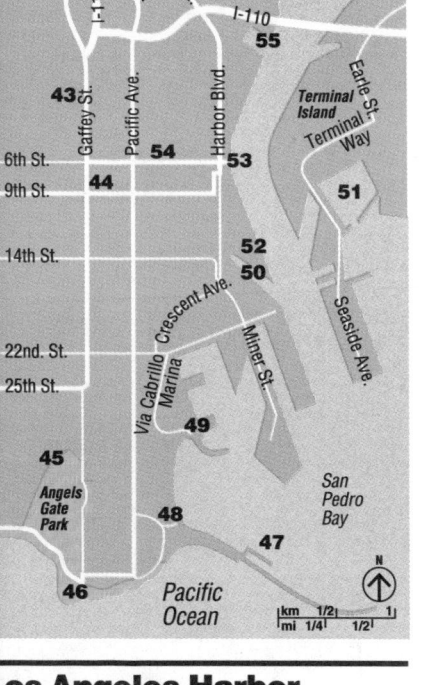

Map labels: Front St., I-110, 55, 43, Pacific Ave., Gaffey St., Harbor Blvd., Terminal Island, Earle St., Terminal Island Way, 54, 53, 6th St., 9th St., 44, 51, 14th St., 52, 50, Seaside Ave., Crescent Ave., Via Cabrillo Marina, Miner St., 22nd. St., 25th St., 49, 45, Angels Gate Park, 48, San Pedro Bay, 47, 46, Pacific Ocean, N, km 1/2 1, mi 1/4 1/2

## os Angeles Harbor

1876 the first railroad arrived in Los Angeles, but
e city still lacked access to the sea. Despite its shal-
w, unprotected harbor, **San Pedro** (pronounced by
atives as "San Peedro") outmaneuvered Santa
onica for federal funding and became the main port-
-entry for the emerging metropolis. Work began in
399 on a new breakwater and a major port expan-
on. In 1909 the city of LA annexed San Pedro and
**ilmington,** creating the famous shoestring strip, a
retch of city land (at places only a half-mile wide)
om downtown to the harbor, which provided for a
aport and transportation route entirely within city
mits. Today's harbor is the busiest import and export
ade port in the nation, a hub of industry (notably oil
fineries and aircraft plants), and the foremost port-
-call in Southern California for passenger vessels.

t the center of the harbor is **Terminal Island,** linked
San Pedro by the **Vincent Thomas Bridge** and to
ong Beach by the **Gerald Desmond Bridge.** The
reets of downtown San Pedro retain much of the
avor of their colorful past as a seafarer's port town.
he region's commercial fishing fleet contributes to
e area's economy, employing many mariners of Por-
*guese, Greek, and Yugoslav descent. The strong eth-
c traditions make shopping in the multitude of small
ood stores a delightful experience.

**43 San Pedro Grand Hotel** $$$ A misnamed
Best Western hostelry, this small, European-
style hotel has Victorian decor and prices that
are quite grand. ♦ 111 S. Gaffey St, San Pedro.
514.1414, 800/248.3188; fax 831.8262

"he only culture in LA can be found in the yogurt."
**Johnny Carson**

estaurants/Clubs: Red   Hotels: Blue
hops/ 🌳 Outdoors: Green   Sights/Culture: Black

**44 Babouch Moroccan Restaurant** ★$$
Authentic food, such as couscous, lamb, and
chicken *tajine,* is served in an Arabian nights
tentlike setting with belly dancers. ♦ Moroccan
♦ Tu-Su 5-10PM. 810 S. Gaffey St, San Pedro.
831.0246

**45 Fort McArthur Reservation and Angels
Gate Park** The fort dates back to 1888, and
the US Air Force still occupies part of the reservation, but nearly 65 acres have been turned
into a park and museum. The 20-acre park surrounding the large **Korean Bell of Friendship** (a
replica of a bronze bell made in A.D. 771, presented to the US by Korea during the 1976 bi-
centennial) offers picnic sites and a spectacular
view of the Pacific and Point Fermin. A military
museum preserves the workings (minus the
actual guns) of the historic battery used as the
primary West Coast defense fortification during
World War II. Guided tours of the Port of Los
Angeles control tower are offered by reservation through the museum. ♦ Park: daily 10AM-
6PM. Museum: Sa-Su noon-5PM. 3601 S.
Gaffey St, San Pedro. 548.2631

**46 Point Fermin Park** The 37 landscaped acres
of this park along the palisades overlook the
Pacific Ocean and Los Angeles Harbor. The
lookout point has coin-operated telescopes,
and the whale-watching station offers information on the California gray whales' annual winter migration to the Gulf of California. The Victorian Eastlake-style lighthouse, constructed in
1874 from bricks and lumber brought around
Cape Horn by sailing ship, is not open to the
public. The lighthouse originally used oil lamps
approximating 2,100 candlepower until 1925,
when electric power was installed. ♦ Gaffey St
at Paseo del Mar, San Pedro. 548.7756

**47 Cabrillo Beach Fishing Pier** The 1,500-
foot-long publicly owned fishing pier has a
shop that sells equipment and live bait. No li-
cense or fee is required, and there are no rentals. ♦ End of Stephen White Dr, San Pedro.
832.1179

**48 Cabrillo Marine Museum** Children will love
the imaginative displays of marine life and the
behind-the-scenes glimpses of how they are
maintained in this museum designed by **Frank
Gehry** in 1981. To emphasize the spirit of fun,
Gehry created a villagelike cluster of small
buildings housing an aquarium, classrooms,
offices, and a theater, dramatically enclosed
with chain-link fencing, which suggests a playground to the kids, who are the prime audience.
Museum volunteers are always on hand for
tours and workshops. Visitors can handle the
tidepool creatures in a "touch tank" filled with
sea stars, cucumbers, and urchins. For information on whale-watching tours, from late December through early April, call 832.4444.

**191**

♦ Free. Parking fee. Tu-F noon-5PM; Sa-Su 10AM-5PM. Touch tank: Tu-F 2:30PM, 3:30PM; Sa-Su 11:30AM-3:30PM. 3720 Stephen White Dr, San Pedro. 548.7562

**48  The Point Fermin Marine Life Refuge** Next to the museum is this tidepool community. Brochures for a self-guided exploration of tidepool biology are available at the museum.

**49  Madeo Ristorante** ★★$$$ A larger, more glamorous version of the Westside original, this ristorante serves great pasta, veal, and Florentine steak. ♦ Italian ♦ M-Th, Su 11:30AM-2:30PM, 5:30-10PM; F-Sa 11:30AM-2:30PM, 5:30-10:30PM. 295 Whaler's Walk (take 22nd St to Via Cabrillo Marina), San Pedro. 831.1199

**50  SP Slip** Located on the western side of the main channel, this dock is used as a berthing facility by commercial fishing companies. ♦ Off Harbor Blvd, San Pedro

**51  Fish Harbor** Since many of the commercial fishing operations have moved away from Southern California to the South Pacific, there are only a handful of fish canneries that remain in operation here. ♦ Off Seaside Blvd. Berth 261, San Pedro

**52  Ports O' Call Village** At the harbor's edge is a replica of other times and other places. Nineteenth-century New England, a Mediterranean fishing village, and early California live again in this shopping and eating complex. The **Village Boat House,** located in Ports O' Call Village, offers daily cruises of the harbor area where visitors can see the inner harbor, yacht harbor, freighter operations, scrapping yards, and the Coast Guard base. ♦ Tour hours vary with the season; call for hours and information. Berth 77, San Pedro. 831.0287

**53  Maritime Museum** This nautical history collection is appropriately housed in an old ferry building, refurbished by **Pulliam & Matthews.** Much of the old ferry gear remains, giving visitors a sense of imminent departure. There is a fine view of harbor operations from the promenade deck. Next to the museum, the bow section of the US Navy cruiser *Los Angeles* offers a chance to explore. Museum collections include

**South Bay/Long Beach**

a number of ship models, including a 16-foot scale model of the *Titanic,* built from cardboard and match sticks by a 14-year-old boy. The **Naval Deck** is replete with Navy memorabilia, including the bridge deck of the *Los Angeles.* A timeline history of the harbor beginning in 1840 gives a graphic summary of the dredging and construction. ♦ Free. Tu-Su 10AM-5PM. Berth 84, San Pedro. 548.7618

**54  Papadakis Taverna** ★$$ If the mood is right, the waiters dance in this lively, popular restaurant. ♦ Greek ♦ Daily 5-10PM. 301 W. Sixth St, San Pedro. 548.1186

**55  Terminals** On the western side of the main channel are the container terminals, piled high with steel freight containers, and the passenger liner terminals. The terminal for the *Catalina Steamer* and the Catalina helicopter is located just north of this point.

**55  Vincent Thomas Bridge** Spanning the main channel between San Pedro and Terminal Island, this bridge clears the water by 185 feet so that military planes can fly under it. The 6,500-foot-long turquoise suspension bridge is the most visible landmark in the harbor. Freighters are berthed on the northern side of Terminal Island. Dry docks are located across the back channel in the Long Beach side of the harbor and in the Naval Shipyard on the southeastern end of Terminal Island.

**56  General Phineas Banning Residence Museum** In 1864 Phineas Banning, father of the Los Angeles harbor, built this Greek Revival clapboard home (pictured above) of lumber from the Mendocino coast and colored glass from Europe. The house is now decorated with period furnishings. Tours through the building include the restored kitchen, where food is cooked using **Katherine Banning's** recipes, as well as family and public rooms of the mansion. The museum is located in 20-acre **Banning Park,** which offers picnic facilities and playground equipment. Access to the house is by tour only. ♦ Donation requested. Tours Tu-Th 12:30PM, 1:30PM, 2:30PM; Sa-Su 12:30PM, 1:30PM, 2:30PM, 3:30PM. 401 E. M St, Wilmington. 548.7777

**56  Drum Barracks Civil War Museum** This is the last remaining building of **Camp Drum,** a 7,000-soldier Union Army outpost that closed in 1871. Although California sympathized with the Confederacy during the Civil War, this large Union military presence kept the state in the blue ranks. The barracks have been refurbished as a museum of Civil War memorabilia. ♦ Admission. Open for tours only. Tu-Th 10AM, 11AM, noon; Sa 12:30PM, 1:30PM, 2:30PM. 1052 Banning Blvd, Wilmington. 548.7509

Los Angeles' Dominguez Field, a bean field that once belonged to Don Manuel Dominguez's Rancho San Pedro, was host to the first International Air Meet in 1910, drawing nearly 20,000 spectators. All this attention helped attract small aircraft companies to Southern California that later became the foundation of LA's aircraft construction and aerospace industry.

RIK OLSON

## ong Beach

st of the harbor is the city of Long Beach, which was
unded in 1880 and flourished with the oil boom of
e 1920s and the improvements to the port. A few oil
ells survive in **Signal Hill** to the northeast; for a short
ne this was the world's most productive field. From
e sandy strand south of Long Beach, you can see the
pical camouflage created to conceal the almost 600
l-producing offshore oil wells; each palm-clad fake
and covers 10 acres of soundproofed oil wells. The
ng Beach Harbor opened in 1911 and has been ex-
nding ever since. It is a major port for electric ma-
inery and Alaskan crude oil, and a significant West
ast port of entry.

ng Beach was devastated by the 1933 earthquake;
any of the Art Deco buildings erected in its wake
ve since been destroyed by massive urban redevel-
ment. The city center is currently raw and unappeal-
, but elsewhere historic landmarks and districts can
l be found. The LA Metro Rail's Blue Line light rail
ns 22 miles from Long Beach's Transit Mall at First
reet and Pacific Avenue north to downtown LA, daily
m 5:30AM to 8PM. For more information on the LA
etro Rail, call 213/620.RAIL.

**57 Naval Shipyard** You may tour a Navy ship by
advance reservation, usually the second Saturday of the month, at 9AM and 1PM. Call weekdays eight days in advance. ♦ 547.7219

**58 Port of Long Beach** Cargo handling can be
watched from the observation deck atop the
**Port Administration Building.** ♦ M-F 8:30AM-
4:30PM. 925 Harbor Plaza, port end of Queens
Bay Bridge. 590.4123

**59 Travelodge Hotel, Resort & Marina** $$
Formerly the Viscount, this five-story, 200-
room waterfront hotel close to downtown has
been extensively remodeled. ♦ 700 Queensway
Dr. 435.7676, 800/255.3050; fax 437.0866

**60 Queen Mary** This majestic 50,000-ton pas-
senger liner (illustrated above), the largest
ever built, is berthed in Long Beach Harbor.
Launched in 1934, the vessel epitomized Art
Deco luxury when she and her crew of 1,200
cruised the North Atlantic. In 1964 she was
retired from service, purchased by the City of
Long Beach, and converted into a tourist attrac-
tion and luxury hotel. High maintenance costs
may force its closure very soon. ♦ Pier J at the
end of the Long Beach Fwy. 435.3511

**61 Shoreline Village** Part of the downtown
marina, this is another ersatz historical water-
front shopping village with a few quaint tourist
shops and popular restaurants (including two
fish houses). One authentic piece is the 1906
**Charles Looff** carousel. Boat tours of Long
Beach and Los Angeles harbors and dinner
cruises are available here. (Shoreline Village
Cruises, 495.5884.) ♦ Daily 10AM-9PM. 407
Shoreline Dr. 590.8427

Within Shoreline Village:

**Skyrider Parasails** You can get a bird's-eye
view of the shore in a two-seater parasail with-
out getting wet. Riders are lifted 350 feet in the
air from a custom 35-foot-long boat for a 10-
minute flight. ♦ 407 Shoreline Dr. 493.4979

**62 Hyatt Regency** $$$ This luxurious 502-room
atrium hotel near the Convention Center offers
19 suites with scenic harbor views, two restaurants, an outdoor pool, a spa, and business and
banquet facilities. ♦ 200 Pine St. 491.1234,
800/233.1234; fax 432.1972

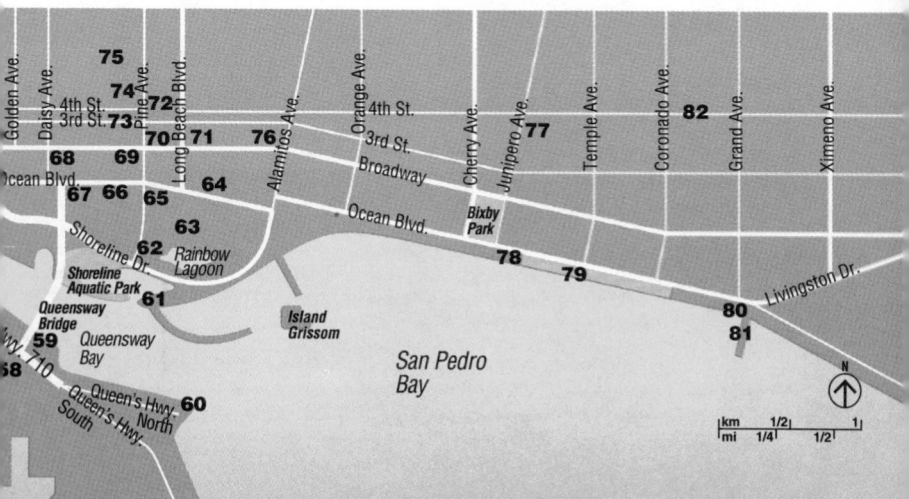

**63 Long Beach Convention and Entertainment Center** The center is home to the acclaimed **Long Beach Ballet, Civic Light Opera,** and **Symphony Orchestra and Opera.** Popular symphony conductor **Joanne Falleta** packs in audiences for both classical and pops concerts, and the opera is one of America's most adventurous companies, noted for innovative staging of rare and classic works and the quality of guest artists. The sports arena is a frequent venue for everything from rodeos to rock concerts. The convention center is being expanded, and its space will triple in size when construction is completed in 1994. ♦ 300 Ocean Blvd. Ticket information: 436.3661. 24-hour recorded event information: 436.3660. Ballet: 427.5206. Civic Light Opera: 432.7926. Opera: 596.5556. Symphony: 436.3203

**64 555 East** ★★★$$$ Located near the waterfront, this is an excellent choice if you're in the mood for traditional American food and a wonderful, old-fashioned dining experience. The dark but inviting interior with generous leather-upholstered banquettes can make you forget about frilly "nouveau anything" restaurants. You won't find pasta with squid ink, but instead juicy cuts of New York, porterhouse, and filet mignon, plus a fine list of side dishes. Start off with dilled jumbo prawns or a pan-fried crab cake appetizer. ♦ American ♦ M 11:30AM-3PM, 5:30-9PM; Tu-Th 11:30AM-3PM, 5:30-10PM; F 11:30AM-3PM, 5:30-11PM; Sa 5:30-11PM; Su 5:30-9PM. 555 E. Ocean Blvd (at Linden Ave). 437.0626

**65 Visitor's Center** Tourist and convention information is available here. ♦ M-F 8:30AM-5PM. One World Trade Center, Suite 300. 436.3645, 436.9982

South Bay/Long Beach

**66 Planet Ocean** Life-size gray whales and dolphins are depicted in this 122,000-square-foot mural—the largest in the world—by internationally acclaimed environmental marine artist **Wyland.** The sea mammals are painted on the curving walls of the **Long Beach Arena.** ♦ 300 E. Ocean Blvd

**67 Giorgio's Place** ★★$$ Innovative food of rare quality is served in this high-ceilinged pink dining room in the **Arco Center.** Salmon in a celery puree, chicken breast with a puree of asparagus, excellent risotto, and *tagliolini al pesto* are a few of the acclaimed dishes. ♦ Italian ♦ M-F 11:30AM-2:30PM, 5:30-10PM; Sa 5:30-10PM. 300 Oceangate. 432.6175

**68 Long Beach Hilton** $$$ This new 397-room mid-rise hotel located in the **World Trade Center** offers a health club, an outdoor pool and Jacuzzi, 14 banquet rooms, a lobby bar, and the **City Grill** restaurant. Free LAX and Long Beach airport shuttles are available. ♦ Two World Trade Center. 983.3400, 800/HILTONS; fax 983.1200

**69 Pine Avenue Fish House** ★★$$ A classic American grill ambience abounds in this corner restaurant, with rich wood textures and comfortable booths. The menu includes a variety of well-prepared fish dishes in unique sauces such as grilled Hawaiian swordfish with papaya salsa. A seasonal highlight is the Maryland soft-shell crab—picatta, blackened, deep fried, and available only from May through September. ♦ American ♦ M 11AM-9PM; Tu-Th 11AM-10PM; F 11AM-11PM; Sa 8AM-11PM; Su 8AM-9PM. 100 W. Broadway Ave (at Pine Ave). 432.7463

**70 Recreation in Long Beach Mural** This 1936 Federal Arts Project mosaic by **Henry Nord** taken from the demolished **Municipal Auditorium** is now installed on the Long Beach Plaza shopping mall parking structure. ♦ Long Beach Plaza at W Third St

**71 Acres of Books** Ray Bradbury acclaims this vast used-book emporium as a treasure. Nearly one million books line the miles of shelves in a 1922 Art Deco-style building. ♦ Tu-Sa 9:15AM-5PM. 240 Long Beach Blvd. 437.6980

**72 Mum's** $$ One of Long Beach's few hip dining spots, this modern, urban restaurant and bar with concrete-like pillars and an uncluttered decor is brisk with professionals at lunchtime and lively on Thursday and weekends, when musicians (usually jazz) play on the sidewalk patio or rooftop—where a dance floor opens during summer weather. Pasta, including the popular chestnut veal ravioli, mesquite-grilled fresh fish—try the jumbo scallops wrapped in sole—and trendy pizza are some of the specialties. ♦ Italian ♦ M-Th 11AM-10PM; F 11AM-midnight; Sa 5PM-midnight; Su 5-9PM. 144 Pine Ave. 437.7700

**73 System M** The spare, high-tech cafe, coffeehouse, and art gallery filled with concrete tables has been renovated with carpets and colorful tablecloths to attract mainstream customers. More upbeat and less industrial, the dress stops short of alienating the musicians, artists, and poets who are regulars. Live jazz and blues music, performance art show, and poetry reading continue in the long storefront space that now offers wine, beer, and California/American cuisine. ♦ Eclectic ♦ M 11AM-3PM; Tu-Th 11AM-midnight; F 11AM-2AM; Sa 5PM-2AM. 213A Pine Ave. 435.2525

# L'OPERA

**74 L'Opera** $$$ This handsome, cosmopolitan restaurant is located in a turn-of-the-century bank building, with heavy green marble pillars

original high recessed ceilings, and modern touches of lighting that give it some contemporary verve. The menu, too, is a mix of old and new, with wonderful Roman fare that is both classic and modern. The vegetarian lasagna and ravioli are excellent. ♦ Italian ♦ M-Th 11:30AM-11PM; F 11:30AM-midnight; Sa 5PM-midnight; Su 5-10PM. 101 Pine Ave. 491.1108

**75 Pavarotti and Stein** $$ Owners **Enrique** and **Cora Borenzstein** have brought their unusual mix of homestyle Italian and gourmet Jewish cuisine from Buenos Aires to Long Beach, where they opened this restaurant in the tile-roofed corner building that formerly housed **Collage.** Comfort food ranges from potato *varenikes* to ravioli and half-roasted chicken. ♦ Italian/Jewish ♦ M 11:30AM-2:30PM; Tu-F 11:30AM-2:30PM, 5:30-10PM; Sa 5:30-10PM. 762 Pacific Ave. 437.3324

**76 Acapulco y Los Arcos** ★$ Though a chain operation, they consistently serve innovative and delicious food. ♦ Mexican ♦ M-Th, Su 11AM-10PM; F-Sa 11AM-11PM. 733 E. Broadway. 435.2487

**77 Carroll Park** The large houses in this historic district were built in the 1910s, and the bungalows in the '20s. ♦ Between Third and Fourth Sts and Junipero and Wisconsin Aves

**78 Long Beach Museum of Art** Located in a 1912 Craftsman-style home, this museum sponsors changing exhibitions that emphasize contemporary Southern California art. The archives of artists' videotapes are the largest on the West Coast. The permanent collection includes work by the **Laguna Canyon School** of the '20s and '30s and regional WPA-sponsored pieces. The carriage house has a bookstore and exhibition gallery. Sculpture by prominent contemporary artists is displayed around the beautifully landscaped site. ♦ Free. W-Su noon-5PM. 2300 E. Ocean Blvd. 439.2119

**79 Bluff Park** This historic district contains diversified houses fronting Ocean Boulevard. On fine days, model plane enthusiasts meet in the park. ♦ Temple Ave (at Ocean Blvd)

**80 Belmont Brewing Company** $ Boasting a patio right on the sandy beach overlooking the pier, the bike path, and the Pacific Ocean—and Long Beach's only brewery—this casual restaurant with modern tropical decor attracts casual diners in shorts. Four types of beer are brewed on the premises. ♦ American ♦ M-Th 11:30AM-10PM; F 11:30AM-11PM; Sa 9AM-11PM; Su 9AM-10PM. 25 39th Pl. 433.3891

**81 Belmont Pier** A bait shop with tackle rentals and a snack bar are located on this 1,300-foot municipal pier. ♦ Bait shop: daily 5AM-10PM. 434.6781. Snack Bar: Tu-Th 11AM-6PM; F-Su 8AM-8PM. End of 39th Pl

---

Restaurants in the Big Yellow House restaurant chain are usually yellow, except in Cerritos. City laws won't permit a big yellow restaurant in the area, so it was painted beige.

# Naples

At the same time **Abbot Kinney** was creating his version of Venice in LA county, another American romantic, **Arthur Parson,** was dredging **Alamitos Bay** to create his picture-perfect pastiche of Italy. He built cottages on curving streets and along canals that were spanned by quaint footbridges. By the end of the '20s, the community now known as Naples was complete. Today, Naples is a residential neighborhood of Long Beach and seems more Americana than Italian, with well-maintained shingled homes and carefully tended gardens. The perimeter of the island is bordered by walkways that overlook the bay and a small beach. In the center, **Colonnade Park** is encircled by the **Rivo Alto Canal.** Although the island is accessible by car, its true charm is seen only by the pedestrian. This is a wonderful place for an afternoon of strolling, picnicking, and boat-watching.

**82 Fourth Street** At the less expensive end of the shopping spectrum, Fourth Street has a number of little shops ranging from chic to modest that carry antiques, Art Deco accessories, gifts, crafts, and clothes. ♦ Between Redondo and Lucille Aves, Naples

**83 Drake Park** Almost every architectural style known to man is found in Drake Park, another Long Beach historic district. ♦ Daisy Ave at Loma Vista (between Seventh and 11th Sts), Naples

**84 Long Beach Firefighters Museum** Open just one day a month, this museum houses five motorized engines, two horse-drawn steamers, handcarts, and memorabilia dating back a hundred years. ♦ Free. Second Sa of every month 10AM-3PM. 1445 Peterson Ave. 597.0351

**85 The Foothill Club** This honky-tonk dance hall is a step back in time. The 1940s club offering live hillbilly music and fried chicken once attracted the likes of **Patsy Cline** and **Buck Owens.** Now faded, it still jams on weekends with an older crowd. ♦ Daily 5PM-2AM. 1922 Cherry Ave, Signal Hill. 494.5196

**86 Shenandoah Cafe** $$ A cozy American restaurant with gingham and graciousness, this place serves down-home Southern cooking

with baskets of apple fritters and fresh rolls. ♦ Southern ♦ M-Th, Su 4:30-10PM; F-Sa 4:30-11PM. 4722 E. Second St. 434.3469

**86 Legends** $ The original rowdy sports bar and restaurant founded by rugby great **John Morris** and Rams all-pro **Dennis Harrah** in 1979, Legends is filled with memorabilia, eight projection screens, and two news tickers. Beer drinking and appetizer eating (buffalo wings) are big here. ♦ American ♦ M-F 11AM-midnight; F 11AM-2AM; Sa 10AM-2AM; Su 10AM-midnight. 5236 Second St. 434.3469

---

**Restaurants/Clubs:** Red
**Shops/ ♣ Outdoors:** Green

**Hotels:** Blue
**Sights/Culture:** Black

**86 Caffè Gazelle** ★$$ This pretty, friendly restaurant is famous for its hefty portions at reasonable prices. The soups, salads, desserts, and cappuccini shine; do try the creamy pinenut soup. ♦ Italian ♦ M-Th, Su 5-10PM; Sa 5-11PM. 5325 E. Second St. 438.2881

**87 The Gondola Getaway** One-hour cruises on authentic Venetian gondolas with costumed gondoliers thread through the canals of Naples. A basket of bread, and salami and cheese is included. BYOB. Reserve months in advance for December (Christmas lights) and February (Valentine's Day), and one month ahead in summer. ♦ 5437 E. Ocean Blvd. 433.9595

**88 Endo's Waterski Werks** Waterskis can be rented here, and lessons are offered for those with their own boats. ♦ Tu-W noon-6PM; Th-F 10AM-6PM; Sa 10AM-4PM. 5612 E. Second St. 434.1816

**88 Justina's** ★$$ "A Celebration of Food," proclaims the awning, and this pretty little restaurant lives up to its motto with well-prepared roasted duck pasta, jalapeño ravioli, and salmon en papillote. ♦ Eclectic ♦ M-F 5:30-9PM; Sa-Su 8AM-2PM, 5:30-10PM. 5620 E. Second St. 434.5191

**88 Russell's** $ This small chain—started in Long Beach in 1930—is tucked in a tiny, busy coffee shop next to a launderette, but offers some of the tastiest burgers and shakes anywhere. They have good pie, too. ♦ American ♦ M-Th 7AM-10PM; F-Sa 7AM-11PM; Su 7AM-9PM. 5656 E. Second St. 434.0226

**88 Morry's of Naples** Wine tastings are offered three nights a week at this long-established wine and liquor store. ♦ M-Th, Su 7AM-10PM; F-Sa 7AM-midnight. Tastings: W-F 6-9PM. 5764 E. Second St. 433.0405

**89 Seaport Village** On this island surrounded by Long Beach Marina boat slips, several large predictable chain restaurants, including the **Rusty Pelican, The Chart House,** and **Windrose,** serve standard steak and fresh seafood fare in seaside wooden buildings. They offer pleasant marina views of the waterways and boats. ♦ 182 Marina Dr. 799.3870

Within Seaport Village:

**Seaport Watercraft** Though located in a marina of sailboats and yachts, this company is set for speed, with Jetski and powerboat rentals. Boats ranging in size—14 to 21 feet—and horsepower—40 to 265—come in both cuddy cruisers and bow riders. Party deck boats for 13, wet suits, water skis, and other equipment are also available. ♦ Daily 9AM-6PM, or by reservation. 799.3870

**Star Party Cruises** Live reggae bands play on weekend cruises, and a Sunday champagne brunch features blues and jazz musicians aboard a hundred-passenger double-decker boat. ♦ 140 Marina Dr. 431.6833

**90 Bogart's** $$ If you liked *Casablanca*, try Bogart's, with its wicker, ceiling fans, potted palms, and live entertainment. ♦ American ♦ W-Sa 8PM-2AM. 6288 E. Pacific Coast Hwy (No of Westminster in Marina Pacifica Mall). 594.8976

**91 Rancho Los Alamitos** Another part of the original 1790 Nieto land grant, this rancho has an adobe house that has been enlarged several times since it was built in 1806. The interior is very much as it was when the **Bixby** family occupied it during the 1920s and 1930s. The grounds contain cow and horse barns, a blacksmith's shop, and a lush five-acre garden planted with native California cacti and succulents, herbs, and exquisite Chinese and Japanese wisteria. Visitors to the buildings must join docent tours. ♦ Free. W-Su 1-5PM. 6400 Bixby Hill Rd. 431.3541

**92 El Dorado Park** This 800-acre recreational facility is divided into two sections. **El Dorado East Regional Park** is an unstructured activity area containing meadows and several lakes where fishing is permitted. The largest lake rents paddleboats. There are more than four miles of bicycle and roller-skate paths and an archery range. **El Dorado West City Park** offers an 18-hole golf course, night-lit tennis courts, tennis shop, roller-skate rentals, six baseball diamonds, a duck pond, a children's playground, a band shell, a branch of the Long Beach Public Library, and a number of game courts. The **El Dorado Nature Center,** located in the east section, is an 80-acre bird sanctuary and native chaparral community. The small museum in the center of one of the two lakes exhibits material about the natural history of Southern California. Maps are available at the museum. ♦ Vehicle admission fee. East Park: daily 7AM-6PM. West Park: daily 7AM-7PM. 429.6310. Nature Center: Tu-Su 10AM-4PM. 421.9431. 7550 E. Spring St

**93 Outdoor Antique and Collectible Market**
More than 800 dealers offer every kind of collectible, from the serious to the silly. ♦ Admission. Third Su of every month, first Su of Nov 8AM-3PM. Long Beach Veteran's Memorial Stadium, Lakewood Blvd at Conant St, Long Beach. 213/655.5703

**94 Long Beach Airport** The airport is served by three commercial airlines. Private bus companies provide transportation between Long Beach Airport and Long Beach, and Los Angeles and Orange counties. ♦ 4100 Donald Douglas Dr. Take Lakewood Blvd exit north from the San Diego Fwy. 421.8293

**95 Bixby House** One of the few remaining examples of English architect **Ernest Coxhead's** residential work, this 1895 shingle-style house was built for a member of the Bixby family. The wood-shingle Victorian house has Craftsman design elements. It's a private residence. ♦ 11 La Linda Dr, Bixby Knolls

**96 Rancho Los Cerritos** The romance of the old rancho days is recalled at this renovated 1844 Monterey-style adobe. The two-story residence was built by **Don Juan Temple** on part of the 1790 Nieto land grant. Subsequently enlarged, the house is furnished as it was between 1866 and 1881, when the **Bixby** family used it as headquarters for their ranching empire. Exhibitions here include the children's room, the foreman's bedroom, and a blacksmith's shop. The exhibition wing features material relating to social and economic aspects of rancho life and a research library of California materials. Some of the original walks and trees planted in the mid-19th century remain in the restored five-acre garden. ♦ Free. W-Su 1-5PM. Tours: Sa-Su 1PM, 2PM, 3PM, 4PM. 4600 Virginia Rd, Long Beach. 424.9423

**97 Johnny Reb's Southern Smokehouse** $
Peanut shells litter the floor of this homey, rustic, and busy restaurant that serves seafood gumbo, barbecued ribs, fried green tomatoes, catfish, and pecan pie. ♦ Southern/Cajun ♦ M-Th, Su 7AM-9PM; F-Sa 7AM-10PM. 4663 Long Beach Blvd. 423.7327

## Bests

### Michael McCarty
Michael's Restaurant

**Mr. Chow's** in Beverly Hills, for lobster and ginger, Peking duck, and Tattinger rosé.

**Spago** in West Hollywood, for the prosciutto pizza, goat-cheese-and-basil calzone, and Joseph Phelps' Insignia.

**Valentino** in Santa Monica, for Friday lunch. Whatever Piero wants, plus *Angelo Gaja Barbaresco, Maurizio Zanella Ca del Basco Reserve.*

**West Beach Cafe** in Venice, only after midnight, for old cabernets and lots of champagne.

**Paul Gurian's,** for barbecued shrimp.

**72 Market Street** in Venice Beach, for Florida stone crabs and a Stoli.

**Michael's** in Santa Monica. Phil Reich's computerized wine list and my food, such as shad roe, roach crabs, white-truffle pasta, Killian's Red, Olympic-size onion rings, foie gras sauté, and all the sauces! Plus the dreaded Health Bar.

**Don Henley's,** for ribs.

**Angeli.** Magnums of everything, whatever John and Evan suggest.

**John's Garden Grocers.** Best fruit and sandwiches in town.

### Dr. Craig C. Black
Director, LA County Natural History Museum

The delight of a family as they slowly discover the ferret popping up behind a log in our Alaskan bear group or first notice the salmon flopping in a pool under a bear's claw.

The wary wonderment of an eight-year-old child when he or she first sees and hears a Triceratops stamping its feet and roaring at a passerby.

Watching the California condor admirers exclaim over the size of the vanishing species.

The incessant quest for more information about dinosaurs from visitors of all ages.

Admiring the fiery beauty of the Hixon ruby in the **Deutsch Gallery of Gems.**

Comparing the **Lando Hall Model of Los Angeles** circa 1940 to Los Angeles today.

**Edwin Deakin** paintings at the **California Museum.**

The **Parson's Discovery Center,** where children of all ages can learn about the diversity of life on our planet.

A jewel among natural history museums is the entire **Page Museum,** which is located at the **Tar Pits.**

### Frank Gehry
Architect

I go to **Firenze Kitchen** on North La Brea because my cousin owns it.

### Laurent Quenioux
Owner, Seventh Street Bistro

Driving in Los Angeles at 7AM on Sunday along **Mulholland Drive.**

One of my biggest thrills is to go shopping at **Irvine Market,** located in the **Beverly Center.** You have to watch out or you may end up buying the whole store...or at least groceries for three months. It's the best food market in Southern California.

My favorite restaurant is a tiny place on the Sunset Strip called **Talesai.** It's a Thai restaurant and a must-see—and one of LA's biggest assets.

Looking at my restaurant when it's empty because it's so neat and beautiful; however, I like it much better when it is full of people laughing, smoking, and grazing on food.

I love the customers who talk to me about my cuisine and tell me how wonderful it is. I know the next day they will delight themselves with a fatty hamburger at the stand next door. That's Hollywood!

# Catalina Island

This island paradise 26 miles offshore lives up to its reputation as a romantic getaway. Arriving by boat, you'll first see the misty green peaks of a mountain range that rises from the ocean floor to form this and the other Channel Islands. Next, your eyes are drawn to the gleaming white buildings climbing the hillside above the Mediterranean-style port of **Avalon** and its round casino on a spur of land. And finally, you'll enter the harbor, which is thronged with pleasure boats and backed by picturesque, winding streets lined with red-tiled houses and shops. The hotel rooms are in short supply and pricey during the summer; most visitors come for the day on ferries, a trip that takes as little as an hour.

Avalon's resident population of 3,000 is far outnumbered by the influx of up to 12,000 visitors a day, and the town, established in 1913, is straining at the seams. There is a plan to ease the pressure by adding houses, small hotels, and civic amenities over the next 15 years, without sacrificing the small-town charm. Fortunately, most of the island has been preserved in its unspoiled natural state, and traffic is generally limited to golf carts and the buses that transport visitors along the back roads. You can see even more of the island if you hike. Catalina is 28 miles long and up to eight miles wide. And the native wildlife in the underdeveloped interior is extraordinary. Catalina is home to more than one hundred species of birds. There are also 400 species of native plant life here, including eight types found only on this island, such as the Catalina ironweed, the wild tomato, and the dudleya hassel, whose generic name means "live forever." Herds of wild bison (left by a movie crew several decades ago), boars, and goats roam free over the back region of the island (and a buffalo joyously rolling over on its back like a big puppy is a sight not quickly forgotten).

Most of the island has been privately owned since the native Indians were resettled on the mainland in 1811. Avalon was named in 1888 by the sister of an

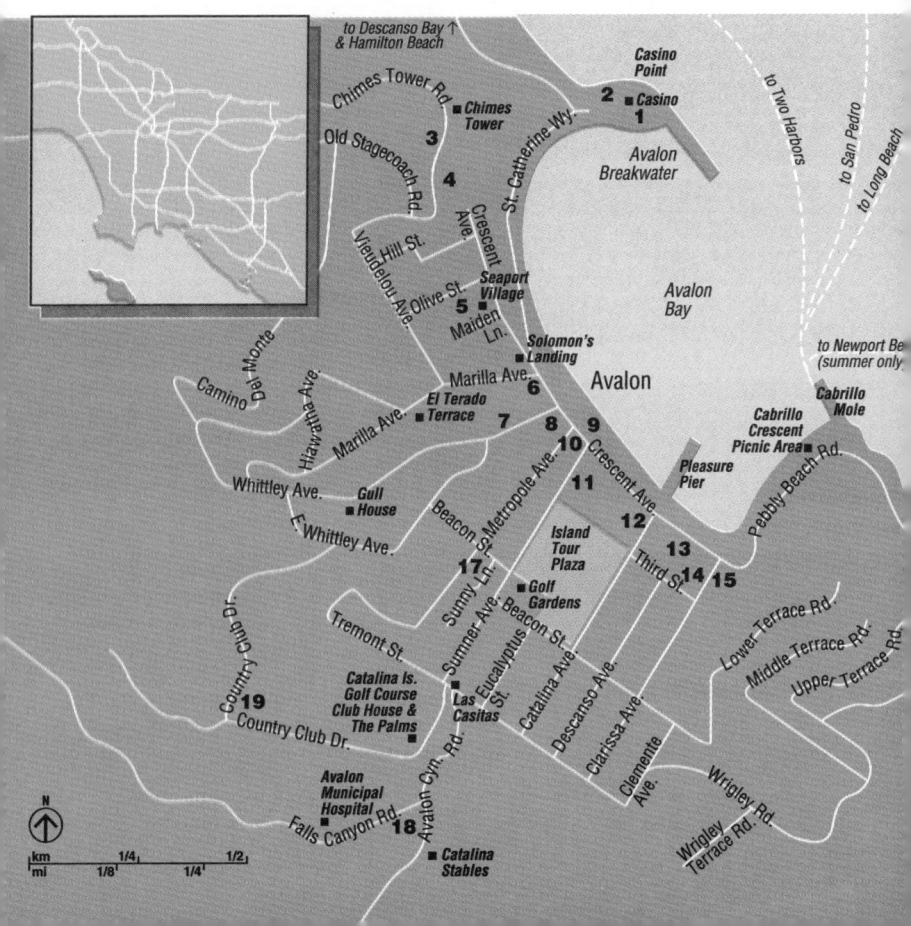

arly developer, **George Shatto**, after the island of Avalon in **Tennyson's** *Idylls f the King,* the refuge of blessed souls in Celtic mythology. In 1919 **William Vrigley, Jr.,** the chewing-gum scion, purchased the Santa Catalina Island Company, built the casino in Avalon and a mansion for himself, promoted deep-sea shing, and established a spring-training camp for his baseball team, the **Chicago ubs.** Avalon became a popular tourist spot during the 1930s, but most of the nterior of the island and much of the coastline remained undeveloped. A nonrofit conservancy acquired the title to about 86 percent of the island in 1975 nd now administers this unique open space in conjunction with the County f Los Angeles. For more visitor information, call 310/510.1520.

---

*rea code 310 unless otherwise noted.*

## low to Get to Catalina Island

**oat** Year-round service is available from the ports f Long Beach and San Pedro. Boats from both ports iake five trips daily from mid-June through mid-eptember, and three trips daily from mid-September irough mid-June. During peak months, service rect to the Two Harbors/Isthmus area is available. eservations for all sailings to the island are advis-ole; call **Catalina Cruises** at 436.5006. The **Catalina hannel Express** offers 55-minute trips daily year-und, from a dock beside the *Queen Mary* in Long each to Avalon; and 90-minute trips from San Pedro nd Redondo Beach to Avalon and Two Harbors are vailable aboard stabilized vessels with airline-style eating (519.1212; group information 519.7957). atalina Passenger Service operates luxury catama-ans from Balboa Pavilion in Newport Beach. *Catalina lyer* departs daily on a 75-minute trip to Catalina land (714/673.5245).

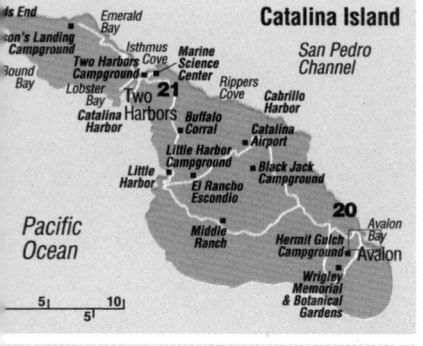

**Catalina Island**

**Helicopter** Charter flights from Long Beach are available, but the most convenient access to Catalina is by helicopter. The flight takes about 18 minutes in fair weather. **Island Express** (510.2525) flies from San Pedro and from the Viscount Hotel in Long Beach.

## Getting around the Island

**Driving** Rental cars are not allowed in the interior. If you have a friend with a car on the island, you may obtain a temporary card key to drive outside of Avalon from Santa Catalina Island Conservancy (for more information, call 510.1421).

**Hiking** Permits are required to hike into the interior and may be obtained free of charge at the County Department of Parks and Recreation Office (213 Catalina Street, 510.0688) in Avalon or at the Catalina Cove and Camp Agency at the Isthmus.

## Recreation

Visit Wrigley's Memorial Botanical Garden, or try fishing, swimming, golf, or tennis. There are all sorts of sight-seeing tours, such as the glass-bottom boat trip, flying-fish boat trip, and scenic terrace drive. Tours range from 40 minutes to four hours. A three-hour "Around the Island Tour" departs Avalon daily at noon. It includes El Rancho Escondido, which is home to some of America's finest Arabian horses. Contact the following for more information: **Catalina Sight-seeing Tours,** 510.2000, 800/428.2566; **Catalina Adventure Tours,** 510.2888; **Catalina Safari Bus** (backpacking tours), 510.2800; and **Island Navigation** (water taxis to all points), 510.0409.

Bikes, horses, baby strollers, fishing tackle, etc., can easily be rented. If you want to bring your bike along, contact your cross-channel carrier for details. **Argo Diving Service** (510.2208) offers rental equipment.

## Accommodations

**Beach Realty** (PO Box 2100, Avalon, CA, 90704; 510.0039) can arrange cottage rentals. Note that most hotels require a two-day or even a one-week minimum stay during the summer. A chamber of commerce information office on the green pleasure pier in Avalon is open daily.

Arrangements for camping at Black Jack or Little Harbor must be made through the County Department of Parks and Recreation (M-F 9AM-1PM, 2-4PM, 510.0688). A brochure describing the trails may also be obtained from the department. Arrangements for camping at Little Fisherman's Cove (Two Harbors) must be made through Catalina Cove and

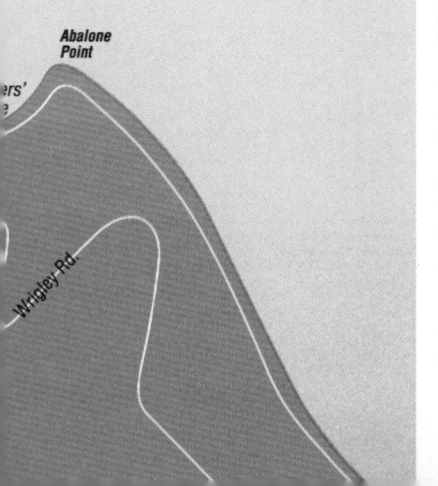

Camp Agency (PO Box 5044, Two Harbors, CA, 90704; 510.0303). All camping is by permit only and advance reservations are required.

**1 Casino** The island's signature building, a circular Spanish Moderne structure (pictured above), designed by **Webber & Spaulding** in 1928, is situated on a rocky promontory at the northwest end of Crescent Bay. It houses one of America's most beautiful movie palaces, a one thousand-seat theater with fanciful underwater murals and a working organ. There's a splendid Art Deco box office, restored tiles, and murals around the entrance. Above the theater is a grand ballroom where thousands can dance to big bands as they did more than 50 years ago. You can reserve the space for a terrific private party. There is also a small museum and art gallery. Daytime tours of the casino and evening showings of new movies are presented daily in summer, and weekends off-season. ◆ 1 Casino Way. Movie schedule: 510.0179. Private parties: 510.0550

**2 Descanso Beach Club** Family cookouts are a popular event here—you barbecue your own steaks or hamburgers and the club provides the salad and trimmings. The beach is a short walk from the Casino. ◆ Saturday only 5:30-9PM. Off Casino Way. Reservations required. 510.2780

**3 The Zane Grey Hotel** $$$ Tahitian teak beams in an open-beam ceiling, a hewn-plank door, a log mantle, and walls of mortar mixed with goat's milk are combined with blessed isolation and an extraordinary view of the ocean and the hills in this former Avalon home of the foremost writer of the American West. The

## Catalina Island

pueblo was originally built for Zane Grey in 1929 as a haven for his literary labors and fishing desires. Amenities here include free taxi pick-up, an outdoor pool, and complimentary tea or coffee throughout the day. The rates are lower in winter. ◆ 199 Chimes Tower Rd. 510.0966

**4 Wolfe House** In 1928 **Rudolph Schindler** created this icon of modernism, comprising a stack of balconied floors that exploit the steep site and extraordinary views. It's a private residence. ◆ 124 Chimes Tower Rd

**5 Seaport Village Inn** $$ One of the island's newer hotels, it's close to the beach and has a spa, suites, and off-season packages. Amenities include color TV with cable, private baths, studio suites with views, fully furnished kitchens, and wet bars. ◆ 119 Maiden Ln. 510.0344

**6 Hotel Villa Portofino** $$$ This 34-room waterfront hotel features the ambitious Italian **Ristorante Villa Portofino** ($$) restaurant. Two-bedroom family units are available. Amenities here include a large sundeck and honeymoon accommodations. ◆ 111 Crescent Ave. 510.0555, 800/346.2326. Restaurant: 510.050

**7 Hotel Catalina** $$ The charm of yesterday lives in this renovated 32-room Victorian hotel only a half-block from the beach. Movies for guests are shown every afternoon, and there's a Jacuzzi. ◆ 129 Whittley Ave. 510.0027; fax 510.1495

**8 Channel House** $ A lunch of a salad or sandwich on the terrace overlooking the harbor is a treat; dinners are forgettable. ◆ American ◆ Daily 11AM-2PM, 5-10PM. Fall and winter: lunch is served only F-Su. 205 Crescent Ave. 510.1617

**9 Armstrong's Seafood Restaurant** ★$$ Specialties include mesquite-grilled swordfish, fresh lobster, and abalone. ◆ Seafood ◆ M-Th, Su 11AM-9PM; F-Sa 11AM-10PM. 300 Crescent Ave. 510.0113

**9 Busy Bee** $ Chinese chicken salad with ginger dressing, hamburgers, and sandwiches are offered in this pleasant cafe. ◆ American ◆ M-Th, Su 8AM-9PM; F-Sa 8AM-10PM. 306 Crescent Ave. 510.1983

**10 Chi-Chi Club** Live jazz and bluegrass tunes keep this club hopping. Call ahead for hours and programs. ◆ Cover charge on weekends during summer. 107 Sumner Ave. 510.2828

**11 Glenmore Plaza Hotel** $$$ This charming redecorated Victorian hotel offers 45 rooms, Jacuzzis, and a tree-filled courtyard. **Clark Gable** slept here and you can rent his suite. Amenities here include whirlpool tubs in most rooms, Continental breakfast, wine and cheese in the afternoon, and a free shuttle ride to the boat area. ◆ 120 Sumner Ave. 510.0017, 800/422.8254; fax 510.2833

**12 Hotel Vista del Mar** $$$ Located right in the center of town, this new beachfront hotel has fireplaces and Jacuzzis. ◆ 417 Crescent Ave. 510.1452; fax 510.2917

**13 Pavilion Lodge** $$ On the beach in the heart of town, this place has a large central courtyard, free cable TV, and group rates. ◆ 513 Crescent Ave. 510.1788, 800/428.2566; fax 510.2073

**14 Garden House Inn** $$$ Guests at this nine-room bed-and-breakfast just off the beach are treated to a cold buffet breakfast daily and wine and hors d'oeuvres every Saturday evening. Amenities include cable TV and VCR. ◆ 125 Clarissa Ave. 510.0356

The first air-conditioned railroad cars began service between LA and Chicago in 1914.

Restaurants/Clubs: Red          Hotels: Blue
Shops/ 🌳 Outdoors: Green      Sights/Culture: Black

**15  Cafe Prego** $$ Old-world warmth and charm are offered here, along with sautéed calamari, linguine with clams, and piccata of veal. ◆ Italian ◆ Daily 5:30-10PM. 603 Crescent Ave. 510.1218

**16  Inn on Mt. Ada** $$$$ The **Wrigley Mansion** has been converted into a luxurious bed-and-breakfast with just six guest rooms, all with ocean or harbor views. Guests enjoy all meals, wine and hors d'oeuvres, a gas-powered golf cart, and a free shuttle to and from the hotel. ◆ 398 Wrigley Rd. 510.2030

**17  Hotel St. Lauren** $$$ Victorian decor and harbor views are two of the attractions of this hotel, located a block from the water. Amenities include 42 guest rooms, Continental breakfast, king-size beds, whirlpool tubs, and oceanfront views. ◆ 231 Beacon Ave. 510.2299; fax 510.1365

**18  The Sand Trap** $ A local favorite, this place serves soup, burgers, and omelets. ◆ American ◆ Daily 7:30AM-3PM. Avalon Canyon Rd, en route to Wrigley Botanical Garden. 510.1349

**19  Catalina Canyon Resort Hotel** $$$ A sauna and pool and adjoining tennis courts and a golf course are offered at this resort in a secluded setting. The courtesy vans are available for your transportation needs, and the hotel has special facilities for meetings. ◆ 888 Country Club Dr. 510.0325, 800/253.9361; fax 510.0900

the **Cove Resort** of catalina

**20  The Cove Resort of Catalina** The luxury villas in this new private community have access to a pool, sauna, Jacuzzi, golf, tennis, a secluded beach, and boat moorings. ◆ Hamilton Cove, north of Avalon. 510.1220; fax 510.2630

**21  Two Harbors** Be sure to pack a picnic for this idyllic day trip destination, by boat or **Safari Bus** (510.2800) from Avalon. ◆ Center of island

**21  Banning House Lodge** $$ This converted classic with 11 rooms is a peaceful retreat with no television. There's a dining room, solarium, and hilltop view of both sides of island. Be sure to book well ahead. ◆ Two Harbors. Reservations required. 510.0303; fax 510.1354

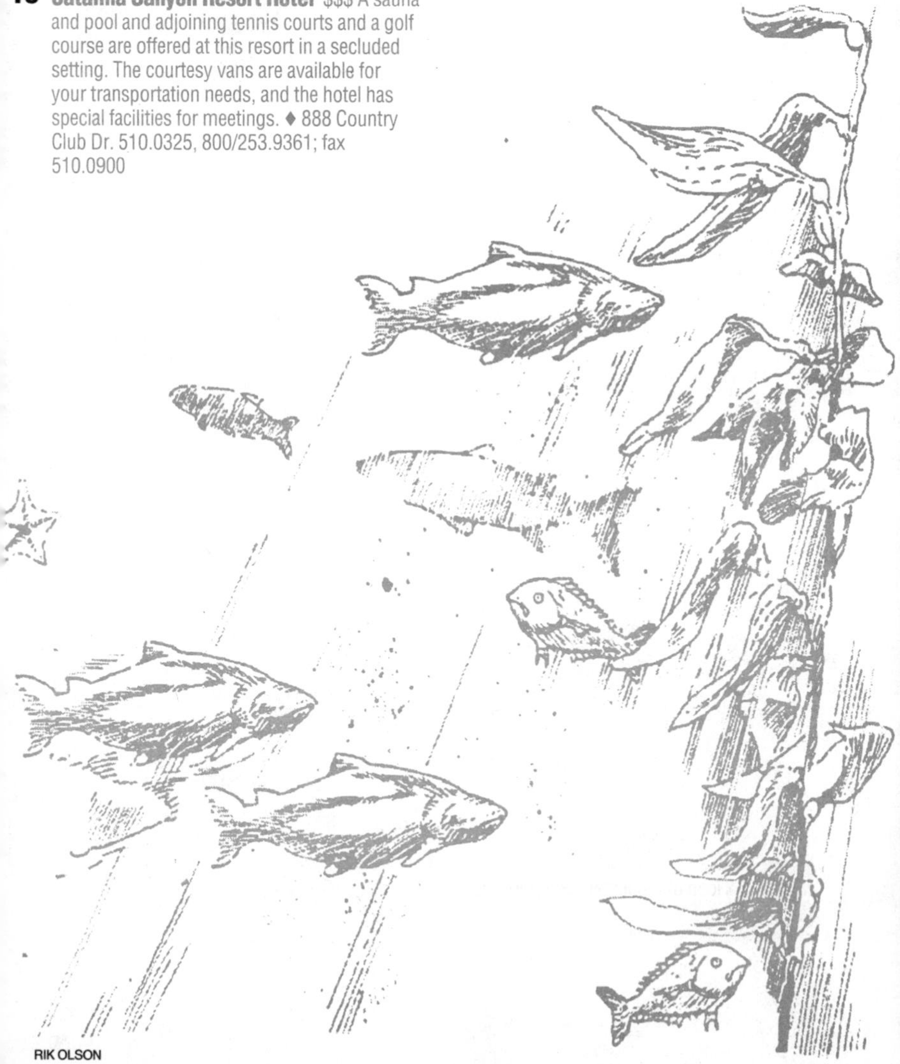

RIK OLSON

# Orange County North/ Disneyland

Like the San Fernando Valley, Orange County has become a separate metropolis of more than two million people and it's still growing. This boom has occurred in the last four decades—since **Walt Disney** opened **Disneyland** in **Anaheim** in 1955 and the **Irvine Ranch** was finally developed in the 1970s. Orange County shares many of the same problems as LA—primarily traffic congestion and deteriorating air quality—but it is set apart by its newness. It is an embryo city, half finished, and only now acquiring the institutions and resources it needs to match its wealth and ambitions. It is a maze of separate communities that can be divided, like Hollywood, into two areas: the less prosperous north, with its ethnic and blue-collar enclaves and huge entertainment parks centered on Anaheim; and the affluent south, with its luxurious homes, hotels, and restaurants, and its burgeoning cultural scene.

The ranchos of the Spanish and Mexican periods became the farms and orchards of the Yankees in the middle of the 19th century. In 1857 a cooperative agriculture

colony was established by 50 Germans, who named their community Anaheim, combining the name of the local river, the Santa Ana, and the German word for home, *heim*. Originally part of Los Angeles County, the area's autonomy was mandated by the California legislature in 1889. For the first 50 years of the 20th century, Orange County seemed a land of milk and honey. Well-tended groves of Valencia orange trees stretched as far as the eye could see, perfuming the air with the fragrance of their blossoms. In the 1950s land values began to skyrocket, fueled by a postwar generation eager for a suburban lifestyle. As land became more valuable for homes and developments, the groves began to disappear. By the next century, the trees will be just a memory, immortalized in the names of streets and condominium tracts.

*Area code 714 unless otherwise noted.*

## Getting around Orange County

Public transportation here is erratic, at best. An unusual way to reach **Disneyland** is the brief (about 35 minutes) and delightful **Amtrak** local to Fullerton from Union Station (for additional information about this

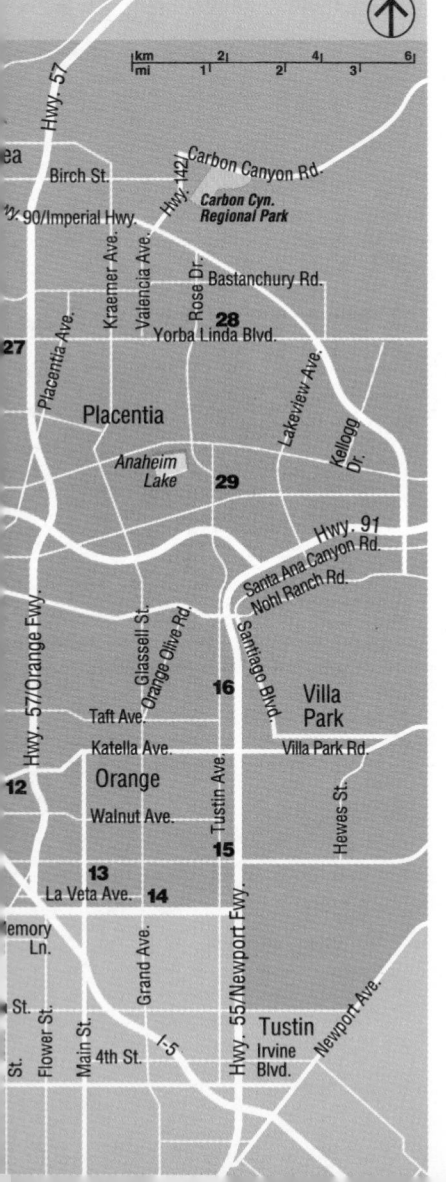

service, call 800/USA.RAIL). From the Fullerton train station, walk about one-and-a-half blocks to Commonwealth and Harbor streets. From there you can board **Orange County Transit Authority (OCTA)** bus No. 435 to get to the **Disneyland Hotel.** The OCTA has extensive service throughout the county, but allow a lot of time; on many routes the buses only run once an hour. Call 636.7433 for more information.

The **Southern California Rapid Transit District** has service from its main terminal at Sixth and Los Angeles streets in LA to major locations in Orange County. **Greyhound** (620.1200) and **Trailways** (742.1200) serve Anaheim and Santa Ana from LA; Greyhound also covers Newport Beach and Laguna Beach en route to San Diego. From the Westside of LA, a convenient way to get to Orange County is the regularly scheduled **Airport Coach Service** from **Los Angeles International Airport.** The coaches take you directly to the major hotels, to Disneyland, and to the **John Wayne Airport.**

A reliable and convenient shuttle service runs between the major amusement parks and hotels in the Anaheim-Buena Park area, **South Coast Plaza,** and **Newport Beach.** Called the **Funbus,** it circulates about every 35 minutes, and its service accommodates the park's hours.

For local transportation, there is **Anaheim Yellow Cab** (535.2211) and **Coast Yellow Cab** (434.8700), but for extensive travel to specific places away from the major tourist sites, a car is the only practical option. For more information about transportation, special events, sight-seeing services, or accommodations, the **Anaheim Area Visitor's and Convention Bureau** has an office at the **Anaheim Convention Center,** 800 West Katella Avenue; 999.8999.

1 **Los Alamitos Race Course** One of LA's top tracks features quarter horse racing from mid-November through January, and May through mid-August. Harness racing is held from late February through April, and mid-August to mid-November. ♦ Admission. Post time 7PM. 4961 Katella Ave, Los Alamitos. 995.1234

2 **Hobby City** This six-acre cluster of old-fashioned collectors' shops has 23 buildings, including a log cabin shop that sells American Indian memorabilia. ♦ Daily 10AM-6PM. 1238 S. Beach Blvd, Anaheim. 527.2323

3 **Anaheim Country Inn** $ This 1910 Queen Anne mansion has been converted to a small, moderately priced bed-and-breakfast with a front porch and a large garden. ♦ 856 S. Walnut St, Anaheim. 778.0150, 800/755.7801

**4 Disneyland** The kingdom where fantasy and magic are around the next turnstile covers 76 acres and has cost more than $200 million to build. New attractions are added almost every year. Expect to spend at least eight hours here. A good way to get an overview of the park is from the **Monorail** or the perimeter **Railroad.**

The Magic Kingdom (illustrated below) is divided into seven areas: **Main Street, U.S.A.; Adventureland; New Orleans Square; Critter Country; Frontierland; Fantasyland;** and **Tomorrowland.**

**Main Street, U.S.A.** Close to the entrance to the park is Main Street, U.S.A., an idealized turn-of-the-century town. Small shops, with wooden floors that resound under your feet and glass display cases at precisely the right height for children's noses, sell a variety of nostalgic merchandise. In the nearby **Opera House,** *Great Moments with Mr. Lincoln* brings our sixteenth president to life through the magic of Audio-Animatronics.

**The Central Plaza,** the hub of the park, is located at the end of Main Street, U.S.A. From this point, the other park areas spread out, and you may enter the land of your choice via its unique theme gate.

**Adventureland** The **Jungle Cruise** takes you down the simulated Nile, Congo, and Amazon rivers in a flat-bottomed boat; elephants bathe and crocodiles guard a ruined temple. More Audio-Animatronic magic is at work in the **Enchanted Tiki Room,** where exotic birds come to life in an amusing show.

**New Orleans Square** On the Rivers of America, filigreed balconies overlook winding streets ablaze with flowers and lined with quaint shops. Every day is Mardi Gras with Dixieland music. Take a ride with the **Pirates of the Caribbean** on flat-bottomed boats that explore a haunted grotto hung with Spanish moss and glide into a seaport for pillage and plunder. Ghosts inhabit the **Haunted Mansion,** which uses holographiclike imagery to bring many of the 999 residents to wonderfully disembodied life.

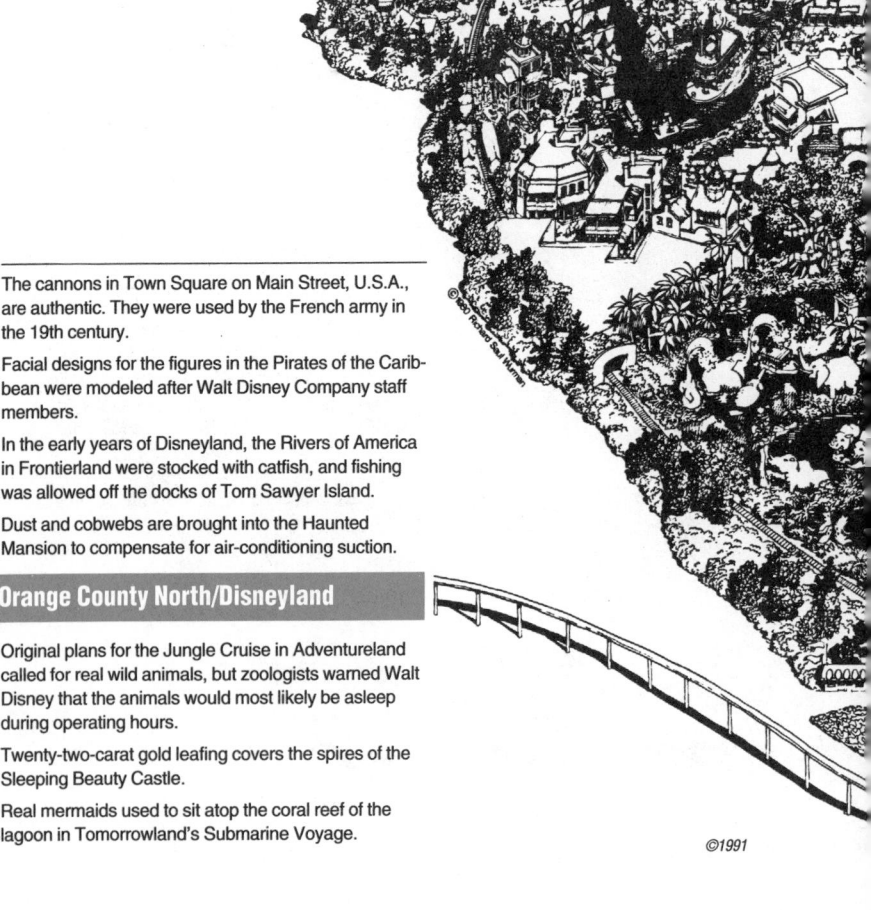

The cannons in Town Square on Main Street, U.S.A., are authentic. They were used by the French army in the 19th century.

Facial designs for the figures in the Pirates of the Caribbean were modeled after Walt Disney Company staff members.

In the early years of Disneyland, the Rivers of America in Frontierland were stocked with catfish, and fishing was allowed off the docks of Tom Sawyer Island.

Dust and cobwebs are brought into the Haunted Mansion to compensate for air-conditioning suction.

## Orange County North/Disneyland

Original plans for the Jungle Cruise in Adventureland called for real wild animals, but zoologists warned Walt Disney that the animals would most likely be asleep during operating hours.

Twenty-two-carat gold leafing covers the spires of the Sleeping Beauty Castle.

Real mermaids used to sit atop the coral reef of the lagoon in Tomorrowland's Submarine Voyage.

©1991

**Critter Country**  Don't miss this Audio-Animatronic jamboree of mechanical bears that will set your toes tapping to country tunes like "Tears Will Be the Chaser for My Wine" and "All the Guys that Turn Me On Turn Me Down." **Davy Crockett's Explorer Canoes** let you paddle along the Rivers of America. A relatively new attraction is **Splash Mountain,** a spectacular log flume adventure.

**Frontierland**  Next to Adventureland, this area has battles, a blazing fort, and the **Golden Horseshoe Jamboree,** which you can enter through the swinging doors of a Western saloon and see cancan dancers. The **Rivers of America** run along the shore and are plied by an amazing assortment of vessels. **Big Thunder Mountain Railroad** is an exciting rollercoaster ride through a deserted mine; riders confront floods, swarms of bats, and fierce animals—and live to tell the tale.

**Fantasyland**  Enter this magical land through the **Sleeping Beauty Castle.** Over the drawbridge and through the stone halls is the world of very familiar storybook characters. The **Casey Jr. Circus Train** chugs past **Cinderella's** castle, **Pinocchio's** village, and the home of the **Three Little Pigs.** The whirling teacups of the **Mad Tea Party** will leave your head spinning. Boats glide through **It's a Small World,** filled with scenes of animated children from many lands all singing the same tune in their own native tongue.

The most popular ride in Fantasyland is the **Matterhorn,** a 14-story replica of the Swiss mountain built for white-knuckle fun. You are hoisted aloft in tandem bobsleds for a thrilling plunge through ice caverns and around hairpin curves that ends with a splashy finale. **Videopolis** is a popular nightspot, featuring live musical revues.

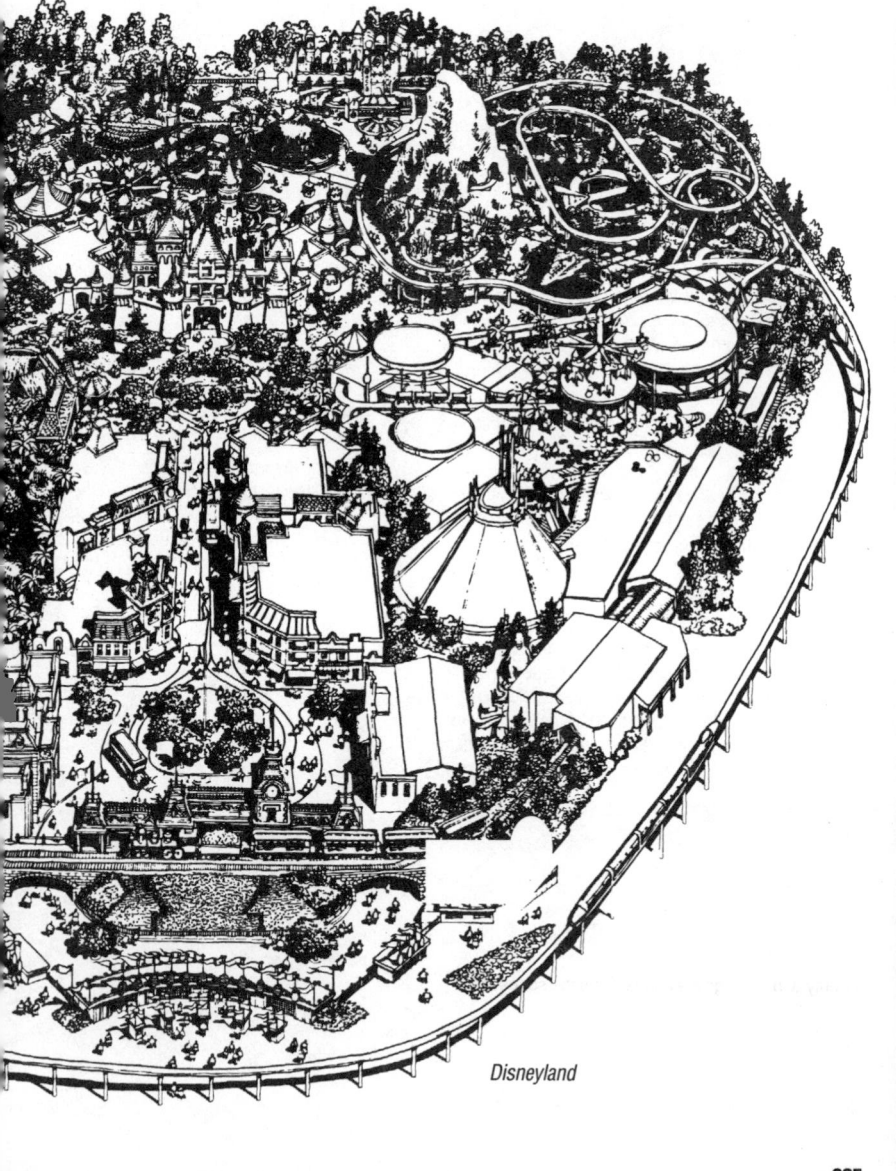

*Disneyland*

**Tomorrowland** Here you'll find science fantasy—and a vision of how the real world may be (with monorails and people-movers now being introduced 25 years after their Disneyland debut). The **Mission to Mars** and **Rocket Jets** may prove equally prophetic. The **Magic Eye Theater** presents **Captain EO**, **George Lucas'** 3-D extravaganza, directed by **Francis Coppola** and starring **Michael Jackson**. Another Lucas production is **Star Tours**, a simulated space flight with an awesome sense of realism. The aquatic world is equally accessible via the **Submarine Voyage.** The perils of outer space will thrill you on **Space Mountain**, a $20 million high-speed journey to the stars. Visitors enter through a simulated NASA control center and board rockets that travel aloft through a series of optical effects. The downward plummet is equally spectacular, with showers of meteors illuminating the ride home.

Summer nights in Disneyland offer a series of special events. The Main Street, U.S.A. **Electrical Parade** is held twice every night, and fabulous floats and Disney characters are illuminated by 100,000 sparkling lights. The parade is capped by a spectacular fireworks display. On nights when park hours are extended, **Fantasmic!** erupts in a special-effects spectacular featuring **Mickey Mouse** conjuring up visions such as **Pink Elephants on Parade,** with the help of lasers, pyrotechnics, and giant props. Music fills the air in almost every corner of the Park. The **Plaza Garden** features big band music and dancing. **Tomorrowland Terrace** has rock concerts and dancing. Continuous Dixieland jazz on the **French Market Stage** enlivens the atmosphere in New Orleans Square.

In addition to formally scheduled concerts, Disneyland is full of roving minstrels, troubadours, and musicians. Food, ranging from nonalcoholic drinks and light snacks to multicourse dinners, is widely available in the more than 25 restaurants and snack centers. The menu in each place is keyed to complement the neighboring attractions. **Harbor Gallery** is a recent addition offering good chowder and grilled fish.

Admission to Disneyland admits you to all rides and shows without further charge, except for the shooting galleries. The park offers numerous services, such as pet kennels, package lockers, baby stroller rentals, a baby-changing station, and a first-aid dispensary. Some rides have height and age minimums. Guided tours

are available for first-time visitors. ◆ Admission. Daily 8AM-1AM, during summer season; M-F 10AM-6PM, Sa-Su 9AM-midnight, the rest of year; extended hours on holidays. Harbor Blvd, exit off Santa Ana Fwy, follow signs to Disneyland. 999.4000, 213/626.8605, ext 4565

**Restaurants/Clubs:** Red　　**Hotels:** Blue
**Shops/ 🌳 Outdoors:** Green　　**Sights/Culture:** Black

**5 Disneyland Hotel** $$$ Three towers surround a marina, **Seaports of the Pacific,** that evokes the spirit of the Magic Kingdom, to which it is linked by monorail. There are 10 tennis courts, three pools, a tropical beach, a shopping mall, and 11 restaurants and lounges. ◆ 1150 W. Cerritos Ave, Anaheim. 778.6600, 800/642.5391; fax 956.6582

**6 Anaheim Convention Center** Across the street from Disneyland, it has an 8,700-seat arena, four 100,000-square-foot exhibition halls (with another near completion), and 35 meeting rooms set in attractively landscaped grounds. The center—the most successful on the West Coast—is used for events ranging from concerts to conventions. ◆ 800 W. Katella Ave, Anaheim. 999.8900

**6 JW's** ★★★$$$ Imaginative, sometimes great cooking by **John McLaughlin,** who has traveled the world in search of fresh inspiration, is offered in a romantic, librarylike dining room. Specialties have included rack of lamb with garlic sauce, veal medallions with mushrooms and Grand Marnier soufflé. JW's is within the **Anaheim Marriott.** ◆ Eclectic ◆ M-Sa 6-10PM. 700 W. Convention Way. 750.8000

**6 Inn at the Park** $$ This 480-room, 14-story hotel is located next to the Convention Center and across the street from Disneyland. ◆ 185 S. Harbor Blvd, Anaheim. 750.1811, 800/421.6662; fax 971.3626

**7 Hansa House** $$ Families will like this Scandinavian all-you-can-eat smorgasbord. The groaning boards feature some unusual dishes like corn fritters and a herring plate, as well as a wide range of entrées and unusually good salads. ◆ Scandinavian/American ◆ Daily 7-11AM, noon-3PM, 4:30-9PM. 1840 S. Harbor Blvd, Anaheim. 750.2411

**8 Hyatt Regency Alicante** $$$ The flamingos, pools, and 60-foot palms in the glass atrium suggest a tropical island in this 17-story, 400-room hotel. There's also tennis, a spa, three restaurants, Camp Hyatt babysitting service, and stylish decor. ◆ 100 Plaza Alicante (between Harbor Blvd and Chapman Ave). 750.1234, 800/972.2929

**9 Belisle** $ Big breakfasts, fresh sandwiches, meat loaf, and pies are served in heaping portions at this country-style restaurant. ◆ American ◆ Daily 24 hours. 12001 Harbor Blvd, Garden Grove. 750.6560

German settlers, who bought land for two dollars an acre to grow grapes and produce wine, founded Anaheim. The city was California's wine capital until the 1880s, when a blight wiped out the vineyards.

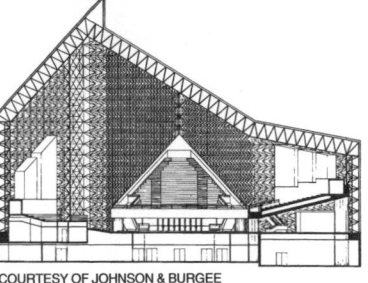

COURTESY OF JOHNSON & BURGEE

**10 Crystal Cathedral** Only a few blocks away from Disneyland is the all-glass Crystal Cathedral of the **Garden Grove Community Church**, designed by **Johnson & Burgee** in 1980, with a new steeple designed by **Philip Johnson** in 1990. Made of white steel trusses and tempered silver glass, the cathedral (illustrated above) is a shimmering extravaganza 415 feet long, 207 feet wide, and 128 feet high that seats 2,862. The 236-foot Crean Tower, made of highly polished stainless steel prisms, has a 52-bell carillon.

The church's previous center was designed by architect **Richard Neutra** in 1961. It is an International-Style steel-and-glass church first used for drive-in services. Passengers in 1,400 cars congregated to go to church without leaving their autos. Neutra's son **Dion** designed the adjacent 15-story **Tower of Hope** for the expanding church administration in 1967. ♦ Tours: M-Sa 9AM-3:30PM every half-hour. Services: Su 8:30AM, 9:30AM, 11AM, 12:30PM (Spanish), 7PM. 12141 Lewis St, Garden Grove. 971.4000

**11 Dover's** ★★$$$ Such highly praised dishes as conch chowder, duck breast with honey and horseradish, and pork noisettes with yellow peppers are served in a soaring, light-filled room. The restaurant is within the **Doubletree Hotel**. ♦ Eclectic ♦ M-F 11:30AM-2PM, 6-10PM; Sa-Su 10:30AM-3PM, 6-10PM. 100 City Dr, Orange. 634.4500

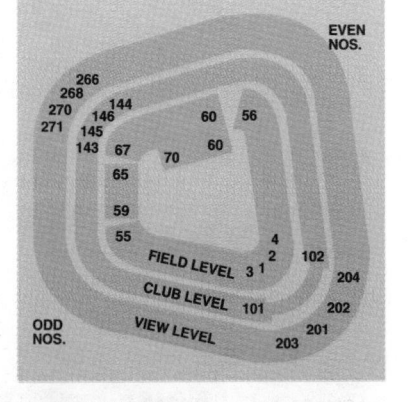

**12 Anaheim Stadium** Home of the **California Angels** baseball team and the **LA Rams** football team, the stadium features comfortable seats and good visibility (see the plan above). ♦ 2000 Gene Autry Way, Anaheim. 254.3000 (stadium), 634.2000 (California Angels information)

**13 La Brasserie Restaurant** ★$$$ This intimate and relaxed bistro specializes in home-style soups, well-prepared fish, and veal. The library dining room is appealing. ♦ French ♦ M-F 11:30AM-2PM, 5-10PM; Sa 5-10PM. 202 S. Main St, Orange. 978.6161

**14 Yen Ching** ★★$$ Wonderful food is served in a cool, modern setting, and the unusually friendly service makes this a consistent favorite. Specialties include crispy duck, pot stickers, and whole fish with garlic sauce. ♦ Chinese ♦ M-Th 11:30AM-2:30PM, 4:40-9:30PM; F 11:30AM-2:30PM, 4:40-10:30PM; Sa noon-10:30PM; Su noon-9:30PM. 574 S. Glassell St, Orange. 997.3300

**15 Caffe Piemonte** ★$$ This sparkling trattoria is hidden in a lackluster shopping center. Polenta, salmon-filled agnolotti, and the rack of lamb have been praised. ♦ Italian ♦ Tu-F noon-1:30PM, 5-9PM; Sa-Su 5-9PM. 1835 E. Chapman Ave, Orange. 532.3296

**16 Doll City USA** Claiming to be the largest of its kind, this 7,700-square-foot store has thousands of dolls, buggies, and related books. ♦ M-Sa 10AM-4PM. 2040 N. Tustin Ave, Orange. 998.9384

**17 Angelo's** $ This classic drive-in, with pert carhops on roller skates and occasional rallies of vintage wheels, has a terrific neon sign. ♦ American ♦ M-Tu, Su 10:30AM-11PM; W-Th 10:30AM-midnight; F-Sa 10:30AM-2AM. 511 S. State College Blvd, Anaheim. 533.1401

**18 Werner's** ★$ Helen Werner has been serving up honest home cooking here since 1955. She still bakes the pies from scratch, and her grandson/chef helps with the chicken and dumplings. ♦ American ♦ Tu-Sa 4:30-8:30PM; Su 11:30AM-8PM. 1001 W. Lincoln Ave, Anaheim. 535.5505

**18 Hansen House** Built in 1857, this white clapboard house with a narrow front porch was designed in the Greek Revival style. Also known as the **Mother Colony House,** this was the first house in Anaheim, built by **George Hansen,** founder of the **Mother Colony,** a group of Germans who left San Francisco to grow grapes in Southern California. Inside the restored home is an exhibition on Anaheim's history. ♦ Free. Tours usually held Wednesday mornings. Call for appointment. 414 N. West St, Anaheim. Library: 254.1850

## Orange County North/Disneyland

In 1923, Walt and Roy Disney established the Disney Brothers Studio in Silverlake.

Of the American cities that have the most per capita ski magazine subscribers, Anaheim/Santa Ana ranks third, and LA is 19th.

"Living in Los Angeles these days is like being in group therapy with eight million people."
**Taylor Negron,** LA Comedian

**19 Knott's Berry Farm** The nation's first theme park (illustrated below) had its start in 1934 when **Mrs. Cordelia Knott** began selling home-made chicken dinners to supplement income from the family's berry farm. Mrs. Knott's chicken kitchen survived the Depression and spawned a 150-acre entertainment facility that emphasizes the wholesome aspects of an ideal-ized and simpler America. There are five theme areas, comprising 165 rides, attractions, live shows, restaurants, and stores.

**Ghost Town** A replica of an 1880s Old West boom town, complete with cowboys, cancan dancers, and gold panning, it includes several authentic buildings culled from real ghost towns. Old-time melodramas are presented in the **Birdcage Theatre.** The **Butterfield Stage-coach** tours the countryside, making riders bless the day that shock absorbers were in-vented. Plan on getting wet if you choose to take a **Log Ride,** where your log boat floats through old sawmill and logging camps before splashing 42 feet in its final descent.

**Roaring '20s** This nostalgic glimpse of a vin-tage amusement park enhanced by the latest technology takes you back in time with **King-dom of the Dinosaurs,** a seven-minute ride through prehistoric times. The 20-story **Sky Jump** allows riders to parachute to the ground at free-fall speeds.

**Camp Snoopy** High in the Sierra Mountains, **Snoopy** and his **Peanuts** friends welcome youngsters to rides, shows, an 1896 merry-go-round, and performing animals.

**Fiesta Village** A tribute to California's Latino heritage, piñatas, mariachis, a *mercado,* and a turn-of-the-century, hand-carved merry-go-round are found within a lushly landscaped and tiled plaza. A dance area features Latin and rock music. The **Marionette Theatre** is particularly artful and appealing to children. One of the most popular rides is **Montezooma's Revenge,** a roller coaster with cars that spin through a 360-degree loop at 55 miles per hour and then shoot backward. Also located in this area is **Dragon Swing,** a Viking ship dangling from a huge A-frame, thrilling riders by swinging back and forth until it achieves a 70-degree arc.

**Wild Water Wilderness** Turn-of-the-century California is featured here, with **Bigfoot Rapids,** a white-water river raft trip. Other thrill rides in-clude **XK1,** in which riders can control their

planes 70 feet above ground; and an extrava-ganza on **Reflection Lake,** *The Incredible Wa-terworks Show.* The **Good Time Theatre** pre-sents live shows daily.

**Knott's Marketplace** Just outside the park is a separate dining and shopping village. Here you can sample the chicken dinners and boy-senberry pies that launched Knott's; enjoy the **Knott's Family Restaurant** or **Cable Car Kitchen,** or a salad, burger, or barbecue. Gifts, baked goods, and clothes are also on sale.

Height and age restrictions apply on some rides. An admission ticket provides access to everything except **Pan for Gold** and the arcades. ♦ Admission. M-F 10AM-midnight, Sa 10AM-1AM, June-Aug; M-F 10AM-6PM, Sa 10AM-10PM, Su 10AM-7PM, Sept-May. 8039 Beach Blvd, Buena Park. 827.1776. Re-corded information: 220.5200

**20 Movieland Wax Museum** More than 270 lifelike replicas of Hollywood stars are dis-played in 150 sets of classic movies. **Madonna, Kevin Costner, Arnold Schwarzenegger, Mel Gibson, Captain Kirk,** and **Spock** have joined the **Marx Bros., John Wayne,** the **Keystone Kops,** and **Shirley Temple.** Bring your camera for a close-up of your favorites, quake in the **Chamber of Horrors,** and shop for Hollywood memorabilia in the gift store. ♦ Admission. Daily 9AM-7PM. 7711 Beach Blvd, Buena Park. 522.1154

**21 Medieval Times** $$ If you haven't overdose on good cheer at one of the theme parks, you might end your day here in a mock castle that offers a tournament with knights on horseback as you are being served dinner (which you eat with your hands) by costumed serfs and wenches. ♦ American ♦ Visits: M-F 9AM-3PM Dinner shows daily. Call for times. 7662 Beach Blvd, Buena Park. 521.4740, 800/899.6600

**21 Ming's Palace Restaurant** $$ Orange County's Chinese residents hold their banquet here. Hong Kong noodles and seafood special-ties such as crispy shrimp in baked salt are served. ♦ Chinese ♦ M-Th 11:30AM-9:30PM;

*Knott's Berry Farm*

F 11:30AM-10:30PM; Sa 10:30AM-10:30PM; Su 10:30AM-9:30PM. 7880 Beach Blvd, Buena Park. 522.8355

**2  International Printing Museum** Working antique printing machines, a printer's office circa 1900, and a myriad of other exhibitions going back to **Gutenberg** are on display. ◆ Admission. Tu-Sa 10AM-5PM. 8469 Kass Dr, Buena Park. 523.2080

**3  La Mirada Theater for the Performing Arts** Broadway shows and concerts of every kind are presented here. ◆ 14900 La Mirada Blvd (north of Buena Park). Box office: 994.6310, 310/944.9801

**4  Muckenthaler Cultural Center** Located in a lovely 1923 Spanish baroque house given to the city of Fullerton by the Muckenthaler family in 1965, the center is used for art exhibitions, classes, and receptions. ◆ Donation suggested. Tu-Sa 10AM-4PM; Su noon-5PM. 1201 W. Malvern Ave, Fullerton (east of Buena Park). 738.6595

**5  Children's Museum at La Habra** Railroad cars, hands-on displays, including a theatre gallery with costumes and props, and a hands-off beehive are housed in a restored 1923 Union Pacific depot. ◆ Admission. M-Sa 10AM-4PM. 301 S. Euclid St, La Habra. 310/905.9793

**26  Ruby Begonia's** A comfortable spot to ease the cares of the day, this intimate dance club is a favorite with locals. It's located within **Days Inn.** ◆ No cover. M-Sa 11AM-midnight (10PM for food); Su 11AM-10PM. 1500 S. Raymond, Fullerton. 635.9000

**27  California State University at Fullerton** This 226-acre campus has 20 buildings and enrolls 25,000 students. It is a branch of the California State University system. ◆ 800 N. State College Blvd, Fullerton. 773.2011

**28  Richard M. Nixon Library and Birthplace** Admirers and haters of the deposed president should be equally rewarded by a visit to the Spanish-style museum designed by **Langdon & Wilson** in 1990. The museum was built around Nixon's boyhood home. A treasure for political junkies, the museum has a Watergate exhibit, but one of the most popular items is the gun **Elvis Presley** presented to Nixon in the Oval Office. ◆ Admission. M-Sa 10AM-5PM; Su 11AM-5PM. Closed Thanksgiving, Christmas, and New Year's Day. 18001 Yorba Linda Blvd, Yorba Linda. 993.3393

**29  Bessie Wall's Fine Food and Spirits** ★$$$ A hideaway restaurant in a revamped Spanish-style home, it serves chicken and dumplings and Jagerschnitzel. Warm hospitality and attention to detail make the extra drive worthwhile. ◆ Continental ◆ M-F 11AM-2:30PM, 5-10PM; Sa 5-10PM; Su 10AM-2:30PM, 5-10PM. 1074 N. Tustin Ave, Anaheim. 630.2812

©1991

# Orange County South

The **California Gold Coast** is an earthly paradise: temperate climate, sandy beaches, rocky promontories, green canyons, and rolling hills, with a touch of the French and Italian rivieras. Along the coast, boating, golf, tennis, and other recreation are the major businesses, while the interior hills are devoted to education and high-tech industry.

The beaches have distinct identities: **Huntington Beach** is a surfer's paradise; **Newport Beach** and **Balboa** are havens for the yachting crowd; **Corona del Mar** is a quiet beachside community; **Laguna Beach** is an artists' colony; **Dana Point**

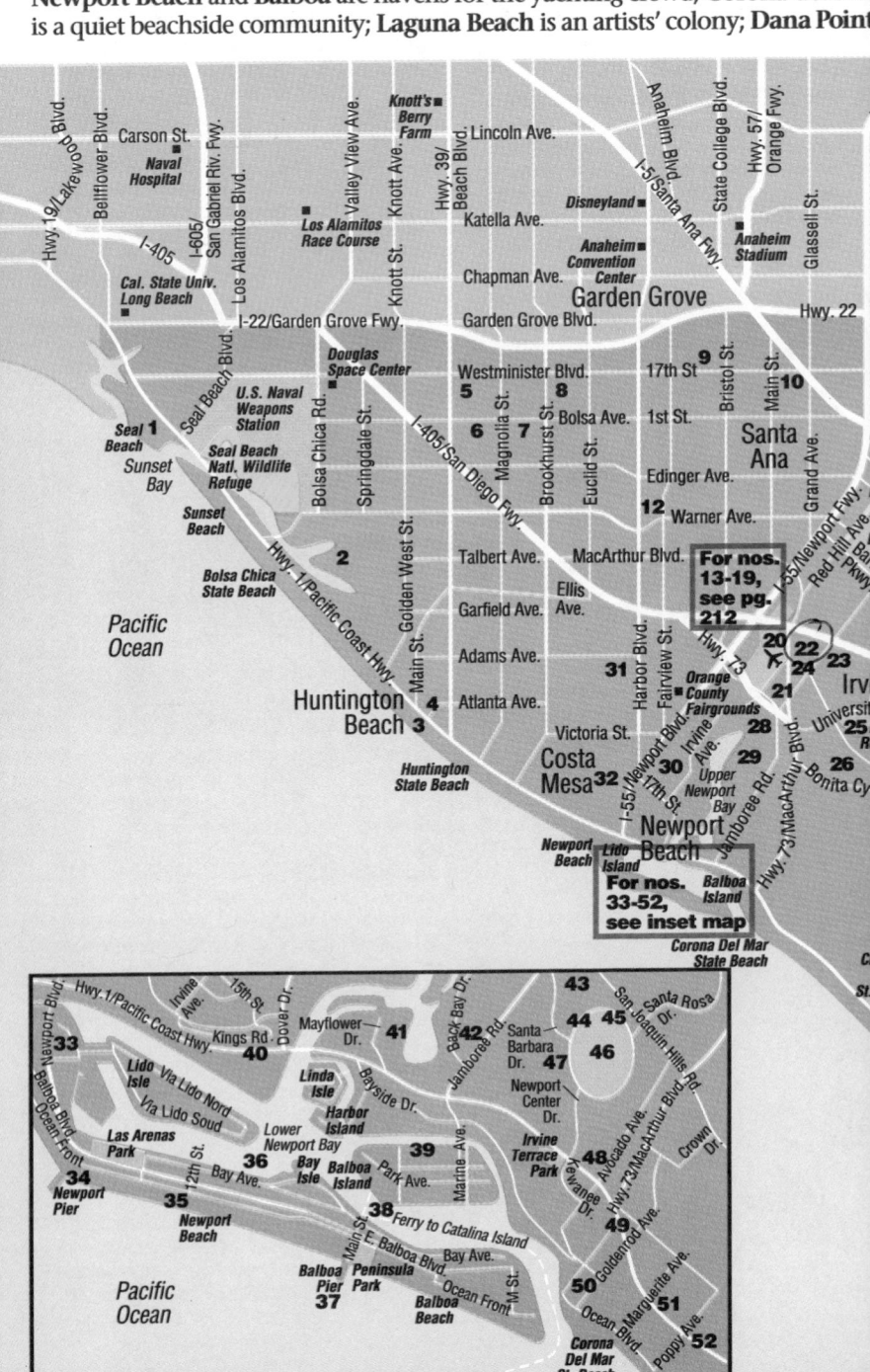

newly developed with a large marina; and **San Juan Capistrano** and **San Clemente** are gracious residential areas.

Thousands of tract homes, developed as planned communities in the '60s, cover the hilly acreage formerly devoted to farming and orange groves on the Irvine Ranch. The relatively new town of **Irvine** surrounds the newest campus of the University of California. Businesses in Orange County South are usually housed in one-story, tilt-up slab concrete buildings, the best examples of which are seen in the **Irvine Industrial Park.** The area is a mecca for high technology, with electronics and computers forming the most important sector of the economy.

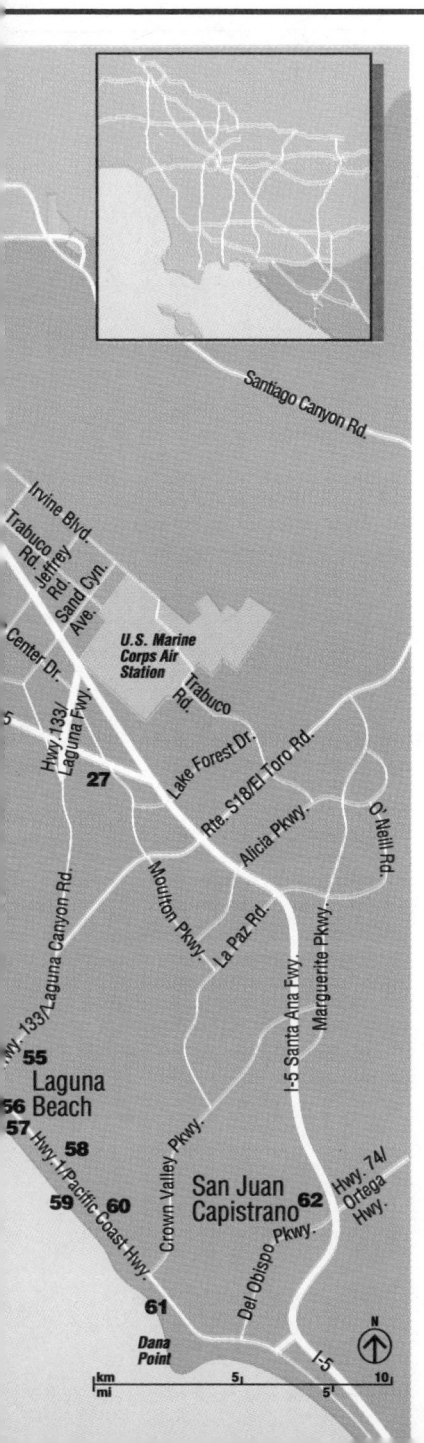

*Area code 714 unless otherwise noted.*

**1  Seal Beach Inn** $$$ Ask for a room facing the flower-filled courtyard in this bed-and-breakfast gem. Nearly all the 24 rooms and suites have period furnishings, a fully-equipped kitchen, and books. The beach and fishing pier are just two blocks away. ◆ 212 Fifth St, Seal Beach. 310/493.2416

**2  Bolsa Chica Ecological Reserve** This wildlife sanctuary offers 200 acres of restored wetlands and bird watching. Guides lead one-and-a-half mile, 90-minute tours at 9AM on the first Saturday of the month. ◆ Entrance and parking inland from Pacific Coast Hwy (between Warner Ave and Golden West St). Huntington Beach. 897.7003

**3  Huntington Pier** The first surfing contests were held at Huntington Beach, and it remains a worldwide haven for surfers. The pier, which was rebuilt and reopened as an all-concrete structure in 1992, is the best place to watch the year-round action. A restaurant, tackle shop, and snack bar will be added by summer 1993. ◆ End of Main St, Huntington Beach

**4  Waterfront Hilton Beach Resort** $$$$ This new 12-story hotel located just across the road from an eight-mile stretch of sandy beach has 300 ocean-view rooms, an outdoor pool, a fitness center, meeting facilities, a nightclub, a restaurant, and a nighttime program for kids. ◆ 21100 Pacific Coast Hwy, Huntington Beach. 960.7873, 800/822.7873; fax 960.7873

**5  Seafood Paradise II** ★★$$ Dim sum for connoisseurs in three dozen varieties are served daily for lunch. The regular Cantonese menu includes such treats as drunken chicken, roast duck, shredded jellyfish, and five-flavor beef. ◆ Chinese ◆ M-Th, Su 10AM-9:30PM; F-Sa 10AM-10:30PM. 8602 Westminster Blvd, Westminster. 893.6066

**6  Grand Garden** ★$ Catfish hot pot, eel braised in coconut milk, and spicy shrimp braised in a clay pot are offered at this modest seafood restaurant. ◆ Vietnamese ◆ M, W-Th, Su 10AM-9:30PM; F-Sa 10AM-10PM. 8894 Bolsa Ave, Westminster. 893.1200

**7  Bahn Cuon Tay Ho** ★$ Sautéed ground meat and shrimp ears, dried shrimp, cold sausage, and barbecued pork are among the fillings for this cafe's sheer, steamed rice sheets. ◆ Vietnamese ◆ Tu-Su 8AM-8PM. 9242 Bolsa Ave, #C, Westminster. 895.4796

**8 Pagolac** ★$ This is a standout in Little Saigon for its seven-course meal of beef—delicate morsels that are chopped, simmered, charbroiled, or rolled in rice paper and served with lettuce, mint, and cilantro. ♦ Vietnamese ♦ Daily 11AM-10PM. 14580 Brookhurst St, Westminster. 531.4740

**9 The Hacienda** ★★★$ This side-street restaurant with a shaded flagstone courtyard and authentic Mexican artifacts is such a popular wedding spot that the owners sell wedding dresses in the back. Try the best margarita in the county, blue-corn chicken enchiladas, and a chile relleno made strictly with chiles grown in New Mexico's Sandia Valley. Everything comes with homemade *sopaipillas*. ♦ Southwestern ♦ M-Tu 11AM-2PM; W-F 11AM-2PM, 5-9PM; Su 11AM-2PM. Call ahead on Saturday, as it is often closed for weddings. 1725 N. College Ave, Santa Ana. 558.1304

**10 MainPlace Santa Ana** The Jerde Partnership remodeled this 1958 indoor mall in 1987 in **Jon Jerde's** trademark style, with colorful tiles, neon, and whimsical signs. The cramped, two-story, skylit center, anchored by the stores **Nordstrom, Bullock's, Robinson's,** and **May Co.,** includes six movie screens and 190 specialty shops. ♦ M-F 10AM-9PM; Sa 10AM-7PM; Su 11AM-6PM. 2800 N. Main St. 547.7800

**11 Zov's Bistro** ★★$ It's located in a drab commercial center, but this little restaurant has the feel of a European bistro. Chef and owner **Zov Karamardian's** menu offers delicious Armenian pizza, fresh fish—try the salmon—rack of lamb, and mouth-watering desserts. The servers are sometimes curt, but meeter-and-greeter **Gary Karamardian** is always there with warmth and a handshake. ♦ Mediterranean ♦ M-Tu 11AM-2:30PM; W-Sa 11AM-2:30PM, 5-9PM. 17440 17th St, Tustin. 838.8855

**12 Gen Kai** ★★$$ Simple wood tables, a long sushi bar, and a lone tatami platform make up the decor, but don't be deterred—this is a favorite eating place for local Japanese chefs, and the rustic dishes taste wonderful. Highlights include marinated squid, asparagus and sausage, stewed fish with vegetables, and hot-pepper eggplant with onion. ♦ Japanese ♦ M-Th 11:30AM-2PM, 5:30-11PM; F 11:30AM-2PM, 5:30-10PM; Sa-Su 5:30-10PM. 16650 Harbor Blvd, Fountain Valley. 775.3818

**13 Horikawa** ★★$$ This versatile branch of the distinguished restaurant in LA's Little Tokyo offers teppan-yaki, sushi, and classic dishes in

**Orange County South**

a setting of elegant simplicity. ♦ Japanese ♦ Tu-Th 11:30AM-2PM, 6-10PM; F 11:30AM-2PM, 6-10:30PM; Sa 5:30-11PM; Su 5:30-9:30PM. 1611 Sunflower Ave (north side of South Coast Plaza Village). 557.2531

---

Restaurants/Clubs: Red    Hotels: Blue
Shops/ 🌿 Outdoors: Green    Sights/Culture: Black

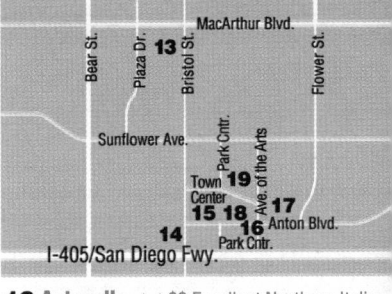

**13 Antonello** ★★$$ Excellent Northern Italian food, including cioppino and scampi in musse sauce, is served with flair in a village street se ting. Owner **Antonio Cagnolo** is a caring host and maintains an excellent wine list. ♦ Italian ♦ M-Th 11:30AM-2PM, 6-10PM; F 11:30AM-2PM, 6-11PM; Sa 6-11PM. 1611 Sunflower Ave (north side of South Coast Plaza Village). 751.7153

**13 Gustaf Anders** ★★★$$$$ Spacious elegar and wonderful food are found in this former L Jolla restaurant. The standouts are the sugar- and salt-cured salmon, smoked salmon and black caviar sandwich, marinated beef, and crusty home-baked breads. ♦ Scandinavian ♦ M-Th 11:30AM-2PM, 5:30-10PM; F-Sa 11:30AM-2:30PM, 5:30PM-midnight; Su 5:3(10PM. 1651 Sunflower Ave (north side of So Coast Plaza Village). 668.1737

**13 Gandhi** ★★$$ Outstanding in looks and cui sine, Gandhi offers terrific *naan* (bread), and e emplary tandoori, *masalas,* and regional dishe ♦ Indian ♦ M-Th 11:30AM-2:30PM, 5:30-10PM; F-Sa 11:30AM-2:30PM, 5:30-11PM; S 11AM-2:30PM, 5:30-10PM. 1621 Sunflower Ave (north side of South Coast Plaza). 556.72

**14 South Coast Plaza** This upscale shopper's heaven has more than 270 stores on the mair landscaped plaza and the adjoining **Crystal, Carousel,** and **Jewel Courts,** including seven department stores (**Bullock's, May Co., Nord strom, Saks Fifth Avenue, Sear's, Broadway** and **Robinson's**). In between is a selection of designer boutiques to rival Beverly Hills: **Gucc Cartier, Channel, Tiffany, Emporio Armani, Polo/Ralph Lauren, Charles Jourdan, Barney New York, Jaeger, Louis Vuitton, Scribner's Books,** and **Godiva Chocolatier,** to name a fe It is also the busiest retail center in Southern California, with more than 18 million visitors a year, as worthy a visit as any theme park. ♦ M 10AM-9PM; Sa 10AM-7PM; Su 11AM-6PM. 3333 Bristol St (off I-405, San Diego Fwy). 241.1700

At South Coast Plaza:

**Rizzoli's Bookstore** The most elegant, liter ate, and beautiful bookstore chain now has a nearby LA address. ♦ M-F 10AM-9PM; Sa 10AM-6PM; Su noon-5PM. Between Jewel ar Crystal Cts. 957.3331

**Spiga** ★$$ Excellent fried mozzarella and un usual pizzas and pastas are served in this trattoria that offers both alfresco and indoor seating. ♦ Italian ♦ M-Sa 11AM-10PM; Su 11AM-7PM. Crystal Ct. 540.3365

**15 Westin South Coast Plaza Hotel** $$$ The weekend specials are a good value at this 17-story hotel that includes tennis and volleyball courts, a pool, and 24-hour room service. ♦ 686 Anton Blvd. 540.2500, 800/228.3000; fax 754.7996

**16 California Scenario** Artworks are scattered throughout South Coast Plaza, but the treasure (worth the drive from LA) is **Isamu Noguchi's** 1.6-acre sculpture garden. Framed by reflective glass towers and the blank white walls of parking structures, this oasis is often overlooked by visitors. Noguchi created a contemporary version of a traditional Japanese garden in which natural rocks, sandstone structures and paving, trees, cacti, and running water symbolize different aspects of the state of California. ♦ Free. Daily 8AM-midnight. 611 Anton Blvd

**17 Plaza Tower** The curved facade and stainless-steel panels of this 1991 **Cesar Pelli** office building gleam in the light and capture the color of the sunset. The sophisticated structure has a formal front, a double grid of round-edged horizontal and vertical ribs, and double loggias and setbacks at the 17th and 21st floors. ♦ 600 Anton Blvd, Costa Mesa

**18 South Coast Repertory Theatre** The **Mainstage** and **Second Stage** present a diversified program of live comedy and drama September through June. ♦ 655 Town Center Dr. Box office: 957.4033

**19 Orange County Performing Arts Center** From the **Kirov Ballet** to *Cats,* from *Fiddler on the Roof* to the **American Ballet Theatre,** the center has become a rival to LA's Music Center since its opening in 1986. The auditorium is named for **Henry T. Segerstrom,** who developed South Coast Plaza and spearheaded the effort to make it a center for the arts. Concerts and opera are also regularly featured. ♦ 600 Town Center Dr. Box office: 556.2787

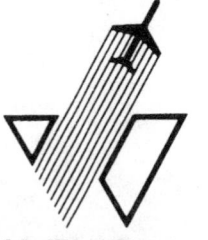

**20 John Wayne Airport** Nine commercial and five commuter carriers serve this busy alternative to LAX. They provide direct service to 19 domestic destinations. As the population of Orange County exploded (from 200,000 in 1950 to well over 2.4 million today), the airport's capacity became strained. Fortunately, major expansion was completed in 1990. The firm of **Gensler & Associates,** taking inspiration from the shape of an airplane fuselage, designed an award-winning new terminal. The rounded, bronze-tinted roofs of its three long, sleek, parallel vaults can be seen running perpendicular to the San Diego Freeway. For ground transportation to LAX, call 973.1100. ♦ 3151 Airway Ave (South of I-405, San Diego Fwy and I-55, Newport Fwy), Santa Ana. 252.5006

**21 Pascal** ★★$$$ Superb seafood, with a hint of Provence in the bold colors and seasonings, is served here. Mussels steamed with saffron, bass with thyme, and chicken with olives are among the signature dishes. ♦ French ♦ M-Th 11:30AM-2:30PM, 6-9:30PM; F 11:30AM-2:30PM, 6-10PM; Sa 6-10PM; 1000 N. Bristol St, Newport Beach. 752.0107

**22 Chanteclair** $$$ The French farmhouse decor offers a romantic setting for such dishes as filet Wellington, veal Oscar, and grilled swordfish. ♦ Continental ♦ M-Th 11:30AM-2:30PM, 5-10PM; F 11:30AM-2:30PM, 5-11PM; Sa 5-11PM; Su 10:30AM-2:30PM, 5-10PM. 18912 MacArthur Blvd (across from John Wayne Airport), Irvine. 752.8001

**22 Bistango** ★★$$ This modern restaurant with a granite bar, rough-slate floor, chic Italian furniture, and nearly a hundred contemporary gallery artworks (they're for sale) is a power-lunch meeting place by day, and a jazz hot spot at night. Master chef **John Waxman,** formerly of **Michael's** in Santa Monica and **Jams** in New York, was a menu consultant for such dishes as inventive pastas, designer pizzas, and grilled meat and seafood. ♦ Eclectic ♦ M-F 11:30AM-3PM, 5-10:30PM. Bar menu: daily 11:30AM-11:30PM. Music nightly. 19100 Von Karman Ave (Atrium building), Irvine. 752.5222

**22 Bistro 201** ★★$$$ Set in a modern office park building, this contemporary **David Wilhelm** restaurant is modeled on sophisticated New York bistros. This time Wilhelm applies his flair for the exotic to traditional bistro fare, with dishes such as roast rack of lamb on garlicky lima beans. The bar is zinc topped and an-

gular, the banquettes covered in raw silk, and the atmosphere cosmopolitan. Jazz musicians play Wednesday through Saturday, and a late-night menu is offered after 11PM. ♦ Eclectic ♦ M-Tu 11:30AM-4PM, 5:30-10PM; W-F 11:30AM-4PM, 5:30PM-1AM; Sa 5:30PM-1AM; Su 5:30-10PM. 18201 Von Karman, Irvine. 553.1122

**22 Prego** ★★$$ Modeled on a Tuscan villa, this happy, crowded place serves innovative pizzas, rabbit, duck, and free-range chicken from the rotisserie, and such special treats as ravioli filled with ricotta, chard, and sage. ♦ Italian ♦ M 11:30AM-10:30PM; Tu-Th 11:30AM-11PM; F 11:30AM-midnight; Sa 5PM-midnight; Su 5-10PM. 18420 Von Karman Ave, Irvine. 553.1333

**23 Park Place** This complex of futuristic glass-clad structures with rooftop pods for air-conditioning equipment—developed by **Fluor Corporation**—has become an Orange County landmark along the San Diego Freeway (I-405). Completed in 1976, it was designed by **Welton Becket & Associates.** It is best viewed from the freeway. ♦ 3333 Michelson Dr, Irvine

**24 Le Meridien** $$$$ This striking ziggurat-shaped member of an international chain of French-owned luxury hotels has a Newport Beach address, but it is located well inland, across from the airport. It has a swimming pool, exercise rooms, good weekend rates, and three restaurants, including **Cafe Fleuri,** a sophisticated coffee shop, and the **Bisttro Terrasse,** which offers exquisite spa cuisine on an outdoor terrace. ♦ 4500 MacArthur Blvd, Newport Beach. 476.2001, 800/543.4300; fax 476.0153

Within Le Meridien:

**Antoine** ★★★$$$$ Serious dining in an opulent setting of silk-covered walls, mirrors, and fine furnishings is found here. The consulting chef is **Gerard Vie** (who follows **Jacques Maximin** of the Hotel Negresco in Nice), and the kitchen has drawn raves for its treatment of silky foie gras, meats, and poultry. There's a superb wine list and polished service. ♦ French ♦ Tu-Sa 6-10PM. 476.2001

**25 Chinatown** ★$$ **Alice Fong** did the brightly colored decor that makes **Michael Chiang's** restaurant such a feast for the eye, despite its uninspiring location. The firecracker lamb, gun-powder scallops, confetti chicken, and aromatic shrimp are as tasty as they sound. ♦ Chinese ♦ M-Th, Su 11:30AM-10PM; F-Sa 11:30AM-11PM. 4139 Campus Dr, Marketplace Mall, Irvine. 856.2211

**26 University of California at Irvine** UC Irvine was founded in 1965 on a thousand acres donated by the **Irvine Company.** Twenty-five buildings house five major schools and a number of

rare exception to the prevailing architectural mediocrity of UC campuses is the **Information Computer Sciences and Engineering Researc Facility**—a splendid complex of buildings by **Frank Gehry** located on the southeast edge of the inner ring—and new work by **Morphosis** and other cutting-edge California architects. Th **Bren Events Center, Fine Arts Gallery** sponso exhibitions of 20th-century art and is open free of charge Tuesday to Sunday from noon to 5PM. Theatrical performances are held in the **Fine Arts Village Theatre,** the **Concert Hall,** and **Crawford Hall.** ♦ San Diego Fwy (I-405) to Jamboree Rd, W to Campus Dr, So. 856.5011

**27 Wild Rivers** The family water park with 40 rides and attractions is set on a lush tropical si formerly occupied by **Lion Country Safari.** Yo can shoot the rapids on an inner tube, be fired over water on the **Wipeout,** or lie back and improve your tan. There are paddling pools for very small children, refreshments, and group picnic sites by advance reservation. ♦ Admission. Daily 10AM-8PM, June-Oct; some weekends off season 11AM-5PM. 8770 Irvine Cente Dr (off San Diego Fwy, I-405), Irvine. 768.9453

**28 Kitayama** ★★★$$ This *kaiseki* restaurant is so authentic that it would help to bring a Japanese friend along to translate the menu—though there is also an excellent and more accessible sushi bar. The fixed-price *omakase kaiseki* (chef's choice) is highly praised, as is the bargain lunch. ♦ Japanese ♦ M-F 11AM-2PM, 6-10PM; Sa 6-10PM. 101 Bayview Pl, Newport Beach. 725.0777

**29 Upper Newport Bay** Surrounded by the bluf of Newport Bay is this remarkable and idyllic 741-acre preserve for ducks, geese, and other avian users of the Pacific Flyway. Paths along the far reaches of the estuary are wonderful for quiet early morning walks. ♦ Backbay Dr (at Jamboree Rd), Newport Beach

**30 Crab Cooker** $$$ This well-loved and always crowded restaurant does not accept reservations, even, as one story has it, from a presiden of the United States who wanted to circumvent the line. Their specialty is mesquite-broiled sea food. ♦ Seafood ♦ M-Th, Su 11AM-9PM; F-Sa 11AM-10PM. Fish market opens at 10AM. 220 Newport Blvd, Costa Mesa. 673.0100

**31 Mandarin Gourmet** ★$$ The showcase of **Michael Chiang,** who also owns **Chinatown** in Irvine, this restaurant serves fine Mandarin and Szechuan dishes in a contemporary setting. Aromatic shrimp is a standout, but the menu is full of interesting discoveries. ♦ Chinese ♦ M-Th 11:30AM-3PM, 4:30-10PM; F 11:30AM-3PM, 4:30-11PM; Sa 11:30AM-11PM; Su 11:30AM-10PM. 1500 Adams Ave, Costa Mesa 540.1937

## Orange County South

interdisciplinary and graduate departments. Full-time enrollment is about 17,000. The campus was laid out as an arboretum; more than 11,000 trees from all over the world form a green grove in the center of the tan hills of the Irvine Ranch. A self-guided tree tour brochure is available at the Administration Building. A

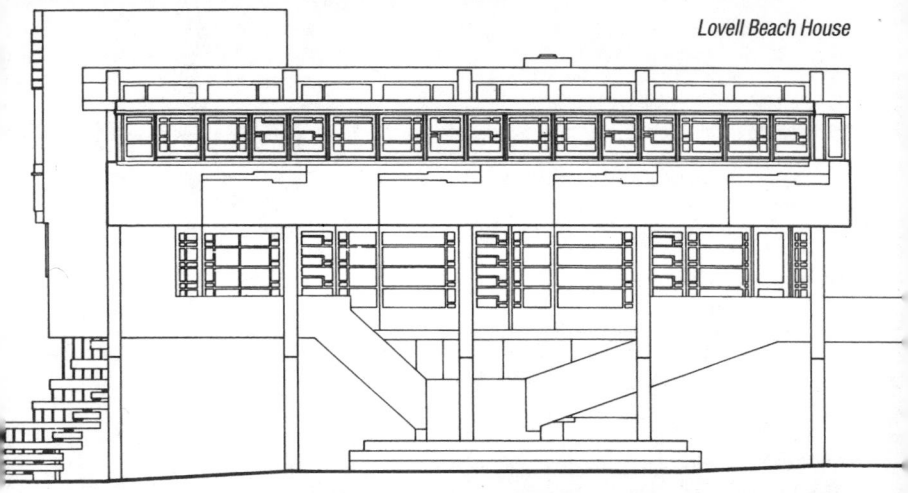

*Lovell Beach House*

**32 The Golden Truffle** ★★$$$ Chef/owner **Alan Greeley's** friendly neighborhood cafe and restaurant offers Caribbean-influenced California cuisine. ◆ Eclectic ◆ Tu-Th 11:30AM-2:30PM, 6-9:30PM; F 11:30AM-2:30PM, 6-10PM; Sa 6-10PM. 1767 Newport Blvd, Costa Mesa. 645.9858

**33 Ho Sum Bistro** ★$ In an all-white space you can enjoy light, delicious chicken, dim sum, noodles, and other snacks. ◆ California/Chinese ◆ M-Th, Su 11AM-10PM; F-Sa 11AM-11PM; Su 4-9PM. 3112 Newport Blvd, Costa Mesa. 675.0896

**34 21 Oceanfront Restaurant** ★★$$$ Though this clublike restaurant (formerly **The Rex**) has changed its name, chef **Luiz Tzorin** is still preparing the especially fine abalone and a popular fresh Colorado rack of lamb. ◆ Continental ◆ Daily 5:30-11PM. 2100 Oceanfront, Newport Beach. 673.2100

**34 Doryman's Inn** $$$ This bed-and-breakfast inn offers ocean views and Victorian decor in a converted 1891 commercial building—the first in the city. ◆ 2102 W. Oceanfront, Newport Beach. 675.7300

**35 Lovell Beach House** One of the great monuments of modern architecture, **Rudolph Schindler** designed this 1926 beach house (pictured above) for the same progressive doctor who was to commission a house by **Neutra** in Los Feliz a few years later. It is a fine example of Schindler's early constructivist style, combining grace, lightness, and strength in a style far ahead of its time. It's a private residence. ◆ 13th St at Beach Walk, Balboa

**36 Newport Harbor** There are 10 yacht clubs and 10,000 boats in this aquatic playground. The exclusive residential area has been a prestige summer resort for many years. The bay includes **Lido Isle, Linda Isle, Harbor Island, Bay Isle,** and **Balboa Island.** Boat slips or moorings can be rented through the county sheriffs' Harbor Division (723.1002). Cruises include **Hornblower Yachts** (brunch and dinner/dancing, 549.8866) and the **Cannery Brunch Cruise** (675.5777) ◆ Newport Beach

**37 Ruby's** $ The lovingly re-created streamline diner helped launch a trend —and a growing chain, now in more than 12 locations—toward white formica, red vinyl, and quilted stainless steel. Cuddle up in a booth to enjoy omelets, mountains of fries, hamburgers, and milk shakes. ◆ American ◆ Daily 7AM-10PM. End of Balboa Pier, Newport Beach. 675.7829

**38 Balboa Pavilion** This historic landmark built as a Victorian bath house and electric Red Car terminal in 1906 was a popular destination for fashionably dressed bathers from around the greater LA area. Now the most visible focal point on the bay, it is outlined by twinkling lights at night, and its harbor-view bar and res-

taurant are popular for wedding receptions. It is also the Newport Terminal for Catalina Island tours, whale-watching expeditions, and harbor cruises aboard the Pavilion Queen, which last 45 to 90 minutes and show you the Newport Harbor. ◆ 400 Main St, Balboa. 673.5245. Sport fishing and skiff rentals: 673.1423

**38 Balboa Ferry** Three tiny ferries take you between the Balboa Peninsula and Balboa Island. ♦ Daily 24 hours. Palm St on Balboa Peninsula or Agate Ave on Balboa Island

**39 Balboa Island** Balboa is actually three islands connected by bridges, and they are, in descending size, the **Big Island**, the **Little Island**, and **Collins Island**. A favorite island pastime is an evening stroll among the luxury homes. ♦ Corona del Mar

**40 Marrakesh** ★$$$ The Hollywood-Arab decor of tiled fountains and pillows on the floor provides a sumptuous setting for elaborate Moroccan dinners that include chicken pie, couscous, and baklava. ♦ Moroccan ♦ M-F 6-10PM; Sa-Su 5:30-11PM. 1100 W. Pacific Coast Hwy, Newport Beach. 645.8384

**41 Newport Dunes** This aquatic and recreational vehicle park on a 15-acre lagoon is not only for campers; visitors may rent watersports equipment and boats, including pedalboats, sailboats, kayaks, windsurfers, boogie boards, skates, and bicycles. There are also meeting facilities, a launching ramp, and dressing rooms. ♦ 1131 Back Bay Dr (Pacific Coast Hwy at Jamboree Rd), Newport Beach. 729.3863. ResortWatersports: 729.3863

**42 Hyatt Newporter** $$$ Located on Newport's Back Bay, this 26-acre resort has 410 rooms and four three-bedroom villas with private pools. The sporting options here include golf, tennis, and swimming, and, of course, there's a spa with Jacuzzis.

**Duke's,** an English pub filled with **John Wayne** memorabilia (he used to frequent the resort and started the tennis club), offers live entertainment Wednesday through Saturday from 9PM to 2AM. Summer concerts are held at 7:30PM on Friday in an outdoor amphitheater. ♦ 1107 Jamboree Rd (at Pacific Coast Hwy), Newport Beach. 644.1700, 800/234.1234; fax 644.1552

**43 Newport Harbor Art Museum** Changing exhibitions of contemporary art and a permanent collection of 20th-century art emphasizing works by California artists are presented in this internationally famous museum. The **Sculpture Garden Cafe** has light meals and snacks; the gift shop sells catalogs and books. ♦ Admission. Tu-Su 10AM-5PM. 850 San Clemente Dr, Newport Beach. 759.1122

**44 Tutto Mare** ★$$ This stylish trattoria serves Northern Italian fare, specializing in seafood and pastas. ♦ Italian ♦ M-Th 11:30AM-11PM; F-Sa 11:30AM-midnight; Su 5-10PM. 545 Newport Center Dr, Newport Beach. 640.6333

The photo-finish camera and automatic timing were first introduced at the 1932 Summer Olympics in Los Angeles.

## Four Seasons Hotel
### NEWPORT BEACH

**45 Four Seasons Hotel** $$$$ The flagship of th luxury hotel chain, this 20-story tower with a four-acre garden is located in Fashion Island. The decor is refined, the art of outstanding quality, and the views spectacular. ♦ 690 Newport Center Dr, Newport Beach. 759.0808, 80C 755.0690; fax 759.0568

Within the Four Seasons:

**Pavilion** ★★★$$$$ Such specialties as crab fritters, lobster ragout, and tenderloin of lamb with turnip pancakes are served amid pale, sophisticated decor in this ambitious restaurant. ♦ California ♦ M-F 6:30AM-2PM, 6-10PM; Sa 6-10PM; Su 10:30AM-2PM, 6-10:30PM. 760.4920

**46 The Ritz** ★★★$$$$ Not to be confused with the Ritz-Carlton down the coast, **Hans Prager'** luxury restaurant draws the same well-heeled crowd. Its bouillabaisse has been acclaimed as the best west of the Mississippi, and the carousel appetizer (with fresh foie gras, sweet smoked trout, and gravlax), the liver with crisp onion sticks, and the classic osso buco have also won devoted fans. ♦ Continental ♦ M-Th 11:30AM-3PM, 6-10PM; F 11:30AM-3PM, 5:30-11PM; Sa 5:30-11PM. 880 Newport Center Dr, Newport Beach. 720.1800

**47 Fashion Island** A $100 million renovation and expansion has breathed new life into this once staid, 1960s shopping center. The **Jerde Partnership's** Mediterranean-themed 1980s design, completed in 1990, is so popular that families come just to stroll through the upscale outdoor mall and its plazas. Located in the center of the spacious 75-acre Newport Center complex, the shopping center has views of the Pacific, 200 specialty shops, four department stores (**Neiman Marcus, Robinson's, I. Magnin,** and **The Broadway**), and the **Atrium Court** a tri-level complex with lush landscaping and balconies. The food court is exceptional, with gourmet take-out restaurants and bakeries, an a farmer's market with the freshest produce and fish. A planned **Hard Rock Cafe** with a 50-foot blinking guitar sign is expected to bring nightlife to the shopping center. ♦ M-F 10AM-9PM; Sa 10AM-6PM; Su 11AM-6PM. Off Pacific Coast Hwy (between Jamboree and MacArthur Blvds), Newport Beach. 721.2022

**48  El Torito Grill** ★$ From the zingy salsa to the creative tortilla fillings, everything is freshly made and served with flair in this casual hot spot. ♦ Southwestern ♦ M-Th 11AM-11PM; F-Sa 11AM-midnight; Su 10AM-midnight. 951 Newport Center Dr, Newport Beach. 640.2875. Also at: 633 Anton Blvd, Costa Mesa. 662.2672

**49  Sherman Library and Gardens** This jewel of a botanical garden and library specializes in the horticulture of the Pacific Southwest. The well-maintained grounds are lush with unusual seasonal flowers and famous hanging baskets. The tea garden serves pastries and coffee. A gift shop sells a variety of horticultural items. ♦ Admission. Gardens: daily 10:30AM-4PM. Library: M-F 9AM-5PM. 2647 E. Coast Hwy, Corona del Mar. 673.2261

**50  Trees** ★★$$$ Three dining rooms, a tree-filled courtyard, and a bar with nightly piano music and a fireplace create a cozy setting for the eclectic cuisine—which ranges from Maryland crab cakes to Thai fried chicken—of chef/owner **Russell Armstrong.** ♦ Eclectic ♦ M-Th, Su 5:30-10PM; F-Sa 5:30-11PM. 440 Heliotrope, Corona del Mar. 673.0910

**51  Carmelo's** ★★$$ The eclectic menu, friendly service, and live music draw crowds to this unpretentious trattoria. Specialties to try include pasta Sorrentina (with fresh porcini mushrooms and zucchini flowers), pumpkin-flavored gnocchi, and Dover sole Milanese. ♦ Italian ♦ M-Th, Su 5:30-10PM; F-Sa 5:30PM-12:30AM. Music and dancing: M-Th, Su until 1AM; F-Sa until 1:30AM. 3520 E. Pacific Coast Hwy, Corona del Mar. 675.1922

**52  Five Crowns** ★★$$$ Fine food, professional service, and a charming ambience account for the popularity of this improved version of England's oldest inn (**Ye Old Bell** at Hurley, AD 1135). Herb-roasted free-range chicken, roast duckling with apple-prune compote, and prime rib are dependable choices. ♦ Continental ♦ M-Sa 5-10PM; Su 10:30AM-2:30PM, 4-10PM. 3801 E. Coast Hwy, Corona del Mar. 760.0331

The Los Angeles Inter-Urban Railroad was built in 1898, and it provided a network of trolleys (affectionately referred to as the Big Red Cars) that serviced Southern California, linking Santa Ana, Whittier, Riverside, Redlands, Newport Beach, and Glendale. The trolleys skirted the coastline from Santa Monica to Balboa, and traveled as far out as San Bernardino to Arrowhead Springs. By 1949 all the trolley lines were discontinued as Angelenos adopted a new mode of transportation: the automobile.

The 1933 Long Beach earthquake claimed the lives of 115 people and caused more than $40 million worth of property damage.

# Laguna Beach

A Mediterranean climate, a beautiful three-mile beach, and an artsy atmosphere have made Laguna Beach a popular resort for years. **John Steinbeck** lived here while writing *Tortilla Flat,* and **Bette Davis** made her home here during the 1940s. Most of the 20,000 year-round residents commute to industrial areas outside of Laguna Beach. The community supports a primarily cottage industry of small shops, crafts galleries, and tourist services.

**53  Hortense Miller Garden**  Docents lead two-hour tours through this spectacular overgrown two-acre private garden that features native flora and fauna and exotic plants. More than 1,200 species are represented. Reservations are required two weeks in advance. ♦ Admission. Tours: W, Sa, and occasionally Tu 10AM. 22511 Allview Terrace, Laguna Beach. 497.0716

**53  Festival of Arts/Pageant of the Masters** Show biz and technical wizardry are combined to simulate great works of art, such as *The Last Supper,* on live models. Using acrylic paints to deflect stage lighting, artists apply innovative makeup on models who must remain motionless for up to a minute-and-a-half during the performance. For seven weeks each year, some 600 volunteers and a small staff of trained professionals draw oohs and aahs from more than 200,000 wide-eyed spectators. So critical is the sophisticated stage lighting that a matinee performance would be unthinkable. Book well ahead for the July and August performances. ♦ Admission. 650 Laguna Canyon Rd, Laguna Beach. 494.1145, 800/487.3378

**54  Laguna Museum of Art** Permanent collection and changing exhibitions of work by California artists are displayed here. ♦ Admission. Tu-Su 11AM-5PM. 307 Cliff Dr. 494.6531, 800/487.3378

**54  242 Cafe** ★★$$ Tasty, healthful breakfasts (try the Norwegian salmon scramble) with fresh-squeezed juices and buckwheat pancakes, and lunch and dinner treats including sautéed eggplant salad, New Mexico fettuccine, and Thai chicken pizza are served in this tiny trattoria. BYOB. ♦ California ♦ M-Th, Su 7:30AM-10PM; F-Sa 7:30AM-11PM. 242 N. Pacific Coast Hwy. 494.2444

**55  Kachina** ★★$$ One of the county's hottest restaurants, this arty spot, with its nouvelle Southwestern cuisine, launched the area's most renowned chef and restaurateur, **David Wilhelm.** Crowded, noisy, and popular, Kachina serves Wilhelm's trademark surprises, such as

goat-cheese rellenos and red-chile linguine. ♦ Southwestern ♦ M-Th, Su 5:30-10PM; F-Su 9:30-11PM. 222 Forest Ave. 497.5546

"God bless the LA police, they were the first Keystone Kops."

**Mack Sennet,** Hollywood director and producer

**55 Cafe Zinc Market** ★★★$ A quiet sidewalk patio fronts this gourmet food market and vegetarian restaurant, where patrons line up to wrap their hands around a tall, hot mug of the county's best cappuccino. Bread from **La Brea Bakery**, homemade granola, plate-size gourmet pizettes, sandwiches, and great salads make this one of the area's best new cafes. ◆ Vegetarian ◆ Tu-W 7AM-6PM; Th-Sa 7AM-11PM; Su 7AM-5PM. Market: Tu-F 7AM-7PM; Sa-Su 8AM-5:30PM. 350 Ocean Ave. 494.6302

**55 Renaissance Cafe** ★$ This popular coffeehouse and restaurant, with brick walls, concrete floors, modern art, cafe tables, and a sidewalk patio, serves everything from crab cakes to smoked-chicken breakfast burritos, pastas, and fish. Their seven-ounce burger is a big seller. There's live music nightly. ◆ California ◆ Meals: M-Th, Su 7AM-10PM; F-Sa 7AM-11PM. Stays open M-Th, Su until 10:30PM and F-Sa until 12:30AM. Nightly music starts at 8PM. 234 Forest Ave. 497.5282

**55 Five Feet** ★★★$$ East meets West in this modern, arty restaurant that is centered on its open kitchen. Chef/owner **Michael Kang** surprises and delights with such dishes as *kung pao* calamari, goat-cheese won tons, and softshell crabs with pineapple cilantro salsa. ◆ Chinese ◆ M-Th, Su 5-10PM; F-Sa 5-11PM. 328 Glenneyre St. 497.4955. Also at: Fashion Island, Newport Beach. 640.5250

**56 Fahrenheit 451 Bookstore and Coffeehouse** The original, small, rustic used bookstore founded by hippies in the 1960s and named for the **Ray Bradbury** novel was a hangout for **Timothy Leary,** and still carries how-to tomes on mushroom and marijuana growing. In 1991 newer owners added a store and coffeehouse with the same name to sell new books in a slick and airy minimall right across the street. Both shops have strong sections on philosophy, religion, poetry, and spirituality. At the coffeehouse, local musicians stop to play, and browsers can eat pastries and vegetable tarts. ◆ Used bookstore: daily 11AM-5:30PM. 509 S. Coast Hwy. 494.9013. Coffeehouse/bookstore: M-Th, Su 8AM-midnight; F-Sa

## Orange County South

8AM-1AM. 540 S. Coast Hwy, Laguna Beach. 494.5151

**57 Vacation Village** $$ This resort with a private beach, pools, whirlpool, recreation, and restaurants has reasonably priced rooms, suites, and studios. Fifty of the 130 rooms have ocean views. ◆ 647 S. Coast Hwy, Laguna Beach. 494.8566, 800/843.6895; fax 494.1386

**57 Eiler's Inn** $$ Warm, personalized service greets you at this charming bed-and-breakfast located a block from the beach. ◆ 741 S. Coast Hwy, Laguna Beach. 494.3004

**58 The Carriage House** $$$ Another charming New Orleans-style bed-and-breakfast near the sea, this one has six suites with private entrances, and four with kitchens. There's a pretty garden, a friendly dining room, and it's just three minutes from the beach. ◆ 1322 Catalina St, Laguna Beach. 494.8945

**59 Surf & Sand Hotel** $$$$ A $26 million remodel of this local standard has updated its Mediterranean decor. One of the few Southern California hotels right on the ocean, it has 160 rooms with seaview balconies and two restaurants overlooking the Pacific—one near the sandy beach, the other nine stories up. The hotel has meeting facilities, an outdoor pool, and excellent service. ◆ 1555 S. Coast Hwy, Laguna Beach. 497.4477, 800/524.8621; fax 494.7653

Within the Surf & Sand Hotel:

**The Towers** ★★$$$ This stunning, mirrored Art Deco restaurant overlooks the ocean from the ninth floor. Northern Italian cuisine is served in an elegant atmosphere. ◆ Italian ◆ Daily 5:30-10PM. 497.4477

**60 Dizz's As Is** ★$$ In a reflection of Laguna's bohemian, laid-back spirit, everyone here dresses to please him or herself, and the plates don't match. Cioppino and filet mignon are standout dishes. ◆ Eclectic ◆ M-Th, Su 6-9:30PM; F-Sa 6-10PM. Closed M during winter. 2794 S. Coast Hwy, Laguna Beach. 494.5250

**61 The Ritz-Carlton Laguna Niguel** $$$$ East Coast style and West Coast atmosphere mix nicely in this luxury resort hotel. How could it be otherwise with a setting on a dramatic bluff overlooking the Pacific? Amenities include two swimming pools, four tennis courts, sailing accommodations at Dana Point, direct access to a two-mile beach, a restaurant, a cafe, a club, and a library where high tea is served in the afternoon. Even if you don't stay in a suite that comes with its own Steinway piano, you can still enjoy music. It's the Ritz-Carlton's policy to have piano music playing somewhere in the hotel from 6AM to 11PM every day of the week. ◆ 33533 Ritz-Carlton Dr, Dana Point. 240.2000, 800/241.3333; fax 240.0829

Within the Ritz-Carlton Laguna Niguel:

**The Dining Room** ★★★$$$$ Specialties have included pheasant mousse with blueberry vinegar sauce, sweetbreads in port and caper sauce, and saddle of rabbit with basil cream sauce. The wine list is outstanding. This is an ideal place if you want to overindulge in formal, grand surroundings and drop a bundle of money. ◆ French ◆ Tu-Th 7-10PM; F-Sa 6-10PM. 240.2000

RIK OLSON

**62** **Mission San Juan Capistrano** Founded in 1776 by **Father Junipero Serra,** this simple adobe (illustrated above) is one of the oldest churches in California. In 1796 Indian laborers under the charge of a Mexican stonemason began a grand stone church that was completed in 1806, only to be destroyed by an earthquake six years later. Instead of rebuilding the monumental stone structure, services resumed in the older adobe church. In the 1890s the **Landmarks Club** saved the adobe from destruction, and in the 1920s it underwent major restoration. The famous swallows that return to Capistrano each 19 March, St. Joseph's Day, are cliff swallows that build their gourdlike nests in the broken arches of the ruins of the stone church. ♦ Admission. Daily 8:30AM-5PM. Camino Capistrano at Ortega Hwy, San Juan Capistrano. 248.2049

**62** **Capistrano Depot** $$$ Take Amtrak direct from Union Station to this refurbished train station, where lunches and dinners feature dishes from the best of the old railroad lines, and jazz music accompanies drinks in the boxcar bar. ♦ American ♦ M-Th 11:30AM-2:30PM, 5-9PM; F-Sa 11:30AM-2:30PM, 5-10PM; Su 10AM-2:30PM. 26701 Verdugo St, San Juan Capistrano. 496.8181

**62** **San Juan Capistrano Library** The harmonious but slightly tongue-in-cheek use of anachronism is a hallmark of celebrity postmodern architect **Michael Graves,** who designed this 1983 library. The buildings are arranged around an arcaded courtyard, a lovely fountain,

gazebos for reading and resting, and the polychrome interior refer to the nearby Spanish mission. ♦ M-Th 10AM-9PM; F-Sa 10AM-5PM. 31495 El Camino Real, San Juan Capistrano. 493.1752

---

The Rams, a professional football team based in Cleveland, moved to LA in 1947.

# Desert Areas

The Southern California desertscape is a vast region where you can ride dirt bikes on the dunes in Lancaster at the mouth of **Antelope Valley**, bungee-jump off a hot-air balloon in **Perris Valley** near **Riverside**, or wander through its many natural splendors. Sun-worshipping collegians and senior citizens tend to gravitate to **Palm Springs**, a popular weekend getaway once punned as a city of "the newly-wed and the nearly dead." It's also a haven for tennis jocks and golf devotees—and not even the recent earthquakes and occasional tremors ever seem to scare them away. If you're a seeker of spiritual self-discovery or splendid isolation, however, visit **Joshua Tree National Monument** located between Riverside and **San Bernardino**, where you can feel free—or lost—among the prickly yuccas.

## Antelope Valley

At the north of LA County is arid high desert, sparsely populated and undeveloped, providing a nearby escape from urban claustrophobia.

**1 Vasquez Rocks County Park** The surrealistic tumble of lacy sandstone rocks, some several hundred feet high, are great for climbing. The area is an outcropping of the San Andreas Fault and is named for the famous 19th-century bandit, **Tiburcio Vasquez**, who used it as one of his numerous hideouts. ♦ Free. Escondido Canyon Rd (off Hwy 14)

**2 Antelope Valley California Poppy Reserve** Two thousand acres have been set aside for the preservation of the golden poppy the California state flower. During the spring, the reserve is carpeted with a solid blanket of flowers. ♦ Free. Open Mar-May only. 17 miles W of Lancaster (off Hwy 138)

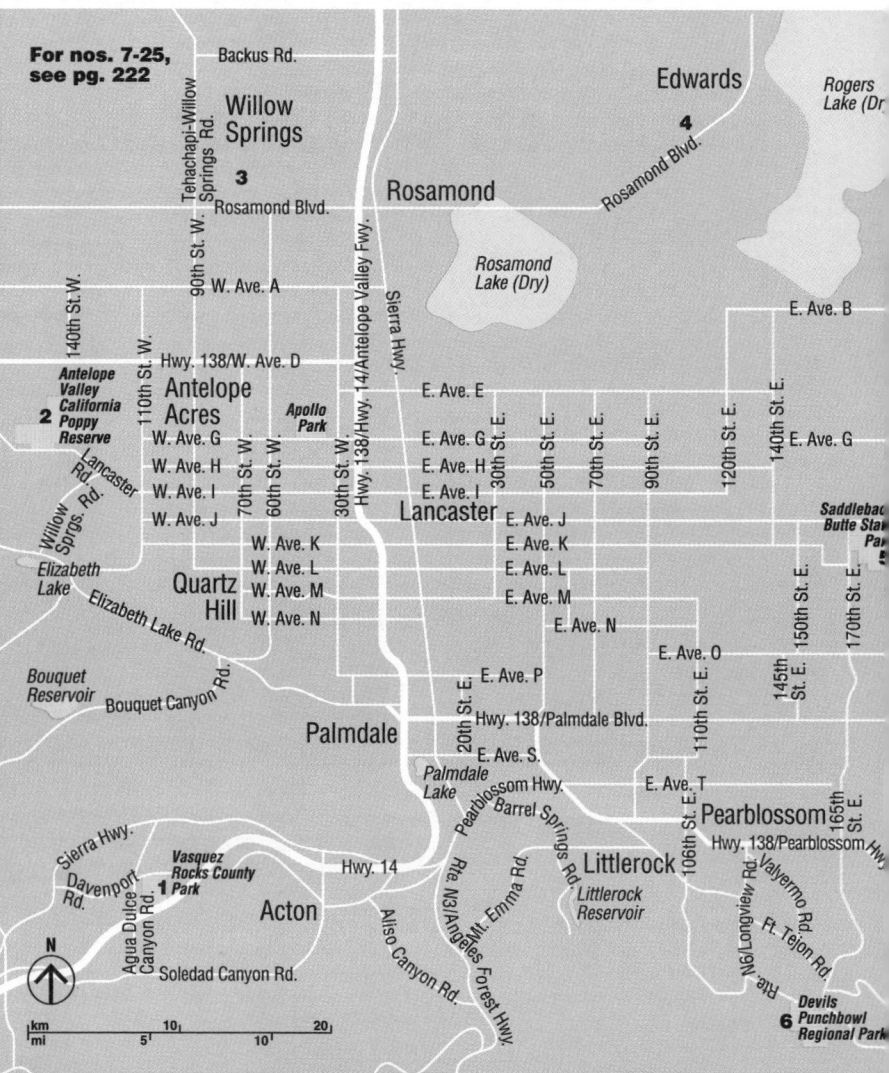

For nos. 7-25, see pg. 222

**3 Willow Springs Raceway** This is one of the best tracks in America for watching top car and motorcycle racing year-round. You can see the entire one-mile track from almost any point. Light refreshments are available. And weekend races last all day long. ♦ Admission. Take the Rosamond exit off Hwy 14 north of Lancaster. 805/256.2471

**4 Edwards Air Force Base** This is the place to see the space shuttle land on the dry surface of **Rogers Lake**. ♦ Free. Daily tours 10:15AM, 1:15PM, except on Federal holidays and during shuttle operation. Rosamond Blvd (off Hwy 14), follow the signs. 805/258.3460

**5 Saddleback Butte State Park** Native chaparral can be seen on a sandstone bluff here. There is also a magnificent stand of Joshua trees, bizarrely shaped plants that are, improbably, members of the lily family. ♦ Admission. Daily 24 hours. 170th St (off California Hwy 138). 805/942.0662

**6 Devil's Punchbowl Regional Park** Located in the high desert area near Pearblossom, the rocky landscape of this 1,310-acre county park is rich in native plants and includes a number of hiking trails. The Punchbowl is a natural depression in a slope of tumbled boulders. The park also includes a lovely stream, the size of which varies greatly with the season, ringed with willows and other water-loving plants. ♦ Free. Daily sunrise to sunset. 2800 Devil's Punchbowl Rd, Pearblossom. 805/944.2743

# San Bernardino and Riverside Counties

To the east of Los Angeles is a vast area, part desert, part mountain, into which humankind has introduced some of the ugliest developments and the worst smog in America. Despite these atrocities, however, there are some things worth seeing here, as outlined in the listings below.

**7 Mount Baldy** Ski Mount Baldy in winter or hike it in summer. By lift or on foot, it's over 10,000 feet to the top and worth it for the view. ♦ Turn off San Bernardino Fwy and follow the signs to Mount Baldy Village. 909/982.2829, 818/335.1251

**8 Sycamore Inn** ★$$$ Built on the site of a historic stagecoach stop, the restaurant continues an old tradition of warm hospitality and service. Prime rib, a huge stone fireplace, and wingback chairs warm the atmosphere. ♦ American ♦ M-Th 11:30AM-2:30PM, 5-10PM; F-Sa 11:30AM-2:30PM, 5-11PM; Su 10AM-2:30PM, 3-10PM. 8318 Foothill Blvd, Rancho Cucamonga. 909/982.1104

**9 Ontario International Airport** This fast-growing alternative to LAX offers 10 major and three commuter airlines. There is long- and short-term parking, plus several privately operated parking lots outside the airport. Public transportation to the surrounding areas is limited. Local hotels operate free shuttles to and from the airport. Baggage claim areas offer information kiosks on local hotel pickups, car

rentals, and shuttle services, including **Inland Express** (909/626.6599) and **SuperShuttle** (714/973.1100). Current terminal expansion and construction may cause some delay, so call ahead. The airport is located about 40 miles east of LA, and 30 miles west of San Bernardino, northwest of Riverside, between the San Bernardino (I-10) and Pomona (I-60) freeways. ♦ Take I-60 (Pomona Fwy) and exit off Grove Ave. 909/988.2700

**10 San Bernardino** There's a city hall (300 N. D Street) designed by **Cesar Pelli**, and to the west on the old Route 66, a marvelous folly: the **Wigwam Village Highway Hotel** (2728 W. Foothill Boulevard, just off the San Bernardino Freeway).

**10 Bobby Ray's Texas BBQ** ★$ Ribs, chicken, and links are slowly cooked in a smoky oven and served with a zesty sauce. ♦ American ♦ W-Th 11AM-8PM; F-Sa 11AM-10PM. 1657 W. Baseline St, San Bernardino. 909/885.9177

*Knickerbocker Mansion*

**11 Big Bear Lake** At 9,000 feet and surrounded by forests, Big Bear Lake has a tranquility that **Lake Arrowhead,** walled off by home sites and full of ear-shattering speedboats, now lacks. You can stay at **Gold Mountain Manor** (909/585.6997), where **Clark Gable** and **Carole Lombard** spent their honeymoon, or at the historic **Knickerbocker Mansion** (illustrated above; 909/866.8221). Hearty German dinners are served at **George & Sigi's Knusperhauschen** (909/585.8640). ♦ Off Hwy 330

"People here still believe. The sun comes out every day and smacks them in the face and they march off gamely to face insurmountable odds. Los Angeles may be the most renewable city in the world."

    **Tom Shales,** *Washington Post* television critic

In 1890 the Santa Fe Railway offered a free train ticket from anywhere east of the Rockies to anyone who purchased property valued at $500 in Lordsburg, now known as LaVerne, California, which is east of Los Angeles.

**12 Mission Inn** $$$ It's difficult to imagine that a two-story, 13-room adobe house built in 1876 became the centerpiece of Riverside's historic downtown, an eclectic ensemble of Mission Revival, Victorian, and Beaux Arts architecture styles. The vision of **Frank Miller,** the inn itself represents many design influences and was inspired by Miller's penchant for travel and collecting. In its golden era, the hotel flourished with a celebrated guest registry, from aviation pioneers **Amelia Earhart** and **Charles Lindbergh** to industry barons **Andrew Carnegie** and **Henry Ford.** But the inn rapidly declined after Miller's death in 1935, and it was dangerously close to demolition until the inn was rescued by the **Riverside Redevelopment Agency.** Furthe[r] protection was guaranteed when the inn entered the **National Register of Historic Places** in 1977. **ELS/Elbasani & Logan** led the painstaking renovation process, which involved extensive seismic upgrading and interior resto[-] ration. Within the 240 guest rooms and 36 suites are several unique architectural elements, some with domed ceilings, wrought iron balconies, tile floors, and leaded-glass windows. There are also two wedding chapels featuring a 17th-century altar (the **Nixons** were married here). The inn has an outdoor swimming pool and a spa, too. ♦ 3649 Seventh St, Riverside. 909/784.0300; fax 909/683.1342

**12 California Museum of Photography** **Stanley Saitowitz** remodeled this downtown Kress store in 1990 to house this photography collec[-] tion, which rivals those of Eastman House and the Smithsonian. Director **Jonathan Green** presents a lively program of exhibitions and events. Researchers may use the study center. ♦ W-Sa 11AM-5PM; Su noon-5PM. 3824 Main St, Riverside. 909/784.3686 (recording), 909/787.4787 (office)

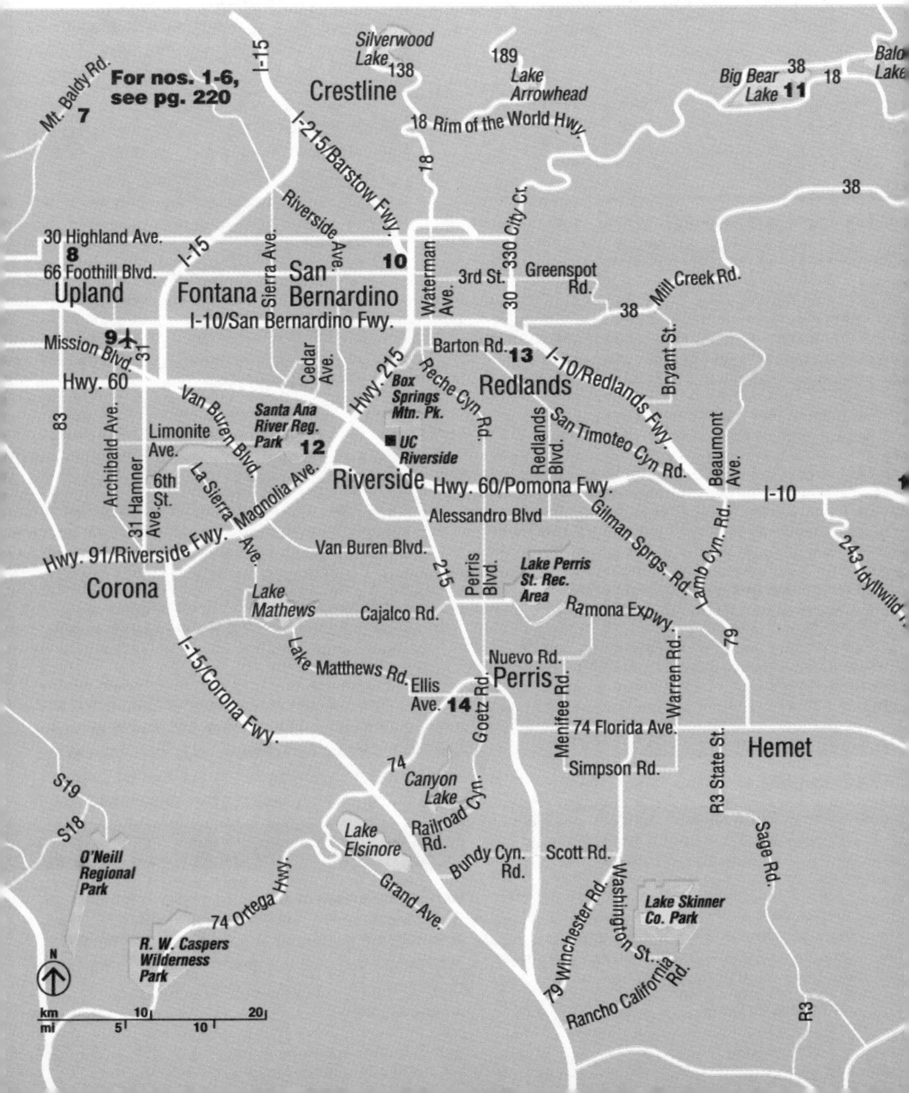

For nos. 1-6, see pg. 220

Mt. Baldy Rd.
**7**
Silverwood Lake 138
189 Lake Arrowhead
Big Bear 38 18
Lake 11
Balo Lake
Crestline
I-15
I-215/Barstow Fwy.
18 Rim of the World Hwy.
18
Riverside Ave.
330 City Ct.
38
30 Highland Ave.
**8**
66 Foothill Blvd.
**Upland**
I-15
Sierra Ave.
**San Bernardino**
**10**
Waterman Ave.
3rd St.
330
30
Greenspot Rd.
Mill Creek Rd.
38
**Fontana**
I-10/San Bernardino Fwy.
Mission Blvd.
**9**
Hwy. 60
31
Cedar Ave.
Hwy. 215
Barton Rd.
Reche Cyn. Rd.
**13**
**Redlands**
I-10/Redlands Fwy.
Bryant St.
83
Archibald Ave.
Van Buren Blvd.
Limonite Ave.
**Santa Ana River Reg. Park**
Box Springs Mtn. Pk.
San Timoteo Cyn. Rd.
Redlands Blvd.
Beaumont Ave.
I-10
**12**
6th St.
31 Hamner Ave.
La Sierra Ave.
Magnolia Ave.
■ **UC Riverside**
**Riverside**  Hwy. 60/Pomona Fwy.
Gilman Sprgs. Rd.
Lamb Cyn. Rd.
243 Idyllwild
Hwy. 91/Riverside Fwy.
**Corona**
Alessandro Blvd
Van Buren Blvd.
215
Perris Blvd.
Lake Perris St. Rec. Area
Ramona Expwy.
Warren Rd.
79
R3 State St.
**Hemet**
Lake Mathews
Cajalco Rd.
Nuevo Rd.
**Perris**
Menifee Rd.
74 Florida Ave.
I-15/Corona Fwy.
Lake Matthews Rd.
Ellis Ave.
**14**
Goetz Rd.
Simpson Rd.
Sage Rd.
S19
74
Canyon Lake
Railroad Cyn. Rd.
S18
O'Neill Regional Park
Lake Elsinore
Bundy Cyn. Rd.
Scott Rd.
Winchester Rd.
Washington St.
Lake Skinner Co. Park
R3
74 Ortega Hwy.
R. W. Caspers Wilderness Park
Grand Ave.
79
Rancho California Rd.

N

km   10   20
mi 5   10

**12 Riverside Art Museum** In this 1929 **Julia Morgan**-designed structure are several gallery spaces that showcase the full gamut of artwork, from historical exhibits to works of contemporary Southern California artists. Located within the museum's courtyard is **A Moveable Feast,** a charming cafe serving light fare for lunch. There's also a gift shop. ♦ Admission. Museum: M-F 10AM-5PM; Sa 10AM-4PM. Cafe: M-F 11:30AM-1:30PM. 3425 Seventh St, Riverside. 909/684.7111

**12 Riverside Municipal Museum** This Renaissance Revival building contains several exhibits on local and natural history, including a variety of flora and fauna, birds, and a gallery devoted to the city's citrus industry. ♦ Free. Tu-F 9AM-5PM; Sa-Su 1-5PM. 3720 Orange St, Riverside. 909/782.5273

**13 Kimberly Crest House and Gardens** The flamboyant 1897 château features Tiffany glass, formal gardens, lily ponds, and citrus groves recalling the city's heyday. ♦ Admission. Tours: Th-Su 1-4PM every 30 minutes. 1325 Prospect Dr (at Highland Ave), Redlands. 909/792.2111

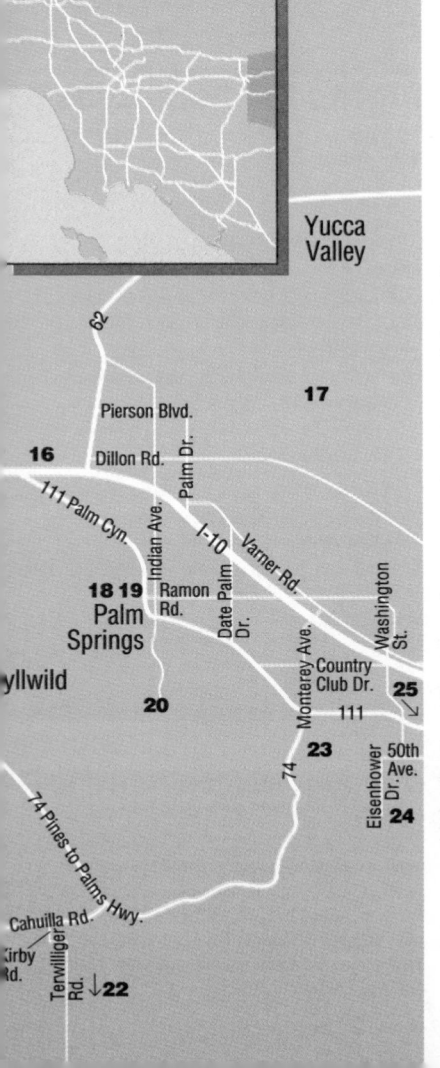

**13 Redlands** An architectural gem discovered during the early citrus-farming period, Redlands is notable for the Tuscan-style loggia of the **Santa Fe Railroad Station** (located on Orange Street, south of Pearl); the picturebook 1890 **Morey House** (140 Terracina Boulevard, 909/793.7970), which is a bed-and-breakfast inn and is open for tours on Sunday from noon to 3PM; and don't miss the grand Victorian mansions along Olive Street.

## Perris

Real estate and railway development helped establish the town of Perris in 1882. It was named after **Fred T. Perris,** the chief engineer of the California Southern Railroad line, which stretched from San Diego to Riverside. The city prospered in the wool trade, however, fortunes eventually soured for its inhabitants in the 1890s when the water system failed to keep up with the demand, and many residents fled westward toward Riverside.

**14 Orange Empire Railway Museum** This museum displays more than 150 steam locomotives and streetcars, including some you can even ride. Perris was once a railroad town, and there's a fine surviving train station here. ♦ Free, except for some special events. Daily 9AM-5PM. Train rides: 11AM-5PM. 2201 S. A St, Perris. 909/657.2605 (recording), 909/943.3020 (office)

**14 Perris Valley Airport** You won't find any commercial airlines landing on the runways here. This airport features gliders, hot-air balloons, ultralight planes, and parachuting. ♦ 2091 Goetz Rd. 909/657.3904

## Palm Springs

A smartly casual resort located at the base of **Mount San Jacinto,** Palm Springs is rapidly building itself into extinction. It is the golf capital of the world, sponsoring more than a hundred tournaments annually, as well as a mecca for tennis players, sunbathers, shoppers, and diners. Mineral hot springs have been an attraction here for millennia; the **Agua Caliente Indians** used the natural spas for ritual and medicinal purposes. Soaking and sunning continue today as favorite Palm Springs pastimes, not only in the hot springs, but also in the city's 7,000 swimming pools.

The region is also known for its beneficial climate. The clean air has a light-as-a-feather quality with an average daytime temperature of 88°F (though it can easily reach 120°F in the summer). Humidity is low, and the yearly rainfall averages 5.39 inches. Around town are some remarkable modern desert houses designed by **Richard Neutra** and **John Lautner**. However, avoid the hideously commercialized, traffic-clogged Route 111,

**Desert Areas**

with its succession of lookalike developments. For information on hotels, restaurants, and other attractions in the greater Palm Springs area, call 619/770.9000, 800/96.RESORT; for hotel and condominium reservations in Palm Springs, call 800/472.3788.

**15  Desert Hills Factory Stores** Clever developers have found a way to attract discount shoppers to the remotest corners of Southern California. There are more than 45 factory outlet stores, offering men's and women's apparel, footwear, home furnishings, toys, and leather goods, and they capture the attention of commuters traveling along Interstate 10 to and from Palm Springs. If the kids are bored, treat them to nearby Dinosaur Gardens. ♦ Daily 9AM-8PM. 48650 Seminole Rd, Cabazon. 909/849.6641

**15  Dinosaur Gardens** Claude Bell designed and built the 150-foot-long apatosaurus and matching tyrannosaurus rex, which occupy a garden in the **San Gorgonio Pass,** 18 miles northwest of Palm Springs, on the north side of Interstate 10. ♦ Nominal admission. Children under 10 free. Hours vary, so call before you go. 5800 Seminole Dr, Cabazon. 909/849.8309

**16  Whitewater Canyon** The canyon offers interesting scenery and a trout farm. Rental tackle and bait are available. You can cook your catch on grills in the picnic area. ♦ Off I-10, near Cabazon

**17  Joshua Tree National Monument** A natural wonder just two-and-a-half hours from LA, Joshua Tree is comprised of 870 square miles of beautiful mountain and desert flora. And the granite monoliths around **Hidden Valley** challenge the skills of rock climbers. Campsites are available. ♦ 74485 National Monument Dr, off Rte 62. 619/367.7511

**18  Palm Springs Aerial Tramway** A spectacular tram ride—the largest single-span lift in the world—travels to an altitude of 8,516 feet on **Mount San Jacinto** for a fantastic view of the surrounding area. At the top is a bar, restaurant, shops, and 54 miles of hiking trails. The cars run every 30 minutes. ♦ Summer: M-F 10AM-9PM; Sa-Su 8AM-9PM. Winter: Daily 10AM-8PM. N. Palm Canyon and Tramway Rd. 619/325.1391 (recording), 619/325.1449 (office). Camping by permit only at **Mount San Jacinto State Park and Wilderness.** Information and reservations: 909/659.2607

**19  Palm Springs Desert Museum** This large cultural facility displays permanent collections and changing exhibitions of contemporary and historical art. There is a fine collection of more than 1,300 American Indian artifacts. ♦ Admission. Tu-F 10AM-4:30PM; Sa-Su 10AM-5PM. 101 Museum Dr. 619/325.0189, 619/325.7186

**20  Indian Canyons** Andreas, Murray, and Palm canyons offer large and unusual rock formations, good hiking trails, and a stand of majestic **Washingtonian Palms** believed to be almost 2,000 years old. ♦ S. Palm Canyon Dr

**21  Idyllwild** A community nestled in mile-high mountains, Idyllwild has tall stands of pines, a tumbled rock formation for climbing, and trails for hiking in summer and cross-country skiing in winter. Drive-in campgrounds for overnight stays are located within Idyllwild and **Stone Creek** parks. ♦ Reservations: 800/444.7275 (ask for C6161 for Idyllwild camp; C6162 for Stone Creek camp)

**22  Anza Borrego Desert** This 470,000-acre state park is a well-maintained desert preserve surrounded with an unusual number of flora and fauna varieties. The striking geological formations resemble a miniature Grand Canyon. ♦ Take Corona Fwy to Hwy 79. 619/767.4205. Park information 619/767.5311

**23  Living Desert Reserve** This 1,200-acre desert interpretive center contains nature trails, a botanical garden, a visitor center, and a gift shop/bookshop. Group tours are available. ♦ Admission. Daily 9AM-5PM. Closed 16 June to 1 Sept. 47-900 Portola Ave, Palm Desert. 619/346.5694

**24  Lake Cahuilla** The lake is great for fishing, swimming, boating, and picnicking. ♦ Daily 6AM-7PM. Off I-10 (east) 25 miles south of Palm Springs in Indio. 619/564.4712

**25  Salton Sea** Swimming, boating, and water skiing are available at this 38-mile-long inland sea, which lies 235 feet below sea level. A **National Wildlife Refuge** is located at the southern end. The **Visitors Center** has wildlife exhibitions and offers tourist information. ♦ Off Hwy 111. 619/394.4112

# Sights for Sore Eyes

On a clear day in LA (granted, that's a rarity) you may not be able to see *forever* in this city so famous for smog, but you can get some great views from these vantage points:

- The Los Angeles basin from Griffith Park Observatory
- Century City from the San Diego Freeway (I-405) transition southbound to the Santa Monica Freeway (I-10) eastbound
- Santa Monica Bay from Toppers restaurant in the Radisson Huntley Hotel in Santa Monica
- Whales, dolphin schools, and San Nicolas Island from the cliffs of Malibu
- Airplanes landing and taking off from Los Angeles International Airport from the observation deck of the Theme building
- Downtown Los Angeles from the Tower Restaurant in the Transamerica building
- The Los Angeles basin and the Hollywood Bowl from Mulholland Drive between Outpost Drive and Cahuenga Boulevard
- The Westside, Century City, and the San Gabriel Mountains from the rooftop parking garage of Westside Pavilion shopping mall
- Palos Verdes Peninsula on the South Bay Bicycle Trail southbound from Playa del Rey
- The San Fernando Valley from Fryman Canyon's overlook lookout on Mulholland Drive

The oldest route in California, the Indian Bear Trail, was renamed El Camino Real by the Spaniards and later formed the route of what is now the Ventura Highway (Interstate 101).

## rry Norris

ntemporary Art Consultant,
rry Norris Contemporary Art

anged as a series of pavilions with gardens and
rtyards, the dazzling **Cerritos Center for Perform-**
**Arts** provides a wondrous theater experience.

**Gas Company** tower is a supremely elegant,
histicated, and intelligent addition to the down-
vn skyline. I particularly appreciate the insistence
fine, detailed craftsmanship.

e lobby of the **Regent Beverly Wilshire Hotel**
tures a soothing dining experience in a luxurious
ng-room setting.

n Sedlar's **Bikini** restaurant is an adventurous
roach to a pancultural, global cuisine—all in a
matic interior by designer Cheryl Brantner.

ry exhibition in **Angles Gallery** on Main Street in
nta Monica is a quietly satisfying experience.

## iro Shimizu

vertising Designer/Art Director, T&S Associates

za Bakery at Yaohan Plaza (at First and Alameda
eets) makes the best thick-sliced Japanese bread.
great for morning toast and green-tea mousse,
awberry shortcake, and chestnut cake; it also has
e tables and you can sit and watch the pedestrians
ittle Tokyo walk by.

ross from the bakery is **Asahi Bookstore,** which
ers a great selection of Japanese books, maga-
es, art books, and literature, as well as children's
oks and learning materials for foreigners who want
learn Japanese.

a Saturday afternoon, shop at **Yaohan Plaza** for
authentic Japanese supermarket experience—and
ff yourself with free samples.

## bert Cates

n Director/Producer, Cates Doty Productions, Inc.;
ducer of the 62nd, 63rd, 64th, & 65th Academy
ards Programs; Dean of the UCLA School of
eater, Film & Television

ving up the **Pacific Coast Highway** and turning
st through any of the wonderful canyons. The
mbination of the view of the Pacific Ocean and the
y drive is breathtaking.

lking through Westwood and the UCLA campus. It
he smallest and the most complete metropolis I've
er seen, with dozens of eating places and shops.
erwards, seeing a film. There are more than 30
vie screens in this idyllic territory.

d finally, eating at **La Bruschetta** on Westwood
ulevard. The food is incomparable, especially a
te of carpaccio followed by a super spaghetti
*ognese*. What a day!

## aig Turner

tropolitan Editor, *Los Angeles Times*

ummer evening's chamber music concert at the
n Anson Ford Amphitheater, located near the
Ilywood Bowl.

A night game at **Dodger Stadium**—and be sure to
catch the view of the downtown skyline from the
parking lot.

Drive the length of **Sunset Boulevard**—from downtown to the Pacific. On it, or just off it, you'll see the
immense diversity of LA: Olvera Street, Chinatown,
Echo Park, Hollywood, the Strip, Beverly Hills, Westwood, UCLA, and the beaches.

If you're here on the right weekend, take the Blue Line
Trolley to the **Long Beach Grand Prix,** where the race
takes place on the city streets. On the way back, stop
off and visit the **Watts Towers.**

Sunday brunch at the **Ritz-Carlton Huntington Hotel**
in Pasadena. It's a trip back to the '30s, and the surrounding neighborhood will remind you of the rich
and dangerous clients Philip Marlow collected in *The*
*Big Sleep.*

Horseback riding in the **Santa Monica Mountains** or
around **Big Bear Lake.**

A burrito at **Yuca's Hut** on Hillhurst.

The galleries, film programs, and free Sunday concerts at the **LA County Museum of Art.**

A spring visit to the **Antelope Valley California Poppy**
**Reserve** in Lancaster for an endless view of a carpet
of flowers.

Anything made at the **La Brea Bakery.**

Reading the Sunday *Los Angeles Times* at a Santa
Monica sidewalk cafe.

## Cesar Pelli

Architect

**Watts Towers** (Rodia)
**Bradbury Building** (Wyman)
**Horatio West Court** (Gill)
**Lovell House** (Neutra)
**Gamble House** (Greene and Greene)
**Eames House** (Eames)
**Barnsdall House** (Frank Lloyd Wright)
**Wayfarers' Chapel** (Lloyd Wright)
**Schindler House** (Schindler)

## Christine and Joachim Splichal

Owners, Patina Restaurant

Playing tennis at the **Los Angeles Tennis Club.**
Walking our dog Coco around **Hollywood Lake.**
Eating sushi at **Katsu.**
Drinking great Burgundies with dinner.
Going to the fish market early in the morning.
Attending old-car auctions and rare-wine auctions.

### Desert Areas

Playing the stock market (this is Joachim's pastime).
Visiting LA's art galleries.

**Restaurants/Clubs:** Red          **Hotels:** Blue
**Shops/ 🍃 Outdoors:** Green          **Sights/Culture:** Black

# Beaches: Northern Tours

**Area:**  A drive up and down the Pacific Coast Highway past some of the loveliest beaches in Los Angeles County

**Mileage:**  53 miles round-trip from the intersection of the Santa Monica Freeway (I-10) and the Pacific Coast Highway (1)

Take the Santa Monica Freeway (I-10) to its end at Santa Monica, where it will merge into the Pacific Coast Highway (1). Go north on this road for the tour. Although much of the beachfront is public, you will notice numerous private homes; many are elaborate residences of the rich and famous. Almost all of the beaches are free and open to the public. A parking fee is charged in lots adjoining beach areas. On summer weekends, parking may be difficult to find. Getting across the Pacific Coast Highway (PCH) on foot or turning around in a car is dangerous; extreme caution is advised.

The first major public beach is **(1) Will Rogers Beach State Park,** named for the famous cowboy humorist. This beach stretches for several miles along the Coast Highway and is well-provided with parking, facilities, and volleyball areas. Surfers congregate along the area opposite Sunset Boulevard.

You may detour up Sunset Boulevard to visit **(2) Will Rogers State Historic Park** or the **(3) Self-Realization Fellowship Lake Shrine.** See page 103.

At the corner of Coastline Drive is the **(4) J. Paul Getty Museum.** For more information, see page 123.

At Topanga Canyon Boulevard, a right turn will take you to the semirural community of **(5) Topanga, Topanga State Park** (see page 124), or a drive to the **(6) San Fernando Valley** over a winding and scenic canyon. For more information, see the "San Fernando Valley" chapter on page 130.

**(7) Malibu** is a long stretch of beach with homes pressed against the ocean edge and dotting the chaparral-covered hills. The area on the right side of the PCH is subject to landslides; you will notice retaining walls holding back the earth. Much of the beach is walled off by the "cottages" of the affluent and famous, but there are about 10 public access paths, with minimal parking, that are posted on the PCH. You also can walk or jog down from the pier. Malibu is one of the most famous of the seaside communities, as much for its residents as for its scenery.

The **(8) Malibu Sportfishing Pier,** located about 10 miles along this route, is a charming spot for surfer-watching and reviving breaths of ocean air.

**Surf Riders State Beach,** located just east of **(9) Malibu Point,** is a favorite with surfers. About 12 miles out, you may take a detour right on Malibu Canyon Road, which traverses the Santa Monica Mountains to the San Fernando Valley, following the edge of a colorful and rugged canyon with some vista turnouts along the way. **(10) Malibu Creek State Park** is located beside this road. This is also the road to **(11) Pepperdine College.**

**(12) Paradise Cove** is located just east of **Point Dume,** approximately 16 miles along this route. It is a sheltered beach with white sand, tumbled sandstone cliffs, and fishing and boat launching facilities. Admission is charged.

**(13) Zuma Beach** is on the west side of Point Dume. This broad, flat beach is one of the most popular, offering volleyball, picnic facilities, easy parking, miles of smooth sand, and good body- and board-surfing.

**(14) Leo Carrillo Beach** is beautiful and secluded, located in a wide cove that is slightly sheltered by rock at either end. The northern portion of the beach is very popular with surfers. Swimmers should go to the center of the cove to avoid underwater rock formations.

Across the Pacific Coast Highway, approximately 26 miles from the start of this tour, is **(15) Point Mugu State Park,** an expanse of rolling hills and sycamore-shaded canyons that is a perfect spot for an easy hike or a picnic. For more information on this park, see the "Malibu/The Canyons" chapter on page 122.

To return, retrace your route on the Pacific Coast Highway to the Santa Monica Freeway.

---

**Area:**  Santa Monica, Ocean Park, Venice, and Marina del Rey, the most popular and colorful of the southland beach areas

**Mileage:**  Four miles round-trip from Santa Monica Pier

The Santa Monica/Marina del Rey area is a compact neighborhood best seen on foot or by bicycle. The use of a car is preferable only to get from neighborhood to neighborhood. The bike path begins just north of the **Santa Monica Pier** and parallels the beach south to **Palos Verdes,** a distance of some 30 miles. A short ride through the marina to **Playa del Rey** is highly recommended. The best walking and skating sites are on **Oceanfront Walk,** between the Santa Monica and Venice piers, and along **Main Street.**

Begin at the **(1) Santa Monica Pier** at Colorado and Ocean avenues in Santa Monica. You might want to stop here for a carousel ride to get into the proper

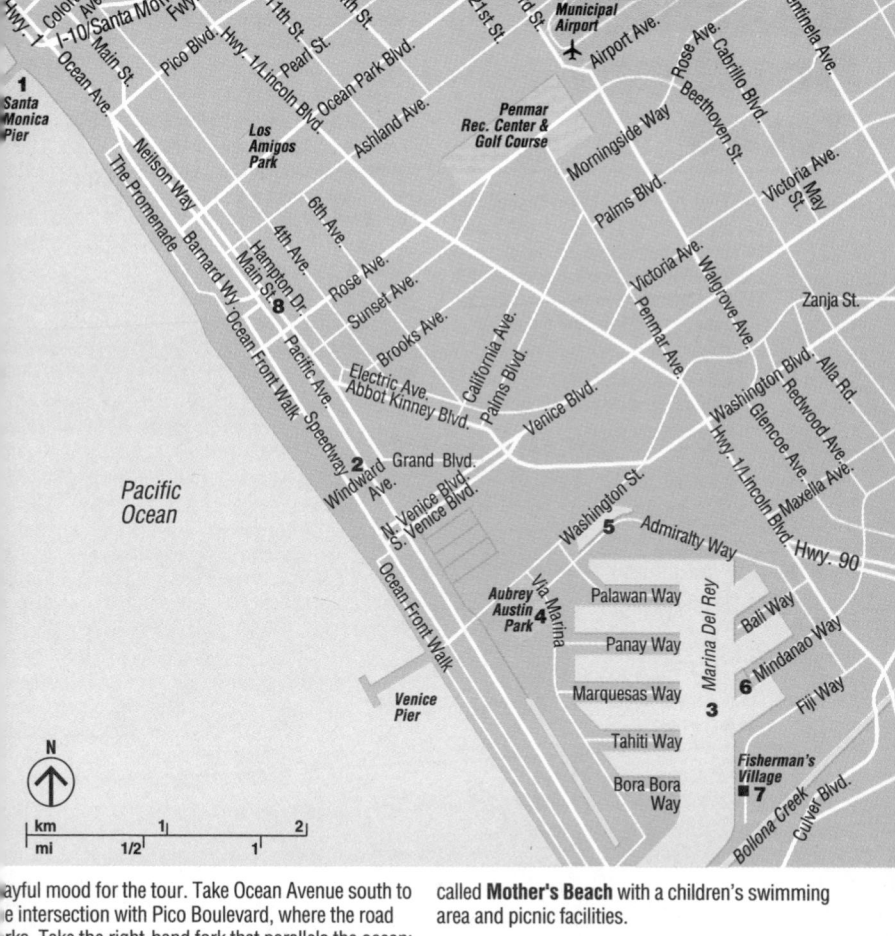

ayful mood for the tour. Take Ocean Avenue south to e intersection with Pico Boulevard, where the road rks. Take the right-hand fork that parallels the ocean; is is Barnard Way. Follow Barnard around to the left ntil it rejoins the former Ocean Avenue, which has een rechristened Neilson Way. Turn right at Neilson nd continue. The street changes names again in the ext block as you enter Venice Beach, becoming Pa-fic Avenue.

ontinue down Pacific past the corner of **(2) Wind-ard Avenue,** the last remnant of old Venice, whose eachfront is now a frenetic mixture of skaters, cy-ists, joggers, entertainers, and assorted eccentrics. ikes and roller skates can be rented here.

t Washington Street, a short stroll takes you to the **enice Pier** for views, fishing, people-watching, and nacks. There are several bicycle-rental shops along is street. Continue down Pacific. You are now enter-g **(3) Marina del Rey,** about three miles from the anta Monica Pier. The Marina section of Pacific takes ou past frayed relics of old Venice: canals, bridges, nd a few disguised oil wells.

t the end of Pacific, where it abuts Via Marina, is a mall promenade area and jetty looking out over the arina del Rey entrance channel. This is a fine place stop and watch the sailboats glide by. Via Marina urves around the entrance channel and enters a ensely built area of apartments and condominiums ntil it reaches Admiralty Way.

t the corner of Admiralty Way and Via Marina is the **4) Aubrey Austin Park,** and a small protected beach

called **Mother's Beach** with a children's swimming area and picnic facilities.

Turn right onto Admiralty. At five-and-a-half miles you will pass the **(5) Bird Sanctuary** on the left and the **Marina City Towers** on the right.

Follow Admiralty to Mindanao Way and turn right. Continue to the end of the street, where you will find the entrance to **(6) Burton Chace Park.** The well-main-tained park has picnic areas, barbecues, soft grassy knolls, rest rooms, and a tower to climb to watch the boats in the marina.

Return to Admiralty and turn right to the next penin-sula, Fiji Way. Go right again to **(7) Fisherman's Vil-lage,** a place for shopping, eating, and strolling.

Follow Fiji back to Admiralty and go left. At the corner of Admiralty and Via Marina, turn right. Go to Washing-ton Street and turn left. Go a few blocks to Pacific and turn right. At Rose Avenue, turn right, go one block to Main Street, and turn left.

**(8) Main Street,** beginning near Marine Street and continuing almost to Pico, is a delightful small shop-ping and dining area. Many of the restaurants along this street have rear patios that face the Pacific Ocean. Park in the city lots west of Main Street. To return to down-

town LA on the Santa Monica Freeway (I-10), follow Main Street to Pico, turn right, and at Lincoln Boulevard, turn left. The freeway intersects Lincoln in two blocks.

# Beaches: Southern Tours

**Area:** The Gold Coast beaches of Orange County from Newport Beach to Laguna Beach, and the relatively new planned community of Irvine; an alternate route leads to Mission San Juan Capistrano

**Mileage:** 150 miles round-trip from the downtown LA civic center

Take the Santa Ana Freeway (I-5) south from civic center; or an alternate route is the San Diego Freeway (I-405). At 34 miles, take the Newport Freeway (Hwy 55) south. Go to the end of the freeway, where it becomes Newport Boulevard, a four- to six-lane street. Continue straight through Costa Mesa into **(1) Newport Beach.**

At 44 miles, get into the left lane and go over the bridge onto the **(2) Newport Peninsula.** You'll notice the yacht anchorage in the **Lido Channel** on your left as you pass over the bridge. Continue on Newport Boulevard, which curves to the left as it follows the peninsula. Opposite the **(3) Newport Pier,** Newport Boulevard becomes Balboa Boulevard.

At Palm Street, turn into the parking lot for a visit to the **(4) Balboa Pier** to enjoy the ocean view. You can also rent roller skates here.

Walk across Balboa Boulevard into the **Fun Zone** for some snacking and a visit to the **(5) Balboa Pavilion.**

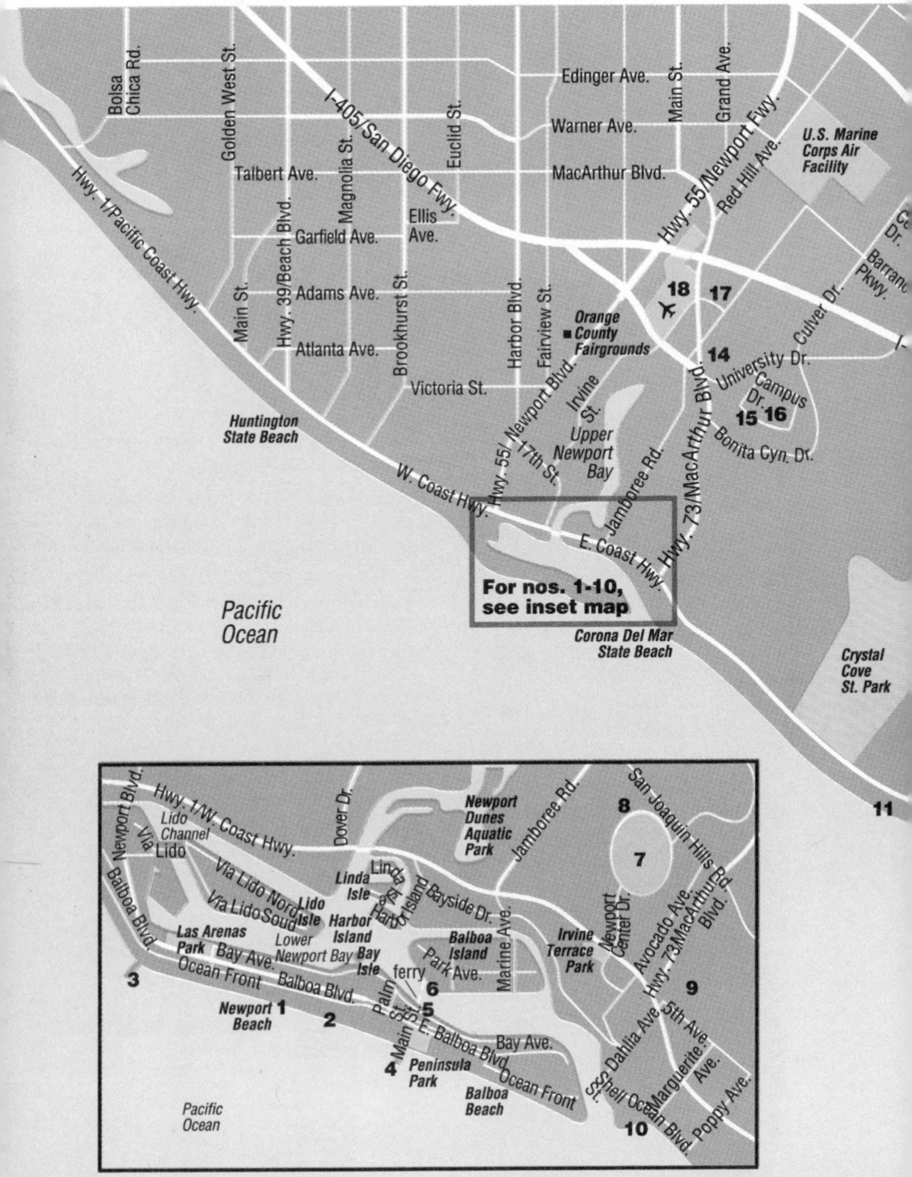

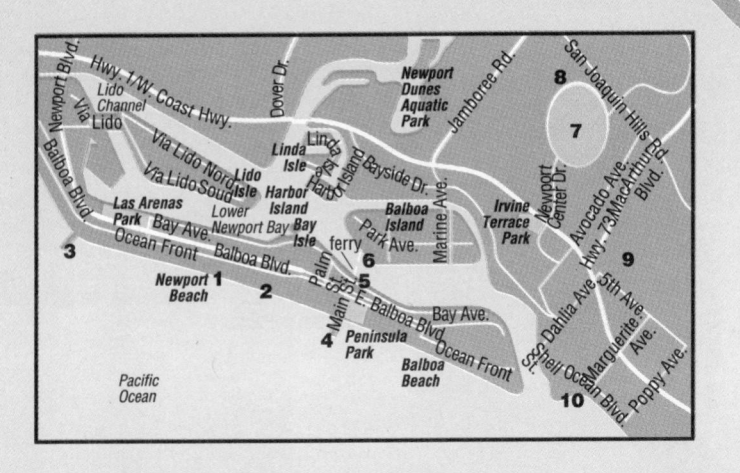

To get to the ferry to **(6) Balboa Island,** follow the signs from the parking lot to the crossing. The three-minute cruise across the **Main Channel** can be made aboard the *Admiral, Commodore,* or *Captain.* When you disembark at Agate Avenue, continue straight for two blocks to Park Avenue. Go right and travel through a neighborhood of shipshape homes to Marine Avenue. Go left on Marine, through the center of the business district, and over Back Bay Channel on a little bridge. Continue straight a short distance to Bayside Drive, veer left, and continue up the hill to the East Coast Highway. Go right, past the **(7) Fashion Island Shopping Center.**

For a detour, turn left at Newport Center Drive and visit the **(8) Newport Harbor Art Museum.**

Continue straight on the East Coast Highway, past the **(9) Sherman Foundation Gardens,** and turn right on

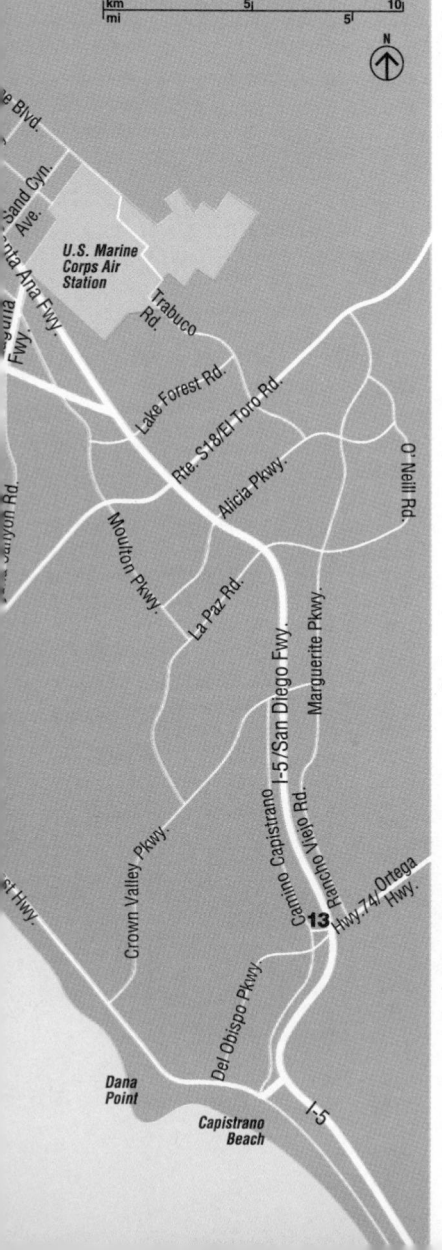

Marguerite Avenue. Go through beautifully manicured residential streets to Ocean Boulevard. Turn left and park near the hilly knoll that tops **(10) Corona del Mar State Beach.** This is a beautiful seaside area, rocky on the south and sandy on the north, with a superb view. There is excellent swimming in the northern waters that are protected by the east jetty of the Newport Harbor entrance.

Follow Ocean to Poppy Avenue and turn left back to the East Coast Highway. Turn right onto Coast Highway and continue south. The stretch between Poppy and Laguna Beach has rolling golden hills coming down to meet the undeveloped beach, giving a last glimpse of what the coast was like prior to the 20th century. **(11) Cameo Cove,** just north of Laguna Beach city limits, is a breathtaking scene of dark rock promontory and emerald-green water.

At approximately 55 miles, you enter **(12) Laguna Beach,** an area known for beautiful scenery and scenic artists. Go left at Forest Avenue. Find a parking spot and spend some time strolling down pleasant shop-lined streets, or cross the Coast Highway to follow the Pacific Ocean along the boardwalk.

To return to LA from this point, go north a short distance on the Coast Highway to Broadway. Go right to Laguna Canyon Road (133), and then to the San Diego Freeway (I-405).

At this point, hardy souls with unflagging energy may wish to continue south to **(13) Mission San Juan Capistrano,** where the famous cliff swallows return annually to this Spanish adobe church. Follow Pacific Coast Highway down to Del Obispo Street, which is just past Dana Point. Go left to Ortega Highway (74). Go right to the mission at the intersection of Ortega Highway and Camino Capistrano. To return to LA from Capistrano, take the San Diego Freeway (I-5) north from its intersection with Ortega Highway.

To continue back up to **(14) Irvine** from Laguna Beach, return north on Pacific Coast Highway to MacArthur Boulevard (Hwy 73). Turn right.

Lovers of trees, education, and/or architecture may wish to detour to the **(15) University of California at Irvine.** From MacArthur, go right on University Drive to Campus Drive. Go right on Campus to Bridge Road. Go right on Bridge to North Circle View Drive, then turn left. The **(16) Administration Building and Visitor Center** are located on the right-hand side of North Circle View Drive.

Meanwhile, the future may be taking shape in the **(17) Irvine Industrial Park,** located on both sides of MacArthur Boulevard. The simple, monolithic shapes of these structures contain businesses whose products vary from computer software to advanced technological systems.

**(18) John Wayne Airport,** located on the left side of MacArthur Boulevard, is a busy commercial and small craft airport. The award-winning terminal designed by **Leason Pomeroy Associates** in 1990 takes its shape from an airplane fuselage: three sleek, parallel vaults with rounded metal roofs.

To return to LA, go to the San Diego Freeway (I-405) off of MacArthur Boulevard and head north.

# Mountain Tours

**Area:** Some of the most scenic but easily driven coastal mountain routes, showing rugged mountains and beautiful ocean views

**Mileage:** Minimum: 47 miles round-trip from Ocean Avenue and the Pacific Coast Highway in Santa Monica

Maximum: 100 miles round-trip with alternate routes from Ocean Avenue and the Pacific Coast Highway

Begin at the Pacific Coast Highway where the Santa Monica Freeway (I-10) ends near the Santa Monica Pier. Follow the Coast Highway north for five-and-a-half miles to Topanga Canyon Boulevard.

Turn right on Topanga Canyon Boulevard. The narrow two-lane highway winds past a sycamore-shaded creek at the base of chaparral-covered cliffs. As the road ascends into the hills you will see spectacular rock formations and abruptly tilted cliffs. The 10,000-acre **Topanga State Park** features 18 miles of bicycle trails and 32 miles of hiking trails. Camping is permitted through special reservations; call 818/880.0350.

At about 10 miles is the main part of the rustic community of **(1) Topanga.** The narrowness of this winding road sometimes slows traffic, particularly on the weekends.

At 15.2 miles, the road descends to a panoramic view of the San Fernando Valley and the **Simi** and **Chatsworth hills.** This is a good place to stop and appreciate the huge expanse of the valley's wide territory.

At 16.9 miles, turn left on **(2) Mulholland Drive.** A great deal of housing construction is going on in this once rural area.

At this point, carsick travelers or those who wish to make only a short trip can continue straight on Topanga Canyon Road to Woodland Hills and the Ventura Freeway (I-101), which takes you back to LA.

For those who wish to continue this tour, at 17.5 miles, make a left near the Woodland Plaza Shopping Center to continue onto **Mulholland Highway.** The road widens to four lanes near Daguerre Road, but narrows back to two soon afterward.

At about 19 miles, the intersection of Old Topanga Canyon Road and Mulholland Highway is confusing, but continue driving straight ahead and soon a sign will appear confirming that you are indeed on Mulholland Highway.

**(3)** Steep rock, jagged hills, and abrupt terrain become an interesting backdrop for the road around 23.7 miles. Breathtakingly beautiful scenery and rock formations with all the drama of an old Western movie—probably because many were filmed out here—begin at around 25.5 miles.

At 27 miles is a stoplight intersection for Las Virgenes Road. Turn left. The two-lane highway passes rugged wide-open vistas of classic western scenery and horseback-riding trails. At Mulholland and Malibu Canyon Road is **Malibu Creek State Park,** a 7,000-acre park featuring more than 15 miles of hiking and equestrian trails; for more information on this park, call 818/880.0350.

At 28.7 miles is **(4) Tapia Park,** a wilderness park along Malibu Creek with great hiking paths through fields and wooded areas. This is an ideal place for picnicking and relaxing.

At about 30 miles, a series of geologically wondrous gorges and steep valley formations begins. Many turnouts provide a chance to stop and examine the intricate stratification of rock layers, all tilted upward in various directions.

At 32.5 miles, several palm trees announce the **(5) Hughes Research Laboratories,** where the first practical laser was built. The lab is at the peak of a hill and just at the other side is a spectacular ocean view.

The road to **(6) Pepperdine University** soon appears. The intersection of the Pacific Coast Highway and Malibu Canyon Road is at 33.4 miles. Turn left to return to Santa Monica.

Alternate routes:

At the intersection of Las Virgenes and Mulholland Highway, continue straight on Mulholland and go west past **(7) Malibu Lake.**

At the intersection of N9 or Kanan Road and Mulholland Highway, a detour can be made through the rugged scenery of **Latigo Canyon** by going south or left for a short while on N9 and then turning left on **(8) Latigo Canyon Road.**

Mulholland Highway (23) loses its state highway designation to **(9) Decker Road.** You can follow Decker (now state 23) south to the ocean from the **(10)** intersection, or continue west on Mulholland, skirting the Ventura County line until Mulholland takes you onto

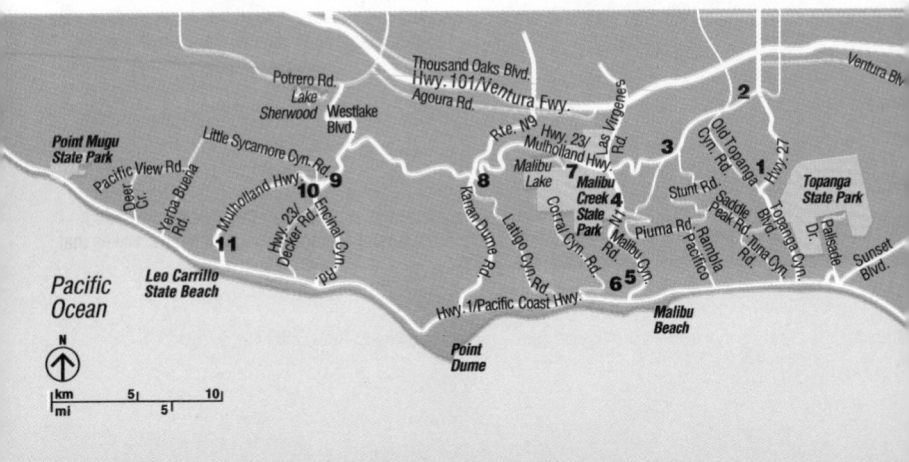

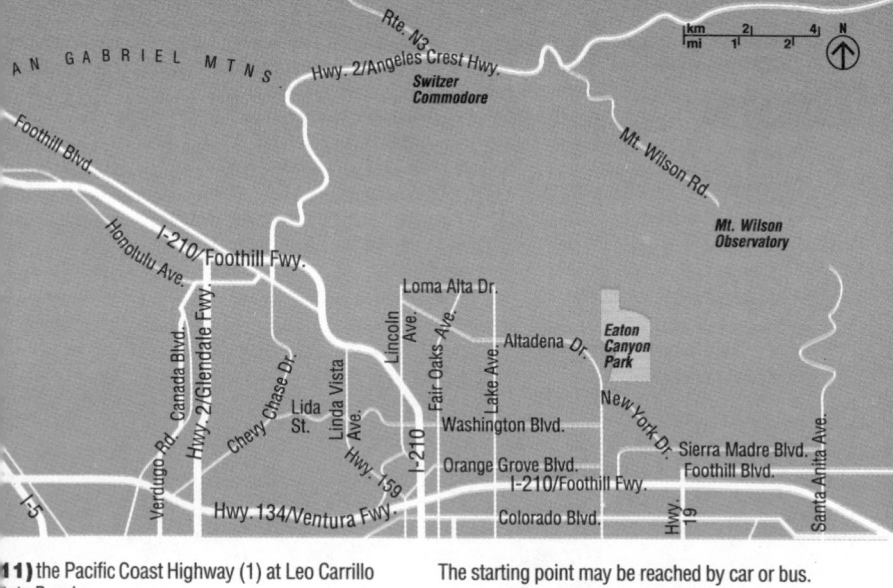

**1 1 )** the Pacific Coast Highway (1) at Leo Carrillo State Beach.

Follow the Pacific Coast Highway back south to Santa Monica. For more information, call the National Park Service at 818/597.9192 or the Santa Monica Mountains National Recreation Area at 818/597.9192.

**Area:** A vigorous driving and hiking expedition that traverses the San Gabriels from La Canada to the Antelope Valley, with a hiking stop at the Arroyo Seco Cascades

**Mileage:** 60 miles by car from the intersection of Routes 210 and 2 to the intersection of Routes 14 and 210; and a four-mile hike on foot

From the Foothill Freeway (I-210), take the Angeles Crest Highway (2) north into the mountains for 10.5 miles. At approximately a half-mile past the intersection of Route 2 and the Angeles Forest Highway (N3), turn right off Route 2 at the Switzer Campground sign. Follow the road a winding quarter-mile and park near the picnic area, following the stream for one mile to the **Commodore Switzer Trail Camp.** For information, call **Clear Creek** station at 818/797.9959. The foot trail then crosses the stream, whose waters abruptly drop off into a 50-foot fall. Follow the trail uphill to a fork. Take the left branch of the fork into the gorge beneath the falls. To return, retrace your steps. Drive back to the intersection of Route 2 and Angeles Forest Highway (N3). Go right for 30 minutes to the intersection with the Antelope Valley Freeway (14). Go west to the Foothill Freeway (I-210), a distance of 20 miles.

**Area:** Hikes within Eaton Canyon, ranging from the one-eighth-mile Arroyo Nature Trail, through the natural rock pools of Upper Eaton Canyon, to a 16-mile overnight jaunt to Mt. Wilson; for information, call 818/398.5420 and see the map above

**Mileage:** 30 miles by car round-trip from the Foothill Freeway (I-210); and a 1/2- to 16-mile hike by foot, depending on the route taken

The starting point may be reached by car or bus.

**Bus:** Take No. 79 north on Olive Street in downtown LA to the intersection of Huntington Drive and San Gabriel Boulevard. Transfer to No. 264. Get off at New York and Altadena drives. Walk one block north on the east side of Altadena to the gate of Eaton Canyon Park. For information, call 800/252.7433.

**Car:** From the Foothill Freeway (I-210), turn on Altadena Drive to No. 1750, which is the entrance to Eaton Canyon Park. Go through the gates to the **Robert M. McCurdy Nature Center,** a quarter-mile down the path. The center has brochures for the self-guided **Arroyo Nature Trail,** as well as information on the other trails in the park and canyon. Among the possibilities are a half-mile hike to **Eaton Falls;** a three-mile climb to the **Henninger Flat Campground and Ranger Station;** a three-mile excursion to the natural stone pools in upper **Eaton Canyon;** and for those who bring their pajamas, a 16-mile overnight to **Mount Wilson.**

The San Gabriel Mountains tower above the city to the north. A century ago, naturalist **John Muir** described them as among the "most rigidly inaccessible" he had ever trod. Today, these guardians are laced with trails and roads. The visitor who tours by car will see spectacular vistas from the Angeles Crest and Angeles Forest highways, but the serenity and majesty of the range is revealed only to those who explore on foot. Roads can be blocked by snow in winter. Information and maps are available from the **Angeles National Forest San Gabriel Canyon** entrance station (Highway 39 and Baldy Road; 818/969.1012), or from the **National Park Service** (30401 Agoura Road, #100, Agoura Hills; 818/597.9192). Hikers are no longer required to have entry permits, but are strongly urged to advise friends of their itinerary in case of an accident. All visitors should bring water and take special precautions during the fire season—from June to December.

Don't touch the shiny clusters of trilobed serrated leaves; they are poison oak. And the rattlesnakes that

live in this wilderness strike only to protect themselves, so if you leave them alone, they will leave you alone.

# Architecture Tours

**LA has always been a mecca for architects** with a strong sense of individualism and style. The following four driving tours take you around LA's best architecture, from high rises to houses, from the cultural to the fantastical.

The architectural heritage of Los Angeles is rich and varied. This day-long pilgrimage will take you on a broad sweep of the area to see some of LA's best landmarks. For this tour, follow the numbers on the map that are colored in red.

This is a rewarding journey and—in typical LA fashion—you hardly have to leave your car to make the tour. The trip is approximately 46 miles long and takes at least five hours. Please bear in mind that the private residences should be viewed only from the street.

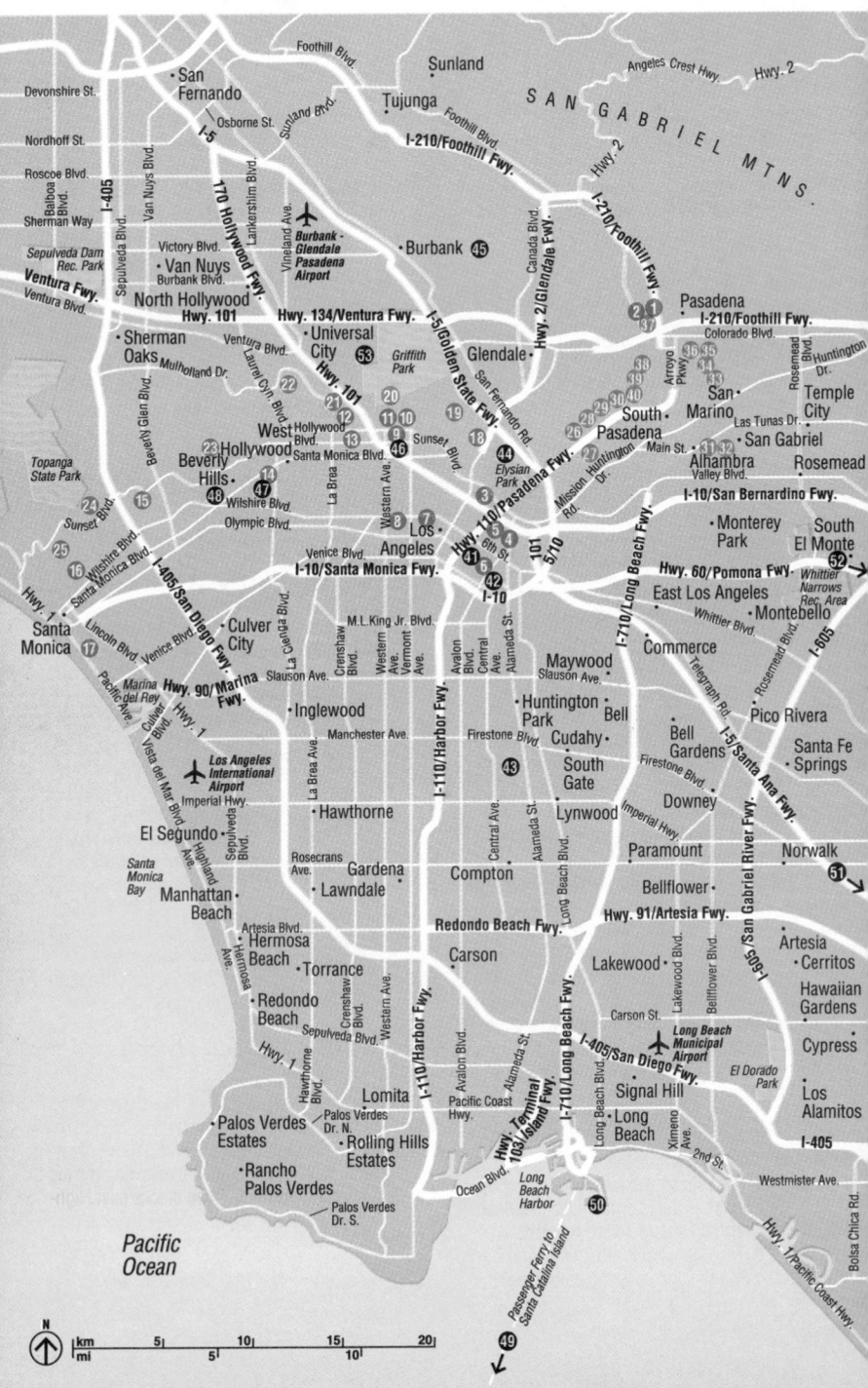

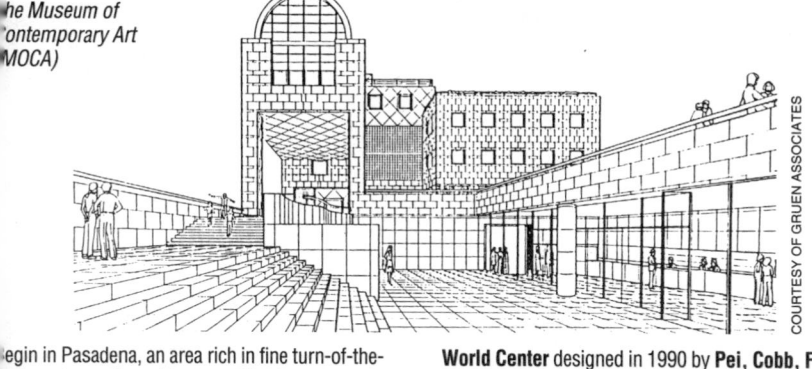

the Museum of
Contemporary Art
(MOCA)

begin in Pasadena, an area rich in fine turn-of-the-century domestic architecture. Slightly north of the interchange of the Long Beach (I-710) and the Ventura (134) freeways, or north from the Orange Grove Boulevard exit of the Pasadena Freeway (110), is the (1) Gamble House at 4 Westmoreland Place, a large vacation bungalow designed in 1908 by Pasadena craftsman architects **Charles** and **Henry Greene** (it's open Thursday through Sunday from noon to 3PM). All along (2) **Arroyo Terrace,** the street to the left of the Gamble House, other houses by Greene and Greene can be seen.

Take Orange Grove Boulevard south to the Pasadena Freeway (110). Head south on the freeway, stay to the right, and connect with the Hollywood Freeway (101) going north. Exit at Echo Park-Glendale Boulevard and turn right at the end of the exit onto Bellevue Avenue. Turn left (north) on Edgeware Road East and turn left again on Carroll Avenue. This is the (3) **Carroll Avenue Historic District:** the 1300 block of Carroll Avenue, lined with late Victorian homes.

Take Edgeware south to Temple Street, turn left (east), continue into downtown and turn right on Broadway. At Third Street on the left is the (4) **Bradbury Building,** which must be seen from the inside to appreciate its interior court. Saturday tours of the lobby are conducted by the LA Conservancy. For more information, call 213/623.2480. To continue the tour, take a right on Third, drive through the tunnel, turn right on Flower Street, and stay left at the fork. The vacant land on your right is the site for the (5) **Walt Disney Concert Hall** designed by **Frank Gehry** (the expected completion date is 1996). Take a right on First Street and a right on Grand Avenue. On your left at 250 Grand Avenue is the (5) **Museum of Contemporary Art (MOCA),** the first major United States project by internationally renowned Japanese architect **Arata Isozaki.** Continue to Fifth Street, and on your left (555 W. Fifth Street) is the (5) **Gas Company Tower** designed in 1991 by **Skidmore, Owings & Merrill/R. Keating, Designer.** On your right, at the southwest corner is the 1926 Beaux Arts landmark (5) **Central Library** by **Bertram Goodhue** and **Carleton Winslow, Sr.** Turn left on Sixth Street and left on Olive Street. On your right is (5) **Pershing Square,** where a $14 million renovation designed by **Ricardo Legorreta** and **Hanna Olin** is underway (and scheduled to be completed by late 1993). On your left is the restored Italianate Beaux Arts (5) **Biltmore Hotel** constructed by **Schultze & Weaver** in 1923. Turn left on Fifth Street and you'll see the **Frank Stella Mural** adjacent to the Gas Company Tower.

Continue to 633 W. Fifth Street and on your right is the tallest building in LA, the 73-story (5) **First Interstate**

**World Center** designed in 1990 by **Pei, Cobb, Freed/ Harold Fredenburg.** Next door are **Lawrence Halprin's** 1990 **Bunker Hill steps.** Continue west and on your right you will see the cylindrical towers of the (5) **Westin Bonaventure Hotel** (404 S. Figueroa Street) designed by **John Portman** in 1976. Turn left on Flower Street (south), right on Eighth Street (west), and right on Figueroa Street. On your left at 777 S. Figueroa you'll see the (6) **777 Tower** designed in 1991 by **Cesar Pelli & Associates.** At the northwest corner of Figueroa Street and Wilshire Boulevard you'll find the (6) **Sanwa Bank Plaza** (601 S. Figueroa) designed in 1991 by **Albert C. Martin & Associates.**

Turn right (west) on Wilshire to see some moderne commercial buildings. Visible at a distance is the tan terra-cotta and green-copper-trimmed tower of the (7) **I. Magnin Bullocks Wilshire Department Store** at 3050 Wilshire Boulevard, which was designed by **John** and **Donald B. Parkinson** in 1929. Farther west is the (8) **Wiltern Center Building** at 3790 Wilshire Boulevard, a zigzag moderne complex of turquoise terra-cotta that includes a theater, shops, and offices and was built in 1931.

Turn right (north) on Western Avenue and turn right (east) at Hollywood Boulevard. Enter Barnsdall Park on the right, before the intersection with Vermont Avenue. Here is **Frank Lloyd Wright's** first Los Angeles project, the (9) **Hollyhock House** constructed in 1917 (tours are offered Tuesday through Sunday at noon, 1PM, 2PM, and 3PM; for more information, call 213/ 662.7272). Return to Hollywood going right (east) and immediately turn left at Vermont Avenue. Turn right on Franklin Avenue (east). Between Myra Avenue and St. George Street is the **Shakespeare Bridge,** a handsome open spandrel adorned with long Gothic arches. Return to a westbound direction on Franklin and turn right at Vermont Avenue. Cross Los Feliz Boulevard, and where Vermont forks, go to the left on Glendower Avenue. At 2607 Glendower Avenue is Wright's stunning concrete-block (10) **Ennis-Brown House** (designed in 1924), with its spectacular setting in the hills.

Return to Vermont and at Franklin Avenue turn right (west). On the right, at 5121 Franklin, is the dramatic (11) **Sowden House** by **Lloyd Wright,** Frank Lloyd Wright's son. Continue on Franklin following the jog to the left at Highland Avenue. Three blocks past Highland Avenue, turn left (south) on Orange Drive and come up the back way to **Meyer and Holler's** extravagant (12) **Grauman's** (now **Mann's**) **Chinese Theatre**

**233**

(designed in 1927), at 6925 Hollywood Boulevard. Turn left onto Hollywood Boulevard to get a better view of it.

Turn right (south) onto Highland and turn left (east) on Sunset Boulevard. At 6671 Sunset Boulevard is the (13) **Crossroads of the World**—international theme shops designed by **Robert Derrah** in 1936 as a tourist attraction. Turn right (south) on Cahuenga Boulevard and right again (west) on Santa Monica Boulevard. Continue on to San Vicente Boulevard and turn left (south). The large blue-and-green glass structures at the corner of San Vicente and Melrose Avenue are the (14) **Pacific Design Center.** The building, with an interior court and shops, was designed in 1975 by **Cesar Pelli** for **Victor Gruen and Associates.**

Return to San Vicente going north to Sunset and turn left (west). Continue on Sunset past the University of California, Los Angeles (UCLA), and turn left at Veteran Avenue. At the first street, turn right on Cashmere Street and right again on Greenfield Avenue. **Rudolph Schindler's** (15) **Tischler House** (designed in 1949), with its angular de Stijl-inspired facade, is at 175 Greenfield Avenue. Take Greenfield to the end of the block and turn left (west) on Sunset. At Bundy Drive turn left (south) and at Montana Avenue turn right. Turn left on 22nd Street. At Washington Avenue and 22nd is the dramatic (16) **Gehry House,** a 1977-1978 remodeling of an older house using corrugated steel, wood, and glass, by architect **Frank Gehry.** Go east on Washington Avenue to 26th Street and turn right. At Broadway turn right and at Ocean Avenue (Neilson Way) turn left. In order to enter the one-way street of Hollister Avenue, take a left turn on Strand Street and right turns on Main Street and Hollister.

To conclude the tour, view the white cubistic (17) **Horatio West Court Apartments** (designed in 1919) at 140 Hollister Avenue by **Irving Gill,** one of California's leading architects of the modern movement. To get back to the Santa Monica Freeway, take Ocean Avenue (Neilson Way) left (west) to Pico Boulevard and turn right. At Lincoln Boulevard turn left and you will see signs for the Santa Monica Freeway, which heads toward downtown.

---

**LA living has been established in style by trendsetting architects. This tour is a sampling of the finest houses designed by modern architects, with the addition of a few excellent Revival-style homes, from Silver Lake west through Hollywood to Santa Monica. For this tour, follow the numbers on the map that are colored in green.**

The tour is approximately 37 miles long and takes at least three hours. The following sites are all private residences and should be viewed only from the street. Begin in Silver Lake. Turn north on Reno Street from Sunset Boulevard onto Silver Lake Boulevard. (The Silver Lake area cannot be entered directly from Sunset.) Follow Silver Lake to the right around the lake. At 2300 Silver Lake Boulevard is the (18) **Neutra House,** an International-style house designed in 1933 and rebuilt in 1963 by Viennese immigrant **Richard Neutra.** Down

the street are a number of other houses by Neutra: Nos. 2250, 2242, 2240, 2238, 2226, 2218, 2210, and 2200.

Continue north on Silver Lake and turn left at its end onto Glendale Boulevard. At the fork go left on Rowena Avenue and at Los Feliz Boulevard turn left. Two blocks farther, at Commonwealth Avenue, turn right (north). Turn left at the third block on Dundee Drive. At the end of the street is Neutra's (19) **Lovell House** (designed in 1929) at 4616 Dundee Drive, a classic International-style house cantilevered on a hillside. Return to Los Feliz and turn right (west). At Vermont Avenue turn right and veer to the left to take Glendower Avenue. Winding up the hill you will reach **Frank Lloyd Wright's** spectacular 1924 concrete-block house, the (10) **Ennis-Brown House** at 2607 Glendower Avenue.

Return to Vermont and turn right at Hollywood Boulevard. On the left is Barnsdall Park. See Frank Lloyd Wright's first Los Angeles project, the (9) **Hollyhock House** designed in 1917-1920 (tours are held Tuesday through Sunday at noon, 1PM, 2PM, and 3PM; for more information, call 213/485.4581).

Return to Hollywood and turn left. At Normandie Avenue turn right (north), and at Franklin Avenue turn left (west). **Lloyd Wright's** dramatic 1926 concrete-and-stucco (11) **Sowden House** is at 5121 Franklin Avenue. Continue on Franklin and turn right (north) on Western Avenue. Take it to its end where it veers right connecting with Los Feliz. Get in the left lane in preparation to turn left at the first street, Fern Dell Drive. Turn left again to Black Oak Drive. Turn left on E. Live Oak Drive and right on Verde Oak Drive. Veer to the left on Valley Oak Drive. At 5609 Valley Oak Drive is Lloyd Wright's spacious copper-trimmed (20) **Samuels-Navarro House,** built in 1922-1924.

Retrace back to Los Feliz and at Western turn left (south). At Franklin turn right and continue past the jog to the left at Highland Avenue. Three blocks past Highland, turn right on Sycamore Avenue and drive up to the (21) **Yamashiro Restaurant** at 1999 N. Sycamore Avenue. This restaurant, designed as an authentic Chinese palace by **Franklin Small** in 1913, was formerly the home of art dealers **Adolphe** and **Eugene Bernheimer.**

Return to Franklin, turn right (west), then left on Sierra Bonita and right on Hollywood. At the end of this street you will automatically enter Laurel Canyon up to Mulholland Drive and turn right (east). At Torreyson Place turn right. From here you can see the (22) **Malin House,** known as the **Chemosphere House,** a residence designed by **John Lautner** in 1960.

Return to Mulholland and turn left (south) on Laurel Canyon. When you reach Sunset, turn right (west). At the intersection of Cory Avenue and Sunset, take the small street to the right on Sunset Boulevard, going straight onto Doheny Road. The (23) **Greystone Mansion** is located at 501 N. Doheny Road (at Loma Vista Drive) in Greystone Park (open daily 10AM to 5PM). The expansive English Tudor mansion, designed by **Gordon B. Kaufmann** in 1923 for oil millionaire **Edward Doheny,** is owned by the city of Beverly Hills. For more information, call the mansion at 310/550.4654.

Return to Loma Vista and head south. At Mountain Drive veer left and turn right (west) at Sunset Boulevard. Continue on Sunset and pass the University of California, Los Angeles (UCLA). Turn left on Veteran Avenue and turn right at Cashmere Street. Turn right on Greenfield Avenue and see Viennese immigrant

architect **Rudolph Schindler's** ingenious(15) **Tischler House** (designed in 1949) at 175 Greenfield Avenue. Continue north on the street to return to Sunset and turn left (west). At the Bundy Drive-Kenter Avenue intersection, turn right onto Kenter, and at the second block on the right, Skyeway Road, turn right. **Frank Lloyd Wright's** redwood-and-stucco 1939(24) **Sturgis House** is at 449 Skyeway Road.

Return to Sunset and turn right (west). One block past Mandeville Canyon, turn right at Riviera Ranch Road. Here and on Old Oak Road are architect **Cliff May's** original "ranch houses," popularized throughout America during the '40s and '50s. Return to Sunset and turn left (east). Turn right at Rockingham Avenue. Across 26th Street and after a slight jog to the right, Rockingham becomes La Mesa Drive. From 26th to 19th streets, La Mesa is draped by huge Moreton Bay fig trees, and in the 2100 to 1900 block of La Mesa are a number of(25) **Spanish Colonial Revival** homes by **John Byers** from the 1920s to 1930s. They are Nos. 2153, 2101, 2034, and 1923 La Mesa Drive.

At the end of the road is San Vicente Boulevard. Take it to the left one block and continue on 20th Street, jogging left at Montana Avenue. Turn left on Washington Avenue. At 22nd Street you will see a dramatic house on the southwest corner, the(16) **Gehry House,** 1002 22nd Street, which will conclude the tour. The Dutch Colonial house was remodeled in 1977-1978 by architect **Frank Gehry,** using corrugated metal, wood, and glass. You can then return to the Santa Monica Freeway by heading west on Washington. At 20th, turn right to connect with the freeway.

---

The strongest cultural influence on Los Angeles architecture has been the Spanish tradition. This tour views a number of Spanish Colonial, Mexican, and Mission Revival buildings. It also concentrates on the Craftsman Movement from the turn of the century. For this tour, follow the numbers on the map that are colored in blue.

The Pasadena area abounds in fine architecture of many styles, but the English-based Arts-and-Crafts Movement found one of its strongest American outlets here. This tour is approximately 19 miles long and takes at least four hours. Private residences should be viewed only from the street. Begin this tour at a location adjacent to the Pasadena Freeway (110). On the west side of the freeway at Avenue 43 exit is the(26) **Lummis House** (built in 1898-1910) at 200 E. Avenue 43. The boulder home was built by **Charles F. Lummis,** enthusiast of the Spanish, Mexican, and Indian heritage of Southern California (tours are held on Saturday and Sunday from 1PM to 4PM). Across the freeway,(27) **Heritage Square** is a bright cluster of Victorian mansions in various stages of renovation (818/449.0193).

Now take Avenue 43 left (west) to Figueroa Street and turn left. At Marmion Way, turn right. On the northwest corner of Marmion and Museum Drive is the **Southwest Museum,** which was designed in 1912 and houses an impressive collection of Southwest Indian art. A monument to the Mission style, it is embellished with architectural references to the Alhambra in Spain. Return to Figueroa and turn left. At 4603 N. Figueroa Street is the(28) **Casa de Adobe,** a 1917 reconstruction of a Mexican adobe house by **Theodore Eisen.**

Continue on Figueroa going northeast to Arroyo Glen and turn right. At 6211 Arroyo Glen is the(29) **San Encino Abbey** (built in 1909-1925), a private residence designed by **Clyde Browne** in a combination of Spanish Mission and European Gothic styles.

Return to Figueroa and turn right, continuing northeast. At York Boulevard, turn right (south). The(30) **Judson Studios** are located at 200 S. Avenue 66. These turn-of-the-century studios are famous for their Craftsman glass and mosaic work. Return to York and turn right. Continue on as the road becomes Pasadena Avenue and then Monterey Road. At Huntington Drive, jog left and turn right (south) on San Marino, and at a fork in the road, go to the right onto Santa Anita Street. At the corner of Santa Anita and Mission Drive is the(31) **Mission Playhouse,** 320 S. Mission Drive, designed in 1927 by **Arthur Benton** to appear similar to the Mission San Antonio in Monterey County. Go east one block to visit the(32) **San Gabriel Mission Archangel** at 537 W. Mission Drive, the fourth mission established by **Father Junipero Serra.** The restored mission was originally built between 1791 and 1805 and is open daily from 9:30AM to 4PM.

Now head north on Serra Drive and turn left on San Marino Avenue. Turn left on(33) **Lombardy Road** and notice the Spanish Revival homes, all private residences, in the 1700 to 2000 blocks, especially No.1750 by architect **Roland E. Coate;** No. 1779 by **George Washington Smith,** at the corner of Allen Avenue; 665 Allen Avenue, another Smith house; and two **Wallace Neff** houses at Nos. 1861 and 2035 Lombardy. Turn right (north) on Sierra Bonita Avenue and go one block to California Boulevard. Before you is the campus of the(34) **California Institute of Technology.** The oldest buildings, from the 1930s, were designed by **Gordon Kaufmann** in the Spanish Renaissance and Spanish baroque styles. Note especially the(34) **Atheneum Club** facing Sierra Bonita and the adjacent dorms seen as you turn left (west) onto California Boulevard. Continue on California to El Molino Avenue and turn right (north).

At 37 S. El Molino Avenue is the Spanish Colonial (35) **Pasadena Playhouse** (designed in 1924-1925) by architect **Elmer Grey.** Turn left at the corner on Colorado Boulevard heading west and at Fair Oaks Avenue turn left. One block away is Green Street. Turn left and then right at Raymond Avenue. You will be in front of the large turretted Spanish Colonial(36) **Hotel Green & Castle Green Apartments** designed in 1890-1899 by architect **Frederick Roehrig.** Head north on Raymond and at Colorado Boulevard turn left (west). Turn right on Orange Grove Boulevard. Just past Walnut Street, you will see a small street flanking Orange Grove Boulevard on the left. This is Westmoreland Place. At No. 4 is the(1) **Gamble House** built in 1908 by famous Pasadena Craftsman architects **Charles** and **Henry Greene** (open Thursday through Sunday from noon to 3PM; you must call in advance for tours, 818/793.3334). To the left of the house is(2) **Arroyo Terrace,** which has a number of Greene and Greene houses. All are private resi-

dences. Pay particular attention to Nos. 368, 370, 400, 408, 424, and 440, which were built between 1902 and 1913.

Return to Orange Grove Boulevard and turn right. At Holly Street, one block away, turn right to Linda Vista Avenue. Turn left and then go one block to (37) **El Circulo Drive,** then turn left. At 95 El Circulo and 825 Las Palmas Road are two rural Spanish Revival homes designed by amateur architect **Edward Fowler** in 1927. Backtrack to Linda Vista Avenue. Turn right (north) to Holly Street and then turn right (east). At Orange Grove Boulevard turn right (south). Turn right at California Boulevard and note the (38) **E.J. Cheesewright House** at 686 W. California Boulevard, a 1910 Craftsman house that looks like an English snuggery with its thatch roof. At Arroyo Boulevard turn left (south). See the (39) **Batchelder House,** 626 S. Arroyo Boulevard, built in 1909 by **Ernest Batchelder,** Pasadena craftsman and renowned tilemaker. Conclude this tour with the finest example of a Spanish Monterey style house, the home at (40) 850 S. Arroyo Boulevard, designed by **Donald McMurray** in 1927.

To return to the Pasadena or Ventura freeways, turn left at Grand Avenue and right on Bellefontaine Street to get to Orange Grove. From Orange Grove you can connect with the Pasadena Freeway (110) by turning right and heading south, and with the Ventura Freeway (134) by turning left.

---

This tour is a sampling of some of LA's fantastic architecture—ranging from the serious to the whimsical. For this tour, follow the numbers on the map that are colored in black.

A bit of fantasy abounds on almost every street of LA, so along the way you might note additional structures that have adopted the styles of other areas and other cultures, or buildings that present straightforward indulgence and delight in commercialism, futurism, and personal eccentricities. This route leads you around the city in an extremely broad sweep from downtown to Watts, and north to Glendale ending in Beverly Hills. The tour is approximately 52 miles long and takes at least four hours. Please keep in mind that the private residences should be viewed only from the street. In downtown LA the shimmering futuristic apparition at 404 S. Figueroa Street is the (5) **Westin Bonaventure Hotel** by architect **John Portman.** Take Figueroa south to Olympic Boulevard and turn left. At Hill Street turn right to see the (41) **Mayan Theater,** now the **Mayan Nightclub** at 1038 S. Hill Street. The pre-Columbian facade was designed by **Morgan, Walls & Clements** in 1927. Continue on Hill to Pico Boulevard and turn left (east). At the end of Pico you will come to Central Avenue and the shiplike (42) **Coca-Cola Building** designed in 1935-1937 by **Robert Derrah** at 1334 S. Central Avenue, which has enormous Coke bottles at the entrance to the plant. Turn right onto Central and follow the signs on the right to enter the Santa Monica Freeway (I-10) going west (to Santa Monica). After a short distance, connect with the Harbor Freeway (110) South (toward San Pedro).

Turn off at the Manchester Avenue exit and go left (east). Manchester turns into Firestone Boulevard. At Elm

Street turn right (Elm turns into Wilmington Avenue), and at the intersection of 107th Street, turn right. There you will see the unique monument (43) **Watts**

**Towers** at 1765 E 107th Street. This is a personal vision made of broken tile, glass, and debris erected from 1921 to 1954 by an Italian immigrant tile-layer, **Sam Rodia.**

Retrace back to the Harbor Freeway (110) and go north on the freeway (toward Pasadena) and connect with the Hollywood Freeway (101). Take the Hollywood Freeway west and get off after a short distance at the Echo Park-Glendale Boulevard exit. Take Echo Park north to Baxter Street and turn right. At Avon Street turn left (driving the streets around here is like taking a roller coaster ride). You will want to park and walk on the right (east) side of Avon to Avon Park Terrace. There you will see what looks like an authentic Indian pueblo, the (44) **Atwater Bungalows** at 1431-33 Avon Park Terrace, built in 1931 by **Robert Stacy-Judd.** Return to your car and at Baxter turn right. At Alvarado Street turn left and at Glendale turn right. Proceed north to Rowena Avenue and turn left. Glendale continues at right and take it to San Fernando Road and turn left. At Grandview Avenue turn right and take it to its end.

At the intersection of Mountain Street and Grandview you will enter the **Brand Library,** formerly the (45) **Brand House** (built in 1902), an exotic East Indian and Moorish mansion that is now a public library. Return to Grandview and at San Fernando turn left. At Los Feliz Boulevard turn right. Turn left at Vermont Avenue and right onto Sunset Boulevard, you will pass the Indian (46) **Self-Realization Temple** at 4860 Sunset Boulevard and the (13) **Crossroads of the World** at 6621 Sunset Boulevard. This 1935 tourist attraction presents a ship sailing into a courtyard of shops representing various European countries. At Highland Avenue turn right and at Hollywood Boulevard turn left. At 6925 Hollywood Boulevard you will see (12) **Mann's** (formerly **Grauman's**) **Chinese Theatre,** an extravagant and exotic Chinese design dating from 1927.

Continue west on Hollywood and at La Brea turn left. At Santa Monica Boulevard turn right and at San Vicente Boulevard turn left (south). On the right, just north of Beverly Boulevard is the (47) **Tail-o-the-Pup** hot-dog stand at 329 San Vicente Boulevard. On the corner of the Beverly Center is the **Hard Rock Cafe,** with a 1959 Cadillac and palm tree on its roof (at San Vicente and Beverly Boulevards). There also is a large digital billboard displaying the diminishing number of the world's rain forest acreage and the alarming rise in the global population.

Turn right on La Cienega Boulevard, right on Wilshire Boulevard, and continue west on it into Beverly Hills. Slightly before the intersection of Wilshire and Santa Monica, turn right on Linden Drive. At Carmelita Avenue turn left. At the corner of Walden Drive and Carmelita is the (48) **Spadena House** at 516 Walden Drive, a 1921 Hansel and Gretel cottage that was originally a combined movie set and production office. From Wilshire going west you can connect with the San Diego Freeway (I-405) to the Santa Monica Freeway (I-10).

This tour by no means covers all the fantasy architecture in Southern California. Interested viewers should also make a point to see the (49) **Avalon Casino, (50) Queen Mary, (51) Crystal Cathedral, (51) Disneyland, (52) Drive-thru Donut,** and the (53) **Hollywood Sign.**

## Restaurants

Only restaurants with star ratings are listed at right. All restaurants are listed alphabetically in the main (preceding) index. Always call to ensure a restaurant has not closed, changed its hours, or booked its tables for a private party. The restaurant price ratings are based on the average cost of an entrée for one person, excluding tax and tip.

★★★★ An Extraordinary Experience
★★★ Excellent
★★ Very Good
★ Good

$$$$ Big Bucks ($45 and up)
$$$ Expensive ($25-$45)
$$ Reasonable ($15-$25)
$ The Price Is Right (less than $15)

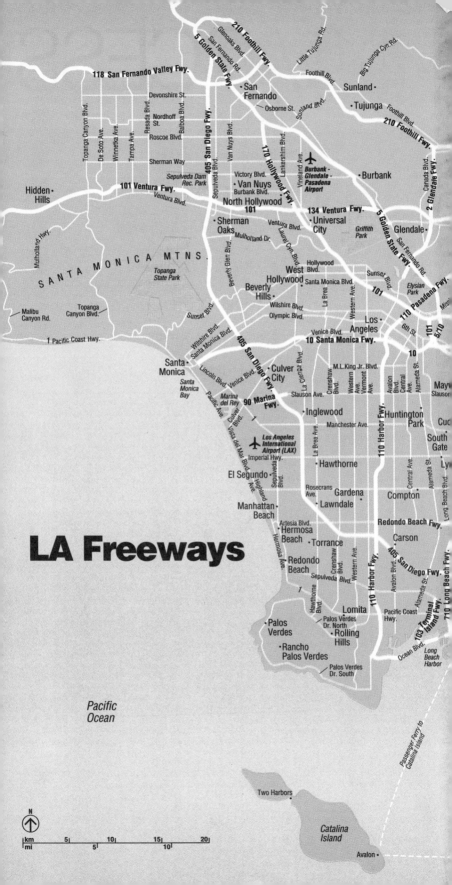
# LA Freeways

S0-AAN-289